LaunchPad for *Choices & Connections* is where video scenarios, adaptive quizzing, activities, and more are available. See the inside back cover for information or visit **bedfordstmartins.com/choicesconnections** for instructions on how to log on.

TRY THESE FEATURES...

LearningCurve	How to Communicate	Making Communication Choices	Activities
e LearningCurve for Ch. 3: Mediated Communication tests your knowledge of competent online messages	▶ "Removing an Embarrassing Post" helps you maintain a positive online face (Ch. 3, pp. 66–67)	"Distorting Online Self-Presentation" helps you handle deceptive practices in online dating (Ch. 2, p. 40)	"Analyzing Your Online Face" provides a chance to self-reflect on your digital identity (Ch. 3, p. 81)
e LearningCurve for Ch. 4: Understanding Culture reviews cultural influences on communication	▶ "Adapting to Cultural Differences" assesses cultural differences in groups (Ch. 4, pp. 100–101)	"When a Friend Is Different" considers how to adapt to a culturally different roommate (Ch. 4, pp. 104–105)	
e LearningCurve for Ch. 7: Active Listening assesses your understanding of the listening process		"To Multitask or Not, That Is the Question" tests how you would handle distracting texting practices (Ch. 7, pp. 171–172)	"The Noise List" examines where you can improve your listening skills (Ch. 7, p. 185)
e LearningCurve for Ch. 8: Managing Conflicts gauges how well you understand approaches to conflicts	▶ "Collaboration in a Conflict" explores how roommates can work together (Ch. 8, pp. 198–199)	"I Wasn't Being Sarcastic" confronts how to handle misunderstood intentions when online (Ch. 6, pp. 152–153)	"Choose Your Own Ending" prompts you to re-evaluate conflicts you've experienced (Ch. 8, p. 209)
e LearningCurve for Ch. 10: Managing Interpersonal Relationships reviews relationships maintenance strategies		"Why Didn't You At Least Text Me?" examines how to handle communication rules in romances (Ch. 3, p. 73)	"Communication Rules" ponders how you can improve your own relationships (Ch. 10, p. 259)
e LearningCurve for Ch. 12: Leadership in Group Communication tests how well you know small group communication skills	▶ "Handling Complaints" helps you balance differing opinions in groups (Ch. 12, pp. 296–297)	"You're Not Funny" deals with handling a group member who is distracting the team (Ch. 11, pp. 280–281)	"Practicing Problem Solving" gives you a chance to be a leader (Ch. 12, p. 311)
e LearningCurve for Ch. 17: Persuasive Speeches tests your comfort with guidelines and practices for persuasive speaking	▶ "Oral Citations" guides you in correctly citing sources in speeches (Ch. 13, pp. 332–333)	"But the Video Went Viral" considers how you can handle humor and appropriate examples in speeches (Ch. 14, pp. 350–351)	"As Seen on TV" asks you to find your own speech models (Ch. 17, p. 455)

More than any current text, *Choices & Connections* immediately engages students with relevant and interesting material. Further, the title says it all; students will better see that they have *choices* in how they communicate. And, the authors do an excellent job in *connecting* course concepts from chapter to chapter.

Ann Vogel
University of Wisconsin, Oshkosh

Absolutely and without question what is most appealing about *Choices & Connections* is the authors' ability to engage the student.

Bruce Bishop
Palomar College

I am EXCITED by the emergence of *Choices & Connections*! It is a flexible textbook that can easily reach a wide variety of potential student audiences with exciting and accessible content.

Ladori Lara
Austin Community College

Choices & Connections is an engaging textbook that effectively presents the essential concepts and skills of human communication through the use of vivid, relevant illustrations while linking all of the chapters so that students can clearly understand that no phase of the process stands alone.

Dante Morelli
Suffolk County Community College

Choices & Connections is succinct, engaging, and challenging. I can't wait to use this text!

Sandra Grayson
Mississippi College

CHOICES & CONNECTIONS

AN INTRODUCTION TO COMMUNICATION

CHOICES & CONNECTIONS

AN INTRODUCTION TO COMMUNICATION

STEVEN McCORNACK
Michigan State University

JOSEPH ORTIZ
Scottsdale Community College

Bedford/St. Martin's
Boston • New York

For Bedford/St. Martin's

Publisher for Communication: Erika Gutierrez
Senior Developmental Editor: Noel Hohnstine
Associate Editor: Alexis Smith
Senior Production Editor: Jessica Gould
Project Manager: Won McIntosh
Production Supervisor: Samuel Jones
Marketing Manager: Thomas Digiano
Editorial Assistant: Joanna Kamouh
Copy Editor: Jamie Nan Thaman
Indexer: Melanie Belkin
Photo Researcher: Susan McDermott Barlow
Art Director: Lucy Krikorian
Text and Cover Design: Jerilyn Bockorick
Composition: Cenveo Publisher Services
Printing and Binding: RR Donnelley and Sons

Manufactured in the United States of America.

9   8   7   6   5   4
f   e   d   c   b   a

For information, write: Bedford/St. Martin's, 75 Arlington Street, Boston, MA 02116
   (617-399-4000)

ISBN 978-0-312-38783-9 (paperback)
ISBN 978-1-4576-4931-8 (loose-leaf edition)

Acknowledgments
Figure 1.4 NCA Credo for Ethical Communication, p. 21 "Credo for Ethical Communication," National Communication Association. Used by permission.

Art acknowledgments and copyrights appear on the same page as the art selections they cover. It is a violation of the law to reproduce these selections by any means whatsoever without the written permission of the copyright holder.

At the time of publication all Internet URLs published in this text were found to accurately link to their intended Web site. If you do find a broken link, please forward the information to Alexis.Smith@macmillan.com, so that it can be corrected for the next printing.

Preface

Choices & Connections *bolsters students' understanding of how their communi-cation choices connect to the personal, relational, and professional outcomes they experience; and empowers them to improve their lives by learning how to skillfully adapt their communication to various contexts.*

Such a declaration might strike you as an unusual beginning for a preface. But this statement embraces the pedagogical goals that guide our teaching and serve as the foundation for our text, *Choices & Connections*, and its associated learning program, LaunchPad. As instructors who have taught introductory communication classes every semester for decades (at both community colleges and four-year universities), the idea of "positive transformation through pedagogy" is central to both of our respective teach-ing philosophies. In simple terms, what we teach can change our students' lives for the better. At the same time, *how* we teach today is far different from when we first embarked upon our careers. Students live lives of technological immersion; fluidly shifting from texting one moment to Tweeting the next. Correspondingly, they learn in myriad ways, from accessing course content on their phones to writing reflective blogs on personal webpages. Because of this, a new text was needed that reflects the different ways in which students communicate and learn, while providing them with the essential concepts and skills they need to improve their lives. *Choices & Connections* is just such a book.

Whether it's delivered online, face-to-face or in some other format, the introductory course presents unique challenges for us as teachers. How do we distill for students the sheer amount of research and theory the discipline has to offer? How do we create connections between domains that—at least in students' eyes—often seem widely disparate? How can we better highlight the practical relevance of this material, thereby boosting student attention *and* retention? What can we do to facilitate their knowledge and skill acquisition, so that students walk away from the class as vastly improved communicators?

Choices & Connections is designed to meet these challenges in ways that optimize student learning and instructor ease-of-use. Throughout the book we inspire students to take ownership of their communication choices, see the connections between seemingly disparate contexts, build adaptive communi-cation skills, and improve their capacity to self-assess. This is accomplished in many ways, including compelling examples, case studies, and annotated visuals throughout the book, and LaunchPad, our dynamic and easy-to-use platform where interactive videos, LearningCurve, a personalized quizzing program, and more are available. And we developed the print and online components together so that they work hand-in-hand, creating individualized learning experiences that adapt to students' needs and encourage practical application. For example, the text of Chapter 6 discusses theory and research regarding how to manage one's nonverbal behavior online, and then students are faced with a video-based skills feature in LaunchPad on how to evaluate one's body language and nonverbal cues while on a Skype video call with a friend.

From the title and chapter content to the online video activities, the importance of making good choices is a consistent theme throughout. But we don't just "finger wag" at students, telling them (like the clichéd parental entreaty) to "make good choices." Instead, through features such as the *Making Communication Choices* case studies and the LaunchPad-based interactive challenges presented in the *How to Communicate* video scenarios, we systematically guide students through *how* they can reason from choices to communication to outcomes; so they can use their skills to better adapt to life's daily demands. For instance, the *How to Communicate* feature in Chapter 9 motivates students to consider how choosing the right time and place to end a roommate relationship can have a measurable, positive effect on the outcome of the interaction. Students can then log on to LaunchPad and see the roommate scenario play out over a series of video clips.

Coupled with this unique emphasis on choice is a focus upon helping students see the connections between various communication contexts. From this, students learn that the knowledge and skills relevant for meeting one type of communication challenge are readily transferable to multiple settings. For example, the critical self-reflection skills covered in Chapter 2 are reintroduced in our coverage of active listening, managing nonverbal impressions, as well as using feedback to improve public speaking skills. By helping students better recognize the links that exist between different communication concepts and forms, they will develop greater adaptability and versatility in their communicative skill set.

For many students, this unique class may be the only point of contact they will ever have with our discipline. As such, every aspect of *Choices & Connections* is constructed to be interesting and memorable for students. We begin each chapter with a compelling narrative, illustrating chapter concepts through a diverse range of examples culled from literature, popular culture, film, television, and history. For instance, the Chapter 1 opener explores how organizers of the annual South by Southwest (SXSW) festival in Austin, Texas, ultimately use communication to bring people together every year. And in LaunchPad, students can craft their own communication plans for the learning activities found throughout the text—making them easy assignments for developing critical thinking.

Finally, to give students the same level of depth and understanding about their online communication that we provide them in all other areas, *Choices & Connections* includes Chapter 3: Mediated Communication—a unique chapter completely dedicated to online communication, which provides students with reliable, current scholarship so they can make better choices when using social media.

No matter if the communication is done in person or through digital channels, the same elements of choice, communication, and outcomes are present. We make choices in planning our messages; these decisions influence the production and presentation of our communication; and others interpret and evaluate our behavior in ways that yield the personal, relational, and professional outcomes we experience. What you will find throughout *Choices & Connections* with LaunchPad is a complete digital and print learning program wholly guided by this mission to enhance students' understanding of their communication *choices and connections*.

Features

Choices & Connections plus LaunchPad seamlessly combine print and digital in this introductory text, empowering students to make better communication choices for better outcomes

- **Emphasis on making informed and adaptive choices.** The central mission of *Choices & Connections* is to help students understand that their communication is rooted in the choices they make. Therefore, the quality of their choices—and their ability to skillfully adapt their communication to different contexts—is largely what distinguishes the times when they experience successful interactions with others from those when they don't. In the LaunchPad-based ⊙ *How to Communicate* online video scenarios, students can easily practice the skills needed to make more informed choices.

- **A multifaceted, immersive digital experience.** *Choices & Connections* with LaunchPad was designed from the ground up to use the best aspects of both print and digital to create a superior and individualized learning experience for students. Online videos ⊙ expand content by bringing concepts to life, modeling speech behaviors, and giving students a chance to reflect on their own communication experiences. Students can further master theories and their application through the adaptive and personalized quizzing program ✅ LearningCurve. Instructors who choose to adopt LaunchPad have a new and easy way to manage courses online, with the content, videos, adaptive quizzing, and activities all in one online space. LaunchPad brings it all together. See p. xi for more information.

- **Intuitive approach to connecting communication concepts.** Based on decades of experience in teaching introductory communication courses, the authors carefully weave together different concepts to provide a holistic view of communication. For example, important cultural and gender influences—a focus of Chapter 4—are integrated in other chapters, videos, and features to give students insight into the complexity of the choices they must consider to competently connect with others. These types of links will reinforce the integrated nature of communication rather than framing it as an ad hoc assortment of disparate topics.

Choices & Connections helps students become knowledgeable and adaptable communicators through self-reflection and skills application

Emphasis on practical communication skills and self-assessment. Whether giving a speech or resolving a conflict, students are consistently reminded to reflect on their own experiences and carefully consider their choices. The *Making Communication Choices* case studies put this idea to the test by connecting research to real-life dilemmas. In LaunchPad, students can respond to the case study to make their own—and informed—communication choices, as well as access the following video scenarios and adaptive quizzes below.

▶ *How to Communicate* **video scenarios promote adaptable skill development.** Working through a series of online videos, students confront a real-life communication challenge and then adapt their messages when things go in unusual directions. Combining thought-provoking questions and compelling videos, this feature takes students' skill development to a new level of understanding.

✓ **LearningCurve creates personalized learning through adaptive quizzing.** Chapter call-outs prompt students to tackle the LearningCurve quizzes to test their knowledge and reinforce learning. Based on cognitive research on how students learn, this adaptive, game-like quizzing program motivates students to engage with course materials. The reporting tools let you see what students understand so you can adapt your teaching to their needs.

Choices & Connections focuses on how students really communicate

Extensive coverage of social media. *Choices & Connections* meets students where they are with a focus on technology and online messages. Whether via an app, text, post, or note, learning appropriate digital communication skills is a necessary component of successful communication. Throughout the text—and especially in the unique, dedicated coverage found in Chapter 3: Mediated Communication—*Choices & Connections* highlights our changing modes of communication to help students refine and improve their pervasive use of communication technologies.

Choices & Connections offers streamlined coverage, engaging examples, and extensive study tools for students

Engaging student experience. Accessible and appealing, *Choices & Connections* provides streamlined content; built-in study aids to guide reading; a variety of pop culture, current event, and real-life examples; and a clean, eye-catching design.

End of chapter materials focus on self-review. Students can test their comprehension of major topics in the Pop Quiz or go to LearningCurve in LaunchPad to access adaptive quizzes and review further. Chapter Recaps pull out main ideas, while the Activities give students opportunities to self-reflect and try out new skills.

Extensive video collection helps students learn concepts and prepare for their speeches. LaunchPad's Key Term videos illustrate important chapter concepts, while Sample Speech Resources and other public-speaking clips provide a start-to-finish look at speech preparation, including full-length speech videos and briefer clips.

Digital and Print Formats

For more information on these formats, please visit the online catalog at **bedfordstmartins.com/choicesconnections/catalog.**

LaunchPad for *Choices & Connections* is a dynamic new platform that dramatically enhances teaching and learning. LaunchPad combines the full e-book with carefully chosen videos, quizzes, activities, instructor's resources, and LearningCurve. LaunchPad offers a student-friendly approach, organized for easy assignability in a simple user interface. Instructors can create reading, video, or quiz assignments in seconds, as well as embed their own videos or custom content. The Gradebook quickly and easily allows you to review the progress for your whole class, for individual students and for individual assignments. *How to Communicate* video scenarios, Key Term videos, and Sample Speech Resources and video clips enhance every unit of Launch-Pad. LaunchPad can be ordered on its own or packaged for *free* with *Choices & Connections*. Learn more at **bedfordstmartins.com/launchpad.**

Choices & Connections is available as a print text. To get the most out of the book, *Choices & Connections* can be packaged *free* with LaunchPad.

The loose-leaf edition of *Choices & Connections* features the same print text in a convenient, budget-priced format, designed to fit into any two-ring binder. The loose-leaf version can be packaged *free* with LaunchPad.

The Bedford e-book to Go for *Choices & Connections* includes the same content as the print book and provides an affordable, tech-savvy PDF e-book option for students. Instructors can customize the e-book by adding their own content and deleting or rearranging chapters. Learn more about custom Bedford e-Books to Go at **bedfordstmartins.com/ebooks**—where you can also learn more about other e-book versions of *Choices & Connections* in a variety of formats, including Kindle, CourseSmart, Barnes & Noble Nook-Study, Know, CafeScribe, or Chegg.

Resources for Students

For more information on these resources or to learn about package options, please visit the online catalog at **bedfordstmartins.com/choicesconnections /catalog.**

LaunchPad for *Choices & Connections*

Every new copy of *Choices & Connections* can be packaged with LaunchPad for free. LaunchPad comes with access to **LearningCurve**, an adaptive online learning tool that helps students study, practice, and apply their communication skills. Chapter call-outs prompt students to the book's LaunchPad, where they can answer questions about the material in each chapter. Learn more at **LearningCurveWorks.com.**

When packaged with LaunchPad, *Choices & Connections* also comes with access to all of the *How to Communicate* video scenarios and over two hundred Key Term and Public Speaking videos that define important terms from the text (see the last book page for a list) and provide speech models for students. Finally, the free companion website Communication Central hosts a variety of resources and study tools, including Web links, sample speeches, and the *Bedford Speech Outliner*.

The Essential Guide to Intercultural Communication **by Jennifer Willis-Rivera (University of Wisconsin, River Falls).** This useful guide offers an overview of key communication areas, including perception, verbal and nonverbal communication, interpersonal relationships, and organizations, from a uniquely intercultural perspective. Enhancing the discussion are contemporary and fun examples drawn from real life, as well as an entire chapter devoted to intercultural communication in popular culture.

The Essential Guide to Rhetoric **by William M. Keith (University of Wisconsin, Milwaukee) and Christian O. Lundberg (University of North Carolina, Chapel Hill).** This handy guide is a powerful addition to the public-speaking portion of the human communication course, providing an accessible and balanced overview of key historical and contemporary rhetorical theories. Written by two leaders in the field, this brief introduction uses concrete, relevant examples and jargon-free language to bring concepts to life.

The Essential Guide to Presentation Software **by Allison Joy Bailey (University of North Georgia) and Rob Patterson (University of Virginia).** This guide shows students how presentation software can be used to support but not overtake their speeches. Sample screens and practical advice make this an indispensable resource for students preparing electronic visual aids.

Outlining and Organizing Your Speech **by Merry Buchanan (University of Central Oklahoma).** This student workbook provides step-by-step guidance for preparing informative, persuasive, and professional presentations and gives students the opportunity to practice the critical skills of conducting audience analysis, dealing with communication apprehension, selecting a speech topic and purpose, researching support materials, organizing and outlining, developing introductions and conclusions, enhancing language and delivery, and preparing and using presentation aids.

Media Career Guide: Preparing for Jobs in the 21st Century **by Sherri Hope Culver (Temple University) and James Seguin (Robert Morris University).** Practical and student-friendly, this guide includes a comprehensive directory of media jobs, helpful tips, and career guidance for students considering a major in communication studies and mass media.

Research and Documentation in the Electronic Age **by Diana Hacker (Prince George's Community College) and Barbara Fister (Gustavus Adolphus College).** This handy booklet covers everything students need for college research assignments at the library and on the Internet, including advice for finding and evaluating Internet sources.

Resources for Instructors

For more information or to order or download these resources, please visit the online catalog at **bedfordstmartins.com/choicesconnections/catalog**.

Instructor's Resource Manual for *Choices & Connections* **by Laura McDavitt (Jackson State University).** This downloadable manual contains helpful tips and teaching assistance for new and seasoned instructors alike. Content includes learning objectives, lecture outlines, general classroom activities, and review questions, as well as suggestions for setting up a syllabus, tips on managing your classroom, and general notes on teaching the course.

Computerized Test Bank for *Choices & Connections* **by Charles Korn (Northern Virginia Community College).** The Computerized Test Bank includes multiple choice, short-answer, essay, true/false, and matching questions for every chapter. In addition, each question is connected to a learning objective, has a difficulty level, and indicates a correlating page reference to the textbook. The questions appear in easy-to-use software that allows instructors to add, edit, re-sequence, and print questions and answers. Instructors can also export questions into a variety of formats, including Blackboard, Desire2Learn, and Moodle. The Computerized Test Bank can be downloaded from the "Instructor Resources" tab of the book's catalog page, and the content is also loaded in the LaunchPad question bank administrator.

PowerPoint slides for *Choices & Connections*. Available as a download, each chapter's slides contain the most important concepts and definitions, including key figures.

***ESL Students in the Public Speaking Classroom: A Guide for Teachers* by Robbin Crabtree (Fairfield University) and David Sapp (Fairfield University) with Robert Weissberg (New Mexico State University).** As the United States increasingly becomes a nation of linguistically diverse speakers, instructors must find new pedagogical tools to aid students for whom English is a second language. This guide specifically addresses the needs of ESL students in the public-speaking arena and offers instructors valuable advice for helping students deal successfully with the unique challenges they face.

Professional and student speeches. Available on DVD, Volume 19 of the esteemed Great Speeches series offers dynamic professional speeches for today's classroom, featuring such compelling speakers as Bill Clinton, Christopher Reeve, and the Dalai Lama. Additional professional videos are available from the Bedford/St. Martin's Video Library. In addition, three videotapes of student speeches (featuring students of varying abilities from Texas Tech and the University of Oklahoma) provide models for study and analysis. These professional and student speech resources are free to qualified adopters. Please contact your sales representative for more information.

***Coordinating the Communication Course: A Guidebook* by Deanna Fassett and John Warren.** This essential resource offers the most practical advice on every topic central to the coordinator/director role. Starting with setting a strong foundation, this professional resource continues on with thoughtful guidance, tips, and best practices on crucial topics such as creating community across multiple sections, orchestrating meaningful assessment, hiring and training instructors, and more. Model course materials, recommended readings, and insights from successful coordinators make this resource a must-have for anyone directing a course in communication.

Acknowledgments

We would like to thank everyone at Bedford/St. Martin's who was involved in this project and whose support made it possible, especially Denise Wydra, Vice President, Editorial Humanities and Publisher Erika Gutierrez who worked with us on the vision for this project and launched us into this adventure. A very special thanks goes to Noel Hohnstine, Senior Development Editor. This project became yours, and you made it happen from start to finish. Without your unflagging optimism, brilliant insights, and indefatigable work ethic, we never would have been able to do this. Thank you to Associate Editor Alexis Smith for all of her efforts and especially her work on the adaptive learning program, LearningCurve, and the *How to Communicate* video project, and to Editorial Assistant Joanna Kamouh for her attention to details across the project, including the book's visual and video programs. We would like to thank the entire *How to Communicate* film crew, especially director Kaliya Warren, for working tirelessly to achieve our vision for these videos, director of photography Zach Kuperstein, sound mixer Joe Pfeil, and photographer Tim Whitney; in addition, we would like to thank all of the actors who brought this feature to life. This book also would not have come together without the efforts of Director of Production, Editing, and Design Sue Brown, Managing Editor Elise Kaiser, Senior Production Editor Jessica Gould, and Project Manager Won McIntosh, who oversaw the book's tight schedule; the watchful eyes of Production Supervisor Samuel Jones; and the beautiful new design by Jerilyn Bockorick and stunning photo research by Susan McDermott Barlow. We credit our copy editor, Jamie Nan Thaman; our proofreaders, Judy Kiviat and Lori Lewis; and our text permission manager, Linda Winters. We would like to thank the team of writers at Publishers Solutions for lending their expertise to our ancillary program, including LearningCurve, and also Lauren Keller-Johnson of Kilo Consulting for her editorial insights throughout the book's development. Finally, the enthusiasm and support from the marketing team is particularly appreciated: Vice President of Sales Craig Bleyer, Vice President of Marketing Susan Winslow, Marketing Manager Tom Digiano, and the entire sales force of Macmillan Education.

On a more personal level, Steve would like to thank his parents, Connie and Bruce, for instilling within him a deep and abiding passion regarding reading and writing; his sons, Kyle, Colin, and Conor, for their unflagging support of "Dad the author"; and—most of all—Kelly, for simultaneously keeping him grounded yet always lifting him up. Joe is deeply grateful to Diana for her unconditional support as he worked on this project. She is both rudder and rock for their family. Many thanks to his children, who in their own unique ways provided amazing support, including keeping him current with popular culture trends. Finally, Joe is indebted to his colleagues and students who animate his thinking and teaching.

Throughout the development of this textbook, hundreds of human communication instructors voiced their opinion through surveys, focus groups, and reviews of the manuscript. A special thank you goes to the dedicated members of the editorial board, whose commitment to the project is surpassed only by their help in shaping the book: Sandra Grayson, *Mississippi College*; Kara Laskowski, *Shippensburg University*; Laura McDavitt, *Jackson State University*; Travice Baldwin Obas, *Volunteer State Community College*; and Ann Vogel, *University of Wisconsin, Oshkosh*.

We would also like to thank everyone else who participated in this process: Jonathan Amsbary, *Virginia Tech*; Kay Barefoot, *College of the Albemarle*;

Bruce Bishop, *Palomar College*; Stephen Braden, *Kennesaw University*; Dana Burnside, *Lehigh Carbon Community College*; Amy Howell Burton, *Northwest Vista College*; Tim Chandler, *Hardin-Simmons College*; Mindy Chang, *Western New England College*; Sarah Clements, *Pulaski Technical College*; Paige C. Davis, *Cy-Fair College*; Tasha Davis, *Austin Community College*; Sherry Dean, *Richland College*; JoRita Defrancesco, *Central Arizona College*; Thomas Downard, *Northeastern University*; Natalie Dudchock, *Jeff State Community College*; Ann Duncan, *McClennan Community College*; Paul Edleman, *Sauk Valley Community College*; Kathleen Edelmayer, *Madonna University*; Rebecca Ellison, *Jefferson Community College*; Brandy Fair, *Grayson College*; Deloris J. Foxworth, *Kentucky State University*; Cole Franklin, *East Texas Baptist University*; Tracy Frederick, *Southwestern College*; Seth Frei, *University of Texas at Austin*; Chris Gurrie, *University of Tampa*; Stacy Gresell, *Lone Star College-CyFair*; Bitrus Gwamna, *Iowa Wesleyan College*; Pamela Hayward, *Georgia Regents University*; James Hikins, *University of Central Arkansas*; David Johnson, *Volunteer State Community College*; Erik Kanter, *Virginia Tech University*; William Kingsley, *Shippensburg University*; Amanda Knight, *Andrew College*; Ladori Lara, Austin Community College; Maureen Louis, *Cazenovia College*; Leigh Makay, *Heidelberg University*; Jennifer McCullough, *Kent State University*; Michael McGill, *University of Pikeville*; Rory McGloin, *University of Connecticut*; Robert Mild, *Fairmont State University*; Diane Millette, *University of Miami*; Dante Morelli, *Suffolk County Community College*; Nichole Morelock, *Texas Tech University*; Eric Morgan, *New Mexico State University;* Ephraim Nikoi, *University of Washington, Superior*; Lori Norin, *University of Arkansas, Fort Smith*; Araceli Palomino, *Germanna Community College;* Miri Pardo, *St. John Fisher College*; Paul E. Potter, *Hardin-Simmons University*; Vonda Powell, *Simmons College*; Devon Powers, *Drexel University*; Laurie Pratt, *Chaffey College*; Marlene Preston, *Virginia Tech*; Tracey Quigley Holden, *University of Delaware*; Janice Ralya, *Jeff State Community College*; Jeff Ringer, *St. Cloud State University*; Sherry L. Rhodes, *Collin County Community College—Spring Creek*; Renee Robinson, *Saint Xavier University*; Kimberly Schaefer, *Baker University*; Pam Secklin, *St. Cloud State University*; Joe Sheller, *Mount Mercy University*; Nick Trujillo, *Sacramento State University*; Mark Woolsey, *Yavapai College*; Kevin Wright, *University of Oklahoma*.

Finally, no textbook is created by one person. Thank you for the human communication discipline and its students.

Brief Contents

Contents

For videos and LearningCurve quizzing to help you review, go to **bedfordstmartins.com/choicesconnections**.

---

(3) Mediated Communication   *56*

For videos and LearningCurve quizzing to help you review, go to **bedfordstmartins.com/choicesconnections**.

4 **Understanding Culture** *82*

⊙ ✔ *For videos and LearningCurve quizzing to help you review, go to* **bedfordstmartins.com/choicesconnections**.

---

5 **Verbal Communication** *110*

◉ ✔ *For videos and LearningCurve quizzing to help you review, go to* **bedfordstmartins.com/choicesconnections**.

⑥ Nonverbal Communication   *132*

◉ ✔ *For videos and LearningCurve quizzing to help you review, go to* **bedfordstmartins.com/choicesconnections**.

 For videos and LearningCurve quizzing to help you review, go to **bedfordstmartins.com/choicesconnections**.

✓ *For videos and LearningCurve quizzing to help you review, go to* **bedfordstmartins.com/choicesconnections**.

PART 2   INTERPERSONAL COMMUNICATION

⑨ Principles of Interpersonal Communication *210*

 ✓ *For videos and LearningCurve quizzing to help you review, go to* **bedfordstmartins.com/choicesconnections**.

For videos and LearningCurve quizzing to help you review, go to **bedfordstmartins.com/choicesconnections**.

---

12 Leadership in Group Communication *286*

▶ ✓ *For videos and LearningCurve quizzing to help you review, go to* **bedfordstmartins.com/choicesconnections**.

PART 4 PUBLIC COMMUNICATION

(13) Preparing Your Speech 312

 For videos and LearningCurve quizzing to help you review, go to **bedfordstmartins.com/choicesconnections**.

(14) Composing Your Speech 340

For videos and LearningCurve quizzing to help you review, go to **bedfordstmartins.com/choicesconnections**.

---

(15) Delivering Your Speech *372*

For videos and LearningCurve quizzing to help you review, go to **bedfordstmartins.com/choicesconnections**.

16 Informative Speeches 400

▶ ✓ *For videos and LearningCurve quizzing to help you review, go to* **bedfordstmartins.com/choicesconnections**.

17 Persuasive Speeches 426

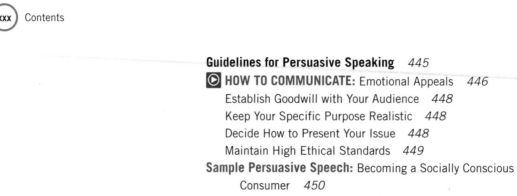

About the Authors

Dr. Steven McCornack,
Michigan State University

Dr. McCornack is an Associate Professor of Communication at Michigan State University, where he also serves as the Director of Undergraduate Studies, Honors Advisor, and Faculty Advisor to the Undergraduate Communication Association. His research interests include deception, message production, and family communication. Dr. McCornack teaches undergraduate and graduate courses on interpersonal communication, relational communication, and language/discourse. Since he began at MSU in 1988, he has received several awards for undergraduate teaching excellence, including the Amoco Foundation Excellence in Teaching Award, a Lilly Endowment Teaching Fellowship, the MSU Teacher/Scholar Award, and the MSU Alumni Excellence in Undergraduate Teaching Award. In 2013, he received the National Communication Association's Donald H. Ecroyd Award for Outstanding Teaching in Higher Education. Dr. McCornack received his BA from the University of Washington and his MA and PhD from the University of Illinois.

Dr. Joseph Ortiz,
Scottsdale Community College

Dr. Ortiz has taught for over 30 years, beginning in 1983 at Clovis Community College (NM). In 1989, he joined the faculty of Scottsdale Community College, where he teaches courses on human communication, interpersonal and small group communication, and digital storytelling. In support of student learning, Dr. Ortiz is heavily involved in the use of classroom assessment tools, service learning, collaborative learning methods, and the use of online technology. A campus leader, he has served as chair of the Fine Arts Division, faculty senate president, and interim Associate Dean of Instruction. Dr. Ortiz holds a BS in Speech from Lamar University in Texas, an MA in Communication from Eastern New Mexico University, and an EdD in Higher and Adult Education from Arizona State University.

CHOICES & CONNECTIONS

AN INTRODUCTION TO COMMUNICATION

1

Introduction to Communication

(**H**)is goal was simple: create a fun forum for talking about bands with other music enthusiasts.[1] As he describes, "I originally decided to host the festival so I could connect and hang with club owners and music lovers I knew in Kansas City and New Orleans." But little did newspaper editor Louis Black know that his brainchild—South by Southwest (SXSW)—would eventually morph into the world's largest multipurpose festival, featuring not just music but every type of entertainment, communication, and media technology imaginable.

Each spring, SXSW draws tens of thousands of musicians, filmmakers, tech designers, and spectators to Austin, Texas. More than 2,500 bands perform, and they are as talented as they are diverse: jazz saxophonist Grace Kelly, hip-hop producer RZA, indie band Vampire Weekend, Chicano rockers Los Lonely Boys. Dozens of films are debuted. Hundreds of games and apps are demoed. SXSW has even become a key way to break into various media industries. John Mayer, James Blunt, and the Polyphonic Spree were all signed by major music labels after appearing at SXSW. Movies debuting at SXSW include *The Hurt Locker*, *Bridesmaids*, and *The Cabin in the Woods*. Even Twitter first gained national (and international) popularity following heavy publicity at SXSW.

At the heart of SXSW, however, is communication. Festival organizers use social media such as Facebook, Vimeo, Twitter, and Google+ to coordinate and conduct the festival. Amid the various musical performances and film screenings, SXSW participants interact face-to-face with industry leaders, socialize at meet-ups with friends and new acquaintances, participate in group workshops, and even interview for jobs. Each day brings opportunities to listen in on panel discussions and presentations hosted by people like Facebook's Mark Zuckerberg,

Rita Quinn/Getty Images for SXSW

---

[1]All content in the opener adapted from Dream Share Project (2011) and http://sxsw.com.

musician Dave Grohl, Wikipedia cofounder Jimmy Wales, and filmmaker Lena Dunham. Many of these events are streamed live online, so people around the world can share in the experience. What began as quiet conversations in the darkened corners of night-clubs is now a multifaceted communication extravaganza.

Despite its size, impact, and global reach, SXSW remains dedicated to Louis Black's original intent: connecting people through communication. As he describes, "We've struggled hard to maintain the integrity of the event. . . . What we love most is the creative community that comes out of the event. SXSW may be huge, but it's fundamentally about people who love music and film and new media; and most importantly people who love to *talk* about it all with each other."

Communication connects us to one another. Whether you're attending a festival like SXSW or spending a normal day at school, work, or home, you interact with people one-on-one, in groups, and in public. You may text, tweet, post, e-mail, call, or talk face-to-face. You might give a presentation to a small or large audience or interview for a job.

Across all of these types and instances of communication, two things are important to keep in mind. First, *the communication choices you make are connected to the outcomes that follow.* When you communicate well, you increase the likelihood of desirable outcomes, such as successful group projects; persuasive presentations; and satisfying, healthy relationships. When you communicate poorly, you are more likely to generate negative outcomes, such as group dissatisfaction, confused audience members, and relationship turmoil.

Second, *different types of communication are connected to each other in fundamental ways.* Sure, texting a close friend is different from sending an e-mail to a work group or giving a speech in front of a class. However, these forms of communication also share similarities. Specifically, they involve presenting yourself to others, planning your messages, and using language to convey your thoughts. Because of these connections what you learn in every chapter of this book will apply to a wide variety of scenarios.

This book will help you build your communication skills by deepening your understanding of communication choices and their connections. In this chapter, you'll learn:

- What communication is and how the communication process works
- The goals that communication helps you achieve
- How the study of communication developed
- The characteristics of communication competence
- The choices and connections underlying your communication

What Is Communication?

LearningCurve can help you review! Go to **bedfordstmartins.com /choicesconnections**.

Lots of people believe that communication is just common sense. But people are not born knowing how to communicate well. Instead, they become good communicators by learning about communication concepts and theories, building skills, and practicing in their everyday lives. You can take the first step toward becoming a competent communicator by learning what communication is and why it matters.

When you think about communication and the role it plays in your life, what may leap to mind are the various challenges you face. For instance, "How can I get along better with my family?" "Why don't the other group members listen to my ideas?" or "What can I do to give better speeches?"

Merrick Morton/Columbia Pictures/Courtesy Everett Collection

Whether you're trying to uncover a mystery like Lisbeth Salander and Mikael Blomkvist in *The Girl with the Dragon Tattoo* or just meeting a friend for coffee, the messages you convey, the context of the situation, and the channel and media through which you interact all have an impact on your conversation.

To answer these questions and meet these challenges, you may rely on your gut sense of what you should do; for example, "I need to be more open about how I feel," "I should be more assertive," or "I should spend more time rehearsing."

Taking a class on communication is different than relying on intuition. When you're formally educated about communication, you learn information based on theory, research, and practice. This empowers you to broaden and deepen your skills as a communicator, allowing you to better handle communication challenges when they arise. Learning about communication begins with this basic question: What exactly is communication?

Defining Communication

The National Communication Association (2002), a professional organization representing communication teachers and scholars in the United States, defines **communication** as the process through which people use messages to generate meanings within and across contexts, cultures, channels, and media. This definition highlights five features of communication.

First, communication is a *process* that unfolds over time through a series of interconnected actions. Imagine you and your roommates are discussing how to set up the common areas in your apartment. If they ask for your opinion on furniture placement, you're likely to give it simply because they've asked. Their action of asking a question creates your action of answering. If they dismiss your suggestion and joke about how stupid it is, their actions may hurt your feelings. Later, when they ask you about how to decorate the living room, you may be more cautious about sharing your ideas out of fear of ridicule. Thinking of communication as a process means realizing that everything you and others say and do during encounters shapes what happens in that moment and in the future.

Second, people engaged in communication ("communicators") use *messages* to convey meaning. A **message** is the "package" of information transported during communication. When people exchange a series of messages, whether face-to-face or online, the result is an **interaction** (Watzlawick, Beavin, & Jackson, 1967).

Third, communication occurs in a seemingly endless variety of **contexts,** or situations. For instance, you communicate with others in class, at parties, at work, and at home. In each context, many different factors affect how you communicate. These factors include how much time you have, how many people are in the situation, and whether the setting is personal or professional. This is why you probably communicate differently with a friend during an intramural basketball game than when the two of you see each other in class the next day.

Fourth, people communicate through various channels. A **channel** is the sensory dimension along which communicators transmit information. The most common channels are auditory (sound), visual (sight), and tactile (touch). For example, your professor smiles at you and says, "You did a great job with your speech!" (visual and auditory channels), or a friend comforts you with a hug during a moment of sadness (tactile).

Fifth, to transmit information, communicators use a broad range of **media,** or tools for exchanging messages. Media can include texting, tweeting, posting, e-mailing, making a phone call, or talking face-to-face. Often people use several different media at once. For example, you text a friend while you're checking Tumblr or Instagram, you call your mother while you're scrolling through her latest e-mail to you, or you Google reviews for a movie you're interested in seeing while Skyping a colleague who's in a different office. Chapter 3 (Mediated Communication) will explore more about how technology influences your communication.

Why You Communicate

Why do you communicate? This question may strike you as silly because the answer seems so obvious. You communicate to share your thoughts and feelings to others, right? Although that is true, communication also helps you meet three types of goals (Clark & Delia, 1979).

The first type is **self-presentation goals,** which involve presenting yourself in certain ways so others will view you as you want them to. For example, suppose you're the president of the electronic dance music (EDM) club on campus. To get a permit to hold a dance at the student union, you have to make a presentation to the student organization council. You want the council to see you as a credible, trustworthy person who will organize the gathering responsibly. Only then will they approve your permit application, so you tailor your communication accordingly.

The second type is **instrumental goals**—practical objectives you want to achieve or tasks you want to accomplish. For instance, if you're leading a meeting to put together the permit proposal for your dance, you'll remind other group members to stay focused if the discussion starts to wander.

The third type is **relationship goals**—building, maintaining, or terminating bonds with others. For example, if you want to build a friendship with another dance club member, you might ask her to join you for coffee before you audition DJs for the dance.

Communication Models

Think about all the different ways you communicate each day. You text your best friend, saying you're done with your exam and are ready to be picked up. You present awards at your soccer team's end-of-season banquet, acting more animated when you see people's attention start to wander. You spend the evening with your brother, reliving and retelling stories from your childhood.

But how does the communication process differ in each scenario? Sometimes you create messages and send them to receivers (like your text message). Other times you present messages to recipients, and they indicate their understanding and interest (like the audience members at the soccer banquet). Or you may mutually create meanings with others, with no one serving as "sender" or "receiver" (like you and your brother sharing family stories). These scenarios reflect three different ways of viewing the communication process: the *linear model*, the *interactive model*, and the *transactional model*.

As you continue reading about these models, keep a few things in mind. First, communication scholars developed these models to examine and describe how communication works. Second, the models represent a historical evolution of scholarly thought, from a relatively simple depiction of communication as a linear process (the linear model) to one that views communication as a complicated process that is mutually crafted (the transactional model). Finally, each model doesn't necessarily represent a good or a bad way of thinking about communication. Instead, each offers a different way of identifying the important elements affecting the communication process.

Linear Communication Model. The linear model was the first formal model of communication and was created more than sixty years ago by engineers at Bell Labs to explain how information is transmitted across telephone lines (Shannon & Weaver, 1949). According to the **linear communication model,** communication is an activity in which information flows in one direction, from a starting point to an end point. The linear model contains several components. In addition to a *message* and a *channel*, there is a **sender** (or senders)—the individual who generates the information to be communicated, packages it into a message, and chooses one or more channels for sending it. The person (or people) for whom a message is intended is the **receiver.** The transmission of the message is often affected by **noise**— distractions that change how the message is received. Noise may originate outside the communicators—such as poor reception during a cell-phone call. Or it can come from the communicators themselves, such as when distracting thoughts cause senders' or receivers' attention to drift. (See Figure 1.1.)

Although the linear model was conceived more than six decades ago, it still accurately illustrates the broad range of communication forms you experience every day. For example, much of your online communication—including tweets, texts, e-mails, and wall posts—reflects this model. Certain public-speaking contexts may also fit, especially those in which you present prepared scripts to audiences who are expected to sit quietly and listen without responding to or challenging you. But the linear model doesn't accurately

FIGURE 1.1
LINEAR MODEL OF COMMUNICATION

MESSAGES COMMUNICATED THROUGH CHANNELS

SENDER

RECEIVER

NOISE

explain other communication forms, such as face-to-face conversation. For example, when you converse with a friend face-to-face, you may speak in partial sentences and rely on the other person to mentally fill in the missing information. The linear model doesn't account for the back-and-forth flow of such encounters.

Interactive Communication Model. The **interactive communication model** also views communication as a process involving senders and receivers. However, according to this model, communication is influenced by two additional factors: feedback and fields of experience (Schramm, 1954). **Feedback** consists of the verbal and nonverbal messages coming from recipients in response to messages. For example, by nodding and saying, "Uh-huh" or "That's right," recipients let senders know they've received and understood messages. Feedback also lets receivers indicate their approval or disapproval of messages. **Fields of experience** consist of the beliefs, attitudes, values, and experiences that each participant brings to a communication event. People with similar fields of experience are more likely to understand each other than are individuals with dissimilar fields of experience. (See Figure 1.2.)

Like the linear model, the interactive model accurately describes a range of communication forms that you experience. For example, while you're giving a speech in your class, you may notice the reactions of your classmates—such as fidgeting or lack of eye contact—and then modify your message on

FIGURE 1.2
INTERACTIVE MODEL OF COMMUNICATION

MESSAGES COMMUNICATED THROUGH CHANNELS

FEEDBACK

SENDER

RECEIVER

FIELD OF EXPERIENCE

FIELD OF EXPERIENCE

NOISE

Kira Kuznetsova/Shutterstock

the spot as needed, to capture their attention and get your message across. Classroom instruction, group presentations, and weekly team meetings among coworkers are often viewed as interactive.

Also like the linear model, the interactive model presents communication as a process in which there is both a clearly designated and active sender and a receiver. But it overlooks the active role that receivers often play in constructing the meaning of communication events, as well as instances in which people jointly create meaning. At a family reunion, for example, your uncle starts droning on as usual his most recent round of golf. You and your sister glance at each other and immediately understand the meaning of your shared look. If you were to put words to this meaning, you would both be saying, "Oh no, here he goes again!" But neither of you is the sender or the receiver in this instance; instead, you *collaboratively* create communication meaning. The transactional communication model can help explain such encounters.

Transactional Communication Model. The **transactional communication model** views communication as multidirectional; that is, participants mutually influence one another's communication behavior (Miller & Steinberg, 1975). According to this model, there aren't senders or receivers. Instead, participants constantly exchange verbal and nonverbal messages and feedback to collaboratively create meanings. (See Figure 1.3.) This may be something as

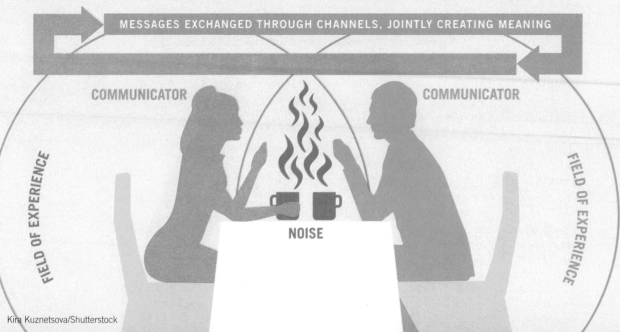

FIGURE 1.3

TRANSACTIONAL MODEL OF COMMUNICATION

MESSAGES EXCHANGED THROUGH CHANNELS, JOINTLY CREATING MEANING

COMMUNICATOR   COMMUNICATOR

FIELD OF EXPERIENCE   FIELD OF EXPERIENCE

NOISE

Kira Kuznetsova/Shutterstock

simple as a shared look, as in the preceding example with your sister and your uncle. It may be an animated and intense conversation between you and a friend, in which the meanings exchanged go way beyond the words that are said. It may even involve people jointly creating acts of communication. Sociologist Jurgen Streek (1980), in discussing the transactional nature of communication, describes a classroom roll call he once observed. The teacher asked, "Now, where is . . ." and before she could complete her query, a student chimed in "Ernesto?" knowing just who the teacher was seeking. Such instances illustrate how we often build communication collaboratively rather than simply receiving or sending messages.

The transactional communication model intuitively captures encounters that seem interpersonal in nature. These include instances such as you and your romantic partner having a phone conversation in which the words seem secondary to the feelings being conveyed, as well as conversations with close friends, in which a few key words or looks instantly convey a wealth of shared information (we discuss interpersonal communication in more detail in Chapters 9 and 10). But the transactional model doesn't fit certain types of online communication, such as e-mails, wall posts, tweets, and texts, in which senders and receivers are more clearly designated, and the communication is better described as either linear or interactive.

Studying Communication

> Now that you have a better understanding of what communication is, let's look at how people have studied communication throughout the ages, and the types of communication that teachers and scholars focus on today. Understanding the past, present, and future of the communication field will help you apply what you learn to your everyday life.

The authors of this book, Steve and Joe, both started college with the goal of becoming lawyers. But their plans—and their lives—changed when they began to study communication. For Joe, the turning point came during an afternoon jog with an attorney named Tom Roebuck, who occasionally trained with Joe's university cross-country team. While talking about classes and potential majors, Tom told Joe, "I can't think of any better preparation for law school than a communication degree." The next day, Joe switched his major. As he continued his course work, he grew fascinated with communication as a field of study and ultimately decided to pursue a teaching career instead of going to law school.

Steve's story is similar. As an undergrad at the University of Washington, he visited his professor, Mac Parks, during office hours. While chatting about communication research, Mac suddenly asked Steve, "Have you ever thought about going into the field?" Steve admitted that he didn't even know what "the field of communication" was. When Mac told him, Steve realized that communication—not the law—was his calling.

Studying communication fosters real-life skills that are valuable in the workplace. Whether you're a nurse, an athlete, or an author and businesswoman like Facebook COO Sheryl Sandberg, knowing how to competently communicate can make or break your success.

(Clockwise from top left) Hero Images/Getty Images; Imaginechina via AP Images; John Rhodes/Fort Worth Star-Telegram/MCT via Getty Images

For some of you, the communication class you're taking (for which you are reading this book) will be your only exposure to the field. For others, this class—and other courses in communication—may inspire you to become communication majors. You might even experience the same thing Joe and Steve did: the realization that you want to devote your life to studying and teaching communication. But regardless of whether you take one communication class, make communication your college major, or build a career involving communication, learning about communication connects you to a scholarly field that dates back thousands of years.

A Brief History of Communication

The field of communication is undeniably modern, with its attention to topics like social media, online relationships, and the effects of video games. But it has ancient roots. By understanding a little about the field's history, you can see how the concepts and practices you'll learn about in this book evolved from the past into their present-day forms.

Communication in Antiquity. Communication is an academic discipline that goes back thousands of years and traverses many different cultures. For example, one of the earliest books ever written—the maxims of the Egyptian sage Ptahhotep (2200 B.C.E.)—offers suggestions for improving your communication (Horne, 1917). In this ancient guidebook, Ptahhotep encourages people to be truthful, kind, and tolerant in their communication. He urges readers to practice active listening, especially in situations in which people lack experience, because "to not do so is to embrace ignorance." He also emphasizes mindfulness in using language, noting that "good words are more difficult to find than emeralds."

Almost 2,000 years after Ptahhotep, the communication tradition known as rhetoric emerged. **Rhetoric** is the theory and practice of persuading others through speech (Dues & Brown, 2004), and it became a formal discipline of study in ancient Greece and Rome (Kennedy, 1999). In Greece, Socrates and his student Plato were among the first to debate the nature of rhetoric. Socrates thought of rhetoric not as a philosophy but as a practical skill that people could gain through experience (Kennedy, 1999). Socrates and Plato also knew that people could use communication skills in unethical as well as ethical ways, and they argued strongly against using words to manipulate or exploit others. But it was Aristotle—perhaps the best-known ancient Greek scholar—who taught that ethical persuasion required a speaker to demonstrate credibility, provide logical reasoning, and appeal to the emotions of the listeners. As you'll learn in Chapter 17, Aristotle's teachings are still very relevant today in understanding how to develop a persuasive speech.

The study of rhetoric was also a concern of ancient Romans. Statesman and orator Cicero noted three practical objectives of public speaking: to instruct, to persuade, and to honor (Clarke, 1953). These goals are still discussed in modern public-speaking courses as informative, persuasive, and special occasion speeches. Cicero also outlined five requirements of speech crafting and presentation that are still in use today: invention (reasoning out truth to make your case compelling), arrangement (organizing the information you want to present), style (selecting suitable words to convey the information), memory (knowing your subject and remembering your words), and delivery (controlling your body and voice when presenting your speech). In Chapters 13–17, you'll learn how these requirements guide the preparation and delivery of speeches.

Communication in the Early 20th Century. Throughout the era stretching from ancient Rome to the close of the 19th century, communication scholars stayed focused on rhetoric. In the 1900s, however, things started changing. Stimulated by philosophical interest in the human mind and behavior, scholars across a broad range of disciplines began studying forms of communication other than rhetoric (Knapp, Daly, Albada, & Miller, 2002). For example, in 1927, political scientist Harold Lasswell detailed the four persuasive aims of governmental propaganda: to create hatred against the enemy, to preserve friendship with allies, to gain the cooperation of neutral parties, and to demoralize the enemy. Harvard business professor Elton Mayo examined the effects of coworker interactions on productivity, giving rise to the human relations movement and the recognition that supportiveness is crucial for competent workplace communication (Roethlisberger & Dickson, 1939). Psychologist Jean Piaget (1926) analyzed the role that children's ability to *perspective-take* (see things from others' viewpoint) played in shaping their communication. By World War II, dozens of scholars in several different disciplines were studying communication and communication-related topics, such as the effect of environments on interaction, empathy, and conflict.

Communication after World War II. Immediately following World War II, interest in the field of communication exploded, mostly owing to the use of mass media propaganda during the war. Countries on each side had harnessed film and radio to send messages on a massive scale to their respective populations, convincing them that their cause was just and that the enemy was "evil." With so many professors wanting to research communication, and so many students wanting to learn about it, universities began creating dedicated communication departments. Some schools housed communication studies researchers alongside rhetorical scholars, creating departments focused on speech communication.

By the early 1970s, dozens of communication and speech communication departments existed in the United States. Colleges and universities taught classes in the traditional areas of public speaking and rhetoric, but they also introduced new areas, such as mass media effects, communication in relationships, group discussion, and organizational communication. As the discipline became further unified, it attracted even more interest among scholars and students. Topics of interest diversified further. By the end of the 20th century, nonverbal communication, gender and communication, communication across cultures, health communication, and communication technologies became standard offerings in undergraduate curricula at hundreds of American colleges and universities, and institutions outside of the United States began to offer communication classes as well.

Today, tens of thousands of students around the world graduate each year with majors in communication, and millions more take communication classes. These students learn about cutting-edge research, examining such things as how others' online posts about you influence people's perception of you (discussed in Chapter 3), verbal aggression and cyberbullying (Chapter 5), how to work productively in a virtual group (Chapter 11), and how to deal with speech anxiety (Chapter 15). Armed with a broad knowledge of communication theory and practical skills, students majoring in communication go on to pursue careers in areas as diverse as human resource management, public relations, sales, marketing, sports broadcasting, media production, news media, advertising, community relations, and political consulting. To see how being skilled in communication may apply to your career path, see Table 1.1.

TABLE 1.1

CAREERS IN COMMUNICATION[2]

CAREER PATH	WHAT CAN I DO?	HOW CAN I GET THERE?
BUSINESS	• Sales • Human Resources • Insurance • Real Estate • Entrepreneur	• Develop strong verbal and written communication, interpersonal, and analytical skills. • Seek leadership roles in other campus organizations. • Learn to work well on a team.
PUBLIC RELATIONS & ADVERTISING	• Public Relations • Advertising • Marketing • Creative Directing	• Develop excellent writing and public-speaking skills. • Serve as public relations officer of an organization. • Develop a portfolio of writing samples, ad campaigns, and other relevant work.
MEDIA	• Writing • Editing • Copywriting • Publishing • Broadcasting	• Take courses in journalism, broadcasting, public relations, and advertising. • Develop excellent interpersonal, presentation, and research skills. • Work for campus or local newspaper, radio station, or television station.
 **GOVERNMENT & LAW**	• Community Affairs • Campaigning • Lobbying • Social Services • Prosecution • Defense • Nonprofit or Public Interest	• Develop strong research skills and attention to detail. • Participate in debate or forensic team to hone communication skills. • Take courses in conflict management and develop negotiation skills.
EDUCATION	• Teaching • Research • Information/Library Science • Administration and Student Support Services	• Develop strong interpersonal communication and public-speaking skills. • Get involved in campus leadership roles in residence halls, student unions/activities, programming boards, orientation, admissions, etc. • Learn to work well with a variety of people.

[2]Table 1.1 data from "What Can I Do With This Major?" retrieved from: http://whatcanidowiththismajor.com/major /communication-studies/

Types of Communication

As the preceding history illustrates, communication is a diverse field with a rich past. Although many specific topics are currently being studied and taught (such as doctor-patient communication, information flow within organizations, and deception), the field as a whole can be divided into four broad types: mediated communication (Chapter 3), interpersonal communication (Chapters 9–10), small group communication (Chapters 11–12), and public communication (Chapters 13–17). Throughout this book, we explore the differences and connections between these types.

Mediated communication is separated ("mediated") by some type of technological device. You use mediated communication when you make phone calls, send text messages or e-mails, tweet, use FaceTime or Skype, and post messages online. As you'll see later in this book, mediated communication is best used to meet certain types of goals. For example, text messaging is fine for planning a meeting location for your study group (instrumental goal). However, you probably wouldn't want to use texting to resolve a disagreement with your romantic partner (relationship goal).

Interpersonal communication is communication between two people in which the messages exchanged have a significant impact on the participants' thoughts, emotions, behaviors, and relationship. Through interpersonal communication, you build, maintain, and end bonds with your friends, family members, lovers, and other relationship partners.

Small group communication involves three or more interdependent persons who share a common identity (such as membership on a team) and who communicate to achieve common goals or purposes. For example, a group might come together to complete a class project, organize a fund-raiser, or produce music. Small group communication involves unique challenges, such as the need to coordinate group members' responsibilities, build group unity, clarify expectations, and accommodate members' diverse communication styles.

Public communication is the process of preparing and delivering a message to an audience to achieve a specific purpose (also known as public speaking). For instance, you will probably have to give a speech for this class. (This may sound scary, but don't worry—we have advice in Chapter 15 to manage your anxiety.) You might also need to communicate publicly in other situations, such as giving a talk to a youth group or presenting a project idea to your coworkers by videoconference.

These four types of communication differ in terms of their main purpose, the number of people involved, and their nature (linear, interactive, or transactional). Yet they also are *connected* to one another—in history and in current practice. Specifically, in all four types, people use messages to generate meanings. In addition, all four types are affected by views of self, perceptions of others, communicators' cultural backgrounds and listening skills, and the use of verbal and nonverbal communication. (We will explore these areas together in Chapters 2, 4, 5, 6, and 7.) In addition, you can use the four types of communication to pursue self-presentation, instrumental, and relationship goals.

Perhaps most important, the choices you make when using any type of communication strongly influence the outcomes you experience. When you make good choices, you're more likely to get positive outcomes. When you make poor choices, negative outcomes often follow. What does it mean to make "good" choices and communicate "well"? We tackle that question in the next section.

DOUBLE TAKE

MEDIATED & PUBLIC COMMUNICATION

Whether you're sending a text or making a speech, different types of communication are often connected. In addition to what is pointed out below, what connections can you make between the different types of communication you participate in each day?

Mediated devices aid in relationship maintenance (interpersonal communication)

Group texts help teammates organize (small group communication)

Presentations can motivate teams to take action (public communication)

Speeches viewed by online audiences can have a global reach (mediated communication)

Cavan Images/Getty Images

Hill Street Studios/Blend Images/Corbis

Communication Competence

Communication is a choice. How you choose to phrase your messages, exhibit facial expressions, and even approach a conflict is up to you. Each time you make such a choice, you have the opportunity to strive for competence. This can help you set the stage for success in your own life.

Cesar Chavez transformed the lives of thousands by persuading powerful people to act on behalf of the poorest laborers in America.[3] How? He mastered the art of *communication competence*: consistently interacting with others in an appropriate, effective, and ethical fashion. A compelling public speaker, Chavez effectively rallied migrant laborers to organize strikes protesting horrific work conditions in the fields, eventually leading to the creation of the United Farm Workers (UFW) organization. He was equally skilled at appropriately adapting his language to lawmakers, communicating the plight of farmworkers in poignant terms to those who controlled the laws governing them. Although landowners attacked him and his fellow workers with shotguns and dogs, he remained steadfastly committed to ethical communication, never lashing back at those who subjected him and others to violence. His competence ultimately paid off in an enormously positive and profound outcome: the creation of new laws ensuring better working conditions and higher wages for field laborers.

Chavez used his communication competence to manage groups and move audiences to action. But he was equally talented at interpersonal communication. For example, after delivering a speech in Washington, D.C., Chavez was ushered away by his bodyguards. When he spied UFW workers who had been volunteering to help with the event, he veered toward them, even as his guards tried to force him toward his car. Chavez shook the workers' hands, saying, "I noticed how you stayed here all day and worked so hard. It is because of you there is a movement. I may be the one who does the speaking, but it is you who make the movement what it is!"

Cesar Chavez received many honors, including the Águila Azteca—the highest civilian award in Mexico—and the U.S. Presidential Medal of Freedom. His legacy is about justice, nonviolence, and help for the needy. It's also proof that communication can change the world.

Communication is the means through which you achieve your goals (Burleson, Metts, & Kirch, 2000). But it is the *competence* of your communication that determines the *quality* of your outcomes. Competent communicators report higher levels of educational and professional achievement, more satisfaction with their relationships (including happier marriages), and better psychological and physical health (Spitzberg & Cupach, 2002).

Throughout the book, we explore the knowledge and skills necessary for strengthening your competence in all types of communication. In this chapter,

---

[3]All information regarding Cesar Chavez is excerpted from the California Department of Education (n.d.) and the County of Los Angeles Public Library (n.d.).

Jason Laure/The Image Works

Cesar Chavez's ability to adapt his language to connect with both migrant laborers and lawmakers was crucial for his success in the United Farm Workers organization. How does your manner of speaking change according to the person receiving your message?

we lay the foundation for your learning by explaining how to achieve communication competence.

Understanding Communication Competence

Communication competence means consistently communicating in ways that are *appropriate* (your communication follows accepted norms), *effective* (your communication helps you achieve your goals), and *ethical* (your communication treats people fairly) (Spitzberg & Cupach, 1984; Wiemann, 1977).

Appropriateness. **Appropriateness** is the degree to which your communication matches expectations regarding how people should communicate. In any setting, norms govern what people "should" and "shouldn't" say, and how they "should" and "shouldn't" act. For example, telling jokes or personal stories about your love life isn't appropriate during a job interview, but it might be appropriate when you're hanging out with close friends who know you and your sense of humor. Competent communicators understand when such norms exist and adapt their communication accordingly.

Competent communicators also know that overemphasizing appropriateness can backfire. If you *always* adapt your communication to what others want, you may end up making poor choices. For example, you might give in to peer pressure (Burgoon, 1995). Think of a friend who always does what others want and never argues for his own desires. Is he a competent communicator? No, because he'll probably seldom achieve goals that are important to him. How

When Piper Chapman began her one-year sentence at a women's prison in *Orange Is the New Black*, her idea of appropriateness quickly changed as she assimilated to her new surroundings. How do you deal with situations where what you deem as appropriate doesn't line up with what's occurring around you?

Jessica Miglio/© Netflix/courtesy Everett Collection

about the boss who tells employees that their work is fine even when it isn't? Is she competent? No, because she's withholding information her employees need to improve their job performance. Competence means striking a healthy balance between appropriateness and other important considerations, such as achievement of goals and the obligation to communicate honestly.

Effectiveness. **Effectiveness** is the ability to use communication to accomplish the three types of goals discussed earlier (self-presentation, instrumental, and relationship). Sometimes you have to make trade-offs—prioritizing certain goals over others, even if you want to pursue all of them. For instance, to collaborate effectively with groups, you have to know when to stay on task and when to socialize. Say that you and several other students form an intramural softball team to compete in a campus league. At the first team meeting, you may want to come across as athletic, funny, and likable (self-presentation goal) and begin building friendships with others on the team (relationship goal). But if you don't focus your communication during the meeting on creating a practice schedule (instrumental goal), the team won't be ready to play its first game. Chapter 12 discusses how you can be an effective leader and communicator in such situations.

Ethics. **Ethics** is the set of moral principles that guide your behavior toward others (Spitzberg & Cupach, 2002). At a minimum, you are ethically obligated to avoid intentionally hurting others through your communication. By this standard, communication that's intended to erode a person's self-esteem, that expresses intolerance or hatred, that intimidates or threatens others' physical well-being, or that expresses violence is unethical and therefore incompetent (Parks, 1994).

However, to be an ethical communicator, you must go beyond simply not doing harm. During every encounter—whether it's interpersonal, a small group, or a public presentation—you need to treat others with respect and communicate with them honestly, kindly, and positively (Englehardt, 2001). As you'll see in Chapter 3, mediated communication presents unique challenges for ethical communication. To help you make ethical choices in all situations, consider the guidelines in the National Communication Association's Credo for Ethical Communication (1999) in Figure 1.4.

In communication situations that are simple, comfortable, and pleasant, it's easy to behave appropriately, effectively, and ethically. True competence, however, develops when you consistently communicate competently across *all* situations that you face—even ones that are uncertain, complex, and unpleasant. A critical goal of this book is to equip you with the knowledge and skills you need to handle those more challenging communication situations. For example, the How to Communicate: Competent Conversations feature on pages 22–23 asks you to adapt your understanding of communication competence to an unpleasant encounter.

FIGURE 1.4

NCA CREDO FOR ETHICAL COMMUNICATION

Questions of right and wrong arise whenever people communicate. Ethical communication is fundamental to responsible thinking, decision making, and the development of relationships and communities within and across contexts, cultures, channels, and media. . . . Therefore we, the members of the National Communication Association, endorse and are committed to practicing the following principles of ethical communication:

- We advocate truthfulness, accuracy, honesty, and reason as essential to the integrity of communication.
- We endorse freedom of expression, diversity of perspective, and tolerance of dissent to achieve the informed and responsible decision making fundamental to a civil society.
- We strive to understand and respect other communicators before evaluating and responding to their messages.

- We promote access to communication resources and opportunities as necessary to fulfill human potential and contribute to the well-being of families, communities, and society.
- We promote communication climates of caring and mutual understanding that respect the unique needs and characteristics of individual communicators.
- We condemn communication that degrades individuals and humanity through distortion, intimidation, coercion, and violence, and through the expression of intolerance and hatred.

- We are committed to the courageous expression of personal convictions in pursuit of fairness and justice.
- We advocate sharing information, opinions, and feelings when facing significant choices while also respecting privacy and confidentiality.
- We accept responsibility for the short- and long-term consequences for our own communication and expect the same of others.

COMPETENT CONVERSATIONS

 One way to improve your communication competence is by adapting your messages to others' behaviors. Learn how to navigate difficult conversations by going to LaunchPad at **bedfordstmartins.com/choicesconnections** and completing the **How to Communicate video scenario** for Chapter 1 to practice your skills.

CONSIDER THIS:
Your professor assigns you to work with Jacob, your ex's best friend. When you and your ex were dating, Jacob was friendly and supportive, and the two of you got along well. But the breakup was ugly, and you and Jacob haven't talked since. As you meet with Jacob to brainstorm ideas, there's obvious tension. You decide to break the ice and ask him how he's doing. Jacob responds with an icy "Fine," then says, "So, have you destroyed any new lives recently?"

WHAT WOULD YOU DO?
The following advise illustrates how competent communication skills can keep the encounter productive. As you watch the video, consider how the dialogue reflects each element of competence. Then, test your knowledge of key skills, and create your own responses to the **What if? video prompts**.

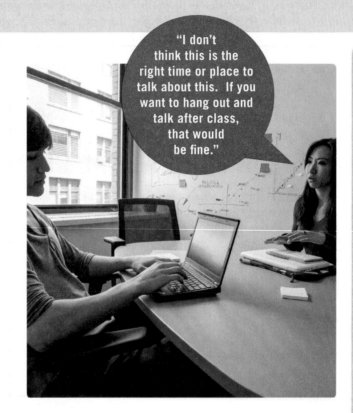

"I don't think this is the right time or place to talk about this. If you want to hang out and talk after class, that would be fine."

1 **KEEP YOUR COMMUNICATION APPROPRIATE,** given the setting, by not responding angrily to Jacob's taunt and by offering an alternative encounter for personal discussion.

② COMMUNICATE EFFECTIVELY

by keeping your conversation focused on the task at hand and by encouraging Jacob to do the same.

"I've got a couple of ideas for the project, but I'd like to hear your ideas first."

③ MAKE YOUR MESSAGES ETHICAL

by treating Jacob with kindness and respect, despite his rudeness.

"I know you're really angry with me, and I admire you for that, because it shows you're loyal and devoted to your friend. But I'm hoping we can put the past behind us for the sake of the project. What do you think?"

 WHAT IF? But what if things don't work out as shown? Test your ability to adapt your communication by watching the What if? videos and planning a response for each situation.

1. What would you say when Jacob attempts to end the encounter by saying, "I have no interest in talking to you—whether it's now or later"?

2. How would you get Jacob's focus off the past when he says, "Yeah, I can see why you'd want to leave the past behind. That's what you do, isn't it: destroy people, bail, and then say, 'Can't we leave the past behind?'"

Putting Competence into Practice

Competent communicators know how to translate their knowledge into **communication skills**—repeatable goal-directed behaviors and behavioral patterns that they routinely practice (Spitzberg & Cupach, 2002). Throughout this book, we provide you with skills you can use in all of the communication challenges you'll face in life, so you can produce positive outcomes. To illustrate, consider two of the most important skills you'll need in your communication toolbox: knowing when and how to use mediated communication competently; and knowing how to appropriately, effectively, and ethically interact with people whose cultural backgrounds differ from your own. As Chapter 3 discusses, using mediated communication competently means making wise choices regarding when to communicate online versus off, recognizing the three Ps of mediated communication (powerful, public, and permanent), and adapting your messages to ensure clarity. In a similar fashion, Chapter 4 will teach you intercultural competence: how to appropriately adapt your communication to the other communicators, effectively balance their goals with your own, and treat them with the same dignity and respect that you want for yourself.

Of course, to use your knowledge and skills to improve your communication, you must also be motivated to do so. If you do not believe your communication needs improvement, or if you believe that competence is unimportant or no more than simple common sense, your competence will be difficult, if not impossible, to refine. But if you are strongly motivated to improve your communication, you can master the knowledge and skills necessary to develop competence.

Choices and Connections

When you're communicating, everything you say and do counts—and is connected to what comes after. There are no "take-backs" or "do-overs." That's why it's so important to know how to make good communication choices.

In season three of the IFC skit-comedy series *Portlandia*, an investigative journalist exposes the city's mayor as the biggest "energy hog" in Portland—a city known for its environmental sensibilities. Searching his apartment with his assistants, the mayor discovers the source of his energy consumption: he has left his home printer running continuously in test mode for 10 years because he didn't know it could be turned off. Hosting a press conference to explain his error to an outraged public, the mayor gets caught up in the moment and hurls the offending printer into the Willamette River. Of course, this only makes matters worse. Now he's not only an energy hog but also a polluter. He resigns in shame and becomes a goat-herding recluse.

Though the skit is meant to poke fun at politicians and environmentalists, it illustrates two serious points that together form the central theme of this book. First, every choice you make as a communicator is connected to the outcomes that follow. Second, the different types of communication you engage in are connected to each other by similarities that vastly outweigh their differences.

Scott Green/© IFC/Courtesy: Everett Collection

The incompetent choices made by Kyle MacLachlan's character in *Portlandia* quickly got him demoted from mayor of Portland to secluded goatherd. When have you made a poor communication choice? How did you recover?

Communication Choices

As we've said before in this chapter, your communication choices affect the outcomes you experience. Take something as simple as how you respond to an angry text message from a family member. If you fire back an equally hostile response, the situation escalates, and the two of you are now fighting. What's more, the conflict will likely spread to other family members, as each person weighs in on what happened and takes sides in the battle. Think about what might happen if you respond competently instead. For example, you take the time to craft a message asking why the other person is upset, making sure to avoid sarcastic or accusatory responses. Then you offer to help, and reassure him or her of your support. These choices are far less likely to lead to a fight or spread conflict to others.

The fact that your communication choices affect your outcomes means your communication is irreversible. When you post a message online, send a text or tweet, leave a voice-mail message, or express a thought out loud during a group meeting, you set in motion the series of outcomes that follow. Once you've communicated something, you can't take it back. That's why it's important to think carefully before you communicate, asking yourself, "Is what I'm about to say going to lead to outcomes I want?" If the answer is no, then you'll want to revise your message.

Of course, communication (by definition) involves interaction with others, and the choices *they* make influence your outcomes as well. But you can't control how others choose to behave toward you—only how you behave toward them. Consequently, the best—and only—path you have for improving your outcomes is to take control of your communication and improve your

MAKING COMMUNICATION CHOICES
TIME FOR PAYBACK?

① CONSIDER THE DILEMMA

You dated Riley for over a year. You were in love and thought the two of you might even get married someday. But last week you discovered that Riley had been cheating on you for the last two months. You were so furious and hurt that you broke it off, and you haven't spoken with Riley since. Riley has been texting and e-mailing you, begging forgiveness, but you haven't responded.

One night you're studying with your roommate when you get a text from Riley. But instead of being another apology, it's a request. Riley let you borrow a thumb drive last week, which apparently contains all of Riley's notes for an important project, and Riley's hard drive just crashed—making the thumb drive the only copy of these materials. Riley wants to come by and get it. You're just about to text "OK" when your roommate interjects, "Are you insane!? After what Riley did to you? You should throw it away and tell Riley you can't find it." The more you think about it, the more the idea appeals to you. You're still angry and sad, and you want to make Riley suffer! This would be a little payback. Just then, Riley texts you again, "Do u have my drive? I really need it! Please text me back!"

② CONNECT THE RESEARCH

There's no question that betrayal in a close relationship is one of the worst experiences you can have. Unfortunately, some people respond to betrayal by seeking revenge. Revenge comes in many forms, most of which are as unethical and destructive as the behavior triggering the vengeance. Canadian researchers Susan Boon, Vicki Deveau, and Alishia Alibhai (2009) found that vengeful partners commonly exact their revenge online, by posting negative photos of their lovers on Facebook or blogging about their lovers' deficient sexual attributes. In extreme cases, vengeance may involve sabotaging partners at work so they get fired, or de-enrolling them from their college or university.

Partners who seek revenge report a host of motives for doing so, but the most common involve a desire to "have power over a partner" and "to make the partner suffer" (Boon, Deveau, & Alibhai, 2009). People seeking revenge often presume they will feel better once "justice has been served." However, research by communication scholar Stephen Yoshimura (2007) examining the aftermath of revenge suggests that people not only continue to feel angry about the betrayal but also feel remorseful and anxious about repercussions from their vengeful acts. So although you may be tempted to seek vengeance in the wake of a betrayal, keep this in mind: not only is such behavior unethical (two wrongs do not make a right), but you may suffer even more if you behave in this way.

③ COMMUNICATE

Before making a communication choice, consider the facts of the situation, and think about the revenge research. Also, reflect on what you've learned so far about the connections between communication choices and outcomes (pp. 24–27), ethics (pp. 20–21), and communication competence (pp. 18–24). Then answer these questions:

❶ Is it ethical to throw away the thumb drive and tell Riley you can't find it?

❷ If you follow your roommate's suggestion, what will be the outcomes? Will you feel better? Will your relationship with Riley be improved? What about the long-term consequences of your choice?

❸ What are you going to text Riley?

choices. When you recognize that your communication is a choice and then elect to communicate appropriately, effectively, and ethically, you'll have done all that you can to foster satisfying communication outcomes in your personal and professional lives. This book shows you how to make competent communication choices in a wide range of situations—even when others do not.

✓ **LearningCurve** can help you review! Go to **bedfordstmartins.com /choicesconnections.**

Communication Connections

In addition to recognizing the link between communication choices and outcomes, your communication competence will be boosted by learning the connections that exist between the different types of communication. Yes, communicating face-to-face is different from interacting online, just as conversing within a group is different from presenting in front of an audience. Yet many similar skills connect them. Consider, for example, what it means to be a "good listener." It matters little whether you're listening to an audience member's question following a presentation or Skyping with your sister who is overseas. The characteristics that constitute being a good listener (and that we discuss in Chapter 7) transcend communication type and context. Becoming a competent communicator means understanding the connections between different forms of communication, as well as the skills that are unique to each.

Throughout this book, we will provide you with numerous examples illustrating the connections between different communication types. For instance, you'll see how determining your communication purpose is important whether you're planning a group meeting or preparing a speech; realize how the skills used for managing interpersonal conflict can help when problems arise in teams; and discover that sharing appropriate and relevant information about yourself (known as *self-disclosure*) is important for both creating small group bonds and establishing rapport with an audience during a speech.

But perhaps even more important than these specific points of connection is the fact that *your communication and your communication skills connect you to other human beings.* Communication is your primary vehicle for exchanging meaning, achieving goals, connecting with others emotionally, and building personal and professional relationships with others.

The importance of communication for connecting you to others makes it essential that you base your communication choices on the best knowledge you have. No one would consider making a decision about collegiate majors, future careers, or major purchases without first gathering the most trustworthy information available. Communication should be no different. That's where this book—and the class you're taking—come in. We (your authors: Steve and Joe) will provide you with the best research, theory, and practical skills training that the field of communication has to offer. As you absorb this knowledge and start applying these skills in your own life, you'll position yourself to make the best communication choices. As a result, you'll boost the odds of creating positive outcomes in your personal and professional lives, including healthy, satisfying connections with others.

CHAPTER ① REVIEW

CHAPTER RECAP

- **Communication** is the process through which people use **messages** to generate meanings within and across **contexts**, cultures, **channels**, and **media**.
- You can use communication to help you achieve three types of goals: **self-presentation, instrumental,** and **relationship.** Various *communication models* (**linear, interactive,** and **transactional**) help you understand how this communication takes place.
- Although the field of communication began with the study of **rhetoric** in ancient Greece, today it is composed of four main types: **mediated, interpersonal, small group,** and **public communication**.
- **Communication competence** determines the quality of your communication and is a combination of **appropriateness, effectiveness,** and **ethics**.
- There are two key axioms to keep in mind when building your communication skills: the communication choices you make are connected to the outcomes that follow, and different types of communication are connected to each other in fundamental ways.

LAUNCHPAD

LaunchPad for *Choices & Connections* offers unique video scenarios and encourages self-assessment through adaptive quizzing. Go to **bedfordstmartins.com /choicesconnections** to get access.

✓ LearningCurve adaptive quizzes

▶ How to Communicate video scenarios

▶ Video clips that illustrate key concepts

KEY TERMS

Communication, p. 5

Message, p. 6

Interaction, p. 6

Contexts, p. 6

▶ Channel, p. 6

Media, p. 6

Self-presentation goals, p. 7

Instrumental goals, p. 7

Relationship goals, p. 7

▶ Linear communication model, p. 8

Sender, p. 8

Receiver, p. 8

▶ Noise, p. 8

Interactive communication model, p. 9

Feedback, p. 9

Fields of experience, p. 9

▶ Transactional communication model, p. 10

Rhetoric, p. 13

Mediated communication, p. 17

Interpersonal communication, p. 17

Small group communication, p. 17

Public communication, p. 17

Communication competence, p. 19

Appropriateness, p. 19

Effectiveness, p. 20

Ethics, p. 20

Communication skills, p. 24

Looking for more review questions? **LearningCurve** can help you master key concepts from this chapter. Go to **bedfordstmartins.com /choicesconnections.**

❶ Which of the following is *not* one of the five features that define communication?

a. Contexts   **c.** Channel
b. Ethics   **d.** Media

❷ If you convince your sister to lend you her car by describing your clean driving record and devotion to speed limits, you are accomplishing what type of goal?

a. Rhetorical   **c.** Self-presentation
b. Relationship   **d.** Instrumental

❸ According to the _____ model, there aren't senders or receivers; instead, participants constantly exchange verbal and nonverbal messages and feedback to collaboratively create meaning.

a. transactional   **c.** linear
b. interactive   **d.** instrumental

❹ Which feature of competent communication requires you to treat others with respect and communicate with them honestly, kindly, and positively?

a. Effectiveness   **c.** Appropriateness
b. Ethics   **d.** Connections

❺ Repeatable goal-directed behaviors and behavioral patterns that you routinely practice and that reflect knowledge of competent communication are known as _____.

a. communication skills
b. communication competence
c. fields of experience
d. feedback

❶ **Tracking Your Media Meter**

As a way to compare how you use different communication media, create a log of your communication patterns across various media for just one day. Track how often you text, tweet, e-mail, post, call, talk face-to-face, and so on. For each communication encounter, include a brief note regarding what it was about. Then, analyze your log based on the following questions: Which communication media did you use most often? Why? What guided your decision in choosing certain media over others? Do certain media seem more intimate or less personal than others? Were some more enjoyable or more demanding? How do you think your choice of communication media influenced the outcomes you experienced?

❷ **Exploring Competent Communication**

Call to mind a recent communication encounter that you found difficult or problematic. This could be a conflict, an awkward interaction, or an instance in which you regretted what you said or someone misinterpreted you. With a partner, recall exactly what you said and what happened as a result. Now, revisit the components of competence discussed on pages 18–24. What aspects of your communication were appropriate, effective, or ethical? Which were not? What could you have done to be more competent in the situation? How would that have changed the outcomes you experienced? What does this tell you about the benefits or limits of competent communication?

2

Self and Perception

"Neither slavery nor involuntary servitude . . . shall exist within the United States."

—13th Amendment to the U.S. Constitution

(T)he movie *Lincoln* (2012) recounts how President Abraham Lincoln succeeded in getting slavery abolished through passage of the 13th Amendment to the U.S. Constitution. Lincoln had very little time to get the bill approved by Congress. Support for the amendment was almost entirely based on the assumption that it would end the Civil War: if the slaves were freed, it would end the confederacy's cause. However, emissaries from the South were coming to Washington, D.C., to propose peace. If a truce were struck prior to the amendment passing, the reason many congressmen had for supporting the amendment would be lost. Lincoln set about getting the needed votes.

Several skills possessed by Lincoln—brought to life by the actor Daniel Day-Lewis—empowered him to prevail. For instance, Lincoln was deeply self-reflective and believed strongly in sharing one's inner reflections and feelings with others. As he noted, "The inclination to exchange thoughts with one another is probably an original impulse of our nature—If I be in pain, I wish to let you know it . . . and my pleasurable emotions also, I wish to communicate to, and share with you."[1] Second, he felt great empathy toward African Americans and recognized how passage of the amendment would end their suffering. As Lincoln described in the movie (and in real life), "Abolishing slavery settles the fate for the millions now in bondage—and the unborn millions to come."

But perhaps most important, Lincoln accurately perceived how others saw him and tailored his communication accordingly. This allowed him to achieve maximum impact in advocating his cause. In the climactic scene of the film, Lincoln meets with a group of congressmen and learns that he is still several votes short. Perceiving that they will be more responsive if he pulls rank on them, he works that into his message: "We are stepped out upon the world stage, now, with the fate of human dignity in our

[1] Excerpted from Shenk (2005, p. xii).

hands. Blood has been spilled to afford us this moment—now, now, now! I am President of the United States, clothed with immense power, and I expect you to procure these votes. I leave it to you to determine how it shall be done." Within days the votes were found, and on January 31, 1865, the bill passed the House. Slavery in the United States was illegal.

More than 150 years ago, a deeply self-reflective president harnessed the power of perception to persuade Congress to abolish slavery. In doing so, he fulfilled the promise made in his speech at Gettysburg two years earlier: "We here highly resolve that these dead shall not have died in vain—that this nation, under God, shall have a new birth of freedom."

The movie *Lincoln* shows how Abraham Lincoln used communication to pass the 13th Amendment. He achieved this through his knowledge of self, willingness to share his feelings with others, accurate perception, empathy, and ability to adapt his communication. By combining a strong sense of self with accurate perceptions, you can set the stage for successful communication in your own life. In this chapter, you'll learn:

- The nature of self and its impact on communication
- How you present yourself to others, online and off
- The perception process and common errors made in it
- Ways to form impressions of others
- The importance of perception-checking and empathy

✔ **LearningCurve** can help you review! Go to **bedfordstmartins.com /choicesconnections**.

The Nature of Self

Your "self" isn't just one thing but many: who you think you are as a person; what your values, attitudes, and beliefs are; and how you feel about your self-worth. Because all of these factors influence how you communicate, the first step to improving your communication is to understand your self.

Who are you? You may answer this question by describing your personality—funny, friendly, or intense—or perhaps by explaining what you do: musician, athlete, or computer geek. You may even identify the various roles you play: "I'm Grace's daughter," "I'm a nursing student," or "I'm the fry cook at Randy's Grill." But who you are—your *self*—isn't a single thing that can be captured in a simple statement. Instead, the **self** is an evolving blend of three components: self-awareness, self-concept, and self-esteem. Your self shapes how you communicate, whether online or off, with friends or in groups, and even before audiences.

Self-Awareness

Self-awareness is the ability to view yourself as a unique person, distinct from your surrounding environment, and to reflect on your thoughts, feelings, and behaviors—in short, asking yourself, "Who am I?" (Rochat, 2003).

But self-awareness isn't only about inward analysis. You also look outward, to others, and compare yourself to them. Through **social comparison**, you assign meaning to others' behaviors and then compare their behaviors against your own. Think of times you've wondered about your own speaking abilities after seeing a classmate deliver a stellar presentation or pondered your interpersonal skills after watching a sibling comfort a friend. When you stack up favorably against people you admire, you think well of yourself ("I'm as fast as the black belts in my karate class!"). When you don't compare favorably, you think less of yourself ("Why can't I be as funny as my brother?").

When communicating, you are always self-aware, constantly considering your thoughts, feelings, and behaviors. But to improve your communication, you must routinely practice **critical self-reflection**, a special kind of self-awareness that focuses on evaluating and improving your communication. To engage in critical self-reflection, consider these five questions:

1. What am I thinking and feeling?
2. Why am I thinking and feeling this way?
3. How am I communicating?
4. How are my inner thoughts and feelings affecting my communication?
5. How can I improve my thoughts, feelings, and communication?

The goal of critical self-reflection is to enhance your communication. By routinely practicing critical self-reflection, you will achieve a deeper understanding of the factors that influence your communication choices, allowing you to make better decisions and achieve improved outcomes as a result.

Self-Concept

If self-awareness asks the question, "Who am I?" **self-concept** is the answer—that is, your overall assessment of who you are ("I'm a _____ person"). Your self-concept is based on the beliefs, attitudes, and values you have about yourself. *Beliefs* are convictions that certain things are true ("I'm a caring person"). *Attitudes* are evaluations ("I'm satisfied with my fitness level"). *Values* are enduring principles that guide your behaviors ("I think it's morally wrong to lie"). Your beliefs, attitudes, and values are often intertwined. For example, if you think that communicating honestly is important (value), you likely also view yourself as an honest person (belief) and evaluate your honest communication positively (attitude). Understanding your beliefs, attitudes, and values and how they may differ from those of others helps you adapt your communication to anyone with whom you are interacting.

Early in life, the people who matter most to you—parents, siblings, teachers—help define your self-concept. Their reactions to you serve as a type of mirror in which you begin to see yourself as others see you (Cooley, 1902). For example, when Steve was young, his folks routinely emphasized his musical ability, leading him to think of himself as a musician. In contrast, Joe's parents constantly praised his academic achievements, causing him to see himself as a scholar.

As you age, the range of people who help shape and maintain your self-concept broadens to include friends, lovers, and coworkers. In fact, according to **Self-Verification Theory** (Swann, Chang-Schneider, & Angulo, 2007), you often choose your relational partners based on how well they support your self-concept. If you see yourself as an aspiring anime artist, you'll probably choose friends, dating partners, and even roommates who support and reinforce this view—for instance, by praising your work (Swann & Pelham,

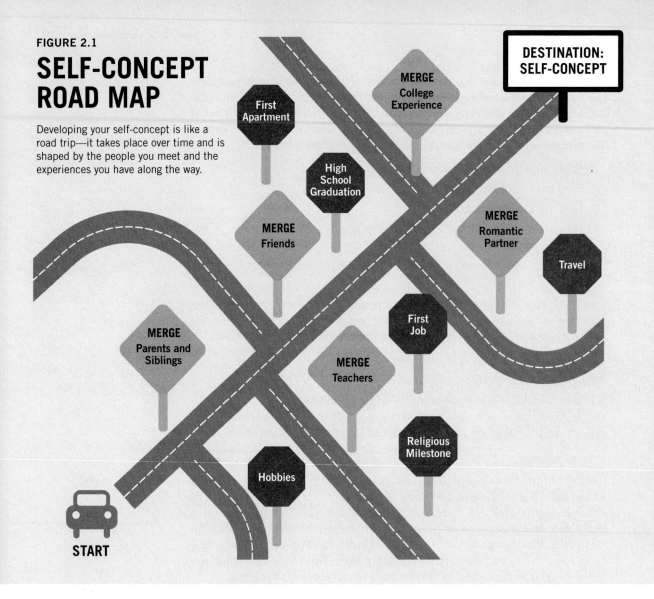

FIGURE 2.1

SELF-CONCEPT ROAD MAP

Developing your self-concept is like a road trip—it takes place over time and is shaped by the people you meet and the experiences you have along the way.

DESTINATION: SELF-CONCEPT

MERGE
College
Experience

First
Apartment

High
School
Graduation

MERGE
Friends

MERGE
Romantic
Partner

Travel

MERGE
Parents and
Siblings

First
Job

MERGE
Teachers

Religious
Milestone

Hobbies

START

2002). This holds true even for negative self-concepts: if you think you're shallow or obsessive, you'll likely be drawn to people who support this view (Swann, Hixon, & De La Ronde, 1992).

Your self-concept often leads to **self-fulfilling prophecies,** predictions you make about interactions that cause you to communicate in ways that make those predictions come true. Say your boss assigns you to a new team whose members strike you as especially creative and intelligent. If you think you're not as talented as they are, you may predict that they'll ignore your contributions to group discussions. As a result of this prediction, you remain quiet during the first team meeting. The other group members interpret your silence as a desire not to contribute and begin excluding you from the discussion. Later, you tell yourself, "See! I knew they wouldn't want my input!" But if you saw yourself as creative and smart, you might predict that the team would welcome your contributions. You would then offer your ideas confidently, and the others would likely make a point of including you in the discussions.

Self-Esteem

Self-esteem is the overall value you assign to yourself. Whereas self-awareness asks, "Who am I?" and self-concept is the answer to that question, self-esteem is the follow-up query, "Given who I am, what's my evaluation of my worth?" Self-esteem strongly shapes your communication, relationships, and general outlook on life. People with high self-esteem report greater life satisfaction, communicate more positively with others, and experience more happiness in their relationships than do people with low self-esteem (Fox, 1997). They also show greater leadership ability, athleticism, and academic performance (Fox, 1992).

According to **Self-Discrepancy Theory**, your self-esteem is determined by how you compare to two mental standards (Higgins, 1987). The first standard is your *ideal self*—all the qualities (mental, physical, emotional, material, spiritual) you want to possess. The second standard is your *ought self*—the person you think others want you to be. Ought self stems from expectations of your family, friends, colleagues, and romantic partners, plus the culture you grow up in. You experience high self-esteem when your self-concept matches your ideal and ought selves ("I'm the kind of person I want to be" and "I'm the kind of person others wish me to be"). By contrast, you may suffer low self-esteem if your self-concept is inferior to your ideal and ought selves. You can work on improving your self-esteem by following these steps:

1. *Assess your self-esteem.* List the beliefs, attitudes, and values that make up your self-concept. Review the list, and determine whether you view yourself positively or negatively.

2. *Analyze your ideal self.* Who do you wish you were? If this ideal self is attainable, how could you become this person?

3. *Analyze your ought self.* Who do others want you to be? What would you have to do to become this person?

4. *Revisit and redefine your standards.* If your ideal and ought selves are realistic and reachable, move to step 5. If they're not (e.g., you'd love to be a multimillionaire by age 20, but it's not likely you'll get there), redefine your standards so they are realistic and reachable. Frame your new standards as a list of goals.

5. *Create an action plan.* List the actions necessary to reach your ideal and ought selves. Establish a realistic time line—perhaps several months or years. Then carry out this action plan, checking your progress as you go.

DOUBLE TAKE

IDEAL (VS) OUGHT SELF

Your self-esteem is determined by how closely your ideal and ought selves align. In which situation do you think the student's ideal and ought selves are more closely matched? Why?

Blend Images/Veer   Kevin C. Cox/Getty Images

Culture, Gender, and Self

Engaging in critical self-reflection, pondering your self-concept, and assessing your self-esteem likely aren't new activities. After all, many people spend time looking inward to get a better sense of their selves. What's more, your self seems to be natural and innate: you were born a certain kind of person, and that's just who you are. But without even realizing it, how you think about your self—and how you communicate that self to others—are shaped by powerful outside forces. Two of the most influential are culture and gender.

Culture and Self. In this text, we define **culture** broadly and inclusively, as an established, coherent set of beliefs, attitudes, values, and practices shared by a large group of people (Keesing, 1974). Culture includes many types of large-group influences, such as nationality, ethnicity, religion, gender, sexual orientation, physical abilities, and age. You learn your culture from parents, teachers, religious leaders, peers, and the mass media (Gudykunst & Kim, 2003).

Culture influences your communication in many ways, as Chapter 4 discusses in detail. But when it comes to your view of self, whether you grew up in an individualistic or collectivistic culture is highly influential. If you were raised in an **individualistic culture,** you likely learned that individual goals matter more than group goals. People in individualistic cultures are encouraged to focus on themselves and their immediate family (Hofstede, 1998), and individual achievement is praised as the highest good. Countries with individualistic cultures include the United States, New Zealand, and Sweden (Hofstede, 2001).

If you were raised in a **collectivistic culture,** you were probably taught the importance of belonging to groups that look after you in exchange for your loyalty (Hofstede, 2001). In collectivistic cultures, the goals, needs, and views of the group matter more than those of individuals, and the highest good is cooperation with others. For example, in China—a country with a collectivistic culture—the concept of "doing your own thing" has no direct translation to the Chinese language (Hofstede, 2001). Other collectivistic cultures include Guatemala, Pakistan, and Taiwan.

Gender and Self. **Gender** is the set of social, psychological, and cultural attributes that characterize a person as male or female (Canary, Emmers-Sommer, & Faulkner, 1997). Your concept of gender forms over time through interactions with others. Thus, it's distinct from the biological sex organs you are born with, which distinguish you anatomically as male or female.

Immediately after birth, you begin a lifelong process of gender socialization, in which societal norms define and assign appropriate behavior for each gender. Within current American culture, for example, many girls are taught that the most important aspects of self include compassion and sensitivity to one's own and others' emotions (Lippa, 2002). Many boys are taught that the most important aspects of self are assertiveness, competitiveness, and independence. As a result, women and men within the culture form very different views of self (Cross & Madson, 1997). Women tend to see themselves as connected to others; men, as separate from others.

Presenting Your Self

Every time you communicate with others, you present a version of your self to them. Sometimes this represents who you really are; other times you may hide your true self. In either case, the self you present is the "you" people know. If you want people to see you in a certain way, it's essential to learn how to present your self skillfully.

Anne Burrell is a rock star in the world of chefs. Easily identifiable from her shock of white-blond hair, charisma, humor, and quirkiness, she draws millions of viewers to her Food Network shows *Secrets of a Restaurant Chef* and *Worst Cooks in America*. But in May 2012, Anne's image was challenged when writer and television personality Ted Allen outed her as a lesbian. During an interview on Sirius XM radio, host Romaine Patterson joked to Allen about Burrell, saying, "I have the biggest crush on her . . . whether or not she's a lesbian, I don't care." Allen responded, "I'm not going to put a label on Anne, but she is dating a woman right now. You've got some competition." Afterwards, many fans expressed surprise, noting that Burrell had never presented herself publicly as a lesbian. But Burrell herself was quick to embrace the disclosure, releasing a statement confirming her sexual orientation and noting that she is in a committed relationship with a woman. Food Network executives supported her

When celebrity chef Anne Burrell was publicly outed, she had to make a decision about how to reconcile her public and private selves. Are there areas of your private self you would need to reconcile if they became public? How would you manage that?

Angela Pham/BFAnyc/Sipa USA/Newscom

"new" self-presentation as well, commenting, "We're always looking to broaden the diversity of our hosts, and we work hard to find talent that has the expertise, charisma, and broad appeal necessary to work on our air."

In addition to your *private self*—the combination of your self-awareness, self-concept, and self-esteem—you also have a *public self*: the self you present to others (Fenigstein, Scheier, & Buss, 1975). You actively create your public self through your communication and behavior.

Sometimes your private and public selves mirror each other. At other times, such as when Ted Allen outed Anne Burrell, it can seem as though your private and public selves are different. But regardless of the nature of your private self, people form impressions about you based on the public self you present. People know and judge the "you" who communicates with them—not the "you" you keep inside. Thus, managing your public self is a crucial part of being a competent communicator.

Creating Faces and Masks

The positive self you want others to see and believe is your **face** (Goffman, 1955). Face doesn't just happen; you actively create and present it through your communication. Your face can be anything you want it to be: perky and upbeat, cool and levelheaded, cynical and detached.

You create different faces for different situations. Sometimes your face is a **mask:** an outward presentation designed to cover private aspects of your self

(Goffman, 1955). For example, suppose you have an interview coming up for a new job. The night before, you and your romantic partner break up. When meeting with your potential new boss, you act upbeat, engaging, and competent—even though you want to curl up on the floor and cry. Sometimes you adopt masks to protect others. Paramedics often do this when they talk in calm, comforting tones to keep severely injured accident victims from going into shock.

Losing Face

When you create a certain face (or a mask) and then do something that contradicts it, you *lose face* (Goffman, 1955). People may perceive you as phony and may feel betrayed by your actions. Losing face can also cause you to experience **embarrassment**—feelings of shame, humiliation, and sadness. For example, when Steve was in high school, he competed at a state public-speaking tournament. During the final qualifying round, he suddenly blanked in the middle of his speech. As he stood there silently for several seconds, feeling and looking incompetent in front of his audience, he contradicted his face of "confident, competitive public speaker." The result was embarrassment that he remembers to this day.

Maintaining Face

Losing face is painful for everyone involved, so maintaining face during communication is critical. For example, when Ted Allen outed Anne Burrell, she succeeded in maintaining her face by immediately acknowledging what happened and noting her commitment to her partner. What's more, the Food Network executives helped her maintain face by making it clear that they considered her lesbian identity to be a welcome part of their diverse network.

How can you maintain your face? First, use words and actions consistent with the face you're trying to create. If you tell members of a project team that you're excited to hear everyone's input, be sure to demonstrate this by actively listening when each member offers suggestions instead of tuning out and texting your friends. Second, make sure your communication meshes with others' existing knowledge about you. If you're giving a speech about the dangers of listening to loud music through headphones and walk into class blasting music through your earbuds, you won't be able to maintain face. Finally, try to anticipate and manage events that could contradict your face. If you tell your dating partner that you haven't been in contact with your ex, you won't want a message from him or her to pop up on your Facebook wall.

Of course, everyone falls from grace on occasion. But remember, most people want you to maintain face, because your face is the positive, public "you" with whom they're most familiar. So when something happens that causes you to lose face, promptly acknowledge that the event happened, admit responsibility for any of your actions that contributed to the event, apologize for your actions and for disappointing others, and move to maintain your face again. Apologies are fairly successful at reducing

MAKING COMMUNICATION CHOICES

DISTORTING ONLINE SELF-PRESENTATION

1 CONSIDER THE DILEMMA

Tired of the local dating scene, you join an online matchmaking service. As you craft your profile, your friends encourage you to "spin" your self-presentation. "Make yourself ten pounds lighter," says one, and another encourages you to "change your age and say you have a master's degree." When you protest that this isn't honest, they say, "Don't worry about it—everyone does it! Besides, do you want to meet people or not?"

After a couple of weeks, you connect with Jordan, who seems to be your soul mate. You two have everything in common, from tastes in movies and music, to religious and political beliefs. Excited to meet offline, you arrange a lunch date.

Jordan proves to be even more desirable in person than online. As you enjoy lunch together, you cover many topics, including your educations, your families, and your life dreams. It is clear that the attraction you shared online exists offline as well. As lunch ends, you tell Jordan, "I'd really like to see you again." However, Jordan frowns and says, "I have to be honest. Although I've really enjoyed our date, I'm a little confused. You're not exactly how I thought you'd be, based on your profile. I mean, as we were talking, you said you are still in school. But that isn't what your description says. Is there stuff you just haven't told me, or did you make things up for your profile?"

2 CONNECT THE RESEARCH

People often present themselves online in ways that amplify positive characteristics, such as warmth and friendliness, while masking characteristics they think are undesirable or unattractive (Gosling, Gaddis, & Vazire, 2007). This is especially true on online dating sites. More than a quarter of online matchmaking members report having lied in their profiles to present themselves as more attractive (Brym & Lenton, 2001).

Communication scholar Jeffrey Hall and colleagues (2010) surveyed over 5,000 online dating service users to examine the specific ways in which they misrepresented themselves. Although both men and women lied about their ages (making themselves younger), men were more likely than women to lie about income and educational

levels, whereas women were more likely to lie about their weight.

Of course, distorting your online self-presentation is ultimately self-defeating if you wish to form offline relationships. Researchers found that 86 percent of dating site users reported having met others who they felt had misrepresented their physical attractiveness (Gibbs, Ellison, & Heino, 2006), and in such situations, they typically felt "lied to" (Ellison, Heino, & Gibbs, 2006).

So, while distorting your self-presentation online is both tempting and commonplace, if your goal is to forge an offline connection, you should present yourself authentically online. Otherwise, people may judge you as dishonest, and that can end a promising relationship before it even begins.

3 COMMUNICATE

Before making a communication choice, consider what the research tells you about online self-presentation. Also factor in what you have learned about face (pp. 38–41), embarrassment (p. 39), and apologies (pp. 39–41). Then answer these questions:

1. Was it ethical to post distorted information in your dating profile? Why or why not?
2. If you were Jordan, what would you be thinking and feeling in this situation?
3. What are you going to say to Jordan?

MAINTAINING FACE

In movies like *Flight*, *Argo*, and *Silver Linings Playbook*, the characters face challenges for which maintaining their public face is crucial to their success. But maintaining your face is not only important in extraordinary circumstances like landing a plane safely. How do you use communication to maintain your face on a daily basis?

(Clockwise from top left) Robert Zuckerman/© Paramount Pictures/Courtesy Everett Collection; Claire Folger/© Warner Bros. Pictures/Courtesy Everett Collection; JoJo Whilden/© Weinstein Company/Courtesy Everett Collection

people's negative impressions and the anger that may have been triggered—especially when such apologies avoid excuses that contradict what people know really happened (Ohbuchi & Sato, 1994). People who consistently deny their inconsistencies or who blame others for their lapses are judged much more harshly.

Perceiving Others

Along with your view of self, your perception of others determines how you communicate. Although it may seem as though your view of other people is both accurate and objective, it is anything but. Understanding the process of perception will help you avoid errors that might cause you to communicate incompetently.

What do you perceive when you see gang graffiti—a colorful jumble of unintelligible symbols? A frightening marker of a threatening subculture? Or complex visual communication indicating group membership and territoriality? In his studies of Chicago street gangs, Northwestern University

What do you perceive when you see graffiti in this style? What about other types of street art (tagging, murals, political messages)? Consider how the different ways people select, organize, and interpret information influences how they perceive not only graffiti but every encounter they have each day.

Steve Shoup/Shutterstock

professor Dwight Conquergood (1994) found that gang members viewed one another like family. To reinforce this bond, they created sophisticated communication systems through hand signals, manner of dress (such as colors or jewelry), and graffiti. These markers enhanced their sense of belonging and created a perceptual boundary from the outside world. Though passersby saw the graffiti as meaningless or intriguing "urban art," gang members saw the designs in a radically different light. For them, graffiti defined territories, reinforced identities, and sent messages to fellow gang members ("You're one of us") and to rivals ("You're the enemy").

The differing views that people have of gang graffiti are a reminder that *all* communication is viewed through the lens of **perception**: the process of selecting, organizing, and interpreting information from your senses. Simply put, perception is the gateway to the world around you.

The Perception Process

Perception occurs when you do the following:

1. *Select* information to focus your attention on
2. *Organize* the information into an understandable pattern, such as words, phrases, ideas, or images
3. *Interpret* the meaning of the pattern

Each step in the perception process influences the others: the information you select determines how you organize it, your mental organization of information shapes how you interpret it, and your interpretation of information influences how you mentally organize it. (See Figure 2.2.) Let's take a closer look at each step.

Step 1: Select Information. During the first step of perception, **selection,** you focus your attention on certain sights, sounds, tastes, touches, or smells in your environment. One estimate suggests that even though your senses take in 11 million bits of information per second, you select only about 40 bits to pay attention to (Wilson, 2002). With so much information out there, how do you decide what to select? You're more likely to focus on something when it is visually or audibly stimulating, deviates from your expectations, or is viewed as important (Fiske & Taylor, 1991).

Consider what this means for your communication. If you're attending a presentation and the speaker talks in a dramatic, impassioned way, you're more likely to pay attention than if the presenter had spoken in a monotone and stood passively behind the lectern. If Tom, a team member who's usually talkative, sits silently during a meeting, he'll defy your expectations—so you'll notice him. And if you hear your child start to cry in an adjacent room, you'll likely consider the situation important and focus your attention on it.

FIGURE 2.2

THE PERCEPTION PROCESS

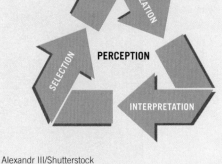

Alexandr III/Shutterstock

Step 2: Organize the Information into a Pattern. Once you've selected something to focus your attention on, you structure the information you receive through your senses into a coherent pattern in your mind. This is the second step of the perception process, known as **organization** (Fiske & Taylor, 1991). For example, once your attention is drawn to Tom (the unusually quiet group member), you begin to observe all that he is doing—his posture, facial expressions, bodily movements, and lack of comments—and organize it within your mind as a coherent package: "This is how Tom is acting right now."

Step 3: Interpret the Pattern. As you organize information you've selected into a coherent pattern, you engage in the third step of perception: **interpretation,** or assigning meaning to the information you've selected. You call to mind familiar information that's relevant, and use that information to make sense of what you're hearing and seeing. Borrowing on the previous example, this is the stage of perception in which you would assign meaning to the behaviors of Tom that you have focused your attention on: "When people who are usually talkative are suddenly quiet, they often have something on their minds. Tom is being unusually quiet. Maybe Tom is upset about something."

Attributions and Perceptual Errors

Following the perception process, you often want explanations for why things are happening the way they are ("Why is Tom not talking during the meeting?"). These explanations are known as **attributions.** Two types of attributions are commonplace. One is that *external* factors or events—things outside of the person—caused the person's behavior ("Tom just heard that

FUNDAMENTAL ATTRIBUTION ERROR

The morning rush at a coffee shop can be equally frustrating for customers and employees. Think about how their interactions might change if they considered external, rather than internal, attributions for one another's behaviors.

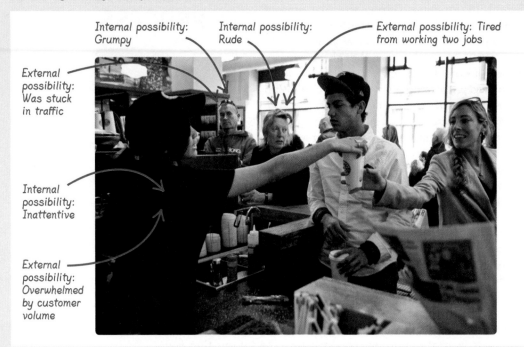

Internal possibility: Grumpy

Internal possibility: Rude

External possibility: Tired from working two jobs

External possibility: Was stuck in traffic

Internal possibility: Inattentive

External possibility: Overwhelmed by customer volume

Ramin Talaie/Bloomberg via Getty Images

his dad is sick, so he's thinking about that instead of taking part in the meeting"). The other is that *internal* factors—personality, character, emotions—caused the person to act as he or she did ("Tom is a moody jerk, and that's why he's not contributing").

Given the number of people you communicate with each day, it's not surprising that you occasionally form invalid attributions. One common mistake is the **fundamental attribution error,** the tendency to attribute others' behaviors to internal rather than external forces (Heider, 1958). The fundamental attribution error is the most prevalent of all perceptual errors (Langdridge & Butt, 2004). When you communicate with others, they—not the surrounding factors that may be causing their behavior—dominate your perception. As a result, when you make judgments about why someone is acting a certain way, you overestimate the influence of the person and underestimate the influence of external factors (Heider, 1958; Langdridge & Butt, 2004).

A related error is the **actor-observer effect,** the tendency to make external attributions regarding your own behaviors (Fiske & Taylor, 1991). During encounters with others, you tend to focus on external factors—especially the people you're interacting with. Therefore, you tend to identify these external factors as causing your behavior. This is particularly prevalent during unpleasant interactions. For example, if you're giving a speech and the audience doesn't pay attention, you might get angry and feel that such anger is a justifiable reaction to audience members' rudeness rather than a lack of self-control on your part.

However, when your actions result in success, you tend to take credit for the success by making an internal attribution ("The audience paid attention because I'm a skilled speaker"). This tendency is known as the **self-serving bias** (Fiske & Taylor, 1991). By crediting yourself for your successes, you feel better about who you are and the skills you possess.

Your attributions directly influence how you communicate with others and the outcomes that result. For example, imagine that your partner forgets to pick up your dry cleaning on the way home from work. If you attribute your partner's forgetfulness to work pressures and a hectic schedule (external causes), you'll probably communicate in a supportive way ("I know how busy you are—I should've texted you a reminder"). But if you make internal attributions ("my partner is self-centered and inconsiderate"), you'll likely communicate in a destructive way ("I'm sure you'd remember if it were your stuff that needed picking up!").

Forming Impressions

Whenever you meet people, you paint pictures in your mind of who they are and what you think of them. These images can be positive or negative, long lasting or subject to change. However, they act as a powerful guide in shaping your communication, for better or for worse.

Although it's hard to believe now, Joe was a competitive distance runner in college. Grueling training runs in the heat and humidity of southeast Texas bonded him and his fellow teammates, helping them overcome differences in their ethnic backgrounds, personalities, lifestyles, and worldviews. But just as they were forming more positive impressions of one another, the runners as a group were perceived differently by other students on campus. At the time, long-distance running was only just starting to gain popularity in the United States. Students who didn't understand the sport viewed the athletes as freaks. Who in their right mind, after all, would run 20 miles a day? In Texas?! The runners' scrawny physiques even led some people to say they were malnourished, creating further skepticism about the sport. Yet many of these same critics were shocked to see how much pizza the runners put away in the dining hall as they loaded up on carbohydrates before a race.

Like those who judged the distance runners, you also use the perception process to form **impressions** of others: mental images of who people are and how you feel about them. All aspects of the perception process shape your impressions: the information you select to focus your attention on, the way you organize this information, the interpretations you make, and the attributions you create.

Because the perception process is complex and everyone organizes and interprets information differently, impressions vary widely. Some take shape quickly: You hear a politician giving a speech and take an immediate dislike to him. Other impressions form slowly, over a series of encounters. Some are intensely positive: "Long-distance runners are amazingly dedicated and disciplined!" Others are neutral. Some are negative: "Long-distance runners are freaks!" Let's look at some ways you form impressions.

Gestalts

One way you form impressions of others is to construct a **Gestalt,** a general impression of a person that's positive or negative. You identify a few traits about the person and then arrive at a judgment ("I like you" or "I don't like you"). For example, audience members begin forming impressions of you the

THE POWER OF GESTALTS

One way to understand the power of Gestalts is to consider how you feel about controversial public figures. For example, do you have a strong opinion about the celebrities pictured here? Chances are you don't personally know any of them, but you still form strong Gestalts about them. Consider how this same process works for people you meet in person or online.

(Clockwise from top left) David Mepham/FilmMagic/Getty Images; James Devaney/WireImage/Getty Images; PBG/PA Photos /Landov

moment you begin a speech. Your clothing, posture, facial expressions, and opening remarks generate an overall impression that can instantly enhance or undermine your credibility.

Gestalts form rapidly and require relatively little mental or communicative effort. This makes them useful for encounters in which you must make quick judgments about others based on limited information. Imagine you need to hire someone and have dozens of résumés to review. Although résumés don't reflect the sum total of what the applicants are like, the Gestalts you create based on them will help you decide whom to interview ("This résumé is well crafted, has no typos, and highlights skills relevant to this job. I *like* her already!").

A disadvantage of Gestalts is that they can distort how you interpret information you later learn about people. Think about someone for whom you've formed a strongly positive Gestalt. Now imagine discovering that this person cheated on his taxes. Because of your positive Gestalt, you may dismiss the significance of this behavior ("He probably made an innocent mistake"). This tendency is known as the **halo effect.**

The counterpart of the halo effect is the **horn effect,** the tendency to negatively interpret the behavior of people for whom you've formed negative Gestalts. Call to mind someone you can't stand. Now imagine that this person has cheated on her taxes. Chances are, you'll chalk up her behavior to bad character or lack of values ("I knew she was a cheat!").

Algebraic Impressions

A second way to form impressions is to develop **algebraic impressions**— analyzing the positive and negative things you learn about someone to calculate an overall impression, then updating this impression as you learn new information (Anderson, 1981). It's similar to solving an algebraic equation, whereby you add and subtract different values to compute a final result. However, when forming algebraic impressions, you don't place an equal value on every piece of information you receive. Instead, information that's important, unusual, or negative is usually weighted more heavily than information that's trivial, typical, or positive (Kellermann, 1989). This happens because people tend to believe that important, unusual, or negative information reveals more about a person's "true" character than does other information (Kellermann, 1989).

Of course, other people form algebraic impressions of you, too. So, when you're communicating—whether in person or online, with a friend or in front of an audience—be mindful of what important, unusual, or negative information you share about yourself. This information will have a particularly strong effect on others' impressions of you.

Algebraic impressions are more accurate than Gestalts because you take time to form them and you consider a wider range of information. They're also more flexible. You can update your algebraic impression every time you receive new information about someone. For instance, you discover through Facebook that the cool classmate you talked to yesterday has political views much different from your own. Accordingly, you become a bit cautious about pursuing a romance with this person while remaining open to seeing where things will lead.

Stereotypes

A final way to form impressions is to categorize people into a social group (like their race, age, or gender) and then evaluate them based on information you have related to this group. This is known as **stereotyping** (Bodenhausen, Macrae, & Sherman, 1999). Stereotypes replace the subtle complexities that make people unique with blanket assumptions about their character and worth based solely on their social group affiliations. Stereotyping is difficult to avoid because it's the most common way we form impressions (Bodenhausen et al., 1999). Why? Social-group categories can be the first things you notice about others when you meet them. So you often perceive people in terms of their social group before it's possible to make any other impression (Devine, 1989).

Stereotyping often leads to flawed impressions. In one workplace study, male supervisors who stereotyped women as "the weaker sex" perceived female employees' work performance as deficient and gave women low job evaluations—regardless of the women's actual job performance (Cleveland, Stockdale, & Murphy, 2000). A separate study examining college students' perceptions of professors found a similar biasing effect for ethnic stereotypes. Euro-American students who stereotyped Hispanics as "laidback" perceived Hispanic professors who set high expectations for classroom performance as "colder" and "more unprofessional" than Euro-American professors who set identical standards (Smith & Anderson, 2005).

Despite claims of being the most democratic and equalizing mass medium, the Internet actually enables stereotyping. During online communication, people don't have the nonverbal cues and other information that can distinguish someone as a unique individual. As a result, people communicating online are more likely than those communicating face-to-face to form stereotypical impressions of others (Lea & Spears, 1992; Spears, Postmes, Lea, & Watt, 2001; P. Wallace, 1999).

Because stereotyping fails to consider the intricate complexities that distinguish individuals from broad group affiliations, it often leads to flawed impressions. To avoid an overreliance on stereotypes, always adapt your communication to the person, not the group.

Chris Carlson/AP Images

Though stereotypes are used to form impressions, they should not reflect rigid attitudes toward groups and their members. This is known as *prejudice* and can cause you to communicate in destructive and unethical ways. See Chapter 4 (pp. 82–109) to learn more about prejudice and how you can overcome it.

Improving Your Perception

Even though perception and impression formation occur in specific ways, they are not unchangeable processes. You can improve your perception and impressions by critically questioning your own judgments and routinely considering the feelings, needs, and viewpoints of others.

In the movie *Inception*, Leonardo DiCaprio plays Dom Cobb, a master at "extraction"—entering people's unconscious minds while they're asleep and stealing their thoughts. Since he spends much of his time living inside others' dreams, Cobb often has difficulty telling what's real and what isn't. To help with this, he uses a spinning top to tell whether he's dreaming or awake. Within a dream state, Cobb's top spins smoothly and endlessly. When he's awake, it spins for a few moments, then wobbles and falls. In either case, the top allows Cobb to quickly perceive the truth.

Of course, in the real world, you don't have a top to tell you if your perceptions are accurate. Instead, you must rely on your own perceptual abilities. Two skills can help you improve your perception and the resulting communication choices you make: perception-checking and empathy.

Perception-Checking

Perception-checking is a five-step process for testing your impression of someone and avoiding errors in judgment. First, review your knowledge about the person. Your impression of this individual is only as accurate as the information you have. Never presume that you know the "truth" about someone.

Second, assess attributions you've made about this individual. Avoid attributing the person's behavior exclusively to internal causes. Remember that all behavior stems from a blend of internal and external forces.

Third, question your impression. Make sure you're not basing it solely on a Gestalt or a stereotype.

Fourth, share your impression with the individual. Present it as "here's my viewpoint," not as the "right" or "only" perspective.

Fifth, check your impression with the person: "Do you see it the same way?" As communication teachers, we can't count the number of times students have asked us, "Do you think he meant this?" or "Do you think she was trying to . . . ?" We always say, "Why don't you ask them?"

EMPATHY FOR
A GROUP MEMBER

 One way to improve your communication competence is by adapting your messages to others' behaviors. Learn how to express empathy by going to LaunchPad at **bedfordstmartins.com/choicesconnections** and completing the **How to Communicate video scenario** for Chapter 2 to practice your skills.

CONSIDER THIS:
You're assigned to lead a group project for a class. One team member, Alex, has missed two of the first three meetings. When you meet with Alex to discuss this, you discover that she has a three-year-old she is raising as a single mother and that she is working full-time to put herself through school. She genuinely wants to contribute to the project but is struggling to juggle all of the competing demands in her life.

WHAT WOULD YOU DO?
The following advice illustrates how to express empathy for Alex's situation while still keeping the group's goals in mind. As you watch the video, consider how the dialogue reflects perspective-taking and empathic concern. Then, test your knowledge of key skills, and create your own responses to the **What if? video prompts**.

"We've missed you at the last couple of meetings . . . I am concerned about how you're doing personally. Is everything OK? . . . I'm here to listen, if you need someone to talk to."

(1) OPENLY EXPRESS CONCERN for Alex as a person, not just as a group member.

2 **LEGITIMIZE HER SITUATION,** letting her know that feeling overwhelmed when faced with such demands is perfectly understandable.

"I can't even imagine dealing with all that you've got going on right now. It's totally understandable that you're feeling stressed."

3 **REAFFIRM THE IMPORTANCE** of her contribution, making it clear that you want her to stay in the group.

"The insights you've contributed to the project so far have been awesome. We don't want to lose you as a group member. What can we do to help you out, so we can make this work as a team?"

WHAT IF? But what if things don't work out as shown? Test your ability to adapt your communication by watching the What if? videos and planning a response for each situation.

1. How would you respond to Alex when she says, "Why would I talk to you about my problems? It's not like we're friends or anything."

2. What can you do to show empathic concern when Alex says, "Yes, you're right: you can't imagine, or understand, what I'm going through."

TABLE 2.1

PERCEPTION-CHECKING

SITUATION   Imagine that you are working on a group project for your communication class. Your group leader, Heather, doesn't take suggestions from other members and only moves forward with her own ideas. What steps should you take before confronting Heather about her leadership style?

1 Review your knowledge.
What do you know about Heather as a classmate?

I know that Heather:
- Is a dedicated student
- Is on an academic scholarship
- Usually works alone

2 Assess attributions.
What combination of internal and external attributions may Heather's behavior stem from?

Internal: Heather is controlling.
External: Heather has a lot of pressure to succeed academically.

3 Question your impression.
Is your conclusion fair?

Is it correct to conclude that Heather is simply a bossy leader?

4 Share your impression.
Present your impression to Heather in an open manner to invite conversation.

"To me, it seems the discussions are a little one-sided. I think all the group members would like to contribute."

5 Check your impression.
See if Heather understands your viewpoint and discuss a way to make it better.

"That's my viewpoint. Do you agree? Can we make discussions more inclusive?"

TAKE AWAY   Instead of jumping to conclusions, it's important to remember that both internal and external attributions affect a person's behavior. Once you understand that the external pressure to keep her academic scholarship is causing Heather to control the group, you can more competently approach improving communication within the group.

Mastering perception-checking takes practice, but the effort is worthwhile. Perception-checking helps you make fewer communication blunders. It also enables you to tailor your communication to people as they really are. Thus, your messages become more sensitive and effective. Ultimately, others will see you as a more competent communicator if you use perception-checking.

Empathy

✓ **LearningCurve** can help you review! Go to **bedfordstmartins.com /choicesconnections**.

Empathy is among the most valuable tools for communicating more effectively with others (Campbell & Babrow, 2004). The word *empathy* comes from the Greek word *empatheia*, meaning "feeling into." When you experience **empathy,** you "feel into" others' thoughts and emotions, making an attempt to identify with them (Kuhn, 2001).

Empathy consists of two components: perspective-taking and empathic concern (Davis, 1994). *Perspective-taking* is the ability to see things from other people's point of view without necessarily experiencing their emotions (Duan & Hill, 1996). *Empathic concern* means becoming aware of how other people are feeling and experiencing compassion for them (Stiff, Dillard, Somera, Kim, & Sleight, 1988). For example, imagine your friend John texts you that his boyfriend just broke up with him. In experiencing empathy for your friend, you would put yourself in his shoes and call to mind instances in which a romantic partner left you. Then you'd envision the emotional pain and turmoil you've felt on such occasions, and use these memories to feel compassion toward John.

But experiencing empathy isn't enough. You must also convey your empathy to others. To do so, let others know you're genuinely interested in listening to them ("I'm here to listen if you want to talk"). Tell them you think their views are valid and understandable ("I can totally understand why you would feel that way"). Express your concern about them ("I care about you and am worried that you're not OK"). And, finally, share with them your own emotions regarding their situation ("I feel terrible that you're going through this").

When expressing empathy, avoid using "I know" messages ("I know just how you feel"). Even if you make such comments with kind intentions, the other person will likely be skeptical, particularly if they suspect that you don't or can't feel as they do. For example, when people suffer a great loss—such as the death of a loved one—many don't believe that anyone else could feel the depth of anguish they're experiencing. Saying "I know how you feel" isn't helpful under these conditions. To see how you can competently display empathy, see How to Communicate: Empathy For a Group Member on pages 50–51.

When you express empathy to others, be sure you validate their feelings and share your concern for them, but also— perhaps most important—really listen to what they need, and offer to help as you can. After all, if the roles were reversed, isn't that what you would want from others?

Helder Almeida/Shutterstock

CHAPTER ② REVIEW

CHAPTER RECAP

- Your **self** is an evolving blend of three components: **self-awareness, self-concept,** and **self-esteem.** These shape how you communicate in all situations and contexts.
- The positive self you want others to see and believe is your **face;** your face is a **mask** when you hide parts of it. To avoid **embarrassment,** work on maintaining your face.
- **Perception** is how you view the world around you. You use **attributions** to explain why things happen.
- There are many ways to form **impressions** of others, including constructing **Gestalts,** forming **algebraic impressions,** and **stereotyping.**
- You can improve your perception by practicing **perception-checking** and **empathy.**

LAUNCHPAD

LaunchPad for *Choices & Connections* offers unique video scenarios and encourages self-assessment through adaptive quizzing. Go to **bedfordstmartins.com /choicesconnections** to get access.

✅ LearningCurve adaptive quizzes

▶ How to Communicate video scenarios

▶ Video clips that illustrate key concepts

KEY TERMS

Looking for more review questions? **LearningCurve** can help you master key concepts from this chapter. Go to **bedfordstmartins.com /choicesconnections**.

❶ According to Self-Discrepancy Theory, you are more likely to experience high self-esteem if _____.
  a. your self-concept matches your ideal and ought selves
  b. you prioritize your ought self over your ideal self
  c. your relational partners support your self-concept
  d. you strive for your most idealistic self at all times

❷ What is the difference between your face and a mask?
  a. Your face is private, composed of your deeply held beliefs.
  b. A mask covers the private aspects of your self.
  c. You can have only one face but several masks.
  d. You recover from embarrassment by creating a new mask.

❸ The overwhelming tendency of people to attribute others' behaviors to internal rather than external forces is known as _____.
  a. self-serving bias
  b. stereotyping
  c. actor-observer effect
  d. fundamental attribution error

❹ Which of the following impressions form over time?
  a. Halo effect   **c.** Algebraic
  b. Horn effect   **d.** Gestalts

❺ Which of the following is *not* one of the five steps of *perception-checking*?
  a. Review your knowledge about the person
  b. Compare your impressions with a neutral source
  c. Question your impression
  d. Check your impression with the person

ACTIVITIES

❶ **Applying Self-Discrepancy Theory**

Revisit Higgins's Self-Discrepancy Theory on page 35 and consider how it applies to you and your feelings about your self. Then, write a brief paper describing your self-esteem: overall, how do you feel about your self? Briefly explain your self-concept, your ideal self, and your ought self. Where did your ideal and ought selves come from? When you compare them to your self-concept, are there any self-discrepancies? If not, how is the lack of discrepancies related to your esteem? If there *are* discrepancies, how might they be overcome? Be specific. If you resolved these discrepancies, would your esteem improve? Why or why not?

❷ **Recovering from Embarrassment**

Either individually or in groups, find an example of an embarrassing moment from a TV show, Web series, or movie. (You can revisit Goffman's discussion of face and embarrassment on pp. 38–39.) If possible, find a clip online to share with your class; if not, describe it in detail. How did the character communicate in response to his or her embarrassment? Did he or she maintain or "save" face? Now consider the three practices suggested for maintaining face, and the recommendations for recovering from losing face. Based on these, how would you evaluate the character's handling of the situation? What specific advice would you give to him or her on how to better recover from losing face?

3

Mediated Communication

Growing up in St. Louis, Jack Dorsey was fascinated by the radio conversations of police and firefighters. Listening in with a scanner, what most struck him was that everyone talked in short bursts, providing constant updates on their activities—what they were doing and where they were going. Years later, this emergency-personnel eavesdropping inspired him to invent Twitter, the social networking platform designed to quickly share small amounts of information. As he describes, "Twitter is instant—now, we all can update others about where we're going, what we're doing, what we're thinking, how we're feeling, and what we care about—and it can go out to the entire world."[1]

Dorsey's invention has changed how the world connects and communicates. After all, expressing yourself in 140 characters or less is now part of our cultural fabric. But Dorsey believes that instead of replacing face-to-face interactions, online and offline communication habits influence each other. For example, he struggles with competent communication in his own life. "I have a tendency to be silent at times, which unsettles people a bit, because they don't know what I'm thinking. The biggest thing I've learned is that I need to communicate more—be more vocal." This recognition led him to change how he sends out messages in his newest start-up company, Square. The company practices an open communication system that keeps employees in the loop at all times. Dorsey uses e-mail and other communication technologies to share all information—including decision-making processes and sensitive documents on company goals and profits that are normally restricted to higher-level management. In addition, Dorsey doesn't have an office or a desk—unheard of for someone in his position. Instead, he spends his days roaming around the building, talking with employees

Tomohiro Ohsumi/Bloomberg via Getty Images

---

[1]All information in this opener from Logan (2013).

face-to-face, and using his tablet to connect with people who are offsite via e-mail, text, and (of course) Twitter. To Dorsey, this is one of the benefits of technology and social media: people can connect and communicate no matter where or who they are.

Hundreds of millions of people worldwide now use Twitter every day. In the summer of 2012, Arab revolutionaries used it to organize protests. When Pope Benedict XVI resigned in 2013, his final message to his followers was a tweet. Celebrities and sports personalities feed the curiosity of millions of their followers by tweeting both the trivial and the significant details of their lives. Asked about whether it is easier to communicate in person or online, Dorsey is reflective regarding the benefits and limitations of media. "I guess my natural state is to communicate through technology. But do I appreciate it as much as face-to-face communication? No. Do I feel like I'm an expert in having a normal conversation face-to-face? Absolutely not. It's just not my natural state. I'd rather be walking . . . and thinking about things. . . . And Tweeting."

☑ **LearningCurve** can help you review! Go to **bedfordstmartins.com /choicesconnections**.

Whether you actively use Twitter or not, technology plays a major role in how you communicate with others. As Chapter 1 states, communication occurs when people use various tools and media for exchanging messages, including sending texts, making video presentations, and posting to social media sites. Given the many tools for transmitting messages, how do you choose what media to use when communicating with others? After all, communicators do not always agree on the use of media for exchanging messages (Ingram, 2013). Twitter may be appropriate for staying connected with your friends, but your grandparents may not tweet. Understanding how media affect your communication will help you communicate more competently. In this chapter, you'll learn:

- The functions and characteristics of mediated communication
- Ways to present your identity through mediated communication
- The challenges of using mediated communication
- Guidelines for competently using mediated communication

What Is Mediated Communication?

Technology is so prevalent in our lives, it is easy not to think about it much. Phone, laptop, app—what does it matter? Indeed, technology helps with everything from family chats to late-night study sessions, but it also has unique considerations of its own. For starters, technology changes your communication, including what kind of feedback you receive and how you process it.

Think about all the ways you communicate each day. How much do you talk to other people in person or on the phone? How many texts and Tweets do you send? How often do you check in or post to social networking sites? Who are you communicating with at school or work? What types of messages are you sending? Chances are, you do most of your communicating through communication technologies—texting, Facebook, Twitter, Tumblr, Instagram, Skype, Vine, Snapchat, WhatsApp, or any of the hundreds of sites, apps, and tools that become available each day (and that disappear as quickly!).

It's common to spend many of your waking hours on the phone and computer—often at the same time. When you use these technologies to talk, text, post, tweet, e-mail, and chat, you engage in **mediated communication:** communication with others that is separated, or "mediated," by some type of technological device.

Types of Mediated Communication

The phrase *mediated communication* may make you think about "the media"—that is, online news and entertainment sites, video games, television channels, movies, radio stations, newspapers, and magazines. These

USING MEDIATED COMMUNICATION

Every text, tweet, post, video, pin, or note you send through mediated channels (whether personal, professional, or for fun) is as much of a communication choice as the words you use in a face-to-face conversation. How much do you consider the functions and characteristics of your messages before sending them?

(Clockwise from top left) Csondy/istockphoto; Take A Pix Media/agefotostock; PYMCA/UIG via Getty Images

are examples of **mass media:** mediated communication vehicles that involve the sending of messages from content creators to huge, relatively anonymous audiences (Chaffee & Metzger, 2001). The content in such media is created for public consumption and is mostly one-directional; that is, you don't directly interact with anyone by reading or watching this content.

Although mass media are an important area of research for communication scholars, this chapter focuses on **social media,** which enable communicators to directly send and receive messages in real time or across time intervals. Increasingly, people use media devices—such as mobile phones and computers—to manage their relationships, communicate in school and work groups, and deliver presentations. At work, for instance, most interactions take place over e-mail, texts, or phone calls. Many businesses use Skype (or other videoconferencing systems) to conduct employment interviews. Daily communication with friends, family, and romantic partners happens through social media—dropping parents a quick "Hi" by text

TABLE 3.1
DIFFERENCES BETWEEN MASS MEDIA & SOCIAL MEDIA[1]

	MASS MEDIA	SOCIAL MEDIA
EXAMPLES	New York Times National Public Radio Whitehouse.gov Fox News	Text messaging Facebook Twitter Instagram
COMMUNICATION FLOW	One-way	Two-way
PURPOSE	Information (news) Entertainment Advertising Public service	Information Self-presentation Relationship building Managing work tasks Alleviating boredom
FAMILIARITY WITH THE AUDIENCE	Mostly unknown	Mostly known
CONTENT CONTROL	Source provider	Senders and receivers
TYPE OF FEEDBACK	Viewer ratings and comments, page view counts	Immediate and/or delayed responses or replies

[1]Adapted from Chaffee & Metzger (2001).
VLADGRIN/Shutterstock

message or catching up with friends through Facebook or video chat. As a student, you might participate in online discussion groups and make online presentations for classes. For an overview of the differences between mass media and social media, see Table 3.1.

Functions of Mediated Communication

Even though the specific platforms, sites, and apps you use to communicate via social media change constantly, there are still established ways in which these tools meet your communication needs. As Chapter 1 discusses, communication helps you meet three types of goals, and these apply to mediated communication as well:

- *Instrumental goals* are the practical objectives you want to achieve or tasks you want to accomplish. This includes using social media to find information, coordinate schedules, and confirm reservations.

- *Relationship goals* include how you build, maintain, or terminate bonds with others. This is a popular way to use social media, allowing you to get in touch with people you haven't spoken to in a while, share your own news, and even block or defriend people you aren't close to anymore. Such tools are often at the center of our social lives. In one study, college students reported that online posts are the easiest way to find out about upcoming social events (Quan-Haase & Young, 2010).

- *Self-presentational goals* involve presenting yourself in certain ways so others view you as you want them to. Through photos, updates, posts, and comments, you create a public self. As Chapter 2 discusses, a *public self* is the self you present to others (Fenigstein, Scheier, & Buss, 1975). In this chapter, we'll explore how you use *online self-presentation* to create that self.

In addition to fulfilling such goals, mediated communication serves two other important functions:

- *Participating in professional and public communities* means you can engage with people outside of your intimate networks of family and friends. For example, e-mail can be used to express your concerns about proposed new laws to government officials. Or you could deliver a virtual presentation to work team members at offsite locations. (We'll discuss more about delivering speeches online in Chapter 15.)

- *Alleviating boredom* through social media is a common experience (Quan-Haase & Young, 2010). People often seamlessly integrate mediated communication into the less stimulating moments of their lives. You might text with coworkers during slow work shifts ("Are you as bored as I am?") or chat online with friends when you need a break from studying.

Characteristics of Mediated Communication

Since mediated communication serves different functions, you have choices in the types of media you use to communicate with others. Imagine that you've just received a great job offer. Would you share the good news with your roommate in person or through a text message? In either format, your message is essentially the same: "I got the job!" But the characteristics of your communication—including how you interact with your roommate, the nonverbal cues exchanged, and how long your message endures—will differ depending on the format you choose.

Synchronous versus Asynchronous Communication. When you talk with someone face-to-face, you're engaged in **synchronous communication:** a back-and-forth exchange of messages that occurs in real time. Additional forms of synchronous communication include phone conversations, instant messaging, and videoconferences. By contrast, in **asynchronous communication**, there are time lapses between messages. If you send an e-mail, leave a voice mail, or post to a forum, there is a delay before a response arrives or you may get no response at all.

It's best to use synchronous communication when you need to communicate a difficult or complicated message. For example, you may want to use the phone or Skype to tell your family that you won't be coming home for the holidays as planned. If you text them with the news, they may think you're insensitive or incompetent ("What kind of daughter cancels holiday plans through a text?"). However, synchronous communication requires all the communicators to be available at the same time. That's not always possible, especially when people live in different time zones or have conflicting work or life schedules. In these situations, asynchronous communication may be best. It is also appropriate for nonurgent, quick, and simple messages, such as letting a friend know you're running a few minutes late for a lunch date.

Restriction of Nonverbal Information. Communicating face-to-face with others provides immediate access to *nonverbal* cues, such as facial expressions and tone of voice, which help you understand other people's thoughts and feelings. When your roommate responds with a smile and a high-five after you tell her you got a new job, she clearly feels happy for you. As Chapter 6 explains, nonverbal behaviors are undeniably an important part of your communication with others.

In mediated communication—especially those forms that involve text only—you get little or no nonverbal information. According to the **cues-filtered-out model**, in this type of communication, many of the cues vital for making sense of messages are not available; they are "filtered out" (Culnan & Markus, 1987). This makes mediated communication more difficult to understand than face-to-face communication. If you're texting with someone, it's almost impossible to tell if they're being sarcastic or sincere. In one study, 27 percent of respondents agreed that e-mail is likely to result in miscommunication of the senders' intended meaning, and almost 54 percent agreed that it's relatively easy to misinterpret an e-mail message (Rainey, 2000). To help minimize such confusion, communicators use acronyms (LOL, TIC) or emoticons (or emoji) to convey their intent more clearly. But even these symbols are a poor substitute for the nonverbal cues available when communicating face-to-face.

The fact that nonverbal information is restricted during most mediated communication doesn't necessarily mean that the interaction is less important or personal. According to **social information processing theory** (Walther, 1992), people communicating through social media compensate for the lack of nonverbal cues by taking more care when choosing their words. The result is that mediated communication, though "cue filtered," can be just as personal as face-to-face interaction (Walther & Parks, 2002).

http://support.apple.com/kb/ht4976

To help neutralize the cues-filtered-out model, a common practice is to use emoticons or emoji (like the ones shown here) to provide some nonverbal cues about the message's intent. In what types of scenarios do you use such images to clarify the meaning of your text messages?

Message Life Span. A basic principle of communication is that there are no "take-backs" or "do-overs." Everything you say becomes part of the permanent record of your relationship with others. So when you snap at your parents or insert a tasteless joke into a speech, you can't turn back time and erase your error.

This is especially true in mediated communication. Every time you send a digital message (text, e-mail, tweet, video, or post), it stays in your account *and* in the accounts of those who received it. It also stays in the servers of companies hosting the accounts. Deleting a text, an e-mail, a post, or the entire account doesn't make the information go away. Anyone with the right access can find it. Even apps that promote disappearing messages or pictures (like Snapchat) can be easily saved with a little know-how.

Digital messages thus have a long life span and are easily searchable, retrievable, and replicable (boyd, 2007). Why does this matter? One reason is because many employers check job applicants social media profiles to get a sense of what the applicant is really like. Some even ask for applicants' passwords to closely examine their accounts (Garber, 2012). Although that is an extreme (and possibly illegal) case, it is commonplace for employers to Google potential new hires. If you Google your own name, what comes up? Search engines can easily find your digital trail and deliver it to anyone who wants it. Be mindful when sending text messages and e-mails or posting online, because you're creating an enduring record of your communication that is easy to find and to share.

Self-Presentation and Mediated Communication

Take a moment to think about how you're dressed today. Are you wearing casual clothes or something more professional? You select your clothing to make a specific impression, based on what you'll be doing and who you'll be seeing. Likewise, when you select photos, post updates, and share information online, you create an impression that influences how others see you.

If you have a social network account, look at your profile: the photos, status updates, or links you've posted and your list of friends. What does all this say about you? Are you fun and outgoing? A hard partier? Deeply philosophical? A humanitarian? A shopaholic? In a study of almost 400 Facebook profiles, researchers found that 92 percent of users posted a personal photograph, 83 percent made their wall public, and 55 percent indicated their sexual orientation (Nosko, Wood, & Molema, 2010). You could learn a lot about someone just from that information alone!

When you set up a social network profile, you make a series of decisions about how to present your self. Such choices determine your online *face*, or the positive self you want others to see (Goffman, 1955). Creating your online face is an important part of your online self-presentation, and it requires as much careful planning and management as does your in-person self-presentation.

DOUBLE TAKE

ONLINE FACE & SELF-PRESENTATION

Imagine you saw the images below posted to two new acquaintances' Facebook pages. Based on the photos, what would you perceive about the online face each is presenting? Why?

Izf/Shutterstock

Sam Edwards/Getty Images

Creating Your Online Face

Scholars studying mediated communication suggest that three elements largely determine your online face: your posted content, your e-mail and screen names, and your friends and professional connections.

Posted Content. Everything you post online communicates information about who you are and how you wish to be seen. A status update like, "Monster trucks one night, demolition derby the next—Gotta love the county fair!" or a tweet that reads, "$1 oysters until 7 pm at Harpers—come hang with the gang!" communicates powerful messages about your tastes, interests, and social identity (you're a "country" person; you're a "foodie"). The same goes for posting, sharing, and tagging photographs and videos.

Online faces are far from objective, however. People post content to amplify positive personality characteristics, such as warmth, friendliness, and extraversion (Vazire & Gosling, 2004). For instance, photos on social networking sites typically show groups of friends, giving the impression that the person in the profile is likable, fun, and popular (Ellison, Steinfield, & Lampe, 2007). These positive and highly selective depictions of self generally work. When viewing someone's profile, you tend to believe what you see and form the same impressions about the person that he or she intended (Gosling, Gaddis, & Vazire, 2007).

Of course, it's not just what you post about yourself that determines your online face—it's also the content that others post about you. Research shows that when friends, family members, coworkers, or romantic partners post information about you, their content shapes others' perceptions of you even more powerfully than your own postings do—especially when their postings contradict your self-description (Walther, Van Der Heide, Kim, Westerman, & Tong, 2008).

Why do others' posts have so much power? When assessing someone's online description, you consider the **warranting value** of the information presented—that is, the degree to which the information is supported by other people and outside evidence (Walther, Van Der Heide, Hamel, & Schulman, 2009). Information that was obviously crafted by the person, that isn't supported by others, and that can't be verified offline has *low warranting value*, and most people don't trust it. Information that's created or supported by others and that can be readily verified through alternative sources (online and off) has *high warranting value*, and is seen as valid. So, if you post news about how well you played in a lacrosse game and the news is featured on your school newspaper's Web site, its warranting value increases (Walther et al., 2009).

The research on warranting value suggests that you need to manage online content posted by others that contradicts the self you want to present—even if you think such content is cute or funny. If you want to track what others are posting about you, set up a Google Alert or regularly search for your name and other identifying keywords. If anyone posts information about you that doesn't match how you want to be seen, politely ask that

REMOVING AN EMBARRASSING POST

 One way to improve your communication competence is by adapting your messages to others' behaviors. Learn how to manage your online self-presentation by going to LaunchPad at **bedfordstmartins.com/choicesconnections** and completing the **How to Communicate video scenario** for Chapter 3 to practice your skills.

CONSIDER THIS:
While hanging out with friends, you imitate how your boss flirts with customers, totally unaware that your friend Tim is shooting a video of your performance. The next day, you're horrified to discover that Tim has posted the video online. You want him to take it down immediately, and ask him to meet with you right away.

WHAT WOULD YOU DO?
To maintain a positive relationship, you'll want to avoid sending a text message simply demanding that Tim remove the post. Instead, arrange to meet face-to-face or over the phone to talk about the post. As you complete the video activity, consider how the dialogue protects the in-person and the online face. Then, test your knowledge of key skills, and create your own responses to the **What if? video prompts**.

"I saw that you posted a video of me imitating how my boss flirts with some of her customers . . . I'm so embarrassed."

① **BE SPECIFIC.** Describe the exact post and your feelings about it. Avoid attacking or blaming language.

② EXPLAIN WHY IT MATTERS TO YOU. State the personal impact of the post and other potential consequences.

"I'm really worried that my boss will see it and be hurt. I also feel like it makes me look mean."

③ POLITELY REQUEST that the post be removed. Use language that saves face for your friend.

"I know you meant no harm by it, but I would like for you to remove it."

WHAT IF? But what if things don't work out as shown? Test your ability to adapt your communication by watching the What if? videos and planning a response for each situation.

1. When Tim downplays your feelings—"I don't see why you're mad about it. No one knows who you're imitating, and it's funny"—how can you still maintain your online face?

2. What can you say if Tim reminds you of a time you embarrassed him? "You weren't too concerned about being 'mean' when you posted a photo of me passed out after AgFest last year."

Your online self-presentation is also influenced by the people you follow, the tags you use, and the posts you like. One advantage of social media is that these markers make it easy for you to find and follow people with similar interests.

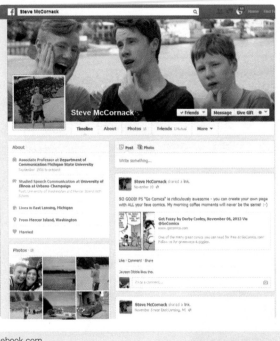

facebook.com

person to delete it. For more on managing your online face, see How to Communicate: Removing an Embarassing Post on pages 66-67.

E-mail and Screen Names. The name you use for your e-mail address, online profiles, or Web site tells others how you want to be perceived (Baym, 2010). Although it is tempting to underestimate their impact, these names create powerful impressions. On dating Web sites, for example, screen names that are playful or represent physical traits ("Fun2bwith," "Blueeyes") are rated by viewers as attractive (Whitty & Buchanan, 2010). Neutral screen names ("0257") or names suggesting wealth ("Silverspoon") convey a sense that the individual is boring or arrogant (Whitty & Buchanan, 2010).

However, what works for one site may not be a good idea in other contexts. You wouldn't want to use your dating profile name ("Fun2bwith") for an e-mail address on a job application. For example, Joe maintains a professional identity through his academic e-mail address (joseph.ortiz@ scottsdalecc.edu), which states his full name and the school where he teaches. But in fantasy baseball forums, his screen name—joeStros13—reflects a more casual identity. Carefully choose screen names based on the audience to which you are trying to appeal.

Friends and Professional Connections. Lists of your friends on Facebook, of your professional connections on LinkedIn, or of your followers on Twitter can also give impressions about your social status, political ideology, and other interests (Donath & boyd, 2004). For example, if you're linked to people who post frequently about animal rights, someone looking at your profile might assume that this cause is important to you, too. Even the number of friends listed on your profile creates impressions. In one study, individuals with about 300 friends on Facebook were viewed as more likable than those with 100 friends or a lot more than 300 friends (Tong, Van Der Heide, Langwell, & Walther, 2008). Why? Having "too few" Facebook friends made people seem unpopular. Having "too many" made them appear to spend too much time online or seem indiscriminate in their choice of friends.

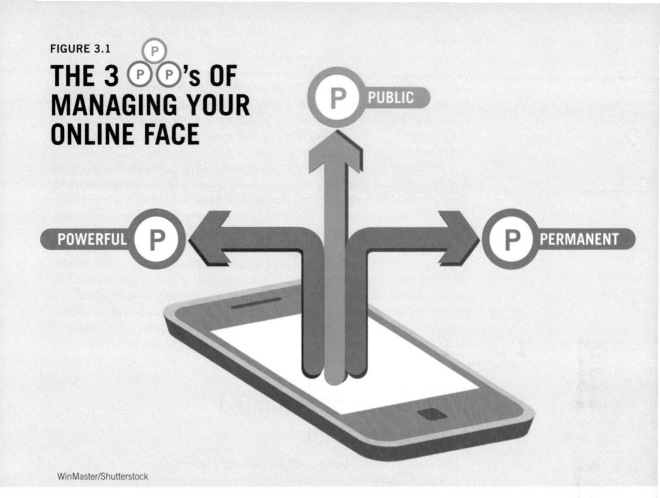

FIGURE 3.1

THE 3 P P P's OF MANAGING YOUR ONLINE FACE

PUBLIC

POWERFUL P

P PERMANENT

WinMaster/Shutterstock

Managing Your Online Face

Given how much communication occurs through social media, it's essential to competently manage your online face. The three Ps of mediated communication—*powerful*, *public*, and *permanent*—can help you do just that.[3]

Mediated communication is *powerful* in shaping others' impressions of you. When you communicate with others through social media, they're more likely to think that your communication reflects your "true" self than they would of your face-to-face communication (Shedletsky & Aitken, 2004). For example, if you e-mail a job application to a potential employer and don't include a proper subject line, greeting, or message, they could conclude that you're unprofessional.

Mediated communication is *public*. Always assume that the self you present to others through social media is going to be viewed by a much larger

[3] Personal communication with authors, May 13, 2008. This material was developed specifically for this text and published with permission of Dr. Malcolm Parks; it may not be reproduced without written consent of Dr. Parks and the authors.

audience than you intended. E-mails, texts, tweets, photos, videos, comments, and status updates can be downloaded, saved, edited, copied, captured, and forwarded by recipients to others. Even if you have privacy settings enabled, there's nothing stopping authorized friends from downloading posts and photos and distributing them to others.

Mediated communication is *permanent*. Blog posts, status updates, tweets, photos, and e-mails don't "go away" when you send or delete them; they are saved by recipients and stored on servers and can be retrieved later. Assume that anything and everything you and others post about you online may still be available long into the future.

Keeping the three Ps of mediated communication in mind will help you create and maintain the online face you want others to see. Additionally, there are unique challenges for maintaining positive face when you communicate online in work groups—known as *virtual teams*—and when you deliver online presentations. Chapter 11 (Small Group Communication) considers specific skills for communicating in virtual teams, and Chapter 15 (Delivering Your Speech) addresses steps for making online presentations.

Challenges of Mediated Communication

Sometimes it just happens. Without thinking, you send a sarcastic or rude message, forgetting about how it might affect the person receiving it. Although technology is convenient and useful, it also makes it easier to make poor communication choices, such as using harsh language, lying, and even harassing.

In the movie *Catfish*, New York photographer Nev Schulman meets Megan Faccio through Facebook. He quickly falls for her, attracted by her photos and apparent musical talent. Over eight months, they develop an online romance through messages, e-mails, and phone calls. An aspiring singer, Megan impresses Nev with files she sends of her music. But Nev's infatuation with Megan soon cools when he finds that her cover of the country standard "Tennessee Stud" was lifted from another artist on YouTube. When Nev finally decides to visit Megan at her home in rural Ishpeming, Michigan, what he discovers is a web of lies and fantasy. There is no Megan. She is the creation of another woman named Angela who pieced together a fictional Megan from the pictures, interests, and music of other people's online profiles.

Nev fell for a common pitfall of mediated communication: people misrepresenting who they are for personal gain or satisfaction. In fact, online deception is so common that Nev went on to host a *Catfish* TV show on MTV, on which he helps people find out if their online relationships are based on reality or lies. More often than not, the relationships are based on some form of deception. (Additionally, some people believe Nev himself to be deceptive—claiming he made up the scenario for the movie and none of it was real.)

MTV/Courtesy: Everett Collection

MTV's show *Catfish* chronicles one of the most common challenges of mediated communication: people using deception to lie about their identity and intentions when forming relationships online. Have you ever interacted with someone online who turned out to be not what they seemed?

The harsh truth is that some people use mediated communication to lie, deceive, harass, and bully. Of course, these challenges aren't limited to mediated messages, but certain characteristics of such communications make them especially likely to be used in this way.

Causes of Mediated Communication Challenges

The limited amount of nonverbal information available in mediated communication, especially social media, can impact behavior in two ways: communicating in a more unconstrained or open fashion and experiencing difficulty in feeling empathy.

Online Disinhibition. When using mediated communication, especially text-only social media, people often feel free to say things—good and bad—that they'd never say to someone face-to-face. This effect is known as **online disinhibition** (Suler, 2004). As noted earlier, much of mediated communication is *asynchronous*—you don't interact with others in real time but exchange messages that are read and responded to later. When you're communicating asynchronously, it's almost as if time gets magically suspended (Suler, 2004). You know you'll get responses to your messages, but you can choose when (and whether) to view those responses. This can make you more willing to openly express emotions that you might otherwise conceal if you knew you'd get an immediate response.

Mediated communication also provides a sense of *invisibility*. When you're not sharing physical space with your communication partners, you feel as if they can't really see or hear you. This makes you feel detached from the consequences of your messages. This sense is enhanced when you use screen names or identities that aren't traceable to your offline self.

Even if you don't mean to, online disinhibition increases the likelihood that you will use language that is more harsh, profane, rude, and blunt than you'd normally use. Similarly, when receiving messages via social media, you should expect others to use language that is more direct and unedited than would be used when talking face-to-face.

Empathy Deficits. As Chapter 2 discusses, *empathy* is the ability to "feel into" others' thoughts and emotions. When nonverbal cues are restricted, it can be hard to experience empathy. That's because the same part of your brain that controls empathy also monitors nonverbal feedback (Goleman, 2006). During face-to-face encounters, you constantly track feedback from others, watching their facial expressions, eye contact, and gestures, and listening to their tone of voice. This feedback enables you to feel empathy for them—to imagine what they're thinking and feeling about your communication.

When you see or hear people react negatively to something you're saying, you can instantly modify your communication to turn the interaction in a more positive direction. So if you say to your roommate, "Hey, let's invite all our friends over this weekend for a *Game of Thrones* marathon! We can watch all of season 3," and, in response, she rolls her eyes and says, "Oh, great," in a sarcastic tone of voice, you know to ask what's wrong. When she expresses concerns about the work involved in hosting such an extended party, you two have the opportunity to talk it over and agree to a compromise, like inviting fewer friends for just one night to watch a movie instead.

Now consider what happens when you don't get nonverbal feedback during communication—such as when you're texting, e-mailing, tweeting, or posting online. If you can't perceive others' immediate nonverbal feedback, you can't experience empathy and adjust your communication accordingly (Goleman, 2007). You might be confused by a WhatsApp message from your roommate saying, "oh, great ;)" to your idea about the *Game of Thrones* marathon. In this situation, you are less able to *perspective-take*—that is, to see the situation and your communication from your partner's point of view. Is your roommate excited? Sarcastic? Annoyed?

This experience can lead to **empathy deficits:** a dramatic reduction in your ability to experience the other person's feelings. Consequently, you may express yourself in blunt, tactless, and inappropriate ways—like "shouting" by using capitalized words or communicating things you'd never say over the phone or face-to-face. For example, you assume that your roommate's text means she's dismissing your idea for a *Game of Thrones* marathon, and you reply, "FINE! You don't have to be involved!!!" Complicating matters further, people on the receiving end of your communication have the same deficit. Their online messages are less sensitive and less tactful as well, even if they don't mean it any more than you do.

MAKING COMMUNICATION CHOICES

WHY DIDN'T YOU AT LEAST TEXT ME?

1 CONSIDER THE DILEMMA

It was only a weekend trip, but Peyton's leaving still bothered you. The two of you were inseparable since you started dating four weeks ago. Adding to your uneasiness was the thought of Peyton traveling to Las Vegas—aka "Sin City." As you part ways at the airport, you wave your phone and say, "Don't forget to stay in touch." "Of course!" Peyton replies.

Shortly after Peyton's scheduled arrival time, you send a text: "Did you make it in ok?" No response. After waiting 30 minutes, you send another text, "Hey, make it to Vegas?" An hour later, Peyton finally texts back, "yes, flt was on time. Training til 5. Call then."

The day passes quickly as you run errands and study. When you finally notice the time, it's after 7:00 p.m. and Peyton still hasn't called. Since Las Vegas is in your same time zone, you're certain the training is done by now. Around 8:30 p.m. you text Peyton, "Still training? What's going on?" No response. When you try to call, Peyton's voice mail greets you immediately. You don't leave a message.

Just after midnight your phone rings. It's Peyton. "I'm sorry I didn't call earlier. We went to dinner and ended up walking the strip afterwards, and . . ." Angrily you interrupt, "Yeah, whatever. It's not hard to text and let me know. Hope you're having a good time. I'll talk to you tomorrow," and then hang up.

2 CONNECT THE RESEARCH

Romantic couples use mobile phones to stay in contact, coordinate their plans, and flirt with each other (Miller-Ott, Kelly, & Duran, 2012). When couples cannot be physically together, mobile phones provide ongoing availability for staying connected. But the ongoing availability comes at a price. Phones can be a way of checking up on your partner, and they can create unnecessary interruptions or cause hurt feelings when a text message does not get an immediate reply.

Couples experience tension when they lack clear rules about using mobile phones in their relationship (Miller-Ott et al., 2012; Duran, Kelly, & Rotaru, 2011). Rules are mutually understood

agreements about the appropriate use of cell phones for communicating with each other. Romantic partners often argue about excessive phone calling and texting or the failure to answer phone calls or texts (Duran et al., 2011). Although they are not written, rules emerge when couples communicate their expectations and preferences about how to use cell phones in the relationship.

Negotiating rules is important to keeping couples happy about their ongoing availability and use of cell phones. One study found that romantic couples who mutually agreed that they would not fight through cell-phone conversations or texts reported high relationship satisfaction (Miller-Ott et al., 2012).

3 COMMUNICATE

Before making a communication choice, consider the facts of the situation and the research on rules for using mobile phones in romantic relationships. Also, reflect on what you've learned about synchronous and asynchronous communication (pp. 61–62), online disinhibition (pp. 71–72), flaming (p. 75), and mediated communication competence (pp. 76–79). Then answer these questions:

1. What factors could influence Peyton's responses to your text messages? How might your self-esteem affect your view of the situation?

2. Would you consider your text messages and phone call excessive? Were Peyton's delayed responses disrespectful? If you had negotiated some rules for being in touch before Peyton left, what would be some reasonable expectations?

3. What are you going to say to Peyton the next day?

When you communicate face-to-face, you have the advantage of getting real-time feedback from the other person. But communicating online restricts feedback, which can lead to empathy deficits. This is a common problem at work, where busy schedules and deadlines cause people to use mediated communication channels incompetently.

RUTH FREMSON/The New York Times/Redux Pictures

Types of Mediated Communication Challenges

When people experience online disinhibition and **empathy deficits**, they're more likely to encounter challenges in mediated communication. The most common of these are digital deception, flaming and trolling, and online harassment and cyberbullying.

Digital Deception. Anyone who sends messages that intentionally mislead or create a false belief in recipients is committing **digital deception** (Hancock, 2007). Digital deception can take several forms. One form is **identity-based digital deception,** whereby someone falsely misrepresents his or her identity or gender (Hancock, 2007). Some people exaggerate or enhance aspects of their identity online. In the movie *Catfish*, Angela deceived Nev by lying about her name, age, physical appearance, and musical abilities. Although that was a special case, similar deception is common on dating sites, where people exaggerate their education and income levels and lower their weight and age (J. A. Hall, Park, Song, & Cody, 2010).

Another form of digital deception is **message-based digital deception,** which is the manipulation of information with the intent of misleading recipients (Hancock, 2007). This type of deception can include **butler lies,** which people use to avoid conversation, prevent embarrassment, or simply be polite (Hancock &

Toma, 2009). For example, you ignore a friend's text but later reply saying you "just got her message." Message-based digital deception also includes serious lies that can devastate personal, social, and work relationships (De-Paulo, Kirkendol, Kashy, Wyer, & Epstein, 1996). Examples include texting your spouse that you're in a work meeting to cover up an affair, or e-mailing a professor that you missed an assignment due to illness, when in fact it's just because you were unprepared.

Flaming and Trolling. If you've ever received mediated messages that are hostile, insulting, or profane, you know they can be hurtful. When people say vicious and aggressive things online that they would never say in person, they are **flaming**. Flaming is a direct outcome of online disinhibition and empathy deficits: when you feel little empathy toward others and also feel comparatively "invisible," you're more likely to communicate in inappropriate, destructive ways.

To reduce the likelihood of flaming in your own mediated communication, draft text messages, e-mails, and posts and then reread them before sending, asking yourself, "Would I say the same thing to this person's face?" If your answer is no, then don't send the message. Instead, delete it and consider more constructive ways to express your thoughts.

Some people post flame messages on purpose to start fights, a practice known as **trolling**. People troll for their own enjoyment or because they're bored (Donath, 1999). Read the comments for popular YouTube videos, and you'll see trolling at work ("My 3-year-old sings and plays better than this sucky band!"). The best response to trolls is to ignore them. But this is often easier said than done. Trolls can be very disruptive to online communities because their intent is to cause discord and they will often continue to post until disruption is achieved. When a hostile comment is posted online, it's not unusual to see the acronym *DNFTT* (Do not feed the trolls) soon follow, as a warning not to "take the bait."

Online Harassment and Cyberbullying. Some texts, e-mails, or postings constitute **online harassment**: mediated messages perceived by the recipient as disturbing, threatening, or obsessive (Walker, Sockman, & Koehn, 2011). For instance, your roommate—much to your embarrassment and against your direct requests not to—repeatedly takes pictures of you drinking at parties and then posts them on Instagram. Or a coworker forwards e-mails with

In addition to not engaging with anyone trolling or flaming online, you can also take measures to report inappropriate or obscene messages. Most platforms (like Instagram, shown) allow you to report or block users—an unfortunate but necessary function.

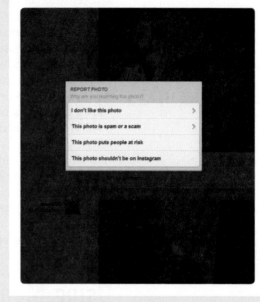

www.instagram.com

sexist humor and images to you at work, even after you ask him to stop. Never ignore this kind of communication. If it happens, directly and clearly ask the person to remove the post or to stop sending the e-mails. If the person refuses, contact people in positions of authority (managers, resident advisers, professors, parents) and ask for advice on what to do.

Online harassment can turn into **cyberbullying** if the communication patterns become persistent and are used to exert power over you (Walker et al., 2011; Wolak, Mitchell, & Finkelhor, 2006). Much like face-to-face bullying, cyberbullying is intended to cause social embarrassment, inflict emotional pain, or damage a person's reputation. Although cyberbullying largely occurs among teens, it can also happen in the workplace in the form of threatening e-mails or voice mails and sexually charged material (White, 2010). If you believe you're being cyberbullied, firmly tell the bully to stop, and keep written records of the offending messages. If the bullying doesn't stop, meet with an authority figure (such as a school or human resource administrator) to describe what's taking place and to ask for help. Most important, if the bullying has you fearing for your physical safety, immediately report it to local law enforcement. Many states have laws to protect victims of cyberbullying. If you need help with handling cyberbullying, refer to www.stopbullying.gov.

Using Mediated Communication Competently

You probably spend a lot of time playing with the various features of a new phone or tablet, but it's just as important to learn how to communicate competently using technology. Otherwise, you might make some missteps— like sending lengthy text messages when a phone call would've been easier or sounding more aggressive than you intended.

Concerned about inflammatory and uncivil discussion in online public forums, computer science researcher Travis Kriplean developed Reflect, a free Web-based program that seeks "better discussion through restatement" (http://engage.cs.washington.edu/reflect/). The program works in the comment section of online forums and requires you to briefly summarize a person's comment before you can share your response to it. This forces commenters to show that they've "listened." According to Reflect's mission statement, this will help people avoid conflicts due to misunderstandings and thereby build stronger online communities.

By trying to minimize conflicts and encourage open discussions online, Kriplean is encouraging competent mediated communication. In addition to your taking the time to really listen to what others are saying, the following suggestions can help you improve your own mediated communication.[4]

---

[4] Material for the first four points is published with permission of Dr. Malcolm Parks; it may not be reproduced without written consent of Dr. Parks and the authors.

1. **Know when to communicate online versus face-to-face.** In many situations, online communication is more time efficient than in-person communication. For instance, messaging a friend to remind her of a coffee date makes more sense than dropping by her workplace, and it's probably quicker and less disruptive than calling her. But online communication is not the best medium for giving in-depth, lengthy, and detailed explanations of professional or personal dilemmas or for conveying weighty relationship decisions. As the chapter's opening story illustrates, Jack Dorsey places so much value on meeting face-to-face with employees that he doesn't even have an office.

   Since it isn't practical (or necessary) to deal face-to-face on every issue, there are some guidelines to consider in determining the best medium for your message. First, consider the message itself. Handle emotional messages face-to-face. If this isn't possible, use synchronous communication (a phone call or video chat) so you can better monitor and respond to the other person's reactions. With complex and difficult messages, consider using more than one medium. For example, hold a meeting to explain work policy changes and then follow up by e-mailing a summary of your main points or additional details to the meeting attendees. Second, consider the recipient of your message. Does he or she prefer certain means of communication? If so, adapt your format accordingly. For instance, your aunt may not respond to an Evite for a graduation party, but she will open an invitation she receives in the mail.

2. **Remember the three Ps.** Always remember that mediated communication is *powerful*, *public*, and *permanent*. The things you say and do online

---

The Reflect program seeks to minimize trolls and flaming by requiring visitors to follow competent communication practices like remembering the three Ps, using clear language, and respecting others.

Before responding to a comment, a new poster first explains how he understands what was said.

Asking questions allows the commenters to engage with each other in a civil debate.

Con:: The constitutional right to bail is critical for many poor defendants.

James B But the only people that this amendment would apply to--those charged with crimes that might put them away for life, AND who have demonstrated a propensity for violence--are already having their bail set at extremely high levels. Which means that only the poor defendants are waiting around in jail, the rich ones get bailed out.

Vin Hill This amendment would allow wealthy defendants to be denied bail. The

- Are you saying that you believe this law would not be applied to wealthy and poor defendants equally? *Vin Hill*
  - I meant that the CURRENT law does not treat the wealthy and the poor equally, since the wealthy can afford levels of bail that the poor cannot. *James B.*
- What do you hear James saying?

- What do you hear Vin saying?

Travis Kriplean

FIGURE 3.2

PRACTICING COMPETENT COMMUNICATION ONLINE

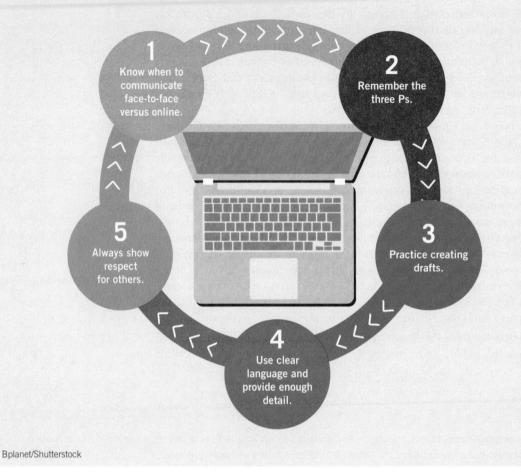

1 Know when to communicate face-to-face versus online.

2 Remember the three Ps.

3 Practice creating drafts.

4 Use clear language and provide enough detail.

5 Always show respect for others.

Bplanet/Shutterstock

endure. Old e-mails, photographs, videos, messages, and blogs—all of these may still be accessible years after you first send them. Think before you post.

3. **Practice creating drafts.** Because online communication makes it easy to flame, many of us impulsively fire off messages that we later regret. Instead, get into the habit of saving posts, texts, and e-mail messages as drafts. Then revisit the drafts later and edit them as needed for appropriateness, and effectiveness. You may be surprised at how a little time can give you perspective on a message. And don't forget that sometimes the most competent online communication is none at all. If you are reviewing a draft and realize it's only going to cause unnecessary damage, delete it.

4. **Use clear language and provide enough detail.** Without feedback, people often misinterpret online messages. To avoid misunderstandings, try to use the clearest words possible. Avoid slang, jargon, and abbreviations unless you know the receiver will understand them and interpret them correctly. This is especially true when giving online presentations or participating in videoconference meetings, when it is important that your audience understand your messages clearly.

   In addition, provide enough detail in your messages. In the rush of texting, we often resort to the simplest, shortest messages possible. Take a bit more time to provide enough detail so that the other person has some context for your message. If you text your spouse "home 2 hrs late," he might wonder if something bad has happened. If your text says, "Still working. Be home 2 hrs late," he can relax, knowing that you're OK. For more on how to create understandable messages, see Chapter 5, pages 116–118.

5. **Always show respect for others.** Empathy deficits can make it hard to communicate in sensitive, respectful ways. So when you're communicating online, put extra energy into *perspective-taking*, or seeing things from other people's point of view, and *empathic concern*—becoming aware of how other people are feeling and experiencing compassion for them. As Chapter 2 explains (pp. 49–53), this will help you experience and express *empathy* for other people. This is at the heart of Kriplean's Reflect program—expressing understanding of and respect for others' viewpoints. Demonstrating similar kindness, caring, and concern in other forms of mediated communication will go far to reduce tensions, build rapport, and create more positive outcomes in all your communication.

✓ **LearningCurve** can help you review! Go to **bedfordstmartins.com /choicesconnections**.

Fancy Collection/SuperStock

The convenience of mediated communication sometimes makes it easy to forget its specific challenges and the time it can take to use it competently. Before sending out your next quick text or multitasking between several apps, take a moment to be sure you are sending the message you intend.

CHAPTER ③ REVIEW

CHAPTER RECAP

- There are two types of **mediated communication: mass media** and **social media.** Social media help you meet your instrumental, relationship, and self-presentational goals.
- Since social media can limit the amount of nonverbal information you receive, the **social information processing theory** suggests that you compensate for this by taking more care with the words you choose to use.
- When creating and managing your online face, remember the three Ps of mediated communication for any content you post—*powerful*, *public*, and *permanent*.
- **Online disinhibition** and **empathy deficits** are two possible causes of mediated communication challenges, such as **digital deception, flaming, trolling, online harassment,** and **cyberbulling**.
- Knowing how to competently use mediated communication can help you improve your relationships, your work life, and your online presentation skills.

LAUNCHPAD

LaunchPad for *Choices & Connections* offers unique video scenarios and encourages self-assessment through adaptive quizzing. Go to bedfordstmartins.com /choicesconnections to get access.

 LearningCurve adaptive quizzes

 How to Communicate video scenarios

 Video clips that illustrate key concepts

KEY TERMS

Mediated communication, p. 58

Mass media, p. 59

Social media, p. 59

Synchronous communication, p. 61

Asynchronous communication, p. 62

Cues-filtered-out model, p. 62

Social information processing theory, p. 62

Warranting value, p. 65

Online disinhibition, p. 71

Empathy deficits, p. 74

Digital deception, p. 74

Identity-based digital deception, p. 74

Message-based digital deception, p. 74

Butler lies, p. 74

Flaming, p. 75

Trolling, p. 75

Online harassment, p. 75

Cyberbullying, p. 76

1 If you want to have an important conversation with a family member, you should first try to engage in a real-time conversation, or _____.

a. asynchronous communication

b. synchronous communication

c. public communication

d. nonverbal feedback

2 When evaluating someone's online face, which of the following do you consider as part of the content's warranting value?

a. If it is supported by others

b. If it can be verified by alternative sources

c. If it is obviously crafted by the person posting it

d. All of the above are correct

3 Which of the following is a main cause of *empathy deficits*?

a. Increased feeling of online disinhibition

b. Sense of invisibility when online

c. Lack of nonverbal feedback

d. Use of identity-based digital deception

4 _____ occurs when people say or do negative things online that they would never do in person.

a. Flaming

b. Butler lie

c. Cyberbullying

d. Deception

5 Which of the following is *not* one of the chapter's suggestions for competently using mediated communication?

a. Avoiding misunderstandings by using clear language and appropriate amounts of detail

b. Creating message drafts and revisiting them later before sending

c. Using perspective-taking and empathic concern when communicating online

d. Limiting mediated communication to a couple of messages per day

ACTIVITIES

1 Analyzing Your Online Face

Look at one of your online profiles for a social media site—Facebook, Tumblr, Twitter, Google+. (If you don't have one, use the profile of a family member or friend.) Working with a classmate, use the three Ps of mediated communication—powerful, public, and permanent—to evaluate each other's online face. What face do you perceive your partner to have? Is it accurate? Based on what your partner perceived, how can you improve your own online face?

2 Flaming and Trolling in Action

Look at the discussion thread in the comment section of a recent online news article about a controversial topic (e.g., www.washingtonpost.com or www.nytimes.com). Identify any instances of flaming, trolling, or harassment and analyze how other commenters responded to these posts. Work with a small group of classmates to prepare a group report on how these comments worked with or violated the guidelines for mediated communication competence suggested in this chapter. Present the report in class.

4

Understanding Culture

elen Torres was born in Puerto Rico but spent her early childhood in a diverse Detroit neighborhood of Polish, Hispanic, Lebanese, and Euro-American families. The summer before she entered third grade, her family moved. Now in a suburb populated mostly by white families, the Torreses were the only Hispanic family in the area.[1] Excited about the change, Helen's mother immediately volunteered to help out with activities at Helen's new school, including fund-raising and school parties.

Soon an incident occurred that changed Helen's view of communication and culture forever. A parent called Helen's mother and asked her to bake cupcakes for an upcoming school event. Helen's mother, a bilingual but dominantly Spanish speaker, didn't know what "cupcakes" were. Why would anyone want a *cup*-sized cake? Concluding that the caller must be confused, Helen's mom baked a beautiful full-sized cake and brought it to school. Seeing the cake, the other kids teased Helen. "I shut them up," Helen explains. "I said, 'My mom can speak two languages. *Can yours?*'"

The cupcake incident quickly faded from Helen's classmates' memories, but for Helen's mother it fostered a sense of insurmountable difference between her and the other mothers. She stopped volunteering for school functions, afraid of embarrassing her daughters. For Helen, the misunderstanding inspired an intense curiosity about communication and cultural difference. This curiosity would eventually lead her to earn a master's degree in communication, and to become a national activist on behalf of Hispanic civil rights.

Years later, Helen hosted a roundtable for a federal agency looking to expand its reach and service to underrepresented communities. One participant was a woman who ran a nonprofit

[1]All information that follows was provided to the authors by Helen Torres in a personal interview, December 5, 2012. Published with the permission of Helen Torres.

organization helping victims of eastern European war crimes establish themselves in the United States. The woman spoke slowly and nervously, with a thick accent. Helen immediately sensed that the other group members were getting irritated with how long the woman was taking to express herself. As Helen describes, "I kept imagining my mother and the cupcake. So I told the other group members to be patient with her and allow her extra time to speak. She had great ideas, and the fact that she was willing to share these with us meant that we should support her."

Today, Helen Torres is executive director and CEO of Hispanas Organized for Political Equality (HOPE), an influential nonprofit committed to achieving political and economic equality for Latinas through leadership, advocacy, and education. But she still recalls the cupcake incident and its impact on her life. "Some may think it's a silly story, but it illustrates a profound point: communicating competently with people from other cultural communities is an essential skill. We must be able to bridge cultural divides through our communication to ensure that all people have their voices heard, understood, respected, and valued, and that no one feels the sense of alienation that my mother once did."

☑ LearningCurve can
help you review! Go to
**bedfordstmartins.com/
choicesconnections**.

Have you been in situations in which, like Helen's mother, you felt distant
from others because of cultural differences? How did you bridge such divides? One way to approach such situations is through your communication.
By understanding cultural influences and improving your ability to communicate competently with people from other cultures, you can build more
positive and mutually satisfying connections with them. In this chapter,
you'll learn:

- The defining characteristics of culture
- What co-cultures are, and their role in communication
- The impact of ingroups, outgroups, and prejudice on communication
- The ways cultural differences influence how people communicate
- How to improve your intercultural communication competence

What Is Culture?

> Whether you realize it or not, your culture affects your communication all the
> time. More than just your race or ethnicity, cultural traits like age, physical
> abilities, social class, and even your values and beliefs influence how you view
> yourself as well as how you perceive others.

In the United States, cultural diversity is rapidly increasing. In 2011, for
example, more than 50 percent of all U.S. births were nonwhite—including
Latino, Asian, African American, and mixed-raced children (U.S. Census
Bureau, 2012). International student enrollments in the country are also
on the rise (Institute of International Education, 2011), so your classmates are just as likely to be from Seoul as Seattle. Plus, with all the
smartphones, tablets, and laptops available, there is easy access to people
all over the world. This enables you to conduct business and personal relationships on a global level in a way never possible before. As your daily
encounters increasingly cross cultural lines, the question arises: What
exactly *is* culture?

Culture Defined

In this book, we take a broad and inclusive view of **culture,** defining it as an
established, coherent set of beliefs, attitudes, values, and practices shared by
a large group of people (Keesing, 1974). Culture includes many types of
influences, such as your nationality, ethnicity, religion, gender, sexual orientation, physical abilities, and age. But what really makes a culture a "culture"
is that it's widely shared. This happens because cultures are learned, communicated, layered, and lived.

Culture Is Learned. You learn your cultural beliefs, attitudes, and values
from many sources, including your parents, teachers, religious leaders,

WHAT IS YOUR CULTURE?

Culture is so integrated into your everyday life, it is easy to overlook how it can inform everything you see, hear, or believe. How do the activities and images shown relate to your culture or not? What other aspects of your culture make you *you*?

(Clockwise from top left) Asia Images Group/Getty Images; NARINDER NANU/AFP/Getty Images; Hero Images/Corbis; susafri/istockphoto.com; Robert McGouey/Getty Images; Mario Tama/Getty Images

peers, and the mass media (Gudykunst & Kim, 2003). This process begins at birth, through customs such as choosing a newborn's name, taking part in religious ceremonies, and selecting godparents or other special guardians. As you mature, you learn deeper aspects of your culture, including the history behind certain traditions—for example, why unleavened bread is eaten during the Jewish Passover or why certain days are more auspicious than others. You also learn how to participate in rituals—everything from blowing out the candles on a birthday cake to carving pumpkins on Halloween. In most societies, teaching children to understand, respect, and practice their culture is considered an essential part of child rearing.

Culture Is Communicated. Each culture has its own practices regarding how to communicate (Whorf, 1952). Imagine you're part of a group project and the other members decide to do the assignment in a particular way. If you grew up in Singapore, you'd be expected to support the group's decision even if you thought another approach would be better. Withholding your dissenting opinion would be considered competent communication because the culture in Singapore emphasizes group harmony over personal preferences. American culture, however, stresses the importance of individual expression. So if you grew up in the United States, you'd probably feel that it's perfectly acceptable—and perhaps even your duty—to voice your concerns about the group's decision.

Culture Is Layered. Many people belong to more than one culture simultaneously. This means they experience multiple "layers" of culture, as various traditions, heritages, and practices are recognized and held to be important. Steve's Uncle Rick, for example, is originally from Canada but is now an American citizen. Rick is passionate about being an American: he played hockey for a U.S. collegiate team, is deeply patriotic, sings the national anthem at ball games, and celebrates the Fourth of July. But every four years, when the Winter Olympics roll around, his Canadian cultural allegiance emerges from beneath the American layer, and he cheers the Canadians over and above everyone else—especially when it comes to hockey!

Culture Is Lived. Culture affects everything about how you live your life. It influences the neighborhoods you live in; the means of transportation you use; the way you think, dress, talk, and even eat. Its impact runs so deep that it is often taken for granted. At the same time, culture is often a great source of personal pride. Many people consciously live in ways that celebrate their cultural heritage—through such behaviors as wearing a Muslim hijab, placing a Mexican flag decal on their car, or greeting others with the Thai gesture of the wai (hands joined in prayer, heads bowed).

FIGURE 4.1

CULTURAL INFLUENCES

Many factors combine to form your culture. Here is a sample of some influences, but what other aspects do you consider part of your culture? Are some aspects more important than others?

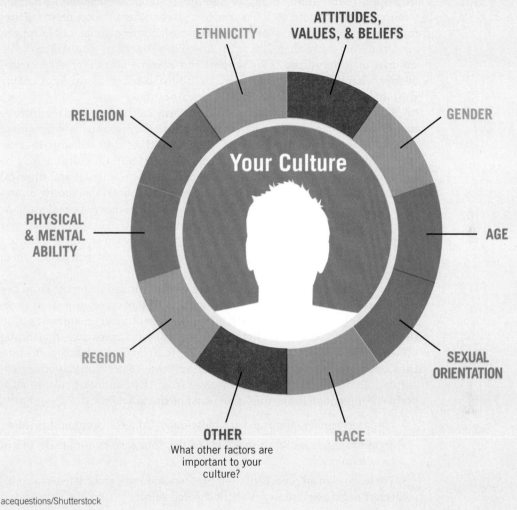

ETHNICITY

ATTITUDES, VALUES, & BELIEFS

RELIGION

GENDER

Your Culture

PHYSICAL & MENTAL ABILITY

AGE

REGION

SEXUAL ORIENTATION

OTHER
What other factors are important to your culture?

RACE

acequestions/Shutterstock

Co-cultures

As societies become more culturally diverse, there is also an increased awareness of how various cultures, and groups of people within them, interact. In any society, there's usually a group of people who have more **power** than everyone else—that is, the ability to influence or control people and events (Donohue & Kolt, 1992). Having more power in a society comes from controlling major societal institutions, such as banks, businesses, the government, and legal and educational systems. According to **co-cultural communication theory,** the people who have more power within a society determine the *dominant culture*, because they get to decide the prevailing views, values, and traditions of the society (Orbe, 1998). Consider the United States. Throughout its history, wealthy Euro-American men have been in power. When the country was first founded, the only people allowed to vote were landowning males of European ancestry. Now, more than 200 years later, Euro-American men still make up the vast majority of the U.S. Congress and Fortune 500 CEOs. As a consequence, what is thought of as "American culture" is tilted toward emphasizing the interests, activities, and accomplishments of these men.

Members of a society who don't conform to the dominant culture—by way of language, values, lifestyle, or physical appearance—often form what are called **co-cultures**; that is, they have their own cultures that *co-exist* within a dominant cultural sphere (Orbe, 1998). Co-cultures may be based on age, gender, social class, ethnicity, religion, mental and physical ability, sexual orientation, and other unifying elements, depending on the society (Orbe, 1998). U.S. residents who are not members of the dominant culture—people of color, women, members of the LGBTQ community, and so forth—exist as distinct co-cultures, with their own political lobbying groups, Web sites, magazines, and television networks (such as Lifetime, BET, Telemundo, and Here TV).

Because members of co-cultures are (by definition) different from the dominant culture, they develop and use numerous communication practices that help them interact with people in the culturally dominant group (Ramirez-Sanchez, 2008). There are three types of approaches, depending on whether the co-cultural members wish to *assimilate* (be accepted) into the dominant culture, get the dominant culture to *accommodate* their co-cultural identity, or *separate* themselves from the dominant culture altogether. For example, they might do some of the following:

- Use overly polite language with individuals from the dominant culture
- Suppress reactions when members of the dominant culture make offensive comments
- Try to excel in all aspects of their professional and personal lives to counteract negative stereotypes about their co-culture
- Act, look, and talk as much as possible like members of the dominant culture
- Openly disparage their own co-culture
- Quietly but clearly express their co-cultural identity through appearance, actions, and words
- Conform to negative stereotypes in an exaggerated way to shock and scare members from the dominant culture

How might these communication practices work in real life? Imagine that an African American couple moves to a largely Euro-American suburb. They socialize primarily with their white neighbors—never displaying any indication of their African American heritage other than their skin color. Meanwhile, their son dresses in sagging pants, wears a do-rag, and blasts gangsta rap through Beats headphones. Through these behaviors, he actively strives to conform to stereotypes about young black males. Despite their differences, all these behaviors have the same goal: managing the tension between African American co-culture and the dominant Euro-American culture.

Ingroups and Outgroups

Culture has an enormous and powerful effect on your perceptions. When you grow up with certain cultural or co-cultural beliefs, attitudes, and values, you naturally perceive those who share these with you as similar to your-self—people you consider **ingroupers** (Allport, 1954). You might think of individuals from many different social groups as ingroupers if they share important cultural commonalities with you, such as nationality, religious beliefs, ethnicity, age, socioeconomic class, or political views (Turner, Hogg, Oakes, Reicher, & Wetherell, 1987). In contrast, you may view people who aren't culturally similar to yourself as **outgroupers**.

DOUBLE TAKE

INGROUPS OR OUTGROUPS

Would you classify the people and activities shown below as ingroupers or outgroupers? What specific aspects in each image make someone seem similar or dissimilar to you? How does this classification influence your communication?

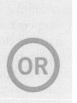

Bob Sacha/Corbis   Kevin R. Morris/Corbis

People often feel passionately connected to their ingroups, especially when they reflect central aspects of their self-concept, such as sexual orientation, religious beliefs, or ethnic heritage. This feeling of connection means you're more likely to give your money, time, and help to ingroupers than to outgroupers (Castelli, Tomelleri, & Zogmaister, 2008). For example, if two volunteers show up at your door asking you to donate money and time to a fund-raising effort, which one are you more likely to support: the volunteer working for a group you feel connected to, or the volunteer representing a group you feel no link to? Many people would pick the ingrouper.

You're also more likely to form positive impressions of people you perceive as ingroupers (Giannakakis & Fritsche, 2011). For instance, in one study of 30 ethnic groups in East Africa, members of each group perceived ingroupers' communication as more trustworthy, friendly, and honest than outgroupers' communication (Brewer & Campbell, 1976). When people communicate in rude or inappropriate ways, you're more inclined to form negative impressions of them if you see them as outgroupers (Brewer, 1999). If a customer at your job snaps at you but is wearing a T-shirt that advocates your cultural beliefs and values, you're likely to make the attribution, "He's just having a bad day." The same communication coming from someone wearing a shirt attacking your cultural beliefs will likely provoke a negative, internal attribution: "What a jerk!"

One of the strongest determinants of ingroup and outgroup perceptions is race. **Race** classifies people based on common ancestry or descent and is judged almost exclusively by a person's physical features (Lustig & Koester, 2006). Perceiving someone's race almost always means assigning him or her to ingrouper or outgrouper status (Brewer, 1999) and communicating with that person based on that status.

When categorizing other people as ingroupers or outgroupers, it's easy to make mistakes. Even if a person seems to be the same race as you (e.g., white), she may have a very different ethnic, religious, and cultural heritage (you're Irish Catholic; she's Russian Jewish). Likewise, even if someone dresses differently than you do, he might hold cultural beliefs, attitudes, and values that are very similar to your own. If you assume that people are ingroupers or outgroupers based on surface-level differences, you may mistakenly perceive that you don't share anything in common. As a consequence, you might never discover that you do share important qualities and thus could miss out on an opportunity to make a new friend, work productively with a colleague, or form a romantic bond.

Prejudice

As the section on impressions in Chapter 2 explains (pp. 45–49), *stereotypes* are a way to categorize people into a social group and then evaluate them based on information you have related to this group. Stereotypes play a big part in how you form impressions about others during the perception

In April 2013, the students of Wilcox County High School took matters into their own hands and organized the school's first integrated prom, overcoming the prejudice that had previously resulted in years of racially segregated celebrations.

Maria Izaurralde/Zuma Press

process. This is especially true for racial and gender characteristics, since they are among the things you notice first when encountering others. But when stereotypes reflect rigid attitudes toward groups and their members, they become **prejudice** (Ramasubramanian, 2010).

Because prejudice is rooted in stereotypes, it can vary depending on whether those stereotypes are positive or negative. According to the **Stereotype Content Model** (Fiske, Cuddy, Glick, & Xu, 2002), prejudice centers on two judgments made about others: how warm and friendly they are, and how competent they are. These judgments create two possible kinds of prejudice: *benevolent* and *hostile*.

Benevolent Prejudice. *Benevolent prejudice* occurs when people think of a particular group as inferior but also friendly and competent. For instance, someone judges a group as "primitive," "helpless," and "ignorant" but attributes their "inferiority" to forces beyond their control, such as lack of education, technology, or wealth (Ramasubramanian, 2010). Thus, although the group is thought of negatively, it also triggers feelings of sympathy (Fiske et al., 2002). People engaging in benevolent prejudice might think that members of a group of people are "inferior" but could improve themselves "if only they knew better."

Hostile Prejudice. *Hostile prejudice* happens when people have negative attitudes toward a group of individuals whom they see as unfriendly and incompetent (Fiske et al., 2002). Someone demonstrating hostile prejudice might see the group's supposed incompetence as intrinsic to the people: "They're naturally lazy," "They're all crazy zealots," or "They're mean and violent." People exhibiting hostile prejudice often also believe that the group has received many opportunities to improve ("They've been given so much") but that their innate limitations hold them back ("They've done nothing but waste every break that's been given to them").

Overcoming Prejudice. Prejudice, no matter what form, is destructive and unethical. Benevolent prejudice leads to condescending and disrespectful communication. Hostile prejudice is the root of every exclusionary "ism": racism, sexism, ageism, classism, ableism, and so on.

The root of prejudice is deeply held negative beliefs about particular groups (Ramasubramanian, 2010). If you think you have prejudiced beliefs, your communication skills can help you confront them and permanently give them up. Use the perception-checking and empathy guidelines discussed in Chapter 2 (pp. 49–53) to help you evaluate and change your own beliefs. Also, learn about the cultures and groups you have prejudiced beliefs about. During interactions, ask members of these groups questions about themselves, and listen actively to the answers. This will ease the uncertainty and anxiety you may feel around others who are culturally different from you (Berger & Calabrese, 1975). Finally, be open to new people and experiences; this can result in quality relationships that break down prejudicial barriers.

On the other hand, if you've been on the receiving end of prejudice, try not to generalize your experience with that one person (or persons) to all members of the same group. Just because someone of a certain age, gender, ethnicity, or cultural group behaves badly doesn't mean that *all* members of that group do. One of the bitter ironies of prejudice is that it often triggers a reaction of prejudice in the people who have been unfairly treated. This is not to excuse the prejudice or poor communication of others but to help you avoid adding to the vicious cycle of prejudicial communication.

Cultural Influences on Communication

Your cultural background differs from that of other people in many ways. One way those differences are expressed is through your communication—such as how you deal with power structures, share emotions, and even view time. Understanding and adapting to such factors will help you communicate more competently.

The hit TV show *Modern Family* focuses on a California clan whose members have different cultural backgrounds. Euro-American patriarch Jay is married to the (much younger) Gloria, who is originally from Colombia. In addition to their child together, Jay serves as stepfather to Gloria's son, Manny. Jay's

ABC/Photofest

Gloria Delgado-Pritchett, played by Sofia Vergara, is a Colombian woman whose cultural norms often conflict with those of her American-born family members. How do you navigate situations where culture blurs the line of understanding between yourself and others?

children from a previous marriage also have families of their own. His son, Mitchell, and Mitchell's partner, Cam, have an adopted daughter from Vietnam, while Jay's daughter, Claire, and her goofy husband, Phil, have three children. Given this diversity, interactions between the characters routinely cross lines of age, gender, ethnicity, and sexual orientation—often at the same time. Not surprisingly, there's a lot of miscommunication stemming from these differences. For example, Gloria speaks with a Colombian accent and often tangles up her English words. On Halloween, she tells Jay he's "going to be a gargle." Manny chimes in to clarify, "She means 'gargoyle.'" Later, when a box of Jesus figurines is mysteriously delivered to their house, Jay realizes the error: he had told Gloria to call his secretary and order a box of baby *cheeses*.

Shows like *Modern Family* poke lighthearted fun at cultural differences. However, the real-world communication distinctions between cultures can be profound. Scholars suggest that six cultural characteristics shape our communication: individualism versus collectivism, high and low context, uncertainty avoidance, emotion displays, power distance, and views of time.

Individualistic versus Collectivistic Cultures

In **individualistic cultures,** people tend to value independence and personal achievement. Members of these cultures are encouraged to focus on themselves and their immediate family (Hofstede, 2001), and individual achievement is

The emergence of social media platforms like Facebook, Twitter, Ask.fm, and Instagram gave rise to the popular trend of posting selfies. How does this exemplify the individualistic culture that exists in American society?

Anna Bryukhanova/Getty Images

praised as the highest good (Waterman, 1984). Individualistic countries include the United States, Canada, New Zealand, and Sweden (Hofstede, 2001).

By contrast, in **collectivistic cultures** people emphasize group identity ("we" rather than "me"), interpersonal harmony, and the well-being of ingroups (Park & Guan, 2006). If you were raised in a collectivistic culture, you were probably taught that it's important to belong to groups, or "collectives," that look after you in exchange for your loyalty. In collectivistic cultures, people emphasize the goals, needs, and views of groups over those of individuals and define the highest good as cooperation with others rather than individual achievement. Collectivistic countries include Guatemala, Pakistan, Taiwan, and Japan (Hofstede, 2001).

Differences between individualistic and collectivistic cultures can powerfully influence people's behaviors—including which social networking sites they use and how they use them. For instance, people in collectivistic cultures tend to use sites that emphasize group connectedness, whereas those in individualistic cultures gravitate to sites that focus on self-expression (Barker & Ota, 2011). American Facebook users devote most of their time on the site describing their own actions and viewpoints as well as events that are personally important to them. They also post controversial status updates and express their personal opinions—even if these trigger debate. Japanese users of Mixi, meanwhile, carefully edit their profiles so they won't offend anyone (Barker & Ota, 2011). Whereas American Facebook users often post photos of themselves alone doing various activities,

Mixi users tend to write in diaries that are shared with their closest friends, boosting ingroup solidarity (Barker & Ota, 2011).

High and Low Context

Cultures can also be described as *high* or *low context*. In **high-context cultures,** such as in China, Korea, and Japan, people use relatively vague and ambiguous language and even silence to convey important meanings. (High-context cultures are often collectivistic as well.) People in such cultures often talk indirectly (using hints or suggestions) because they presume that members of their ingroup will know what they're trying to say. As a result, they don't feel a need to provide a lot of explicit information.

In **low-context cultures,** people tend *not* to presume that others share their beliefs, attitudes, and values. Thus, they strive to be informative, clear, and direct in their communication (E. T. Hall & Hall, 1987). Many low-context cultures are also individualistic; as a result, people openly express their views and try to persuade others to accept them (E. T. Hall, 1976, 1997a). Within such cultures, which include Germany, Scandinavia, Canada, and the United States, people work to make important information obvious, rather than hinting or implying.

How does the difference between high-context and low-context cultures play out in real interactions? Consider the experiences of Steve's friend, Naomi Kagawa, a Japanese communication professor. Growing up in Japan—a high-context culture—Naomi learned to reject requests by using words equivalent to "OK" or "sure." The Japanese reject requests this way because it maintains the harmony of the encounter. These words, however, are accompanied by subtle vocal tones that *imply* no. Because all members of the culture know this practice, they recognize that such seeming assents are actually rejections. In contrast, in the United States—a low-context culture—people don't share such a practice. Instead, people often come right out and say no, then apologize and explain why they can't grant the request. When Naomi first visited the United States, this difference caused misunderstandings in her interactions. She rejected unwanted requests by saying, "OK," only to find that people presumed she was consenting rather than refusing. And she was surprised, even shocked, when people rejected her requests by explicitly saying no.

Uncertainty Avoidance

Cultures vary in how much they tolerate and accept unpredictability, known as **uncertainty avoidance.** As scholar Geert Hofstede explains, "The fundamental issue here is how a society deals with the fact that the future can never be known: should we try to control the future or just let it happen?" (Hofstede, 2009a). In *high-uncertainty-avoidance cultures* (such as Mexico, South Korea, Japan, and Greece), people place a lot of value on control. They define rigid rules and conventions to guide all beliefs and behaviors, and they feel uncomfortable with unusual or innovative ideas. People from such cultures want structure in their organizations, institutions, relationships, and everyday lives (Hofstede, 2001). For example, a coworker raised in a high-uncertainty-avoidance culture would expect everyone assigned to a project to have clear roles and responsibilities, including a designated leader. In his research on organizations, Hofstede found that in high-uncertainty-avoidance cultures, people commit to organizations for long periods of time, expect their job responsibilities to be clearly defined, and strongly believe that organizational rules should not be broken (2001, p. 149). Children raised in such cultures are taught to believe in cultural traditions and practices without ever questioning them.

In *low-uncertainty-avoidance cultures* (such as Jamaica, Denmark, Sweden, and Ireland), people put more emphasis on "letting the future happen" without trying to control it (Hofstede, 2001). They care less about rules, tolerate diverse viewpoints and beliefs, and welcome innovation and change. They also feel free to question and challenge authority. In addition, they teach their children to think critically about the beliefs and traditions they're exposed to rather than automatically following them. There is, however, some middle ground. Both the United States and Canada are considered moderately uncertainty avoidant.

Emotion Displays

In all cultures, norms exist regarding how people should and shouldn't express emotion. These norms are called **display rules:** guidelines for when, where, and how to manage emotion displays appropriately (Ekman & Friesen, 1975). Display rules govern very specific aspects of your *nonverbal communication*, such as how broadly you should smile, whether or not you should scowl when angry, and the appropriateness of shouting in public when you're excited. (For more on nonverbal communication displays, see Chapter 6, pp. 137–138.) Children learn such display rules and, over time, internalize them to the point where following these rules seems "normal." This is why you likely think of the way you express emotion as natural, rather than as something that has been socialized into you through your culture (Hayes & Metts, 2008).

Because of differences in socialization and traditions, display rules vary across cultures (Soto, Levenson, & Ebling, 2005). Take the two fastest-growing ethnic groups in the United States—Mexican Americans and Chinese Americans (Buriel & De Ment, 1997). In traditional Chinese culture, people prioritize emotional control and moderation; intense emotions are considered dangerous and are even thought to cause illness (Wu & Tseng, 1985). This belief even shapes communication in close relationships. Chinese American couples don't openly express positive emotions toward each other as often as Euro-American couples do (Tsai & Levenson, 1997). Meanwhile, in traditional Mexican culture, people openly express emotion, even more so than those in Euro-American culture (Soto et al.,

2005). For people of Mexican descent, the experience, expression, and deep discussion of emotions provide some of life's greatest rewards and satisfactions.

When families immigrate to a new society, the move often provokes tension over which display rules they should follow. People more closely oriented to their cultures of origin continue to communicate their emotions in traditional ways. Others—usually the first generation of children born in the new society—may move away from traditional forms of emotional expression (Soto et al., 2005). For example, Chinese Americans who adhere strongly to traditional Chinese culture openly display fewer negative emotions than do those who are Americanized (Soto et al., 2005). Similarly, Mexican Americans with strong ties to traditional Mexican culture express intense negative emotions more openly than their Americanized counterparts.

It's important to be aware of these differences when communicating with others. An emotional expression—such as a loud shout of intense joy—might be considered shocking and inappropriate in some cultures but perfectly normal and natural in others. At the same time, don't presume that all people from the same culture necessarily share the same expectations. As much as possible, adjust your expressions of emotion to match the style of the individuals with whom you're interacting.

Comedy writers often play with display rules, purposely enlarging the characters' reactions or going against the norm to create humor. The outlandish expressions and antics from Seth Rogen and Jay Baruchel in *This Is the End* are an example. When it comes to display rules, where is the line between funny and wrong?

Suzanne Hanover/© Sony Pictures/Courtesy Everett Collection

Power Distance

The degree to which people in a particular culture view the unequal distribution of power as acceptable is known as **power distance** (Hofstede, 1991, 2001). In *high-power-distance cultures*, it's considered normal and even desirable for people of different social and professional status to have different levels of power (Ting-Toomey, 2005). In such cultures, people give privileged treatment and extreme respect to those in high-status positions (Ting-Toomey, 1999). They also expect individuals of lesser status to behave humbly, especially around people of higher status, who are expected to act superior.

In *low-power-distance cultures*, people in high-status positions try to minimize the differences between themselves and lower-status persons by interacting with them in informal ways and treating them as equals (Oetzel, Ting-Toomey, Matsumoto, Yokochi, Pan, Takai, & Wilcox, 2001). For instance, a high-level marketing executive might chat with the cleaning service workers in her office and invite them to join her for a coffee break. See Figure 4.2 for examples of high- and low-power-distance cultures.

Power distance affects how people deal with conflict. In low-power-distance cultures, people with little power may choose to engage in conflict with high-power people. What's more, they may do so *competitively*: confronting high-power people and demanding that their goals be met. For instance, employees may question management decisions and suggest that alternatives be considered, or townspeople may attend a meeting and demand that the mayor address their concerns. These behaviors are much less common in high-power-distance cultures (Bochner & Hesketh, 1994), where low-power people are more likely to either *avoid* conflict with high-power people or *accommodate* them by giving in to their desires. Chapter 8 discusses more ways people approach conflict and how power affects those choices.

Power distance also influences how people communicate in close relationships, especially families. In traditional Mexican culture, for instance, the value of *respeto* emphasizes power distance between younger people and their elders (Delgado-Gaitan, 1993). As part of *respeto*, children are expected to defer to elders' authority and to avoid openly disagreeing with them. In contrast, many Euro-Americans believe that once children reach adulthood, power in family relationships should be balanced—with children and their elders treating one another as equals (Kagawa & McCornack, 2004). To learn how you can handle cultural factors like power distance in group settings, see How to Communicate: Adapting to Cultural Differences on pages 100–101.

Views of Time

Cultures vary in terms of how people view time. Scholar Edward Hall (1997b) distinguished between two time orientations: monochronic (M-time) and polychronic (P-time). People who have a **monochronic time orientation** view

FIGURE 4.2

POWER DISTANCE ACROSS COUNTRIES

HIGH-POWER-DISTANCE COUNTRIES	MODERATE-POWER-DISTANCE COUNTRIES	LOW-POWER-DISTANCE COUNTRIES
Malaysia	Spain	Norway
Panama	Pakistan	Sweden
Guatemala	Italy	Ireland
Philippines	South Africa	New Zealand
Mexico	Hungary	Denmark
Venezuela	Jamaica	Israel
China	United States	Austria

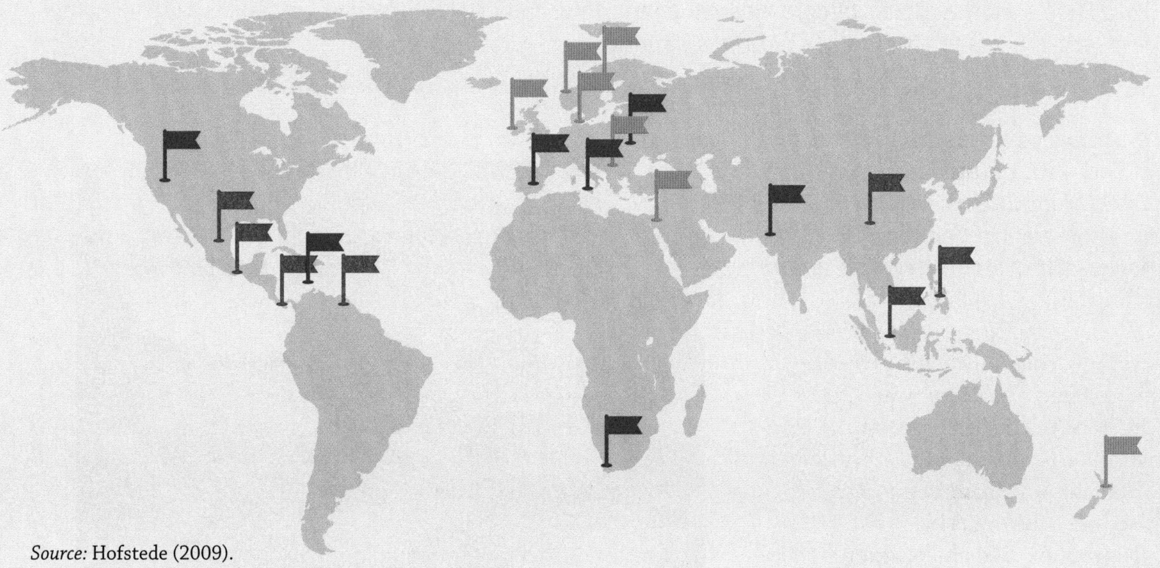

Source: Hofstede (2009).

time as a precious resource. It can be saved, spent, wasted, lost, or made up, and it can even run out. If you're an M-time person, "spending time" with someone or "making time" in your schedule to share activities with him or her sends the message that you consider that person—and your relationship—important (E. T. Hall, 1983). You may view time both as a gift you give others to show your affection and as a tool for punishing someone ("I no longer have time for you").

People who have a **polychronic time orientation** don't view time as a resource to be spent, saved, or guarded. They don't consider time of day (what time it is) as especially important or relevant to daily activities. Instead, they're flexible when it comes to time, and they believe that

ADAPTING TO CULTURAL DIFFERENCES

 One way to improve your communication competence is by adapting your messages to others' behaviors. Learn how to better handle cultural differences in group settings by going to LaunchPad at **bedfordstmartins.com/choicesconnections** and completing the **How to Communicate video scenario** for Chapter 4 to practice your skills.

CONSIDER THIS:

You're assigned to a group project with several class-mates from collectivist, low-emotion-display, and high-power-distance cultures. The group chooses one of them, Lily, as group leader. At your first meeting, Lily begins by suggesting a topic for the project. All the other group members immediately agree. This makes you angry because you had a different idea that you were excited about and wanted the group to pursue.

WHAT WOULD YOU DO?

The following advice illustrates how to communicate in a way that recognizes the cultural preferences of Lily and the other group members. This includes factors like power distance, collectivism, and emotion displays. As you watch the video, consider how the dialogue reflects each cultural factor. Then, test your knowledge of key skills, and create your own responses to the **What if? video prompts**.

"I'm glad you were selected to be our group leader. I think you'll do a great job overseeing everything."

① **OPENLY SUPPORT LILY'S AUTHORITY** as group leader, even though you may see her as an "equal" rather than someone who has power over you.

② AVOID AN OPEN DISPLAY OF ANGER, instead keeping your face neutral or smiling, and complimenting her on the quality of her idea.

"I like your idea for the project—it's really smart."

③ SUPPORT THE GROUP SENTIMENT, even though it may mean sacrificing your own desires.

"As there is obviously a consensus, I'm happy to support what everyone else in the group wants to do."

WHAT IF? But what if things don't work out as shown? Test your ability to adapt your communication by watching the What if? videos and planning a response for each situation.

1. What if you realize Lily is trying to adapt to you when she says, "Don't let my position as group leader keep you from expressing your own opinions. What do you really think about my idea?" What would you say?

2. How would you respond to Lily's encouraging question, "I want to make sure everyone is happy. Is there something you would rather do instead?"

harmonious interaction with others is more important than "being on time" or sticking to a schedule.

Differences in time orientation can create problems when people from different cultures make appointments with each other (E. T. Hall, 1983). For example, those with an M-time orientation, such as many Americans, Canadians, Swiss, and Germans, often find it frustrating if P-time people show up for a meeting after the scheduled start time. In P-time cultures, such as those in Arabian, African, Caribbean, and Latin American countries, people think that arriving 30 minutes or more after a meeting's scheduled start time is perfectly acceptable, and that it's OK to change important plans at the last minute.

You can improve your communication by understanding other people's views of time. Learn about the time orientation of a destination or country before you travel there. Also, respect others' time orientation. If you're an M-time person interacting with a P-time individual, don't suddenly dash off to your next appointment because you feel you have to stick to your schedule. Your communication partner will likely think you're rude. If you're a P-time person interacting with an M-time individual, realize that he or she may get impatient with a long, leisurely conversation or see a late arrival to a meeting as inconsiderate. In addition, avoid criticizing or complaining about behaviors that stem from other people's time orientations. Instead, accept the fact that people view time differently, and be willing to adapt your own expectations and behaviors accordingly.

Creating Intercultural Competence

Even when you understand what culture is, how co-cultures work, and the ways culture influences communication, you can still have trouble communicating with people from different backgrounds. To work toward competence, be mindful of the differences discussed so far, actively seek to understand other cultures, and adapt your communication as needed.

In the award-winning movie *Gran Torino*, Clint Eastwood plays Walt, a bitter, racist widower who lives alone in Michigan, estranged from his sons. Despite his bigoted attitudes, Walt strikes up a friendship with two Hmong teens who live next door—Sue and Thao—after he saves Thao from a gang beating. To help Walt communicate more effectively with the Hmong, Sue teaches him some simple rules: Never touch a Hmong on the head, because they believe that the soul resides there. Don't look a Hmong straight in the eye; they consider it rude. Don't be surprised if a Hmong smiles when he or she is embarrassed; that's how they handle that emotion. In return, Walt teaches Thao how to communicate during a job interview with an American construction foreman: "Look him straight in the eye, and give a firm handshake!" He even instructs Thao on the art of trading teasing insults

In the film *Gran Torino*, Walt realizes his previous beliefs were racist only when he allows himself to experience his neighbor's culture. How has learning about someone's culture changed or enhanced your impressions for the better?

with American male friends. As these unlikely friendships deepen, Walt (to his astonishment) realizes he has more in common with his neighbors than with his own family.

Like Walt, Thao, and Sue, you will likely form lasting bonds with people who come from cultures vastly different from your own. The gateway to such connections is **intercultural competence,** the ability to communicate appropriately, effectively, and ethically with people from diverse backgrounds. You can strengthen your intercultural competence by applying the following practices: world-mindedness, attributional complexity, and communication accommodation.

World-Mindedness

When you possess **world-mindedness,** you demonstrate acceptance and respect toward other cultures' beliefs, values, and customs (Hammer, Bennett, & Wiseman, 2003). You can practice world-mindedness in three ways. First, accept others' expression of their culture or co-culture as a natural element in their communication, just as your communication reflects your cultural background (Chen & Starosta, 2005). Second, avoid any temptation to judge others' cultural beliefs, attitudes, and values as "better" or "worse" than your own. Third, treat people from all cultures with respect.

MAKING COMMUNICATION CHOICES
WHEN A FRIEND IS DIFFERENT

1 CONSIDER THE DILEMMA

During your second semester at school, you move into a house with several other people. One of your housemates, Adoni, is an international student who differs from you in ethnicity, religion, and socioeconomic status. Having never lived with anyone but family members before, you are often amazed at Adoni's beliefs and experiences. When Adoni shares stories about life growing up in a small village that lacked what you consider basic essentials, you can't help but think, "How could anyone live like that!?" The more Adoni shares, the more you feel superior. Your culture and upbringing just seem so much better than Adoni's.

However, you also quickly learn that Adoni is kind and generous. When you were stuck on a series of calculus proofs, Adoni took two hours to help you work through them. Then, when you came down with mono, Adoni helped you stay caught up in your classes, even sitting in on lectures and taking notes for you.

As the months go by, you find your mixed feelings toward Adoni intensifying. On the one hand, Adoni is honest, direct, and supportive. The two of you even share a lot of the same interests and tastes. But you're not sure whether you could ever be close, because Adoni is so culturally different. Although you like Adoni, you still feel that Adoni's cultural beliefs and traditions are silly and backwards.

One night, when the two of you are studying, Adoni says, "You know, it's been really hard for me, adjusting to life here. Everything is so different. But your friendship has really helped. I consider you my best friend. How do you feel about me?"

2 CONNECT THE RESEARCH

Scholars Lily Arasaratnam and Smita Banerjee (2007) looked at the impact that *ethnocentrism*—the belief that one's own cultural beliefs, attitudes, values, and practices are superior to those of others—had on the development of friendships. They surveyed over 400 African American, Asian American, Euro-American, and Hispanic college students, measuring ethnocentrism, the students' desire to form friendships with culturally diverse others, and the number of close friends students had from culturally dissimilar backgrounds.

Arasaratnam and Banerjee found that the more people believed things like "my culture is superior to all others" and "most cultures are backwards compared to my culture" (i.e., ethnocentrism), the less interested they were in learning about other cultures. Those with ethnocentric beliefs were also substantially less motivated to form new friendships with culturally different others and reported considerably fewer cross-cultural friends. In short, ethnocentrism acts as a powerful barrier against forming such relationships.

This research shows that although it's important to possess pride in your cultural heritage, believing that your culture is *superior* to all others can cause you to avoid relationships with diverse others. Consequently, be mindful of the degree to which you judge others as culturally inferior, and always keep in mind that *most* people feel as strongly about their own cultural backgrounds as you feel about yours.

Before making a communication choice, consider the facts of the situation, and think about the ethnocentrism research. Also, reflect on what you've learned so far about culture (pp. 84–92), intercultural competence (pp. 102–107), and perception (pp. 41–45). Then answer these questions:

❶ What are your thoughts and feelings toward Adoni? How is your view of your own culture's superiority impacting your thoughts and feelings?

❷ How does Adoni view you and *your* culture? Does Adoni have the characteristics you look for in a good friend? Why or why not?

❸ What are you going to say to Adoni?

This can be especially challenging when differences seem impossible to bridge or when the other person's beliefs, attitudes, and values conflict with your own. But practicing world-mindedness means more than just tolerating cultural differences you find perplexing or problematic. Instead, treat all people with respect by being kind and courteous in your communication. You can also preserve others' personal dignity by actively listening to and asking questions about viewpoints that may differ from yours.

World-mindedness is the opposite of **ethnocentrism,** the belief that one's own cultural beliefs, attitudes, values, and practices are superior to those of others. Ethnocentrism is not the same thing as pride in your cultural heritage or patriotism. You can be culturally proud or nationally patriotic and not be ethnocentric. Instead, ethnocentrism is a *comparative evaluation*; ethnocentric people view their own culture or co-culture as the standard against which all other cultures should be judged, and they often have contempt for other cultures (Neuliep & McCroskey, 1997; Sumner, 1906). Consequently, such people tend to see their own communication as competent and that of people from other cultures as incompetent.

Attributional Complexity

When you practice **attributional complexity,** you acknowledge that other people's behaviors have complex causes. To develop this ability, observe others' behavior, and analyze the various forces influencing it. For example, rather than deciding that a classmate's reserved demeanor or limited eye contact means she's unfriendly, consider the possibility that these behaviors might reflect cultural differences.

Also, learn as much as you can about different cultures and co-cultures, so you can better understand people's communication styles and preferences. Experiencing other cultures through observation, travel, or interaction is a great way to sharpen your intercultural communication competence (Arasaratnam, 2006).

In addition, routinely use *perception-checking* to avoid attributional errors, and regularly demonstrate *empathy* to identify with others. In situations in

One way to enhance world-mindedness, practice attributional complexity, and try communication accommodation is to travel and experience other cultures firsthand. What experiences do you have with traveling in other cultures, and what did you learn from these interactions?

bikeriderlondon/Shutterstock

which the cultural gaps between you and others seem impossibly wide, try to see things from their perspectives, and consider the motivations behind their communication. Examine how people from diverse backgrounds make decisions, and compare their approaches to yours. Finally, ask others to explain the reasons for their behavior, and then accept and validate their explanations ("That makes sense to me") rather than challenging them ("You've got to be kidding!"). Avoid making statements such as, "I know that people like you act this way because you think that . . ."; you'll only come across as presumptuous.

Communication Accommodation

A final way to enhance your intercultural competence is to adjust your communication to mesh with the behaviors of people from other cultures. According to **communication accommodation theory,** people are especially motivated to adapt their communication when they seek social approval, when they wish to establish relationships with others, and when they view others' language usage as appropriate (Giles, Coupland, & Coupland, 1991). In contrast, people tend to accentuate differences between their communication and others' when they wish to convey emotional distance and disassociate themselves from others. Research suggests that people who use communication accommodation are perceived as more competent (Coupland, Giles, & Wiemann, 1991; Giles et al., 1991).

How does this work in practice? Try adapting to other people's communication preferences (Bianconi, 2002). During interactions, notice how long a turn people take when speaking, how quickly they speak, how direct they are, and how much they appear to want to talk compared to you. You may also need to learn and practice cultural norms for nonverbal behaviors—including eye contact, head touching, and handshaking—such as those Sue taught Walt in *Gran Torino*.

You can even do this during public presentations. For example, find out about your listeners' preferences during your audience analysis, and try to adapt your communication accordingly while developing your speech. So if you'll be speaking to an audience whose first language is not English, avoid slang; your listeners may not understand it. At the same time, avoid imitating other people's dialects, accents, or word choices. Most people consider such imitation inappropriate and insulting.

To help you boost your own intercultural communication competence, consider the five suggestions in Table 4.1, which pulls together what we've discussed in this chapter.

✓ **LearningCurve** can help you review! Go to **bedfordstmartins.com/choicesconnections**.

TABLE 4.1

CREATING INTERCULTURAL COMMUNICATION COMPETENCE

1 Understand the many factors that create people's cultural and co-cultural identities.

2 Be aware of the different cultural influences on communication: individualism and collectivism, high and low context, uncertainty avoidance, emotional displays, power distance, and views on time.

3 Embrace world-mindedness to genuinely accept and respect others' cultures.

4 Practice attributional complexity to consider the possible cultural influences on your and others' communication.

5 Use communication accommodation when building and maintaining relationships with people from different cultural backgrounds.

VLADGRIN/Shutterstock

CHAPTER ④ REVIEW

CHAPTER RECAP

- A **culture** is a set of widely shared beliefs, attitudes, values, and practices; cultures are learned, communicated, layered, and lived.
- Judging someone as a member of a shared **co-culture,** as an **ingrouper,** or as an **outgrouper** influences how you perceive and communicate with that person.
- Cultures vary in terms of where they fall in certain spectrums. Whether people identify as being from an **individualistic** or a **collectivistic culture,** or from a **high-** or **low-context culture,** as well as their tolerance for **uncertainty avoidance,** can influence their communication styles.
- Additional cultural influences on communication include emotion displays, **power distance** preferences, and views of time. Considering these factors can help you better communicate with others.
- You can strengthen your **intercultural competence** through **world-mindedness, attributional complexity,** and communication accommodation.

LAUNCHPAD

LaunchPad for *Choices & Connections* offers unique video scenarios and encourages self-assessment through adaptive quizzing. Go to **bedfordstmartins.com /choicesconnections** to get access.

 LearningCurve adaptive quizzes

 How to Communicate video scenarios

 Video clips that illustrate key concepts

KEY TERMS

Culture, p. 84
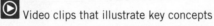 Power, p. 87
Co-cultural Communication
    theory, p. 87
Co-cultures, p. 88
Ingroupers, p. 89
Outgroupers, p. 89
Race, p. 90
Prejudice, p. 91
Stereotype Content Model, p. 91
Individualistic cultures, p. 93
Collectivistic cultures, p. 94
High-context cultures, p. 95

Low-context cultures, p. 95
Uncertainty avoidance, p. 95
Display rules, p. 97
Power distance, p. 98
Monochronic time orientation, p. 98
Polychronic time orientation, p. 99
Intercultural competence, p. 103
World-mindedness, p. 103
Ethnocentrism, p. 105
Attributional complexity, p. 105
Communication accommodation
    theory, p. 106

POP QUIZ

✓ Looking for more review questions? **LearningCurve** can help you master key concepts from this chapter. Go to **bedfordstmartins.com /choicesconnections**.

1 According to co-cultural communication theory, the people with the most _____ within a society determine the *dominant culture*.

a. ethnocentrism   **c.** prejudice
b. world-mindedness   **d.** power

2 When people communicate in rude or inappropriate ways, you're more inclined to form negative impressions of them if you see them as _____.

a. ingroupers   **c.** outgroupers
b. M-time followers   **d.** P-time followers

3 In _____ cultures, people tend not to presume that others share their beliefs, attitudes, and values; thus, they strive to be informative, clear, and direct in their communication.

a. individualistic   **c.** high-context
b. low-context   **d.** collectivistic

4 In high-uncertainty-avoidance cultures, what do people place a lot of value on?

a. Innovative ideas   **c.** Comparative evaluation
b. Control   **d.** Change

5 According to the chapter, which of the following is *not* a way to create inter-cultural competence?

a. Practicing attributional complexity
b. Employing benevolent prejudice
c. Using communication accommodation
d. Considering cultural influences on communication

ACTIVITIES

1 Exploring Your Cultural Layers

A basic truth about culture is that we all exist as multiple layers of cultural influences—including age, class, nationality, ethnicity, sexual orientation, gender, and religion. To better understand how your varied cultural and co-cultural identities impact your communication, list what you think are your most important cultural markers (e.g., "I'm an upper-middle-class, Evangelical, Latina female from the Southwest United States"). Then, write a brief comment (no more than one to two sentences each) explaining how exactly each culture or co-culture impacts your communication with others, both positively and negatively. Finally, connect your layered cultural identities to outcomes in your life. What personal and professional challenges and benefits have you experienced? How do those challenges and benefits influence your communication with others? If you feel comfortable, present this information to your class in a two- to three-minute speech.

2 Culture in the Media

Many TV shows and movies base their jokes on stereotypical communication problems between men and women or between people from different cultures. For example, think about how shows like *New Girl* or movies like *The Hangover* trilogy get a lot of their laughs. With a partner, find an example from the media that uses culture and communication in this way. Discuss how the example embodies or violates principles discussed in this chapter. How could the media better represent communication between people from different cultures?

5
Verbal Communication

As a poet, motivational speaker, and actor, Ed Mabrey spends his life carefully crafting his words. His hard work has paid off. Mabrey is a two-time winner of the Individual World Poetry Slam Championship (2007 and 2012).[1] In this annual competition featuring dozens of the world's best performance poets—each of whom is a champion in his or her home region— Mabrey and others get to show off their unique talents. Mabrey's recent victories have cemented his status as one of the finest performance poets ever: two-time Haiku slam champion, 2012 Poetry Slam Artist of the Year, and four-time National Poetry Slam Finalist.

Poetry slam is the competitive art of performance poetry. Unlike written poetry, which is designed to be read, performance poetry is created to be spoken in front of a live audience. At poetry slams, judges assess poets and award them points. Although slams vary in their rules, most require that the poems be brief and that poets perform without props, costumes, or musical instruments. Poets are judged solely on their choice of words and the emotion with which these words are communicated to the audience.

The poetry performed at slams varies widely in topic—everything from comedy to social commentary, inner reflection to outward expression of love. Champion Ed Mabrey's poetry focuses on his view of world events, his close relationships, and even casual encounters. His poem "Pursuit of Happyness," for example, is about a conversation with a homeless person at a Subway restaurant.

No longer limited to coffee shops or bookstores, poetry slams also exist online. Poetry Slam, Inc., which organizes national and international competitions, hosts a video slam contest, in which poets submit videotaped

AP Photo/Bebeto Matthews

---

[1]All content that follows adapted from Poetry Slam, Inc. (www.poetryslam.com), and Seattle Poetry Slam (2013).

performances and have online audience members vote for the one they like best. A recent winner of the video slam was Kait Rokowski, who provided a blistering performance regarding gender roles and sexual assault (you can see Kait's poem on YouTube).

But despite the diversity among poets, poetic content, and medium, the common theme that runs throughout all performance poetry is the importance of carefully choosing clear, honest, and understandable language packed with powerful meaning. Poets seeking to win slams can't just craft language into small, elegant poems. They must verbally communicate their creations to audiences in a competent fashion. Although poetry slams are highly competitive—poets intensely vie with one another for points and tenths of points—they are ultimately about celebrating the communicative power of the spoken word. As poet Allan Wolf describes, "The points are not the point; the point is poetry."

You may not be a performance poet like Ed Mabrey or Kait Rokowski, facing audiences and judges who evaluate you through points. But you are judged just the same, every single day, based on the words you choose. If you competently communicate to others, you're awarded "points" in the form of people liking you, being influenced by you, or judging you to have desirable skills—like being "an amazing speaker" or "a skilled conversationalist." Regardless of your personal rhyme or reason, your words pack a potent punch in shaping others' impressions of you. As a consequence, it's important to understand the power of verbal communication and how to use it competently. In this chapter, you'll learn:

- The four defining features of language
- Strategies for creating understandable messages and taking responsibility for your words
- How to use language that avoids gender bias and is mindful of cultural differences
- Ways to manage the challenging aspects of verbal communication

☑ **LearningCurve** can help you review! Go to **bedfordstmartins.com /choicesconnections**.

The Nature of Verbal Communication

Whenever you write, speak, sign, tweet, or text, you're using language to convey meaning to others. But the words you choose also communicate powerful messages about who you are in relation to your listeners. Understanding how verbal communication works will help you use language more competently in every area of your life.

Your days are filled with verbal communication. You talk with your professor during her office hours, then text your roommate to see if you can get a ride home. You e-mail group members about an upcoming project, then give a speech in front of your communication class. You chat with coworkers after your shift, then Skype with your partner stationed overseas. Through all of these exchanges, you employ **verbal communication**—the use of spoken or written language to interact with others. Because language is the basis of verbal communication, understanding the nature of language is key for improving your verbal communication skills. Language has four defining features: it is symbolic, it is rule governed, it conveys meaning, and it is intertwined with culture.

Language Is Symbolic

When Steve was in sixth grade, his friend Ed would play an annoying word game with people. Ed would point to a table and say, "What's that?" The unwitting victim would answer, "It's a table, duh!" Ed would say, "No, that's just the *word* we use to represent it. What's it *really*?" The person would pause, then respond, "Oh, I see. OK, it's wood and metal and plastic." "No," Ed would laugh, "those are just *words* that we use to *represent* what it is. What is it *really*?" About this time the person would get fed up with Ed's game and walk away.

Ed's game illustrates the first defining feature of language: it is symbolic. When items are used to represent other things, they are considered **symbols.** In verbal communication, words are the primary symbols used to represent people, objects, events, and ideas (Foss, Foss, & Trapp, 1991). Thus, the word *table* refers to an object with a flat surface and legs to support it. You could just as well call it a "cotknee" or some other term. If you did, nothing about the actual object would change—just its name. As psychologist Erich Fromm noted, words only point to our experience of the world; they are not the experience. All languages are collections of symbols in the form of words people use to communicate.

Language Is Rule Governed

Two types of rules govern the use of language. The first type is **constitutive rules,** which define words' meanings. Constitutive rules tell you what words "count as" what objects (Searle, 1965). For example, in the English language, *dog* represents a four-legged domesticated animal that is a common household pet. In Spanish, the word *perro* represents this same animal. Constitutive rules involving informal or metaphorical expressions can make things challenging when you're trying to learn a new language. For example, someone new to English may get confused when a friend says, "My dogs are tired," if the speaker really means, "My feet hurt."

The second type comprises **regulative rules,** which control how you use language. Regulative rules guide everything from spelling to grammar to conversational structure. Examples in the English language include "Add an 's' or an 'es' to a noun to create its plural form" and "When someone asks you a question, you should answer."

Language Conveys Meaning

Language enables you to convey meaning to others in two ways. The first is the literal meaning of your words, as agreed on by members of your culture. These are known as **denotative meanings.** Such meanings are what you find in dictionaries; for example, *family* means "a group of individuals related through common ancestry, legal means, or other strong emotional or social bonds." But the word *family* evokes different meanings for different people. Some may hear the word and immediately think, "Individuals I can count on for love and support." Others may hear it and think, "People who are always judging me!" Such variations represent **connotative meanings**—the meanings you associate with words based on your life experiences. What does the word *family* mean to you?

Denotative and connotative meanings can create confusion if you don't manage them carefully. For example, suppose your friend aces an exam that you flunked. You text her, "I hate u!" The denotative meaning suggests you

DOUBLE TAKE

Depending on your personal experiences, the word *gambling* can have vastly different connotative meanings. When a friend says she is going gambling, do you think that sounds fun, boring, wasteful, or something else entirely?

Tim Pannell/Corbis

Ken Seet/Corbis

feel hatred toward your friend. But the connotative meaning—your real message—is "I'm envious but proud of you." If you and your friend have a history of communicating with each other in this way, your friend will probably read your message as you intend. But with a person you don't know as well, an "I hate u!" text could backfire. To use verbal communication competently, choose your words carefully and clarify connotative meanings if there's a chance someone could misunderstand your message.

Language and Culture Are Intertwined

Members of a culture use language to communicate their thoughts, beliefs, attitudes, and values with one another, and thereby reinforce their collective sense of cultural identity (Whorf, 1952). Consequently, the language you speak (English, Spanish, Mandarin, Urdu), the words you choose (proper, slang, profane), and the grammar you use (formal, informal) all announce to others: "This is who I am! This is my cultural heritage!"

Each language reflects distinct sets of cultural beliefs and values. However, a large group of people within a particular culture who speak the same language may (over time) develop their own variations on that language, known as **dialects** (Gleason, 1989). Dialects may include unique phrases, words, and pronunciations (such as accents). Dialects reflect the shared history, experiences, and knowledge of people who live in a particular geographic region (the American Midwest or the Deep South), share a common socioeconomic status (urban working class or upper-middle-class suburban), or possess a common ethnic or religious ancestry (Irish English or Yiddish English) (Chen & Starosta, 1998).

People often judge those who use dialects similar to their own as ingroupers and are thus inclined to make positive judgments about them (Delia, 1972; Lev-Ari & Keysar, 2010). As Chapter 4 discusses, this is a cultural influence; ingroupers are people you perceive to be culturally similar to yourself. In a parallel fashion, people tend to judge those with dissimilar dialects as outgroupers (people who are culturally dissimilar to you) and make negative judgments about them. Keep this tendency in mind when you're speaking with people who don't share your dialect, and resist the temptation to make negative judgments about them. For additional ideas on managing ingroup or outgroup perceptions, see Chapter 4.

Verbal Communication Skills

Even though people use language all the time to verbally communicate, not everyone does so skillfully. Knowing the difference between words that are understandable, inclusive, and respectful, and those that aren't—and putting this knowledge to use when speaking with others—is essential to competent verbal communication.

While attending his nephew's graduation ceremony at the University of Washington, Steve expected to hear a formulaic keynote address extolling "the importance of being successful" and "having a competitive edge." But William Gates Sr.—father of Microsoft billionaire Bill Gates, and cochair of the Bill & Melinda Gates Foundation—didn't give the usual graduation speech. Instead, he said, "My favorite axiom is this: 'We are all in this together.'" He talked about how important family and friendships are for life happiness. Then he broadened his discussion to global citizenship: "Citizenship means that we behave according to the belief that every person matters just as much as every other person." As Gates spoke, the crowd quieted. Students and parents

William Gates Sr.'s commencement speech shows how powerful language can impact an audience. Have you ever been similarly affected by a speech? Why?

Courtesy of the University of Washington

alike stopped texting and chatting and began listening. At the climax of his speech, Gates declared:

> People suffering in poverty are human beings. They are not national security assets. They are not markets for our exports. . . . They are human beings who have infinite worth in their own right without any reference to us. They have mothers who love them, children who need them, and friends who cherish them, and we simply ought to help them.[2]

When he finished, 43,000 students and family members rose to give a standing ovation. Immediately after, people in the stadium began texting and chatting again. But this time, their messages and comments were uniform: "That was an amazing speech!"

Undoubtedly, the profound nature of Gates's topic helped make his speech memorable. But a person can talk about important things in vague, wordy, or distorted ways that make listeners tune out. In Gates's case, it was his *choice of words* that created the biggest impact: understandable, honest, and inclusive language that crossed gender and cultural boundaries. Gates made an audience of thousands feel as though they were joined together in something bigger and better than simply sitting in a stadium, listening to a speech.

How can you harness the power of language in similar ways? Try four things: (1) create understandable messages; (2) use "I" and "we" language; (3) avoid gender-based presumptions; and (4) be mindful of cultural differences.

Create Understandable Messages

In his exploration of language and meaning, philosopher Paul Grice noted that in order for people to have competent interactions, they tailor their messages so that others can understand them. To produce understandable messages, you can apply the **cooperative principle:** making your verbal communication as *informative*, *honest*, *relevant*, and *clear* as required for a particular situation (Grice, 1989).

Be Informative. Being *informative* means presenting all of the information that is appropriate and important to share. It also means avoiding providing information that isn't appropriate or important. For example, suppose your sister is getting married and you are in the wedding party. When you make a toast at the reception following the ceremony, everyone will expect you to comment on how the couple met and how their love for each other is inspiring. To *not* say these things would be remiss. On the other hand, you won't want to be *too* informative by sharing inappropriate details (such as stories about their sex life) or unimportant details (such as what was on the menu at the restaurant where they first met).

---

[2]Speech excerpt from Bill & Melinda Gates Foundation (2010).

UNDERSTANDABLE MESSAGES

Shows like *Girls*, *Scandal*, and *Newsroom* feature characters who constantly struggle with creating understandable messages, whether talking to friends, lovers, or coworkers. How do such messages impact not only the communication in the moment but also the relationships of the people involved?

(Clockwise from left) Jessica Miglio/© HBO/Courtesy: Everett Collection; SHONDALAND/THE KOBAL COLLECTION; John P. Johnson/©HBO/Courtesy: Everett Collection

Be Honest. **Honesty** is the single most important characteristic of competent communication, because other people count on the fact that the information you share with them is truthful (Grice, 1989). Being honest means not sharing information you're uncertain about and not presenting information as true when you know it's false. For example, let's say that during a meeting, someone asks you a question you're unable to answer. Rather than fumbling through a potentially incorrect response, acknowledge that you don't know the answer, and determine a way to get the required information. Dishonesty in verbal communication violates standards for ethical behavior and leads others to believe false things (Jacobs, Dawson, & Brashers, 1996).

Be Relevant. You are *relevant* when you present information that's responsive to what others have said and applicable to the situation. As examples of responsiveness, when people ask you questions, you provide appropriate answers. When they make requests, you explicitly grant or reject those requests. Dodging questions or abruptly changing topics is uncooperative and may be seen as deceptive. In the wedding toast scenario, a relevant speech would cover the couple's relationship. Going off on tangents regarding your own relationships would be irrelevant ("Seeing them together reminds me of my own love life; just last week I . . .").

Be Clear. Using *clear language* means presenting information in a straightforward fashion rather than framing it in vague or ambiguous terms. This was one of the most impressive aspects of Gates Sr.'s commencement speech: he used clear, concise language that everyone easily understood: "People suffering in poverty . . . have mothers who love them." (Check out Chapter 15 for suggestions on how to use clear language in your own speeches.)

At the same time, using clear language doesn't mean being brutally frank or dumping offensive or harmful information on others. When you find yourself in situations in which you have to deliver bad news ("Your project report needs serious revision"), tailor your message in ways that consider others' feelings ("I'm sorry for the inconvenience this may cause you"). Similarly, you'll improve the likelihood of positive outcomes during conflicts by expressing your concerns clearly ("I'm really upset") while avoiding language that attacks someone's character or personality ("You're such an idiot") (Gottman & Silver, 1999).

Misunderstandings. Of course, just because you use informative, honest, relevant, and clear language doesn't guarantee that others will understand you. When one person misperceives the meaning of another's verbal communication, **misunderstanding** occurs.

Misunderstanding occurs frequently online, owing to the lack of nonverbal cues that help clarify intended meaning. One study found that 27.2 percent of respondents agreed that e-mail is likely to result in miscommunication of intent, and 53.6 percent agreed that it is relatively easy to misinterpret an e-mail message (Rainey, 2000). The tendency to misunderstand communication online is so prevalent that scholars suggest the following practices: *If a particular message must be absolutely error-free or if its content is controversial, don't use e-mail or text messaging to communicate it.* Whenever possible, conduct high-stakes encounters, such as important attempts at persuasion, face-to-face. Never use e-mails, posts, or texts for sensitive actions, such as professional reprimands or dismissals, or relationship breakups (Rainey, 2000). To learn how to create understandable messages and avoid misunderstandings during conflicts, see How to Communicate: Disagreement with Family on pages 120–121.

Mediated communication platforms like FaceTime and Skype help eliminate the possibility of misunderstanding someone when you're not able to talk in person. How does the language you use online differ from the language you use through text?

David Malan /Getty Images

Use "I" and "We" Language

When verbally communicating, avoid using **"you" language**—phrases that place the focus of attention and blame on other people, such as "You let me down" or "You make me so angry!" Instead, use **"I" language**—phrases that emphasize ownership of your feelings, opinions, and beliefs. "I" language makes it clear that you're expressing your own perceptions rather than stating unquestionable truths, making it less likely to trigger defensiveness in others (Kubany, Richard, Bauer, & Muraoka, 1992). For instance, imagine you're involved in a group project, and some group members are working harder than others. If you bring up this topic with the group, saying "I think it's important that the workload be evenly distributed" will seem less threatening than "You guys aren't doing your fair share!"

At the same time, strive to build solidarity through **"we" language**—phrases that both emphasize inclusion and enhance feelings of connection and similarity (Honeycutt, 1999). In the group project example, you might say "We all want this project to be a success" in order to emphasize how the whole group is working together. One study found that married couples who used "we" language maintained more positive emotions during disagreements and had higher overall marital satisfaction than couples who did not (Seider, Hirschberger, Nelson, & Levenson, 2009). To compare and contrast the differences between "you," "I," and "we" language, see Table 5.1.

TABLE 5.1

"YOU," "I," AND "WE" LANGUAGE

SITUATION	"YOU" LANGUAGE	"I" LANGUAGE	"WE" LANGUAGE
A friend blows up at you when you cancel dinner plans.	"You really hurt my feelings."	"I'm feeling really hurt."	"We need to work harder on not hurting each other's feelings."
A classmate forgets to make a main point during a group presentation.	"You totally messed up our presentation."	"I feel like our presentation has some mistakes."	"Although we made some mistakes in our presentation, we totally rocked the paper."
A coworker isn't filling out order sheets correctly.	"You need to do a better job on your order sheets."	"I think the order sheets could be done a bit better."	"We can improve the quality of our order sheets with better inventory management."

VoodooDot/Shutterstock

DISAGREEMENT WITH FAMILY

 One way to improve your communication competence is by adapting your messages to others' behaviors. Learn how to navigate a disagreement with a family member by going to LaunchPad at **bedfordstmartins.com/choicesconnections** and completing the **How to Communicate video scenario** for Chapter 5 to practice your skills.

CONSIDER THIS:

Your mom decides that a great way for your family to reconnect is to take a two-week road trip next summer, driving across the country to see your grandparents. She sends you and your siblings an e-mail, highlighting the sights you'll see and how much "fun" it will be. Everyone is excited—except you. Although you get along well with your family, the idea of being trapped in a car with them for half a month sounds like a nightmare! What's more, you'd planned on working full-time over the summer to earn money for school.

WHAT WOULD YOU DO?

The following advice illustrates how to use your verbal communication skills when handling sensitive topics. As you watch the video, consider how the dialogue reflects the cooperative principle and properly uses "I" and "we" language. Then, test your knowledge of key skills, and create your own responses to the **What if? video prompts**.

"I'd like to talk with you about our plans for next summer. When would be a good time for me to call? Or can we talk at home this weekend? I'll be there on Saturday morning."

① SCHEDULE AN OFFLINE ENCOUNTER with your mom by sending her an e-mail or text, asking when she can talk with you on the phone or meet with you in person.

"I know how excited everyone is about the trip, especially you. But I just can't take two weeks off from work. I need those hours to afford school next year. I hope you can understand my situation, and that I'm not disappointing you too much with my decision."

(2) **EXPRESS YOUR OPINION** informatively and honestly, being careful to use "I" language to take accountability for your feelings.

"Why don't we invite Grandma and Grandpa to fly out and join us for the Fourth of July? I have that weekend off, so we can all be together and reconnect as a family."

(3) **USE "WE" LANGUAGE** to emphasize family inclusion, offering alternatives for a family gettogether.

 WHAT IF? But what if things don't work out as shown? Test your ability to adapt your communication by watching the What if? videos and planning a response for each situation.

1. What would you say when your mom doesn't want to talk in person and writes back, "I'm really busy with work right now—let's just chat over e-mail"?

2. How would you handle your mom's anger at your reluctance to go? "This may come as a shock to you, but the whole world doesn't revolve around you and your work schedule! You need to make a decision about what's more important: your work or your family."

Avoid Gender-Based Presumptions

Many people believe that men and women have different verbal communication preferences and practices. Specifically, they assume that women use and prefer "indirect" and "flowery" language, whereas men use and prefer "direct, clear, and concise" language (Spender, 1990). But scientific research has found that men and women are actually more similar than different when it comes to language. For example, after reviewing data from more than 1,000 gender studies, researchers Dan Canary, Tara Emmers-Sommer, and Sandra Faulkner (1997) found that if you consider all of the factors that influence communication and compare their impact, only about 1 percent of people's verbal communication behavior is related to gender. The researchers concluded that during verbal communication, "men and women respond in a similar manner 99% of the time."

Why do people think that men and women use language differently? Perception. Because people *believe* that men and women are different, they *perceive* differences in their communication—even when such differences don't exist. In a well-known study documenting this effect, researchers gave two different groups of participants a copy of the same speech (Mulac, Incontro, & James, 1985). One group was told that a man had authored and presented the speech; the other group, that a woman had authored and presented it. Participants who thought the speech was female in origin perceived it as having a more "artistic quality" and complimented the language for being "pleasing, sweet, and beautiful." Participants who were told that a man had authored the speech viewed it as having more "dynamism" and complimented the language as "strong, active, and aggressive." Yet both groups read the same speech.

The lesson? You don't need to adjust your verbal communication to your listeners' or readers' gender. Men and women appreciate language that is informative, honest, relevant, and clear. Everyone prefers talking with people who avoid placing blame through "you" language, and who use "I" language to take responsibility for their own actions and feelings. Additionally, using "we" language creates a sense of unity with others, regardless of their gender.

Be Mindful of Cultural Differences

As Chapter 4 discusses, different cultures often have different ideas about what constitutes competent verbal communication. To help you communicate competently with people from other cultures, consider the following guidelines.

First, think about whether the people you are communicating with are from a high- or low-context culture. As Chapter 4 notes, in *high-context cultures* (China, Korea, Japan), people presume that listeners share extensive knowledge in common with them. As a result, they don't feel a need to provide a lot of specific details in their messages. In *low-context cultures* (Germany, Scandinavia, the United States), people tend not to presume that listeners share their beliefs, attitudes, and values, so they tailor their verbal communication to be informative, clear, and direct (E. T. Hall & Hall, 1987).

Consider what this cultural difference means for expressing constructive criticism. If you told a classmate from a high-context culture, "I thought your presentation had several problems," he or she would likely perceive your comment as intolerably direct and rude. A more comfortable comment for this classmate might be, "What issues do you think arose in your speech?" But if you asked a classmate from a low-context culture this question, he or she might interpret it as cryptic. To avoid such confusion, try to tailor the directness of your language to your listeners' cultural preferences.

Second, adjust your verbal communication to match others' speech rates and desired balance of "turn taking" (Bianconi, 2002; Coupland, Giles, & Wiemann, 1991). Observe how rapidly the person you're talking with speaks, and how long a turn he or she takes when talking. Then match the person's speech rate, and use similar turn lengths. Monitor any feedback while you're conversing (such as nodding or fidgeting) to see whether your conversation partner wants you to continue or stop. (For more details on accommodating, see pp. 106–107 in Chapter 4.)

Third, and most important, don't change your language or voice in substantial ways just because you're speaking to someone from another culture. For example, many Euro-American college students switch to simplistic language and talk slower and louder when interacting with Asian and Asian American students, as if they were talking with small children. This change in speech behavior is viewed as both patronizing and insulting by recipients (Jimenez & McCornack, 2011).

Verbal Communication Challenges

"Sticks and stones may break my bones, but words can never hurt me." Nonsense. The words you choose have the power to cause grievous injury to the emotions and self-esteem of others. But by learning to identify and avoid destructive forms of language—and constructively respond when others use them—you can become a more competent verbal communicator.

He is the most prejudiced, verbally aggressive, deceptive, and slanderous character ever to show up on television screens. He has been described as "a bundle of pure, unadulterated evil." He's *South Park*'s Eric Cartman—a boy plagued by greed, hatred, and an unquenchable thirst for power. Through hundreds of episodes, Cartman has tried to reignite the Civil War, feigned disability, tricked another boy into eating his own parents at a chili cook-off, and released an almost endless anti-Semitic verbal assault on his classmate Kyle.

Importantly, however, Cartman's terrible communication choices often have disastrous outcomes. His manipulation of and cruelty to others only occasionally nets him happiness, and he never learns from his mistakes. This makes him endearing in a strange way: his communicative failings make viewers feel good about their capacity to change and improve. So whether you love Cartman or loathe him, laugh at his offensive antics or recoil from them, he reveals an essential truth about the dark side of verbal communication: when you use prejudiced, aggressive, deceptive, or defamatory language, you sow the seeds of your own destruction.

South Park's Eric Cartman is the cartoon definition of how *not* to communicate. His unabashed bad behavior is shocking but also shows viewers the consequences of poor communication skills. How do you handle dealing with any real-life "Cartmans" you run into?

Comedy Central/Courtesy: Everett Collection

Prejudiced Language

As Chapter 4 discusses, *prejudice* means presuming negative things about other people based on their group affiliation (ethnicity, religion, age, gender, sexual orientation). It is a negative form of *stereotyping*. People who use **prejudiced language** speak in ways that display contempt, dislike, or disdain for a group or its members. In *South Park*, for example, Cartman uses prejudiced language almost constantly when he talks with his Jewish friend Kyle and when he sees "hippies"—anyone with long hair and tie-dyed clothing.

There are as many types of prejudiced language as there are groups. A person can use language that's prejudiced toward men or women (*sexist language*) or toward gays, lesbians, bisexuals, or transgendered persons (*homophobic language*). It can also be used to criticize various ethnicities (*racist language*), people of different ages (*ageist language*), and even socioeconomic groups (*classist language*). Some people use prejudiced language when discussing physical or mental disabilities, political affiliations, social or religious groups, and even collegiate majors.

Most of us readily recognize racist, sexist, and disability-related slurs. But prejudiced language can be less obvious—for example, when people use ethnic and gender-specific modifiers to describe others even when such descriptors are unnecessary to the point they're making ("the Hispanic doctor" or "a male nurse"). Subtle prejudiced language also shows up in the use of such expressions as "That's so gay," to mean that something isn't "cool" or "acceptable." Such expressions are hurtful and perpetuate negative stereotypes.

What can you do if another person's language is prejudiced and offensive? As we discuss in Chapter 8 about managing conflict, confronting others is rarely easy, but it can be done. Consider the following suggestions:

- Determine the risk of confrontation. Is the person likely to be open to your point of view? A friend, family member, or peer may be willing to listen. However, if it's a stranger or someone with power over you (like your boss), it might be best to ignore the comments or to leave the situation.

- If you choose to confront the person, avoid an approach that causes the person to lose face, creating embarrassment. Instead, talk with the person privately, and open with an affirming statement ("I know that you probably mean no harm when you say, 'That's so gay'").

- Next, state your feelings about the prejudiced language, and politely ask the person to revise his or her language ("I feel uncomfortable with this phrase because I have a brother who's gay; I would appreciate it if you didn't use it").

- Finally, listen to and acknowledge what the person says in response. If necessary, reassert your request that the prejudiced language be avoided ("I understand that you mean nothing by it, but I would still appreciate it if you wouldn't use it").

Verbal Aggression

Verbal aggression is the use of language to attack someone's personal attributes, such as their weight, looks, intelligence, or physical ability (Infante & Wigley, 1986). Verbal aggression is distinct from prejudiced language in three respects: the goal is to intentionally injure a particular person's feelings, the attack targets unique personal attributes rather than group affiliation, and the message often includes profanity.

Verbal aggression can take the form of **cyberbullying:** habitually attacking a person using the Internet, interactive and digital technologies, or mobile phones.[3] Individuals engage in cyberbullying by sending numerous insulting text messages, such as "u r so fat and ugly!" or writing Facebook wall posts denouncing someone as a "whore" or "loser." The impact of cyberbullying can be devastating. Such was the case with Phoebe Prince—a high school student in Massachusetts—who killed herself following repeated acts of verbal aggression by her fellow female students via text messages, Facebook posts, and face-to-face encounters.

Why are people verbally aggressive? Sometimes the behavior is triggered by a temporary state of stress, anger, or exhaustion. Other times it's in reaction to real or perceived slights. In the Phoebe Prince case, the girls attacked her because they felt Phoebe had "crossed a line" by befriending and dating their boyfriends (Bazelon, 2010). Still others act that way because they believe that using profanity, insults, and threats will get them what they want, like Cartman from *South Park*.

It's hard to communicate competently with verbally aggressive people. Imagine giving a speech in a public forum such as a student union meeting and having someone stand up and yell, "Shut up, you loser!" What would you

---

[3]Adapted from www.stopcyberbullying.org (2010).

TABLE 5.2

HOW TO HANDLE VERBAL AGGRESSION ONLINE

If you receive a text, e-mail, or online post that is aggressive or hostile toward you, try the following steps to respond competently and not escalate the situation:

1. Consider the intent of the message carefully to help you determine whether you should respond. Is the sender intentionally trying to provoke you? Did the sender just get carried away with emotion? Is the sender aware of the tone of the message?

2. If you choose to respond, create a draft message first, save it, and then revisit it in a few hours. Do not send the message yet.

3. Later, check your response. Is it informative, honest, relevant, and clear?

4. Did you avoid "you" language, and use "I" and "we" language where appropriate, to minimize defensiveness and bridge your differences?

5. Make sure your message is respectful and polite, avoiding any hint of personal attack or retaliation.

6. Only once you are sure the message fits these requirements should you send it.

1. VLADGRIN/Shutterstock; 2. Max Griboedov/Shutterstock

say and do? To manage verbally aggressive individuals, researcher Dominic Infante (1995) offers three suggestions:

- Avoid communicating in ways that may trigger aggression in the first place, such as teasing, baiting, or insulting others.

- If you know someone who is *chronically verbally aggressive*—meaning he or she is verbally aggressive most of the time—avoid or minimize contact with that person.

- If you can't avoid such interactions, try to remain polite and respectful during them. Don't interrupt the aggressive person. Stay calm, and acknowledge the other person's perspective if possible. Avoid retaliating with personal attacks of your own; they'll only escalate the aggression.

For ideas on how to handle verbal aggression online, see Table 5.2.

Deception

Deception is the deliberate use of uninformative, untruthful, irrelevant, or vague language for the purpose of misleading others. Deception takes many forms. People may be overly vague in what they say, trying to "veil" the truth. They may dodge a question or change the topic to avoid embarrassing or problematic disclosures. The most common form of deception is *concealment*: leaving important and relevant information out of messages (McCornack, 2008). Table 5.3 explains other types of deception, including avoidance, lying, and being vague.

Deception is especially commonplace online. People can easily hide and distort information in chat or e-mail messages, and recipients of messages have little opportunity to check accuracy. Some people provide false information about their backgrounds, professions, appearances, and gender online to amuse themselves, to form relationships unavailable to them offline, or to take advantage of others through online scams (Rainey, 2000). However, most people provide accurate information on social networking sites like Tumblr or Instagram, because close friends will hold them accountable for what they post (Back et al., 2010).

Whether it's face-to-face or online, deception is unethical, impractical, and destructive. It exploits the message recipients' belief that speakers are

TABLE 5.3

TYPES OF DECEPTION

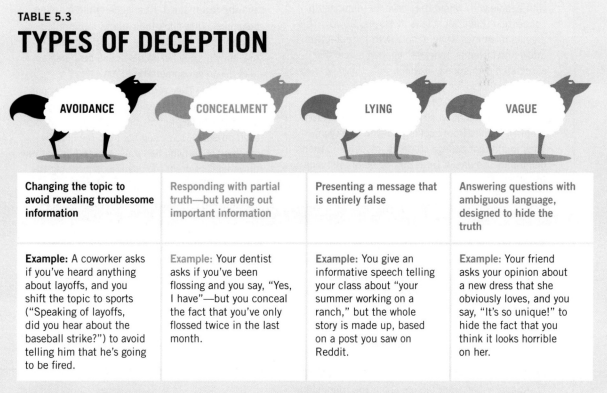

AVOIDANCE	CONCEALMENT	LYING	VAGUE
Changing the topic to avoid revealing troublesome information	Responding with partial truth—but leaving out important information	Presenting a message that is entirely false	Answering questions with ambiguous language, designed to hide the truth
Example: A coworker asks if you've heard anything about layoffs, and you shift the topic to sports ("Speaking of layoffs, did you hear about the baseball strike?") to avoid telling him that he's going to be fired.	Example: Your dentist asks if you've been flossing and you say, "Yes, I have"—but you conceal the fact that you've only flossed twice in the last month.	Example: You give an informative speech telling your class about "your summer working on a ranch," but the whole story is made up, based on a post you saw on Reddit.	Example: Your friend asks your opinion about a new dress that she obviously loves, and you say, "It's so unique!" to hide the fact that you think it looks horrible on her.

Adrian Niederhaeuser/Shutterstock

MAKING COMMUNICATION CHOICES
PROTECTING A FRIEND FROM HARM

1 CONSIDER THE DILEMMA

Aliana is your best friend on campus. She is attractive, funny, and outgoing. She's also stubborn; once her mind is made up, she'll do what she wants.

It's a Friday night, and you and Aliana decide to go out dancing. You both take turns as the designated driver, and tonight is your turn to drive. Shortly after arriving at the club, Aliana is approached by a guy who asks her to dance. You figure she'll be back after one or two songs, but a half hour passes, and she is still with him. Irritated, you signal to her, and when she walks over, she says, "OMG! He is *so* hot!" You, however, have a different impression. "Do you

know him?" you ask, "because he seems kind of sketchy." Aliana laughs and says, "I've had classes with him before—he's fine."

As the hours slide by, it's clear that "Mr. Sketchy" (as you now call him) is making a serious play for your friend. Worse, you note that he's feeding her drinks, one after the next, and she is now wasted. You decide to intervene, but when you tell her it's time to go, she says she's going home with Mr. Sketchy. When you tell her you don't think that's a good idea, Aliana snaps, "Don't tell me what to do! You're not my mother!" Worried about her safety, you're uncertain about your next move.

2 CONNECT THE RESEARCH

Research suggests that more than one-third of college students drink heavily, and that such drinking contributes to a "hookup culture"—an environment in which students engage in risky sexual behavior with people with whom they have no relationship connection (Paul, McManus, & Hayes, 2000). This creates dilemmas when people wish to protect their intoxicated friends from the negative outcomes associated with such behaviors.

Researchers Lisa Menegatos, Linda Lederman, and Aaron Hess (2010) looked at college students' verbal communication strategies for trying to stop drunken friends from hooking up with strangers. They found that college students in such situations commonly use one of three strategies to intervene (p. 383):

- **Persuasion:** They try to convince their friend to not go home with the guy, emphasizing the potential health and social consequences, such as the risks of pregnancy and sexually transmitted disease, and the regret she'd experience in the morning.
- **Deception:** They trick their friend into not leaving with the guy. For example, they might tell her that they'll drive her to his house but, instead, take her to get something to eat.
- **Confrontation:** They verbally or physically discourage their friend from leaving with the guy, by assertively telling her it's time to leave the club or even physically removing her from the club by grabbing or carrying her, if necessary. Alternatively, they might confront the guy who is pursuing the hookup, telling him to leave her alone.

3 COMMUNICATE

Before making a communication choice, consider the facts of the situation, and think about what the research tells you about communicating with an intoxicated friend who is engaging in risky behavior. Also reflect on what you have learned about deception (p. 127), verbal aggression (p. 125), and verbal communication skills (pp. 115–123). Then, answer these questions:

1 What ethical obligation do you have to protect Aliana? What other factors about the friendship

and the situation should you consider when deciding what to do next?

2 Of the three communication approaches researchers have identified for such a situation, which would you most likely try? What other approaches would you consider?

3 What would you say to Aliana next?

communicating cooperatively by tricking them into thinking that the messages are informative, honest, relevant, and clear (McCornack, 2008). Deception is unethical because it denies others information they may need to make personal or professional decisions, and it demonstrates disrespect (LaFollette & Graham, 1986). Deception is also impractical: a lie typically leads to more lies (McCornack, 2008). Even something as simple as telling a friend that you like his new jacket when you don't can get you into trouble. When you're with your friend or mutual acquaintances, you have to remember to always praise it rather than criticize it. Otherwise, he will discover your lie. Finally, deception is destructive; when discovered, it has unpleasant personal and professional consequences (McCornack & Levine, 1990), such as conflicts among friends or romantic partners, loss of trust from an audience, or even dismissal from a job.

LearningCurve can help you review! Go to **bedfordstmartins.com /choicesconnections**.

Defamation

Defamation is intentionally false communication that harms a person's reputation. In written form, defamation is called *libel*; in spoken form, it's *slander*. Defamation isn't just ineffective verbal communication; it can result in legal charges against the person who commits it. But whether such charges will stick depends largely on whether the target of the defamation is a public figure (politician, celebrity, famous athlete) or a private citizen. For public figures, the legal system counts criticism as "free speech." To have defamation charges upheld, public figures must demonstrate that the person who made the statements *acted with malice* and *knew that their claims were false*.

In cases involving private citizens, such as gossip or online rumors, legal action is more likely. Private citizens don't have the same access as public figures to media outlets that can counter defamatory statements; they also don't open themselves up to criticism by being a public figure. Consequently, private citizens' rights to protect their reputations outweigh free-speech rights to criticize and defame.

What does this mean in practical terms? When communicating with others—especially online (which is permanent) or in a speech (which is public)—don't write or say anything that could harm a private citizen's reputation. For example, blogging about a coworker engaging in sexual harassment, or giving a speech in which you denounce a local businessman as racist, may result in someone filing a lawsuit against you. Although you have free-speech rights to (fairly) criticize public figures, you do *not* have the right to publicly assail private citizens in ways that damage their reputations. When it comes to verbal communication, the old adage is true: if you don't have something nice to say about someone, don't say anything at all.

CHAPTER ⑤ REVIEW

CHAPTER RECAP

- **Verbal communication** is the use of written or spoken language to interact with others. Language is symbolic, is rule governed, conveys meaning, and is intertwined with culture.
- You can increase your verbal communication skills by creating messages that adhere to the **cooperative principle** and by using **"I" and "we" language.**
- Although there are many common stereotypes about how men and women communicate, studies show that men's and women's verbal communication is more similar than different.
- Consider how cultural factors like *high-* or *low-context* culture, preferred speech rates, or desired balance of turn taking can influence interactions, and try to adapt as best you can.
- Avoiding verbal communication pitfalls such as **prejudiced language, verbal aggression, cyberbullying, deception,** and **defamation**—and learning how to handle situations when others use them—will help you improve your communication competence.

LAUNCHPAD

LaunchPad for *Choices & Connections* offers unique video scenarios and encourages self-assessment through adaptive quizzing. Go to **bedfordstmartins.com/choicesconnections** to get access.

✅ LearningCurve adaptive quizzes

▶ How to Communicate video scenarios

▶ Video Clips that illustrate key concepts

KEY TERMS

Verbal communication, p. 112

Symbols, p. 113

Constitutive rules, p. 113

Regulative rules, p. 114

 Denotative meanings, p. 114

 Connotative meanings, p. 114

Dialects, p. 114

Cooperative principle, p. 116

Honesty, p. 117

Misunderstanding, p. 118

▶ "You" language, p. 119

▶ "I" language, p. 119

▶ "We" language, p. 119

Prejudiced language, p. 124

Verbal aggression, p. 125

Cyberbullying, p. 125

Deception, p. 127

Defamation, p. 129

Looking for more review questions? **LearningCurve** can help you master key concepts from this chapter. Go to **bedfordstmartins.com /choicesconnections**.

1 You and your sister using the phrase "blue moon" to signal to each other when your mom is in a bad mood is an example of _____.

a. regulative rules

b. constitutive rules

c. connotative meanings

d. denotative meanings

2 Which of the following is *not* one of the four characteristics of understandable language, according to the cooperative principle?

a. Honest

b. Symbolic

c. Clear

d. Informative

3 Phrases that both emphasize inclusion and enhance feelings of connection and similarity are known as _____.

a. "we" language

b. understandable messages

c. "I" language

d. cooperative principle

4 According to researcher Dominic Infante, how can you competently communicate with verbally aggressive people?

a. Avoid teasing, baiting, or insulting others.

b. Minimize contact with people who are chronically verbally aggressive.

c. Remain polite and respectful, and don't retaliate with your own attacks.

d. All of the answers are correct.

5 According to Table 5.3, Types of Deception, which of the following refers to revealing only part of the truth while leaving out important information?

a. Vague

b. Avoidance

c. Lying

d. Concealment

ACTIVITIES

1 What Went Wrong?

Think of a recent conflict or unpleasant encounter you've had. It can be with anyone: a professor, a friend, a roommate, a family member, a coworker. Write out exactly what you and the other person said, to the best of your recollection. If it was a text-based interaction, use the e-mails, texts, or tweets for reference. Now, look at the language that you and your partner used. How did specific things that each of you said contribute to the unpleasantness of the interaction? Revisit the coverage of the cooperative principle and "I" and "we" language on pages 116–119. What could you have said differently to help the situation be more positive or to better explain your point of view?

2 Just a Little White Lie

With a partner, discuss the definitions and differences between the types of deception outlined in Table 5.3: avoidance, concealment, lying, and vague. Do you consider some of these types more deceptive than others? When, if ever, is it acceptable to use these forms of deception? Is it ever ethical to deceive? Provide examples and rationales for each.

6

Nonverbal Communication

Serene smiles. Goofy grins. Contorted grimaces. Giant posters of people making such faces have been popping up all over the globe for the last several years—from southern Sudan to the Standing Rock Indian Reservation in North Dakota. Most are pasted illegally onto the sides of buildings, bridges, and walls; on public staircases; and even on trains and buses. Who's behind these displays? Renegade French artist JR.[1] When asked about the meaning of his work and what he is hoping to achieve through it, he notes that his work can change people's perceptions of one another in powerful, positive

ways. How? When you see these people making faces, you also see their humor, personalities, and willingness to poke fun at themselves. You see them using nonverbal behaviors to communicate. Suddenly, people who might have seemed strange and different from you seem silly, similar, and likable.

JR's art installations are collaborative group projects. For a project entitled *Face2Face*, JR photographed Israelis and Palestinians who did the same jobs— taxi drivers, lawyers, and cooks. He then pasted the images side by side in various Israeli communities. As he describes, "The experts said no way—the people will not accept it. But they did. When you paste an image it's just paper and glue. People can tear it, tag on it, the people in the street are the creator. The rain and the wind will take them [the images] off anyway. They're not meant to stay. But it's now four years after, and most of them are still there. *Face2Face* demonstrated that what we thought was impossible was possible."

Wherever they are pasted, JR's installations are immediately recognizable, because they focus on close-up images of the human face. JR uses a wide-angle lens to photograph his subjects, which requires

David Silverman/Getty Images

[1]All content that follows adapted from Khatchadourian (2011) and JR (2011).

him to stand just a few inches away from them—an intimate distance requiring trust. He then has people "make faces" that represent themselves—communicating vivid and intense messages of identity and emotion. As he describes, "I ask people to make a face as a sign of commitment—not a smile that really doesn't tell who you are or what you feel."

In 2011, JR received the prestigious TED Prize, which recognizes "an extraordinary individual with a creative and bold vision to spark global change"

(ted.com, n.d.). His latest project, *Inside Out*, involves people submitting self-portraits, which he then prints on enormous posters and sends back, so that contributors can paste them wherever they want. Inherent to *Inside Out* is JR's ongoing recognition of the power of nonverbal communication to impact people's impressions. As he notes, "The idea is that you have to stand for what you care about. It is easy on Facebook to say 'I love this' or 'I'm against that.' But to stand for your own image in the street? That's another level."

✓ **LearningCurve** can
help you review! Go to
**bedfordstmartins.com
/choicesconnections**.

As the artwork of JR spotlights, your nonverbal communication powerfully impacts people's impressions of you. Something as simple as a grin or a scowl can make the difference between people liking or not liking you, approaching or avoiding you. This makes learning about, taking control of, and improving your nonverbal communication incredibly important. When you take the time to better understand nonverbal communication and strengthen your skills, the potential payoff is enormous. Nonverbal communication ability is related to higher levels of self-esteem and life satisfaction, perceptions of attractiveness and popularity, greater interpersonal influence in situations requiring persuasive ability, and higher relationship satisfaction (Burgoon & Hoobler, 2002; Carton, Kessler, & Pape, 1999; Hodgins & Belch, 2000). In this chapter, you'll learn:

• The characteristics that define nonverbal communication
• How to use different types of nonverbal communication
• The functions of nonverbal communication
• Ways to improve your nonverbal communication skills

Characteristics of Nonverbal Communication

> Although the words you choose are important, your nonverbal communication has more impact because it conveys more meaning. Thus, your nonverbal communication is the most important tool in your communication competence toolbox. The starting point for using this tool skillfully is understanding the characteristics that define it.

Nonverbal communication is the transmission of meaning through an individual's nonspoken physical and behavioral cues (Patterson, 1983, 1995). This includes instances in which you intentionally mean to communicate—such as rolling your eyes to convey annoyance when arguing with your sister—and times when you unintentionally send a message, such as yawning during class. You may just be tired that day, but your teacher could interpret it as a sign that you're bored by her lecture. In addition to being both intentional and unintentional, nonverbal communication has several distinguishing features: it uses multiple channels, conveys more meaning than verbal communication, blends with verbal communication to create meaning, and is influenced by gender and culture.

Nonverbal Communication Uses Multiple Channels

Nonverbal communication conveys information through multiple channels, including auditory, visual, and tactile. Consider what happens when a classmate presents an idea during a discussion. As she speaks, you listen to and interpret the meaning of her words (verbal communication). But at the same time, you're noticing various nonverbal channels—her vocal pitches and tones (auditory);

her facial expressions, gestures, postures, and appearance (visual); and possibly physical contact (tactile), if she's sitting next to you and happens to touch you. You receive all of this information simultaneously and use it to interpret her meaning: Is she excited about her idea? Unsure? Tired? Her nonverbal communication helps you make sense of the words she says and the meaning she intends.

Nonverbal Communication Conveys More Meaning Than Verbal Communication

Because it uses multiple channels, nonverbal communication conveys more meaning than verbal. This is especially evident when people send **incongruent messages**, in which their verbal and nonverbal behaviors contradict each other—for example, saying "I'm fine" while frowning. In such situations, people overwhelmingly trust the nonverbal messages more than they trust the verbal (Burgoon & Hoobler, 2002). An essential part of competent nonverbal communication is producing **congruent messages,** in which your verbal and nonverbal communications match. Congruent messages are perceived as direct and honest, and they create less confusion for others. For example, if you're mad at your sister, you scowl when saying, "Yes, I'm angry!" instead of smiling. Or when you're giving a speech, you reinforce the strong statement "Incidents like this cannot happen again!" by pounding your fist on the lectern rather than standing there motionless.

DOUBLE TAKE

INCONGRUENT (VS) CONGRUENT MESSAGES

When your verbal communication ("I'm so happy for you!") doesn't match your nonverbal behavior, people are more likely to believe your nonverbal communication. In the following photos, which woman is sending congruent messages?

Andrew Hobbs/Getty Images   Diego Cervo/Veer

Nonverbal Communication Blends with Verbal Communication

When interacting with others, you don't just use either verbal or nonverbal communication. Instead, you blend both to create and interpret messages (Birdwhistell, 1970; Jones & LeBaron, 2002). You can do this in five ways:

- *Replace* verbal expressions with nonverbal, such as shrugging your shoulders and turning your palms upward instead of saying, "I don't know."

- *Repeat* verbal messages—for instance, saying, "It's up there" and then pointing upward.

- *Contradict* verbal messages with nonverbal communication deliberately—for example, using sarcasm by telling a friend "I love that song" while rolling your eyes, to indicate that you really don't like the song at all.

- *Enhance* the meaning of verbal messages, such as telling a cousin about a professor who kept blinking her eyes while lecturing—and blinking your own eyes repeatedly to demonstrate the teacher's nervous behavior.

- *Spotlight* certain parts of verbal messages—for example, elevating the volume of your voice on a single word: "I did NOT mean it that way!"

Nonverbal Communication Is Influenced by Gender

Stereotypes about gender suggest that men and women communicate nonverbally in different ways. Men are often thought to be powerful and aggressive, while women are conceived of as more demure or meek. But these are just ill-informed notions. What's the *truth* about gender and nonverbal communication? Data from hundreds of studies suggest four consistent differences between the sexes (J. A. Hall, 1998; J. A. Hall, Carter, & Horgan, 2000). First, women are better than men at communicating nonverbally in ways receivers can correctly interpret and are more accurate than men in interpreting others' nonverbal expressions. Second, women show greater facial expressiveness than men, and they smile more. Third, women gaze at others more than men do during interpersonal interactions, especially during same-sex encounters. Indeed, women are more likely than men to find speakers persuasive when the presenters maintain eye contact with them (Bailenson, Beall, Loomis, Blascovich, & Turk, 2005). Fourth, men are more territorial than women in terms of personal space. Men maintain more physical space between themselves and others while talking, tolerate intrusions into their personal space less than women do, and are less likely to give way to others if space is scarce. Correspondingly, women enjoy closer proximity during same-sex encounters than men, prefer side-by-side seating more than men do, and perceive crowded situations more favorably.

Of course, not all women and men show these differences. Understanding that such differences *may* exist can help you improve your cross-sex nonverbal communication. For example, if you're hosting a presentation in which the audience is largely male, arrange the seating to provide ample space between audience members. When you're talking with a female friend, she may desire shared gaze and prefer to sit in close proximity to you.

Nonverbal Communication Is Influenced by Culture

The culture in which you were raised plays an enormous role in molding your nonverbal communication behaviors (Matsumoto, 2006). Different cultures have very different **display rules**—guidelines for when, where, and how to appropriately express emotion (Ekman & Friesen, 1975). As Chapter 4 discusses, people from Asian cultures are often taught to control their display of intense emotions (grimacing, scowling, large smiles) much more so than are Americans (Matsumoto, Takeuchi, Andayani, Kouznetsova, & Krupp, 1998). Within traditional Mexican culture, however, people are encouraged to openly express emotions, both positive and negative (Matsumoto, 2006).

Cultures also vary in the degree to which they emphasize close physical space, shared gaze, and physical contact during interaction. People from **high-contact cultures** prefer frequent touching, shared gaze, close physical proximity, and direct body orientation (facing each other while talking). Examples of high-contact cultures include Brazil, Mexico, Italy, and Spain. Those from **low-contact cultures** prefer infrequent touching, little shared gaze, larger physical distance, and indirect body orientation (angled away from each other during interaction). Low-contact cultures include Britain, Canada, the United States, and Japan. (See Figure 6.1.)

FIGURE 6.1

HIGH- & LOW-CONTACT CULTURES

LOW-CONTACT CULTURES

United States
Canada
Northern Europe
Australia & New Zealand
Asia

HIGH-CONTACT CULTURES

South America
Latin America
Southern Europe
Africa
Russia
Middle East

1. Michael D. Brown/Shutterstock;
2. Michael D. Brown/Shutterstock

Understanding cultural differences in nonverbal expression can help you improve your overall communication competence. For example, if you're on a first date with someone from a low-contact culture, give him or her plenty of room during your date and avoid unnecessary touching. If you're giving a presentation to a small group consisting of people from a high-contact culture, stand close to your audience and don't be hesitant to touch nearby listeners to emphasize a point, if it's relevant to do so.

Types of Nonverbal Communication

Your use of body movement, voice, touch, personal space, appearance, beliefs about time, and environmental features work together to create your nonverbal communication. This influences how others perceive your messages, who you are, and how you feel. Understanding the different types of nonverbal expression and how they work will help you make sure these impressions are the right ones.

At age 16, Tyra Banks began doing fashion shows in Europe for designers such as Chanel, Valentino, and Fendi. She subsequently appeared in *Elle* and *Vogue*, and was the first African American woman to grace the cover of *GQ*. But what catapulted her to the top of the global modeling industry was not just her beauty—it was also her unique self-awareness of, and control over, the various types of nonverbal communication. For example, Tyra distinguishes 275 different smiles she uses when modeling, including seven basic smiles she teaches protégés on her show, *America's Next Top Model*.[2] One of these smiles doesn't involve the mouth at all, just the eyes—which Tyra calls a *smize*. Another smile uses body posture and movement—specifically, shifting her shoulder position sideways and downward, and turning her head toward the listener. These and the 273 other smiles all reflect specific emotions or situations, from anger to surprise.

Tyra Banks has built a media empire from her uncanny ability to manipulate her nonverbal communication on fashion runways, on television, and in photographs. But the types of nonverbal communication she uses—and coaches other models how to modify—are the very same ones you use in your daily life. Scholars of communication identify seven such types: body movement, voice, touch, personal space, appearance, beliefs about time, and environmental features. Although you experience these collectively as a whole, understanding how each type influences your own and others' communication can make the difference between successful and unsuccessful interactions.

---

[2]T Screen Test Films: Tyra Banks (2008).

Body Movement

Communication scholars refer to body movement as **kinesics,** from the Greek word *kinesis*. This broad category encompasses most of the cues people typically think of as nonverbal communication: facial expressions, eye contact, gestures, and body postures.

Facial Expressions. Think back to the story of French artist JR in our chapter opener. Why would he focus on people's *faces* as the centerpieces of his art installations? Because of all the behaviors people display when communicating, facial expressions have the most impact (Knapp & Hall, 2002). Everything from the arch of an eyebrow to the curl of a lip can convey information about mood and emotion (Ekman, 2003). Facial expressions are so important that you may feel compelled to use emoticons (☺ ☹) when texting to clarify your intentions. In fact, one of the reasons for the popularity of Skype, videoconferencing, and video chat is that these technologies allow people to see and interpret their communication partners' facial expressions.

Eye Contact. You use eye contact to show attention, interest, affection, and even aggression. Looking directly at your audience while giving a speech, for example, conveys concern for their reactions and affiliation with them. Eye contact conveys the same message within group and interpersonal settings as well. When you look at people directly, you're attentive to them, and when you avoid eye contact, you signal that you're disinterested, bored, or ready for the encounter to end. Of course, eye contact can also be used aggressively. When you want to convey dominance over someone—something we talk about later in this chapter—you may try to "stare them down" (Matsumoto, 2006). Since eye contact can show a variety of emotions and intentions, it can be challenging to make sure you perceive others' communication correctly. For ideas on how to handle such situations, see How to Communicate: Perceiving Nonverbal Messages on pages 140–141.

Tyra Banks believes that just a simple manipulation of your eyes and smile can cause a drastic change in the attitude you portray to the world. How do you use nonverbal communication to express your emotions?

Kevin Mazur/Child11/WireImage/Getty Images

PERCEIVING NONVERBAL MESSAGES

 One way to improve your communication competence is by adequately understanding others' behaviors. Learn how to handle incongruent messages in nonverbal communication by going to LaunchPad at **bedfordstmartins.com/choicesconnections** and completing the **How to Communicate video scenario** for Chapter 6 to practice your skills.

CONSIDER THIS:
While on a Skype video call with a long-distance friend, you describe your new romantic partner—explaining why the two of you get along so well. During your story, your friend frowns, rolls her eyes, and looks down at the floor.

WHAT WOULD YOU DO?
The following advice illustrates how to use perception-checking to ask if you are interpreting nonverbal messages correctly. As you watch the video, consider how the dialogue incorporates the characteristics of nonverbal communication and the functions of each type. Then, test your knowledge of key skills, and create your own responses to the **What if? video prompts**.

1 DESCRIBE YOUR OBSERVATIONS in neutral terms, being as specific as possible and using "I" language in explaining your perceptions.

② EXPRESS YOUR CONCERNS

about her nonverbal communication, framing her behavior as "it" rather than "your actions" and emphasizing that your concern derives from admiration.

"I respect you and your opinion enormously, and so I'm concerned that it might have been in response to what I was sharing with you."

"Were the behaviors I noticed because of what I was saying or something else entirely?"

③ DIRECTLY ASK

her about the meaning of her nonverbal communication, making sure to use "I" language and suggesting several possibilities so that it's not a "yes/no" question.

WHAT IF? But what if things don't work out as shown? Test your ability to adapt your communication by watching the What if? videos and planning a response for each situation.

1. What would you do when your friend denies that she made the nonverbal behaviors in question, saying, "I don't know what you are talking about. I didn't do anything"?
2. How would you handle your friend when she says that her nonverbal behaviors were unrelated? "I was just checking the time. I have to get going or I'll be late for my shift."

Gestures. People use four types of *gestures* (hand motions) to communicate nonverbally:

- **Emblems** substitute for verbal statements—for example, waving your hand at a friend to communicate "Hi!"
- **Illustrators** accent verbal messages—for example, holding your hands a certain distance apart while saying, "The fish I caught was this big."
- **Regulators** help control turn taking during interpersonal encounters, group discussions, and question-and-answer sessions following presentations. You may point your finger, hold your palm up, or twirl your hands to "tell" people to keep talking, repeat something, hurry up, or wait longer before beginning their turn.
- **Adaptors** are touching gestures that serve a psychological or physical purpose, such as rubbing your chin when thinking about a tough question or playing with a paper clip when you're bored during a long meeting.

Body Postures. The straightness of your back (erect or slouched), your body lean (forward, backward, or vertical), the straightness of your shoulders (firm and broad or slumped), and your head position (tilted or straight up) all communicate information to the people with whom you're interacting. For example, Steve's karate instructor interviewed convicted muggers regarding what they looked for in potential victims. The most popular response? Body posture. The muggers perceived people who walked with shoulders slumped, back slouched, and heads drooping as "weak" and "good targets." They saw people who walked with shoulders back, spines erect, and heads up as "confident and strong," and avoided them. The ability of your posture to make such strong impressions is important to remember not only when you are making a presentation, as it will influence how the audience perceives you, but when you are interviewing for a job, as the interviewer will take your nonverbal communication into account when forming an impression of you.

Voice

Vocal characteristics used to communicate nonverbal messages are known as **vocalics**. When you interact with others, you typically think of their voice as one thing—for example, shrill, loud, deep, or nasal—but voices are actually made up of several characteristics. The four qualities of voice—tone, pitch, loudness, and speech rate—create distinct impressions for listeners in any interaction.

Tone. *Tone* stems from the resonance and breathiness of your voice. You can create a rich vocal tone—conveying authority and confidence—by allowing your voice to resonate deep in your chest and throat. Alternatively, restricting your voice to your sinus cavity ("talking through your nose") creates a whiny tone—often judged as unpleasant. How much you breathe while

DIFFERENT TYPES OF GREETINGS

How you greet others reflects many aspects of your nonverbal communication. Think about how your greetings use facial expressions, eye contact, gestures, touch, personal space, and even beliefs about time. What messages are you sending through your greetings?

(Clockwise from top left) Jeremy Woodhouse/Blend Images/Aurora Photos; EyesWideOpen/Getty Images; GoGo Images/age fotostock; Suchit Nanda/age footstock; Yellow Dog Productions/Getty Images; Getty Images

speaking also affects tone. If you expel a great deal of air when speaking, you convey sexiness. If you constrict airflow when speaking, you create a thin, hard tone, which may communicate nervousness or anxiety.

Pitch. *Pitch* is the frequency range of your voice—how high or low it is. People tend to associate lower pitches with strength and competence, and higher pitches with weakness (Spender, 1990).

Loudness. *Loudness* is the volume of your voice. You can increase loudness to emphasize certain words, phrases, or points. When texting, tweeting, or posting online, people indicate loudness (i.e., shouting or yelling) with CAPITAL LETTERS.

Speech Rate. *Speech rate* is how quickly you speak. Although it is commonly believed that talking at a moderate and steady rate is the best choice, research shows that speaking fast or slow by itself doesn't seem to determine speech effectiveness (Krause, 2001). Instead, it's whether you correctly pronounce and clearly articulate your words. Keep this in mind if you are making a public speech; if you're a fast talker, take care not to slur or blur your words.

Touch

Communication scholars refer to touch as **haptics,** from the ancient Greek word *haptein.* The meaning of such physical contact with others depends on the duration, part of the body being touched, strength of contact, and surrounding context (Floyd, 1999). For example, *functional-professional touch* is used to accomplish some type of task, such as touch between physicians and patients during examinations, or between coaches and athletes while "spotting" a workout activity. *Social-polite touch* derives from social norms and expectations, the most common form being the handshake, which has served as a form of greeting for over 2,000 years (Heslin, 1974). You use *friendship-warmth touch*—for example, gently grasping a friend's arm and giving it a squeeze—to express liking for another person. *Love-intimacy touch*—cupping a romantic partner's face tenderly in your hands, giving him or her a big, lingering hug—lets you convey deep emotional feelings. *Sexual-arousal touch,* as the name implies, is intended to physically stimulate another person. Finally, *aggressive-hostile* touch involves forms of physical violence, such as grabbing, slapping, and hitting—behaviors designed to hurt and humiliate others.

People differ widely in their personal preferences for giving and receiving touch, with some liking less contact than others. For example, both Steve and Joe are low-contact people: Joe isn't much of a hugger, and Steve dislikes handshakes. Yet both have family members who are "high contact" and enjoy sharing lots of touch. This makes for interesting—and occasionally awkward—interactions at family get-togethers, where the parties involved struggle with whether hugs and handshakes should be shared or avoided.

Keep such individual preferences in mind when you interact with others, and adapt your touch behaviors to match their desires.

Personal Space

How close or far away you position yourself from others while communicating is known as **proxemics,** from the Latin word *proximus*, meaning "near." Proxemics often illustrates the nature of the encounter and how you feel about the people with whom you're interacting. There are four different zones for physical distance, and each is used in specific kinds of settings (E. T. Hall, 1963):

- *Intimate space* ranges from 0 to 18 inches. Most people use this only with people to whom they feel extremely close. (see Figure 6.2.)
- *Personal space* ranges from 18 inches to 4 feet and is often used during encounters with friends.
- *Social space* ranges from about 4 feet to 12 feet. Many people use it when communicating in the workplace or with acquaintances and strangers.
- *Public space* ranges upward from 12 feet—including great distances—and is used during formal occasions, such as public speeches or college lectures.

Of course, these distances aren't absolute; different people have different preferences for space. You may feel crowded if people sit closer than two feet from you, whereas your best friend may be perfectly comfortable sitting

FIGURE 6.2

SPATIAL DISTANCE

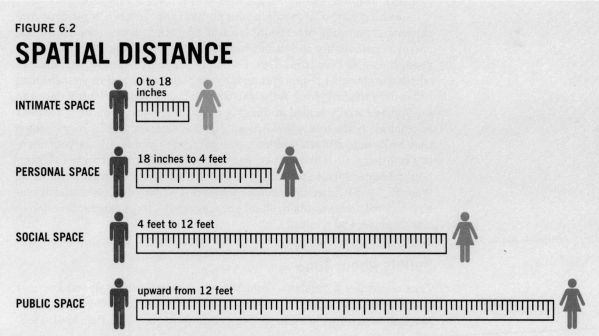

INTIMATE SPACE — 0 to 18 inches

PERSONAL SPACE — 18 inches to 4 feet

SOCIAL SPACE — 4 feet to 12 feet

PUBLIC SPACE — upward from 12 feet

1. Michael D. Brown/Shutterstock; 2. Michael D. Brown/Shutterstock

shoulder-to-shoulder with others. Space preferences also vary widely across cultures (Chen & Starosta, 2005). For example, during casual conversations, most North Americans feel comfortable an arm's-length distance apart. Latin Americans, North Africans, and those from the northern and western Middle East tend to prefer a closer distance. Japanese and Chinese tend to keep a larger distance. Failure to appreciate these differences can cause awkwardness and anxiety during cross-cultural encounters. People from cultures emphasizing closer distance may keep edging closer to their conversation partner and may judge the other person as "aloof" and "standoffish" if he or she keeps backing away. Correspondingly, people from cultures emphasizing larger distances will be baffled by and uncomfortable with perceived invasions of their space. Because violations of space expectations can cause discomfort, try to adjust your use of space in accordance with others' preferences whenever possible.

Appearance

The way you look speaks volumes about who you are because people use your *physical appearance*—visible attributes such as hair, clothing, body type, and other features—to make judgments about you. For example, people who judge you as attractive may also see you as intelligent, persuasive, poised, sociable, warm, powerful, and successful (Hatfield & Sprecher, 1986). Such perceptions are made online as well. If your friends post attractive photos of themselves on your Facebook page, people will perceive you as more physically and socially attractive. If your friends post unattractive photos, you'll seem less attractive to others (Walther, Van Der Heide, Kim, Westerman, & Tong, 2008).

Clothing plays a large role in your physical appearance. People draw conclusions about your profession, level of education, socioeconomic status, and even personality and values based solely on what you're wearing (Burgoon, Buller, & Woodall, 1996). So before leaving the house, ask yourself whether your outfit is appropriate for your plans and whether your clothing will convey the image you want it to convey. If you want a job interviewer to see you as socially skilled and highly motivated, wear something business appropriate to the interview (Gifford, Ng, & Wilkinson, 1985). Your clothing choices include **artifacts**—objects you possess to communicate your identity to others, such as watches, jewelry, and handbags. Artifacts can communicate your affluence, influence, and attractiveness (Burgoon, Buller, & Woodall, 1996). American men, for instance, typically don't wear much jewelry, so a man who wants to stand out may sport a large expensive watch to convey power and wealth.

Beliefs about Time

Time seems like a constant—something that exists outside of you and that everyone views in exactly the same way as you do. But as noted in Chapter 4, people around the globe differ in their beliefs about time (E.T. Hall, 1981, 1983,

NONVERBAL COMMUNICATION IN CONTEXT

Whether it's through body language, facial expressions, or environmental features, all forms of nonverbal communication influence your perception of the situation. What do the nonverbal cues in the photos tell you about each workplace?

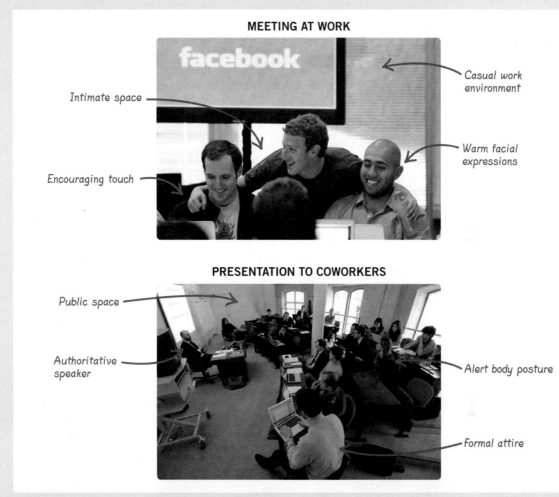

MEETING AT WORK

Intimate space

Encouraging touch

Casual work environment

Warm facial expressions

PRESENTATION TO COWORKERS

Public space

Authoritative speaker

Alert body posture

Formal attire

(Top) Justin Sullivan/Getty Images; (Bottom) PATRICK HERTZOG/AFP/Getty Images

1997b). Those who have an **M-time orientation** (for "monochronic time") value careful scheduling and time management. They view time as a precious resource: it can be saved, spent, wasted, lost, or made up; it can even run out. People who have a **P-time orientation** ("polychronic time") value interpersonal interaction and don't view time as a resource to be spent, saved, or guarded.

How you perceive, orient to, and structure your time communicates powerful nonverbal messages to others. If you show up substantially late to a lunch with an M-time friend, for example, you communicate "lack of caring." In contrast, being 10minutes *early* for a lunch date might convey being "uptight" or "rigid" to a P-time friend. Similarly, if you opt to spend time with your family in the morning—making you an hour late for your work shift—an M-time boss will likely view this as being irresponsible. You might even get fired. A P-time boss, on the other hand, will likely view you as having the right priorities in life. To improve your own competence, keep time orientation differences in mind and be willing to flexibly adapt your behaviors to others as needed.

Environmental Features

Two types of environmental features shape nonverbal communication: fixed features and semi-fixed features (E. T. Hall, 1981). *Fixed features* are relatively stable parts of the environment—for example, walls, ceilings, floors, and doors in a building. Fixed features send powerful nonverbal messages to others. For example, what do luxury homes and cars share in common with first-class seating in airplanes? *Bigger size*. Simple differences in the fixed features of room size, ceiling height, and (in the case of cars and airplanes) seat size and legroom convey greater wealth and prestige. People recognize this and use such features to nonverbally communicate stature to others (by driving big cars, building huge houses, and so forth).

Semi-fixed features are impermanent and usually easy to change. They include things like furniture, lighting, and color. Hard, uncomfortable furniture shortens interactions, just as soft, plush seating encourages relaxed, lengthy encounters. Bright lighting is associated with action-filled environments, whereas soft lighting goes with calm, intimate environments. Color

Consider how environmental features in these two living rooms send nonverbal messages. What do you perceive about the people who live there based on the fixed features and semi-fixed features? What messages are you trying to send through environmental spaces you have control over?

PlusONE/Shutterstock

krsmanovic/Shutterstock

also makes a difference; people experience blues and greens as relaxing, yellows and oranges as arousing and energizing, reds and blacks as sensuous, and grays and browns as depressing (Burgoon et al., 1996).

You can make choices about fixed and semi-fixed factors to send a nonverbal message. For example, if you want to convey a sense of formality while conducting your monthly sales meeting, have attendees sit at a large, rectangular conference table in rigid high-backed chairs, in a room adorned with portraits of the company founders. If you want to convey a sense of creativity and relaxation, have the meeting at a local coffee shop, where salespeople can lounge in comfy chairs in front of a fireplace.

Functions of Nonverbal Communication

Although nonverbal communication seems like something that just happens, it isn't random, nor is it a pointless companion to verbal messages. Instead, it is purposeful and serves many functions. By understanding these functions, you can better match your nonverbal communication to the demands of different situations.

Walking into the kitchen, Steve found his son Kyle laughing over his laptop: "Look at how many people joined my Rave!" Moving closer to the screen, Steve was stunned to see Kyle's *World of Warcraft* character thrusting his hips and gesturing in a bizarre dance, surrounded by other dancing characters. Suddenly there was an on-screen flash, and Kyle's character fell to the ground. "*That* was rude!" Kyle exclaimed. Another player had killed Kyle's character, ending the impromptu dance festival.

In *World of Warcraft* (*WoW*), a massively multiplayer online role-playing game, characters don't just wage war, acquire abilities, advance through levels, and pursue quests. They communicate. Unlike online games of old, where such communication was limited to text, *WoW* allows players to convey a broad range of nonverbal expressions. To communicate nonverbally, players use "emotes"—pregenerated actions you trigger by typing in

Acknowledging the importance of nonverbal communication in real life, *World of Warcraft* allows characters to gesture, move, and produce a wide range of facial expressions to perform actions and build relationships within the online game.

Sean Gallup/Getty Images

FIGURE 6.3

NONVERBAL BEHAVIORS

When communicating, you combine different nonverbal behaviors together to provide specific functions. Depending on the interaction and your communication goals, you adjust these behaviors. For example, what other nonverbal behaviors might you employ (or avoid) in each situation listed below to achieve your communication goals?

COMFORT A FRIEND	CELEBRATE AN ANNIVERSARY	CONFRONT A SIBLING	GIVE A PRESENTATION
Lowered voice pitch	Leaning in closer	Direct gaze and staring	Watching for head nods
Furrowed brow	Expelling air when speaking	Larger-than-life claiming of space	Using regulators
Nodding	Smiling more	Speaking loudly	Standing with your shoulders back
Sharing more touch	Sharing more gaze	Scowling	Posture shifts
Takeaway: Nonverbal behaviors can convey emotional support	Takeaway: Nonverbal behaviors can communicate intimacy	Takeaway: Nonverbal behaviors can convey dominance	Takeaway: Nonverbal behaviors can help manage interactions

1. VoodooDot/Shutterstock; 2. Ekler/Shutterstock; 3. Liskus/Shutterstock; 4. Introwiz1/Shutterstock

certain code words. Most emotes are purely nonverbal. For example, players can wave good-bye ("/farewell"), raise an eyebrow inquisitively ("/eyebrow"), scowl ("/scowl"), point at a target ("/point"), make taunting gestures ("/taunt"), or offer congratulatory high fives ("/highfive").

These virtual nonverbal messages serve a host of functions. Players can directly *convey meaning* ("you motion for everyone to follow"), *express emotion* ("you run around in a frenzied state of panic"), *present themselves* to others in a specific way ("you bow down graciously"), *manage interactions* ("you tap your foot—hurry up already!"), and *define relationships* ("you blow a kiss to another person"). They can even present themselves to others as a fun person to dance with—at least until another character "rudely" attacks them! In the real world, nonverbal communication utilizes these five functions as well.

Conveying Meaning

Nonverbal communication conveys meaning both directly and indirectly. Sometimes you directly communicate, such as flashing a thumbs-up sign to a friend who performed well during a play. At other times, your nonverbal communication is comparatively indirect—for example, wearing black to signal sadness or grief rather than openly crying.

Although you regularly use nonverbal communication to convey meaning, be careful about presuming particular meanings from the nonverbal displays of others. Consider deception, for example. Around the world, people believe that liars fidget nervously, play with their hair or clothes, and smile too much (Global Deception Research Team, 2006). The most commonly believed deception cue is eye contact: "Liars can't look you in the eye," or so we're told by movies, TV shows, Web sites, books, and magazines. But these beliefs are false. Across hundreds of scientific studies involving tens of thousands of participants, not a single nonverbal behavior has been found that consistently indicates deception (DePaulo et al. 2003; Sporer & Schwandt, 2006). So, if someone doesn't look you in the eye while speaking, don't presume that it means deception.

Expressing Emotion

You also use nonverbal communication for **affect displays:** intentional or unintentional behaviors that depict actual or feigned emotion (Burgoon, Buller, & Woodall, 1996). Affect displays are presented primarily through the face and voice. You communicate hundreds, if not thousands, of real and faked emotional states with your face. You may grin in amusement, grimace in disgust, furrow your brow in concern, or lift one eyebrow in suspicion. Your voice also conveys emotions. For instance, most people express emotions such as grief and love through lowered vocal pitch, and hostile emotions such as anger and contempt through loudness (Costanzo, Markel, & Costanzo, 1969).

Presenting Self

Consider all the ways you can use nonverbal communication to present different aspects of your self to others. You can wear religious artifacts to convey your spiritual beliefs. You can select clothing to present your self as Goth, gangsta, preppy, or punk. You can walk slouched and hunched over to communicate dismay, or stand with your head up and shoulders back to demonstrate confidence. Smiling presents you to others as friendly and approachable, while scowling presents you as threatening. An important part of being a competent nonverbal communicator is recognizing the demands of the situation (formal/informal; intimate/impersonal), then shifting your nonverbal communication quickly to present your self in appropriate ways.

Managing Interactions

Your nonverbal communication helps you manage interactions. For example, during conversations or question-and-answer sessions following presentations, you use regulators (such as pointing to the person you want to hear from next), eye contact, touch, smiling, nodding, and posture shifts to

MAKING COMMUNICATION CHOICES

I WASN'T BEING SARCASTIC!

① CONSIDER THE DILEMMA

Chelsea is the top student in your communication class. Although she is brilliant and talented, she knows it and goes out of her way to show off. You admire her, but her arrogance irks you.

Your professor feels strongly that peer assessment—having students critique one another—is an important part of the class. This has worked out well—except for your group project. Chelsea gave you low marks, which impacted your overall grade. Granted, you didn't invest as much effort as you could have, but you were still angry. In the aftermath, the two of you fought over her assessment, and you haven't spoken since.

Now it's time for public speech evaluations, and sure enough, your professor assigns Chelsea to critique you. She must analyze a video of your speech, then send comments to you and the professor. Your speech goes well, but you're worried about Chelsea's assessment. Just before leaving for work, you see that Chelsea's review is posted. Reading it, you're stunned to see that her comments are complimentary, detailed, fair, and extremely insightful. Relieved and excited to receive her praise, you type a hasty message: "Just wanted to say I REALLY appreciate your BRILLIANT and INSIGHTFUL comments!"

Getting home from work, you find another message from Chelsea. It reads, "You know, after the group project I thought you were kind of a loser. But I gave you the benefit of the doubt and approached your speech with an open mind. I spent two hours on my review. The least you could have done was thank me straight up, instead of being sarcastic. I guess my initial impression was right after all. Don't bother writing back—I'll just delete."

② CONNECT THE RESEARCH

To understand sarcasm, people rely primarily on nonverbal communication (Bryant & Fox Tree, 2005). Facial expressions (smirking), eye movements (rolling eyes), and vocal cues (varying pitch) all indicate that speakers mean the opposite of their spoken words.

Because sarcasm is conveyed nonverbally, dealing with sarcasm online can be tricky (Eisterhold, Attardo, & Boxer, 2006). Researchers Whalen, Pexman, and Gill (2009) found that college students use sarcasm in only 7.4 percent of their e-mail. However, when sarcasm is used, it is almost always marked by online nonverbals, such as capped letters, emoticons (winks), or parenthesized statements ("not!" or "sarcasm!").

Whalen, Pexman, and Gill (2009) warn that regardless of such markers, using sarcasm online is risky because of the potential for misunderstanding. Despite this, people typically have high confidence that their online messages will be understood correctly (Kruger, Epley, Parker, & Ng, 2005).

This research suggests three practical tips for better understanding sarcasm and online nonverbal communication:

❶ Given that understanding sarcasm requires nonverbal communication, avoid using sarcasm online.

❷ Because people typically use markers for online sarcastic messages, do not use such nonverbal markers when you want online messages to be interpreted literally. This is especially important when communicating with people who might think you're being sarcastic (e.g., complimenting a person you've previously fought with).

❸ When there's any doubt about someone understanding your meaning, take the encounter offline—by calling on the phone or talking face-to-face—so the person can see and hear your nonverbal communication.

Before making a communication choice, consider the facts of the situation, and think about the sarcasm research. Also, reflect on what you've learned so far about characteristics of nonverbal communication (pp. 134–138) and functions of nonverbal communication (pp. 149–154). Then answer these questions:

❶ What aspects of your message triggered Chelsea's attribution of sarcasm? If you were in

Chelsea's shoes, would you have interpreted your e-mail in the same way? How would you have responded?

❷ What challenges do you face in reaching out to Chelsea and explaining this misunderstanding to her? How can they be overcome?

❸ How are you going to respond to Chelsea?

signal who gets to speak and for how long (Patterson, 1988). You also read your partner's or audience's nonverbal communication while you're speaking—watching for eye contact, smiles, and head nods to ensure that they're listening and engaged. If someone raises an eyebrow after you make a statement, you may pause to see if the listener has a question or comment.

Defining Relationships

A final function that your nonverbal communication serves is to help define two important interpersonal dynamics in your relationships with others: the level of intimacy that you share, and the power balance—that is, who is dominant and who is submissive (Burgoon & Hoobler, 2002; Kudoh & Matsumoto, 1985). Let's explore each of these dynamics individually.

Intimacy. The feeling of bonding or union between yourself and others is known as **intimacy** (Rubin, 1973). Nonverbal communication helps convey and confirm intimacy during interpersonal encounters. Think about how your nonverbal communication differs depending on whether you're interacting with a romantic partner or a close family member—versus an acquaintance. Chances are, with your intimate relationship partner, you likely share more touch (and more intimate forms of touch), sit closer together, share more gaze, use more relaxed postures, lean in toward each other more, smile more, and (of course) share more time with that person than you do with acquaintances (Floyd & Burgoon, 1999; Floyd & Morman, 1999).

Power Balance. In any encounter, communication partners negotiate the balance of power in two ways. **Dominance** involves behaviors used to exert power and influence over others (Burgoon & Dunbar, 2000). To nonverbally communicate your dominance, you would use direct gaze and staring, frowning, and scowling; larger-than-normal claiming of space; invasion of others' space; and indirect body orientation. In contrast, **submissiveness** is the willingness to allow others to exert power over you. To communicate submissiveness, you would smile more, look down and away, take up as little space as possible, and allow others to invade your space without complaint or protest.

Nonverbal communication of dominance or submissiveness sends messages about how you perceive the power balance between you and others. Displays of dominance are most appropriate when you're in a position of power (such as group leader, manager, or team captain) and when you're trying to actively assert your authority to control the behavior of others. Dominance is inappropriate when dealing with people who have power over you or those who are equal to you (e.g., friends, coworkers, and romantic partners). Similarly, be wary of conveying submissiveness to those whom you are supposed to be leading, as it will foster impressions of weakness and incompetence. Submissiveness is most appropriate when faced with others who have authority over you, such as law enforcement officers, military unit leaders, or upper-level managers.

Strengthening Your Nonverbal Communication Skills

Using nonverbal communication competently is as much about learning to better express your intentions as it is about suppressing inappropriate responses. Knowing when to employ nonverbal behaviors, when to control them, and how to better interpret others' use of them will lead you to more competent communication.

Nonverbal communication often seems automatic, something that just naturally occurs while interacting with others. But nonverbal communication is just as controllable as verbal communication if you invest the time and energy into learning how to do so. Focusing on three areas will strengthen your nonverbal communication skills: enhancing your nonverbal expressiveness, inhibiting your nonverbal behaviors when necessary, and checking your nonverbal attributions (Riggio, 2006).

Enhancing Your Nonverbal Expressiveness

Nonverbally expressive people accurately convey their feelings and attitudes through their nonverbal communication (Riggio, 2006). You know when they are happy, worried, or excited, because they smile, wrinkle their brows, or increase their speech rate (respectively). On the other hand, people who have trouble expressing themselves nonverbally are difficult to read and may often be misunderstood. For instance, if you have a blank facial expression during a romantic crisis, your partner may conclude that you don't care

NONVERBAL EXPRESSIVENESS

Consider the role of nonverbal communication on popular television shows like *Parenthood*, *The Mindy Project*, and *New Girl*. In many situations, the main characters' nonverbal expressiveness or displays of inappropriate emotions lead to poignant, awkward, and funny moments—and sometimes get them into trouble. What can you tell about the characters shown here just from their nonverbal expressiveness?

(Clockwise from left) Danny Feld/NBC/NBCU Photo Bank via Getty Images; Jordin Althaus/© Fox/Courtesy Everett Collection; 20th Century Fox Licensing/Merchandising/Everett Collection

about what's happening. Or if you fail to gesture decisively and speak loudly enough while making a sales pitch to potential clients, they may assume that you're not enthusiastic about the product you're selling.

To improve nonverbal expressiveness, strengthen your awareness of your own behavior (Knapp & Hall, 2002) by soliciting feedback from others and observing yourself. For example, ask a trusted friend, mentor, or teacher how your nonverbal behavior comes across when you're communicating inter-personally, in small group settings, or while giving a speech. Do you project confidence or seem nervous? What does your posture say about your level of involvement with the conversation, the other person, or the topic of your presentation? How does your voice sound, and what messages does it send? If you are giving a speech, you can improve your expressiveness by rehearsing in front of a mirror or by viewing video of your performance. Chapter 15 explores specific nonverbal behaviors to use during presentational speaking.

Inhibiting Your Nonverbal Behaviors

To communicate competently, you sometimes need to *inhibit*, or control, your nonverbal behaviors. Many contexts and cultures require that you limit nonverbal expression of intense emotions. For example, leaders during crisis situations are expected to demonstrate calm instead of openly displaying their anxiety or fear (Riggio, 2006). A calm leader is less likely to trigger panic in his or her followers during a crisis. Imagine how you'd feel if the president of the United States, during a national crisis, gave a speech while nervously looking around, fidgeting uncontrollably, and gesturing with trembling hands. It wouldn't matter what was said; your confidence would be swiftly eroded simply by the lack of nonverbal control. Keep this in mind whenever you occupy leadership positions. Similarly, many cultures—especially those emphasizing collectivism (such as China)—have *display rules* discouraging direct expressions of powerful emotions, such as anger. Within such cultures, you'd want to suppress those kinds of expressions, such as the urge to scowl, shout, or shake your fist in response to a group member's argument.

The key to learning nonverbal inhibition is to practice *critical self-reflection*. Identify situations that evoke strong emotional reactions in you. Perhaps these include job interviews, class presentations, and interactions with difficult family members. Then, reflect on how your thoughts and feelings affect your nonverbal communication in these situations. What is it that sets you off in these encounters? How might you think about each situation differently, and what changes could you make to get better results?

For instance, suppose you dread spending time with your brother because you think he resents your success and is therefore angry with you. This fear triggers nervous behaviors—such as avoiding eye contact and fidgeting with your hair—when you get together with him. The behaviors in turn create a sense of distance between you. How might you think about the situation differently to control this fear and avoid unwanted nonverbal behaviors? Perhaps you could envision your brother's attitude toward you as stemming from pain, not resentment. If you reframe the situation that way, you may feel less fearful when you're with your brother and more compassionate instead—an emotion that's less likely to trigger nervous behaviors. Then you could practice actively making changes to your nonverbal behaviors to increase intimacy, such as making more eye contact. Mastering this process can help you inhibit nonverbal emotion displays when it's important to do so.

Checking Your Nonverbal Attributions

Another valuable nonverbal communication skill is correctly interpreting the meaning and intent behind others' nonverbal communication—in other words, making accurate nonverbal attributions. To do this, carefully consider the context as well as factors that may be influencing the other person's behaviors. Always keep in mind the most important rule of attributional accuracy: *People's behavior rarely, if ever, stems from just one simple cause*. For example, many people believe that crossed arms indicate a closed, defensive person. This attribution is touted as truth on TV talk shows and in self-help and advice blogs. But for many people, crossed arms is a relaxed posture. For others, this behavior could simply mean that they're cold. Similarly, if you're conducting a performance evaluation with an employee who makes little eye contact with you, does that mean he's lying? Not necessarily. It could be a culturally learned behavior indicating deference or respect for authority.

Rather than trying to attribute specific meanings to isolated behaviors, consider the cultures and genders of the people involved as well as the communication context. If you're confused about someone's behavior, or if it's important to make accurate attributions about another person's nonverbal communication, practice *perception-checking*. As Chapter 2 explains, figuring out the meaning behind someone else's nonverbal communication can be as simple as asking the person about it. For example, if your roommate comes home and goes straight to her room without greeting you—an unusual behavior for her—you could later ask her, "I was confused by your quietness this afternoon; are you OK?" Rather than assuming she was mad at you about something, you can share your observation of her nonverbal behavior with her, and ask her to clarify what the behavior meant.

✓ **LearningCurve** can help you review! Go to bedfordstmartins.com /choicesconnections.

arek_malang/Shutterstock

When on the phone, you rely mostly on vocalics to understand what your conversational partner really feels or means. The absence of facial expressions, eye contact, gestures, and even posture make it more difficult to properly perceive messages. But using *perception-checking* can help you clear up any potential misunderstandings with just a question or two.

CHAPTER ⑥ REVIEW

CHAPTER RECAP

- Because it uses multiple channels, **nonverbal communication** conveys more meaning than verbal communication. However, it also works with verbal communication to create messages.
- According to some studies, men and women actually do differ in their use of nonverbal expression. Similarly, **display rules** vary from culture to culture, and **high-** and **low-contact cultures** have varying degrees of comfort with regard to touch, space, and shared gaze.
- The different types of nonverbal communication include **kinesics, vocalics, haptics, proxemics,** appearance, beliefs about time, and environmental features.
- Nonverbal messages serve a host of functions: conveying meaning; presenting **affect displays;** creating self-presentations; managing interactions; and displaying levels of **intimacy, dominance,** and **submissiveness.**
- Knowing how to use nonverbal behaviors, when to control them, and how to interpret others' use of them will help you communicate competently in any situation.

LAUNCHPAD

LaunchPad for *Choices & Connections* offers unique video scenarios and encourages self-assessment through adaptive quizzing. Go to **bedfordstmartins.com/choicesconnections** to get access.

 LearningCurve adaptive quizzes

 How to Communicate video scenarios

 Video clips that illustrate key concepts

KEY TERMS

Nonverbal communication, p. 134
Incongruent messages, p. 135
Congruent messages, p. 135
Display rules, p. 137
High-contact cultures, p. 137
Low-contact cultures, p. 137
 Kinesics, p. 139
Emblems, p. 142
Illustrators, p. 142
Regulators, p. 142
Adaptors, p. 142

Vocalics, p. 142
Haptics, p. 144
Proxemics, p. 145
Artifacts, p. 146
M-time orientation, p. 147
P-time orientation, p. 147
Affect displays, p. 151
Intimacy, p. 153
Dominance, p. 153
Submissiveness, p. 154

1 People from _____, such as _____, prefer frequent touching, shared gaze, and close physical proximity.

a. low-contact cultures; Japan
b. high-contact cultures; Canada
c. low-contact cultures; Italy
d. high-contact cultures; Spain

2 Gestures that substitute for verbal statements—for example, giving a thumbs-up to communicate "good job!"—are known as _____.

a. emblems   **c.** regulators
b. illustrators   **d.** adaptors

3 In terms of nonverbal communication, you can express your identity, affluence, and influence through your use of _____.

a. artifacts   **c.** social-polite touch
b. personal space   **d.** fixed features

4 Which of the following is not a way to show dominance through nonverbal communication?

a. Directly staring   **c.** Looking down
b. Frowning or scowling   **d.** Invading others' space

5 One way to improve your nonverbal competence is to evaluate the accuracy of your attributions through _____.

a. inhibition control   **c.** submissiveness
b. perception-checking   **d.** affect displays

ACTIVITIES

1 Communicating Deception

Write down four facts about yourself and your background (hometown, major, profession, personal interests and activities, family history, significant memories). Two of these facts should be true, and two should be false (i.e., two "facts" are made up or lies). In a small group, present these "facts" to your classmates. While others in your group are presenting, note which "facts" you think are truths and which are lies based on the presenters' nonverbal communication. Afterwards, check the accuracy of your observations as well as which facts about you your classmates thought were false. What nonverbal signals seemed more deceptive? Were there any common deceptive expressions in the group? How did your observations align with the chapter content on deception and nonverbal communication (p. 151)?

2 Eye Contact and Intimacy

To test how intimacy is fostered by nonverbal communication, pair up with a classmate you don't know. This activity is timed, so have a phone or watch ready to count 60 seconds. Stand face-to-face, two to three feet from each other. At the start, stare directly into each other's eyes. Hold this direct mutual gaze, without speaking, for the entire 60 seconds. Afterwards, discuss your impressions with your partner. How intimate did the shared gaze feel? Did this activity change how intimate or familiar you feel with others? How? What does this illustrate about intimacy and nonverbal expression?

7

Active Listening

When Command Sergeant Major Joseph Allen speaks with troops about the roles of soldiers and noncommissioned officers, he says something not normally heard from superiors: "I work for you; if there's something I need to do, you need to tell me" (Dey, 2010). Though that message is unusual, Allen sees it as essential. Along with high expectations for his own duties, Allen believes that "listening is a powerful tool for leaders, and it's a big part of [my] approach to dealing with service members" (Dey, 2010). Such a view has worked well for Allen, whose successful military career spans over 35 years.

Although many civilians may assume that interactions in the U.S. military consist only of commands and assents, the emphasis that Allen places on actively listening to others is far from unique. Officers increasingly stress listening as the cornerstone of communication. In fact, Navy Admiral Mike Mullen describes the three *L*s of leadership as "listening, learning, and leading" (Garamone, 2011). As Mullen tells it, "The more senior I've become, the more I try to listen to others and to see challenges and problems through other people's eyes, whether they are service chiefs, combatant commanders, or military leaders throughout the world." Of course, it isn't just U.S. military officers who feel this way. The NATO (North Atlantic Treaty Organization) guide on leadership and command specifically mentions that listening skills are essential for successful military command around the world (Febbraro, McKee, & Riedel, 2008).

During combat operations, active listening can even mean the difference between life and death. Soldiers must be able to hear, understand, and respond immediately to commands so that everyone takes the actions needed to come out of the engagement safely. The benefits of active listening are not solely tactical, however. In helping soldiers recover from combat-related injuries or deal with depression, *the* most important communication skill family and friends can display is a willingness to listen. As the Web site Couragetotalk.org describes (2012), letting soldiers know that you're available to listen—when they are ready to talk—is crucial in aiding recovery, because it powerfully conveys comfort, support, and caring. The same holds true for anyone struggling with everyday concerns. As Command Sergeant Major Allen concludes, "Everyone has something significant going on in their lives that might affect them. Sometimes people just need an ear; they just need somebody to listen to their problems."

Being a good listener is hard work. Whether you're in the military or a civilian, in a public or a private setting, it takes a lot of mental energy to keep your attention focused on other people, follow what they are saying, and make sense of it. Yet many people think of listening as something that just happens. Nothing could be farther from the truth. People spend more time listening than engaging in any other type of communication activity (Jalongo, 2008). Moreover, the ability to listen actively has been shown to improve academic success (Brigman, Lane, Lane, Lawrence, & Switzer, 1999) and can increase your ability to provide emotional support to others (Bodie & Fitch-Hauser, 2010). Employers also value listening skills, identifying them as a key consideration when making decisions about pay raises and promotions (Janusik, 2002). Learning to improve your *active listening* skills can have a significant impact on all areas of your life. In this chapter, you'll learn:

- How the listening process works
- Why people use different listening styles
- The barriers to active listening
- Ways to strengthen your active listening skills

✓ LearningCurve can help you review! Go to **bedfordstmartins.com /choicesconnections**.

The Listening Process

Before you can strengthen your listening skills, it's important to explore the foundation of listening: how you listen, why you listen, and the potential pitfalls of multitasking when trying to listen.

When you listen to someone, you're not engaged in a single act. Instead, you are taking part in a process—a series of separate yet linked actions. As you'll see in the text that follows, how you listen is guided by your motives for listening. What's more, each step of the listening process can be disrupted if you try to engage in other tasks while listening.

Stages of the Listening Process

The process of **listening** involves six stages: hearing, understanding, interpreting, evaluating, remembering, and responding to others' communication. As you learn about each stage, consider why it is critical to becoming a more active listener.

Hearing. Listening begins with **hearing:** physically processing the sound that others have produced, and mentally focusing your attention on it. Hearing occurs when sound waves enter your inner ear, causing your eardrum to vibrate. These vibrations travel along special nerves to your brain, which interprets them as words and sounds. For people who are hearing impaired or deaf, "hearing" means visually noticing that someone else is communicating

K.C. Bailey/© FX Network/Courtesy: Everett Collection

On his hit TV show *Louie*, comedian Louis CK struggles to correctly listen to and engage with the people he encounters. Whether with his own children, a new girlfriend, or strangers on the street, Louie often doesn't interpret messages correctly or allows his mind to wander during conversations. How can you be better prepared to focus your attention when listening to others?

by seeing either the person's lips move or the person's hands gesture in signs (if they are using American Sign Language). In such cases, you can hear with your eyes rather than with your ears.

During this stage of the listening process, the mental side of hearing also begins, as you actively concentrate your attention on the sounds or signs of the other person. If you don't notice the person's messages, or if you are distracted and not paying attention, you can't go on to understand, interpret, evaluate, remember, and respond. This latter scenario often happens when you are multitasking (something we'll discuss in more detail later) or have a low interest in what someone is saying.

The link between hearing and attention implies a critical truth about listening: if you want to become an active listener, you need to give people your undivided attention when they are speaking (Beall, 2010). To boost your attention level, try to recognize the forces that negatively affect it. Throughout the day, notice how your ability to pay attention naturally strengthens and weakens depending on what's happening within or around you. For example, when you're hungry or under a lot of stress, you may have a harder time paying attention to what someone is saying. You can also try to control the factors that make it harder to focus your attention. Avoid situations that call for careful listening when you are overly stressed, hungry, ill, or fatigued— all of which can leave your brain foggy. If you've noticed that you have higher energy levels in the morning or early in the week, schedule attention-demanding activities, meetings, and encounters during those times.

THE LISTENING PROCESS

Listening involves a series of stages that work together. Consider how the entire process is interrupted when one stage isn't completed, like if you get distracted and fail to correctly interpret what was said to you.

Hearing includes both recognizing spoken words and any gestures or lip movements that communicate meaning.

Understanding, Interpreting, and Evaluating happen almost simultaneously.

Remembering provides context for what you hear.

Responding completes the listening process and lets others know you've heard them.

Monkey Business Images/Shutterstock

Understanding, Interpreting, and Evaluating. After hearing, the next three stages of the listening process take place almost simultaneously. You begin **understanding** what you've heard; that is, you recognize the literal (or *denotative*) meaning of the words the other person has said. At the same time, you work on **interpreting** the full meaning of the message. You identify any implications (or *connotative meanings*) suggested in the person's words, and consider what action the person is trying to perform (Is she asking you a question? Issuing a command? Cracking a joke?). To interpret the full meaning of something you've heard, you consider nonverbal cues, such as the speaker's tone of voice, posture, and facial expression. You also take into account the situation and the background knowledge that you and the speaker share.

Even as you're understanding and interpreting the meaning of a message, you're also **evaluating** it: comparing the newly received information against your past knowledge to check its accuracy and validity. Evaluating the message helps you draw conclusions, such as "He's lying" or "She knows what she's talking about."

How do these three stages happen so quickly yet simultaneously? Consider the following example: A student in your class gives a speech on class warfare in politics. At one point in his presentation, he laughs and says, "Most homeless people are that way by choice; why don't they just get a job!?" Once you *hear* this comment (you process the sound of his voice and focus your attention on his message), you immediately do three things. You *understand* the literal meaning of his words, "Most/homeless/people/are . . ." You also *interpret* his intended meaning: Is he serious? Joking? Being sarcastic? At the same time, you *evaluate* the validity of what he said: Is it true that homeless people are that way by choice?

This example highlights an important insight regarding how you understand, interpret, and evaluate messages while listening. *Your mental processing of messages—and eventual responses—are influenced by your own knowledge, attitudes, beliefs, and values.* You don't listen objectively; instead, your listening is guided by what you already think. For instance, if you believe that homeless people aren't homeless by choice and that your classmate was ridiculing homelessness, you might take offense. Alternatively, if you think that homeless people choose their own plight, you might find his remark humorous.

How can you use this insight to improve your understanding, interpretation, and evaluation of messages? Use the *critical self-reflection* and *perception-checking skills* we discuss in Chapter 2 (pp. 33 and 49). First, practice critical self-reflection while listening. Specifically, get into the habit of asking yourself the following questions: What am I thinking and feeling in response to what is being said? Why am I thinking and feeling this way? How am I listening? and How are my thoughts and feelings affecting my listening—especially my understanding, interpretation, and evaluation of the message? Then, perception-check your conclusions by asking yourself the most important question of all: Is my understanding, interpretation, and evaluation of the message accurate? When in doubt, don't hesitate to ask the source of the message to verify your assessment ("I may be completely off, but my interpretation of what you said is this. . . . Is that right?").

Remembering. Once you've understood, interpreted, and evaluated a message, it gets stored in your memory. Later, you can call it back into your conscious mind, a process known as **remembering** (or *recalling*). Remembering is a crucial part of the listening process. Just imagine not being able to remember anything you've heard others say. Merely carrying out daily tasks would be virtually impossible—you couldn't remember a teacher's instructions on how to complete an assignment or even what time your roommate said she would be home. When you can accurately recall information after you've heard, understood, interpreted, and evaluated it, then you've successfully listened to the message (Thomas & Levine, 1994). Indeed, almost every scientific measure of listening uses remembering to measure listening effectiveness.

How can you boost your ability to remember? One way is to use **mnemonics,** devices that aid memory. Mnemonics are abbreviations, words, simple phrases, ideas, or images associated with what you're trying to recall. Alternatively, you might think of an image, an idea, or a song that goes with what you're trying to remember. When creating mnemonics, follow two simple rules: *keep it simple*, so the information is easy to remember, and *repeat the device often*, so you lock it down. For instance, when Steve teaches yoga classes, he needs five items: music to accompany and inspire the class, water to stay hydrated, keys to open the stereo system and equipment room at the health club, his yoga mat, and his book with choreography notes. For the first year he taught, however, he would inevitably forget one of these items, causing chaos before his classes. Finally, after much frustration, Steve created a simple mnemonic: "music-water-keys-mat-book." He said this again and again until it was firm in his mind. Now, every time he has to teach, he says "musicwaterkeysmatbook" out loud to himself before leaving his house—then checks to make sure he has each item.

Responding. The outcome of listening is **responding**—communicating your attention and comprehension to the speaker. Skillful listeners do more than simply attend and comprehend; they convey the results of their listening to speakers by using verbal and nonverbal behaviors known as *feedback.* Scholars distinguish between two kinds of feedback: positive and negative.

When you use **positive feedback,** you look directly at the person who is speaking, smile, position your body so that you're facing him or her, and lean forward. You might also offer *backchannel cues.* These are verbal and nonverbal behaviors, such as nodding and making comments ("Uh-huh," "Yes"), that signal that you're paying attention to and comprehending specific comments. All of these behaviors combine to show speakers that you're listening.

In contrast, people who use negative feedback send a very different message—namely, that they're not listening to the speaker. **Negative feedback** behaviors include avoiding eye contact, turning your body away, looking bored or distracted, and not using backchannel cues.

Feedback can have a powerful effect on speakers. For example, if you're giving a presentation, receiving positive feedback from your listeners can

DOUBLE TAKE

POSITIVE (VS) NEGATIVE FEEDBACK

In the images below, consider how positive or negative feedback is being conveyed. How do distractions like your phone or other devices influence the feedback you give and receive?

Helen King/Corbis

enhance your confidence, generate positive emotions within you, and convince you that your audience members are skilled listeners (Purdy & Newman, 1999). Negative feedback can cause you to hesitate, make mistakes, or stop talking in order to figure out why your audience members aren't listening.

Motives for Listening

When communicating with others, you listen for a variety of reasons. These different purposes are known as **listening functions**, and they powerfully shape how you choose to listen in specific situations. There are five common listening functions:

- When you *listen to comprehend*, you focus on accurately interpreting and storing the information you receive, so that you can correctly recall it later.
- When you *listen to provide support*, you take in what someone else says without evaluating it, and openly express empathy in response.

TABLE 7.1

MATCHING LISTENING FUNCTION TO SITUATIONS

	LISTENING SITUATION	APPROPRIATE LISTENING FUNCTION
	A friend texts you to cancel your dinner plans because he has the flu.	☑ comprehend ☑ support
	Your manager gives a presentation detailing an upcoming project and how to best approach the client.	☑ comprehend
	A classmate challenges your position on a controversial topic during a group discussion.	☑ comprehend ☑ support ☑ analyze
	Your romantic partner, who is very insecure about his or her singing ability, sings your favorite song for you at your birthday party.	☑ support ☑ appreciate
	A classmate with whom you're delivering a class presentation inquires as to whether her voice "still sounds funny" after she received Novocain during a dental checkup.	☑ support ☑ analyze ☑ discern

- When you *listen to analyze*, you carefully evaluate and critique the messages you're receiving.
- When you *listen to appreciate*, you concentrate on enjoying the sights and sounds you're experiencing.
- When you *listen to discern*, you focus your attention on distinguishing specific sounds—for instance, trying to figure out whose phone is ringing at a large and noisy party.

These five functions are not mutually exclusive: you might use two or more within the same encounter, or shift suddenly from one to another as circumstances change. In fact, you *should* demonstrate such flexibility. A key step in becoming an active listener is learning how to adapt your listening to the situation in which you find yourself (Teo, 2005). For example, while at a concert you may listen to appreciate, until your campus newspaper editor texts you a reminder that your review of the show is due the next morning— at which point you'll listen to analyze. (See Table 7.1 on p. 167 for examples of how different listening functions can work together.)

To strengthen your ability to adapt your listening function, practice noticing the listening demands that different situations call for. Routinely ask yourself, What is my purpose for listening? Keep in mind that for some situations, certain types may be inappropriate or even unethical—like listening to analyze when your friend is clearly seeking emotional support.

Multitasking and Listening

Many forms of social media—especially on phones—create hard-to-ignore distractions that make it difficult to stay focused on listening when someone else is speaking. For example, when you're sitting in class and receive a text message, what do you do? If you're like a lot of students, you stop listening to your professor so you can read and respond to the message. This situation is not unique to texting. You may also be tempted to check Twitter or Instagram; play online games; or use other apps while chatting with a friend, family member, or coworker. However, the research on multitasking and listening is clear: people who **multitask**—shift their attention back and forth between many different things at once—are poor listeners and are more likely to mishear messages or miss them completely (Ophir, Nass, & Wagner, 2012). This is true even if you think you are a skilled multitasker; people who consider themselves good at multitasking are just as bad at listening while multitasking as everyone else (Ophir et al., 2012).

Multitasking has a devastating impact on all aspects of the listening process. Because you fail to hear, understand, interpret, and evaluate information correctly in the first place, you can't accurately remember or competently respond to it after the fact. In simple terms, if you multitask, you won't be able to listen well; and if you don't listen well, you can't recall and respond well. This is especially crucial for settings such as college classes and

Michael Weber/imagebroker.net/SuperStock

It's easy to multitask when using various media—watching a video lecture while checking Twitter, or texting during a conversation. But shifting your attention between elements makes it more likely you will misunderstand or not hear messages. What problems have you encountered while trying to listen and multitask?

workplace presentations, in which you receive lots of important information very rapidly—all of which needs to be remembered.

Fortunately, a simple solution to this dilemma exists: *avoid multitasking while listening*. Whenever you're in an environment in which you need to be able to hear, understand, interpret, evaluate, remember, and respond to information, turn your phone off (don't just put it on vibrate or silent), put away other work, close your laptop or shut off your tablet, and actively focus on the person who is speaking.

Listening Styles

Everyone has preferred ways of listening. Do you like listening to long stories told by friends, or do you urge them to "get to the point"? Do you ask for detailed instructions on how to complete tasks at work, or do you just want a brief overview? Your preferred listening style determines how you listen and is shaped by both your gender and your culture.

"If the person you are talking to doesn't appear to be listening, be patient. It may simply be that he has a small piece of fluff in his ear."[1]

---

[1]The quote and information that follows are adapted from the following sources: A. A. Milne (1926), A. A. Milne (1928), and J. Milne (2007).

Though characters from children's books, Pooh and his friends illustrate the different styles of listening. Do you know people in your life who characterize the styles in similar ways? Which style best represents you?

Walt Disney/Courtesy: Everett Collection

He is a billion-dollar-a-year industry, and one the few fictional characters to have a star on the Hollywood Walk of Fame. His insights have been used to help introduce Taoism to Western cultures. Books about him have been translated into 34 languages. He is such a popular character in Poland that residents of Warsaw have named a street after him. But at the heart of the stories about Edward Bear—or as he is commonly known, Winnie-the-Pooh—is a cast of characters who have very different listening styles.

In the original books by playwright and poet A. A. Milne, Christopher Robin is a young boy who is presented as a consistently empathic listener. All the other characters turn to him for comfort and a compassionate ear. Whenever Pooh worries about his own ineptitude ("I am a bear of no brain at all"), Christopher Robin listens sympathetically and offers emotional support: "You're the best bear in all the world." Pooh tries desperately to adopt Christopher Robin's listening style but instead finds himself nodding off or daydreaming about honey (his favorite treat) when someone comes to him with problems.

In contrast to Pooh, Owl is Mr. Analytical. He prides himself on being wise and encourages others to bring detailed information and dilemmas to him, even if he often doesn't know the answers. (He's good at pretending he does, though!) Meanwhile, Rabbit just wants people to get to the point so he can act on it. He tends to interrupt them if they stray from what he considers the purpose of the conversation, sometimes even asking, "Does it matter?" Tigger, for his part, though extremely good-natured, never seems to have the time to listen. For instance, when the group goes adventuring, Tigger can't help but run around in circles excitedly, urging the others to "Come on!" Then he leaves without waiting to hear their responses. Though these characters are fictional, they each demonstrate a listening style that people use in real life.

MAKING COMMUNICATION CHOICES
TO MULTITASK OR NOT, THAT IS THE QUESTION!

① CONSIDER THE DILEMMA

You're attending a weekend seminar for a professional certificate. To qualify, you must pass two tests, one on Saturday and one on Sunday. If you fail the test on Saturday, you have to attend a remedial session that night and retake the test. Passing both tests means you will receive national certification and an immediate pay raise.

Saturday goes well. The presenter is great, and much of the material is familiar. Consequently, you find time—while listening and taking notes—to text your family. Your sister Danielle's softball team is playing in a tournament, and if her team wins, she'll pitch in the finals that night.

Despite your confidence while taking Saturday's test, you fail. Now you must attend the remedial session and retake the test. If you fail the retest, you won't be allowed to proceed, and your chance at certification will be lost. What's more, Danielle's team won, so now you're going to miss seeing her pitch for the championship.

Sitting in the remedial session, you're intent on not missing any of the content. The presenter is going fast, but you're holding your own. So you start texting your mom for game updates. Danielle's team is up by one, but she loads the bases with no outs in the last inning. You're freaking out when suddenly you hear the instructor call your name. Looking up, you see her staring at you. She snaps, "This content is essential for your certification. Please tell me you're not sitting there texting while you're supposed to be listening!"

② CONNECT THE RESEARCH

One of the most important ways you can improve your listening is to limit the amount of time you spend multitasking—especially shifting your attention back and forth between different forms of technology, each of which feeds you unrelated streams of information (Ophir et al., 2012). For example, if you were writing a class paper, would you also be checking Twitter? Watching TV? Playing an online game? Texting? Stanford psychologist Clifford Nass has found that multitaskers are extremely confident in their ability to perform well on the tasks they juggle (Glenn, 2010). Their confidence, however, is misplaced. Multitaskers perform substantially worse on tasks, compared with individuals who focus their attention on only one task at a time (Ophir et al., 2012).

Why is limiting multitasking important for improving listening? Because multitasking erodes your capacity for sustaining focused attention (Jackson, 2008). Cognitive scientists discovered that our brains adapt to the tasks we regularly perform, an effect known as brain plasticity (Carr, 2010). In simple terms, we train our brains to be able to do certain things through how we live our daily lives. People who spend too much time shifting attention rapidly between multiple forms of technology train their brains to only be able to focus attention in brief bursts. They lose the ability to focus attention for long periods of time on just one task (Jackson, 2008). Not surprisingly, habitual multitaskers have grave difficulty listening, as listening requires extended attention (Carr, 2010). Limiting your multitasking and spending at least some time each day focused on just one task (such as reading, listening to music, or engaging in prayer or meditation), with no technological distractions, helps train your brain to sustain attention—and you to listen more effectively.

Before making a communication choice, consider the facts of the situation, and think about the multitasking research. Also, reflect on what you've learned so far about listening and multitasking (pp. 168–169), listening functions (pp. 167–168), and feedback (pp. 166–167). Then answer these questions:

1 If you were in the presenter's shoes, what attribution would you be making about your behavior? Would you react in the same way?

2 What challenges do you face in explaining your situation to the presenter? In balancing your family interests with the weekend seminar? How can they be overcome?

3 What are you going to do for the rest of the session?

Four Listening Styles

Like the characters in Milne's beloved tales, we all tend to listen in the same way, regardless of the situation. A habitual pattern of listening behaviors, which reflects your attitudes, beliefs, and predispositions about listening, is known as a **listening style** (Barker & Watson, 2000). In general, there are four different listening styles.

People-oriented listeners view listening as an opportunity to establish bonds between themselves and others. When asked to identify the single most important aspect of competent listening, people-oriented listeners say that it's empathy for other people's emotions (Barker & Watson, 2000). Because of their ability to empathize, others perceive them as being caring and concerned.

Content-oriented listeners prefer to be intellectually challenged by the messages they receive. They thoroughly evaluate what's been said before they draw conclusions, and they enjoy hearing all sides of an argument.

Action-oriented listeners (or task-oriented listeners) like focused and organized information, and they want clear, to-the-point messages from others. They use that information to quickly make decisions and plot courses of action.

Time-oriented listeners prefer brief encounters. They tend to let others know in advance exactly how much time they have available for each conversation. Individuals using this style are more likely to interrupt speakers and signal lack of interest through negative feedback than people using other styles (Barker & Watson, 2000).

Listening styles are learned early in life, from watching and interacting with parents and caregivers, gender socialization (learning about how men and women are "supposed" to listen), and cultural values regarding what counts as skilled listening (Barker & Watson, 2000). Through constant practice, your listening styles become deeply entrenched in your communication routines. As a

FIGURE 7.1

WHAT'S YOUR LISTENING STYLE?

When a friend comes to you with a problem, do you . . .

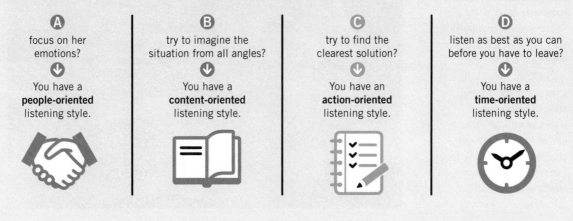

A
focus on her emotions?
⬇
You have a **people-oriented** listening style.

B
try to imagine the situation from all angles?
⬇
You have a **content-oriented** listening style.

C
try to find the clearest solution?
⬇
You have an **action-oriented** listening style.

D
listen as best as you can before you have to leave?
⬇
You have a **time-oriented** listening style.

1. Introwiz1/Shutterstock; 2. WonderfulPixel/Shutterstock; 3. Fenton one/Shutterstock

consequence, you may rely on one or two styles for all of your interactions, and resist switching from your dominant styles—even when those styles are inappropriate for the situation (Chesebro, 1999). This may result in people perceiving you as an inflexible and even incompetent communicator. To be an active listener, you have to use all four styles and strategically deploy them as needed. If you need to provide emotional support—perhaps a friend is going through a breakup—you should use a people-oriented listening style (Barker & Watson, 2000). But if you are listening to a professor present lecture recaps for a midterm, you would want to use an action-oriented style to quickly pick out the information you will need to study.

Gender and Listening Styles

Many people think that women and men have very different listening styles. Women are presumed to be people-oriented listeners; men, action-oriented listeners (or sometimes unable to listen at all!). If this sounds like *stereotyping* to you, you're right. But interestingly, this is one of those rare instances in which stereotypes contain a kernel of truth. Research comparing male and female preferences suggests that men show a small preference for action-oriented listening, while women show a strong preference for people-oriented listening (Bodie & Fitch-Hauser, 2010). Among individuals who use more than one style, men tend to favor action- and time-oriented styles; women favor people- and content-oriented styles.

These findings have led researchers to conclude that men (in general) tend to have a task-oriented and hurried approach to listening, while women

In the best-selling book and movie *Eat Pray Love*, the main character, Liz (played by Julia Roberts in the film), travels to Bali, Indonesia, and meets Ketut, a spiritual medicine man. As their friendship develops, one thing Liz learns from Ketut is how to slow down her listening style to better match Balinese culture—taking lots of time to listen to others and prioritizing the concerns of friends and family over her own schedule.

Francois Duhamel/© Columbia Pictures/Courtesy Everett Collection

perceive listening as more of a relational activity. Keep these differences in mind during interpersonal interactions, group discussions, and presentations. When interacting with men, observe the listening styles they display, and adapt accordingly. Don't be surprised if time- or action-oriented styles emerge the most. When conversing with women, follow the same pattern, and be prepared to quickly shift to more people- or content-oriented styles if needed. On the other hand, don't automatically assume that just because someone is female or male she or he will always listen—or expect you to listen—in certain ways. Instead, take your cue from the actual person you are talking with.

Culture and Listening Styles

Like gender, culture influences people's preferred listening styles, as well as perceptions of styles. For example, in *individualistic cultures* such as the United States and Canada (and particularly in the American workplace), time- and action-oriented listening styles dominate. People often approach encounters with an emphasis on time limits ("I have only 10 minutes to talk" or "I'm going to keep this presentation short and to the point"). Many people also feel and express frustration if others don't communicate their ideas efficiently ("Just say it!"). By contrast, individuals living in *collectivistic cultures* often emphasize people- and content-oriented listening styles.

Always keep in mind that what's considered competent listening in your culture may be perceived as incompetent by others. When communicating with people from other cultures, adapt your listening style accordingly. If you're communicating with someone from a collectivistic culture, try to adopt a people-oriented listening style, and provide positive feedback while the person is speaking. Express interest in his or her feelings, opinions, and concerns, and emphasize points of commonality. More than anything else, avoid hurrying the interaction. Similarly, if you're communicating with someone from an individualistic culture, be prepared to embrace a time- or action-oriented approach to listening. Expect quicker, blunter reactions, and less patience with extended explanations. Of course, always match your style to the individual person, and don't assume someone will have a certain listening style just because he or she has certain cultural affiliations.

Barriers to Active Listening

Being a good listener isn't easy—it's hard work. Numerous challenges exist that can drive you away from active listening and toward incompetence. Overcoming these challenges is essential to improving your listening skills.

In the Golden Globe–winning Showtime series *Episodes*, characters Beverly and Sean Lincoln are British television writers with a hit BBC comedy series. Encouraged to remake their show in the United States for an American audience, things go terribly wrong when they meet Matt LeBlanc (of *Friends* fame) for lunch to discuss the project. While they're describing their show to Matt, he proceeds to tweet and text on his phone, not even looking at them. Concerned that he's not listening, they stop talking, and Beverly asks, "Do you want

Taking a call in the middle of a business meeting on *Episodes* is only one of several barriers to active listening that Matt LeBlanc engages in during the scene. When you have encountered someone so inept at listening, how have you handled the situation?

Colin Hutton/© Showtime Network/Courtesy: Everett Collection to finish that before we . . ." "No, no," Matt responds dismissively, "I'm with you—you're English, you have some sort of show . . ." and rolls his eyes. As they continue their description, he attacks their every comment, at one point sarcastically interjecting, "So, you want me for the 'old fat guy's' part—*thanks*." When Sean tries to salvage the encounter by saying, "We are huge admirers of your work . . . ," Matt's phone goes off, and he waves the couple to be quiet so he can take the call—leaving them to sit awkwardly, waiting for him to finish.

Everyone experiences barriers to active listening. Perhaps audience members were obviously texting while you were giving a presentation. Maybe you were politely pretending to listen during a group discussion but were actually tuned out. Or maybe during a heated discussion with your brother, he seemed more interested in aggressively "scoring points" than truly listening to what you had to say (like the *Episodes* example). In this chapter so far, we've discussed a number of listening pitfalls, including failing to identify the right purpose for listening, multitasking, and neglecting to adapt your listening style to the situation. But in this section, we focus on three of the most common and substantial barriers to active listening—selective listening, pseudo-listening, and aggressive listening—and how you can overcome them.

Selective Listening

Perhaps the greatest challenge to active listening is overcoming **selective listening,** taking in only bits and pieces of information from a speaker (those that attract your attention the most) and dismissing the rest. For example, you pay attention when your manager explains new menu options during a weekly meeting because you work as a server. But you tune out after that and miss an important update on requesting time off. When you selectively listen, you lose out on the opportunity to learn information from others that may affect important personal or professional outcomes.

Selective listening is difficult to avoid because it is the natural result of fluctuating attention. To overcome selective listening, you shouldn't strive to listen to everything all at once. Instead, seek to slowly and steadily broaden the range of information you can actively attend to during your encounters with others. You can do this by practicing the suggestions for enhancing attention discussed earlier in this chapter (p. 163). The most important technique is to avoid multitasking with mediated communication—such as phone calls and text messages—which splits your attention when listening to others.

Pseudo-Listening

You were up most of the night, prepping for an important exam. Now the test is over and you're sitting outside, talking to your best friend on the phone. As he tells you about his latest romantic woes, you find your attention wandering. But you don't want to embarrass yourself or your friend, so you do your best to act the part of an active listener—saying, "Uh-huh," and "Oh, that's too bad," when needed.

In such a scenario, you're engaging in **pseudo-listening**—behaving as if you're paying attention though you're really not. Pseudo-listening is an incompetent way to listen because it prevents you from really attending to or understanding information coming from other people. Thus, you can't accurately recall the encounter later. Pseudo-listening is also somewhat unethical because it's deceptive. Although occasional instances of pseudo-listening to veil fatigue or protect a friend's feelings (such as in our example) are understandable, if you continually engage in pseudo-listening, people will eventually realize what's going on and conclude that you're dishonest or disrespectful. In the *Episodes* example, Matt LeBlanc's pseudo-listening was what made the encounter so awkward and uncomfortable: he obviously wasn't really listening, even though he insisted he was.

Aggressive Listening

People who engage in **aggressive listening** attend to what others say solely to find an opportunity to attack their conversational partners. (This is also known as *ambushing*.) For example, your friend may routinely ask for your opinions regarding fashion and music, but then disparage your tastes whenever you share them with her. Or a guest lecturer may encourage questions and comments following his presentation, but then mock your opinions when you volunteer them.

FOX/Photofest

Even on a show known for its absurdity and self-centered characters, **Gob Bluth** on *Arrested Development* stands out for his aggressive listening style. A constant schemer, he often tries to solicit information from his siblings (like Michael, shown) to use for his own advantages and plots. However, this rarely works in his favor as he is also a poor listener and misunderstands what others are trying to tell him.

The costs of aggressive listening are substantial. People who consistently use listening to ambush others typically think less favorably of themselves (Infante & Wigley, 1986), experience lower marital satisfaction (Payne & Sabourin, 1990), and may experience more physical violence in their relationships (Infante, Chandler, & Rudd, 1989).

If you find yourself habitually listening in an aggressive fashion, you can combat it by discovering and dealing with the root cause of your aggression. Often, external pressures such as job stress, relationship challenges, or family problems can play a role, so be careful to consider all possible causes and solutions for your behavior. Don't hesitate to seek professional assistance if you feel it would be helpful. If you're in a personal or professional relationship with someone who uses aggressive listening against you (such as Matt LeBlanc in *Episodes*), limit your interactions when possible, be polite and respectful, and use a people-oriented listening style. Avoid retaliating by using aggressive listening yourself, because it will only escalate their aggression.

Improving Your Active Listening Skills

Although it sounds like a cliché, improving your active listening skills will improve your life. If you're a skilled listener, people will perceive you as a more competent communicator overall, and you'll benefit both professionally and personally as a result.

Sources as varied as CNN, *Vanity Fair*, and Bill O'Reilly have described Oprah Winfrey as "the world's most powerful woman."[2] She has won 35 Emmys, was nominated for an Oscar, and is the wealthiest African American in history. But though her rise to the top was undoubtedly powered by her brilliance, charisma, and work ethic, Oprah herself cites a different source for her success: listening. She built her media empire on her talent as a talk-show host, and the central skill she wielded within that role was active listening. As she explains, "Everybody wants to be heard. Toni Morrison said that what every child wants to know is, 'Do your eyes light up when I enter the room? Did you hear me and did what I say mean anything to you?' That's all they're looking for. That's what everybody is looking for. . . . And the reason I think my ability to communicate with people around the world has been so rewarded is because I actually understand that. If I am sitting at a restaurant, people come up to me, sit down, bring their children. The reason people open up so much is because they know that I am going to really listen to them, I'm not going to ridicule them, and they're going to leave with a sense of dignity" (Academy of Achievement, 1991).

Oprah's testimonial reminds us of the importance and impact of *active listening*: how listening to others can make them feel valued and respected.

---

[2]All information that follows is adapted from the following sources: Academy of Achievement (1991), LaGesse (October 31, 2005), and Sherr (December 26, 2010).

George Burns/Oprah Winfrey Network via Getty Images

Oprah Winfrey credits her success to her ability to engage in active listening and make people feel comfortable and cared about. When people feel you are truly listening to them, they are more likely to respond in kind, strengthening your relationships and ability to achieve your own communication goals.

How can you listen in such powerful, positive ways? At the heart of active listening are three skills: managing nonverbal and verbal feedback, adapting listening to speakers and situations, and recognizing the value of silence.

Manage Your Feedback

The starting point for active listening is, as Oprah puts it, making people feel as though you're really listening to them. Regardless of your listening style, listening function, or the situation, active listening always includes attentiveness to the speaker (Purdy & Newman, 1999). When speaking, you look for nonverbal and verbal signs that your listeners are paying attention, such as those that signal positive feedback. When listening, you can provide speakers with the same signals. For example, eye contact is an especially powerful indicator of active listening. In fact, if you break eye contact while someone else is talking, that person is likely to assume that you've stopped listening. He or she may even stop and say something like, "Am I boring you?" or "Do you need to leave?" (Goodwin, 1981).

To improve your listening skills, you can manage your feedback by following four guidelines. First, *make your feedback positive*. Lean forward, sit or stand in a position that lets you directly face the speaker, and use your facial expressions to mirror the emotions of what's being discussed. Above all else, look at the speaker while he or she is talking. Avoid behaviors that might be mistaken as negative feedback. For example, something as simple as glancing at your cell phone or someone who's walking by could give the impression that you're bored or that you want the encounter to end.

ACTIVE LISTENING

 One way to improve your communication competence is by learning how to really listen to others. Learn how to support others through listening by going to LaunchPad at **bedfordstmartins.com/choicesconnections** and completing the **How to Communicate video scenario** for Chapter 7 to practice your skills.

CONSIDER THIS:
Reynaldo, a close friend, asks you to critique an informative speech he's preparing for class. However, during the rehearsal, he breaks down emotionally, confessing that his father—who has been increasingly forgetful—has been recently diagnosed with Alzheimer's.

WHAT WOULD YOU DO?
The following advice illustrates how active listening skills can help you communicate with and comfort someone in distress. As you watch the video, consider how the dialogue incorporates skills like adapting listening functions, managing feedback, and recognizing the value of silence, when appropriate. Then, test your knowledge of key skills, and create your own responses to the **What if? video prompts**.

"I am so sorry to hear this. My thoughts go out to you and your father. How are you both holding up?"

1 **ADAPT YOUR LISTENING FUNCTION** from analytical to support and adopt a people-oriented style that expresses empathy for your friend and his family.

(2) MANAGE YOUR FEEDBACK

by making your attentiveness obvious. Put away your phone, provide eye contact, and lean toward him.

"What can I do to help out?"

(3) RECOGNIZE THE VALUE OF SILENCE

by not rushing to fill the conversational space with your own talk ("My grandmother also had Alzheimer's . . ."). Instead, let your friend speak as he wishes.

WHAT IF? But what if things don't work out as shown? Test your ability to adapt your communication by watching the What if? videos and planning a response for each situation.

1. How can you still listen actively when Reynaldo mocks his momentary lapse by saying, "Never mind, I'm just being stupid"?
2. When Reynaldo reacts defensively and says, "There's nothing you can do to help," what do you say next?

Second, *make your feedback obvious*. No matter how attentively you listen, unless speakers notice your feedback, they won't know you're listening. To ensure that speakers can perceive your feedback, make sure your vocal feedback ("Uh-huh," "Yes") is loud enough for them to hear, and that your visual feedback (smiling, head nodding) is visible to them.

Third, *make your feedback appropriate*. Some situations call for intense, almost aggressive feedback—for example, a musician urging the audience to participate during a concert, or a coach trying to pump her team up before a big game. In situations like these, you're expected to use dramatic behaviors—clapping, jumping up and down—to show that you're interested and paying attention. In other settings, it's more appropriate to use quieter feedback, such as sustaining eye contact when listening to a romantic partner or nodding when listening to a group member describe the budget for a fund-raising dance.

Finally, *make your feedback immediate*. Always provide feedback as soon as you can. If you wait too long to provide the feedback, the speaker may not recognize the response as feedback, or may even infer that you're not listening (such as when you say "Uh-huh, yeah" several seconds after he or she has finished talking). To see how managing your feedback and other active listening skills can influence an encounter, go to How to Communicate: Active Listening on pages 180–181.

Adapt Your Listening

A key theme that runs throughout this chapter is the importance of quickly and flexibly adapting your listening styles and functions, depending on the speaker to whom you're listening and the demands of the situation. When it comes to listening actively, one size (or approach) does *not* fit all. For example, and as discussed earlier, people of different genders or from different cultures often have very different expectations about what counts as competent listening. This is why it's important to take these differences into consideration when communicating, and adapt your listening as needed.

In addition, situational demands are dynamic, not static. Communication encounters are always changing, and with these changes come varying demands in what is expected of your listening. For instance, imagine that you're having a group meeting, and the discussion is focused on critiquing the research the group is including in the final presentation. Suddenly, one of the group members, who has been grinning throughout the meeting, says, "Hold on a second. I can't stand it anymore. I just have to tell you guys: I got engaged last night!" Continuing to listen in an analytical fashion at this point (saying, "That's nice, but let's stick to assessing the research. There's a problem with . . .") would be completely inappropriate. Instead, you instantly shift to *listening to provide support* and *a people-oriented style* ("I am so excited for you! Congratulations!"). To be an active listener, be mindful of the situational demands, the purpose of the encounter, and the needs and wants of the speaker—and then adapt your listening skills accordingly. For additional hints on how to be an active listener, see Table 7.2.

TABLE 7.2

ACTIVE LISTENING

To be a more active listener, try these strategies:

Concentrate on important aspects of encounters and control factors that impede your attention.

Communicate your understanding to others in competent and timely ways by providing polite, obvious, appropriate, clear, and quick feedback.

Improve your recall abilities by using mnemonics or linking new information to other senses, visuals, or features.

Develop an awareness of your primary listening functions in various situations.

Practice shifting your listening style quickly, depending on the demands of the encounter.

Gst/Shutterstock

Recognize the Value of Silence

A final, often unappreciated, quality of being an active listener is recognizing the value of silence. Sometimes people just want someone to quietly listen so they can share their thoughts, feelings, and emotions—a sympathetic ear or a shoulder to cry on. If you're listening to someone who has this need, maintain good eye contact, as always, but avoid frequent use of more obvious forms of positive feedback, such as comments like, "I know what you mean" or "I can see why you're upset." For someone who just wants an ear or a supportive shoulder, these behaviors could come across as intrusive.

In fact, research on grief management has found that the two listening behaviors identified as most helpful by people who are grieving are quietly allowing the griever to vent, and providing a sense of presence and attentiveness while the griever talks (Bodie & Fitch-Hauser, 2010). In such situations, it's not just a matter of adopting a people-oriented listening style and listening to provide comfort. In addition, you must dial down your conversational participation so that the other person feels free to fill the silence with what he or she wants to say. By listening in this way, you'll not only help the person work through his or her grief but also make it clear that you're there for him or her.

✓ **LearningCurve** can help you review! Go to **bedfordstmartins.com /choicesconnections**.

CHAPTER ⑦ REVIEW

CHAPTER RECAP

- The process of **listening** involves six stages. In addition to **hearing** a message, you also **understand, interpret,** and **evaluate** it, before **remembering** and **responding** to it.
- Although knowing how the different **listening functions** work and how to switch between them is important, try not to **multitask** when listening or you might completely miss information.
- Your **listening style** is influenced by your personal preference, gender, and culture. However, being an active listener also means using all four styles as needed.
- Though common, try to avoid listening pitfalls, such as **selective, pseudo-,** or **aggressive listening.**
- By managing your feedback, adapting your listening, and recognizing the value of silence, you can improve your active listening skills.

LAUNCHPAD

LaunchPad for *Choices & Connections* offers unique video scenarios and encourages self-assessment through adaptive quizzing. Go to bedfordstmartins.com /choicesconnections to get access.

 LearningCurve adaptive quizzes

 How to Communicate video scenarios

 Video clips that illustrate key concepts

KEY TERMS

Listening, p. 162
Hearing, p. 162
Understanding, p. 164
Interpreting, p. 164
Evaluating, p. 164
Remembering, p. 165
Mnemonics, p. 165
Responding, p. 166
Positive feedback, p. 166
Negative feedback, p. 166

Listening functions, p. 167
Multitask, p. 168
Listening style, p. 172
People-oriented listeners, p. 172
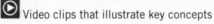 Content-oriented listeners, p. 172
Action-oriented listeners, p. 172
Time-oriented listeners, p. 172
Selective listening, p. 176
Pseudo-listening, p. 177
Aggressive listening, p. 177

POP QUIZ

✓ Looking for more review questions? **LearningCurve** can help you master key concepts from this chapter. Go to **bedfordstmartins.com /choicesconnections**.

1 During which stage of the listening process do you compare new information against your existing knowledge?

a. Evaluating   **c.** Interpreting

b. Understanding   **d.** Responding

2 If your sister is giving you detailed directions to her new apartment during a phone call, you are listening to _____.

a. analyze   **c.** comprehend

b. appreciate   **d.** discern

3 During which of the following activities are you mostly likely to mishear messages?

a. Positive feedback   **c.** Interpreting

b. Negative feedback   **d.** Multitasking

4 Which of the following types of listeners view listening as an opportunity to establish bonds between themselves and others?

a. Content-oriented   **c.** People-oriented

b. Action-oriented   **d.** Time-oriented

5 Though possibly caused by stress, people who use _____ may think less favorably about themselves and experience lower marital satisfaction.

a. aggressive listening   **c.** pseudo-listening

b. selective listening   **d.** action listening

ACTIVITIES

1 **The Impact of Negative Feedback**

Recall an encounter in which you were saying something important but the other person gave you negative feedback. Perhaps the person made fun of what you were saying or clearly ignored your message via text or e-mail. Write a brief paper explaining what happened and how the negative feedback affected your communication during the interaction. Did this influence any other communication between the two of you? Is negative feedback ever competent? If so, when?

2 **The "Noise List"**

To examine how your attention wavers when listening, choose two people— a classmate, a friend, a family member, a coworker, a romantic partner—and engage each of them in a conversation of at least 10 minutes. Afterwards, record as many details as you can about each conversation—whom it was with, topics covered, time of day, and location. Then come up with a "noise list," detailing the distractions you faced in each conversation. What impeded your ability to actively listen? Did you ever multitask during the conversations? Did you experience similar noise challenges in both conversations? How could you overcome such distractions, or noise, during future conversations?

8

Managing Conflict

A) fter a brief breakup following a bitter fight, Ronnie and Sammi talk about their romance.[1] "I miss you," Ronnie says, "and I think we should work things out." "You're my best friend, and I love you," confesses Sammi. What Sammi doesn't tell Ronnie, however, is that during their breakup she was hitting on another guy, Arvin, through text messages.

Later that night, while they and the other cast members of MTV's iconic show *Jersey Shore* are out at a bar, Arvin shows up and tells one of the *Jersey* housemates, Mike, about Sammi's flirty text messages. When Mike expresses doubt, Arvin shows him the texts on his phone—complete with Sammi's ID. Busted!

Mike then shares the news with the other women from the house, who warn Sammi.

Upon being alerted, Sammi refuses to admit wrongdoing and instead blames Arvin for sharing the texts. She then accosts Ronnie, who refuses to talk to her. When she insists on having the conversation, it turns into a nasty screaming match, with Ronnie shouting, "We're finished!" Later, at home, the conflict spreads to the other housemates. Sammi confronts Mike about "stirring things up" by sharing the texts, and she and Mike trade accusations about who's "the shadiest." Then, while the other roommates chime in with jokes and taunts, the fight between Sammi and Ronnie explodes again. With both of them shouting and swearing, the credits roll. Another episode of *Jersey Shore* wraps up, filled with misperceptions, poor communication choices, and destructive outcomes.

Conflicts on reality shows—like now-canceled *Jersey Shore*—seem surreal, almost comical. It is easy to tune in weekly and watch just for fun, as the characters call each other names, escalate the tensions, and endure the inevitable pain that disagreements bring. But the conflicts you experience in your own reality are both different and similar to those involving Sammi, Ronnie,

MTV Networks/Photofest

---

[1]All information adapted from MTV.com (March 10, 2011).

Snooki, and Mike. They are different in that you experience them firsthand, so the pain is deep and personal. They are similar in that there's a firm connection between the communication choices you make and the personal, relational, and professional outcomes that result. Dealing with conflicts the way the crew on *Jersey Shore* did—by exclusively blaming others, refusing to acknowledge their own accountability, and communicating in hostile and demanding ways—inevitably leads to negative outcomes. But when you approach conflict as a communication challenge, best solved by being respectful, flexible, and mutually oriented, you create the possibility of successfully resolving dilemmas in ways that leave you and others satisfied.

Although the interpersonal, group, and public encounters that fill your days bring with them bountiful rewards, they also provide fertile ground for conflict (Malis & Roloff, 2006). Why? Everyone has his or her own goals, preferences, and opinions, so when we deal with each other, clashes inevitably occur. The starting point for understanding conflict is to recognize that conflict will always be a part of life. The challenge isn't how to *avoid* conflict but how to *manage* it.

Dealing with conflict is difficult because most disagreements occur between people who know each other, are involved in close relationships, or work together (Benoit & Benoit, 1990). Thus, conflicts feel like intense, negative, emotional events (Berscheid, 2002). Yet conflicts can also be constructive, giving people the opportunity to openly confront and solve problems that may have simmered for a long time. Properly managed, conflicts can even help clarify your own and others' viewpoints and goals, as well as teach you how to adapt your communication to live and work more constructively with one another (Donohue & Kolt, 1992). In this chapter, you'll learn:

- What conflict is and how it unfolds as a process
- Which approaches to managing conflict are least—and most—competent
- How the conflict-management approach you use affects the outcomes that result
- What barriers exist to managing conflict well, and how they can be overcome

☑ **LearningCurve** can help you review! Go to **bedfordstmartins.com /choicesconnections**.

Defining Conflict

How do the conflicts in your life happen? Are they "out of nowhere" blowups? Do they contain heated language? Do you avoid them at all costs? No matter the type, all conflicts are a process involving people who perceive incompatible goals or actions. Knowing what conflicts are empowers you to recognize them when they exist, and manage them more constructively.

Consider all the things that have triggered conflict in your life: jealousy, betrayal, stress, perceived slights, sex, time, money, work, politics, religion, personal habits—or even combinations of these. Now think about the people with whom you've shared these disputes: family, friends, coworkers, classmates, roommates, neighbors, strangers, romantic partners. And don't forget the setting. You've likely clashed with others while chatting online or texting, during phone calls, while engaged in face-to-face group discussions, or perhaps even during formal talks or presentations. Yet despite the seemingly limitless variation in causes, participants, and contexts, all conflicts have surprisingly similar defining elements. A **conflict** is a communication process between people who perceive incompatible goals or interference in achieving their objectives (Wilmot & Hocker, 2010). Almost all conflicts you'll experience follow this definition: they begin with perceptions, involve clashes in goals or actions (or both), and are processes that unfold over time.

Conflict Begins with Perception

Conflict doesn't begin with communication. It doesn't even begin when goals or actions collide. Instead, conflict begins when people *perceive* incompatible goals or actions (Roloff & Soule, 2002). Because conflict begins with perception, the perceptual errors and biases Chapter 2 discusses play an active role in shaping how conflicts unfold. For example, during conflicts, you're more likely to place blame on others than on yourself, perceive others as uncooperative and yourself as helpful, and believe you're acting reasonably and others are behaving irrationally. These self-enhancing perceptual errors may lead you to make incompetent communication choices when managing the conflict.

Conflict Involves Clashes between Goals or Actions

At the heart of conflicts are clashes between people's goals or actions. Some conflicts revolve around goal disputes, ranging from disagreements between group members (whether or not a presentation should start with a funny story) to arguments between romantic partners regarding relationship desires (whether or not they should be exclusive). Other conflicts break out when the actions of certain people interrupt or interfere with the actions of others: someone takes the parking space you were waiting for, or a roommate repeatedly texts you while you're trying to study.

DOUBLE TAKE

DEALING WITH CONFLICT IN PERSON (&) ONLINE

Understanding and managing a conflict with a friend can change dramatically depending on whether it occurs face-to-face or through a mediated form of communication. In the images below, how might the setting influence perceptual errors or the conflict process?

Henglein and Steets/Getty Images   Peter Cade/Getty Images

Conflict Is a Process

Conflicts often seem as if they're single, isolated events: "I had a terrible fight with my mom via texts this weekend" or "Our group meeting turned in to an all-out war last night." Sure, a single communication, such as a comment, text message, e-mail, or post, can *trigger* conflicts. But conflicts are never just one event. Instead, they are a communication process that unfolds over time. Most conflicts proceed through several stages, each involving decisions and actions that affect what direction the conflict will take and what consequences it will ultimately have for the individuals involved. Thinking of conflict as a process means embracing this fact: *The approach you choose for managing conflict will directly determine whether the conflict is resolved and whether you will be satisfied in the aftermath.*

Selecting an Approach to Conflict

When conflict erupts, you make choices about how to deal with it. You may avoid the issue, accommodate the wishes of others, compete to get what you want, or collaborate to solve the problem. All of these choices have consequences—determining whether the conflicts endure, escalate, or are resolved, and whether your relationships with the people involved are damaged, destroyed, or preserved.

"And the Moonman goes to . . . Taylor Swift!"[2] At the now infamous 2009 Video Music Awards, 19-year-old Taylor Swift beat out Beyoncé for "Best Female Video." As Swift took the stage to begin her acceptance speech— "Thank you so much; I always dreamed what it would be like to maybe win one of these someday, but I never actually thought it would happen!"— rapper and producer Kanye West sat in the audience stewing, believing that Beyoncé, not Swift, should have won. Rather than avoiding the issue, or commenting on it quietly to his entourage, he got up and stormed the stage. Grabbing the microphone from a stunned Swift, West shouted, "Gonna tell ya, I'm really happy for you, I'm gonna let you finish, but Beyoncé had one of the best videos of all time, *one of the best videos of all time!*" He then handed the mike back to Swift, who stood there in shock for 30 seconds, silently holding her award. Audience members booed West, who made an obscene gesture at them off camera.

Within hours, the incident was the top-trending topic on Twitter. Industry insiders spoke out publicly against him, and even President Obama chimed in on the criticism, calling West a "jackass" for his misbehavior.

---

[2]Information that follows is from the following sources: *Us Weekly* (September 14, 2009) and France (September 14, 2009).

Christopher Polk/Getty Images

Although West blogged an apology ("I'm sooooo sorry to Taylor Swift and her fans and her mom"), he received so much flak that he ended up taking several months off from recording and performing.

Few (if any) of us will have to deal with a conflict in front of millions of television viewers. But when you do experience disagreements, the same conflict process unfolds as the one between West and Swift. First, choices are made regarding how to manage the conflict. Second, outcomes follow from these choices. In this section, we discuss four common approaches to conflict—avoidance, accommodation, competition, and collaboration—and their outcomes.

Avoidance

When you select **avoidance,** you approach a conflict by *not* managing it. You ignore or avoid talking about the conflict, or you communicate about it in indirect ways, by dropping hints, cracking jokes, or making sarcastic remarks. Avoidance is the most frequent approach to conflict (Sillars, 1980). People often use it because it seems easier and safer than directly engaging in disputes with others.

Although people opt for avoidance because it seems safe, it actually poses substantial risks (Afifi, McManus, Steuber, & Coho, 2009). First, routinely avoiding conflict can create **cumulative annoyance,** in which your

The characters who appear in director Woody Allen's films are often neurotic overthinkers who imagine situations that do not exactly exist in reality. For decades, Allen has used pseudo-conflict as a driving force for plot and character development in everything from *Annie Hall* to *To Rome with Love*. How do you fare when you assume something to be true based on your perceptions rather than actual facts? Are the results positive, or does it create more conflict?

repressed resentment grows as your mental list of complaints about other people builds up (Peterson, 2002). Eventually, cumulative annoyance overwhelms your ability to suppress it, and you explode. Imagine you're working on a group project, but the other members reject every suggestion you make. You manage this by not saying anything; after all, you don't want to make waves. But your irritation intensifies. Then, when planning the group's final presentation, you realize the perfect way to hook your audience's attention. When you suggest it to the group, they shoot you down yet again. "THAT'S IT! I don't care what you all do; I'll handle my part by myself," you scream. Such an angry outburst may destroy any possibility of working further with the group. Perhaps it's no surprise, then, that people who use avoidance are less satisfied with their relationships than people who engage more directly in conflict (Caughlin & Golish, 2002).

Second, avoidance raises the risk of **pseudo-conflict,** the perception that there's a conflict between you and others when there really isn't. For example, you think your new manager at work dislikes you because she never chats with you. Since you assume she doesn't like you, you worry that she'll give you a negative performance review (or worse, fire you). So you start searching for a new job. But the manager actually *does* like you; she's just stressed out by her new job demands. If you never bother to talk with her about this ("Gayle, I was wondering why we never chat"), you might end up leaving a much-loved job because of your misperception.

Despite the risks, avoidance can be a wise choice for managing conflict in situations where emotions run high (Berscheid, 2002). If you and the other people involved are angry to the point where no one can control their emotions, yet you continue the interaction, you risk saying things that will permanently hurt the relationship. To prevent that unhappy outcome, it's best to leave the room, hang up, or hold off on responding to texts or e-mails until your temper has cooled. If you choose this route, be sure to provide a brief explanation for your departure ("I'm sorry, but I've got to leave for a while and sort out my thoughts"), and give an approximate time when you will contact the person again ("I'll call you tonight" or "I will text you in a half hour to let you know how I'm doing"). This lets people know that you aren't abandoning them and are planning on returning. When you've calmed down, you can reestablish contact and try another approach.

Accommodation

If you choose **accommodation**, you manage conflict by abandoning your own goals or actions and giving in to others' desires. Taylor Swift took this approach when she allowed Kanye West to take the microphone away from her and challenge her victory. Similar to avoidance, accommodation may result in positive or negative outcomes, depending on the situation and your relationship with the others involved. For example, accommodating close relational partners is a hallmark of healthy relationships (Hendrick & Hendrick, 1992). Putting their needs before your own, at least on occasion, shows them that you love them and you're willing to make sacrifices to ensure their happiness. But if accommodation runs in only one direction—one person always giving in to the other, never the other way around—the person who always gives in will probably build up resentment and grow dissatisfied with the relationship (Sprecher, 2001).

Whether you choose accommodation depends in part on your **power** in the situation and the relationship—that is, your ability to influence or control important resources, people, and events (Donohue & Kolt, 1992). Powerful people can choose whether they wish to accommodate others or not, without fear of reprisal. People without power must accommodate those who have power—or they could suffer harmful consequences. For example, suppose you work as a barista at a coffee shop and are an "at-will" employee, meaning that your manager has the authority to fire you at any time, for any reason, without cause or notice. Your manager has enormous power over you, so when he asks you to stay late and work an extra shift, you'll probably accommodate his request—even if you have to give up your plans for the evening. After all, if you don't accommodate him, you might lose your job. Correspondingly, if *you* are the manager—and have the power—you have the freedom to pick and choose whether you want to accommodate employees who ask favors of you (such as a night off), without fear of repercussion from your decision. People have different types of

TABLE 8.1

TYPES OF POWER

	RESOURCE	EXPERTISE
DESCRIPTION	Power derived from material things such as money, property, and food	Power based on special skills or knowledge
EXAMPLE	Most bosses have resource power over employees since they control workers' employment and compensation.	People with specialized degrees or a lot of experience in an area—like software developers or nurses—have power since they know or can do things others can't.

1. WinMaster/Shutterstock; 2. Introwiz1/Shutterstock

power that they can use in various ways. For an overview of the different types of power, see Table 8.1.

Competition

Another way to approach conflict is **competition**—confronting others and pursuing your own goals to the exclusion of theirs. This was the approach taken by Kanye West when he ran onto the stage, grabbed the microphone, and declared Beyoncé the rightful winner at the VMAs. Competition has two defining characteristics: open and clear discussion of the conflict, and pursuit of one's own goals without regard for others' goals (Sillars, 1980).

As with accommodation, whether you'll choose competition depends on your power in the situation and the relationship. Simply put, if you have power, you'll be more likely to use competition than if you don't (Peterson, 2002). Because you control important resources, you can withhold those resources from others (if you feel you must) to serve your own desires. Consider how this works between parents and children. If parents wish to vacation at one destination, but the kids want to go somewhere else, the parents can just say, "Too bad, we're going where *we* want to go," and the matter is finished. After all, they control the money needed to fund the trip.

The competitive approach raises the risk of **escalation** in a conflict—a dramatic rise in emotional intensity and unproductive communication. If you and the others involved in the conflict refuse to back down from the dispute, the conflict becomes a test of wills, virtually guaranteeing that tensions will escalate. Even conflicts that start out as minor can quickly explode into major disputes. When this happens, conflicts can intensify into something

SOCIAL NETWORK 	PERSONAL	INTIMACY 
Power that comes from having an extensive network of friends, family, acquaintances, or business partners with substantial influence	Power based on desirable personal characteristics such as beauty, intelligence, charisma, communication skills, or sense of humor	Power acquired from a close and unique bond you share with another person
People with lots of connections have power if they can help others get access to jobs, schools, material goods, etc.	"Social butterflies" or other charming people have power when their personalities or other social skills attract others to them.	Accommodating to or doing favors for close family or romantic interests that you wouldn't do for other friends demonstrates power based on intimacy.

called **kitchen sinking** (from the expression "throwing everything at them but the kitchen sink"), in which combatants hurl assorted accusations at each other that have little to do with the disagreement at hand: "You didn't like my presentation? Well, nobody here at work can stand you! We all wish you'd quit!" The goal of kitchen sinking is to hurt the other person's feelings in whatever way you can, rather than manage the conflict constructively. The result is often irreparable damage to the relationship.

Technology can inadvertently foster escalation in conflicts. When you communicate through social media, you can't see or hear your communication partners and their reactions (Shedletsky & Aitken, 2004). This lack of feedback makes it harder to understand what others are feeling. Known as *empathy deficits*, this puts you at risk for incompetent communication. When you are unaware of the full impact your communication choices have on your partners, it's easier to bully them or use hostile personal attacks that escalate the conflict. Also, as Chapter 3 explains, people on the receiving end of your communication experience the same empathy deficits. Their online messages are less sensitive and less tactful as well, even if they don't mean it any more than you do.

Collaboration

The most constructive approach for managing conflict is **collaboration**— treating conflict as a mutual problem-solving challenge. Often, the result of using a collaborative approach is *compromise*, in which everyone involved modifies his or her individual goals to come up with a solution to the conflict. (We'll discuss compromise more on p. 201.) You're most likely to use collaboration when you respect the other people involved and are concerned

MAKING COMMUNICATION CHOICES
I DIDN'T LIE!

CONSIDER THE DILEMMA

You're dating Casey, who is wonderful and whom you love very much. One issue, however, is Casey's jealousy toward your ex, Jaden. You are still close friends with Jaden, and you tease each other about everything, including your relationships. This has gotten you into trouble with Casey, who recently saw a text message from Jaden to you that joked, "When are you going to dump Casey and come back to me?" Casey was livid, and the two of you got into a huge fight. Casey wanted you to end all contact with Jaden, but you convinced Casey otherwise. Even now, Casey doesn't fully trust you and hates Jaden.

It's Wednesday night, and Casey is working, so you head to the library to study. You send a text telling Casey this. Then you get a message from Jaden: "Huge party at my place!" You decide to skip studying and head to Jaden's. You don't tell Casey of your change in plans because you don't want to trigger a fight while Casey's at work. Jaden's party is awesome, and you end up staying until early in the morning.

Heading home, you check your messages, only to find a missed call and voice mail from Casey. Apparently, one of Casey's friends took photos of you and Jaden dancing at the party and posted them online. Casey is furious, saying that you lied, you can't be trusted, and it's over between the two of you.

CONNECT THE RESEARCH

Communication scholars Brandi Frisby and David Westerman (2010) studied conflict within romantic relationships—specifically, whether partners communicated face-to-face or through technology, and the outcomes that resulted.

Nearly two-thirds of their sample reported managing conflicts through technology (texts, e-mail, instant messaging, and social networking sites). The most common tool was texting; more than half of the sample dealt with conflicts this way, usually because of a lack of proximity and the convenience of texting.

Although participants commonly used technology to manage their conflicts, they also realized the superiority of dealing with conflicts face-to-face. People reported that face-to-face conflict "is so much better" because you can see the person and read his or her nonverbal communication. As one person described, "I want to know how the other person feels with their facial expressions" (Frisby & Westerman, 2010, p. 975).

The choice of medium for communicating about conflict substantially influenced the approaches to conflict, as well as subsequent outcomes. People who chose to manage conflicts via technology were more likely to compete. In contrast, people who met face-to-face chose collaboration and were substantially happier with their relationships afterwards.

COMMUNICATE

Before making a communication choice, consider the facts of the situation, and think about the research on technology and conflict. Also, reflect on what you've learned so far about conflict approaches (pp. 190–197) and escalation (pp. 194–195). Then answer these questions:

❶ If you were Casey, would you have interpreted the situation in the same way? How would you have responded?

❷ What challenges do you face in reaching out to Casey and explaining your side of the story? How can they be overcome?

❸ What are you going to do?

about their desires as well as your own (Keck & Samp, 2007; Zacchilli, Hendrick, & Hendrick, 2009).

When collaborating, try to meet face-to-face, rather than through mediated channels, if at all possible. Meeting in person makes it more likely that the people involved will seek constructive solutions and consider everyone's goals and desires (Frisby & Westerman, 2010). If this isn't an option, arrange a phone call instead.

To manage conflict through collaboration, try the following four suggestions (Wilmot & Hocker, 2010). First, *attack problems, not people*. When talking about the conflict, keep your language courteous, respectful, and positive—avoiding personal attacks. Treat the source of the conflict as separate from the people who are involved, using *"I" and "we" language* to emphasize this: "*I* can see that this disagreement is bothering *us*; let's try to figure out how *we* can solve it." As Chapter 5 on verbal communication explains, avoid *"you" language*, which can place blame on others.

Second, *focus on common interests and long-term goals* ("I know we all want this group project to be a success"). Arguing over positions ("I want this" or "I want that!") may just escalate things, as the conflict becomes a test of wills about who will back down first.

Third, *create options before arriving at decisions*. Identify different possible routes for resolving the conflict, and then combine the best parts of them to come up with a solution. Don't get bogged down searching for the one "perfect" solution—it may not exist.

Fourth, *critically evaluate your solution*. Carefully consider this question: Is it equally fair for everyone involved?

Because collaboration focuses on respectful and ethical communication, and on satisfying everyone's interests rather than just one person's, it tends to net more positive outcomes than the other approaches to conflict. Collaboration increases people's relationship satisfaction (Frisby & Westerman, 2010), and individuals who regularly use collaborative approaches are more likely to resolve their conflicts and experience shorter and fewer disputes overall (Caughlin & Vangelisti, 2000). To see how you can collaborate, check out How to Communicate: Collaboration in a Conflict on pages 198–199.

FIGURE 8.1

COLLABORATION

1. Attack problems, not people.

2. Focus on common interests and long-term goals.

3. Create options before arriving at decisions.

4. Critically evaluate your solution.

pking4th/Shutterstock

COLLABORATION IN A CONFLICT

 One way to improve your communication competence is by adapting your messages to others' behaviors. Learn how to collaborate during a conflict by going to LaunchPad at **bedfordstmartins.com/choicesconnections** and completing the **How to Communicate video scenario** for Chapter 8 to practice your skills.

CONSIDER THIS: Your roommate, Tim, hasn't been doing his share of the housework. He leaves dirty dishes and clothes lying around and never helps with the cleaning. It's been a source of frustration for you when you walk into the kitchen and see—yet again—that he has created a mess. Even worse, you have friends coming over soon and are embarrassed by the state of your apartment.

WHAT WOULD YOU DO? The following advice illustrates how a collaborative approach to the conflict can satisfy you both. As you watch the video, consider how the dialogue consistently keeps the focus on collaboration rather than sniping or avoidance. Then, test your knowledge of key skills, and create your own responses to the **What if? video prompts**.

① ATTACK PROBLEMS, NOT PEOPLE, by being respectful and polite. Describe the problem without assigning blame, and use "I" language.

"I feel like our apartment is always disorganized, and it's really bothering me."

② FOCUS ON COMMON INTERESTS AND GOALS. Use "we" language to emphasize shared benefits.

"If we divide up the housework equally, we could easily keep it clean. Then we could have people over whenever we wanted, without worrying about the mess."

CREATE OPTIONS ③ before arriving at decisions, making sure to suggest a range of choices for solving the situation and not clinging to any one in particular.

"I could do the kitchen and the vacuuming if you take care of the bathroom. Or you could do the kitchen—whichever you want. What do you think?"

CRITICALLY EVALUATE ④ your solution, making sure that others find it fair and equal.

"Would that work for you? Or is there something else we could do that's better?"

WHAT IF? But what if things don't work out as shown? Test your ability to adapt your communication by watching the What if? videos and planning a response for each situation.

1. How would you respond when Tim tries to avoid the conversation? "I think things are fine the way they are. You're just obsessed with neatness."

2. What if Tim doesn't want to collaborate and says, "I'll take care of my room, and you can do everything else. You're better at cleaning than I am anyway, and I really don't care." What would you say?

Conflict Endings

When you're in the middle of a conflict, it seems to last forever. But conflicts do end. The approach you choose for dealing with conflict affects not only your future communication with those involved but also the speed with which your conflict will conclude, and the type of ending that will occur.

Some conflicts are brief—they quickly flare up and just as quickly burn out—but others are more enduring and go on for extensive periods of time (even years!). But eventually, most conflicts reach some sort of conclusion. Since conflicts usually occur between people who are close—whether group members, friends, lovers, family, or coworkers—these conclusions are necessary for the relationships to continue. The approach used to manage a conflict directly determines how it will end. Most conflicts end in one of five ways: separation, domination, compromise, integrative agreements, or structural improvements (Peterson, 2002).

Separation

Some conflicts end when one or more of the people involved terminate communication contact, known as **separation.** Separation can take many forms. It might be *technological*: you ignore texts, turn your phone off, and delete incoming e-mails. It might be *physical*, such as when you stop showing up for team meetings or start avoiding family reunions. Or it might be *communicative*, such as when you are still living with a roommate but refuse to talk to each other.

Separation ends conflict encounters but doesn't solve them. Although you might temporarily feel better—having detached yourself from the source of stress—the conflict isn't resolved; it's just temporarily on hold. On the other hand, separation isn't always negative. As noted in the *competition* discussion, if your conflict has escalated to the point that you or others might start kitchen sinking, it's probably best to separate. Temporary separation may help everyone cool off; then you can regroup later and consider how to collaborate.

Domination

When one person or group of people get their way by influencing others to accommodate and abandon their goals, **domination** has occurred. Conflicts that end with domination are often called *win-lose solutions*. The people who get their way "win," while the others who accommodate "lose." The strongest predictor of domination is the power balance between the people involved. In cases in which one person or group has substantial power and opts to use competition, others with less power will likely back down, allowing those with power to dominate.

Domination isn't always destructive, however. Consider, for example, medical or military decisions. In emergency situations in which multiple parties are disputing options, having people in positions of authority enforce

Murray Close/Lionsgate/Courtesy Everett Collection

Most of us won't experience the heightened conflicts that appear in *The Hunger Games*, such as fighting to the death in a dystopian future or finding friends in former enemies. But, regardless of such extremity, when conflicts end you may experience changes in your relationships and communication, just like Katniss and Peeta. In your own conflicts, where have such transformations led?

decisions while other people accommodate solves conflict efficiently, enabling swift action.

Compromise

Conflicts end in **compromise** when the parties involved change their goals and actions to make them compatible. This typically results from people using a collaborative approach and is most effective in situations in which people have relatively equal power and the clashing goals aren't especially important.

In cases in which everyone considers their goals important, however, compromise tends to foster resentment and regret (Peterson, 2002). Why? Imagine that you're leading a meeting in which a team of nurses will plan next month's work schedule. If everyone comes to the meeting not really caring about whether they work days or nights and weekdays or weekends, you all can collaborate and easily compromise on who works when. But if people have strong preferences about their schedule ("I absolutely cannot work Friday nights"), then compromising on these plans will most likely lead to bitterness, as team members compare who got their way and who sacrificed the most.

Integrative Agreements

When people in conflict forge **integrative agreements**, they generate creative solutions that enable all sides to keep and reach their original goals. Such agreements are commonly called *win-win solutions*, and people can arrive at them only through collaborative approaches. To create integrative agreements, the parties remain committed to their individual goals but are flexible in how they achieve them (Pruitt & Carnevale, 1993). Borrowing from the previous example, imagine that you and a coworker both want the same night off. Rather than arguing about who has to sacrifice their night-out plans, you could work together to find two other nurses who are qualified to cover for both of you.

Structural Improvements

Sometimes conflicts end with **structural improvements:** the parties involved change their relationship rules to prevent further disputes. For example, Steve and his wife, Kelly, used to fight whenever he neglected to tell Kelly about Facebook messages he received from his ex, Michelle. After several clashes ("You should have told me she messaged you!"), they created a new agreement: *Whenever Michelle contacts Steve, he must tell Kelly.* Now they both know the ground rules regarding Michelle's messages, and this prevents further arguments.

In structural improvement cases, the conflict itself becomes a vehicle for reshaping relationships in positive ways—clarifying rules (as with Steve and Kelly), improving the balance of power, or redefining expectations about who will play what roles (for instance, members of a student organization deciding to divide authority between co-presidents after two candidates tie in the presidential election). But as with compromise and integrative agreements, you and others can arrive at structural improvements only by choosing to manage your conflicts through collaboration.

Barriers to Constructive Conflict

It's not easy to resolve conflicts. There are powerful barriers that get in the way and they are often ones you create: blaming others but not yourself, using words as weapons, and failing to recognize cultural differences. Overcoming such challenges will help you improve your conflict-management skills.

On *Degrassi: The Boiling Point*, Holly J and Declan are struggling to make their long-distance romance work. Then, while visiting Declan's sister, Fiona, Holly J sees Facebook photos of Declan and another girl on Fiona's computer. One even includes the girl kissing Declan's cheek. "He's *cheating* on me!" Holly J concludes. Furious, she confronts him, only to find that the girl is a friend, and the kiss happened during a birthday party. Later, when Declan abruptly ends a Skype session, Holly J can clearly hear a girl's voice in the background of his room. Rather than talk with him about it, she selects a time when she knows he won't pick up his phone and leaves a voice-mail message breaking up with him. When Declan subsequently surprises her by visiting, Holly J discovers that "the affair" has all been in her mind; the conflict between her and Declan was fueled by her misperceptions.

By this point, you might think that constructive conflict management is simple. You adopt a collaborative approach and work with those involved to forge healthy compromises, satisfying integrative agreements, and positive structural improvements. But it's not that easy. Instead, like the conflict between Holly J and Declan on *Degrassi*, a wide range of barriers keeps us from choosing effective approaches. Three of the toughest barriers are attributional errors, destructive messages, and cultural differences.

Attributional Errors

Recall the most recent serious conflict you've had. Who was to blame? Who behaved cooperatively? When you said or did something negative, what caused your behavior?

If you're like many people, your answers to these questions will be self-serving—designed to make you feel better about yourself. As we discuss in Chapter 2, this happens because human *perception* is subjective, not objective: people see what they want to see, not what is really true. This frequently leads to errors in your *attributions*: the explanations you create for why things are happening the way they are. Consequently, when conflicts erupt, you don't judge yourself, others, or the situation objectively. Instead, you perceive these things subjectively, in ways that paint yourself in a positive light and make others look bad (Sillars, Roberts, Leonard, & Dun, 2000). This is exactly what Holly J did—presume that Declan betrayed her without hearing his side first.

Like many comedies, *The Best Man Holiday* builds its conflicts, resolutions, and laughs around attributional errors, with characters misunderstanding one another, situations, and intentions. Such scenarios—though entertaining—could be greatly helped if the characters engaged in perception-checking immediately instead of letting conflicts fester.

Michael Gibson/© Universal Pictures/Courtesy Everett Collection

TABLE 8.2

TIPS FOR MANAGING CONFLICT ONLINE

Nearly two-thirds of college students (61.2 percent) use mediated channels to engage in conflicts, most commonly via text messaging (Frisby & Westerman, 2010). While managing conflicts offline reduces attributional errors and boosts empathy, that isn't always possible or desirable. When you must deal with the conflict online, try these suggestions (Munro, 2002):

WAIT AND REREAD. When you receive a message that provokes you, don't respond right away. Instead, take a break and then reread it. This gives you a chance to reassess it and reply when you are calmer.

ASSUME THE BEST AND WATCH OUT FOR THE WORST. Presume that the sender meant well, but didn't express him- or herself competently. Remember all the challenges of online communication such as *online disinhibition* and *empathy deficits*. At the same time, realize that some people enjoy conflict. Firing back a nasty message may be what they want.

SEEK OUTSIDE COUNSEL. Before responding, discuss the situation (ideally, face-to-face) with someone whose opinion you trust. Having an additional viewpoint will enhance your ability to perspective-take and will help you make wise communication choices.

WEIGH YOUR OPTIONS CAREFULLY. Choose cautiously between engaging or avoiding the conflict. Consider the consequences associated with each option, and which is most likely to net you the long-term outcomes you desire.

COMMUNICATE COMPETENTLY. Use "I" language, incorporate appropriate emoticons, express empathy and perspective-taking, encourage the other person to share relevant thoughts and feelings, and make clear your willingness to collaborate. Importantly, start and end your message with positive statements that support rather than attack the other person.

During a conflict, it is easy to blame other people for causing it and consider yourself faultless (Schutz, 1999). At the same time, the individuals with whom you're fighting do the exact same thing—think *they're* in the right and *you're* in the wrong. Such one-sided blaming is an attributional error, because in most conflicts, one person isn't the sole cause. Instead, conflicts are mutually created by two or more people, based on differing goals, opinions, or desires. Consider, for example, what happens during conflicts between spouses (Schutz, 1999). Most marital conflicts stem from differing opinions regarding money, housework, sex, or child care. Yet spouses don't attribute mutual blame for these conflicts ("We created this dispute because we disagree on this issue"). Instead, they typically blame each other for causing the conflict. What's more, they even blame each other for their *own* negative remarks made during the fight. So, when terrible things are said during the heat of battle, participants rarely think, "I said that horrible thing because I was angry and out of control." Instead, they typically think, "*You* provoked me into saying it!" Spouses also consistently attribute their own communication to "good intentions" and describe their partner's communication as "irrational" and "inconsistent."

Of course, such attributional errors aren't limited to romantic partners. Everyone makes attributional errors during disagreements, which in turn prevent participants from using collaborative approaches. For example, people typically perceive those they are in conflict with as uncooperative and themselves as cooperative (Sillars et al., 2000). This comparison discourages collaboration. Moreover, people tend to attribute conflicts to long-term differences that can't be overcome ("You've never understood me, so why bother even talking about it?").

To improve your conflict-management skills—and get the best possible outcomes from conflicts—practice analyzing the attributions you're making during disputes and adjusting them to compensate for any potential errors. This will influence your approach to conflict and how you communicate (and is a form of *perception-checking*). Get into the habit of asking yourself three questions:

- Is my partner *really* being uncooperative, or am I just imagining it?
- Is my partner *really* the only one to blame, or have I also done something to cause the conflict?
- Is this conflict *really* due to ongoing differences between us, or is it due to temporary factors, such as stress or fatigue?

Destructive Messages

The problem with attributional errors is that they don't just stay inside your head; you express them. When you perceive others as uncooperative and blame them for conflicts (as well as your own bad behavior), you may say things that make them feel bad, escalate conflicts further, and damage the relationship. Known as destructive messages, these usually take one of three forms: *sniping*, *sudden-death statements*, and *dirty secrets*.

During conflicts, some people resort to **sniping**—communicating in a negative way and then leaving the encounter. When you snipe, you shoot a remark at others, then immediately hide, so the others can't shoot back. For example, your dad waits until he knows you're too busy to answer your phone, then leaves you a voice mail filled with complaints about how you've been neglecting him. Needless to say, sniping is disrespectful, unethical, and destructive. It serves no purpose other than hurtfulness; thus, it only fuels conflicts.

If conflicts spiral out of control, **sudden-death statements** can occur: spontaneous declarations that the relationship is over, even though the people involved did not consider termination a possibility before the conflict. A fight between romantic partners about "friending" an ex on Facebook morphs into, "Maybe we should date other people!" A disagreement between roommates about who's responsible for which household chores escalates into, "Fine—I'm moving out!" Or a dispute over how best to approach a group project results in, "Forget it—we'll all just work separately on our own ideas!" People can "walk it back" after issuing sudden-death statements. However, this is hard to do without looking foolish and impulsive, causing them to *lose face* or experience *embarrassment*. For that reason, many people stand behind their threatening statements, even if the consequences aren't really what they want. If you need to maintain your face after losing it, see the suggestions in Chapter 2 on pages 39–41.

But of all the destructive things that can come out during conflicts, by far the worst (in terms of personal and communicative costs) are **dirty secrets**—messages that are honest in content but have been kept hidden to protect someone's feelings. Examples of dirty secrets include criticism of a romantic partner's physical appearance ("You'll never be as hot as my ex!"), a revelation about workplace attitudes ("Don't you know that most people here think you are terrible at your job and overpaid?"), and lack of maternal feelings ("I wish you'd never been born!"). Similar to sniping, dirty secrets are designed to hurt. But they do far worse damage because the content is true. Therefore, they have the power to permanently damage recipients' feelings and destroy relationships. Although you may be tempted to reveal a dirty secret in the heat of the moment, it's usually not worth it. Instead, leave the encounter and return later, after you've cooled down.

Cultural Differences

A final consideration in competently managing your conflicts involves cultural differences. People from individualistic and collectivistic cultures perceive and approach conflicts in radically different ways. Specifically, people raised in *collectivistic cultures* often view direct discussion of the causes behind a conflict as personal attacks and see such discussion as disruptive to the "harmony" of encounters (Kagawa & McCornack, 2004). Consequently, they tend to approach conflict through avoidance or accommodation. In contrast, many people raised in *individualistic cultures* feel more comfortable openly discussing disputes and don't necessarily perceive such arguments as personal affronts (Ting-Toomey, 1997). As a result, they often compete or collaborate.

Consider how these differences might play out in a culturally diverse workgroup. When a disagreement erupts, the individualists in the group would be inclined to say something like, "There's a problem here," and perhaps even assign blame or express dismay ("I can't believe you don't agree"). The collectivists would be mortified by such behavior, perceiving it as "blunt" and "discourteous" and avoiding further discussion of the issues. When individualists suggest or demand specific solutions, the collectivists would likely

Working on group projects can be difficult—balancing personalities, workload, time constraints, and leadership responsibilities. Having to manage conflicts as well makes the experience even more complicated. In such situations, remember to consider any cultural differences affecting the communication. For example, how can you help everyone feel comfortable while being respectful of differing opinions?

Troy House/Corbis

give in to those solutions—just to restore harmony. The individualists might then conclude that the conflict has been "resolved," even though it hasn't.

Given these differences, how can you manage conflict competently across cultures? If you're an individualist embroiled in a dispute with people from collectivistic cultures, consider these suggestions (Gudykunst & Kim, 2003):

- Maintain the face of everyone involved. Avoid humiliating or embarrassing collectivists, especially in public.

- Use indirect verbal messages more than you usually do. For example, sprinkle your comments with "maybe" and "possibly," and avoid blunt responses such as an outright no.

- Recognize that collectivists may prefer to have a third person mediate the conflict. Mediators allow those in conflict to manage their disagreement without direct confrontation. This lack of confrontation helps maintain harmony in the group or relationship, which is especially important to collectivists.

If you're a collectivist in contention with someone from an individualistic culture, the following tips may help:

- Manage conflicts when they arise, even if you'd much rather avoid them.

- Use an assertive style and be more direct than you usually are. For example, use "I" messages, and directly state your opinions and feelings.

- Recognize that individualists often separate conflicts from people. Just because you're in conflict doesn't mean that the situation is personal.

✓ LearningCurve can help you review! Go to bedfordstmartins.com /choicesconnections.

CHAPTER ⑧ REVIEW

CHAPTER RECAP

- A **conflict** is a communication process between people who perceive incompatible goals or interference in achieving their objectives.
- How you approach a conflict—whether through **avoidance, accommodation, competition, or collaboration**—affects the outcomes.
- The approach you choose is influenced by several factors, including the **power** of those involved and whether people are willing to collaborate.
- Most conflicts end in one of five ways: **separation, domination, compromise, integrative agreements,** or **structural improvements.**
- Managing any conflict runs the risk of dealing with attributional errors, destructive messages, or cultural differences. You can minimize these obstacles by engaging in *perception-checking*, *maintaining face*, and practicing *intercultural competence*.

LAUNCHPAD

LaunchPad for *Choices & Connections* offers unique video scenarios and encourages self-assessment through adaptive quizzing. Go to **bedfordstmartins.com /choicesconnections** to get access.

 LearningCurve adaptive quizzes

 How to Communicate video scenarios

 Video clips that illustrate key concepts

KEY TERMS

POP QUIZ

✓ Looking for more review questions? **LearningCurve** can help you master key concepts from this chapter. Go to **bedfordstmartins.com /choicesconnections**.

1 A pseudo-conflict may result from using a(n) _____ approach to conflict.

  a. avoidance   **c.** competition
  b. accommodation   **d.** collaboration

2 When you respect the other people involved in the conflict, and are concerned about their desires as well as your own, you're more likely to use _____ as an approach to conflict.

  a. avoidance   **c.** competition
  b. accommodation   **d.** collaboration

3 Some conflicts end with creative solutions that enable all sides to keep and reach their original goals. This is known as _____, or *win-win solutions*.

  a. separation   **c.** structural improvements
  b. integrative agreements   **d.** compromise

4 Of all the destructive things that can be communicated during conflicts, the type that is most likely to permanently damage a relationship or all future communication is _____.

  a. kitchen sinking   **c.** sniping
  b. dirty secrets   **d.** sudden-death statements

5 Which of the following is *not* one of the suggestions for handling a conflict with a person from a collectivistic culture?

  a. Maintain the face of everyone involved.
  b. Use indirect verbal messages.
  c. Use "I" messages, and directly state your opinions and feelings.
  d. Involve a third person to mediate the conflict.

ACTIVITIES

1 Checking Your Attributions

To see how attributional errors can influence conflicts, write a brief essay describing a recent conflict you experienced, and answer these questions: Who was to blame? Who behaved cooperatively? When you said or did something negative, what caused your behavior? Then, analyze your answers and communication by responding to these prompts: Are you apportioning blame equally, or is some bias apparent? What impact did your judgments have on your communication choices and the way the conflict ended? How might different attributions have led you to communicate differently in the conflict?

2 Choose Your Own Ending

With a partner, determine a common, important conflict you both experience (e.g., conflicts with roommates over room rules, or with parents over family obligations). Then, decide what each type of conflict ending (identified on pp. 200–202) would look like for this example. For instance, given your conflict, what would a structural improvement look like? How would a compromise work out? Once you've identified each ending, which ones are optimal? Why? Which approaches would result in those endings? What does this tell you about approaches and endings for different conflict situations?

9

Principles of Interpersonal Communication

It was touted as the "most controversial" season finale ever. When Ben Flajnik proposed to Courtney Robinson at the end of season 16 of *The Bachelor*, millions of Americans were outraged. Robinson had become the contestant they loved to hate. But if viewers thought about the communication that took place between Flajnik and Robinson in the weeks leading up to the proposal, they might not have been so surprised. During those weeks, the two experienced the growth of a friendship and then a romance, as well as the rough patches and emotional upheaval that often come with such developments.

The Bachelor is a dating game show that matches a single man with more than two dozen female contestants.[1] The women are eliminated over a series of episodes, based on the bachelor's interactions with them. The show's goal is to have the bachelor propose marriage in the final episode to the "winner" (though not all seasons end with proposals).

The show involves strong expectations regarding communication and relationships. The bachelor evaluates each contestant's potential as a spouse based on physical attractiveness; similarity; strength of attraction toward him; and how well she rises to such challenges as bungee jumping, cliff climbing, and swimming with sharks. Because the goal of the show is for the bachelor to find love, there is an expectation that some of the relationships will progress steadily through the stages of development, with one eventually culminating in marriage (or at least a proposal). The creation of closeness is fostered by relentless pressure on contestants to openly share their thoughts and feelings with the bachelor.

Though the contestants are competing with one another for the chance to "win," they also live together and are expected to form friendships. Those who don't act like a friend—who don't share their thoughts and feelings with

[1] All information that follows is from Rice (2011).

and provide emotional support to other contestants—invite scorn from both their rivals and the viewers. This is the main reason why viewers hated Courtney Robinson in season 16—she refused to communicate supportively toward the other women. Instead, she treated them competitively, going so far as to taunt them with snarky remarks, such as "Winning!" when she received a rose, which guaranteed her protection from elimination.

The Bachelor is one of the most successful reality shows in television history and has sparked two spin-offs as well as sister shows in Canada, Britain, and Chile. But though *The Bachelor* is framed as a show about finding love, at its heart it's about what happens when people are thrown together, attraction sparks, and relationships form and disband. What's at the core of all these processes? Interpersonal communication.

Reality shows like *The Bachelor* aren't reality. Instead, they're heavily edited forms of entertainment, dressed up to look like real life. At the same time, these shows mirror the communication and relationship dramas that many people face. Watching them provides a reflection of how your own communication choices directly correspond to the relational outcomes that follow—whether for good or bad. They are also reminders of the importance of positive, healthy relationships—not only with romantic partners but also with friends, family members, and coworkers (Myers, 2002).

This chapter is the first of two exploring the primary tool you use to create, maintain, and end your relationships—*interpersonal communication*. This chapter covers its basic principles, whereas Chapter 10 provides a close look at how to manage and sustain the relationships you build during your life. In this chapter, you'll learn:

- The defining characteristics of interpersonal communication
- What compels you to form relationships in the first place
- Four types of relationships and their key characteristics
- The stages relationships may progress through

✔ **LearningCurve** can help you review! Go to **bedfordstmartins.com /choicesconnections**.

What Is Interpersonal Communication?

As the name implies, interpersonal communication is "inter-person," or between two people. But what makes interpersonal communication "interpersonal" goes way beyond numbers. Interpersonal communication is how you connect with other human beings in meaningful ways; it's what makes up the moments that matter.

Interpersonal communication is communication between two people in which the messages exchanged significantly impact the thoughts, emotions, behaviors, and relationships of the people involved. As this definition highlights, one difference between interpersonal communication and other communication types is that it is **dyadic**—that is, it involves pairs of people, or *dyads*. For example, when you text back and forth with your roommate between classes, exchange Facebook messages with a long-distance cousin, or chat with a co-worker when on break, you are engaging in interpersonal communication.

In addition, interpersonal communication is your primary tool for building, maintaining, and ending relationships. These relationships include friends, family members, coworkers, and romantic partners, but they also include anyone with whom you have meaningful interactions, such as classmates or group members. (In Chapters 11 and 12, we discuss communication between team members in small groups.) Because interpersonal communication impacts relationships, sharpening your interpersonal communication skills is one of the best ways to improve your relationship health and happiness. To enhance your skills, it's helpful to first understand the four defining characteristics of interpersonal communication.

INTERPERSONAL RELATIONSHIPS

Interpersonal communication can help you forge meaningful bonds with others—whether friends, coworkers, romantic partners, or family.

(Clockwise from top left) Sam Edwards/Getty Images; Hill Street Studios/Blend Images/Corbis; Tim Klein/Getty Images; PictureIndia/SuperStock

Interpersonal Communication Is Transactional

Typically, interpersonal communication is *transactional*: both parties contribute to the meaning created during the communication. As Chapter 1 explains, this covers everything from a shared glance to an intense conversation. For example, if you and your brother spend an evening together, talking about your shared past, you will both likely chime in with contributions and thus construct the stories together. This is very different from most linear forms of communication, such as public speaking, in which a speaker creates and presents messages to audience members who receive and interpret them.

However, interpersonal communication can also be linear, depending on the situation. For instance, suppose you know that a coworker is feeling sad about a recent breakup. You send her a consoling text message in the middle of her workday ("So sorry about what happened. I'm here if you need anything"). You don't expect her to respond because you know she's busy—and she doesn't. In this communication, there is a sender (you), a message (your expression of support), and a receiver (your coworker). It is a linear encounter, but it's also interpersonal, because it's dyadic, and it makes your coworker feel supported and therefore strengthens your connection with her.

Interpersonal Communication Is Dynamic

Interpersonal communication also differs from such events as formal group presentations and public speeches because it's *dynamic*—that is, constantly changing. When you interact with others, your communication and everything that influences it—your perceptions, thoughts, feelings, and emotions—are continually shifting.

For this reason, no two moments within the same interaction will ever be identical. Imagine that your friend starts a conversation by sharing exciting news about receiving a job offer. The encounter starts on a positive note but changes when you learn that it's the same job you wanted—making you happy for your friend but also sad and envious that you didn't get it.

Moreover, because interpersonal communication is dynamic, no two interactions with the same person will ever be identical. So though you were comfortable talking with your father last Sunday on the phone, things may feel more awkward the next time you talk because he seems preoccupied.

Interpersonal Communication Is Relational

Interpersonal communication is relational because it builds bonds with others—easing the distance that naturally arises from differences between people. Philosopher Martin Buber (1965) argued that you can make that distance seem thinner by embracing the fundamental similarities that connect you with others, trying to see things from others' points of view, and communicating with honesty and kindness. You don't have to agree with everything another person says and does, but you do need to approach that individual with an open mind, giving the person the same attention and respect you expect for yourself. According to Buber, only then can you build a meaningful relationship with that person. When you forge relationships in this way, you view your connections to others as **I-Thou.**

Contrast this with when people focus on their differences with others, refuse to accept or even acknowledge others' viewpoints as legitimate, and communicate in ways that emphasize their own supposed superiority over others. This approach views interpersonal connections with others as **I-It**—regarding people as "objects which we observe, that are there for our use and exploitation" (Buber, 1965, p. 24). The more you see others as objects, the more likely you'll communicate with them in disrespectful, manipulative, or exploitative ways. By treating others this way, you can't build meaningful, healthy relationships with them.

Interpersonal Communication Is Impactful

Interpersonal communication *impacts* (influences) the thoughts, emotions, behavior, and relationships of the people taking part in it. When you communicate interpersonally with others, it matters. As a result of the interaction, you may change how you feel and think about yourself and others; alter others' opinions of you; and create, maintain, or dissolve relationships. Thus, interpersonal communication contrasts sharply with **impersonal communication**—exchanges that have a negligible perceived impact on your thoughts, emotions, behaviors, and relationships. For example, you lean over to a classmate and ask her what time it is, and she shows you the display on her phone. Although you are glad to have found out the time, this exchange has no further influence on you, your classmate, or your relationship with this person.

Why Form Relationships?

Whether it is one of life's big moments or an everyday encounter, interpersonal communication is how you share experiences with others and form the bonds that anchor any relationship. Knowing how and why you create such relationships is the first step toward understanding how you communicate within them.

Think about all the people you interact with and meet, online and off, every day—acquaintances, neighbors, service providers, lovers, family members, classmates, friends, coworkers. Across all of these encounters, how many people do you make the effort to get to know well? How many would you consider "relationship worthy"? It's likely that only some of these people reach such a status and that you feel "close" to even fewer.

The friendships and romantic entanglements depicted in the film *The Perks of Being a Wallflower* represent many of the common ways people form relationships—attraction, resources, and proximity. How much did such factors influence a recent relationship development in your life?

John Bramley/©Summit Entertainment/Courtesy Everett Collection

What leads you to form relationships with only a select few individuals, given the vast number of people you interact with every day? To answer this question, let's first define relationships. **Interpersonal relationships** are the emotional, mental, and physical involvements that you forge with others through communication. Scholars suggest that five factors influence whether these interpersonal relationships form or not: proximity, resources, similarity, reciprocal liking, and physical attractiveness (Aron, Fisher, Strong, Acevedo, Riela, & Tsapelas, 2008). These factors influence your relationship choices regardless of gender or sexual orientation (Felmlee, Orzechowicz, & Fortes, 2010).

Proximity

The first factor influencing relationship development is one of the most obvious yet often overlooked: proximity. You're more likely to pursue relationships with people with whom you have frequent contact, whether face-to-face or online. This phenomenon is known as the **mere exposure effect** (Bornstein, 1989). For example, a coworker who works in a cubicle near yours is more likely to become a friend or romantic partner than is one who works on a different floor. Similarly, if you have a cousin whose activities you regularly follow on Twitter, you'll be more likely to think of her as "a close family member" than "a distant relative you see only at annual family gatherings."

Resources

Another factor that compels you to pursue relationships with others is their **resources**—the valued qualities people possess. Resources range from personality traits and physical skills to social status and material wealth. Most people consider certain resources—such as a sense of humor, intelligence, kindness, supportiveness, and whether the person seems fun—to be valuable regardless of gender or sexual orientation (Felmlee et al., 2010).

What leads you to view a particular person's resources as desirable? According to **social exchange theory,** you'll feel drawn to individuals who offer you substantial *benefits* (positive things you like and want) with few *costs* (negative things demanded of you in return). So, you'll be interested in a potential lover who is smart, is attractive, has lots of money, and knows many interesting people, as long as this person isn't also jealous, demanding, possessive, and untrustworthy. In addition, social exchange theory predicts that you will pursue a particular relationship with someone if you think that person offers you rewards you believe you deserve, but only if those rewards seem better than rewards you can get elsewhere (Kelley & Thibaut, 1978). For example, in choosing which neighbor to befriend in your apartment complex, you're more likely to pursue a relationship with one who is funny and friendly than one who is aloof.

Similarity

Research suggests that people seek romantic partnerships, close family involvements, friendships, and coworker relationships with those whom they see as similar to themselves (Miller, Hefner, & Scott, 2007). This is known as the **birds-of-a-feather effect** (from the saying "Birds of a feather flock together"). Say that you have two sisters. Both of them have lived with you since birth (proximity), and both have many attributes that you appreciate (resources). But one sister has interests and personality traits very similar to yours. The birds-of-a-feather effect suggests that you'll feel closer to this sister than you will to your other sister.

At the same time, differences in surface-level tastes and preferences, such as foods, music, and movies, won't hurt your relationship as long as you and the other person are similar in other, more important ways (Neimeyer & Mitchell, 1988). For example, Steve loves the band Radiohead; he even has a RADIOHD vanity plate on his car. His close friend Mac doesn't like the band. However, they have other musical tastes in common (John Coltrane, Dave Brubeck, Miles Davis), and—more important—they have very similar personalities, senses of humor, and political views; thus, their friendship endures.

TABLE 9.1

INFLUENCES ON RELATIONSHIP FORMATION

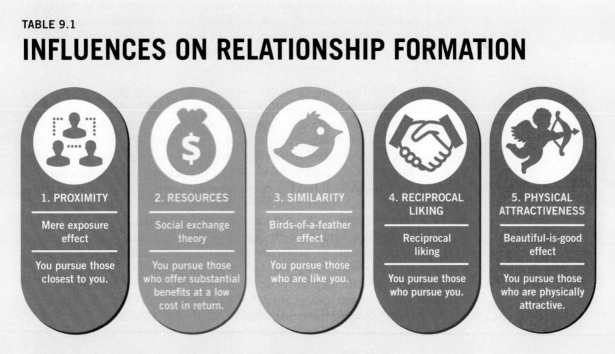

1. PROXIMITY	2. RESOURCES	3. SIMILARITY	4. RECIPROCAL LIKING	5. PHYSICAL ATTRACTIVENESS
Mere exposure effect	Social exchange theory	Birds-of-a-feather effect	Reciprocal liking	Beautiful-is-good effect
You pursue those closest to you.	You pursue those who offer substantial benefits at a low cost in return.	You pursue those who are like you.	You pursue those who pursue you.	You pursue those who are physically attractive.

1. Domofon/Shutterstock; 2. WinMaster/Shutterstock; 3. Introwiz1/Shutterstock; jossnat/Shutterstock

Reciprocal Liking

If someone you're interested in makes it clear that he or she is also interested in you, this is known as **reciprocal liking** (Aron et al., 2008). Reciprocal liking increases the chance that you and the other person will forge a relationship. For example, you're much more likely to become friends with a coworker who strikes up conversations with you and laughs at your jokes—showing that she likes you—than with a coworker who expresses no interest in you. When it comes to romantic involvements, studies examining people's narrative descriptions of "falling in love" have found that reciprocal liking is *the* most commonly mentioned factor leading to love (Riela, Rodriguez, Aron, Xu, & Acevedo, 2010).

Physical Attractiveness

Finally, you're more likely to get involved with people you perceive as physically attractive. Although it might seem obvious that people would naturally be drawn to beauty and good looks, there is another reason for its appeal. Attractive people are often assumed to offer other valued resources, such as competent communication skills, intelligence, and well-adjusted personalities—a phenomenon known as the **beautiful-is-good effect** (Eagly, Ashmore, Makhijani, & Longo, 1991).

Types of Relationships

Of all the relationships you experience, four usually stand out as the most impactful: lovers, family members, friends, and coworkers. But as important as these involvements are, they are also widely different from one another. Knowing the unique characteristics of each relationship type can improve your communication within them.

In Kaui Hart Hemmings's novel *The Descendants* (2011), attorney Matt King faces daunting challenges in the relationships that fill his life. On the professional front, he must make a business decision involving billions of dollars and affecting thousands of people. As the descendant of native Hawaiian royalty and the controlling heir to a massive land holding, Matt must decide whether to sell the land to developers or preserve it. But the decision isn't purely professional; it has family implications as well. The other heirs to the property—Matt's cousins and their families—want him to sell, so they can share in the profits. What's more, they make it clear that if he doesn't sell, there could be a permanent rift in the family. Meanwhile, on the home front, Matt's wife, Joanie, has suffered a devastating brain injury while boat racing and is in an irreversible coma. Suddenly a single parent, Matt must try to reconnect emotionally with two daughters from whom he has long been detached. He must also let friends and family members know that Joanie is dying. Complicating matters further, he discovers that Joanie—whom he had considered his best friend, sparring partner, and closest confidante—was cheating on him before the accident and had planned to divorce him. In the climactic scene of the book, he puts the pain of her betrayal to rest:

> I bow my head and speak to Joanie softly. "I'm sorry I didn't give you everything you wanted. I wasn't everything you wanted. You were everything I wanted. Every day. Home. There you are. Dinner, dishes, TV. Weekends at the beach. You go here. I go there. Parties. Home to complain about the party." I can't think of anything else. Just our routine together. "I forgive you," I say. Why is it so hard to articulate love, yet so easy to express disappointment? (Hemmings, 2011, pp. 235–236)

Throughout *The Descendants*, Matt King juggles the love and pain he feels toward his dying wife, the demands of being a single parent, his encounters with friends and family members, and his dealings with business partners. Similarly, all our lives are filled with these same relationship types: romantic, family, friendship, and workplace.

These relationships differ in many respects, but they share one critical point of commonality: *interpersonal communication*. It may sound cliché, but interpersonal communication is the lifeblood of all your relationships, no matter the type. It's how you initiate relationships, build and sustain them, and end those that have run their course. No matter the variety of channels used to interact within them—online, over the phone, and face-to-face—the focus is always interpersonal.

Given the central role of interpersonal communication in your relationships, let's explore each type of involvement and its defining characteristics.

The Descendants shows how Matt King communicates with various people in his life—showing compassion and forgiveness to those he feels closest to or pulling rank as needed in business dealings. When you consider your own communication, how does it differ depending on the type of relationship you have with the other person?

Ad Hominem Enterprises/The Kobal Collection

Romantic Relationships

Romantic relationships are interpersonal involvements in which the participants perceive the bond as romantic. As this definition suggests, romantic relationships are rooted in *perception*: a romantic relationship exists whenever the two partners believe that it does. As perceptions change, so, too, does the relationship. For example, a couple may consider their relationship "casual dating" but still define it as romantic (rather than friendly). But if one person feels romantic and the other does not, they don't have a romantic relationship (Miller & Steinberg, 1975).

In addition to being affected by the partners' perceptions, romantic relationships can vary in terms of the emotions that the partners feel toward each other.

Liking and Loving. Being in love is arguably the biggest distinction between romances and other relationship types, which center more on liking. What does it mean to be "in" love, and how does this differ from liking?

Most scholars agree that liking and loving are separate emotional states, with different causes and outcomes (Berscheid & Regan, 2005). **Liking** is a feeling of affection and respect that we often have for our friends, extended family members, and coworkers (Rubin, 1973). *Affection* is a sense of warmth and fondness toward another person, while *respect* is admiration for another person, regardless of how he or she treats or communicates with you.

Loving is a more intense emotional connection, consisting of intimacy, caring, and attachment (Rubin, 1973). *Intimacy* is a feeling of closeness and "union" between you and another person (Mashek & Aron, 2004). *Caring* is the concern you have for another person's welfare and the desire to keep him or her happy. *Attachment* is a longing to be in another person's presence as much as possible; in romantic involvements, this often takes the form of sexual desire. Although we may experience intimacy, caring, and attachment with close friends and family members, within romantic involvements, these feelings have a special intensity.

DOUBLE TAKE

PASSIONATE (VS) COMPANIONATE LOVE

At opposite ends of the spectrum, passionate and companionate love are just two of the types of love you may experience in your romantic relationships. How would you describe other types of love? What experiences do you have with how love can change over the course of a relationship?

ROB & SAS/Corbis

Blend Images/SuperStock

Passionate and Companionate Love. Many people believe that to be in love, you have to feel constant and consuming sexual attraction toward a partner. In fact, the experience of romantic love covers a broad range of emotions. At one end of the spectrum is **passionate love,** a state of intense emotional and physical longing for union with another (Hendrick & Hendrick, 1992). Passionate love is experienced across cultures, genders, and ages. Men and women in all cultures report experiencing this type of love with equal frequency and intensity. Moreover, for adults, passionate love is integrally linked with sexuality and sexual desire (Berscheid & Regan, 2005). In one study, undergraduates were asked whether they thought there was a difference between "being in love" and "loving" another person (Ridge & Berscheid, 1989). Eighty-seven percent of respondents said that there was a difference and that sexual attraction was the critical distinguishing feature of being in love. However, passionate love is *negatively* related to relationship duration. Like it or not, the longer you're with a romantic partner, the less intense your passionate love will feel (Berscheid, 2002).

At the other end of the romantic spectrum is **companionate love:** an intense form of liking defined by emotional investment and the close intertwining of two people's lives (Berscheid & Walster, 1978). Many long-term romantic relationships begin as passionate love and then slowly evolve into companionate love, as the "fire" of passion cools with age and familiarity. For example, in *The Descendants*, Matt reflects on how his love for Joanie changed over the course of their relationship from passionate to companionate: "At weddings we roll our eyes at the burgeoning love around us, the vows that we know will morph into new kinds of promises: I vow not to kiss you when you're trying to read; I will tolerate you in sickness and ignore you in health; I promise to let you watch the stupid news show about celebrities" (Hemmings, 2011, p. 46).

Family Relationships

Families today are incredibly diverse. Since 2010, only 20 percent of U.S. households consist of married couples with biological children; within Canada, it is only about 35 percent. Couples are increasingly living together rather than getting married, and rising divorce and remarriage rates have led to blended arrangements featuring stepparents and stepchildren. Adding to this complexity, individual families are constantly in flux, as children leave home, then move back in with parents while looking for work; as grandparents join the household to help with day care or receive care themselves; and as spouses separate geographically to pursue job opportunities (Crosnoe & Cavanagh, 2010).

To embrace this diversity, we use a broad and inclusive definition of family. A **family** is a network of people who share their lives over long periods of time and are bound by marriage, blood, or commitment; who consider themselves a family; and who share a significant history and an anticipated future of functioning in a family relationship (Galvin, Brommel, & Bylund,

Will Smith and Jada Pinkett Smith may be best known for their successful acting careers, but being an entertainer is an identity shared by their children, Jaden and Willow Smith, who also perform in the music and movie industries.

Evan Agostini/Invision/AP Images

2004). This definition highlights three characteristics that distinguish families from other relationship types: shared identity, multiple roles, and emotional complexity.

Shared Identity. Families possess a strong sense of shared identity: "We're the MacTavish clan, and we've always been adventurous" or "We Singhs have a long history of creative talent." This sense of shared identity is created by three factors, the first of which is how the family communicates (Braithwaite et al., 2010). The stories you exchange and the way members of your family deal with conflict and talk with one another all contribute to a shared sense of what your family is like (Tovares, 2010). For instance, our friend Lorena's great-grandparents emigrated from their farm in Sicily to the United States. To build a life in their adopted country, they learned English, worked in textile mills, and eventually bought their own home. But they also endured taunts and mistreatment from people who looked down on immigrants. Lorena remembers attending multigenerational family dinners at their home on Sundays, where everyone recounted stories about how tough and resilient her "Nana and Nano" were to succeed in America—and how they passed on these same qualities to the next generations.

In addition to how a family communicates, genetic material can further foster a sense of shared identity (Crosnoe & Cavanagh, 2010). This can lead to shared physical traits—such as distinct hair colors, body types, and facial characteristics—as well as similar personalities, mental abilities, and ways of relating to others.

Finally, a common history can also help create a sense of shared identity (Galvin et al., 2004). Such histories can stretch back for generations and may feature family members from a broad array of cultures. In *The Descendants*, for instance, Matt King's family is incredibly diverse but bonded by their heritage as native Hawaiian royalty. The history you share with your family is created jointly, as you go through time together. For better or worse, everything you say and do becomes a part of your family history.

Multiple Roles. Family members constantly juggle multiple roles (Silverstein & Giarrusso, 2010). When you're a lover, a friend, or a coworker, you're just that: lover, friend, or coworker. Within your family, however, you're not just a daughter or a son—you may also be a sibling, a spouse, and an aunt or an uncle. By the time you reach middle age, you may simultaneously be parent, spouse, grandparent, daughter or son, *and* sibling. Each of these roles carries its own expectations and demands, forcing you to learn how to communicate effectively in each one, often at the same time.

Emotional Complexity. It is commonly thought that people should feel only positive emotions toward their family members (Berscheid, 2002). As psychologist Theodor Reik (1972) notes, people are "intolerant of feelings of resentment and hatred that sometimes rise in [them] against beloved persons—we feel that such an emotion has no right to exist beside our strong affection, even for a few minutes" (pp. 99–100). Yet members of the same family typically experience both warm and antagonistic feelings toward one another (Silverstein & Giarrusso, 2010). That's because family members get into conflicts, just as do people in any other type of relationship. Personality differences, contrasting interests and priorities—all of these can create tensions that fuel resentment and other unpleasant emotions among family members. But if you believe you're not *supposed* to feel angry or frustrated with your family, this sense of wrongness can make these emotions seem even more intense. Thus, two things you can do to improve your family relationships are to realize that it's perfectly normal to not always get along, and to accept the complexity of emotions that will naturally occur within such involvements.

Friendships

Friendships play a crucial role in your life. In addition to being one of the most common types of relationships you experience, they are also an important source of emotional security and self-esteem (Rawlins, 1992). They provide a sense of belonging when you're young, help you solidify your identity during adolescence, and provide satisfaction and social support when you're elderly (Miller et al., 2007).

What exactly are friendships? **Friendships** are voluntary interpersonal relationships characterized by intimacy and liking (McEwan, Babin Gallagher, & Farinelli, 2008). Whether casual or close, short– or long–term, friendships have three distinguishing characteristics: they are based on liking, they are created by choice, and their bonds are strengthened through shared interests.

Liking. People feel affection and respect for their friends; in other words, friends are people whom you *like* (Rubin, 1973). You also enjoy spending time with them (Hays, 1988). At the same time, because friendships are rooted in liking rather than love, you're not as emotionally attached to your friends as you are to your romantic partners, and you don't put as many emotional demands on them. Indeed, many people assume that they should be more loyal to and more willing to help romantic partners and family members than their friends (Davis & Todd, 1985). Imagine a friend calls you at work, in tears because her boyfriend has just dumped her. She's extremely depressed, and

As you can see on TV shows like *How I Met Your Mother*, no two friendships are exactly the same. Though they may be based on shared interests, each friendship you have likely tests your interpersonal skills in a different way. Do you notice that some of your friends are better listeners than others? Who do you turn to when you want to let loose?

RON P. JAFFE/CBS/Landov

you're worried about her, but you hesitate to leave work early to see her. If it had been your sister who called in the same predicament, you might have been more willing to leave work to make absolutely sure she was OK.

Choice. You have more freedom in choosing your friendships than you do in any other relationship category (Sias et al., 2008). Whether you decide to become friends with someone is a pretty straightforward process: if you both want to be friends, you form a friendship. It's not always that simple in romantic, family, and workplace involvements. For example, in some cultures, people can choose whom they date or marry. But in others, there may be rules governing such matters—including arranged marriages. In your family, you may be bound to others through involuntary ties, including birth, adoption, or the creation of a stepfamily. In the workplace, you have to work with certain people, whether you like them or not.

Shared Interests. Similarity in interests is the primary force that draws you to your friends (Parks & Floyd, 1996), no matter what your age, gender, sexual orientation, or ethnicity. As a result, friendships are less stable, more likely to change, and easier to break off than family or romantic relationships (Johnson, Wittenberg, Villagran, Mazur, & Villagran, 2003). Why? When your interests and activities change, your friendships may change, too. If you adopt different political or religious beliefs or suffer an injury that prevents you from playing a beloved sport, friendships that were built on previous similarities may evaporate. Of course, some friendships will endure—if you and your friend find new points of commonality—but others will fade away. Indeed, a change in shared interests is one of the most common reasons friendships end (Miller et al., 2007).

Workplace Relationships

Affiliations you have with professional peers, supervisors, subordinates, or mentors are **workplace relationships**. These involvements vary along three dimensions: *status*, *intimacy*, and *choice* (Sias & Perry, 2004). First, most workplaces are structured hierarchically in terms of status, with some people ranked higher or lower than others in organizational position and power. Thus, a defining feature of workplace relationships is the equality or inequality of relationship partners. For example, you may work side by side every day with your coworker Katelyn, doing food prep, inventory, and cleanup in a restaurant. But if Katelyn is also your supervisor—she decides whether you keep your job and whether you get promotions and raises—she has power over you. That affects how you and she communicate. If Katelyn asks you to stay late or do additional work, it isn't simply a request: it's a professional demand. However, you can't make similar demands of her because you don't have the same level of authority.

Workplace relationships also vary in intimacy. Some remain strictly professional, with interpersonal communication restricted to work-related concerns. Others become deeply intimate. If you spend three nights a week sharing the same shift with Erin and Dante, you'll likely get to know them both. But if you only share the same tastes, attitudes, beliefs, and values with Dante—not Erin—you may end up forming a deeper bond with Dante than with Erin.

Finally, workplace relationships are defined by varying degrees of choice— the degree to which participants willingly engage in them. As noted earlier, you don't get to pick your coworkers. This can be especially challenging when you're expected to work closely and productively with people you don't like or don't get along with. On the other hand, you *do* get to choose which coworkers become your friends—and sometimes, even which become romantic partners.

WORKPLACE RELATIONSHIPS

No matter the type of work environment, the relationships you have at work are defined by status, intimacy, and choice.

Intimacy: Open office environments can provide more opportunities for you to get to know your coworkers.

Status: Coworkers of equal standing can collaborate on new ideas before presenting them to a supervisor.

Choice: You must work with all your colleagues, but who becomes your friend is entirely up to you.

Robert Schlesinger/picture-alliance/dpa/AP Images

MAKING COMMUNICATION CHOICES
WHEN A GOOD FRIEND CHANGES

1 CONSIDER THE DILEMMA

Raisa has been your friend for years. She's a first-generation Guatemalan American, and her family is very strict. Growing up, Raisa prioritized grades over play, but the payoff came when she was admitted to elite universities. Thrilled, her family now wants her to attend law school.

You've always liked Raisa, because although she's kind of uptight (perfectly groomed and ridiculously polite), she's also very supportive. She's the one friend you can always count on for good advice, whether you're fighting with a family member or suffering a romantic breakup.

Recently, Raisa travels to Guatemala to build houses with Habitat for Humanity. Although you initially stay in touch with her by Skype, as the months pass, it becomes too much of a hassle to schedule chats, and so you switch to occasional e-mails. You still feel close to her, but you also can tell from the tone of her messages that her experiences there are having a substantial impact on her.

When Raisa returns, you pick her up at the airport because her parents are working. Raisa is unrecognizable. She's lost fifteen pounds, and her hair is wild. Gone is the uptight Raisa you've always known, and in her place is a person who wears more dirt than makeup. There's a gleam in her eye, and she greets you with a big hug. As you drive home, she talks nonstop about her passion for her culture and how she wants to work full-time for Habitat. She also tells you that her family doesn't approve, and that they have complained that she has "become a hippie." You're so stunned that you don't know what to say. After a while, Raisa notices your silence. "I know I've changed," she says, "but I've finally figured out who I am. My family can't accept this. Can you?"

2 CONNECT THE RESEARCH

An essential part of building and sustaining close relationships is providing support for *valued social identities*: the aspects of your self you consider most important in defining who you are—musician, nurse, athlete, charity worker, teacher, mother, and so on. Within close relationships, communicating in ways that convey understanding, acceptance, and support for these identities is crucial, even if these identities change over time.

Scholars Carolyn Weisz and Lisa Wood (2005) studied friendships across a span of four years, looking at the impact that identity support, amount of communication, and general emotional support had on these relationships. They found that friends who reported high levels of identity support at the beginning of their study were more likely to describe each other as *best* friends four years later. In fact, identity support proved to be the strongest determinant of closeness—even more so than how often people communicated with each other.

3 COMMUNICATE

Before making a communication choice, consider the facts of the situation, and think about the identity support research. Also, reflect on what you've learned about why you form relationships (pp. 215–218) and the characteristics of friendships (pp. 223–224). Then answer these questions:

1. How do you think and feel about Raisa's transformation? What does her family think?

2. Put yourself in Raisa's shoes. How would you feel if you were in her position, facing family opposition? What does she want from you?

3. What are you going to say to Raisa?

Relationship Stages

Although there's no set rule for how relationships progress, most go through certain stages, marked by differences in communication and intimacy. These turning points provide a sense of where the relationship is going. Sometimes these are positive—such as when good friends become best friends. Other times they're less pleasant, such as when you break off a romance. Knowing about these stages will help you recognize the status of your own relationships and communicate better within them.

Think back to *The Bachelor* TV show, which we discussed in our chapter opener. On that show, relationships between the women and the man grow closer or further apart, depending on what each learns about the other and how they perceive their interactions. Relationships among the female contestants also change, evolving into strong friendships or unraveling into heated conflicts depending on how they communicate with each other.

In those regards, *The Bachelor* mirrors real life. As people spend more time together communicating and interacting, relationships develop as well as decay. Most relationships—including romantic, family, friendships, and coworker involvements—go through various stages. At each stage, the partners' communication, thoughts, and feelings demonstrate distinctive patterns. Communication scholar Mark Knapp (1984) identified 10 relationship stages, 5 of them relating to "coming together" and 5 having to do with "coming apart."

Coming Together

Knapp's stages of coming together illustrate one possible flow of relationship development. As you read about the stages, keep in mind that these suggest benchmarks or turning points in relationships and are not fixed rules for how involvements should progress. Your relationships may go through some, none, or all of these stages. They may skip stages, jump backward or forward in the sequence, or follow a completely different trajectory.

Initiating. During the **initiating** stage, you size up a new person to decide whether you want to get to know that person better. You consider how attractive or interesting he or she seems by drawing on any information you can find, such as an online profile or impressions from other people who know him or her. You also work out an appropriate way of greeting the individual. You might do this in person—for instance, walking up to a classmate and saying, "Hi, I'm Jonas; would you like to get a coffee sometime?" Or you might do it online, such as when you connect with a long-lost family member through a genealogy Web site like Ancestry.com. In North America, people interested in initiating romantic relationships often use online dating sites to meet new partners (Heino, Ellison, & Gibbs, 2010).

Experimenting. Once you've initiated an encounter with someone, you enter the **experimenting** stage: exchanging demographic information (names, majors, hometowns). As you disclose these details, you look for points of commonality to foster further interaction. For instance, meeting a distant cousin for the first time at a family gathering, you might say, "You were an Army brat? So was I! Wasn't it tough to keep changing schools?" In a romance, this is the "casual dating" phase; in a friendship, it's the "making an acquaintance" stage. Most involvements never progress beyond this stage. You are likely to go through life experimenting with many people but forming deep connections with relatively few of them.

Intensifying. Occasionally, you'll find yourself feeling strongly attracted to or interested in another person. When this happens, your verbal and non-verbal communication becomes increasingly more intimate. During this **intensifying** stage, you and the other person begin to share much more personal information about yourselves, such as secrets from your past ("My father was an alcoholic") or your most cherished dreams and goals ("I've always wanted to raise a family"). Within friendships, you might develop private nicknames for each other (e.g., calling your friend Benjamin "BangBang"). With coworkers, you begin discussing challenges you've faced in your personal life, such as a failed marriage or family tragedy (Sias & Cahill, 1998). In romantic relationships, you may begin expressing commitment verbally ("I think I'm falling for you") and online (marking your status as "in a relationship" rather than "single").

Integrating. During the **integrating** stage, your and your partner's personalities seem to blend. Twins may experience this stage, as do very close or "best" friends. In romantic relationships, partners integrate through engaging in sexual activity and sharing belongings, such as items of clothing, music, and photos. You and your partner engage in activities and interests that clearly join you together as a couple and use language expressing your new identity—"*Our* favorite movie is . . . ," "*We* love that restaurant!" Friends, colleagues, and family members begin treating you as a couple— for example, always inviting the two of you to parties or dinners.

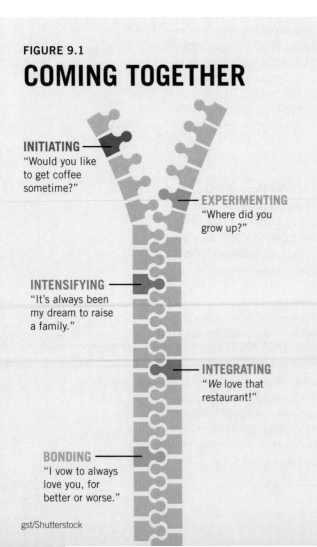

FIGURE 9.1

COMING TOGETHER

INITIATING
"Would you like to get coffee sometime?"

EXPERIMENTING
"Where did you grow up?"

INTENSIFYING
"It's always been my dream to raise a family."

INTEGRATING
"*We* love that restaurant!"

BONDING
"I vow to always love you, for better or worse."

gst/Shutterstock

Bonding. For romances, the ultimate stage of coming together is **bonding,** a public ritual that announces to the world that you and your romantic partner have made a commitment to each other. Bonding is something you'll share with very few people—perhaps only one—during your lifetime. The most obvious example of bonding is a wedding or commitment ceremony.

Coming Apart

In most of your relationships, you will also experiences stages of coming apart—getting less intimate with your relationship partners. One study of college-age dating couples found that across a three-month period, as many as 30 percent of the couples broke up (Parks & Adelman, 1983). Friendships are even less stable than romantic relationships (Johnson et al., 2003). Why? Consider the differences in depth of commitment between friendships and romantic attachments. Friendships are rooted in shared interests, but people's interests frequently change. So, if you switch your major from biology to music, it's likely you will grow apart from the friends you made in your biology lab, as you no longer share the same academic interests or take the same classes. In comparison, romantic relationships are forged from more powerful bonds, such as deep emotional and sexual attachment.

Like coming together, coming apart unfolds over stages marked by changes in the partners' thoughts, feelings, and communication. Many romantic partners, family members, friends, and coworkers experience some of these stages at various points in their relationships. Again, your relationships may go through some, none, or all of these stages. In fact, not all relationships that begin to come apart result in a permanent ending of the relationship. Sometimes, with enough effort, people can resolve their differences. Other times, ending the relationship is the right thing to do because the people involved have either grown apart or permanently lost interest in each other. No matter the situation, the stages of coming apart often involve intense emotional pain that can make it difficult for the individuals involved to communicate competently with each other. This is why it is important to know and understand these relationship stages, so you can better handle them as they come up.

Differentiating. In all relationships, partners share differences as well as similarities. But during the first stage of coming apart, **differentiating,** the beliefs, attitudes, and values that distinguish you from your partner come to dominate your thoughts and communication ("I can't *believe* you think that!" or "We are *so* different!").

Most healthy relationships experience occasional periods of differentiating. These moments can involve arguing over what the partners see as conflicting viewpoints, tastes, or goals. But you can move your relationship through this difficulty—and thus stop the coming-apart process—by openly discussing your points of difference and working together to resolve them.

ENDING A RELATIONSHIP

 One way to improve your communication competence is by adapting your messages to others' behaviors. Learn how to navigate difficult relational stages by going to LaunchPad at **bedfordstmartins.com/choicesconnections** and completing the **How to Communicate video scenario** for Chapter 9 to practice your skills.

CONSIDER THIS:
The close connection that once existed between you and a relationship partner, Alex, has faded. You no longer share anything in common, and you bicker and fight more than you get along. You decide to end the relationship and now must inform Alex of your decision.

WHAT WOULD YOU DO? The following advice illustrates how competent communication skills can help you terminate a relationship. As you watch the video, consider how the dialogue reflects various skills from across this book. Then, test your knowledge of key skills, and create your own responses to the **What if? video prompts**.

"I need to talk with you. It's important and it's going to take a while. Do you have to be anywhere? Is now a good time to chat?"

① **CREATE A CONTEXT** for the conversation by choosing the right time and place, making sure you're face-to-face, in a comfortable environment, and have plenty of time to talk. Don't discuss termination if your partner has important obligations in the near future that might be negatively impacted by your interaction, such as exams or interviews.

2 USE CLEAR, POSITIVE, HONEST "I" LANGUAGE; avoid blame and negativity; keep the focus squarely on you and your feelings; and ask for his or her viewpoint.

"I don't feel that there's a solid connection between us anymore. I think we are going in different directions, and we each should just move on with our lives. Are you feeling the same things?"

3 OFFER EMPATHIC CONCERN and emotional support, being careful to legitimize (rather than challenge) his or her reaction, and framing your decision in a desire for mutual happiness.

"I'm really sorry. I totally understand that this is hurtful and you might be angry and sad. But I just want us both to be happy, and it seems to me that neither of us is really happy anymore."

WHAT IF? But what if things don't work out as shown? Test your ability to adapt your communication by watching the What if? videos and planning a response for each situation.

1. How would you counter Alex's denial that there's a problem in the relationship? "We're just fine! I know we disagree a lot, but so what? You think other people don't argue?"

2. If Alex blames you for the failure of the relationship, and attacks you personally ("This is all your fault anyway! You never really gave us a chance, you know that?"), what would you say?

Circumscribing. If one or both of you respond to problematic differences by ignoring them and spending less time talking, you enter the **circumscribing** stage of coming apart. You actively begin to restrict the quantity and quality of information you exchange in the relationship, creating "safe zones" in which you discuss only topics that won't provoke conflict. Common remarks made during circumscribing include "Don't ask me about that" and "Let's not talk about that anymore."

Stagnating. If circumscribing becomes so severe that you and the other person have almost no safe topics to talk about, communication slows to a standstill, and the relationship enters the **stagnating** stage. You both presume that communicating is pointless because you believe it will only lead to further problems. People in stagnant relationships often experience a sense of resignation; they feel stuck or trapped. However, some stay in the relationship for months or even years. Why? They may believe that it's better to leave things as they are than to put in the enormous effort needed to end or try to rebuild the relationship, or they simply may not know how to repair the damage done to their earlier bond.

FIGURE 9.2
COMING APART

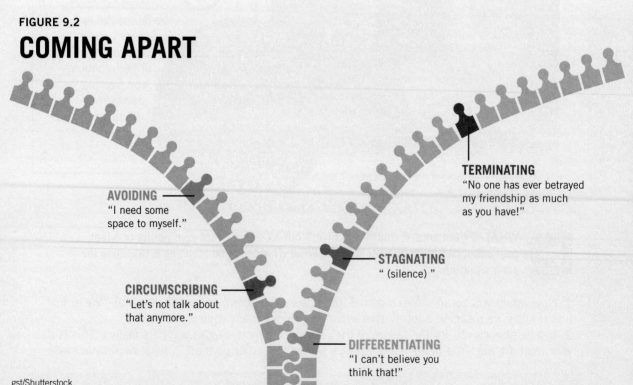

TERMINATING
"No one has ever betrayed my friendship as much as you have!"

AVOIDING
"I need some space to myself."

STAGNATING
" (silence) "

CIRCUMSCRIBING
"Let's not talk about that anymore."

DIFFERENTIATING
"I can't believe you think that!"

gst/Shutterstock

Avoiding. During the **avoiding** stage, one or both of you decide that you can no longer be around the other, and you begin distancing yourself physically. Some people communicate avoidance directly and verbally ("You are no longer my son, and I want no further contact with you!" or "We're no longer friends"). Others may do it by spending more and more time away from their partner—for example, by avoiding family get-togethers or moving out of a shared apartment because "I need some space to myself." Some avoid the other person indirectly—for example, screening the individual's calls, ignoring his or her texts, changing their Facebook status from "in a relationship" to "single," or "de-friending" or "un-following" someone.

 LearningCurve can help you review! Go to **bedfordstmartins.com /choicesconnections**.

Terminating. In ending a relationship, some people want to come together for a final encounter that gives a sense of closure and resolution. During the **terminating** stage, former partners might discuss the past, present, and future of the relationship. They often describe their past relationship by making accusations ("No one has ever betrayed my friendship as much as you have!") or expressing sadness over what's been lost ("I'll never be able to find someone as perfect as you"). Their verbal and nonverbal behaviors reveal a lack of intimacy—for instance, standing far apart and making little eye contact. The partners may also discuss the future status of their relationship. Some may agree to end all contact going forward; others may choose to maintain some type of contact, like an occasional phone call, even though the relationship is officially over.

Many people find terminating a relationship painful or awkward. It's hard to tell someone that you no longer want to be involved with him or her, and it's equally painful to hear it. But by drawing on all you've learned about communication, you can survive this dreaded moment. Use skills from Chapter 2, such as *empathic concern*—being aware of how your partner is feeling and experiencing compassion for him or her—and *perspective-taking*—the ability to see things from your partner's point of view—to handle the situation competently. See How to Communicate: Ending a Relationship on pages 230–231 for additional advice on handling a breakup conversation. You may also find it useful to remind yourself that relationship endings are a kind of death and that it's normal to experience grief, even when terminating is the right thing to do. The suggestions offered in the section on supportive communication in Chapter 10 can help you manage this aspect of termination (see pages 256–257).

CHAPTER ⑨ REVIEW

CHAPTER RECAP

- **Interpersonal communication** is **dyadic** and is your primary tool for building, maintaining, and ending relationships.
- The four defining characteristics of interpersonal communication are that it is transactional, dynamic, relational, and impactful.
- Scholars suggest that five factors influence how people form interpersonal relationships: proximity, **resources**, similarity, **reciprocal liking**, and physical attractiveness.
- Though each type is unique, people build and maintain their relationships—**romantic, family, friends,** and **workplace**—through interpersonal communication.
- Many relationships progress through certain stages, marked by differences in communication and intimacy. These turning points can be positive—**initiating, experimenting, intensifying, integrating,** and **bonding**—or negative—**differentiating, circumscribing, stagnating, avoiding,** and **terminating**.

LAUNCHPAD

LaunchPad for *Choices & Connections* offers unique video scenarios and encourages self-assessment through adaptive quizzing. Go to bedfordstmartins.com /choicesconnections to get access.

✓ LearningCurve adaptive quizzes

▶ How to Communicate video scenarios

▶ Video clips that illustrate key concepts

KEY TERMS

Interpersonal communication, p. 212	Passionate love, p. 221
Dyadic, p. 212	Companionate love, p. 221
I-Thou, p. 214	Family, p. 221
I-It, p. 214	Friendships, p. 223
Impersonal communication, p. 215	Workplace relationships, p. 224
Interpersonal relationships, p. 216	Initiating, p. 227
Mere exposure effect, p. 216	Experimenting, p. 228
Resources, p. 216	Intensifying, p. 228
Social exchange theory, p. 216	Integrating, p. 228
Birds-of-a-feather effect, p. 217	▶ Bonding, p. 229
Reciprocal liking, p. 218	▶ Differentiating, p. 229
Beautiful-is-good effect, p. 218	Circumscribing, p. 232
Romantic relationships, p. 219	Stagnating, p. 232
Liking, p. 220	Avoiding, p. 233
Loving, p. 220	Terminating, p. 233

1 According to philosopher Martin Buber, when you embrace the fundamental similarities that connect you with others, and try to see things from others' points of view, you're communicating in a(n) _____ fashion.

a. dyadic

b. loving

c. I-Thou

d. I-It

2 When it comes to romantic involvements, studies have found that _____ is *the* most commonly mentioned factor leading to love.

a. proximity

b. resources

c. physical attractiveness

d. reciprocal liking

3 The stories that family members exchange, the way they deal with conflict and talk with one another, and their common history all contribute to a sense of _____.

a. shared identity

b. shared interests

c. emotional complexity

d. companionate love

4 Which of the following is *not* a factor in determining how workplace relationships develop?

a. Attachment

b. Choice

c. Intimacy

d. Status

5 During the _____ stage, you become so close to someone else that your personalities seem to blend.

a. bonding

b. integrating

c. experimenting

d. intensifying

ACTIVITIES

1 Interpersonal vs. Impersonal

Working with a partner, come up with your own definition of interpersonal communication based on how you use it daily. Include what distinguishes it from impersonal communication. Then, discuss how mediated forms of communication such as Twitter, e-mails, and texts can be interpersonal and when they can be impersonal. What makes the difference? Does the number of people impact whether an encounter is interpersonal? How? Come up with examples for each, and discuss how the technology can influence whether the communication is interpersonal or impersonal.

2 Love, Hollywood Style

Identify three of the most romantic movies you've seen (e.g., *The Notebook*, *Love and Basketball*, *Love Actually*, *Brokeback Mountain*). For each, assess how passionate love and companionate love are depicted. Is passionate love depicted as superior to companionate love? How do the movies deal with love over time? How do these depictions contrast with your own views of passionate and companionate love? What factors of loving and liking are shown, and which are ignored? What effect does this have on showing "real" romantic relationships in the movies?

10
Managing Interpersonal Relationships

What will make you happy? This seems to be a simple question, with obvious answers: Fame. Being remembered as someone who did something great. Or perhaps fortune. In one survey of college students, 75 percent of respondents rated "being very well off financially" as their top goal in life, and 78 percent said, "It's important to have a beautiful home, a new car and other nice things."[1]

Thinking about what makes you happy is important, because happiness matters. Studies show that happy people are healthier, more energized, more confident, and more socially connected than are unhappy people. Moreover, the pursuit of happiness is the driving force behind most people's decisions: they choose colleges, majors, and careers based on what they believe will help them become happier. But there's a catch: what people *think* will satisfy them often doesn't.

What *really* makes people happy? Psychologist David Myers has devoted much of his career to gathering and interpreting scientific findings on "enduring joy." What he has found is both obvious and surprising. Decades of research involving hundreds of studies and thousands of people in dozens of countries show that human beings are happier when they have meaningful activities to consume their time (challenging jobs, passionate hobbies), exercise regularly, have spirituality in their lives, and get sufficient sleep. It turns out that age, gender, parenthood status (whether you have kids or not), and physical attractiveness have little impact on happiness. What else *doesn't* guarantee happiness? Money. As Myers describes, "Wealth is like health: its utter absence breeds misery, but having it doesn't ensure happiness."

But among all the factors that shape enduring joy, one leaps out

William Perugini/Shutterstock

---

[1]All findings and quotes that follow adapted from Myers (2000, 2002, 2004, 2013).

as the most important in Myers's analysis: *the quality of your interpersonal relationships*. Consider these facts. The happiest college students are those who have satisfying romantic relationships, family bonds, friendships, and workplace attachments. People who report close interpersonal relationships are better able to cope with life's inevitable stresses, which can range from unemployment and illness to the deaths of loved ones. In the previously noted survey of college students, most reported financial gain as their top goal; however, when asked, "What is *necessary* for your happiness?" they answered, "Satisfying interpersonal relationships."

Your life is filled with relationships—so many that you often don't give them a second thought. Maybe you have a neighbor whom you wave to on your way to school and occasionally chat up, a barista who makes your morning coffee, a checkout clerk at the grocery store who has rung up your purchases every Sunday for years. Then there's your inner circle of lovers, family members, friends, and coworkers—the people you consider "close" to you, and with whom you interact every day. Collectively, your connections to all of these people directly determine how you feel as you go through your life. When these relationships are harmonious, you go through your days feeling happy and supported. When they fracture, your days darken with pain and sadness.

Given that satisfying interpersonal relationships are essential for your life happiness, it's important to know how to manage these relationships in a way that best sustains them. In this chapter, you'll learn:

- Ways to use self-disclosure to build relationships
- How to manage relationship tensions
- Successful strategies for sustaining your relationships
- How to support your relationship partners in times of need

☑ LearningCurve can help you review! Go to bedfordstmartins.com /choicesconnections.

Self-Disclosure in Relationships

When you share private information with others, you open up your innermost self to them. Such sharing, known as self-disclosure, is the foundation for intimacy in a relationship. But it's not as simple as "sharing equals closeness." Instead, you must know what, why, and when to disclose in order to build happy and enduring relationships.

The novel *The Help* by Kathryn Stockett (2009) tells the story of a literary collaboration and friendship that cuts across ethnic lines in early 1960s Mississippi. At the center of the story are three women: affluent white author Skeeter and two African American maids, Aibileen and Minny. Aibileen cleans houses and cares for the children of various white families. Minny serves as a maid when she can but frequently gets fired for refusing to let her white employers bully her. Witnessing the racism and discrimination these maids face, Skeeter decides to write a book about their experiences and to frame it as a fictional novel. Skeeter persuades Aibileen to share her stories, who agrees in part to honor her dead son, who loved writing.

Eventually Minny and other maids join in the project. The women know that they are in danger of retaliation from the townspeople, who resent the maids' revealing such sensitive information. But the women feel that their collaboration is worth the risk, because it will help ensure that their voices are heard and possibly make things better for future generations. As the women spend hours together, sharing innumerable tales of pain and suffering, they begin forming tentative bonds. Over time, this solidifies into firm

Dale Robinette/©Walt Disney Studios Motion Pictures/Courtesy Everett Collection

In the movie *The Help*, the friendship between Skeeter, Aibileen, and Minny deepens as they share their thoughts and experiences. How have such personal disclosures influenced relationships with friends and coworkers in your life?

friendships, founded on their long talks and the sharing of their most profound secret of all: they authored the book together.

The Help reminds us of the importance of taking a stand against prejudice. Equally valuable, it shows the role of interpersonal communication in creating relationships. When people disclose their innermost thoughts to one another, they forge a strong emotional bond.

Self-Disclosure and Relationship Development

Revealing private information about your self to others is known as **self-disclosure** (Wheeless, 1978). Self-disclosure is a key part of building and sustaining relationships (Reis & Patrick, 1996). When you disclose to someone, you reveal aspects of your self that you previously kept hidden. Psychologists Irwin Altman and Dalmas Taylor (1973) think of self-disclosure as similar to peeling back layers of an onion. According to their **social penetration theory,** the self is an "onion-skin structure" consisting of three sets of layers. The *outermost layers* of your self are demographic characteristics, such as your birthplace, age, gender, and ethnicity (see Figure 10.1). When you meet someone for the first time, you typically focus the conversation on these characteristics: What's your name? What's your major? Where are you from? The *intermediate layers* contain your attitudes and opinions about things like music, politics, food, and entertainment. Deep within the onion are the *central layers* of your self—core characteristics such as self-awareness, self-concept, self-esteem, personal values, fears, and distinctive personality traits. As Chapter 2 discusses, this is what makes up your *self*.

This notion that the self consists of layers helps explain how to distinguish between casual and close involvements. As relationships progress, partners start peeling down to the deeper layers of the onion, disclosing increasingly personal information to each other. But in addition to *depth*, the revealing of selves that occurs during relationship development involves *breadth*—sharing more aspects of your self at each layer. For example, when you're sharing your attitudes and opinions (the intermediate layers of your self), you would be demonstrating breadth if you covered a relatively wide range of topics instead of discussing in detail only your taste in music.

The deeper and broader self-disclosure becomes, the more it fosters **intimacy**—feelings of closeness between you and others (Mashek & Aron, 2004). Intimacy is self-perpetuating: the more intimacy you feel, the more you disclose; and as you disclose more, feelings of intimacy deepen (Shelton, Trail, West, & Bergsieker, 2010). But for self-disclosure to create intimacy, several conditions must be met (Reis & Shaver, 1988). For one thing, *both* partners must disclose. If one person shares previously private thoughts and feelings, and the other person doesn't, the relationship isn't intimate—it's one-sided.

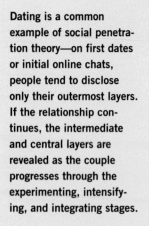

Dating is a common example of social penetration theory—on first dates or initial online chats, people tend to disclose only their outermost layers. If the relationship continues, the intermediate and central layers are revealed as the couple progresses through the experimenting, intensifying, and integrating stages.

Beau Lark/Corbis

FIGURE 10.1
THE LAYERS OF SELF-DISCLOSURE

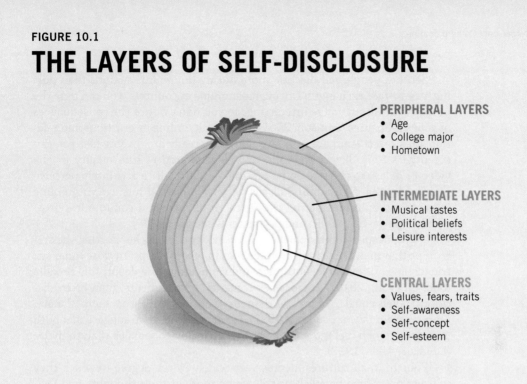

PERIPHERAL LAYERS
- Age
- College major
- Hometown

INTERMEDIATE LAYERS
- Musical tastes
- Political beliefs
- Leisure interests

CENTRAL LAYERS
- Values, fears, traits
- Self-awareness
- Self-concept
- Self-esteem

The partner who is listening to someone self-disclose must also respond supportively. Have you ever shared something deeply personal with a friend, who then commented with something like "I can't believe you did something so stupid!" If so, how did this response make you feel? Chances are it created a feeling of distance rather than one of closeness between the two of you.

Finally, to foster feelings of intimacy with others, it's important to disclose information that people view as appropriate. Sharing information that is perceived as problematic or peculiar can damage relationships (Planalp & Honeycutt, 1985). Imagine that a coworker tells you he's obsessed with serial killers. You probably won't feel closer to him—unless you share the same obsession!

Communicating Self-Disclosure

Researchers have conducted thousands of self-disclosure studies over the last 40 years (Tardy & Dindia, 1997). These studies suggest five important facts about self-disclosure. First, self-disclosure appears to promote mental health and relieve stress (Tardy, 2000). Especially when information is troubling, keeping it inside can lead to obsessing about the secret, as you constantly monitor what you say so you don't disclose it (Kelly & McKillop, 1996). This can raise stress levels, causing immune-system problems, ulcers, and high blood pressure (Pennebaker, 1997).

Second, people self-disclose more during online interactions than during face-to-face exchanges. During most online encounters, you can't see the people with whom you're interacting, so you don't notice the consequences of your disclosures (Joinson, 2001). As a result, online interactions and relationships can seem more intimate than they really are. Even when you can see others—via Skype, webcam, or videoconference—the quality of the video or delays in the streaming can make it difficult to accurately perceive their responses. As Chapter 3 discusses, you can better manage your online interactions by remembering the three Ps of mediated communication—that it is powerful, public, and permanent (see pp. 69–70).

Third, despite common beliefs, little evidence exists supporting the stereotype that men can't share their feelings in relationships. In close same-sex friendships, for example, both men and women disclose deeply and broadly (Shelton et al., 2010). In cross-sex romantic involvements, men often disclose at levels equal to or greater than those of their female partners (Canary, Emmers-Sommer, & Faulkner, 1997). However, studies do suggest that both men and women feel more comfortable disclosing to females than to males (Dindia & Allen, 1992).

Fourth, in all cultures, people vary widely in the degree to which they self-disclose. Some people naturally share more of their thoughts and feelings whereas others don't (Jourard, 1964). Trying to force someone with a different idea of self-disclosure to match your style of self-disclosure—for example, to open up or to share less information—not only is unethical but can also damage the relationship by causing resentment (Luft, 1970).

Fifth, different cultures have distinct overall patterns for self-disclosure. For instance, individuals of Asian descent tend to disclose less than do people of European ancestry (Barnlund, 1975). In fact, Euro-Americans generally tend to disclose more frequently than do almost any other cultural group, including Asians, Hispanics, and African Americans (Klopf, 2001).

Self-Disclosure Skills

Given the importance of self-disclosure in building your interpersonal relationships, putting energy into strengthening your self-disclosure skills is enormously worthwhile. These practices can help:

- **Know your thoughts and feelings.** When you disclose to others, you affect their lives and relationship decisions. Consequently, you're ethically obligated to be certain about the truth of information before you share it. This is especially important when disclosing intimate feelings, such as romantic interest. For instance, don't tell someone you are dating that you love him or her unless you're sure that's how you really feel.

- **Know your audience.** Whether it's a text message or an intimate conversation, think carefully about how others will perceive your disclosure and how it will impact their thoughts and feelings about you. If you're unsure about a disclosure's appropriateness, don't disclose. Instead, talk more generally about the issue or topic first, gauging the person's level of comfort with the conversation before deciding whether to disclose. For example, suppose you decide that you do love your new boyfriend, but you're not sure how he feels about you. Instead of blurting out "I love you!" broach the subject gently, by saying something like "I've really been enjoying spending time with you. We seem to have so much in common, and I have to admit—I'm starting to have some strong feelings for you." If he seems happy to hear this, it may be OK to say "I love you." If he appears uncomfortable, you may want to hold off disclosing your love.

- **Don't make assumptions about gender.** Just because someone is a woman doesn't mean she will disclose freely, and just because a person is a man doesn't mean he's incapable of discussing his feelings. Even though men *and* women tend to feel more comfortable disclosing to women, don't assume that when you're talking with a woman, she'll expect you to share your innermost self. Instead, be aware of how individual people respond to your disclosures, and adjust accordingly.

- **Be sensitive to cultural differences.** When you're interacting with people from cultural backgrounds different from yours, disclose gradually to test their responses. Don't make assumptions about what another person will disclose based on his or her ethnicity. For example, just because a new acquaintance is Italian American doesn't mean she will want to openly share her innermost thoughts and feelings. Likewise, just because someone is Chinese American doesn't mean he will be reluctant to disclose.

- **Don't force others to self-disclose.** Though it's perfectly appropriate to let someone know you're available to listen, it's unethical and destructive to try to make others share personal information with you if they don't want to. People have reasons for not wanting to share certain things about themselves—just as you have reasons for protecting your own privacy.

FIGURE 10.2

SELF-DISCLOSURE SKILLS

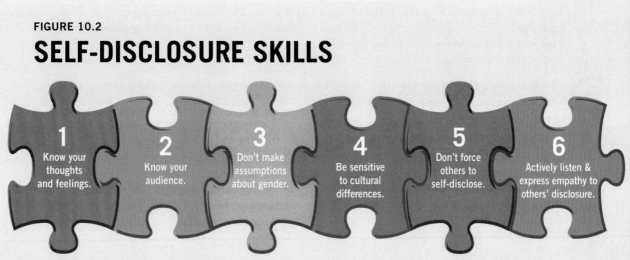

1 Know your thoughts and feelings.
2 Know your audience.
3 Don't make assumptions about gender.
4 Be sensitive to cultural differences.
5 Don't force others to self-disclose.
6 Actively listen & express empathy to others' disclosure.

PointaDesign/Shutterstock

MAKING COMMUNICATION CHOICES

I DON'T WANT TO HEAR THIS!

1 CONSIDER THE DILEMMA

Growing up, your parents fought constantly, and the bitterness of their relationship tore you apart because you love each of them dearly. Now they are divorced, and you live with your mom, who bad-mouths your dad all the time. You try to be a supportive listener, but it's hard because you love your dad, and her comments are so toxic.

The situation escalates when your mom starts dating John. She and John get along really well, but the contrast between their relationship and your parents' former marriage makes things worse. When you visit your dad, he says horrible things about your mom and John, and your mom is still slandering your dad. There seems to be no escape from the negativity, and you're stressed, exhausted, and unhappy.

One night you're at your mom's, and she's on the phone with John. After she hangs up, she says to you, "I'm so glad to have John in my life. He supports me in ways your father never did. And he's a better lover and friend than your father ever was. I can't believe I wasted all those years with your dad!" Listening to her, you feel sick to your stomach. Noticing your reaction, she says, "I'm sorry for always dumping this stuff on you. It's just I've felt so out of control recently. And you're such a good listener—it means so much to me to be able to tell you everything!"

2 CONNECT THE RESEARCH

Communication scholars Tamara Afifi, Tara McManus, Susan Hutchinson, and Birgitta Baker (2007) studied divorced parents' *inappropriate disclosures* to their children: comments that insulted the other parent; were age–inappropriate; or placed the child in an uncomfortable position as mediator, counselor, or friend.

The most frequent type of inappropriate parental disclosure was insults. Parents who slandered one another to their children often felt justified saying such things to support "their side of the story" regarding the breakup. Parents who believed their lives were out of control were more likely to dump inappropriate information on their kids.

Parents' inappropriate disclosures had destructive effects on their children. Kids who said "My parent tells me negative things that my other parent has done" or "My parent tells me things that a child shouldn't have to hear" reported poorer physical and mental health, less psychological well-being, and increased stress.

What can you take away from this research? Although self-disclosure is essential for building and sustaining intimacy, sharing inappropriate *negative* information can be devastating. When you are in a position to share negative information, consider what is appropriate, effective, and ethical given the situation and relationships involved.

3 COMMUNICATE

Before making a communication choice, consider the facts of the situation, and think about the negative disclosure research. Also, reflect on what you've learned so far about self-disclosure in relationships (pp. 238–245) and dynamics of family relationships (pp. 221–223). Then answer these questions:

1 If you were in your mom's place, would you be thinking and talking in similar ways?

2 How is your mom making you feel? What challenges do you face in explaining your feelings to her? In getting her to stop her behavior? How can they be overcome?

3 What are you going to say to your mom?

- **When others disclose to you, actively listen and express empathy.**
  In situations in which people opt to share personal information with
  you, be sure to treat their disclosures with the same respect you expect
  from others when you share such information. Show them that you're
  listening by providing *positive feedback* and using a *people-oriented listening style*, as discussed in Chapter 7. You can demonstrate that you care
  about what they're saying by expressing *empathy*—trying to see things
  from their perspective and showing compassion for them (see Chapter 2
  for more tips on empathy).

Managing Relationship Tensions

Self-disclosure can create positive outcomes, including a sense of trust and
increased intimacy. But it also brings with it challenges, such as how to avoid
feeling vulnerable, and how to retain a sense of your separate self as you get
closer to others. Learning how to resolve such tensions is critical for maintaining healthy, happy interpersonal relationships.

As you engage in relationships, competing impulses or tensions often arise
in your feelings toward your relational partners. These tensions are known
as **relational dialectics** (Baxter, 1990). For example, you may want to "bare
your soul" to your partners, but you don't want to be vulnerable. Or, though
you want to feel close, you also want to remain independent. Sometimes
you want your partners to be predictable, but then again, you don't want
things to get boring. Such dialectics aren't necessarily bad for relationships;
rather, they occur naturally as you become more intimate. At the same time,
competently managing these tensions will help you better sustain your
relationships.

Relational dialectics take three common forms: openness versus protection, autonomy versus connection, and novelty versus predictability. Let's
consider how each develops and how you can deal with them.

Openness versus Protection

The first relational dialectic is *openness versus protection*. As we discussed
earlier in this chapter, when you mutually share private information with
others, relationships naturally develop. Most of us enjoy the feeling of connection and mutual insight that such self-disclosure creates. But although
people want to be open with their relationship partners (whether lovers,
family members, friends, or coworkers), they also desire to keep certain
aspects of their selves—such as their most private thoughts and feelings—
protected. Too much openness can give people an uncomfortable sense that
they've lost their privacy, which can make them feel vulnerable.

According to **communication privacy management theory** (Petronio, 2000),
individuals create *information boundaries* by carefully choosing the kind of

Reality TV shows that feature families, like *Keeping Up with the Kardashians*, often reveal the intimate communication that takes place between parents and children as well as siblings. The Kardashians, for example, made their mark by having almost no communication rules, discussing all topics with one another and, therefore, sharing these disclosures with viewers. How do you think so much openness can affect family communication?

Toby Canham/Getty Images

private information they reveal and the people with whom they share it. These boundaries are constantly shifting, depending on the degree of risk associated with disclosing information (Afifi & Steuber, 2010). The more comfortable people feel disclosing, the more likely they are to reveal sensitive information. Inversely, people are less likely to share when they expect negative reactions to the disclosure.

Think about how people manage information boundaries in romances and friendships. Over time, most lovers and friends learn that it's best not to talk about certain issues, topics, or people; otherwise, conflicts may occur (Dainton, Zelley, & Langan, 2003). As a result, partners negotiate **communication rules**— conditions governing what they can (and can't) talk about, how they can discuss such topics, and who else should have access to this information (Petronio & Caughlin, 2006). Such rules can be perfectly healthy as long as both people agree on them and as long as the avoided issues aren't central to the relationship's survival.

For example, when Steve and his wife, Kelly, were engaged but living in different cities, Kelly would go out dancing with her friends on the weekends. Often, she and her friends would meet handsome, charming, and funny men, and spend the evening chatting and dancing with them. Kelly—being scrupulously honest—would then call Steve and tell him all about it. But Steve was stressing about getting his graduate school work done, so hearing details about these men would make him mad, and the conversation would sour. After several of these unpleasant encounters, they negotiated a new rule: when Kelly goes out dancing with her friends, just tell Steve whether the evening was fun or not, and leave it at that. Because Steve trusted Kelly, he was fine with her providing a general assessment while leaving out the details that would spark his jealousy.

Now consider how communication rules governing openness versus protection are negotiated within families. In some families, members feel free to talk about any topic, at any time, and in any situation. In other families, discussion of sensitive topics—such as politics, religion, or money—may be considered appropriate only in certain settings. For instance, some parents might discuss their finances with a child planning how to pay for college but would not discuss such matters with their younger children. In other families, people never, under any circumstances, talk about topics the family has defined as completely off-limits, such as sex, recreational drug use, legal or financial woes, or serious health problems. Breaking a family communication rule by forcing discussion of a "forbidden" topic can cause intense emotional discomfort among other family members. It may even prompt the family to exclude the "rule breaker" from future family interactions. Keep this in mind before you force discussion of an issue that other family members consider off-limits. If you believe that breaking a communication taboo in your family is essential for a family member's health, consider doing it with the help of a mediator, such as a family therapist or a family-intervention specialist.

Managing openness versus protection through communication rules is also essential within the workplace. Communication rules in the workplace govern whether communications are formal or informal, whether they are personal or impersonal, and even which channels (e-mail, instant messaging, texting, printed memos, face-to-face conversations) are the most appropriate for use among coworkers.

Autonomy versus Connection

The second relational dialectic is *autonomy versus connection*. People form close relationships mostly out of a desire to bond with other human beings. Yet if you come to feel *so* connected to your partners that your own identity seems to dissolve, you may choose to pull back and reclaim some of your autonomy, or independence.

The tension between autonomy versus connection is especially pronounced in romantic and family relationships. When you're in a romantic relationship and enter the *integrating* stage (see Chapter 9), family members, friends, and colleagues start treating you as a couple—for example, always inviting the two of you to social events. This may cause you to start wondering if you have an identity separate from that of your partner. As a student of ours once told his partner when describing this feeling, "I'm not me anymore; I'm *us*."

As with openness versus protection, honest discussion of the issue and relationship rules can help people better balance autonomy versus connection. For instance, a couple may establish a weekly "date night" to reinforce their connection to each other as well as a weekly "me night," during which

DOUBLE TAKE

AUTONOMY (VS) CONNECTION

Spending time with friends can be one of life's great joys. Even though you choose friends based on your similarities and shared interests, spending time pursuing personal hobbies can help you maintain your separate sense of self.

manley099/istockphoto   Rob Tringali/SportsChrome/Getty

each person can get together with other friends or spend time on a hobby or another interest.

Within families, managing autonomy versus connection is even harder. As children move through their teen years, they begin to assert their independence from parents (Crosnoe & Cavanagh, 2010). Their peers eventually replace parents and other family members as having the most influence on their interpersonal decisions (Golish, 2000). This "pulling away from the family" can be difficult for parents or caregivers, who have come to count on the connection with their children.

Connections with family can also cause stress when family members seem blind to who you really are. For example, suppose your mother still treats you as the baby of the family when you get together with older siblings during the holidays—even though you're in your 20s or 30s. In this case, you may want to try spending some time alone with her, discussing your latest professional achievements. This will help remind her that you're not only "her baby" but also an independent, successful adult.

Novelty versus Predictability

The final relational dialectic is the tension between people's need for excitement and change and their need for stability—known as *novelty versus predictability*. We all like the security that comes with knowing how our lovers, family members, friends, and coworkers will behave, how we'll behave, and how our relationships will unfold. For example, romances are more successful when partners act in predictable ways that reduce uncertainty (Berger & Bradac, 1982). However, predictability can also trigger boredom. As you get to know people better, the excitement you felt when the relationship was new wears off, and things can start to feel boring. Reconciling the desire for predictability with the need for novelty is one of the most profound emotional challenges facing relationship partners, especially those involved in romances.

No one perfect solution exists for maintaining a balance between novelty and predictability. But your best bet for dealing with this dialectic is to share novel experiences with your partner—activities that keep your relationship from growing stale. For example, you might go on an adventurous vacation once a year that requires learning new skills together, such as scuba diving. Or you might seek out different activities to share with a friend or sibling, such as hiking, a road trip, or a baking class. Regardless of the particulars, the key is exposure to interesting, new experiences that you can share with each other.

Sustaining Your Relationships

Some relationships make it, and some don't, and there's not much you can do about it, right? Wrong. Relationships don't survive because of fate or magic; they survive because people invest time and energy into making them work. You can help your relationships endure by learning relational maintenance tactics and by providing support when others need it.

In the Google Chrome ad "Jess Time," a father and daughter work through the transition of her living at home to her being away at college. To compensate for the loss of proximity, they use IM and video chat to support each other, share their day-to-day feelings, and keep each other upbeat. Although it's just an advertisement selling Google software, it reflects a reality that many of us experience. When Steve's oldest son, Kyle, left for college, their day-to-day efforts to support and sustain their closeness didn't change—just the means through which they communicated them. Rather than hanging out together in Kyle's room in the evenings, listening to music and talking, they now text each other daily and Skype weekly.

Many people believe that relationships just happen—that love affairs, family bonds, friendships, and professional affiliations arise on their own, run their natural course, and then succeed or fail according to fate. But a core principle of this book is that *you control the destiny of your relationships through the communication choices you make.* When you use all available means—online and off—to communicate positively, assure partners of your commitment, share your feelings, and support partners in times of need, your relationships thrive. When you communicate negatively, keep partners guessing about your degree of commitment, hide your feelings, and fail to support partners, your relationships wither.

Over the course of the one-minute ad "Jess Time," a father and daughter discuss issues big and small, from what tie he should wear to how she can handle the stress of college. Their use of IM and video chat allows them to remain close despite being physically apart. How do you maintain long-distance relationships?

Courtesy of Google

Relational Maintenance

Relational maintenance refers to the use of communication behaviors to keep a relationship strong and to ensure that each party continues to draw satisfaction from the relationship (Stafford, Dainton, & Haas, 2000). Across years of research, communication scholar Laura Stafford has observed three strategies that help romantic partners, family members, friends, and co-workers maintain their relationships: *positivity*, *assurances*, and *self-disclosure* (Stafford, 2010).

Positivity. Arguably the most powerful maintenance tactic in sustaining healthy relationships is **positivity**—communicating in a cheerful and optimistic fashion, doing unsolicited favors, and giving unexpected gifts (Stafford, 2010). Cross- and same-sex partners involved in romantic relationships, and family members, friends, and coworkers all routinely cite positivity as the most important maintenance tactic for ensuring happiness (Dainton & Stafford, 1993; Haas & Stafford, 2005; Stafford, 2010). You use positivity when you[2]

- try to make interactions with others enjoyable;
- make an effort to build others up by giving them compliments;
- strive to be fun, upbeat, and optimistic with others.

---

[2]All bulleted items that follow adapted from the revised relationship maintenance behavior scale of Stafford (2010).

You undermine positivity when you

- constantly look for and complain about problems in your relationships with others without offering solutions;
- whine, pout, and sulk when you don't get your way;
- criticize favors and gifts you've received from others.

How can you implement positivity in your interpersonal relationships? Start doing favors for your relationship partners without being asked, and surprise them with small gifts that show you care. Invest energy into making each encounter enjoyable. Avoid complaining about problems that have no solutions, ridiculing others, whining or sulking when you don't get your way, and demanding favored treatment from others. Show appreciation when someone does something nice for you. Positivity can be especially helpful at work, since it can help offset the stresses you and your coworkers will inevitably face. (See Table 10.1.)

TABLE 10.1

STRATEGIES FOR MAINTAINING RELATIONSHIPS

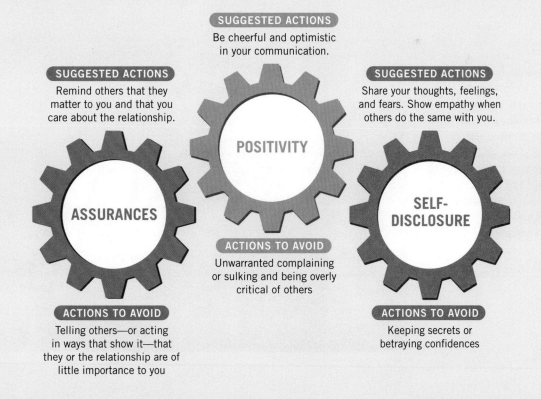

SUGGESTED ACTIONS
Be cheerful and optimistic in your communication.

SUGGESTED ACTIONS
Remind others that they matter to you and that you care about the relationship.

SUGGESTED ACTIONS
Share your thoughts, feelings, and fears. Show empathy when others do the same with you.

POSITIVITY

ASSURANCES

SELF-DISCLOSURE

ACTIONS TO AVOID
Unwarranted complaining or sulking and being overly critical of others

ACTIONS TO AVOID
Telling others—or acting in ways that show it—that they or the relationship are of little importance to you

ACTIONS TO AVOID
Keeping secrets or betraying confidences

Assurances. Another powerful maintenance tactic in boosting relationship satisfaction is the use of **assurances**—messages that emphasize how much your relationship partners mean to you, point out how important the relationships are to you, and show that you see a secure future together. You use assurances when you

- regularly tell your partners how important they are to you;
- talk about future plans and events that you'll share together;
- do and say things to demonstrate the depth of your feelings.

You undermine assurances when you

- suggest that other relationships and things in your life are more important than your relationship partners;
- tell your partners not to count on anything long-term;
- systematically avoid expressing any type of enduring relationship commitment to your partners.

In romantic relationships, family relationships, and friendships, you may express assurances directly by saying things like "I love you" or "You're my closest friend." You may also emphasize how much you value your time

Mediated communication provides lots of ways to maintain your relationships. Sending a text to tell your girlfriend you are thinking of her, posting a funny picture to brighten a friend's day, or sending a short video to your grandparents are easy ways to let others know you care.

Jordan Siemens/Getty Images

together—for example, sending a text message saying "c u soon; can't wait!" Assurances offered to close coworkers can boost intimacy and demonstrate that your relationships are based on choice rather than professional assignment. For example, inviting professional peers to join you in activities outside of the workplace shows that you consider them friends rather than just coworkers.

Self-Disclosure. As we discussed earlier, *self-disclosure* is the revealing of private information about yourself to others in interpersonal communication. Self-disclosure can foster intimacy with another person—for example, when you share increasingly personal information with a new friend as you get closer to him or her.

However, when you use self-disclosure as a relational maintenance tactic, the focus is on creating a climate of security and trust with others. You want to help your relationship partners feel that they can disclose their fears and other feelings to you without you judging, criticizing, or rejecting them. To encourage others to self-disclose, you must behave in ways that are predictable, trustworthy, and ethical. Over time, such behavior convinces your relationship partners that you'll welcome personal information from them. You use self-disclosure for relational maintenance when you

- tell your partners about your own fears and vulnerabilities;
- share your thoughts and emotions with them;
- encourage them to disclose their thoughts and feelings, and offer them empathy in return.

You undermine self-disclosure when you

- make fun of or criticize your relationship partners' perspectives;
- routinely hide important information from them;
- betray them by sharing confidential information about them with others.

To foster disclosure with your lovers, family members, and friends, routinely make time just to talk. Encourage them to share their thoughts and feelings about issues that matter to them, whether it's online, face-to-face, or by phone. When they share their feelings and concerns with you, respond in a respectful way by both showing that you've heard and understood them and not interrupting or letting other events distract you from listening. Avoid betraying secrets that your relationship partners have confided in you, and don't hide relevant information from them.

In your workplace relationships, you can use self-disclosure to create feelings of trust between you and your colleagues. This means following through on your promises, respecting confidences, and demonstrating honesty and integrity in your behavior. (See How to Communicate: Relationship Maintenance at Work on pp. 254–255.)

RELATIONSHIP MAINTENANCE AT WORK

 One way to improve your communication competence is by learning how to adapt to changing circumstances. Learn how to maintain your workplace relationships by going to LaunchPad at **bedfordstmartins.com/choicesconnections** and completing the **How to Communicate video scenario** for Chapter 10 to practice your skills.

CONSIDER THIS: For the last two years, you've worked side by side with Hannah. She is your closest friend at work, and she's funny, smart, and supportive. Recently, Hannah was promoted. Starting next week, she will be working in a different location and you will see her only occasionally.

WHAT WOULD YOU DO? The following advice illustrates how relational maintenance skills can allow your relationship to continue to thrive. As you watch the video, consider how the dialogue incorporates elements of positivity, assurances, and self-disclosure. Then, test your knowledge of key skills, and create your own responses to the **What if? video prompts**.

"I am so excited for you! I know how much this promotion means to you, and how hard you worked to get it. We should go out and celebrate sometime soon— my treat."

(1) USE POSITIVITY in your communication to let her know that your excitement about her good fortune outweighs your disappointment about not working with her anymore.

2 OFFER ASSURANCES TO HER,

emphasizing how much you value her friendship and making plans for continuing the relationship into the future.

"You know, you're really my best friend here. Don't think that just because you're moving that will end. We should set up a regular lunch date so we can stay caught up on all the stuff that's going on in our lives."

3 DISCLOSE YOUR FEELINGS to her, and encourage her to do the same in return.

"Although I'm thrilled for you, I'm sad for me. I'm really going to miss you. How are you feeling about it all?"

WHAT IF? But what if things don't work out as shown? Test your ability to adapt your communication by watching the What if? videos and planning a response for each situation.

1. What would you say when Hannah is noncommittal about continuing the relationship? "I don't think that's going to be possible. I'm going to be ridiculously busy the next few months and won't have time to get together."

2. How can you support Hannah when she says, "I'm terrified! I don't feel prepared at all for the new responsibilities I'm going to be facing. What have I gotten myself into?"

Supportive Communication

Positivity, assurances, and self-disclosure can be powerful tools for sustaining interpersonal relationships. But sometimes you need to do more. When you provide **supportive communication,** you express emotional support and offer personal assistance to lovers, family members, friends, or coworkers who need it (Burleson & MacGeorge, 2002). The need for such support can arise from a wide range of events—everything from being dumped by a romantic partner, getting laid off, or suffering a serious injury, to losing a loved one or failing an important exam. Skillful supportive messages convey sincere sympathy, concern, and encouragement. Messages are not supportive when they mock another person's need for support ("Don't be so dramatic"), tell the individual how he or she should feel ("Come on, snap out of it!"), or indicate that the person is somehow inadequate or blameworthy ("You brought this on yourself, you know").

Communication scholar and social support expert Amanda Holmstrom offers the following suggestions for providing competent supportive communication:[3]

1. *Make sure the person is ready to talk.* If the person appears too upset to talk, don't push it. Instead, make it clear that you care and want to help, and that you'll be there to listen when he or she needs you.

2. *Find the right place and time.* Once the person is ready to talk, find a place and a time where you can have a quiet conversation. Avoid distracting settings, such as parties, where you won't be able to focus. Find a time of the day when neither of you has other pressing obligations. If you are chatting online, be sure not to multitask (checking Twitter or WhatsApp, playing games), so you can devote your full attention to the person.

3. *Ask good questions.* Start with open-ended questions (those that don't require just a yes or no answer), such as "How are you feeling?" or "What's on your mind?" Then follow up with more targeted questions, such as "Are you eating and sleeping OK?" (If the person says no, that may indicate depression.) Don't assume that because you've been in a similar situation, you know what someone is going through. Resist any urge to say "I know just how you feel."

4. *Legitimize, don't minimize.* Don't dismiss the problem or the significance of the person's feelings by saying things like "It could have been worse" or "Don't worry; you'll find someone else!" Research shows that these comments are unhelpful. Instead, let the person know that whatever he or she is feeling is OK ("It's terrible that you are going through this and completely understandable that you are upset").

5. *Listen actively.* Drawing on your listening skills from Chapter 7, show interest in what the person is saying. Make eye contact, lean toward the individual, and provide feedback—such as "Uh-huh" and "Yeah"—when appropriate.

---

[3]Content that follows provided to the author by Dr. Amanda Holmstrom and published with permission. The authors thank Dr. Holmstrom for her contribution.

6. *Offer advice cautiously.* Everyone wants to help someone who is suffering, so you may feel compelled to jump right in and start offering advice. But often that's not helpful, and it may not be what the person wants. He or she may only need a sympathetic ear at the moment. Only give advice when the individual asks you for it, if you have relevant expertise or experience, and if it suggests an action that the person can actually do. When in doubt, ask if the person would like your advice—or just hold back until asked.

7. *Show concern and give praise.* Let the person know you genuinely care and are concerned about his or her well-being ("I am *so* sorry for your loss" or "You're really important to me"). Build the person up by praising his or her strength in handling this challenge ("You've got a lot going on, and you've done so well dealing with it"). Showing care and concern helps connect you to the person, and giving praise can help him or her feel better and gather strength that will be needed to tackle the problem at hand.

✓ **LearningCurve** can help you review! Go to **bedfordstmartins.com /choicesconnections**.

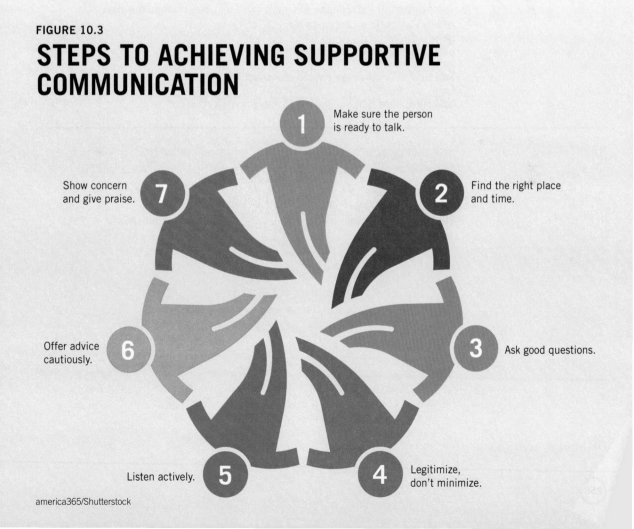

FIGURE 10.3

STEPS TO ACHIEVING SUPPORTIVE COMMUNICATION

1. Make sure the person is ready to talk.
2. Find the right place and time.
3. Ask good questions.
4. Legitimize, don't minimize.
5. Listen actively.
6. Offer advice cautiously.
7. Show concern and give praise.

america365/Shutterstock

CHAPTER ⑩ REVIEW

CHAPTER RECAP

- According to **social penetration theory,** people use **self-disclosure** to reveal themselves to others.
- **Self-disclosure** builds **intimacy** in relationships. Intimacy is self-perpetuating: the more intimacy you feel, the more you disclose; and as you disclose more, feelings of intimacy deepen.
- Though **relational dialectics** can bring challenges to relationships, competent communication can help you manage these tensions.
- You can sustain your relationships through **relational maintenance,** which includes **positivity, assurances,** and **self-disclosure**.
- Providing competent **supportive communication** can help you convey sincere sympathy, concern, and encouragement to your interpersonal relationship partners.

LAUNCHPAD

LaunchPad for *Choices & Connections* offers unique video scenarios and encourages self-assessment through adaptive quizzing. Go to **bedfordstmartins.com /choicesconnections** to get access.

✔ LearningCurve adaptive quizzes

 How to Communicate video scenarios

 Video clips that illustrate key concepts

KEY TERMS

Self-disclosure, p. 239

Social penetration theory, p. 239

Intimacy, p. 240

 Relational dialectics, p. 245

Communication privacy management theory, p. 245

Communication rules, p. 246

 Relational maintenance, p. 250

Positivity, p. 250

Assurances, p. 252

 Supportive communication, p. 256

✓ Looking for more review questions? **LearningCurve** can help you master key concepts from this chapter. Go to **bedfordstmartins.com /choicesconnections**.

1 Which of the following is *not* true about how people communicate self-disclosure?

a. People disclose more online than in person.

b. Women tend to disclose more than men.

c. Disclosure can help relieve stress.

d. People in all cultures disclose at equal rates.

2 In close relationships, partners often negotiate conditions governing what they can (and can't) talk about. This is known as _____.

a. communication rules

b. intimacy

c. communication privacy management theory

d. supportive communication

3 Family members can experience the _____ relational dialectic when children grow up and become less dependent on their guardians for emotional support.

a. novelty vs. predictability   **c.** autonomy vs. connection

b. openness vs. connection   **d.** passiveness vs. argumentativeness

4 Constantly criticizing someone or complaining about problems but not offering solutions undermines _____ in relationships.

a. self-disclosure   **c.** positivity

b. assurance   **d.** intimacy

5 When providing competent supportive communication, you can _____ by commenting on the person's strength in handling a crisis.

a. ask good questions   **c.** offer advice

b. listen actively   **d.** give praise

ACTIVITIES

1 Communication Rules

With a partner, revisit the discussion of the openness versus protection relational dialectic and communication privacy management theory on pages 245–247. Discuss how you think this applies to romantic relationships. First, identify topics or issues that "must" be talked about (i.e., topics about which romantic partners must be open). Then, consider more complicated topics, as well as topics that "should absolutely not" be discussed (attraction to a coworker, flirting with strangers, sexual infidelity). Finally, analyze how these categories affect communication in relationships. How does keeping things from a partner impact intimacy? How would you deal with differences in topics that must or should not be discussed?

2 Relationship Reflection

Write a brief reflection paper analyzing how you engage in relationship maintenance. Pick a close relationship in your life (romance, family member, or friendship), and describe typical interactions that you have with that person. How often do you communicate in ways that bolster and undermine positivity, assurances, and self-disclosure? Provide specific examples. How does this communication impact the relationship—positively and negatively? How can the relational maintenance tactics help you improve your relationship?

11

Small Group Communication

In a cabin called Poet's Loft 50 miles north of San Francisco, a group of filmmakers brainstorm ideas for a movie plot. After two days of debates and discarded suggestions, they settle on a single question: How would the toys feel if Andy, their owner, left for college? (Lehrer, 2010). This simple premise would guide the team from Pixar Animation Studio over the next three years while making the movie *Toy Story 3*.

Since Pixar released its first feature-length animated film (the original *Toy Story* in 1995), the company has produced a string of critically and commercially successful films, including *Finding Nemo*, *The Incredibles*, *Wall-E*, and *Up*. As other major studios lose money on the majority of their films, Pixar cranks out blockbuster after blockbuster, averaging revenues of over $550 million per film and grossing over $7.2 billion total worldwide (Lehrer, 2010; The Walt Disney Company, n.d.). How does the company do it? By turning over insightful story ideas to small groups of dedicated, talented employees who then work together to produce films that capture the hearts and imaginations of children and adults alike.

Whereas most animation studios rely on freelance artists to develop movies, Pixar cultivates employee teams that work together year after year on different projects. According to Ed Catmull (2008), Pixar cofounder and president, the company's commitment to ongoing teams is integral to the studio's success because it "construct[s] an environment that nurtures trusting and respectful relationships and unleashes everyone's creativity. If we get that right, the result is a vibrant community where talented people are loyal to one another and their collective work, [and] everyone feels that they are part of something extraordinary."

Everyone who works on a Pixar film—illustrators, animators, producers, technicians, directors, and more—is responsible for some part of the creative effort. When all team members have a stake in the success of the film, they are more likely to support one another, provide useful feedback, and come together to help solve problems.

Even the Pixar campus layout fosters such collaboration. The late Steve Jobs, a Pixar cofounder, insisted on designing spaces where people could easily meet and interact. He knew "that the real challenge of Pixar was getting people from different cultures—computer scientists and cartoonists—to work together, to really collaborate" (NPR Staff, 2012). The result is Pixar's large, central atrium, which contains employees' mailboxes, the company's meeting rooms, the cafeteria, the coffee bar, and even the main bathrooms.

According to Brad Bird, director of *The Incredibles* and *Ratatouille*, "The atrium initially might seem like a waste of space . . . But Steve realized that when people run into each other, when they make eye contact, things happen" (Lehrer, 2011).

Thanks to its commitment to teamwork in everything from the original idea for a movie to the layout of its buildings, Pixar consistently produces innovative films that set new standards for technical, creative, and financial success. In the case of *Toy Story 3*, the group's collaborative effort resulted in a movie that won Academy Awards for Best Animated Feature and Best Original Song in 2011, and is the top-grossing animated film of all time.

Pixar is not the only company to score great successes by using small groups (or *teams*, as they are often called in the workplace) to conduct its business. Most businesses rely on small groups and teams to manage key assignments and tasks, including designing smartphone apps (product development), developing customer satisfaction surveys (customer relations), creating presentations about new products (sales), and organizing sponsorships of local charity events (marketing) (Kozlowski & Bell, 2003). Yet small groups aren't limited to the workplace; they exist in many different areas of your life. For instance, you might meet with your family to decide where to go on vacation next year, or work with a group of classmates on a school project. Maybe you're part of a homeowners association or a town council. In all of these cases and countless more, you are communicating in small groups. To generate the most value from these experiences, you need to know how small groups operate and how to best communicate within them. In this chapter, you'll learn:

- The defining characteristics and various types of small groups
- How effective small groups communicate
- How individual characteristics affect small groups
- Ways to address the challenges of participating in virtual small groups

✓ **LearningCurve** can help you review! Go to **bedfordstmartins.com /choicesconnections**.

Defining Small Groups

> Participating in groups can help you accomplish tasks that would be difficult to do on your own. But working in groups is not always easy. In order to increase the chances for a group's success, it helps to know why small groups form and what stages they go through.

What makes a collection of individuals a small group? Would three friends planning a bridal shower constitute a small group? What about parents talking outside a dance studio as they wait for their children's lesson to end? Although it may seem as though the people in both of these situations would be considered a small group, only the former matches how communication scholars define the term. A **small group** is three or more interdependent people who share a common identity and who communicate to achieve common goals. Let's take a closer look at the defining characteristics of small groups, the different types, and the phases of small group development.

Characteristics of Small Groups

A small group has four defining characteristics. First, it is made up of inter-dependent persons. This means each person's behavior influences the entire group. If one person doesn't follow through on an assigned job, the other members could fall behind schedule or fail to accomplish their shared goals. For example, planning a friend's bridal shower requires coordinating various

Whether you're working on a project in person, planning a trip with friends virtually, or coming together to create music, like the band fun., it is important that all members share an identity as a group. When have you been part of groups or teams that had a strong identity? How did members create this sense?

(Clockwise from top left) Chris Schmidt/Getty Images; Kevin Mazur/WireImags/Getty Images; Debbie Noda/Modesto Bee/ZUMAPRESS/Alamy

responsibilities. One person forgetting to order the cake causes a problem for the whole group.

Second, small groups have at least three people. After that, scholars disagree about when a group is no longer considered "small." For example, communication scholar Thomas Socha (1997) suggests that a small group is 3–15 people. In practice, however, the upper limit on the number of people in a small group depends on how the communication changes as the group gets larger. Imagine that 30 people will be attending a bridal shower. It would be very hard—even messy—to involve all 30 attendees in planning the event. Instead, you'd want to have a smaller group take over the effort, then share the plan with the other attendees. For the purposes of this book, we will say that a group must be small enough to allow all members to have input in coordinating its activities (Socha, 1997).

Third, members of a small group share a common identity—they see themselves as a group. This makes small groups different from a random assortment of people—say, seven strangers standing together and chatting while waiting to cross a street. After being together for a while, small groups develop rituals, inside jokes, and stories that further strengthen their identity. A friend planning the bridal shower might say, "I spoke to Mr. Spandex today about the menu, and he said . . . ," evoking laughter from other group members who share knowledge of the food caterer's fondness for wearing spandex. As a group develops, its common identity gives members a strong sense of belonging and pride. Dwight Conquergood's (1994) studies of urban gang life in Chicago—discussed in Chapter 2—found that gang graffiti, hand signs, dress, and manner of speech all maintain gang identity. Similarly, a small group will have unique verbal and nonverbal codes that reflect its common identity.

Finally, members in a small group communicate to achieve common goals. Suppose a handful of friends are waiting for a yoga class to start. If they're communicating to pass the time ("How's your week going?"), they're not a small group. But once they decide to plan the bridal shower together, they've created a common purpose and would be considered a small group.

Today, technology makes it increasingly likely that you will work in a team that rarely or never meets in person. A team of three or more people who communicate primarily through technology to achieve common goals is known as a **virtual small group**. This could include working with classmates on a project for an online course or planning a vacation with family members who reside in different states or countries.

Two additional characteristics are unique to virtual small groups. First, team members are separated by physical distance; in some cases, they may be on entirely different continents (Bell & Kozlowski, 2002). Second, virtual small groups rely mainly on technology to manage information, data, and personal communications (Bell & Kozlowski, 2002). If you primarily use discussion boards and Wikis to develop a course project with a few classmates and meet only occasionally in person, you're in a virtual small group.

Types of Small Groups

There are two basic types of small groups. **Primary groups** are the individuals who meet your basic life, psychological, and social needs. For instance, your family and friends protect you from harm and loneliness. (Or at least you hope they will!) Interpersonal communication skills—such as self-disclosure and relational maintenance—are important for developing and maintaining primary group relationships.

Secondary groups consist of people with whom you want to achieve specific goals or perform tasks. Some secondary groups have a short life, such as neighbors brainstorming ideas for a Fourth of July block party. Other secondary groups work together over long periods of time, like the teams at Pixar. Table 11.1 lists different types of secondary groups you might be part of at school,

TABLE 11.1

TYPES OF SECONDARY GROUPS

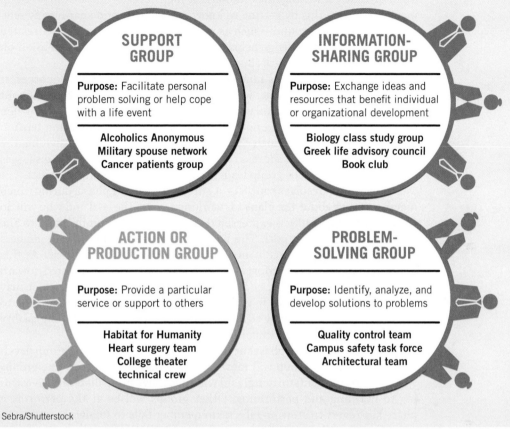

SUPPORT GROUP

Purpose: Facilitate personal problem solving or help cope with a life event

**Alcoholics Anonymous
Military spouse network
Cancer patients group**

INFORMATION-SHARING GROUP

Purpose: Exchange ideas and resources that benefit individual or organizational development

**Biology class study group
Greek life advisory council
Book club**

ACTION OR PRODUCTION GROUP

Purpose: Provide a particular service or support to others

**Habitat for Humanity
Heart surgery team
College theater technical crew**

PROBLEM-SOLVING GROUP

Purpose: Identify, analyze, and develop solutions to problems

**Quality control team
Campus safety task force
Architectural team**

Sebra/Shutterstock

in your community, or at work. In this chapter, we explore the concepts and skills you need to communicate competently in secondary groups.

Development of Small Groups

When you first join a group, it's natural to wonder how the group will work together. How will it decide on a plan? How will members get to know one another? How will the group handle disagreements? What will be the group identity? Although each group is unique, in general, groups go through five phases—forming, storming, norming, performing, and adjourning (Tuckman, 1965; Tuckman & Jensen, 1977). You can tell what phase a group is in by how members communicate with one another, which changes over time.

A small group starts in the **forming** phase—during which members become acquainted with one another and seek to understand the task. When a group first comes together, there is a high level of uncertainty. Group members relieve this by getting to know one another and sharing any relevant personal background—such as prior experiences or interests—related to the task. This knowledge helps the group start to focus its attention on discussing goals for the task (Bushe & Coetzer, 2007).

As the group becomes familiar with its task and with one another, it moves to the **storming** phase, when members express different ideas about how to approach the task and who will take on leadership roles. This is when personality differences and power struggles may surface, creating tension in the group. To prevent such clashes from stalling progress or dividing the group, members should address conflict immediately. Chapter 12 discusses the principles and skills group leaders can use to manage such conflict.

As the group resolves conflicts, it enters the **norming** phase, during which members agree about the plans for working toward the goal and who will do what. The group's unity is expressed through members' commitment to one another and the team goal. The next phase is **performing**, when members actually make the required contributions for completing the task. At this phase, group members' efforts are well coordinated and directed toward achieving the goal. Finally, once the group completes its objectives, it may enter the **adjourning** phase, in which it disbands. Members take this time to evaluate and reflect on how well they accomplished the task and the quality of their relationships (Tuckman & Jensen, 1977).

Although these five phases are insightful for understanding group development, not every group will move in this orderly sequence. Some groups will have no conflict (storming) and will thus move immediately from forming to norming and performing. Other groups will be at the performing phase but revert to storming if a team member fails to follow through with an assignment. Occasionally, groups don't officially adjourn but continue on to a new task or just separate with no review. Paying attention to a group's developmental phase can help you adapt your communication to the needs of the group.

How Small Groups Communicate

Groups achieve their stated goals when members communicate in a cooperative and productive fashion. You can help the group build and maintain positive relationships by understanding how group roles work and adapting your communication to foster group unity.

If you look beyond the romantic scandals and friendship betrayals in most televised medical dramas—such as *House* or *Grey's Anatomy*—you can gain important insights as to how medical teams work. Doctors are the leaders who direct nurses, anesthesiologists, and lab technicians in emergency and

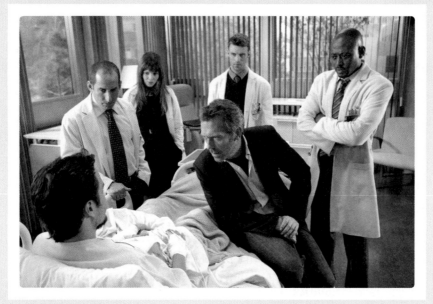

Fox Broadcasting Co./Photofest

Shows like *House* depict how important each role in a medical team is in creating the best possible outcomes for patients. How do the big and small roles you fulfill impact the groups or teams in your life?

operating rooms. Although there is a clear chain of command, everyone still communicates as a team, with nurses and technicians performing tasks and giving opinions. With everyone pitching in, the groups on these shows always seem to catch potential errors or find the correct diagnosis right in time.

But in real life, these groups communicate in much more complicated ways—and the consequences are more severe. If medical teams fail to clearly communicate, they risk making errors that can hurt patients (Healy, 2008). Consider this case: A patient in Tampa, Florida, went to the hospital for a routine stomach test. Instead, he was wrongly prepped for a cardiac catheterization, a complex procedure that involves inserting a thin tube into the groin, threading it to the heart, and then injecting dye so a cardiologist can look for potentially life-threatening blockages.[1] Shortly after the procedure started, a surgical team member realized the error and spoke up, preventing the mistake from going any further. But what if that person hadn't said anything? Though rare, these types of mix-ups do happen in hospitals. One study of medical errors in Colorado found that miscommunication—from surgeons or support staff—was the primary cause of such mistakes (Gardner, 2010).

---

[1]All information in this example from Greene (2008).

When communication breaks down in a small group, problems can occur. Even in a technically skilled medical team, success or failure is largely attributable to how members communicate with one another. Within any small group, members can set the stage for competent communication—and their own success—in five ways: balance group roles, build cohesiveness, establish positive norms, share leadership responsibilities, and manage physical space.

Balancing Group Roles

Within a small group, members fulfill different types of roles. **Formal roles** are assigned positions that members take on by appointment or election (Myers & Anderson, 2008). For example, a doctor is the "leader" of a surgical team. Other small groups, like project teams, often have formal roles—such as "chairperson" and "meeting recorder"—that bestow members with unique responsibilities, such as leading meetings and taking notes on group decisions.

In addition to formal roles, there are **group roles** (also known as *informal roles*)—specific patterns of behavior and communication that members develop from interacting over time. These roles help groups achieve goals, split the workload, organize tasks, and keep relations between group members effective. Group roles are classified in two ways: *task roles* support the group in achieving its goals; *maintenance roles* help strengthen and secure relationships among group members. Unlike formal roles, both task and maintenance roles are generally unassigned. Instead, various group members fulfill these roles as needed, depending on the situation.

Task Roles. When you're exchanging information about duties or goals important to your group, you are fulfilling **task roles.** For example, an interior designer who's remodeling a hotel lobby might share the following information during a design meeting: "The blueprints show that the lobby is 2,250 square feet." Another member of the group could ask, "Do you know how much natural lighting is available in the lobby entrance?" This exchange of messages about the task at hand helps the group carry out its work. Individuals serving task roles may provide ideas, clarify points, summarize discussion, and coordinate information.

Maintenance Roles. Through **maintenance roles,** group members communicate to build trusting and appreciative interpersonal relationships. Teams can achieve high levels of performance when members trust one another and feel personally valued (Campany, Dubinsky, Druskat, Mangino, & Flynn, 2007). Group members can create this environment by listening to one another, appropriately self-disclosing, and managing conflict. For example, some group members may be good at noticing when others are unusually quiet during a discussion and try to involve them ("Analise, what do you think about this proposal?"). Or perhaps another member knows how to spot and deal with tension in the group ("I think we've been at this too long. How about we take a break?"). Members who fill maintenance roles can sustain harmony and satisfaction within the group.

Group Role Flexibility. The group role each member plays changes depending on what is needed. For example, during the forming phase of a group project, you might be the person who makes sure everyone is acquainted by engaging in small talk (maintenance role). Later on, you might ask questions about decision alternatives (task role). The roles that members play depend on their personality and the situation. Extraverted individuals tend to naturally fall into maintenance roles. During a stressful situation, someone in the group may say something funny to relieve the tension (maintenance role) but then try to bring the group back to a productive conversation (task role).

In order for a group to be effective, members must take on both task and maintenance roles. Neglecting one or the other can create problems. If members focus only on getting the task done, they can exhaust themselves, which erodes morale. On the other hand, if they spend all their time building strong interpersonal bonds, they'll soon fall behind in completing tasks. By paying attention to both roles, a group becomes more productive, and its members can draw more satisfaction from working together.

Egocentric Roles. Successful groups also watch for and address the emergence of **egocentric roles,** which occurs when one team member's communication disrupts the group's efforts. For example, an overly aggressive group member can make others afraid to offer their ideas. One common egocentric role is the teammate who relies on other members to do all the work, a phenomenon known as **social loafing** (Harkins, 1987). This can spark resentment among other group members. For ideas on how to handle such behavior, see the How to Communicate: Social Loafing feature on pages 270–271.

Members of a small group can neutralize egocentric roles by establishing positive expectations for behaviors when the group first forms (this is known as *norms*; we discuss them later in the chapter) and by directly confronting disruptive behaviors (Druskat & Wolff, 2001). So if a teammate's constant joking becomes a distraction, someone in the group needs to tell that person that the behavior is keeping the group from doing its work. Otherwise, the group could lose focus and members could become upset, making it harder for the group to achieve its goals (Druskat & Wolff, 2001).

SOCIAL LOAFING

 One way to improve your communication competence is by adapting your communication in unpleasant encounters. Learn how to handle social loafing by going to LaunchPad at **bedfordstmartins.com/choicesconnections** and completing the **How to Communicate video scenario** for Chapter 11 to practice your skills.

CONSIDER THIS: As an assignment for your human communication course, you are part of a group that is making a 15-minute presentation explaining the cultural factors that influence communication. One group member, Paul, did not prepare his slides for the meeting in which the group is putting together the final presentation.

WHAT WOULD YOU DO? The following advice illustrates how addressing egocentric roles is important for a group to stay on task. As you watch the video, consider how the dialogue reflects both task and maintenance roles. Then, test your knowledge of key skills, and create your own responses to the **What if? video prompts**.

"At the last meeting we agreed that we all would have our parts of the presentation ready for today."

① **NOTE INSTANCES** of social loafing and use "we" language to remind Paul of his responsibility to the group.

2 REMAIN OPEN-MINDED

to possible reasons for why Paul is withholding effort, and remind him of how much you value his participation.

"I'm sure you've had a lot of other things going on that have kept you from getting your part done. But your contribution is still essential."

3 PRESENT A CLEAR PLAN

for what you'd like Paul to do, making sure to check whether it works for him, so he feels like a solution has been mutually agreed upon rather than him being told what to do.

"How about e-mailing us your slides by Friday so we can get the presentation set up? Does that work for you?"

 WHAT IF? But what if things don't work out as shown? Test your ability to adapt your communication by watching the What if? videos and planning a response for each situation.

1. How would you respond when Paul shifts blame to another group member? "Why don't you ask Jacob? He never sent me the information that I needed to finish the graph."

2. What if Paul avoids you and rushes off, saying, "Hey, can you just text me? I have to get to my cinema class"? How can you make sure he does his work?

Building Cohesiveness

One reason people join groups is that they fulfill a human need to belong (Baumeister & Leary, 1995). This need is best met when you are part of a **cohesive group,** in which members like one another and have a sense of camaraderie. In highly cohesive groups, members feel a strong sense of unity and commitment to the group's work. In groups that lack cohesion, members may feel disconnected from the group and have difficulty committing to group goals (Johnston, 2007). Members of a small group can build cohesiveness by appropriately self-disclosing, constructively managing conflict, and reserving time for external activity (such as having lunch together).

Establishing Positive Norms

Norms are the expectations about behavior within a group. For example, your work team may expect everyone to be on time for meetings and to arrive prepared. To have the most impact, norms should be clearly communicated. Members can establish positive norms by following a few simple steps:

- *Create ground rules.* When the group first comes together, take time to develop *ground rules*, or written expectations about behavior. For example, "Notify the group if you're going to miss a meeting, silence your phone during meetings, and don't interrupt when someone else is talking."
- *Begin and end meetings on time.* Waiting for everyone to arrive before you start a meeting sends a message that it's OK to arrive late. Similarly, regularly allowing meetings to go over their scheduled time is frustrating for group members with busy schedules.
- *Confront problem behaviors immediately.* Use the conflict-management skills discussed in Chapter 8 to confront behaviors that disrupt the group's interpersonal relationships or goals. For example, avoid making hurtful attacks ("Quit acting like such a baby!") and focus on collaboration.
- *Evaluate the group regularly.* To ensure the group is adequately working toward its goals, conduct regular evaluations (e.g., at the end of each meeting or month). Members can do this by openly identifying what's going well in the group and what needs to be changed. For instance, a group may be meeting its project deadlines, but if members are arguing over workload and responsibilities, that problem needs to be addressed.

Sharing Responsibility

As the previous example illustrated, everyone involved in a medical procedure—nurses, lab technicians, anesthesiologists, and doctors—plays an important role in its success (or failure). In addition to their specific task

Columbia Pictures/Courtesy Everett Collection

In *The Avengers*, a group of self-involved superheroes are forced to band together to take on a common enemy. Although an action movie may seem unrelated to small group communication, the characters actually take on a variety of roles—both maintenance and task—throughout the film, while also establishing norms (especially about behavior!) and sharing leadership responsibilities in order to fulfill their goal: defeat Loki.

roles, members are also committed to the group's mission: delivering proper and safe patient care. So when the surgical staff member realized the patient was getting the wrong procedure, the staff member felt a responsibility to speak up. When group members behave in this way, it is known as *shared leadership*; members influence one another's work, and they each feel a sense of ownership about their contributions and the group's goals. To encourage a sense of shared leadership, the formal leader of a small group should communicate in ways that help members accomplish their tasks, maintain strong interpersonal bonds, and encourage all members to engage in honest (but respectful) dialogue. Chapter 12 explores the concept of shared leadership in more detail.

Managing Physical Space

In any interaction, the physical environment affects the communication process. In small group situations, *semi-fixed features* of the environment—those that can be easily moved or changed, such as furniture and chairs—influence how group members communicate with one another (Sommer, 1965). For example, members of highly cohesive groups tend to sit closer together than do those in less cohesive groups. Additionally, those who occupy seats at the head of a table or in a center position are more likely to be perceived as leaders.

To manage physical space in ways that support communication, teams should look for a space that fits their needs, such as a quiet, comfortable environment for meetings, or a room with whiteboards so they can list ideas generated during brainstorming sessions. In a virtual small group, members should make sure everyone can be seen on videoconference and has access to a microphone. If you plan accordingly, the physical space you meet in can positively influence your group's communication.

The Self's Influence on Small Group Communication

Your self-concept shapes how you communicate in small groups. Everything from your personality to your gender and cultural background affects your communication choices and other group members' perceptions of you. By enhancing your self-awareness, you can communicate more competently in small groups and teams.

In the movie *Moneyball*, Peter Brand (played by Jonah Hill) is a young, newly hired assistant general manager for the Oakland A's. A Yale-educated economist, Peter uses obscure game-performance statistics to evaluate players' talent. His unconventional approach contrasts with the established baseball scouting practice of judging a player's potential by running speed, game techniques, and gut impressions. When he attends his first draft planning meeting, Peter is treated with resentment and hostility by the other (and older) Oakland A's scouts.

Jonah Hill's character in *Moneyball* has to overcome his communication apprehension in order to express his ideas to the other recruiters during meetings. When you're feeling unsure of yourself, how do you maintain an active role in group discussions?

Melinda Sue Gordon/© Columbia Pictures/Courtesy Everett Collection

Visibly intimidated by the more seasoned scouts sitting around the table, Peter is afraid to speak up about how he determines a player's value. Only after general manager Billy Beane (played by Brad Pitt) uses his overpowering personality to silence the grumbling scouts does Peter try to take part in the meeting. But he's unsure of himself and speaks haltingly. As a result, he fails to convince the stubborn scouts that his statistic-based methods will work. Much to the scouts' disbelief and despite their protests, Billy follows Peter's recommendations.

Although all small group members work toward a common goal, each person brings his or her own unique self, experiences, and communication preferences to the group. In the preceding example, Peter's youth, inexperience, and communication style set him apart from the more experienced scouts. These differences initially made it difficult for them to take his ideas seriously. Fortunately for Peter, and for the Oakland A's, Billy Beane was willing to push for Peter's new way of selecting players.

Knowing how certain factors—such as your own communication traits, gender, and culture—influence small group behavior will help you communicate more competently within groups.

Communication Traits

You possess certain enduring traits that affect your communication no matter what the situation. For example, if you are an extravert, you are generally social, outgoing, and seeking out interpersonal interactions, whether you are chatting with your sister or making a speech (Littlejohn & Foss, 2010). However, when it comes to small groups, there are two communication traits that are especially important: communication apprehension and argumentativeness.

Communication Apprehension. Have you ever been afraid to speak up and say what's on your mind, like Peter Brand was with the baseball scouts? If so, you may have experienced **communication apprehension**—fear or anxiety about real or anticipated communication (McCroskey, 2008). Most people experience a small amount of communication apprehension from time to time—for example, when giving a speech. (We discuss how to handle speech anxiety in Chapter 15.) But some individuals experience apprehension on such a regular basis that it becomes part of how they communicate. Known as *high communication apprehension*, this can be so paralyzing that it prevents a person from communicating in everyday situations, such as chatting with coworkers. Naturally, this can result in negative consequences. For example, college students with high communication apprehension experience less academic success in classes that require a lot of discussion compared to students who aren't as fearful about communication (McCroskey & Andersen, 1976). In groups, someone who's nervous and silent may appear to other members as aloof, stiff, withdrawn, or restless (McCroskey, Daly, & Sorensen, 1976). As a result, the other members may wrongly assume that the apprehensive person doesn't care about the group's goals, and they may stop trying to elicit contributions from him or her.

If you experience communication apprehension in groups, you can try to reduce your fear with focused practice. Start by asking simple questions to clarify points made during group discussions. Provide brief comments of support for others when it's appropriate ("Yes, I think that's a good idea"). Try to anticipate what topics may be under discussion or what questions might be asked, and prepare messages you can contribute in advance. Knowing what to say ahead of time will make it easier to speak up. If you believe your communication apprehension is really holding you back, find the courage to talk with an instructor who can direct you to resources that may help.

Argumentativeness. Whereas high communication apprehension can make small group communication challenging, a trait that can enhance it is argumentativeness. **Argumentativeness** is the willingness to take a stance on controversial issues and verbally refute others who disagree with you (Infante & Rancer, 1982). Although the word *argument* carries negative connotations, it can be a positive form of communication in small groups. That's

ARGUMENTATIVENESS (VS) VERBAL AGGRESSION

Group projects can often lead to conflicts among its members. It's important to know how to vocalize your different opinions, because there's a big difference between argumentativeness and being verbally aggressive. Which of these scenarios do you think ended on better terms? Why?

Westend61/Getty Images   Goodluz/Shutterstock

because argumentativeness fosters the exchange of ideas, which is valuable for group decision making. Being highly argumentative is not the same as being *verbally aggressive*, which is characterized by hostile personal attacks on others (Infante, 1987). Instead, someone who is argumentative openly disagrees with ideas without making it personal. If you disagree with your teammate and say, "I see where you're coming from, but I'm not sure we can meet that deadline with our current resources," you are showing argumentativeness. But if you say, "That's a stupid idea! Don't you have any understanding of how limited our resources are?" it's verbal aggression. Since highly argumentative individuals separate issues from people, they tend to communicate well in groups and often emerge as group leaders (Limon & La France, 2005).

Argumentativeness encourages groups to think through and debate ideas, something the Pixar teams do when creating their successful films. This boosts the chances that a group will end up choosing the best possible ideas to act on. Constructive arguing also strengthens bonds in a group. When group members are argumentative, they are more likely to be satisfied with the group relationship and to believe that the group has reached consensus on decisions (Anderson & Martin, 1999). Despite the advantages of argumentativeness, there's a constructive way to argue and a not-so-constructive way, which can lead to unproductive conflict. Chapter 12 presents strategies for effectively dealing with conflicts in small groups.

Gender

Popular stereotypes suggest there are big differences in how men and women communicate. According to these, men are unemotional, dominant, and achievement oriented, whereas women are nurturing, caring, and emotional. However, men and women actually communicate similarly in many ways, including levels of talkativeness, assertive speech, and self-disclosure (Cameron, 2009; Hyde, 2005).

So what does this mean for communication within a small group? You need to be aware of these stereotypes when interpreting your teammates' communication behaviors. People have a tendency to negatively judge men and women who communicate in ways that defy gender stereotypes (Hyde, 2005). For example, you might dismiss an overly emotional male teammate during a heated debate if you think he's not acting the way a man "should" act. Conversely, you may decide that a female team member who doesn't smile often or talk much is cold, because women are supposed to be warm and open with their feelings. If you think gender-based stereotypes are affecting your perception of team members, use *perception-checking* to form more accurate impressions. As Chapter 2 discusses, you can do this by reviewing your knowledge about the other person, assessing any attributions you've made about the individual, and questioning your impression to make sure you're not basing it solely on a stereotype.

Culture

Your culture affects all your communication, but three factors are especially relevant when interacting within small groups (see Figure 11.1). The first is whether you see your individual needs as more or less important than the group's needs. As Chapter 4 discusses, people raised in an *individualistic culture* (the United States and Australia) will place greater importance on their individual achievement and personal happiness than will those from a *collectivistic culture* (China and West Africa). People with a collectivistic orientation place greater importance on group goals, and they especially value cooperation and interpersonal harmony.

A second important cultural dimension is *power distance*, the degree to which people expect inequality between persons of low and high power (Hofstede, Hofstede, & Minkov, 2010). In high-power-distance cultures (such as Mexico and Saudi Arabia), an individual of low power wouldn't disagree with a leader during a discussion. In low-power-distance cultures (including the United States and Canada), many people expect leaders to treat those below them with respect and to invite everyone's input on certain decisions.

A final cultural factor affecting small group communication is *uncertainty avoidance,* or how much tolerance people have for risk (Hofstede et al., 2010).

FIGURE 11.1

CULTURE AND SELF-AWARENESS

In groups, it is important to be aware of how cultural preferences affect all members' communication, even your own.

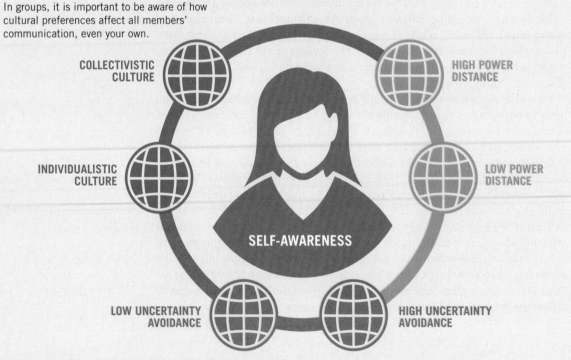

COLLECTIVISTIC CULTURE

HIGH POWER DISTANCE

INDIVIDUALISTIC CULTURE

LOW POWER DISTANCE

SELF-AWARENESS

LOW UNCERTAINTY AVOIDANCE

HIGH UNCERTAINTY AVOIDANCE

1. VoodooDot/Shutterstock; 2. Bplanet/Shutterstock

In cultures with high uncertainty avoidance (such as Germany and Finland), individuals expect structure and rules. In those with low uncertainty avoidance (including the United States and China), people feel more comfortable with change and with having relatively few rules.

Understanding how your cultural orientation affects your communication in small groups is a component of your *self-awareness*. Let's say you have been oriented to collectivistic ways of thought and embrace a high power distance. In this case, you may avoid disagreeing with a group leader or offering your opinion during a discussion. Or suppose you have high uncertainty avoidance; you might become frustrated when a group lacks clear goals or ground rules. By knowing how cultural factors influence your own group behavior, you can be mindful of communicating your ideas in ways that maintain the self-worth, or face, of culturally different teammates (Oetzel & Ting-Toomey, 2003). For example, if you're part of a group in which many members are from a high-power-distance culture and you disagree with something the senior person in the group said, how would you handle it? Voicing your opinion mid-meeting may cause other team members embarrassment. Instead, you could approach the high-status person during a break, and ask, "Are you open to hearing another opinion?" Choosing to raise your objection privately shows respect for the senior person and avoids a potentially embarrassing situation.

Virtual Groups and Teams

Social media and videoconferencing help virtual groups organize their work and communicate. However, as with all online interactions, remember that the three Ps of mediated communication—powerful, public, and permanent—from Chapter 3 still apply. Your self-presentation matters just as much (if not more) when you're working in virtual small groups as it does when you're communicating online with close friends and family.

In our technology-saturated culture, it's easy to think that communicating online with virtual groups should be second nature to us all. However, as the following anecdote from a *Wall Street Journal* article points out, that isn't always the case:

> Jason Walker was in the middle of presenting fourth-quarter earnings to his bosses when an unwelcome surprise popped up on his screen—and the screens of five other people logged on remotely for the virtual meeting. "I love you Teddy Bear," read the instant message from Mr. Walker's significant other. For the next month or so, Mr. Walker was known around the office as "Teddy Bear." (Mattioli, 2008)

Professionals are increasingly working on teams that have members all over the country—even around the globe. Perhaps not surprisingly, an entire industry has sprung up to teach people how to avoid embarrassing situations like the one "Teddy Bear" found himself in. Almost any career you choose—from video game design to public relations—or class project you participate in, you could be working in a virtual small group. As mentioned earlier, a *virtual small group* is any team of three or more individuals who

MAKING COMMUNICATION CHOICES

YOU'RE NOT FUNNY

You had a sinking feeling in your stomach the moment you discovered that Derek was part of your project group in sociology. Professor Bradley had randomly assigned groups to work on a semester project. Derek and three other class-mates—Sylvia, Greg, and Jamie—make up your group. Since the first day of class, Derek has been the typical "funny but annoying guy," and you've been frustrated that Professor Bradley has played off Derek's humorous comments during lectures.

During your first group meeting in the campus library, Derek immediately starts talking about a *Family Guy* episode. Jamie and Greg laugh along with Derek, reciting lines from the episode. Since you don't watch much television, you feel left out and notice that Sylvia is quiet, too.

Deciding to refocus the group to the task, you say, "OK, enough about *Family Guy*. Who's had a chance to review the project requirements?" Derek replies, "I didn't download the assignment. Anyway, did you guys see the episode when Stewie . . ." Unsure of what to do next, you silently review the class assignment while making some notes. Sylvia is now preoccupied with looking over the assignment, too.

After several more minutes, you make up an excuse to interrupt the *Family Guy* conversation by telling the group you have to leave for an appointment. As you get up, you ask, "Is everyone OK with meeting here at the same time on Thursday?" When they all nod in agreement, you continue, "Great. Then let's read the assignment requirements, and come with project ideas to talk about then. See you later."

Driving home, you are fuming, and worry about the potential effects of Derek's comedic behavior on the group's performance. You give serious thought to asking Professor Bradley to move you to another group.

One exciting aspect of working in groups is encountering others with different personalities and life experiences. But some communication behaviors cause stress, lead to destructive conflict, and divide teams (Felps, Mitchell, & Byington, 2006). Known as *bad apple behaviors*, these include withholding effort, displaying excessive negativity, and violating important interpersonal norms (Felps et al., 2006). The inability to effectively control bad apple behavior can negatively affect team motivation and perfor-mance, or "spoil the barrel."

In reviewing numerous studies of bad apple behavior in small groups, Felps et al., (2006) identified three ways teammates respond most often:

1 *Motivation intervention* is an attempt to change the negative behavior through some manner of influence or verbal assertion ("C'mon, Derek, we need to focus on the assignment"). Indi-viduals will likely respond this way when they believe the disruptive person has control over the behavior.

2 *Rejection* consists of ignoring or avoiding the bad apple behavior. Group members would most likely take this route when efforts to change the behavior through influence or assertion have failed.

3 *Defensiveness* is communicating in a manner that protects your sense of self, including withdrawing yourself or being verbally aggres-sive toward the offending party. When direct or indirect attempts to change bad apple behavior are unsuccessful, or you have limited power in the group, you may respond defensively.

The first two strategies can be competent ways of dealing with "bad apples" in a group (Felps et al., 2006). However, the third response, though tempting, may make the problem worse, because the offending person may respond defensively.

Before making a communication choice, consider the facts of the situation, and think about the bad apple behavior research. Also, reflect on what you've learned so far about group roles (pp. 268–269), cohesiveness (p. 272), norms (p. 272), and communication traits (pp. 275–276). Then answer these questions:

❶ What ethical obligation do you have to keep Derek from disrupting the group project?

❷ What do you gain and risk by responding to Derek in each of the three most common ways? What might you gain or lose by asking Professor Bradley to be assigned to another group?

❸ What are you going to do?

work together to achieve a common goal, and who communicate primarily through technology instead of face-to-face encounters.

Working in a virtual small group presents both challenges and advantages. In this section, we'll discuss pitfalls to watch out for and suggest strategies for improving communication in your next virtual group experience—so you can avoid your own "Teddy Bear" moment.

Challenges of Virtual Groups

Lack of face-to-face interactions presents virtual small groups with several challenges. First, the physical distance separating members restricts their nonverbal communication. If you can't see your team members' facial expressions and body postures, you don't know if they're smiling and nodding in agreement or if they're confused or bored. This lack of feedback makes it hard to know how the team feels about what is being said. Even when using videoconferencing and webcams, people can still feel cut off from the group, which can lead to their getting caught up in other behaviors during a virtual meeting that disrupt their concentration, such as eating or checking e-mail (Mattioli, 2008).

Second, it's hard to build cohesion in a virtual team. In interviews with members of a virtual group working for a travel company, one study found that the group experienced mistrust, limited rapport, and feelings of isolation (Kirkman, Rosen, Gibson, Tesluk, & McPherson, 2002). To offset these problems, virtual team members should occasionally meet face-to-face if at all possible. These interactions are essential for building interpersonal relationships and strengthening cohesion. When it's not possible to arrange face-to-face meetings, virtual teams can benefit from icebreaker activities early in a meeting, such as introducing themselves by self-disclosing a fact that others may find surprising (Nunamaker, Reinig, & Briggs, 2009), or engaging in small talk in later meetings once everyone knows one another.

Third, it's difficult to communicate complex information and to make decisions during online meetings. Even with lots of different resources to enable interaction—including instant messaging, Skype, and sophisticated

TABLE 11.2

COMMON TOOLS FOR VIRTUAL SMALL GROUP COMMUNICATION[2]

✉ E-MAIL
(e.g., Gmail & Microsoft Outlook)

Advantages

Easily accessible

Low cost

Useful for exchanging routine information and brainstorming ideas

Disadvantages

Lacks nonverbal information

Less effective for conveying complex information

☎ TELECONFERENCE
(e.g., conference calls & instant messaging)

Advantages

Easily accessible

Useful for exchanging routine information and increasingly complex information

Disadvantages

Lack of visual nonverbal information (i.e., facial expressions and gestures)

Difficult to maintain team members' attention and engagement

◎ VIDEOCONFERENCE
(e.g., Skype & Cisco WebEx)

Advantages

Provides access to verbal and nonverbal information

Useful for communicating complex information and decisions

Disadvantages

Requires all team members to have the same technology

Subject to technical difficulties (user error or equipment failure)

▤ PROJECT MANAGEMENT TOOLS
(e.g., Google Docs & wikis)

Advantages

Low cost

Useful for compiling research findings and collaborating on reports

Disadvantages

Requires moderate training

Team members must continually check the site to contribute and view others' contributions

[2]Except where noted, information in this table is from Bell & Kozlowski (2002).

videoconferencing systems—groups can suffer from missed or delayed messages, misinterpretations, and other issues. Some media are better than others for overcoming these challenges. Table 11.2 considers the advantages and disadvantages of common tools intended to support virtual small group communication. Use this table to determine the best way to reach out to other members of a virtual group, depending on your communication goals.

Finally, team members may vary greatly in their ability to use the group's chosen communication technology. Perhaps a member lacks access to high-speed Internet, or another member's computer crashes during a web conference. All virtual groups need backup plans in case such problems occur. They should also make sure that every member knows how to participate in any conferencing programs, such as those developed by WebEx or Citrix. If you're forming a virtual team, take steps early on to see that everyone has both access to and the ability to use any necessary technology.

Improving Communication in Virtual Small Groups

To help any virtual small group you're part of communicate better, consider the following guidelines:

1. *Determine the best communication method.* Virtual teams often use different technologies for communicating and sharing information. E-mail may be a primary way that routine messages are communicated. File-hosting Web sites like Dropbox and Google Docs allow virtual teams to share meeting notes and reports. Phone calls, videoconferencing, or collaborative platforms are appropriate for discussing complex matters and making decisions. Team members should understand what technologies to use for handling routine communication, managing group documents, and conducting meetings. Importantly, be sure that every team member has the proper login details and the capability to use the technologies.

2. *Provide specific directions before meetings.* Take time-zone differences into account when scheduling a meeting. If group members are from vastly different time zones, schedule meetings so that members take turns being inconvenienced. It's not fair to expect any one person to always be available during very early morning or very late evening hours. Also identify the purpose, expectations, and desired outcomes of each meeting (Nunamaker et al., 2009).

3. *Involve all group members.* Make sure all participants have a chance to contribute to group discussions and meetings. You can do this by asking everyone to share something at the start of a meeting or by asking each person to give a response to questions posed at different points in the meeting (Nunamaker et al., 2009).

4. *Use the cooperative principle.* It's especially important to craft informative, honest, clear, and relevant messages when you're taking part in a virtual group interaction. That's because team members have few or no nonverbal cues to interpret your communication. (See Chapter 5 for more on the cooperative principle.)

5. *Attend to the group's social needs.* Whenever possible, virtual teams should have face-to-face meetings to promote team identity and foster group cohesion (Siebdrat, Hoegl, & Ernst, 2009). When costs, time, or distance get in the way of such gatherings, help your team develop other ways of attending to members' social needs. Make time for conversations about things other than work, such as group members' interests or hobbies. Or create a team Web site that contains pictures of each member and information about their backgrounds and interests. Getting to know one another can help team members feel more of a social connection.

CHAPTER ⑪ REVIEW

CHAPTER RECAP

- A **small group** is composed of three or more interdependent persons who share a common identity and come together to achieve a common goal.
- Small groups develop in stages that include **forming, storming, norming, performing,** and **adjourning.**
- To achieve their goals, members of small groups balance group *roles*, build *cohesiveness*, establish **norms,** share responsibility, and manage physical space.
- Your *self* influences how you communicate in a group, specifically your levels of **communication apprehension** or **argumentativeness** and even your culture and gender.
- **Virtual small groups** are increasingly common at work or school. Though they have specific challenges, you can overcome them by carefully planning the tools and messages you employ.

LAUNCHPAD

LaunchPad for *Choices & Connections* offers unique video scenarios and encourages self-assessment through adaptive quizzing. Go to **bedfordstmartins.com /choicesconnections** to get access.

 LearningCurve adaptive quizzes

 How to Communicate video scenarios

 Video clips that illustrate key concepts

KEY TERMS

Small group, p. 262
Virtual small group, p. 264
Primary groups, p. 264
Secondary groups, p. 264
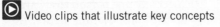 Forming, p. 265
Storming, p. 266
Norming, p. 266
Performing, p. 266
Adjourning, p. 266
Formal roles, p. 268

Group roles, p. 268
Task roles, p. 268
Maintenance roles, p. 268
Egocentric roles, p. 269
Social loafing, p. 269
Cohesive groups, p. 272
Norms, p. 272
Communication apprehension, p. 275
Argumentativeness, p. 276

1 The _____ phase of group development occurs when members of a small group agree about the plans for working toward the group's goals.

  a. forming

  b. norming

  c. storming

  d. performing

2 Which of the following is an example of a task role?

  a. Electing the president of a debate team

  b. Mediating an argument between two group members

  c. Collecting and distributing contact information for all members

  d. Consistently telling jokes to add humor to meetings

3 All of the following ways can help establish positive norms *except* _____.

  a. starting each meeting with an icebreaker activity

  b. making sure to always begin meetings on time

  c. asking members to not multitask during meetings

  d. identifying what is going well in the group and what isn't

4 If group members have different levels of _____, they may have varying expectations for how much structure the group should have.

  a. self-awareness

  b. power distance

  c. uncertainty avoidance

  d. argumentativeness

5 Members of virtual groups may experience _____ if they are unable to see one another's nonverbal behaviors, such as smiles, nods, or looks of confusion.

  a. restricted small talk

  b. a limited sense of cohesion

  c. difficulty making decisions

  d. a lack of feedback

ACTIVITIES

1 **What's Your Role?**

Choose a small group to which you belong (student club, community organization, or work group), and identify the formal and group roles you take on when you participate in the group (task, maintenance, and egocentric). In a one-page paper, explain when you take on different roles in the group, and how your role behaviors impact the group.

2 **Defining Group Norms**

In a small group (in person or online), brainstorm a list of ground rules that would be appropriate for a school study group. For example, "Be on time." As a group, agree to the five most important ground rules. Present and critique the final lists with the rest of the class. What seems to be common in the lists? Did any group have a ground rule that you find surprising?

12
Leadership in Group Communication

(M)ario Sepúlveda fed his coworkers a tuna-based broth that he had cooked in a pot made out of an oil filter from a work truck.[1] Cooking more than 2,000 feet under the earth's surface, he was one of 33 Chilean men who were trapped when the mine they were working in collapsed on August 5, 2010. The miners had only enough food to sustain 10 people for two days. Given the natural instinct to survive, the miners might have started fighting over the food and hoarding it. But Sepúlveda stepped in and helped manage the supply. His efforts ensured that everyone shared the food fairly and that the supply would last as long as

possible—boosting the men's chances of survival. His upbeat personality further helped keep the miners' hopes up, even as their ordeal dragged on. Sepúlveda's actions made him a leader among his starving coworkers.

However, Sepúlveda wasn't the only leader in the group. In order for the men to make it through the ordeal, they were going to have to work together and share various responsibilities. The miners' shift foreman, Luis Urzúa, retained his formal role as leader. Compared to the outgoing Sepúlveda, Urzúa was mild mannered and soft-spoken. But with over two decades of mining experience and a background as an amateur soccer coach, Urzúa had knowledge and skills the other miners respected. He set up systems to help the group endure and to organize structure. For instance, he established daily meetings in which the men voted on how to ration the food; how to send information to rescuers; and who was best suited to handle which work duties, such as removing loose rocks from the ceiling before they could fall and injure the men.

Additional leaders emerged by taking responsibility for other aspects of the group's welfare. Mario Gómez set up a makeshift chapel in the mine. Victor Segovia

RODRIGO ARANGUA/AFP/Getty Images

---

[1]This account of the Chilean miners is summarized from Franklin (2011).

started a written record of the men's daily duties and challenges. Yonni Barrios—who had taken a nursing course—provided medical attention. Thanks to this sharing of leadership duties, no one person had to bear the total responsibility for all the group's needs—physical, emotional, and spiritual.

The miners' hopes soared on the 17th day after the accident, when a drill probe broke through the cavern wall. At last, they could easily communicate with rescuers and get sufficient oxygen and food until their evacuation. It took another 52 days to get them out. But in the end, all the miners survived—in large part because several people were willing to step up and offer various forms of leadership to the group.

In the collapsed mine, Luis Urzúa was the group's formal leader as shift foreman. But it was the sharing of leadership roles and responsibilities among several of the men that helped the group survive extremely challenging circumstances. When it comes to small group communication, we define **leadership** as the ability to influence and direct others to meet group goals. Even when a group has a designated leader—like Urzúa—other members can still provide leadership within the group. That's because *the ability to influence and direct* stems from communication behaviors—which anyone in a group can either initiate him- or herself or foster in others. Since no one person can provide a group with everything it needs, in all situations, other group members—like Mario Sepúlveda—must also step up as leaders. Known as **shared leadership**, each group member has the capacity to influence and direct the group in achieving its goals (Pearce & Conger, 2002).

Developing your leadership capacity is certainly important for being a competent designated leader, but small groups benefit when all members possess and exercise leadership skills. In this chapter, you'll learn:

- Different perspectives on understanding leadership
- Ways to encourage productive communication in a group
- Strategies for leading group problem solving
- How to support effective group decision making
- Ideas for planning, running, and evaluating meetings

Perspectives on Leadership

☑ **LearningCurve** can help you review! Go to **bedfordstmartins.com /choicesconnections**.

> Who are leaders? Are leaders naturally born, or are they created in crisis? Are they tough? Compassionate? Laid back? Powerful speakers? All of the above? By understanding how researchers study and view leadership, one thing becomes clear: leaders are not one thing but a mix of different communication skills and styles.

Before exploring how leadership functions in groups, it is important to have a basic understanding of what leadership really is. Scholars have long explored critical questions about leadership, such as, What personal qualities do effective leaders have? What distinctive behaviors do they demonstrate? and Why do some leadership approaches work in some situations but not others? The research resulting from such questions reflects four primary perspectives on leadership. Together, these perspectives clarify what it means to be a leader in a variety of group situations.

VARIATIONS IN LEADERSHIP STYLES

Examples of competent leaders abound in real life and in the media. Yahoo! CEO Marissa Mayer; TOMS founder Blake Mycoskie; and *Homeland*'s director of counterterrorism, David Estes, all look and carry themselves differently but still assert themselves as strong leaders. Their different but effective leadership styles exemplify the notion that there is no one formula for being a successful leader.

(Left to right) Brian Ach/Getty Images; Zodiac/Splash News/Newscom; Kent Smith/© Showtime Network/Courtesy Everett Collection

Traits View

If someone asked you to identify the defining characteristics of a good leader, you might say things like "smart," "decisive," "sociable," and maybe even "physically attractive" or "tall." A **traits view of leadership** assumes that all talented leaders share certain personal and physical characteristics. For instance, a CareerBuilder.com interview with business professionals suggested that effective leaders are honest, passionate, confident, caring, engaging, humble, fearless, genuine, and supportive (Farrell, 2011). Other studies have shown that in the business world, successful leaders possess drive, knowledge of the business, self-confidence, and integrity (Kirkpatrick & Locke, 1991).

Although the traits view helps us think about the desirable qualities we look for in leaders, a person who has the "right" leadership traits may still not perform well as a leader. For example, extraversion (being sociable and outgoing) is a quality found in many leaders (Judge, Ilies, Bono, & Gerhardt, 2002). But an extravert who is unable to make decisions may have trouble being a group leader. Similarly, it's just as likely that a person who is quiet or shy—traits not normally associated with leaders—could be a valuable leader if he or she has expertise crucial to the group's goals. It's important to remember that the traits view is not an "all or nothing" perspective. Each individual member of a group may possess different leadership traits that contribute to a group's success.

Style View

The **style view of leadership** focuses on the behaviors leaders use to influence others. This perspective identifies three basic behavioral styles. Someone who exhibits an **autocratic leadership style** directs others, telling them what to do. Leaders displaying this style accept limited input from others in the group. Think of a community theater director. For each production, she may choose a script, cast actors in roles, and determine how the actors should interpret the script, with no input from anyone else. Although the cast members are critical for a production's success, the director retains ultimate authority over the play.

On the other end of the spectrum are leaders who provide little direction or structure to their teams. They use what's known as the **laissez-faire leadership style.** When leaders use this style, the group maintains control of what happens. If the theater director were to use this style, she might let cast members make production decisions, such as how the costumes will look or where each actor should stand during particular scenes (Kramer, 2006).

Finally, leaders who invite input from group members and encourage shared decision making are exercising a **democratic leadership style.** A theater director with a democratic style might start production planning by asking the cast and crew for ideas about set design and other matters related to the play. As the production unfolds, the director may remain open to suggestions and feedback.

The style view of leadership gives us a way to talk about leaders. For example, if you tell your dad that the new director is "really autocratic," he'll probably know what you mean. This view can also help you decide how to approach a leadership situation. Do you see yourself as laid-back, forceful, or somewhere in between? If you see yourself as democratic in your approach, how would you handle a group that seemed reluctant to give input when planning an event?

Like the traits view of leadership, the style view has some limitations. Specifically, it doesn't address the question of which style will be most useful in a given situation. The situational view of leadership, which we cover next, can help with this.

Situational View

The **situational view of leadership** maintains that effective leadership is determined by the group's readiness to take on a task, including its motivation and individual group members' experience and knowledge (Hersey & Blanchard, 1988). A group that has been together for a long time and has a lot of experience with, say, raising funds for a local charity would probably need different leadership than a group with little experience or motivation. For example, a team that has just been assembled and that has little experience with fund-raising would benefit from a leader with a *telling*, or autocratic, style. The leader would need to establish structure, provide specific direction about the task, and give frequent feedback to the group about performance. When a group has a moderate degree of experience and motivation with fund-raising, a *selling* style might be the best leadership choice. The leader would give encouragement to group members while maintaining control over how the work is done. As experience and motivation with fund-raising increases within a group, a leader's style may become more *participating*, encouraging shared decision making and providing less specific direction. Finally, a team with a lot of fund-raising experience and motivation would likely require a leader who leads by *delegating*, whereby group members have complete responsibility for organizing and doing the work.

© Eric Audras/Onoky/Corbis

The relationship you have with fellow group members is a big factor in deciding the most effective leadership style to use. Do you take charge differently with friends than you do with classmates? How do shared experiences and motivations affect the way you lead?

The situational view of leadership explains two important things. First, a leader's skills and style must fit the needs of the group. For example, an autocratic leadership style can be successful in some situations (such as if the group is new) and fail miserably in others (if members are used to having more control over tasks). Second, groups change over time as motivation fluctuates, new challenges emerge, or members gain confidence with the task at hand. Effective leaders adapt their style to changing circumstances.

A limitation of the situational view is that—much like the trait and style views—it focuses on *characteristics and approaches* of individuals who are leading others. Each of these views asks a common question: What do effective leaders look like? But none of the three views can account for how *communication* helps a group share responsibility in leading the group. Just as the Chilean miners counted on various members to help them survive, members in any small group can make contributions that help lead the group at a particular moment. The next view of leadership considers the role communication plays in influencing and directing groups.

Functional View

The **functional view of leadership** considers the types of communication behaviors that help a group work toward its goal (Morgeson, DeRue, & Karam, 2009). As Chapter 11 explains, in any group, some communication behaviors help get the job done (*task roles*), while others help build interpersonal bonds within the group (*maintenance roles*). In the functional view, all of these communication behaviors count as a form of leadership, because they are all helping the group function. For example, if you volunteer to put together the slide deck for a group presentation, you are providing useful task leadership. If another group member steps in to help resolve a conflict between two team members, he or she is bringing valuable maintenance leadership to the group.

The functional view sees leadership as a responsibility of each group member rather than a quality that's inside a single person or position. Through *shared leadership*, groups draw on the different skills, experiences, and talents of each member to manage tasks and relationships. Accordingly, group success depends on all members—not just the designated leader.

As you read the rest of this chapter, you will learn communication skills that build leadership capacity. So whether you are the appointed (or elected) leader of a group or simply a member, improving your communication competence in these areas will contribute to effective group leadership.

Leading with Communication

Competent communication within a group doesn't just happen; it takes work. This is not the responsibility of a single, designated leader, however. Instead, if all group members communicate openly and competently respond to conflicts, the group can create and maintain a supportive environment.

In the 2012 season premiere of the reality show *Survivor: One World*, the cast is divided into two tribes—men (the Manonos) versus women (the Salanis). A power struggle quickly erupts within the Salani tribe when Christina, acting alone, makes a deal with the men to trade woven palm fronds for fire. When Christina's teammate, Alicia, learns of the trade, she verbally attacks Christina. Their argument fractures the group, and the Salanis are required to submit to a tribal council that will determine who will get voted off the team.

Survivor host Jeff Probst begins the tribal council by asking the women who is leading their team. Almost immediately, Alicia and Christina start shouting at each other, revealing a lack of coordination and structure within the team. Another teammate, Monica, describes the tribe as "crazy, total anarchy." Probst advises the women to coordinate their leadership or face continued trouble within their team.

MONTY BRINTON/CBS/Landov

The drama between members of the Salani tribe on season 24 of *Survivor* shows how weak leadership skills can cause a group's sense of unity to unravel. How can shared leadership skills create a supportive communication climate?

Although Alicia wasn't wrong to voice her opinion, the way she communicated her anger only made things worse. Moreover, as things began to spiral out of control, no other Salani tribe member stepped in to manage the conflict. A skillful leader would have encouraged better communication among members and dealt with disagreements before they escalated. This would have helped the Salanis avoid such chaos in the group.

Leading groups requires careful attention to maintaining satisfying relations among members while monitoring and evaluating progress toward completing the given task (Morgeson et al., 2009). To encourage this, group leaders can create a supportive climate, prevent groupthink, and help group members constructively work through the inevitable conflicts that arise.

Creating a Communication Climate

Take a moment to consider your recent experiences as a member of a group. What emotions did you have when you were with the group? Did you feel defensive and concerned about what the other members thought of your ideas? Did you feel supported, even when you disagreed with other group members? Your answers to these questions describe the group's **communication climate,** or the emotional tone established within the group (Gibb, 1961). Every group develops a communication climate, and that climate influences all aspects of the group—from how productive the group is to how well its members get along.

The communication climate arises from the verbal and nonverbal messages group members exchange. For example, if members insult one another's ideas, promise to handle a task and then don't follow up, or gossip behind each other's backs, they create a *defensive communication climate*. In such a climate, team members see the group as threatening (Forward, Czech, & Lee, 2011; Gibb, 1961). This can damage group cohesion.

In contrast, members of a group can create a *supportive communication climate* by exchanging respectful and supportive verbal and nonverbal messages. When groups communicate this way, team members focus on the ideas being expressed rather than the individuals expressing them (Forward et al., 2011; Gibb, 1961). Even during disagreements, members of the team strive to generate ideas that everyone can support instead of shutting down conversations or taking sides in the dispute. To learn more about dealing with disagreements productively, see the How to Communicate: Handling Complaints feature on pages 296–297.

You can provide leadership in a group by creating an open exchange of ideas among group members and encouraging constructive rather than destructive communication. For a comparison between supportive and defensive communication behaviors, see Table 12.1. To foster a supportive communication climate in a group, focus on mastering the behaviors described in the middle column, and avoiding the defensive behaviors listed in the last column.

TABLE 12.1

SUPPORTIVE AND DEFENSIVE COMMUNICATION

SITUATION	SUPPORTIVE COMMUNICATION RESPONSE	DEFENSIVE COMMUNICATION RESPONSE
A committee member argues against every suggestion for a fund-raiser.	Uses descriptive language ("I" language, fact-based statements) "I am sensing a lot of dissatisfaction with our ideas today. What's up?"	Employs evaluative language ("You" language, judgmental statements) "You should quit being such a jerk."
A study group member fails to complete the assigned chapter outlines.	Takes a problem-orientation approach (open-ended questions, collaboration) "We've noticed you haven't completed the outlines. Is something wrong?"	Uses controlling messages (attempts to change or exercise power over the other person) "You need to do your work. If you don't, you are out of the group."
A team member wants feedback on sales presentation slides.	Forms cooperative messages (honest disclosure, relevancy) "They were good, but I find the amount of text on each slide to be overwhelming."	Engages strategy (manipulation, dishonesty) "It's great! Don't change a thing before the presentation."
A work colleague is complaining about another team member's work habits.	Demonstrates empathy (active listening, responding with support) "I know you're upset with Taylor; I'd be frustrated, too."	Lacks concern (neutral viewpoint, apathy) "Look, Taylor's just like that. Get used to it."
A cousin is having trouble completing his portion of duties for a family gathering.	Conveys equality (mutual respect, open to feedback) "How are you feeling about your tasks? Would you like me to help out?"	Shows superiority (arrogance, closed to feedback) "Why do you have to be so helpless?"
A team disagrees about a meeting discussion topic.	Makes provisional assertions (open to alternatives, tentative statements) "I know things were pretty hectic at the end of the last meeting, but I thought we agreed to discuss Ella's proposal tonight. What do you recall?"	Emphasizes certainty (rigid thinking, overgeneralizations) "I know what was said at the last meeting. We agreed that we would discuss Ella's proposal tonight. This group is so forgetful!"

Preventing Groupthink

Chapter 11 notes that a key feature of small groups is the degree of *cohesiveness*, or sense of unity, a team achieves. When a group has trouble building cohesiveness, members may not feel committed to the group's tasks or to one another (Aubert & Kelsey, 2003). As a result, they may not

HANDLING COMPLAINTS

 One way to improve your communication competence is by adapting your messages to others' behaviors. Learn how to handle hostile group members by going to LaunchPad at **bedfordstmartins.com/choicesconnections** and completing the **How to Communicate video scenario** for Chapter 12 to practice your skills.

CONSIDER THIS: You are leading a group at work that is in charge of launching a new line of juices targeted at busy moms. This is your first leadership position at work and there have been a lot of delays, which is stressing your teammates. During a weekly status meeting, one member, Tim, complains about a lack of progress in meetings.

WHAT WOULD YOU DO? The following advice illustrates how you can actively listen to the complaint while also keeping in mind the entire team's goals and needs. As you watch the video, consider how competent communication skills like self-awareness, empathy, and collaboration result in a more productive interaction. Then, test your knowledge of key skills, and create your own responses to the **What if? video prompts**.

① BE SELF-AWARE and suppress any defensive nonverbal reactions (teeth-clenching, arm-crossing, or eye-rolling) while Tim is stating his concerns.

② LISTEN TO THE COMPLAINT without interrupting. Ask questions to gather specific details about why Tim is upset.

 "I'm not really sure what you mean by 'waste of time.' How has our meeting time seemed unproductive to you?"

③ EXPRESS EMPATHY

for Tim's concern by respectfully acknowledging his feelings about the situation.

"I realize how frustrating this is for you, particularly because we've had some unavoidable delays. I can imagine you're getting some pressure."

④ USE COLLABORATION

to ask Tim what he would like to see happen. As a group, negotiate a mutually agreeable action or solution.

"How can we make sure our market research is comprehensive and still move things along?"

 WHAT IF? But what if things don't work out as shown? Test your ability to adapt your communication by watching the What if? videos and planning a response for each situation.

1. When Tim brings up another complaint ("I've done a lot of work on this already and you've completely ignored it"), how would you handle extending the conversation?

2. How would you respond to Tim's unwillingness to collaborate on a solution? "It's not my problem to fix."

follow through on assigned tasks or help out other group members. But *too much* cohesiveness can be just as risky—because group members may hesitate to critically evaluate one another's ideas and decisions. In an overly cohesive group, people want to maintain harmony more than anything else, so they avoid challenging one another's ideas—a phenomenon known as **groupthink** (Janis, 1982). Highly cohesive groups become particularly vulnerable to groupthink when they have a long history of success, are under time pressure, or have a high-status or particularly persuasive individual on their team. In the interest of "not rocking the boat," group members hold back potentially conflicting opinions and information. This prevents the group from gathering the diverse views and knowledge it needs to make smart decisions.

Though all groups need cohesion, leaders must also look for and promptly address symptoms of groupthink (Janis, 1982). When groupthink occurs, members may believe that the group is invincible and can do no wrong. They may come to quick agreement on decisions and ignore information or opinions that go against what has been decided. Or members may put pressure on dissenters to "just go along"—for example, by staring disapprovingly at someone who questions a decision or telling the person to "let it go."

If a team seems to be slipping into groupthink, leaders need to take action—fast. The following steps can help:

1. *Encourage input from everyone.* Ask all members to contribute ideas and opinions. Pay particular attention to quiet members, who may be reluctant to express their feelings ("Peter, you haven't said much; what do you think about this idea?").

2. *Appoint a devil's advocate.* Have someone in the group take responsibility for expressing dissenting points of view ("I sense we're all ready to move on this, but what are the potential drawbacks of this decision?").

3. *Delay the decision.* If at all possible, encourage the group to take time to gather more information or to reflect on the decision in question before committing to a final course of action ("I don't feel comfortable deciding on this until we see more data").

Dealing with Conflict

Just as in any interpersonal relationship, conflict is an inevitable part of working in teams. Small groups experience two forms of conflict. **Substantive conflict** revolves around disagreements about the group's tasks, procedures, or decision options (Rahim, 2002). **Affective conflict** stems from interpersonal or cultural differences between members, power struggles, or simply bad feelings (Rahim, 2002). A moderate amount of substantive conflict can help prevent groupthink, but when groups experience too much substantive conflict or get embroiled in affective conflict, it's time for a group member to assume leadership and manage the situation.

Michael Yarish/© Fox/Courtesy Everett Collection

The characters on the show *Glee* constantly move between substantive and affective conflict, sometimes allowing personal feelings about other members to get in the way of the group's goals. How do you handle conflicts that combine elements of both conflict types?

As Chapter 8 covers, there are several possible approaches to dealing with conflict. Choosing the right approach depends on the nature and severity of the conflict. In situations involving unethical behaviors or clearly "right" courses of action, consider using a *competitive* approach, in which you pursue your own goals to the exclusion of others (Rahim, 2002). For example, your class group might want to ignore an assignment requirement they think is "unimportant." Rather than avoiding a conflict and going along with the group, a leader using a competitive approach would openly listen to the group but ultimately insist that the assignment requirement be met.

In instances with too much substantive or affective conflict, a *collaborative* approach may be best. This approach gives everyone a say in the resolution, so they tend to view the outcome as fair. Taking a collaborative approach to managing a conflict involves applying the following practices:

- Focus on common ground rather than proving who's right ("Gina and Christian, you both care about meeting the deadline; you're just disagreeing about how to get there").
- Use *active listening skills* from Chapter 5 by asking questions and paraphrasing what you've heard someone else say ("So, Martin, it sounds like you're concerned that this option is going to cost too much. Is that correct?").
- State your point of view clearly, and take responsibility for it by using "I language" ("I'm not comfortable with this plan because it doesn't say who's responsible for getting the supplies we need").
- Be consistent in your communication ("As I said earlier, I'm not comfortable with this plan") rather than sending mixed messages ("This plan has problems, but if everyone else is OK with it . . .").

- Stick to the issue at hand, and avoid bringing up unrelated matters ("We need to stay focused on the problems in the plan").

In general, avoiding a conflict is not productive unless the issue is insignificant ("You're sitting in my chair!").

Leading Problem Solving

> A common reason for being part of a small group is to solve a problem. But even with such a direct task, groups still need leaders to provide structure to the process. To lead a group in problem solving, you need to fully understand the problem and thoughtfully consider all possible solutions.

Checking in at most airports can be a frustrating process, consisting of long lines, impatient travelers, and overworked counter attendants. In an effort to make its passenger experience more pleasant, Alaska Airlines set out to correct these problems. The company assembled a group tasked with making the check-in process more efficient. With that goal in mind, the team started by researching customer lines and check-in procedures in other settings, such as theme parks and retail stores (Demerjian, 2008). They noticed that in the most efficient check-in settings, self-service kiosks eliminated long wait lines, while employees stood at key locations to direct customers and answer questions.

DOUBLE TAKE

PROBLEMS (VS) PROBLEM SOLVING

These pictures illustrate how successful, collaborative problem solving at Alaska Airlines completely changed the way airline passengers check in for flights. What other situations can you think of in which groups using the problem-solving method completely changed a situation for the better?

AP Photo/Ted S. Warren

AP Photo/Stephen Brashear

Drawing on these insights, team members brainstormed ideas for redesigning passenger ticketing and bag check-in areas using clusters of self-service kiosks.

When the team tested its design at Ted Stevens Anchorage International Airport, it cut customer wait time in half (Valdes, 2007). Encouraged by this success, the team tried out the same design at the much busier Seattle-Tacoma International Airport. Once again, the design worked. At Seattle-Tacoma, check-in took only about 8 minutes—far less than the 25–30 minutes it was taking at other airlines (Demerjian, 2008). The team's efforts changed the standard for millions of airline passengers. Now, it is common practice for airlines to use self-service kiosks at large airports around the world.

Small groups organize for lots of different purposes, including sharing information, providing support or service to others, and—like the Alaska Airlines team—solving a specific problem. A *problem* is a gap between a current situation (it can take up to half an hour to check in at an airline) and a desired condition (it shouldn't take more than 10 minutes to check in). Some problems require only an individual with the right expertise working alone— like a qualified mechanic fixing a car. Other problems are more complex— like how to make the airline check-in process more efficient. Addressing these complex problems requires the collective thought and input of a team. Problem-solving teams generally use two approaches when searching for a solution: structured problem solving and group brainstorming.

Structured Problem Solving

Groups use a *structured approach* to examine and solve a problem. This helps groups maintain a focused and orderly discussion about the problem. To apply the **structured problem-solving approach,** teams collect information on the nature and scope of the problem facing them. Then they systematically search for a solution (Dewey, 1933). Although there is some variation to this method, a structured approach generally follows these steps:

1. *Define and analyze the problem.* Gather information to understand the nature, scope, causes, and effects of the problem. The Alaska Airlines team did this when it studied customer lines and check-in procedures in other settings. Group leaders are responsible for making sure the team gathers enough information about the problem and critically analyzes that information.

2. *Establish criteria for a solution.* Define the criteria that an acceptable solution must meet. For example, what is the deadline? What results must the solution produce? What is the maximum cost the solution can incur? The Alaska Airlines team identified "reduced check-in time" as a criterion for its solution.

3. *Discuss possible solutions.* Suggest a number of potential solutions. If necessary, conduct additional research to understand how similar problems have been solved. More research can also shed light on unintended consequences of the solutions your group is considering. To design the new ticketing and check-in layout, the Alaska Airlines team identified and analyzed many different layout options for checking in.

4. *Choose the best solution.* Using the solution criteria and the discussion about possible solutions, identify the solution that seems optimal. Watch out for overly quick agreement on a solution; this could suggest that your team is falling victim to groupthink.

5. *Implement the solution, and evaluate the results.* Try out the solution, and assess the results to determine whether it is effectively solving the problem. Don't assume that just because a solution is in place, the work is done. The Alaska Airlines team tested its solution in one location and then tried it in another, more complex setting to better gauge its effectiveness.

Group Brainstorming

Through **group brainstorming,** a team focuses on generating as many ideas as possible to solve a defined problem. This approach is often integrated with step three of the structured problem-solving process described in the *structured approach* section. Brainstorming is also used when an outside person or organization asks a group for input in solving a problem. For example, a college administrator may attend a student organization meeting to seek ideas for increasing student participation in a semiannual blood drive. Brainstorming can help groups think creatively, or outside the box, when coming up with solutions. First introduced in his book *Applied Imagination,* advertising executive Alex Osborn (1953) provided four guidelines for effective brainstorming:

1. *Encourage wild ideas.* Even far-fetched ideas can spark creative, workable solutions. For example, during a brainstorming session about increasing campus blood-drive participation, one student might suggest a vampire theme, including a live bat exhibit.

2. *Avoid judging ideas.* Strive to generate as many ideas as possible without judging them. Premature judging—"That's crazy; don't you know bats can carry diseases?"—can discourage group members from offering additional thoughts that could be valuable. In brainstorming, the goal is to keep coming up with suggestions.

3. *Quantity is important.* The more ideas a group can generate, the greater raw material it has as the basis for designing a good solution.

4. *Combine and elaborate on ideas.* Blend together ideas offered by group members, and build on them to generate new ideas. For instance, another student might build on the vampire theme by recommending that the blood drive be scheduled in late October to include a Halloween theme (minus the live bats!).

Building on Osborn's original recommendations, recent studies have shown that group members can get better ideas from a brainstorming session if they come up with some ideas before the discussion and visibly post them for teammates. This helps trigger additional thoughts in other members during the group brainstorming (Brown & Paulus, 2002).

Group brainstorming does, however, have some limitations. If team members feel overwhelmed by the volume of ideas being offered, they may stop expressing their own ideas. Or if they're afraid others will judge them or their ideas, they may avoid making contributions. In some cases, individuals might just be lazy and let others do all the thinking (Sawyer, 2007).

If you're leading or taking part in a brainstorming group, you can help combat these potential downfalls. How? Share Osborn's four guidelines with the entire group before starting a brainstorming session. If you see any criticism occurring during a brainstorming session, remind group members that the goal is to generate lots of ideas *without judging them*. Finally, encourage all members to participate to avoid *social loafing* during the session.

Leading Decision Making

Small groups make tons of decisions—everything from who should be in the group to how to achieve its goals. How do members make such decisions? Should the leader decide for everyone? Should there be a vote? Or should the group discuss choices until everyone agrees? Depending on the group's goals, the leadership style, and the decision being made, it could be any of these options.

It was a simple ad with a big impact. The 2013 NFL Super Bowl came to a screeching halt when the power went out in the New Orleans Superdome. As players, coaches, sportscasters, and fans were left idling for 34 agonizing minutes, the social media team for Oreo went to work. Seizing the opportunity to create a timely and relevant ad, the 15-person group created, approved, and posted an image of an Oreo cookie to Twitter with this simple caption: "Power out? No problem. You can still dunk in the dark" (Watercutter, 2013). The group did all this in about 10 minutes. If you've ever seen an episode of *Mad Men*, you know this is an exceptionally fast turnaround in terms of designing and publishing an ad. The team was able to move so quickly because the designated leaders—in this case, brand managers for Oreo—made fast and firm decisions, enabling the rest of the team to execute the plan immediately. The result was a highly regarded and memorable ad—and proof that a group with clear decision-making processes can achieve great success.

The quick decisions made by the marketing team at Nabisco allowed them to capitalize on an "at the moment" event during the Super Bowl XLVII blackout.

Considered the most creative response to the blackout, the ad's simple coloring mimicked what was happening at the game.

Datasift.com said the ad reached a potential audience of 13.3 million, making it hugely successful for a tweet.

https://twitter.com/Oreo/status/298246571718483968/photo/1

MAKING COMMUNICATION CHOICES
THE BEARER OF BAD NEWS

CONSIDER THE DILEMMA

"We nailed it! I'm glad that's over. Now it's all about spring break!" Clayton exclaims as the team exchanges enthusiastic nods and smiles. As the community outreach director for the Silver City Parks Department, you and a group of three local college interns—Desiree, Clayton, and JC—just finished presenting to departmental staff a Web site redesign to market after-school recreation programs.

As you watch them talk about how great they think the presentation went, you think back to their first week together. At that time you weren't sure they would ever be a cohesive team. Clayton was the most outgoing but very self-absorbed. Desiree—although extremely shy—came highly recommended by her graphic design teacher. JC was ambitious but preoccupied with recent family troubles. You invested a lot of time getting the students to work as a team, and the Web site redesign had been especially important in bringing them together.

"Do you think the staff liked the design?" JC inquires.

"Hard to tell, but I meet with Mr. Jackson on Monday morning to find out," you reply.

"Text us as soon as you know something," Desiree says, as they walk out of the building to begin their spring break.

Monday morning brings bad news. "The staff hated it," Mr. Jackson says just as you sit down in his office. "Here's a list of things you need to fix ASAP before the site can go live." When you remind Mr. Jackson that the interns are on spring break, he replies, "Not a problem. Have Hernandez help you out."

"But the students put a lot of time into the design, and they're anxious to know what the staff thought. I'd like a chance to . . ." you begin to protest.

Mr. Jackson interrupts, "Send them an e-mail. Tell them it was a good effort, but we're going in a different direction. It happens." Stunned and angry, you get up and leave the office.

CONNECT THE RESEARCH

Being a leader means handling difficult tasks, such as providing negative feedback to group members about their work. In order to competently communicate unpleasant messages, a leader has to successfully balance two goals: (1) help those who receive negative feedback maintain a positive face, and (2) maintain a trustworthy and capable impression with the group. To do this, a leader should carefully consider how to form the message and which communication channel to use to deliver it (Kingsley Westerman & Westerman, 2010).

First, leaders should create face-saving messages, in which they frame unpleasant messages in a way that softens the impact of bad news ("Perhaps the design expectations weren't entirely clear, but the new Web site design needs additional work"). Face-saving messages are more

likely to be perceived as nonthreatening by a receiver than would a message that is too direct ("Your design is unacceptable") (Kingsley Westerman & Westerman, 2010). Such messages can help receivers accept the criticism and move forward.

Second, the communication channel used to deliver the message (face-to-face or online) matters. When leaders give unpleasant feedback in person rather than through mediated communication, they are seen as more competent, and the message is perceived as less threatening. This may be because face-to-face communication provides access to nonverbal cues that are important for developing empathy as well as for giving the recipient an opportunity to ask clarifying questions.

Before making a communication choice, consider the facts of the situation, and think about the research on managing impressions and communication channels. Also, reflect on what you've learned so far about leadership styles (pp. 288–292) and communication climates (p. 294). Then answer these questions:

1 What responsibility do you have to immediately share the feedback with your interns? How would you respond if any of them text-messaged you wanting an update?

2 What is the potential impact on team cohesiveness if you share the feedback via e-mail? What do you risk by waiting until the students return?

3 How are you going to break the news?

Small groups make a series of decisions at various points in their work together. Everything from deciding when your group should meet to choosing a caption for an ad is subject to **decision making**—the process of making choices among alternatives. Groups commonly rely on three methods for decision making: decision by authority, decision by majority, and decision by consensus.

Decision by Authority

Some groups use *decision by authority*, in which an expert or a designated leader makes decisions on behalf of the group. Relying on an authority is appropriate when a group must make a decision quickly or when an individual member has expertise that's especially critical for solving the problem at hand. For example, emergency-department physicians determine treatment priorities for incoming patients, while nurses and other support staff follow those decisions and provide little or no input.

However, this method has its drawbacks. For example, team members who disagree with a decision may feel pressured to go along with it. If a team member sees serious flaws in the thinking behind a decision but doesn't speak up loudly enough, disaster can result. If you are leading a group and making a decision by authority, it is still helpful to listen to any questions or concerns of your group members to ensure your decision is as informed as possible.

Decision by Majority

To use the *decision by majority* method, leaders identify two or more options, and all members of the group vote. In most groups, the option that receives a majority of the votes (the most) is declared the winner. This is a common and familiar way to make decisions in groups. Since leaders pick only a few choices for members to vote on, decision by majority can be efficient—particularly in larger groups, where discussion of various options can take up a lot of time.

However, this is not a good approach to use when a group needs to make a quick decision, as in the situation the Oreo branding team faced at the Super Bowl.

One possible consequence in using this approach is that voting divides a group into winners and losers. Those who voted for an option that "lost" may feel that they wasted their time or that their input wasn't valued. Therefore, they may not feel committed to following through on what the group decided.

Decision by Consensus

When a group is responsible for not only making a decision but also putting that decision into action, leaders may want to strive for *decision by consensus*. Achieving **consensus** on decisions means that all members support a given course of action. For example, your class group may be picking a service-learning project to complete as part of a course requirement. Rather than risk fragmenting the group by voting, a consensus decision secures all group members' commitment to the chosen project. Even group members who have concerns about the decision will still support it (Johnson & Johnson, 2008). In most cases, groups that decide by consensus report greater member satisfaction with the decision than groups relying on majority rule (Sager & Gastil, 2006). This happens because the discussion encourages input from all group members and helps build cohesiveness in a team.

To promote decision by consensus, leaders must encourage open discussion. It takes considerable time to get everyone to agree on a course of action, but the resulting group cohesiveness is well worth it. To help set group members' expectations, leaders should clearly explain that decisions will be made by consensus (Sager & Gastil, 1999). Team members, for their part, must strive to actively listen to all ideas as they are proposed. Leaders should also make sure that team members don't feel pressured to simply go along with the group. Saying something like "If anyone here feels uncomfortable with the decision we're moving toward, please speak up and let us know your concerns. We want everyone's input here," will help minimize that outcome.

Each decision-making approach has its pros and cons and is best used under specific circumstances. Regardless of which approach is used, it's important for the leader to clarify the approach for the group. Otherwise, leaders' actions can sometimes seem arbitrary and unpredictable, which can erode group morale and satisfaction.

Leading Meetings

Small groups do much of their work in face-to-face and virtual meetings. But when meetings are poorly planned or managed, people get frustrated, and time is wasted. When leading a group, you can ensure that meetings run smoothly by developing an agenda, encouraging participation during meetings, and following up afterwards.

MEETINGS GONE WRONG

Whether it's because they're intimidating, bad tempered, or just plain bizarre, the leaders in *The Devil Wears Prada*, *The Office*, and *Entourage* demonstrate how meetings with coworkers or team members can go wrong. When you are leading a meeting or a group discussion, what factors are most important for making sure it goes well?

(Clockwise from top left) 20th Century Fox/Courtesy Everett; Byron Cohen/NBC/NBCU Photo Bank via Getty Images; Claudette Barius/© HBO /Courtesy Everett Collection

Have you ever sat in a meeting that had no apparent purpose? What about a meeting in which people talked on and on about a topic but never arrived at a decision? Or a meeting that got derailed by one person and never got back on track? If you've had these experiences, you're not alone. Although meetings are critical for conducting group work, all too many are hugely unproductive.

What are the culprits behind such meetings? In one study, business professionals identified what they saw as the top five meeting problems: (1) participants get off subject, (2) there is no clear agenda, (3) meetings take too long, (4) team members come unprepared, and (5) no definitive action is taken after the meeting (Romano & Nunamaker, 2001). To combat these problems and get the most out of group meetings, leaders must take responsibility for planning, conducting, and following up on/evaluating meetings.

Planning Meetings

Like speeches, the most useful meetings start with a plan. What is the first step in that plan? Defining the purpose of the meeting. Meetings that don't have a clear purpose waste everyone's time. Teams meet for many different purposes. In *information briefings*, participants get updated on key developments of an event or a situation. For example, Joe's oldest son attends monthly sales meetings at his job to learn about new products and sales incentives. *Problem-solving meetings* address an undesirable situation, such as when microchip engineers gather to analyze defects in their company's manufacturing process and generate ideas for remedying the problem. *Decision-making meetings* entail making a choice about something, such as when your French club meets to choose a date for the annual picnic.

Most meetings incorporate a bit of all three—information briefing, problem solving, and decision making—though one of these purposes may be paramount. Whatever the purpose, identifying it (or them) helps leaders develop the **meeting agenda**—a structured, written outline that guides communication among meeting participants by showing which topics will be discussed, in what order, and (often) for how long. Without an agenda, team members may start talking about different subjects at the same time or go off on tangents. (See Table 12.2 for a sample meeting agenda.)

Identifying a meeting's purpose and developing an agenda help leaders decide who should attend the meeting and what materials participants will need to prepare for and take part in the meeting. Leaders can then make sure to distribute in advance any readings, reports, or other materials that will be discussed in the meeting, so participants can come prepared.

Conducting Meetings

If you're conducting a meeting, start by clarifying its purposes and anticipated outcomes. Ensure that participants are acquainted with one another, and that they understand each member's role and responsibilities. If you're conducting a virtual meeting by videoconference or telephone, make sure to introduce everyone involved so that all participants know who is attending and can identify anyone who speaks.

In addition, carefully manage the group's communication so that everyone sticks to the agenda. If the discussion starts veering away from the agenda, redirect attention back to the plan. Watch or listen for people who are dominating the discussion, and encourage quieter members to provide their input. Pay attention to how much time the group is spending on each agenda item, and keep the discussion moving forward so that all items get covered. If a particular task needs more detailed conversation, suggest covering it in a separate meeting. Finally, end the meeting by summarizing key decisions, identifying actions that must be taken, and clarifying who will be responsible for carrying out those actions.

Following Up On/Evaluating Meetings

Once a meeting ends, team members tend to go about their personal and work lives. They may forget all about the action items and decisions that

TABLE 12.2

SAMPLE MEETING AGENDA

**STUDENT
LEADERSHIP TEAM**

Monday, November 3
2:00–3:00 pm
Location: South Conference Room 211

ITEM	PERSON RESPONSIBLE	REQUIRED ACTION	TIME
1. Discuss personal reflection on last month's service project.	All	None	15 minutes
2. Decide on two applications for new student organizations.	Jean	Vote	20 minutes
3. Brainstorm spring retreat locations.	Jean	Identify top two and assign person to conduct research to present at next meeting.	20 minutes
4. Confirm time and place for next meeting.	Sarah	Follow-up e-mail with reminder about time and place	5 minutes

1. Vector pro/Shutterstock; 2. tele52/Shutterstock

came out of the meeting. To counteract this tendency, follow up on agreed-upon actions, and evaluate the outcome of the meeting.

Within 24 hours of a meeting, send a written record of the discussion, actions, and decisions—often called the **meeting minutes**—to everyone who attended the meeting as well as anyone who needs to know what happened. Include any materials or information that was missing or requested during the meeting.

Then spend some time reflecting on what worked well in the meeting and what could be improved upon at the next meeting. For example, did a number of people come to the meeting unprepared because they didn't have enough time to review the materials you sent ahead of time? If so, consider sending required reading even earlier the next time.

LearningCurve can help you review! Go to **bedfordstmartins.com /choicesconnections**.

CHAPTER 12 REVIEW

CHAPTER RECAP

- Scholars generally agree on four leadership perspectives—the **traits view,** the **style view,** the **situational view,** and the **functional view**—to help clarify how leadership works in small groups.
- In addition to establishing a **communication climate,** productive leaders help prevent **groupthink** and deal with **substantive** and **affective conflict** in a group.
- Two of the most common approaches used for solving problems in groups are **structured problem solving** and **group brainstorming.**
- Groups commonly rely on three methods for **decision making:** decision by authority, decision by majority, and decision by consensus.
- To get the most out of group meetings, leaders must take responsibility for planning, conducting, and following up on/evaluating meetings.

LAUNCHPAD

LaunchPad for *Choices & Connections* offers unique video scenarios and encourages self-assessment through adaptive quizzing. Go to **bedfordstmartins.com /choicesconnections** to get access.

☑ LearningCurve adaptive quizzes

 How to Communicate video scenarios

 Video clips that illustrate key concepts

KEY TERMS

Leadership, p. 288

Shared leadership, p. 288

Traits view of leadership, p. 289

Style view of leadership, p. 290

Autocratic leadership style, p. 290

Laissez-faire leadership style, p. 290

Democratic leadership style, p. 290

Situational view of leadership, p. 290

Functional view of leadership, p. 292

Communication climate, p. 294

Groupthink, p. 298

Substantive conflict, p. 298

Affective conflict, p. 298

Structured problem-solving approach, p. 301

Group brainstorming, p. 302

Decision making, p. 305

Consensus, p. 306

Meeting agenda, p. 308

Meeting minutes, p. 309

Looking for more review questions? **LearningCurve** can help you master key concepts from this chapter. Go to **bedfordstmartins.com /choicesconnections**.

1 How does the concept of shared leadership apply to small group communication?

a. It prevents groupthink.

b. It reflects the traits view of leadership, since members have different skills.

c. It allows all group members to influence and direct the group.

d. It avoids affective conflict.

2 In the situational view of leadership, a group that has high amounts of motivation and experience may benefit the most from a _____ leadership style.

a. telling   **c.** delegating

b. participating   **d.** selling

3 A potential outcome of a defensive communication climate within a group is _____.

a. the avoidance of destructive communication

b. a weakening of group cohesion

c. a demonstration of empathy

d. the formation of cooperative messages

4 Which of the following is *not* a step in the structured problem-solving approach?

a. Evaluate the implemented solution

b. Establish criteria for a solution

c. Discuss possible solutions

d. Determine the cheapest solution

5 A potential drawback to _____ is that members who lost may not feel committed to the group decision.

a. decision by majority

b. decision by consensus

c. decision by authority

d. decision by function

ACTIVITIES

1 Leading Hollywood

Watch a film featuring strong leaders, such as *Captain Phillips*, *Lincoln*, *Argo*, *Dangerous Minds*, or *The Devil Wears Prada*. How did the leaders in the film embody one or more of the views of leadership? Give specific examples. Did they adapt their styles to certain situations or people? How successful were their leadership styles? How do you think their leadership styles could be improved?

2 Practicing Problem Solving

Working with a small group of classmates, choose a campus problem—such as student parking, food services, or student health services—and apply the structured problem-solving approach to identify a potential solution. Share your solution with the rest of the class, and then analyze how well the group worked together using the structured problem-solving approach and what you would do differently in the future.

13

Preparing Your Speech

Everything Apple produces—iPhones, iPads, Mac computers, and even Apple TV—reflects the extraordinary mind of the company's cofounder, Steve Jobs. His vision of personal computing guided Apple's success as it became one of the most profitable technology companies in the world. But Jobs also left his stamp on another thing Apple excels at—using compelling live and online presentations to introduce and demonstrate new products.

Unlike most companies that use television ads and social media to introduce products, Apple consistently turns new-product announcements into captivating public-speaking events. As *Forbes* magazine contributor Carmine Gallow (2012) describes:

> Like most people I don't know what Apple is going to announce before they release the product to the public. But I do know exactly how they will craft and deliver the presentation behind the product announcement. I know because Steve Jobs created the template—the model—for a great presentation and nobody at Apple strays from it.

When Steve Jobs presented, he strolled comfortably around the stage, often teasing his audience and building their anticipation about the newest Apple product offerings. He integrated visually stunning graphics to highlight sales figures and company achievements. Other Apple employees frequently joined Jobs onstage to demonstrate new products, their segments appearing seamless and natural. What the audience did not see, however, was the rigorous preparation that went into each well-scripted and well-choreographed presentation.

Former Apple product manager Mike Evangelist had firsthand experience with the grueling effort Jobs put into getting ready for his presentations.[1] Before sharing the stage with Jobs during one Macworld Conference, Evangelist was required to spend hours

---

[1]Account adapted from Evangelist (2006).

practicing under Jobs's watchful eye. Jobs also gave him pointed criticism—even though Evangelist's contribution to the program would last only five minutes.

Apple continues to follow the same high standards and invest the same rigor in preparing its product presentations today. Executives and designers like Tim Cook and Jony Ive spend considerable time thinking through which new products and services to feature, developing visual aids, planning ways of engaging the audience, and rehearsing the presentation. The presentations are carefully designed and prepared because Apple knows the importance of connecting with its audience—both those who attend in person and the hundreds of thousands who watch the product announcements online.

Few people ever give a speech that attracts as much media scrutiny as does an Apple product announcement. But in the course of your life, you will inevitably give some presentations. Knowing how to properly prepare for such occasions will help you achieve success.

Public speaking is the process of preparing and delivering a message to an audience to achieve a specific purpose. Perhaps you'll deliver a project status briefing at work, or make a presentation asking a group of parents to volunteer for after-school activities at your child's school. At the very least, you will likely give a speech for this class. This idea makes many people nervous, even though the speech may be days or weeks away. Don't worry if you're feeling unsettled at the mere idea of giving a speech; it's perfectly normal to feel this way. We'll help out by discussing strategies for coping with public-speaking anxiety (pages 386–388). For now, try to relax, and take comfort in the fact that you already know many of the communication principles and skills that support strong speech preparation. In this chapter, you'll learn:

- The five steps in speech preparation
- How to select your speech topic
- Ideas for analyzing your audience and adapting your topic to them
- How to develop a strategy for researching your speech
- Ways to conduct your research and evaluate your resources

✔️ **LearningCurve** can help you review! Go to **bedfordstmartins.com /choicesconnections**.

Preparing Your Speech: Five Steps

Think about the speeches you've heard during your lifetime. Some were probably very good, keeping your interest and providing useful information. Some were probably not so good—perhaps they were boring or forgettable or both. What's the difference? Preparation. Public speakers who carefully prepare their speeches engage their audiences the most.

As Apple product presentations show, skilled speakers carefully prepare their messages to engage and inspire their audiences. To do the same, follow five steps of speech preparation: think, investigate, compose, rehearse, and revise. (See Table 13.1.)

First, **think** about your audience and speech topic. Determine the purpose of your speech, choose the topic, and consider how to adapt it to your audience. When working through this step, it will be important to develop *accurate perceptions*, or knowledge, of your listeners so that you deliver an understandable speech.

Second, **investigate** resources to use in developing your presentation. This includes planning your research strategy, conducting your research, and evaluating the resources you find.

TABLE 13.1

FIVE STEPS IN SPEECH PREPARATION

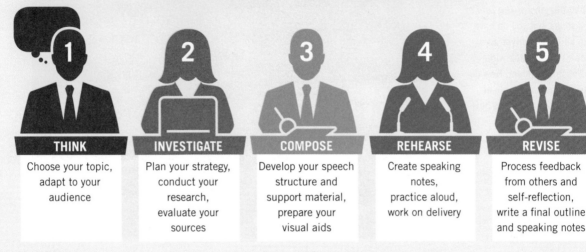

THINK	INVESTIGATE	COMPOSE	REHEARSE	REVISE
Choose your topic, adapt to your audience	Plan your strategy, conduct your research, evaluate your sources	Develop your speech structure and support material, prepare your visual aids	Create speaking notes, practice aloud, work on delivery	Process feedback from others and self-reflection, write a final outline and speaking notes

edel/Shutterstock

Third, **compose** your presentation, outlining your ideas and planning any visual support. You will prepare an introduction to capture your audience's attention, identify your main points, and decide how to conclude the speech. Successful public speakers incorporate the *cooperative principle* (from Chapter 5) into their language, making their message informative, honest, relevant, and clear. They also use "we" language to better connect to and build solidarity with their audiences.

Fourth, **rehearse** your presentation. Apple presentations look easy because of the extensive time the executives and designers spend rehearsing. In this step, you practice your presentation on your own and in front of others, inviting feedback for improvements. This is also the time to work on your *nonverbal skills*—including eye contact, gestures, and facial expressions—to further engage your listeners.

Fifth, **revise** your presentation, adapting it based on the feedback you received while rehearsing. You can further improve your speech content and delivery by being *critically self-reflective*—honestly assessing your communication and considering ways to improve it. You can also use any feedback you receive after the presentation to prepare for your next public-speaking occasion.

In this chapter, we focus on the first two steps: *thinking about your speech* and *investigating your sources*. We discuss steps 3, 4, and 5 in Chapters 14–15.

You may not have the ability to magically disappear at the end of your speech like Bilbo Baggins in *The Lord of the Rings*, but you do have the ability to deliver an interesting speech with purpose and intent. How do the purpose and topic of your speech influence how you deliver it?

NEW LINE/SAUL ZAENTZ/WING NUT/THE KOBAL COLLECTION/VINET, PIERRE

Choosing Your Speech Topic

The first part of Step 1: Think is to identify why you are giving a speech and to choose a speech topic. Although you will want to choose a topic that is appropriate for the situation, it should also be a topic that excites you. You will be spending a lot of time working on the speech, so you might as well enjoy the topic.

J. R. R. Tolkien's timeless adventure *The Lord of the Rings* begins with a speech. At the birthday feast of the hobbit Bilbo Baggins, the guest of honor is making some after-dinner remarks to acknowledge the special occasion and praise his friends. But Bilbo's purpose on this particular evening is to do more than just say "I hope you are all enjoying yourselves as much as I am" and "I am immensely fond of you." Instead, Bilbo's speech catches everyone's attention when, toward the end, he says the following:

> *I have called you all together for a Purpose. . . . I wish to make an ANNOUNCE-MENT. . . . I regret to announce that . . . this is the END. I am going. I am leaving NOW. GOOD-BYE!* He stepped down and vanished. There was a blinding flash of light, and the guests all blinked. When they opened their eyes Bilbo was nowhere to be seen. One hundred and forty-four flabbergasted hobbits sat back speechless.[2]

---

[2]Excerpt adapted from J. R. R. Tolkien (1954; 1994), pp. 28–30.

As fans of *The Lord of the Rings* series know, this speech and Bilbo's sudden disappearance set in motion an extraordinary adventure for his nephew Frodo as he seeks to protect the Ring. Of course, the speeches we give in our lives are rarely as dramatic (or magical!) as this. But no matter the occasion, our speech preparation should always begin in the same way as Bilbo's: by thinking carefully about the general purpose of our speech and considering what topic to discuss.

Identifying Your General Purpose

When preparing a speech, you should first determine your **general purpose**— your reason for giving the presentation. Speeches typically have one of three purposes:

1. *To inform* your audience. **Informative speeches** educate your audience about a topic, describe an object, demonstrate how something works, or explain a concept.

2. *To persuade* your audience. **Persuasive speeches** reinforce or change listeners' attitudes and beliefs and may motivate them to take certain actions.

3. To recognize or celebrate a *special occasion*. **Special-occasion speeches** entertain, celebrate, commemorate, or inspire. These include introducing someone at an event, accepting or giving an award, commemorating an event or a person, or giving a toast.

For the speeches you'll be giving in your communication class, your instructor will probably assign the general purpose. For example, he or she may require you to give an informative or a persuasive speech (or both). When you give speeches in other settings, you will determine your general purpose. For instance, suppose you work as a drug rehabilitation counselor. If you were going to talk to parents of high school students, you could plan an informative speech to explain the warning signs of teen drug use, since that topic would be of interest to the parents. But if you were speaking directly to the teens, you might adapt your plan to give a persuasive speech about why they should resist pressure to use illegal drugs.

However, your general purpose is not always so straightforward. Consider that Bilbo Baggins planned a speech to celebrate his birthday and express admiration to his friends (special-occasion purpose), but he also had an informative purpose: to tell his friends that he would be leaving. Sometimes, like Bilbo, you may blend purposes.

Considering Speech Topics

Once you know the general purpose of your speech, it's time to choose your **speech topic**—the specific content you will present. Most classroom speech assignments allow you to select a topic. When you give a speech outside the classroom, the setting usually determines your topic. If you are invited to speak to student groups about competent conflict resolution, your topic is defined by the invitation; you can't show up and talk about how to design iPhone apps instead!

When you have the freedom to choose your own topic, the choice can sometimes seem overwhelming. So how do you decide what to talk about? With some careful thought, you can come up with a topic that both interests you and will engage your audience. Let's explore three ways for coming up with topic ideas: reflecting on your personal interests/experiences, brainstorming, and developing concept maps.

Interests and Experiences. One of the first things to think about is what interests you. If you have a passion for a certain hobby, cause, or subject, that is a great place to start. You can also consider personal experiences, such as vacations, jobs, or volunteer work. One of our students worked as a limousine driver and used his experience to prepare a speech on when and how to properly tip service workers.

Other ideas for speech topics can be drawn directly from your academic studies. For example, perhaps you learned about eating disorders or social media addiction in a psychology course. Your speech assignment provides the opportunity to share this information with others.

Basing a speech topic on personal interests and experiences has some advantages. Your direct involvement gives you credibility with your audience and opportunities to tell engaging stories. If you feel passionately about your topic, you are more likely to inspire your audience. After all, when audience members see you excited about an issue or a hobby, they can't help but feel curious and interested, too.

Brainstorming. **Brainstorming** is a creative problem-solving strategy that involves coming up with as many ideas as possible in a defined period of time. This is similar to *group brainstorming*, which, as Chapter 12 discusses, is often used in small group communication settings. The most common approach to brainstorming is *freewriting*, or *listing ideas*: writing down all the ideas that come to mind, without judging them, during the allotted time—say, 15 minutes. Some experts maintain that the wilder the ideas are during the brainstorming period, the better the final ideas may be (Kelley & Littman, 2001). After the brainstorming period ends, review your list of ideas and eliminate any that don't interest you. Look over the remaining ideas to see which ones intrigue you the most. This shorter list provides a base for you to further develop your topic by narrowing broad interest areas into more specific ideas. For example, if your brainstorming list has *food* and *health*, you could think further along those lines to *fad diets, fast food, local farming,* or *organic foods*.

Concept Maps. Another way to explore ideas is by creating a **concept map:** a drawing showing connections among related ideas. A concept map helps you expand on one idea with more specific topics. (In contrast, brainstorming helps you generate multiple ideas.) If you came up with a broad topic that

FIGURE 13.1
SAMPLE CONCEPT MAP

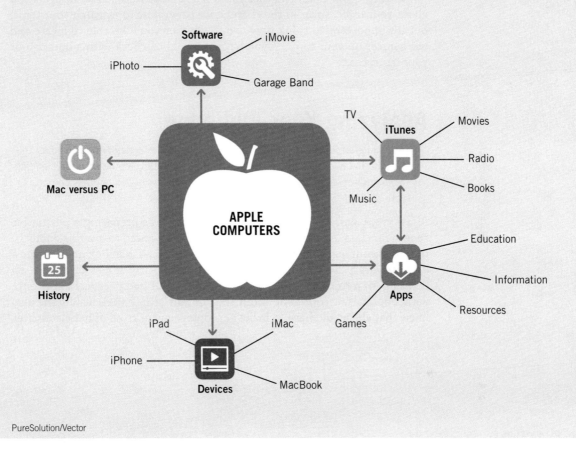

PureSolution/Vector

interests you during brainstorming but are having trouble narrowing it down, a concept map can help you be more specific. For instance, if you're interested in giving a speech about computers, your concept map may look something like Figure 13.1.

Deciding on Your Topic

After you identify a possible topic, ask yourself whether the topic could serve as the basis for a successful speech. The answer could be yes if you find the topic personally or socially important. You want to be interested in and challenged by the topic, since you'll be spending considerable time preparing your speech. You'll also want to consider whether you could complete your speech in the time allotted. For a classroom speech, check whether your topic is acceptable. Your instructor might veto your proposed topic if it's been overdone or inappropriate (such as gun control, abortion, or the legalization of marijuana).

Finally, think about whether you will be able to find quality information about your topic. Later in the chapter, we cover how to research your topic, but it's important to think now about whether you'll be able to locate and use sources on your topic. If you have any doubts, check with a librarian or your instructor.

Analyzing Your Audience

As you determine your speech topic, you should also consider how to adapt the topic to the needs and interests of your audience. Developing an understanding of your audience will guide you in narrowing your topic and actually composing your speech.

A few years ago, one of our students, Paolina, was preparing a persuasive speech for class. As a breast cancer survivor, she wanted to use this opportunity to encourage women to engage in monthly breast self-exams and see a doctor every year, common ways to detect the early stages of cancer. By focusing on a topic she was passionate about and had personal experience with, Paolina felt confident about the content of her speech. But she also knew that she would have to make her topic relevant to all of her classmates

Part of delivering a successful speech is making sure all audience members, not just one demographic, engage with the topic. Paolina's speech was one example of this. But what if the speaker is someone you wouldn't typically associate with the topic? Consider how an audience analysis would help Senator Cory Booker (shown) connect with his mostly female audience at a breast cancer research fund-raising rally.

Matt Rainey/Star Ledger/Corbis

in order to deliver a successful speech. She pondered how to take what's usually considered a women's health issue and make it relevant to the men in the class. While researching her topic, she kept an eye out for ways to make that connection and discovered that men, too, are at risk for breast cancer, although in smaller numbers than women. She also realized that men could encourage the women in their lives to get regular examinations. By taking the time to think about how her topic would relate to her audience, Paolina prepared a speech targeted to *all* of her listeners—men and women alike.

Understanding Your Audience

By thinking about how her topic would connect with her audience, Paolina was using **audience analysis**—a process of identifying important characteristics about audience members, and using this information to prepare a speech.

Audience analysis fulfills three purposes. First, the more you analyze your audience, the better you can adapt your topic to their needs and interests. This is why Paolina's speech on breast cancer prevention addressed men as well as women.

Second, analyzing your audience helps you relate support materials and factual details to your audience's lives and viewpoints. For example, using statistics on local breast cancer rates (as opposed to national or global rates) can make the issue seem more real to listeners.

Third, audience analysis helps shape your nonverbal delivery and language style. Consider how a medical doctor speaking to breast cancer patients about treatment options would use a different manner and vocabulary than when she's explaining the same thing to medical students.

To better understand your audience, you can explore several factors, including demographics; attitudes, beliefs, and values; knowledge; and type.

Audience Demographics. Your listeners' **demographics** include their age, sex, education level, group memberships (religious or political associations), socioeconomic status, family status (single, married, divorced, partnered, with children or without), and cultural background. Depending on your speech topic, some demographic characteristics of your audience will be more relevant than others. For example, imagine that you represent a nonprofit agency and speak frequently to local community groups. The ages and socioeconomic status of your listeners will be important factors to consider as you prepare each speech. College students on a budget may be more interested in learning about volunteering for your agency than donating money, so your speeches to campus clubs would emphasize such opportunities. On the other hand, local business professionals may be willing to donate both service and financial support. Thus, you would adjust your speeches to them accordingly.

Although it's important to take your listeners' demographic characteristics into account when preparing your speech, there are some things you need to consider. As Chapters 2 and 4 describe, people often engage in *stereotyping*—categorizing people into a social group and then forming impressions about them based on information they possess about the group. When conducting your audience analysis, recognize that stereotypes based on demographic characteristics—such as age and sex—can be flawed. For example, Paolina didn't stereotype all the men in her class as being disinterested in the issue. Instead, she found ways to broaden the focus of a "women's health issue" to include the men in her audience. Demographics are best used to develop a sense of possible shared characteristics among your audience that may reflect on their knowledge or interest in your topic. But be careful to not overgeneralize about your audience, because each listener possesses unique attitudes, beliefs, and values that may shape how he or she reacts to your speech.

Audience Attitudes, Beliefs, and Values. Your listeners are not just a collection of demographics; each one also interprets your speech through his or her sense of self. This *self-concept*—or who each perceives him- or herself to be—influences how individual audience members will respond to your message. As Chapter 2 explains, *self-concept* is based on the attitudes, beliefs, and values you have about yourself. An **attitude** is an evaluation that makes a person respond favorably or unfavorably toward an issue, a situation, or a person. If your friend says, "I love Mexican food," he is expressing an attitude.

Each member of your audience has his or her own *self-concept*, which includes individual attitudes, values, and beliefs. All of these affect the way the person perceives incoming information. If you were giving a speech to the rally-goers pictured here, how would you interpret their values and how could that influence your delivery?

Julie Dermansky/Corbis

A **belief** is a conviction regarding what is true and untrue. People develop their beliefs from many sources, including their family, religious or community authorities, education, and life experiences. "There is absolutely life on other planets" is a belief.

Strongly held beliefs that guide our behaviors are known as **values.** How people answer the question, What's important to me? reveals their values. Is it family? Equal rights for all people? Money? Values are strongly shaped by culture—for example, valuing individual freedoms (*individualistic cultures*) over group concerns (*collectivistic cultures*), or vice versa.

By understanding your audience's attitudes, beliefs, and values, you can better adapt your speech topic to connect with them. If you are dealing with controversial social issues, such as stem-cell research, urban poverty, environmental racism, or same-sex marriage, you'll need to demonstrate respect for your audience's attitudes, beliefs, and values regarding your topic, as these may vary from your own. Even when you take a strong stand on a contentious topic, you will need to present your ideas in a way that is civil, is ethical, and doesn't degrade others. You can do this by acknowledging your audience members' views and explaining why you want to present your topic from a particular perspective. For more ideas on accounting for your audiences' attitudes, beliefs, and values, see the Making Communication Choices box on pages 324–325.

Audience Knowledge. Another part of your audience analysis is to consider your listeners' existing level of knowledge about your speech topic. You can make educated guesses about how much your audience members already know or what kind of information they need by reflecting on their demographics (age, education) and their attitudes, beliefs, and values. So though a class of college students will likely know a lot about Twitter or Instagram, a group of senior citizens may be less likely to know about such technologies.

When possible, directly poll your audience while preparing your speech to gauge their knowledge, and adapt your presentation accordingly. Let's say you have video production experience and want to talk about editing video. From an informal poll of your class, you discover that most of your classmates shoot short videos but have no editing experience. This tells you that you'll need to explain and define basic video editing terminology in your speech.

Audience Type. Audiences come in various types. Sometimes you'll be addressing a **captive audience,** meaning that your listeners are required to attend the presentation. Your class is a captive audience because students enrolled in the course have to listen to one another's speeches. Think about how you feel when you're *required* to listen to something versus *choosing* to listen. In general, being forced to listen to a presentation makes you less receptive to its message. So when you're addressing a captive audience, give listeners a reason to pay attention—by explaining early in the presentation how they'll benefit from the information you're providing.

MAKING COMMUNICATION CHOICES

SPEAKING YOUR MIND

1 CONSIDER THE DILEMMA

You decide to attend a campus rally about immigration reform, and you watch, with disappointment, as protesters with opposing views quickly turn the rally into a screaming match and begin trading insults. The turmoil spills over to social media, where students post misinformed and racist comments about the issue. Over the next few days, tensions on campus rise as everyone becomes more devoted to his or her point of view, including you. Your parents immigrated to this country before you were born, and you have very strong feelings about the issue.

Seeking to encourage an open and respectful debate about the issue, your sociology professor, Dr. Levine, plans a campus forum and asks you to make a speech. The forum speeches will provide different perspectives about immigration reform. You would be one of four people to speak at the event, after which Dr. Levine will moderate a discussion about the speeches and the issue overall.

Given your respect for Dr. Levine and your passion about the topic, you want to make the presentation, but you don't want to say something disrespectful, causing you to lose face with the audience or accidentally offend them.

2 CONNECT THE RESEARCH

When presenting to audiences with views different from your own, you can still engage and connect with them by taking the time to create *goodwill*. Establishing goodwill increases the likelihood of maintaining positive face (believability and likability) as a speaker (McCroskey & Teven, 1999). Even in political campaigns, candidates who clearly demonstrate goodwill with voters are more likely to be viewed favorably (Teven, 2008).

Demonstrating goodwill starts with your speech preparation. Maintain fairness and objectivity when conducting research for your speech. When developing your position, try to avoid *polarizing language* (e.g., "those people") and labels (e.g., "conservatives" or "liberals"). Such language can cause your audience to become defensive and quickly dismiss your message.

During the speech, use your opening remarks to establish your goodwill and genuine *empathy*

for your listeners' views. For example, say something like, "I know many of you may disagree with me about this issue, and I respect your viewpoint. But today I'm going to explain why I feel the way *I* do." Audiences are more open to your messages when you show caring, empathy, and fairness (McCroskey & Teven, 1999). Explaining how the information benefits your listeners can also sway those who may initially dislike your topic.

In addition to verbal expressions of goodwill, pay attention to your nonverbal behaviors to ensure that you do not project defensive behaviors (limited eye contact, crossed arms, stiff posture, stern voice) while presenting to your audience. Instead, appropriate smiling, vocal variety, gesturing, and purposeful movement around the room will express caring and goodwill to your listeners (Teven & Hanson, 2004).

Before making a communication choice, consider the facts of the situation, and think about what the research says about establishing goodwill with an audience. Also, reflect on what you've learned so far about audience analysis (pp. 321–325) and preparing speeches in general. Then answer these questions:

1. Do you think it's possible to create goodwill with your audience while being firm in your viewpoint about the topic? Why or why not?

2. What are your ethical obligations to an audience when presenting a controversial topic? How do you balance your family experience and feelings with fairness and objectivity in addressing your audience?

3. What are you going to do when preparing your speech?

In contrast, a **voluntary audience** attends out of self-interest or to fulfill some personal need. These individuals are motivated to listen and may already have some knowledge about your topic. For instance, suppose you go to a tile-laying demonstration at your local home-improvement store because you want to tile your patio. The person conducting the demonstration doesn't need to discuss the benefits of laying your own tile. You're already aware of those benefits; that's why you're there!

Developing Your Audience Analysis

To develop your audience analysis, ask basic questions about your audience, and keep the answers to those questions in mind (or in written notes) while preparing your speech. For example, let's say you're planning a classroom speech. You'll want to make informal observations about your listeners: What's the ratio of men to women? The age ranges? You've probably learned things about your classmates through class activities and discussions, other speech assignments, or any profiles posted to a class Web site. You can also informally poll your class: "How many of you have hiked Copperhead Trail?" Sometimes you can distribute a written or an online questionnaire to identify your listeners' knowledge, attitudes, and beliefs about your topic.

Analyzing a non-classroom audience is trickier. You can briefly interview the person who asked you to make the presentation, to get his or her sense of the audience's demographics; their attitudes, beliefs, and values; and their existing knowledge. You can also ask the person the following questions: What's the purpose of the meeting or event? How many people will attend? Are they required to attend? What other speakers or topics have the group heard recently? What is the group expecting to gain from my presentation? Are there specific needs or challenges you want me to address in my speech? Getting answers to these inquiries will help you narrow your speech topic and determine what content to cover.

Writing Your Specific Purpose Statement

Now that you have your general purpose, a speech topic, and your audience analysis, you're ready to write a specific purpose for your speech. A **specific purpose statement** is one complete sentence summarizing the goal of your speech. It indicates whether you intend to inform or persuade your audience, reflects a narrowing of your speech topic, and is influenced by your audience analysis.

You want to complete your audience analysis before writing your specific purpose statement because what you learn in your analysis will influence your statement. For example, suppose you're preparing a speech to inform your audience about the topic of bullying. Through informal polling, you discover that many of your audience members have experienced or witnessed bullying in the workplace, rather than in school. Therefore, you would want to emphasize that fact in your specific purpose statement: "I want to inform my audience about how to effectively handle bullying in the workplace."

Your specific purpose statement will help you prepare your speech, but it isn't set in stone; you may decide to adjust it while researching your speech. For example, let's say your specific purpose is "I want to persuade my audience to take steps to manage their privacy online." While researching this topic, you discover interesting information about identity theft, including stories of college students as victims. As a result, you could change your specific purpose statement to "I want to persuade my audience to take steps to protect themselves from identity theft."

Planning Your Research Strategy

During Step 2: Investigate, you begin looking for sources for your speech. Although many resources are easily available, not all of them will help you prepare a good speech. After all, Googling your topic is likely to result in thousands of hits. Taking the time to plan a proper search can help you develop a factual speech.

Once you have crafted your specific purpose statement, you may be tempted to start researching your speech by immediately searching online or heading to the library. But this could generate more information than you can possibly sift through, and you may not be sure of exactly what to look for. To manage your time effectively and focus on finding relevant information, plan a strategy for conducting your research. A successful *research strategy* includes (1) identifying your information needs, (2) drawing on your personal knowledge, (3) talking with librarians, and (4) determining how to document and file your research findings.

Identifying Your Information Needs

Your information needs will change as you learn more about your topic and think about your audience. Start by finding general information about your topic, then search for more specific content. Use these questions to guide your research process:

1. *What background information will my audience need?* Depending on your audience analysis, you may need to provide historical background or definitions of key terms in your presentation. If you're giving an informative speech about the benefits of qigong, for example, you should probably provide some history on this ancient Chinese meditative practice. If you don't already have such knowledge about your topic, look for trustworthy resources that provide it, such as organizational Web sites and dictionaries.

2. *What specific information is appropriate for my audience?* Depending on the situation, your listeners may have a lot of expertise with your speech topic or none at all. A communication professor presenting her research to professional peers would include more technical details on her methods and findings than she would when presenting the same research to a lay audience.

3. *How current does my information need to be?* Some speeches cover topics for which the information is fairly stable, such as a speech on the uses of penicillin. For others, information is changing fast—such as a speech on the use of DNA evidence in murder investigations. If your speech topic falls into the latter category, use recent online articles, newspapers, magazines, academic journals, and experts for your research.

FIGURE 13.2

YOUR INFORMATION NEEDS CHECKLIST

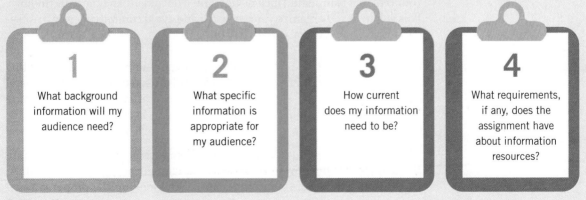

1 What background information will my audience need?

2 What specific information is appropriate for my audience?

3 How current does my information need to be?

4 What requirements, if any, does the assignment have about information resources?

Fenton one/Vector

4. *What requirements, if any, does the assignment have about information resources?* Your instructor may have defined the number and types of resource materials you can use to develop your speech. For instance, some instructors allow *Wikipedia* as a speech resource, while others do not. If you are not sure about the requirements, ask your instructor what is acceptable.

Drawing on Your Personal Knowledge

Although quality research strengthens a speech, don't discount your own knowledge or experiences regarding your topic. Personal stories often make presentations more memorable. Let's say that you recently completed a self-defense class and are preparing a speech to persuade your audience to do the same. Your self-defense training experience is a rich source of relevant information, as are any print materials, Web sites, or videos provided during your training.

If you are developing a speech based on research papers or projects you completed for other classes, the reference lists you created are a good place to start your research. If you choose a topic that's currently getting a lot of media attention, any news sources or reputable blogs you regularly view could make good starting places for your research.

Talking with Librarians

Meet with a librarian at your campus or local library. Some library Web sites even have 24/7 online chat support. Librarians are specially trained to help you find the quality information you need. By talking with a librarian about your specific purpose, you can get ideas for where to start your research and which search terms to use in library databases. Libraries also have extensive collections of print and media resources, periodicals, and special collections that may not be available online.

Documenting Your Research Findings

Your research plan should include how you'll document and file your findings. This will help you organize your research and avoid committing *plagiarism*— misrepresenting others' works as your own.

Organizing Your Research. Develop a consistent approach to documenting and filing the information you find. People tend to keep their research in several forms, including paper, digital, e-mail, and handwritten notes (Jones, Bruce, Foxley, & Munat, 2006). This approach can make it difficult to find specific pieces of information. To better organize your research, follow these guidelines:

1. *Know the documentation style required.* Your instructor will usually require that you document your sources in a standard format, such as APA, MLA, or Chicago. Before you start your research, look up the proper citation

style, and develop the habit of collecting complete bibliographic information for every source you use. If your library's databases provide a source citation option when you download or print an article, use it. Having consistent and accurate citations will help you when you write the references page for your speech outline.

2. *Create a filing system.* Whether for maintaining handwritten notes, printed articles, or online sources, you will need a way to organize your findings. Create a digital or print folder system with meaningful subfolders, so you can easily find the materials you'll need:

General Folder MySpeechStuff

Subfolder Backgrd_Info (documents with background information)

Subfolder Stat_Info (documents with statistical information)

Subfolder Quotes_Ex (documents with useful quotes and examples)

Subfolder VisAid (graphs and charts)

You can also keep notes, documents, and online sources organized in note management apps like Evernote (evernote.com).

3. *Use online bookmarking systems.* To organize information you find on the Web, use **social bookmarking**—free Web-based services that let you save, organize, and keep brief notes about your online resources. Useful social bookmarking services for academic work are Delicious (www.delicious.com), CiteULike (www.citeulike.org), and Diigo (www.diigo.com).

Avoiding Plagiarism. Documenting your research will also help you avoid plagiarism, a major academic, ethical, and legal error. **Plagiarism** is misrepresenting others' works as your own. You commit plagiarism when you use exact words from someone else's work or summarize a unique idea without crediting the source. You have an ethical and a legal responsibility to credit any work that has been created by others, including written texts and spoken words. When you write a paper, you include source information to let your readers know where you found specific information or ideas. You must also do this for speeches by orally citing your sources during a presentation. Even if you unintentionally use others' ideas without proper credit, you're still committing plagiarism. Plagiarizing can have terrible consequences, including receiving a failing grade, being put on academic probation, or—in the professional world—losing a job.

You are more likely to plagiarize when pressed for time and when your source materials are disorganized. To reduce your chances of plagiarizing, use the following strategies:

1. *Start early on the assignment.* Rushing to prepare a speech can lead you to make mistakes in documenting and orally citing your research sources.

2. *Document everything.* Develop the habit of putting clear source documentation on all your research findings. Do this even if you're just

FIGURE 13.3

TIPS TO AVOID PLAGIARISM

1 — Start early on the assignment.

2 — Document everything.

3 — When in doubt, drop it.

SoleilC/Vector

summarizing ideas. You don't want to face a situation in which you have great information to include in your speech but can't recall where you got it.

3. *When in doubt, drop it.* Don't include information in your speech if you've lost the source documentation.

To be an ethical communicator, you want to clearly credit your sources during your speech. The How to Communicate feature on pages 332–333 presents steps for orally citing your sources. When you are unsure about whether to orally cite the source of an idea, it is better to err on the side of caution and give a citation rather than risk plagiarism. Additionally, when preparing your speech, you can ask your instructor for direction if you're confused about whether a particular idea in your speech requires an oral citation.

Conducting Your Research

Once you have determined your research strategy, the next part of Step 2: Investigate is to conduct your research. This includes gathering relevant data from a combination of print resources, Web sites, electronic databases, and conversations with people.

An essential part of responsible and ethical public speaking is making sure the information in your speech is accurate and trustworthy. This is all the more important now, when audiences have easy access to many online resources where they can fact-check your claims. (Think of how often politicians get called out for making false claims in their speeches.) Conducting comprehensive research ensures your presentation is truthful and helps build your credibility with the audience.

Primary and Secondary Resources

There are two types of research resources. **Primary resources** are direct accounts, straight from the original source. These include scientific reports, firsthand descriptions of events, diary writings, photographs of events, congressional-hearing transcripts, and speech manuscripts.

Secondary resources are works that analyze and interpret primary resources. For example, a Web posting that summarizes the results of a study on how treadmill exercise affects the heart rates of people with diabetes and includes additional opinions on the topic is a secondary resource. (The original study published in a medical journal is the primary resource.) Additional examples of secondary sources include magazine articles that report on previous findings, biographies, textbooks, and newspaper articles. Secondary resources can help you interpret complex statistical information and gather alternative opinions.

Whether you use primary or secondary resources depends on your topic and your specific purpose statement. Many classroom speech topics can be developed using only secondary resources. For example, if your specific purpose is to persuade your classmates to vote, you can draw from Web sites and magazine articles that examine the benefits of voting. But if you want to spotlight low turnout among young voters in local elections, you might seek a primary resource, such as a report on voter turnout from your local government office.

Internet Resources

You will probably conduct the majority of your research online (whether at home or in a library). But conducting research online involves more than just Googling your topic and seeing what pops up. Instead, get the most out of your online research by knowing the types of resources available online and how to best use them (see Table 13.2).

Although popular search engines such as Google and Yahoo! help you find information quickly, they can also create *information overload*. For instance, if you are planning to persuade your audience to improve their sleep habits and you enter the search term "sleep habits" into Google, you'll get more than 43 million links. How do you know where to start? Evaluate the information quality of the links, choosing only those sources that have real value for your speech. For example, among the links produced by the Google search, many are selling medication or books. Avoid such sites; if the site is selling you something, it is likely to include biased information. Sites ending in .com can provide quality information if they are objective, such as articles from reputable newspapers and magazines.

Sometimes the most popular sites (those that appear at the top of the search results) aren't the best to use for research purposes. For example, *Wikipedia*'s popularity is driven by the vast amount of material available on the site as well as its high visibility through search engines (Rainie & Tancer, 2007). It is often the first stop for many people doing research online. However, *Wikipedia* has its critics, especially in college and university settings. Such critics claim that *Wikipedia* is not always accurate and that

ORAL CITATIONS

One way to improve your public-speaking skills is by knowing how to properly cite your sources during a speech. Learn how to do this by going to LaunchPad at **bedfordstmartins.com/choicesconnections** and completing the **How to Communicate video scenario** for Chapter 13 to practice your skills.

CONSIDER THIS:

For your communication class, you are giving a speech about why it's important to develop good sleep habits. Your professor wants you to incorporate at least three academic sources. You know how to write source citations for research papers, but you're not sure how to go about crediting your sources in a speech.

WHAT WOULD YOU DO?

The following advice illustrates how to properly cite your sources. As you watch the video, consider how planning a research strategy, conducting appropriate research, and evaluating your sources will help you compose your citations. Then, test your knowledge of key skills, and create your own responses to the **What if? video prompts**.

1 **AVOID PLAGIARISM** by giving proper credit to the sources of quotations, testimony, unique facts, and statistics that you use in a speech. Unlike written reports, there is no standard format for orally citing your sources in a speech. However, you should give enough detail to allow your audience to evaluate the information.

② **USE AN INTRODUCTORY PHRASE** to begin crediting your source. This alerts your audience to the citation. Avoid awkward, forced phrasing, such as ". . . that statistic came from an article in the January 8, 2012, edition of the *New York Times* newspaper."

"The CDC also reports that drowsy-driving-related accidents are most common among young people ages 16–29, especially males."

"In 2012, the Health Center at the University of Georgia posted some of these consequences on its Web site."

③ **PROVIDE INFORMATION** about the credibility of the source, including the author, title of the work, and date. It's not necessary to give page numbers or volume details. If the author and/or title of the work are not well-known, provide additional information to prove the credibility of the source.

 WHAT IF? But what if things don't work out as shown? Test your ability to adapt your communication by watching the What if? videos and making a plan for each situation.

1. How would listing all your sources together influence your audience's view of you? "Before continuing, I would like to say that my sources for this next part of my speech include the Centers for Disease Control, the National Institutes of Health, and . . ."

2. If you give too many details on your source information—"The National Heart, Lung, and Blood Institute, which is part of the National Institutes of Health, a division of the U.S. Department of Health and Human Services, a government agency . . ."—how would this affect your audience's understanding of your speech?

TABLE 13.2

HELPFUL ONLINE RESEARCH SOURCES

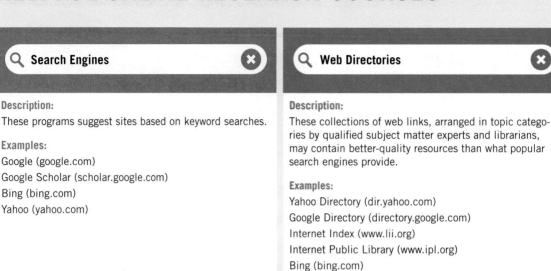

Q Search Engines ⊗

Description:
These programs suggest sites based on keyword searches.

Examples:
Google (google.com)
Google Scholar (scholar.google.com)
Bing (bing.com)
Yahoo (yahoo.com)

Q Web Directories ⊗

Description:
These collections of web links, arranged in topic categories by qualified subject matter experts and librarians, may contain better-quality resources than what popular search engines provide.

Examples:
Yahoo Directory (dir.yahoo.com)
Google Directory (directory.google.com)
Internet Index (www.lii.org)
Internet Public Library (www.ipl.org)
Bing (bing.com)
Yahoo (yahoo.com)

Q U.S. Government Sites ⊗

Description:
The U.S. government produces and archives huge amounts of useful research and information that is considered trustworthy.

Examples:
Directory of U.S. Government sites (www.usa.gov)
Census data (www.census.gov)
Federal statistics (www.fedstats.gov)

Q Nonprofit and Civic Agency Resources ⊗

Description:
Usually designated as .org, these are good sources of information on social or community issues.

Examples:
American Cancer Society (cancer.org)
United Nations (un.org)
826 National (826national.org)

it's too easy for contributors to include biased or incorrect information. Some academic departments even ban its use for student assignments (Educause, 2007). Before using any Web site in your research, make sure it is trustworthy and fulfills the research requirements of the assignment.

Library Resources

A typical academic library invests thousands, if not millions, of dollars annually to provide students with online resources for conducting research. Some popular online library resources include EBSCOhost, LexisNexis Academic, and ProQuest. These databases enable you to search newspapers; primary source documents; periodicals; scholarly journals; government, business, and legal documents; and even televised news transcripts. Moreover, most academic databases allow you to search for photographs, graphs, and other images you may want to use in your speech.

Libraries also offer print and online versions of generalized and specialized encyclopedias and dictionaries. Dozens of subject-specific encyclopedias and dictionaries exist, ranging from *Ancient Europe, 8000 B.C. to A.D. 1000: Encyclopedia of the Barbarian World* to *The Dictionary of Cell and Molecular Biology*. Many encyclopedia entries reference other key sources you can use while researching your speech, such as related books and articles.

Finally, many college libraries subscribe to two popular and useful resources for persuasive speech assignments: *CQ Researcher* and Opposing Viewpoints Resource Center. *CQ Researcher* is a database of reports developed by journalists on specific themes, ranging from health care to the economy. Each report provides background on the topic, an objective examination of different perspectives on the topic, and a bibliography. Opposing Viewpoints Resource Center takes several of the best primary and secondary sources available on controversial social issues and organizes them by topic. Each of these resources is a good starting point for gaining a broad perspective on a social issue.

Interpersonal Resources

Although it may not be the first thing that comes to mind, talking with people one-on-one can provide useful information on your speech topic. Faculty members on your campus or experts in your community can provide insights, explanations, and stories different from online and print resources. For example, interviewing an organ-donor recipient produces a powerful personal story about the importance of organ donation.

If you decide to talk with someone as a part of your research, you will need to plan an **information interview**—a meeting in which you ask questions to gain knowledge or understanding about a particular topic. To conduct a successful interview, you will need to arrange an appointment and indicate how much time you will need with the person. Show respect for your interviewee's time by sticking to the agreed-upon time frame and having questions prepared in advance. When you interview the person, maintain a friendly but professional manner. For more details about how to conduct an information interview, check out the appendix on pages A-9 to A-13.

Evaluating Your Resources

Today, anyone can publish a book, an article, or a Web site given a little time and the right equipment. So it's a good idea to maintain a healthy skepticism about the sources you find for your speech. No matter where your research is from, you need to evaluate it by considering these five factors: relevancy, currency, authority, objectivity, and consensual validation.

Relevancy. Consider the degree to which your source is related to your speech's specific purpose. You can waste a lot of time sifting through and reading material that barely touches on your topic. Take, for example, an informative presentation for your art history class about the use of color in French Impressionist paintings. Your research could lead you to hundreds of books, articles, and online materials about French impressionism. To eliminate irrelevant resources, stay focused on your specific purpose—the use of color in such art.

Currency. For some speech topics, it's critical to have the most current information available. Publication dates of magazines, newspapers, articles, and books are relatively easy to determine, but some Web sites present a different challenge. Try to determine when a site was last updated—check for timely commentary, copyright dates on the home page, or dates of individual posts. Avoid relying on information from any Web site that hasn't been updated in several months. Any site with broken hyperlinks is probably outdated.

Authority. For each resource you find, ask yourself, What are the author's credentials? To determine this, find out qualifications the creator brings to the work, such as personal experience, a prolonged professional career, or relevant academic degrees from a respectable educational institution. You can usually find information about an author's credentials within the first few pages of a book or in a footnote or biographical note in an article or another document.

For an online source, consider the reputation of the sponsoring organization. For example, information found on the American Medical Association (AMA) Web site has authority because of the AMA's reputation as a medical organization. You should also look for footnotes or works-cited listings. Check out those sources to see if they look valid. Often, an online post will link to more information about the author, providing you a chance to check out his or her credentials. Finally, use your instincts to judge the look and feel of the site. Although appearance should never be the sole indicator of authority, mistakes and sloppiness suggest a lack of authority.

Objectivity. You want to use *objective* research sources—those based on facts, not bias. Of course, all sources have some degree of bias. But you want to avoid blatantly one-sided or propaganda-like resources, whose sole purpose is to convey the author's point of view or a particular ideology.

If the resource is a Web site, click on the "About" link, which should take you to a page describing the mission and purpose of the group or organization that publishes the site. Review this information to see if the site is pushing a particular agenda. Also, examine any external links on the site to see what types of organizations the group associates with. Do these associations suggest possible bias? Finally, don't over-rely on commercial Web sites (.com); these sites usually exist to sell or promote some product or service.

Consensual Validation. A resource has **consensual validation** when other sources agree with or use the same information you're considering using.

Consensual validation suggests that the information (especially that found on the Web) is reliable. For instance, imagine you're researching drinking in college. You come across a Web site that defines binge drinking as men drinking five consecutive alcoholic drinks or women consuming four consecutive alcoholic drinks. You ask yourself, What kind of alcohol, and over what period of time? What's the original source of this information? As you research a bit further by consulting library databases, you find several studies conducted at Harvard that use the same definition of binge drinking but that provide more details that answer your questions. You now have confidence in the original information as well as additional details to use in your speech.

LearningCurve can help you review! Go to **bedfordstmartins.com /choicesconnections**.

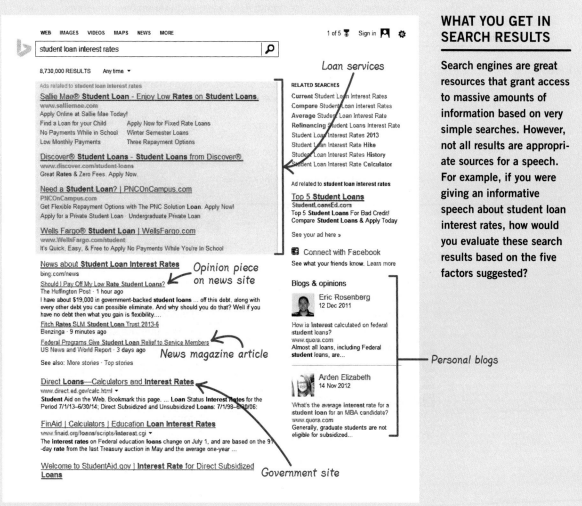

Used with permission from Microsoft.

WHAT YOU GET IN SEARCH RESULTS

Search engines are great resources that grant access to massive amounts of information based on very simple searches. However, not all results are appropriate sources for a speech. For example, if you were giving an informative speech about student loan interest rates, how would you evaluate these search results based on the five factors suggested?

CHAPTER 13 REVIEW

CHAPTER RECAP

- By following the five steps of speech preparation—**think, investigate, compose, rehearse,** and **revise**—you can create compelling public speeches that engage and inspire audiences.
- After determining your **general purpose,** you can select your **speech topic** by reflecting on your personal interests and experiences, **brainstorming,** or developing a **concept map.**
- By conducting an **audience analysis,** you explore several factors, including your listeners' **demographics; attitudes, beliefs,** and **values;** knowledge; and type.
- To manage your time effectively and focus on finding relevant information, plan a research strategy. This not only helps you find and organize information but also helps you avoid **plagiarism.**
- When researching your speech, gather relevant data from a combination of print resources, Web sites, electronic databases, and **information interviews,** and don't forget to evaluate your sources.

LAUNCHPAD

LaunchPad for *Choices & Connections* offers unique video scenarios and encourages self-assessment through adaptive quizzing. Go to **bedfordstmartins.com /choicesconnections** to get access.

 LearningCurve adaptive quizzes

 How to Communicate video scenarios

 Video clips that illustrate key concepts

KEY TERMS

Public speaking, p. 314
Think, p. 314
Investigate, p. 314
Compose, p. 315
Rehearse, p. 315
Revise, p. 315
General purpose, p. 317
Informative speeches, p. 317
Persuasive speeches, p. 317
Special-occasion speeches, p. 317
Speech topic, p. 317
Brainstorming, p. 318
Concept map, p. 318
Audience analysis, p. 321

Demographics, p. 321
Attitude, p. 322
Belief, p. 323
Values, p. 323
Captive audience, p. 323
Voluntary audience, p. 325
Specific purpose statement, p. 326
Social bookmarking, p. 329
Plagiarism, p. 329
Primary resources, p. 331
Secondary resources, p. 331
Information interview, p. 335
Consensual validation, p. 336

❶ During which step of the speech preparation process can you use critical self-reflection to improve your content and delivery?

a. Think   **c.** Rehearse
b. Compose   **d.** Revise

❷ During your audience analysis, you may consider your listeners' demographics in adapting your speech as needed. However, it is important to avoid _____ during this process.

a. brainstorming   **c.** stereotyping
b. captive audiences   **d.** voluntary audiences

❸ Your specific purpose statement is influenced by all of the following *except* _____.

a. research strategy   **c.** audience analysis
b. general purpose   **d.** speech topic

❹ When planning your research strategy, consider which background content—such as definitions or historical context—your audience may need explained. This is part of _____.

a. evaluating your resources
b. documenting your research findings
c. drawing on your personal knowledge
d. identifying your information needs

❺ While researching your speech, check that your sources are _____ to ensure that they aren't providing biased information.

a. accurate   **c.** current
b. objective   **d.** relevant

ACTIVITIES

❶ **Comparing Concept Maps**

Working with a partner, choose one of the following topics. Work independently for 10 minutes to draw your own concept maps of the same topic. Compare your efforts, and discuss what the differences illustrate about selecting a speech topic.

a. Music   **c.** Sports   **e.** Health
b. Washington, D.C.   **d.** Social media

❷ **Clarifying Specific Purposes**

Each of the following specific purpose statements fails to fulfill the guidelines specified in the chapter. For each one, identify the problem, and then rewrite the statement using the guidelines for specific purpose statements on page 326.

a. I want to talk about how to succeed in college.
b. Explain the difference between a curve ball and a slider.
c. Eliminating world hunger.
d. My audience will appreciate classical music and be encouraged to enroll in private music lessons.
e. Pros and cons of starting your own business.

14

Composing Your Speech

A fter hitting her head on a cabinet, Jane McGonigal suffered a debilitating concussion. She experienced long bouts of nausea, headaches, vertigo, and memory loss.[1] Eventually, she began to feel depressed, and her thoughts turned to suicide. But rather than end her life, McGonigal did something quite different. She turned her recovery into a game. As she told an audience assembled at the Technology, Entertainment, Design (TED) Global Conference in Edinburgh, Scotland:

> And these voices became so persistent and so persuasive that I started to legitimately fear for my life, which is the time that I said to myself after 34 days—and I will never forget this moment—I said, I am either going to kill myself or I'm going to turn this into a game.

The game she created—Jane the Concussion Slayer—helped her recovery and saved her life. Wanting to help other people achieve similar results, McGonigal broadened the scope of her game to include a variety of health goals and turned it into a Web site and app entitled SuperBetter (www.superbetter.com).

McGonigal's decision to turn her recovery into a game was a natural outgrowth of her professional work. With a PhD in performance studies from the University of California at Berkeley, she makes her living designing alternate reality–based games that have a positive impact on people by building their resilience, increasing their personal happiness, and helping them develop real-world problem-solving skills.

Addressing the TED audience, McGonigal made a clear point: playing games can extend your life by 10 years. She recounted how a game helped her recover from brain trauma and cited scientific research that shows the benefits of gaming:

> Hundreds of millions of people use social games like FarmVille or Words With Friends to stay in daily contact with real-life

[1]Opener crafted from McGonigal (2012).

friends and family. A recent study from [University of Michigan] showed that these games are incredibly powerful relationship-management tools. They help us stay connected with people in our social network that we would otherwise grow distant from, if we weren't playing games together.

But she did more than quote scientific research to support her point. She also involved her audience in game-like activities. Asking her listeners to follow her directions, McGonigal had them snapping their fingers, using their smartphones to find images of baby animals on the Web, and shaking the hand of another audience member. Each activity was part of a quest game in which the audience earned points toward improving their well-being.

Within the span of a 19-minute speech, McGonigal shared her personal story, provided scientific research, and involved her audience in a game. When it was over, the audience understood not only that playing games can be beneficial to one's physical and mental well-being but that a carefully composed speech can be an event to experience and remember.

✔️ **LearningCurve** can help you review! Go to **bedfordstmartins.com /choicesconnections**.

Even when you know your specific purpose for a speech, determining exactly how to achieve it can be difficult. Jane McGonigal had an important message to share with her TED audience, but deciding how to present her message took work. This process of determining your speech thesis and main ideas and arranging them into a coherent and engaging presentation is the third step of the speech preparation process: **composing**. (See Table 14.1 for the Five Steps in Speech Preparation.) In this chapter, you'll learn:

- How to develop your speech thesis
- Ways to identify and arrange your speech's main points
- Ideas for keeping your audience engaged
- Strategies for introducing and concluding your speech
- How to write preparation and delivery outlines

Developing Your Speech Thesis

> At this point in your speech preparation, you've spent considerable time thinking about your audience, narrowing your topic, and finding quality information to use in your presentation. Now it's time to begin Step 3: Compose by putting all this information together in the central idea—the thesis—of your speech. This will help you structure your presentation.

Your **speech thesis** is one complete sentence that identifies the central idea of your presentation for your audience. This statement is the foundation for composing your speech. Everything from what points you make and which visual aids you use to how you draft your conclusion will relate to it. You will eventually share the speech thesis with your audience as part of the speech's introduction. A compelling speech thesis answers the question, What is the overall point or position I want to convey to my audience? For example, in Jane McGonigal's presentation at the TED conference, her speech thesis was "Playing games can extend your life by 10 years." This central idea helped her compose her main points, stay on topic, and inform her audience about what she wanted them to know.

A good speech thesis meets three requirements. First, it evolves from your specific purpose statement. You adapt the idea based on what you discover during your research and to be more specific to your actual speech. Second, the speech thesis clearly demonstrates to the audience your overall point or position on the topic. Finally, the thesis provides clues as to how your main points will develop. Consider how these requirements are met in the following example:

Specific purpose: I want to inform my audience how to effectively handle bullying in the workplace.

Speech thesis: Workplace bullying is an intolerable situation that can be effectively curbed through specific actions.

TABLE 14.1

FIVE STEPS IN SPEECH PREPARATION

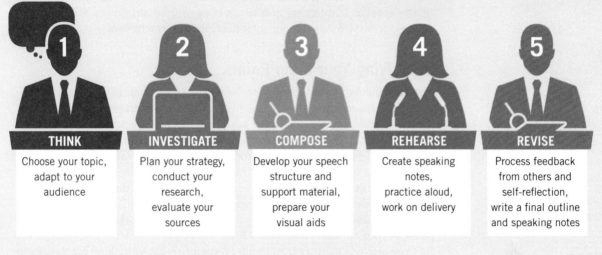

THINK	INVESTIGATE	COMPOSE	REHEARSE	REVISE
Choose your topic, adapt to your audience	Plan your strategy, conduct your research, evaluate your sources	Develop your speech structure and support material, prepare your visual aids	Create speaking notes, practice aloud, work on delivery	Process feedback from others and self-reflection, write a final outline and speaking notes

edel/Shutterstock

Although the speech thesis and specific purpose may seem similar, there is an important difference: the speech thesis is stated directly during the introduction of your presentation, whereas the specific purpose guides your research.

Identifying and Supporting Your Main Points

The speech thesis reflects your point of view or position on the topic. But simply stating your thesis isn't enough; you need evidence to back up your ideas. You do this by identifying your main points and providing appropriate supporting materials. Without such evidence, it is hard to build credibility with your audience.

With your speech thesis drafted, you can begin to structure your speech, or determine what you will say in each part of your presentation. Most speeches have three parts:

- *Introduction:* You lay the groundwork for your speech by connecting with your audience, disclosing your speech thesis, establishing your credibility, and previewing your main points.
- *Body:* You develop your speech thesis with main points and supporting evidence. This is the heart of your presentation.
- *Conclusion:* You summarize your main points and share any final thoughts on your topic.

We will go over all three sections in this chapter, but let's start with the body of the speech. Identifying and supporting your main points will help you figure out what to say in your introduction and conclusion.

Identifying Your Main Points

The **main points** of your speech are the key statements or principles that support your speech thesis and help your audience understand your message. These are the ideas that build the case for why your thesis statement is true.

One way to identify your main points is to ask yourself what essential information is necessary to support your thesis. For example, if you were composing a speech about the dangers of texting while driving, your audience might need to understand why that behavior is dangerous. Let's say that your research uncovered information about the different types of distractions caused by texting. These distractions could make up the first main point of your speech.

You also can identify main points for your thesis by looking for themes in your research. Suppose you have information from your state's department of public safety showing that texting-related traffic accidents have been increasing over the past two years. In addition, by interviewing a state police officer, you found that many accidents he investigates are caused by distracted drivers. Taken together, this information could be used to write a second main point for your speech: accidents caused by texting while driving have been increasing.

Additionally, you might discover that there are several general ideas that will support your thesis. However, you'll only want to include those that are relevant to your audience. If your *audience analysis* (see Chapter 13, pp. 321–326) shows that your listeners are unaware of proposed laws to curb texting while driving, you might decide it is important to explain them in detail. This could also lead you to conclude that the audience could benefit from information about how to change their personal behavior. These two final main points are important because they have a direct bearing on the audience. Table 14.2 reviews how the speech thesis and main points work together.

When developing main points, remember these guidelines:

- *Each main point must support your thesis statement.* You don't want to distract from your speech thesis by including a point that is unrelated to it. A focused presentation increases your chances of keeping the audience's attention.

- *A speech should contain a small number of main points, usually two to five.* You want to keep your information manageable, making it easier for listeners to digest your speech.

- *Each main point should focus on only one idea.* If a point introduces a new idea, then it should appear as a separate main point. As an example, consider how many main points are included in the following sentence: Texting while driving presents three types of distractions, and you can

TABLE 14.2

IDENTIFYING MAIN IDEAS

Speech thesis:
Stopping the dangerous practice of texting while driving must be addressed through new legislation.

Note:
Speech Preparation Step 3: Composing starts with writing the thesis statement. You will mention it in your speech, usually during the introduction.

Main points:

I. Texting while driving presents three types of distractions.

II. Traffic accidents caused by texting while driving have been increasing.

III. New legislation is needed to control the problem.

IV. Individuals must also take responsibility for changing their behaviors.

Note:
Your main points directly support your speech thesis. You will use the supporting materials from your research to fully develop each of the points during the speech.

take steps to stop the practice. (The answer is two; each idea—types of distractions and steps to stop the practice—should be developed as a separate main point.)

Finally, some main points may need to be further divided into **subpoints** to help you explain the idea. Subpoints are especially useful if a particular main point can be broken down into parts or steps. For example, main point I in Table 14.2 could have three subpoints:

I. Texting while driving presents three types of distractions.[2]

   A. Visual distraction

   B. Manual distraction

   C. Cognitive distraction

By using subpoints, you can explain a main point better, and your audience will have an easier time listening to the overall idea. When creating subpoints, make sure they all relate to the main point to avoid confusing your audience.

---

[2]Source: www.distraction.gov/content/get-the-facts/faq.html

Supporting Your Main Points

All your main points and subpoints require *supporting materials* to clarify the ideas and make them memorable for your listeners. Supporting materials include definitions, statistics, examples, and testimony—the proof you need to back up your claims. You can't just tell the audience that texting while driving causes three types of distractions and expect them to take your word for it. Instead, you need to explain what each type is and how that information relates to your thesis. Providing adequate supporting materials lets your audience know the information you are providing is trustworthy.

How do you know what type of supporting materials you need? When conducting your audience analysis, consider questions like the following: How familiar is your audience with your topic? Will they need terms defined or other background information? Do you need to include stories and illustrative examples to interest them in the topic? These types of questions will help you choose appropriate supporting materials that will inform and interest your audience. Although you can base much of your supporting materials on your research, you might also need to do additional research at this point to fill in any gaps.

Definitions. When composing your speech, be aware of when you may have to define terms for your listeners. After all, as Chapter 5 on verbal communication discusses, differences in language use can cause misunderstandings. *Connotative meanings*, for instance, are the meanings you associate with words based on your life experiences. But you can't assume all members of your audience will share those references. Also, your *dialect*—which reflects the language variations you use based on where you live, your socioeconomic status, or your ethnic or religious ancestry—can be a source of misunderstandings if you and your audience use terms differently.

Even within a culture, these differences can cause people who share the same language to not understand each other. For example, what comes to mind when you hear the term "medical errors"? When presenting a U.S. Institute of Medicine report about medical errors to a group, Jennie Chin Hansen (2010) realized she should define the term to make sure her audience understood it in the same way she did:

> The report was based upon analysis of multiple studies by a variety of organizations and concluded that between 44,000 to 98,000 people died each year as a result of preventable medical errors. A simple definition of a medical error is a preventable adverse effect of some form of medical care. (p. 158)

During your audience analysis, get a realistic sense of terms or concepts you may need to define for your audience. This way, you can provide them with all the information they need but not waste time defining words they already know.

Statistics. A **statistic** is a number that summarizes a formal observation about a phenomenon. Statistics can help you make a compelling point, such as Hansen does in the preceding quote by stating "between 44,000 to 98,000 people died each year" to give her audience a sense of the severity of medical errors.

When using statistics, keep a few things in mind. First, think about using a visual chart or graph to summarize statistical information. "Seeing" the numbers in addition to hearing them will help your audience make sense of them. Second, round off large numbers. Instead of listing the exact (but complicated) numbers of medical error deaths in the last few years ("52,861 in 2011; 89,367 in 2010"), Hansen said, "between 44,000 to 98,000 people died each year." Third, when possible, place statistics in a context that will be meaningful to your audience. For instance, Hansen could've said that the 44,000 to 98,000 deaths is comparable to the population of a specific local city or the number of fans that can fit into a professional sports stadium. Finally, although statistics can bring attention to your point, they should be used sparingly. Listeners can get confused trying to understand a lot of abstract statistical information. Try to use statistics only when doing so will have an impact on your audience.

Examples. Main points are made vivid and clear when you use **examples,** or specific references that illustrate ideas. *Real examples* are drawn from actual events or occurrences. Consider how this speaker uses a real example to explain to Congress the benefit of corporate support in the aftermath of Hurricane Katrina:

> As an example of what can be done when public and private interests work together, in Mississippi, industry has helped . . . to meet child care needs. Seeking to hasten the return of its workers, the Chevron Corporation funded the rebuilding of all licensed child care facilities within Jackson County, Mississippi. Certainly this example shows a deep awareness of the link between child care availability and employee availability, and should serve as a model for what could be done elsewhere to help meet this overwhelming need. (Jones-DeWeever, 2007, p. 448)

Sometimes you'll develop a *hypothetical example*—an imagined event or occurrence to make a point. This type of example is helpful when you have difficulty finding an appropriate real example. In a speech about the early warning signs of dating violence, you could develop a hypothetical example to illustrate intentional embarrassment by saying, "Imagine that you're out with friends and your partner starts criticizing your appearance in front of them. This is an act of intentional embarrassment." You should indicate the use of hypothetical examples by using phrases like "Imagine that . . . ," "Suppose . . . ," or "Let's say that . . ." so that your audience knows you're not giving real examples. When developing a hypothetical example, it is important to create one that is realistic and believable. If it is out of the ordinary, your audience may ignore it as an exception.

A special type of example is an **analogy,** which compares something that is familiar to your audience with something that is unfamiliar to them but that you want them to understand. Analogies are useful for illustrating a particularly difficult main point. Here, a speaker uses an analogy to explain that American medical practices involve multiple principles:

> I've often used a simple analogy to explain American medicine to people. I use the idea of the interlocking rings as . . . displayed in the Olympic logo. . . . In my analogy, the first ring is the science of medicine, the evidence-based scientific foundation which determines all that we do. The second ring, interlocked with the first, is the ethics of medicine, the moral underpinning that ensures that what we do is the right thing, morally, ethically, spiritually. And the third ring, equally important and equally interlocked with the other two, is the ring of caring. (Nelson, 2006, p. 239)

When using an analogy, be sure that the comparison you're making is clear and will make sense to your audience. Point out the similarities between the two unlike things, and explain why the comparison works.

Testimony. Relying on the words or experience of others by using **testimony** is a common way that speakers support main points. Speeches incorporate two types of testimony. *Expert testimony* comes from those who, by way of their academic study, work experience, or research, have special knowledge about your topic. *Layperson testimony* is derived from those who have personal experience with the topic. For example, in a persuasive speech on

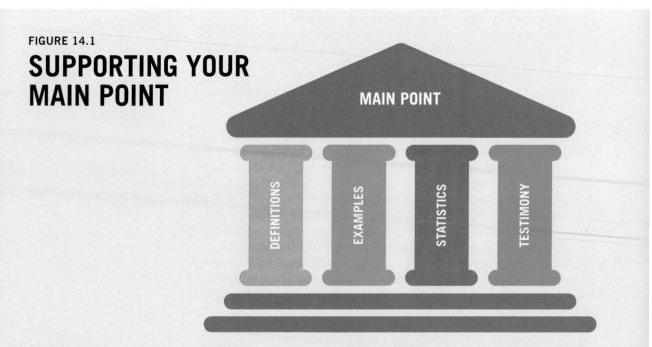

FIGURE 14.1

SUPPORTING YOUR MAIN POINT

MAIN POINT

DEFINITIONS   EXAMPLES   STATISTICS   TESTIMONY

artizarus/Shutterstock

stiffening the laws related to drunk driving, a speaker may draw testimony from police officers who enforce the laws (experts), survivors of alcohol-related traffic accidents (laypersons), or both.

Testimony can be presented in your speech through **direct quotation.** A direct quotation uses the exact words of a person to make your point. This is what William Wallace (2008) does in a speech to football coaches:

> Former LSU, Army and South Carolina football coach, Paul Dietzel, made this interesting observation, "You can learn more character on the 2-yard line than anywhere else in life." He's absolutely right. It is when your back is up against it that the unrelenting determination of the individual and the team are truly tested.

When using a direct quotation, you have an ethical responsibility to accurately convey the words of the person. Don't change the words or take the quote out of context. Be clear in citing the source from which you got the quote, and if necessary, provide some background about the person, such as the professional or personal experience that makes the quote relevant.

Testimony can also be presented by **paraphrasing,** or providing your own summary of another person's words or experience. Paraphrasing is useful when the original words are too complicated, too long, or too confusing to quote directly. When paraphrasing, do not alter the original meaning of what the person said or experienced. You have the same ethical responsibility to properly cite the source when paraphrasing as you do when quoting.

Organizing Your Speech

Considering all the time and energy you put into finding supporting materials for your speech, you want your audience to get the most out of it. One of the best ways to do that is to clearly organize your speech. This will help audience members understand your points and stay engaged while listening.

Our chapter opener on Jane McGonigal mentioned that she gave her speech on the importance of gaming at a TED conference. TED is a nonprofit organization that "believe[s] passionately in the power of ideas to change attitudes, lives and ultimately, the world (ted.com, n.d.)." And what's the best way to spread such ideas? Inspiring speeches! At annual TED conferences, leading thinkers and innovators like McGonigal give presentations on their area of expertise, usually lasting 18 minutes or less. The talks have a reputation for being passionate, engaging, and often exhilarating, as *New York Times* columnist Virginia Heffernan (2009) describes the experience of viewing the speeches online:

> Help. Here I go. My pulse is racing. I'm completely manic. Oh why oh why have I been bingeing on TED talks again? I promised myself I would quit watching the ecstatic series of head-rush disquisitions, available online, from violinists, political prisoners, brain scientists, novelists and Bill Clinton. But I can't. (p. 13)

MAKING COMMUNICATION CHOICES

BUT THE VIDEO WENT VIRAL!

1 CONSIDER THE DILEMMA

You're sitting at your desk when your roommate, Eliza, arrives home and asks what you are up to: "How's it going? Still working on your speech?"

Deciding to use her as a sounding board, you reply, "Yeah. I found this hilarious video that I want to use, but I don't know where to put it in the speech."

"Can I see it?" Eliza asks.

"Sure," you reply, as you pull it up on YouTube. The video shows a prank started by talk-show host Jimmy Kimmel, who challenged viewers to give their children terrible Christmas gifts and record their responses. Among the prank gifts were a rotten banana, a half-eaten sandwich, and a battery. Without fail, each child is stunned at first, and then melts into either a quirky response or a tantrum. Eliza watches quietly, laughing just a few times.

When the video ends, Eliza remarks, "I think it's kinda cruel how parents lied to their own kids just for laughs."

"C'mon," you say, "they were just teasing. Besides, it's funny . . . the class will crack up when I show it. I have a pretty heavy topic." You tell Eliza the specific purpose of your speech—to convince the class to give money or time to their favorite charity during the holiday season. You believe the video can be used to support a main point in your speech: the holiday season is a time when many people think more about themselves than others.

Eliza responds, "Well, that is a pretty serious topic, but there's got to be other ways to make your point without doing it at kids' expense. My dad used to pull a lot of practical jokes like that, and I hated it."

2 CONNECT THE RESEARCH

When speakers use humor thoughtfully in their speeches, they gain credibility and may be more persuasive (Lynch, 2002). Consider the times you've listened to speakers who have told jokes or showed a funny cartoon or video clip. Such comic relief makes speakers appear likable and motivates interest in their messages.

After reviewing decades of research related to humor and public speaking, communication scholar Charles R. Gruner (1985) came up with the following suggestions for using humor in a speech:

- When informing an audience, you are likely to be viewed favorably when you use a small amount of relevant humor. Appropriate and well-placed humor can lead your audience to see you as likable and trustworthy.

- Humor directed at yourself can enhance your image with the audience. Listeners appreciate

speakers who are able to poke fun at themselves.

- Humor may be unnecessary in a speech when you have other interesting forms of support, such as suspenseful or engaging stories. When composing your speech, consider whether humor is important for supporting a point.

- Your audience will likely reject your overall message if you use excessive humor or the humor is inappropriate (sick, racist, or sexist). Don't assume that others will share your sense of humor or see offensive humor as "just a joke."

- Messages involving sarcasm, ridicule, or exaggeration may confuse your audience when you're trying to persuade them. It's more effective to make your case directly rather than by using witty explanations to disparage opposing viewpoints.

Before making a communication choice, consider the facts of the situation, what you know about supporting materials, and the research on using humor in speeches. Also, reflect on what you've learned so far about composing a speech, including supporting your main point (pp. 346–349) and keeping your listeners engaged (pp. 354–355). Then answer these questions:

❶ In addition to considering Eliza's feelings about the video, what other steps can you take to determine whether to use the video in your speech?

❷ What other forms of supporting material (humorous or not) could you use to support the main point: "The holiday season is a time when many people think more about themselves than others"?

❸ Will you use the video in the speech?

TED talks cover everything from online gaming to studying 10,000-year-old ice in Antarctica. (You can watch many of them at ted.com.) But it's not just the interesting topics that inspire such a devoted following. TED talks also grab and hold audiences' attention because they are easy to follow and understand. You don't need to be a leading innovator or scientist to do that; you just need to develop a clear organization for your speech, transition smoothly throughout the presentation, and keep your audience engaged.

Selecting an Organizational Pattern

For your audience to follow the development of your speech thesis, you need to arrange your main points into a logical pattern. There are five common organizational patterns: topical, chronological, spatial, cause-effect, and problem-solution.

Topical. Use a **topical pattern** when your main points can be organized into categories or subtopics. You can arrange the topics in any order—such as least to most important, most to least common, or type (e.g., types of movies: comedy, drama, action, adventure, documentary). Just be sure your order is logical and supports your thesis statement. For example, in a speech about note taking, you could arrange your main points from most common to least common techniques:

Speech thesis: Successful students rely on one of four note-taking techniques.

Main points:

    I. A traditional outline consists of identifying main topics and subtopics.

    II. The fact versus principle pattern lists main points on one side of the page and related facts on the other side.

    III. A mind map creates a diagram to indicate the relationship of ideas as they are presented.

    IV. The précis method involves periodically writing brief summaries of ideas.

Chronological. When your main points suggest a time sequence or a series of steps, you can organize them using a **chronological pattern.** Speeches about a process or how to do or make something often use this pattern:

Speech thesis: Scholar Steven Duck's model of relationship dissolution demonstrates that a relationship breakup involves more than just saying "good-bye."

Main points:

    I. The intrapsychic phase involves thinking about your dissatisfaction.

    II. The dyadic phase happens when you discuss your dissatisfaction with your partner.

    III. The social phase occurs when partners inform immediate family and friends about the relationship breakup.

    IV. The grave-dressing phase consists of the attributions partners make about why the relationship ended.

Spatial. The **spatial pattern** shows listeners how things are related within a physical space. For example, if you were briefing a group that's about to visit Las Vegas for the first time, you'd have an arrangement like the following:

Speech thesis: The excitement of the Las Vegas strip is increased when visitors know the unique attractions found along the way.

Main points:

    I. The south strip features a lot of themed attractions appropriate for families.

    II. The mid strip has many resorts with appeal for young adults.

    III. The north strip preserves some of the charm of old Las Vegas.

Cause-effect. The **cause-effect pattern** enables you to show how events or forces will lead to (or did lead to) specific outcomes:

Speech thesis: Establishing and maintaining a home garden can benefit your well-being.

Main points:

    I. Creating and tending to a home garden involves physical exercise that burns calories.

    II. Retreating to work in a home garden helps relieve mental stress.

    III. Sharing the products of your home garden builds social connections with others.

Problem-solution. The **problem-solution pattern** helps you motivate listeners to take action to address a challenge. In this arrangement, you describe a problem and then present a solution:

Speech thesis: Getting an annual health screening as a college student can save your life.

Main points:

I. Many common diseases affect college students.

II. The failure to diagnose a treatable disease early can lead to bigger problems.

III. Annual health screenings have the power to detect problems, making them easier to treat.

Using Connectives

Once you've arranged your main points in an organizational pattern, think about how **connectives**—words and phrases that link your ideas together—will help you move from one idea to the next. Using connectives will help your audience accurately receive and understand your speech because they show how your ideas are related. As we will discuss later in the chapter, you should write connective phrases into the outline of your speech. Doing so will help you think through the relationship of your ideas and the flow of your speech. There are four types of connectives: internal previews, internal summaries, transitional phrases, and signposts.

Internal Previews. Sometimes you will want to provide your listeners with a first look at the information you're about to cover with statements known as **internal previews.** These statements let your audience in on what you are going to tell them before you actually do. Consider this internal preview in a speech about why students drop out of school:

Three factors contribute to student dropout. These are a lack of academic readiness, financial need, and poor advisement. Let's look at each of these in turn.

When a main point has subpoints, an internal preview can help your audience follow along as you develop each subpoint.

Internal Summaries. **Internal summaries** provide a short review of information you've discussed within a section of the speech. This connective is especially useful when you have covered a main point with multiple aspects, as in the speech about student dropout rates:

As you just heard, poor academic preparation, inadequate finances, and misguided advice prior to enrollment are contributing causes to student dropout rates.

Providing your listeners with internal summaries will solidify the most essential information about the main point before you move on.

Lucas Jackson/Reuters/Corbis

Transitional phrases. When you want to indicate that you're shifting to another point or idea, you can use **transitional phrases.** These phrases provide a verbal signal that you are moving on:

> *Now that we've examined* the reasons for student dropout, *let's focus* on what you can do to prevent it.

These simple phrases can keep your audience from getting lost when you begin to make a different point.

Signposts. **Signposts** are brief words—often numbers—that quickly introduce a new idea. Words like *First, Second, Next, Additionally,* and *Finally* are signposts, as in the following:

> *Additionally,* students can take action to control the forces causing them to drop out.

These are most helpful when you are covering several steps or examples that your audience will need to keep track of.

Keeping Listeners Engaged

Even when your audience wants to listen to your speech, it is easy for them to get distracted by other people or by their phones, or their minds can simply start to wander. To combat such obstacles, try to present information in a way that stimulates your listeners' senses and provides new or unexpected ideas (Fiske & Taylor, 1991; Medina, 2008). When planning your organizational pattern and use of connectives, also think about ways to keep your audience engaged:

- *Integrate novelty*. People pay attention to information that is *novel* (new), different, or unusual (Silvia, 2008). Look for ways to tell your audience something they don't already know. Also, vary your supporting materials by including appropriate testimony or examples to support your points.

- *Use appropriate humor*. A funny story or joke invites attention and is memorable. After all, most people like to laugh. But use humor sparingly, and make it relevant (Gruner, 1985). Never use humor that is obscene, racist, sexist, or insulting to any group—you'll only offend your audience.

- *Tell a story*. Stories engage listeners and create the sense of a shared experience. They also support your speech thesis by clarifying your main points. Stories work best when they contain descriptive language, evoke emotion, and, of course, are relevant to the points you're making.

- *Integrate presentation aids*. Your audience will pay the most attention to what they *see* (Medina, 2008). Consider how charts, graphs, images, video, animations, and other materials can be brought into your presentation to support a point. We'll take a closer look at how to use presentation aids in Chapter 15.

Keeping your listeners engaged is important even when giving short talks, such as *elevator speeches*, in which you must convey a lot of information is a small amount of time. For more on how you can successfully handle such a situation, see the How to Communicate: Elevator Speeches feature on pages 356–357.

Introducing and Concluding Your Speech

How your speech begins and ends can make or break its success. Your introduction is your chance to grab your audience's attention, and your conclusion has the final impact on how your audience responds to your overall message.

During the 2008 U.S. presidential campaign, Barack Obama faced increasing scrutiny of his past association with the Reverend Jeremiah Wright. A controversial church leader, Wright was accused of making inflammatory statements in his sermons about U.S. race relations. Candidate Obama set out to dispel the criticism of his association with Reverend Wright. But he also wanted to address the larger question of U.S. race relations the controversy brought up. Recognizing that a formal presentation would give him the opportunity and exposure to do both, he made a televised speech from

ELEVATOR SPEECHES

One way to improve your competence in impromptu speech scenarios is by preparing and practicing certain messages in advance. Learn how to compose elevator speeches by going to LaunchPad at **bedfordstmartins.com/choicesconnections** and completing the **How to Communicate video scenario** for Chapter 14 to practice your skills.

CONSIDER THIS: You are a student research assistant for a marine biology professor studying how small fish transport carbon dioxide from the air and ocean surface into the deep sea. One day, you meet the college president in the hallway of your department building. He is on his way to a meeting but asks you to briefly explain your research.

WHAT WOULD YOU DO? In an elevator speech, you quickly and clearly explain your work or ideas in 30–60 seconds (the average time of an elevator ride). This type of speech often occurs before and after meetings, during interviews and career fairs, and at social events when you suddenly have a chance to pitch your story. While elevator speeches are usually spur-of-the-moment, being prepared can help you make a positive impression. The following advice illustrates how to competently compose an elevator speech. As you watch the video, consider how concepts like using an organizational pattern and keeping listeners engaged are relevant. Then, test your knowledge of key skills, and create your own responses to the **What if? video prompts**.

1. **GAIN ATTENTION** by identifying the problem that you're trying to solve, the services you offer, or how you help people.

"We have too much carbon dioxide in our air, which has terrible effects on our climate . . ."

2. **EXPLAIN YOUR WORK** using clear language (i.e. what a high school student would understand).

"My research focuses on small fish, like anchovies, because they feed on excessive carbon dioxide found on the ocean's surface."

③ DISCUSS THE VALUE

of your work and why it is relevant to the person or situation.

"We're hoping that by studying the feeding behaviors of these small fish, we might find . . ."

"Hmmm . . . what else should I say next time?"

④ TAKE TIME TO COMPOSE AND REHEARSE

your elevator speech. Find appropriate opportunities to explain your work or ideas. The more times you give the speech, the better you will get.

WHAT IF? But what if things don't work out as shown? Test your ability to adapt your communication by watching the What if? videos and planning a response for each situation.

1. How could you quickly organize your thoughts when you are unprepared and say, "Well, of course, it's marine biology. Oh, well, you know that. Sorry."

2. When you use complicated or vague language—"This semester we've been running a lot of data correlating levels of CO_2 and the impact on our atmosphere . . ."—how can you adapt to confused listeners?

Well-crafted introductions and conclusions that work together, like in then-Senator Barack Obama's "A More Perfect Union" speech, bring a power to your presentation that your main points cannot do alone. How can you make sure your introductions and conclusions come with a punch?

Wolfgang Kumm/epa/Corbis

Philadelphia titled "A More Perfect Union." Obama began by quoting the U.S. Constitution to remind his fellow Americans of the common history and goals for the nation they all share:

> "We the people, in order to form a more perfect union." Two hundred and twenty one years ago, in a hall that still stands across the street, a group of men gathered and, with these simple words, launched America's improbable experiment in democracy. Farmers and scholars; statesmen and patriots who had traveled across an ocean to escape tyranny and persecution finally made real their declaration of independence at a Philadelphia convention that lasted through the spring of 1787.[3]

He then discussed the complex history of racial tension and inequities in the United States and argued that Americans must first acknowledge the anger and resentment that people of different races feel before trying to confront today's social problems. Only through such open dialogue, Obama concluded, can we move toward the more perfect union envisioned by the framers of the Constitution.

By starting his speech with the familiar language of the U.S. Constitution, Obama created a sense of community among his listeners and hinted at

---

[3]Excerpt from "A More Perfect Union." Retrieved June 22, 2013, from http://constitutioncenter.org/amoreperfectunion.

the thesis of his speech. In his conclusion, Obama returned to the idea of "a more perfect union"—thus reminding listeners of his speech's theme. Let's look at how you can create equally strong and memorable introductions and conclusions for your speeches.

Introducing Your Speech

Your speech introduction is your first chance to connect with your audience and prepare them for what you will say. During this time, you want to gain listeners' attention, disclose your speech thesis, establish credibility, connect to listeners' needs and interests, and preview your main points. Although you will be doing most of this simultaneously, speech introductions often begin with gaining your listeners' attention and end by previewing your main points.

Gain Listeners' Attention. More than anything else, your introduction tells the audience what type of speech you are going to give. If you start your speech with overused phrases like "Hi, my name is . . . and today I'm going to talk about . . . ," you are telling your audience that your speech is going to be boring. Instead, create anticipation for what you have to say with a more creative introduction. Here are some ways to do that:

- *Ask a real question.* Posing a real question makes your speech interactive by involving your audience. For example, "By a show of hands, how many of you have completely public social media accounts?" Exercise caution if you encourage verbal responses, because lengthy answers will cut significantly into your speech time. Be prepared to step in and cut off responses if things get out of hand.

- *Ask a rhetorical question.* Rhetorical questions prompt your listeners to silently reflect on an issue. For example, "If you found out today that you only had six months to live, what would you do tomorrow?" This can work better if you are delivering your speech online and can't see or hear the responses of your audience.

- *Make a startling or suspenseful statement.* Start with a fact or statistic that raises your listeners' curiosity or challenges their worldview. For example, "One in three of you in this class will get it at some point in your lives. It's known as the 'silent killer.'"

- *Tell a story.* Begin your introduction with a compelling, relevant story. This is what Obama did when he summarized the story of the U.S. Constitution. When telling a story, keep it brief. You don't want the story to become the speech itself.

- *Use a brief quotation.* Alert your audience to the speech's theme and grab their attention with a relevant quote. For example, "Gandhi said, 'You must be the change you want to see in the world,'" or "I'm an adopted child, and my mother always told me, 'We chose you.'"

TABLE 14.3

INTRODUCTION CHECKLIST

1 Gain Listeners' Attention

2 Disclose Your Speech Thesis

3 Establish Credibility

4 Connect to Listeners' Needs and Interests

5 Review Your Main Points

file404/Shutterstock

- *Reference the occasion or recent events.* Comment on common ground between you and your audience. For example, "Tonight is a wonderful opportunity to reflect on the significance of 50 years of marriage as we honor Lawrence and Charlene."

Disclose Your Speech Thesis. After grabbing your audience's attention, you can reveal the subject matter of your speech, or your speech thesis. For example, "You can reduce the likelihood of falling victim to cyberstalking by taking steps to protect your privacy online." Sometimes you will need to provide background information or definitions to make sure your audience understands your thesis. In a speech about cyberstalking, you may need to define the term in your introduction so that there is no confusion about what you mean.

Establish Credibility. As you introduce a speech, the audience may wonder about your qualifications or experience with the topic. Listeners are more receptive to your message if they perceive you as credible or trustworthy. Although *credibility* is a key component in persuasive speaking, you also want to be trustworthy and ethical when giving informative and special-occasion speeches. How do you establish your credibility during the speech introduction? Briefly tell listeners about any relevant personal experience, or explain why you're interested in the topic. For example, "Last October I discovered that I had a cyberstalker."

Of course, you must maintain your credibility throughout the entire speech. We discuss how to do this in Chapter 17.

Connect to Listeners' Needs and Interests. People pay more attention to a speech when they think the topic is relevant to their needs and concerns. But it's not always apparent to your listeners how they can benefit from listening to your speech. This is why it is important to clearly state "what's in it for them" during your introduction. For instance, "I know that many of you have Instagram, Twitter, and other social media accounts. What I have to share with you today can lower your chances of becoming a victim of cyberstalking."

Preview Your Main Points. End your introduction by highlighting the main points of your presentation. This signals to your audience that you are transitioning from the introduction of your speech to the body: "I will first discuss the common types of cyberstalking that occur online. Then I'll go over some steps you can take to protect yourself."

Concluding Your Speech

Your conclusion indicates that you have finished presenting your main points and are approaching the end of your speech. Plan your conclusion carefully—it's your last chance to make sure your audience understands your main points. An effective conclusion signals the end of your speech, summarizes your main points, and leaves a memorable impact on your audience.

Signal the End. To signal that your speech is coming to a close, provide your listeners with a signpost or transition. Simple phrases like "In summary" or "Before I close" tell the audience that you're about to end the speech. This transition also gives inattentive audience members one last chance to hear your main points.

Summarize Your Main Points. An age-old saying about how to make a speech is "Tell them what you're going to tell them, tell them, and tell them what you told them." In your conclusion, a quick review of your main points helps your audience remember and understand them. But remember that you're only summarizing. Don't repeat extensive details about your main points. Instead, express each main point in one sentence, and avoid introducing any new material in your conclusion.

Have a Memorable Impact. Just as you opened your speech with an attention-getting statement, your parting words should also be memorable. Some of the same strategies used to gain listeners' attention also work for closing your speech—including asking questions, using quotations, or telling a brief story. Another possibility is to introduce your presentation by telling a story but leave the audience in suspense about its ending. You can then finish the story in the conclusion of your

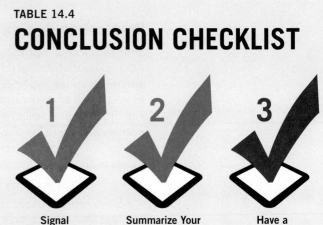

TABLE 14.4

CONCLUSION CHECKLIST

1	2	3
Signal the End	Summarize Your Main Points	Have a Memorable Impact

speech. A particularly effective way to end a speech is to refer back to your opening statement—as Obama did in his speech on race relations when he concluded with a reference to the Constitution and "a more perfect union": "And as so many generations have come to realize over the course of the two-hundred and twenty-one years since a band of patriots signed that document in Philadelphia, that is where the perfection begins."

Putting It All Together: Speech Outlines

The end result of Step 3: Composing is a written outline. All the time you put in toward thinking about your topic, researching it, writing a thesis, drafting your main points, and organizing your ideas is reflected in written outlines that you will use in delivering your speech.

Watch any major awards show, such as the Oscars or the Grammys, and you're bound to see some celebrities take the stage completely unprepared to accept their awards. Fumbling through their acceptance speeches, they make classic mistakes—like forgetting to thank someone or rambling on endlessly. Only on rare occasions do you see celebrities reach into a pocket for prepared notes and speak eloquently and appreciatively about the award. But such planning is crucial for any successful speech.

The last task in composing your speech is to develop your written outlines. A **preparation outline** details your presentation's overall structure. Similar to outlines for essays or research papers, a preparation outline helps you plan the order, flow, and logic of your speech, ensuring that there are no weaknesses or missing elements. A **delivery outline** helps you keep track of your ideas while you're actually presenting your speech to an audience. The following section provides general guidelines for developing both types of outlines. However, since outline formats often vary, be sure to check with your instructor regarding any specific outline requirements for your class.

Preparation Outline

Your preparation outline details your speech's introduction, body, and conclusion. It also lists the references you used to develop your speech and your specific purpose and speech thesis statements. This outline is a great way to keep track of all the information in your speech. You will likely make several drafts of it as you practice your speech and add or delete information as needed. Be sure to keep your outline up to date, so that it reflects your latest thoughts about the speech's structure. You can find an example of a preparation outline on pages 364–367. When creating your preparation outline, keep the following principles in mind:

- Use a consistent set of symbols and indentation. Typically, section headings show the parts of your speech—the introduction, body, and conclusion. Roman numerals (I, II, III) designate your major points for each section; uppercase letters (A, B, C) indicate your subpoints. Additional indentation levels (arabic numbers and lowercase letters) can be used if needed—for example, if you want to include the exact wording for testimony you will quote in the speech. Consistency in symbols and indentation helps you see the relationships among your ideas and make sure those relationships are logical.

- Identify each main point using one complete sentence. This forces you to determine the best way to communicate each point.

- Make certain that all subpoints support the main point they sit under. Known as the **principle of subordination,** this practice ensures that you're making valid arguments and that your claims are well supported and logical.

- Write your connective words and phrases in the outline, but set them off in parentheses ( ) so that they don't get confused with your main points or subpoints. Adding these phrases will help you determine whether your ideas are flowing smoothly.

- Include a works-cited or references section at the end of your outline. This should encompass all the information you'll cite in your speech as well as sources you consulted while preparing the speech. Talk with your instructor about any specific content and formatting requirements for this section.

Delivery Outline

Whereas the preparation outline helps you think through your speech's structure before you give the speech, your delivery outline acts as your "speaker notes" during the actual presentation to remind you of main points and key phrases. Create your delivery outline after you have practiced your speech several times using your preparation outline. Whether you prepare your delivery outline on note cards, sheets of paper, or an iPad, there are some features that are common to all good delivery outlines (see pp. 367–369):

- Write your delivery outline using keywords or phrases. Since the purpose of the delivery outline is to jog your memory while you're presenting, include only words or phrases that trigger the larger ideas you want to convey.

- Type your notes, and use a font (typeface) that is large enough for you to read easily. If you must handwrite your notes, make sure your writing is legible. You don't want your audience to see you struggling to read your own notes!

- Put in time codes and side notes to guide your delivery. Time codes help you stay on track, so you don't rush through your speech or go too slowly. Also, include reminders to use your nonverbal communication skills, such as smiling, looking around the room, and speaking slowly and clearly. Since you are the only one who will see your delivery outline notes, use them in any way that helps you deliver an effective, memorable speech.

SAMPLE PREPARATION AND DELIVERY OUTLINES

Preparation Outline

SPEECH TITLE: PROTECT THE LARGEST ORGAN IN YOUR LIFE

By: Jessica Bordonaro, Scottsdale Community College

• Write your specific purpose and thesis as part of the outline heading to keep the central idea of your speech in mind as you develop your outline.

Topic: Reducing Skin Cancer Risks

Specific purpose: To persuade my audience to take precautionary steps to reduce the risks of skin cancer and other skin-related health issues. •

Speech thesis: By protecting yourself adequately from overexposure to the sun, you lessen your risk of skin damage and skin cancers.

• Section headers are used to identify the introduction, body, and conclusion of the speech. This helps you see the overall speech organization.

INTRODUCTION: •

I. Gain attention: "By a show of hands, how many of you always protect yourselves when you know you are going to be in the sun for a significant amount of time?"

• The outline includes all five components for an effective introduction.

II. Speech thesis: By protecting yourself adequately from overexposure to the sun, you lessen your risk of skin damage and skin cancers.

III. Establish credibility: I have firsthand experience with the negative effects the sun can have on people. •

A. Two family friends died in the past three years from skin cancer.

B. I am very passionate about wanting people to know how to protect themselves from overexposure to the sun.

IV. Connect listeners' need: Living in Arizona, you have exposure to the sun all year round.

• The preview statement links the introduction to the body of the speech.

V. Preview main points: I am going to discuss how not protecting yourself from overexposure to the sun can contribute to skin-health problems, such as sunburn, premature aging, and skin cancer. I am also going to cover some ways you can help protect yourself from these things. •

• Each main point is indicated by a roman numeral and is stated as one complete sentence.

• Subpoints are marked by uppercase letters. Be sure to check for appropriate subordination of all subpoints.

BODY:

I. **Main Point 1:** Your risk for sunburn increases when you don't protect yourself adequately from the sun. •

A. Sunburns happen from overexposure to the sun. •

1. In a 2012 study, dermatologist Jennifer Lin and colleagues observed that among adolescents in the United States, about 83% reported at least one bad sunburn the previous summer.

2. Only about 34% of adolescents reported sunscreen use (Lin, Eder, & Weinmann, 2012).

3. Sunburn doesn't discriminate by skin color.

    a. The Mayo Clinic Web site (2012) states that although lighter-skinned types may burn easily, darker-skinned types can also suffer sunburns. •

    b. All skin types are subject to deep skin damage due to over-exposure to the sun (Mayo Clinic, 2012).

B. According to the National Library of Medicine (2011), "While the symptoms of sunburn are usually temporary . . . , the skin damage is often permanent and can have serious long-term health effects," and that "by the time the skin starts to become painful and red, the damage has been done."

• All supporting material is listed with proper points, including source citations.

(Transition: Sunburn is just the start of much larger issues of skin damage.) •

II. **Main Point 2:** Another issue that can arise when you don't protect yourself well in the sun is premature aging.

A. Intrinsic aging is one type of skin aging.

    1. Intrinsic skin aging is related to natural biological aging.

    2. Intrinsically aged skin appears smooth, pale, and finely wrinkled.

B. Extrinsic aging (or photoaging) is the effect of a lifetime of UV exposure.

    1. According to Fitzpatrick Dermatology, "Many skin functions that decline with age show an accelerated decline in photo-aged skin" (Gonzaga, 2009).

    2. Photoaged skin is characterized by coarse wrinkles, dark spots, and broken blood vessels.

• Connectives are set off in parentheses. They also help show the relationship between main points.

(Transition: Although you might think that sunburns are temporary and aging skin is too far down the road to worry about, there is another damaging effect of the sun to your health.)

III. **Main Point 3:** Overexposure to the sun can contribute to skin cancer.

A. There are different kinds of skin cancer, and some are more aggressive than others.

    1. According to the American Cancer Society Web site (2013), more than 3.5 million cases of non-melanoma skin cancers are diagnosed in the United States each year. •

        a. These include basal- and squamous-cell carcinomas.

        b. These cancers develop on sun-exposed areas of the skin.

        c. These skin cancers are curable when caught early.

    2. Melanoma starts in the particular skin cells that produce our skin color, known as melanocytes.

    3. Melanoma accounted for about 75% of skin cancer deaths in 2012 (Lin et al.).

B. I have had two family friends affected by skin cancer. •

• In composing this speech, the speaker uses a variety of supporting materials, including statistics, examples, expert testimony, and stories.

• The speaker includes a personal story as support-ing material to engage the audience.

(Transition: Given the potentially deadly effects of the sun, what can we do?)

This speech uses four main points to develop the thesis. What organizational pattern does the speech follow?

IV. **Main Point 4:** There are several ways to protect yourself from the sun and its harmful effects. •

    A. Avoid sun exposure during hours of peak sun-ray intensity.

        1. The UV index is a measure of ultraviolet radiation from the sun.

        2. Here is a map of yesterday's UV index.

    B. If you're going to spend extended time in the sun, protect your skin by wearing sunscreen.

        1. Wear generous amounts of at least SPF 30 sunscreen.

        2. Apply 30 minutes before sun exposure to allow absorption.

        3. Remember to reapply, because it comes off in water and from sweat.

    C. You should also protect other exposed areas of your body.

        1. Wear UV-protective sunglasses.

        2. Wear lip balm with a high SPF.

        3. Wear a wide-brim hat.

    D. Even if you don't plan to spend time in the sun, develop the habit of wearing a daily lotion that has sunscreen in it.

        1. This is easy to do if you already put lotion on anyway.

        2. This simple change will ensure you get SPF protection every day.

The conclusion summarizes the main points of the speech and is a final chance to leave the audience with a lasting impression about the topic.

CONCLUSION: •

    I. Summary: Getting too much sun has negative and damaging effects on the body, but you can take simple, specific precautions to protect yourself from the sun's rays.

    II. Summer is approaching, not to mention the fact that we live in Arizona, so do yourself a favor and start buying sunscreen and applying it when you are going to be in the sun.

    III. You don't want to look older than you are or risk dying before your time.

The last part of the outline is a properly formatted list of sources used for preparing the speech.

REFERENCES: •

American Cancer Society (2013). Retrieved from http://www.cancer.org /cancer/cancercauses/sunanduvexposure/skin-cancer-facts

EPA. (n.d.). *UV index.* Retrieved from http://www2.epa.gov/sunwise /uv-index

Gonzaga, E. R. (2009, January). Role of UV light in photodamage, skin aging, and skin cancer. *American Journal of Clinical Dermatology 10*(S1), 19–24. Retrieved from Academic Search Premier.

Lin, J. S., Eder, M., & Weinmann, S. (2011, February). Behavioral counseling to prevent skin cancer: A systematic review for the U.S. Preventive Services Task Force. *Annals of Internal Medicine 154*(3), 190–201. Retrieved from Academic Search Premier.

Mayo Clinic. (2012). *Sunburn: Risk factors*. Retrieved from http://www .mayoclinic.com/health/sunburn/DS00964/DSECTION=risk-factors

National Library of Medicine. (2011, May 13). *Sunburn*. Retrieved from http://www.nlm.nih.gov/medlineplus/ency/article/003227.htm

Delivery Outline ·

INTRODUCTION:

I. "How many of you always protect yourselves when you know you are going to be in the sun for a significant amount of time?"

(Pause briefly)

II. Protecting yourself lessens your risk of skin damage and skin cancer.

III. Firsthand experience: two family friends died. Passionate about protection

(Maintain eye contact) •

IV. Living in AZ

V. Discuss how not protecting contributes to sunburn, premature aging, and skin cancer. Also go over some ways to protect yourself.

(1:00 minute)

BODY:

I. Sun exposure increases sunburn risk.

  A. Sunburn—overexposure to the sun

    1. Among adolescents in the U.S., about 83% had one bad sunburn (Lin, Eder, & Weinmann, 2012). •

    2. Only about 34% of adolescents reported sunscreen use (Lin et al.).

    3. Sunburn and skin color

      a. Lighter-skinned types burn easily; darker-skinned types can suffer sunburns (Mayo Clinic, 2012).

      b. All skin types suffer deep skin damage (Mayo Clinic, 2012).

  B. According to the National Library of Medicine (2011), "While the symptoms of sunburn are usually temporary . . . , the skin damage is often permanent and can have serious long-term health effects," and that "by the time the skin starts to become painful and red, the damage has been done."

* The delivery outline uses phrases and keywords that the speaker can quickly reference to help guide the presentation.

* The notes in parentheses are reminders to stay focused on proper nonverbal and vocal delivery during the presentation. Time codes also help the speaker with pacing the speech.

* The delivery outline includes source citation details so that the speaker gives proper credit to sources during the speech.

(Transition: Sunburn is just the start of much larger issues of skin damage.)

(Move to right side of room)

(3:00 minutes)

II. Another issue is premature aging.

    A. Intrinsic aging

        1. Intrinsic skin aging is natural.

        2. Appears smooth, pale, and finely wrinkled

    B. Extrinsic or photoaging

        1. According to Fitzpatrick Dermatology, "Many skin functions that decline with age show an accelerated decline in photo-aged skin" (Gonzaga, 2009).

        2. Characterized by coarse wrinkles, dark spots, and broken blood vessels

(Transition: Although you might think that sunburns are temporary and aging skin is too far down the road to worry about, there is another damaging effect of the sun to your health.)

(Move to center of room)

(4:00 minutes)

III. Overexposure contributes to skin cancer.

    A. Different kinds of skin cancer; some are aggressive

(Go slowly)

        1. According to the American Cancer Society Web site (2013), more than 3.5 million cases of non-melanoma skin cancers are diagnosed in the United States each year.

            a. Basal- and squamous-cell carcinomas

            b. Develop on sun-exposed areas of the skin

            c. Curable when caught early

        2. Melanoma starts in melanocytes.

        3. Melanoma—75% of skin cancer deaths in 2012 (Lin et al.)

    B. Two family friends affected by skin cancer

(Transition: Given the potentially deadly effects of the sun, what can we do?)

(Move to left of room)

(Maintain eye contact)

(5:00 minutes)

IV. Several ways to protect yourself

(Move back to lectern)

    A. Avoid hours of peak sun-ray intensity.

        1. The UV index

        2. UV index map   (Show map)

    B. Protect your skin by wearing sunscreen.

    1. At least SPF 30 sunscreen   (Show sunscreen container) •

    2. Apply 30 minutes before exposure

    3. Reapply

C. Protect other exposed areas of your body.   (Show each object)

    1. Wear UV-protective sunglasses.

    2. Wear lip balm with a high SPF.

    3. Wear a wide-brim hat.

D. Wear a daily SPF lotion.   (Show everyday lotion container)

    1. Already put lotion on anyway

    2. Simple change ensures SPF protection.

(right margin note) • *Reminders reduce the chance of forgetting to display a visual aid.*

(7:00 minutes)

(Brief pause)

CONCLUSION: •

I. Getting too much sun has negative and damaging effects on the body, but you can take specific, simple precautions to protect yourself from the sun's rays.

II. Summer is approaching.

(Brief pause)

III. You don't want to look older than you are or risk dying before your time.

(right margin note) • *Similar to the preparation outline, all three sections of the speech and connectives are marked to help the speaker stay organized and focused.*

REFERENCES:

American Cancer Society (2013). Retrieved from http://www.cancer.org /cancer/cancercauses/sunanduvexposure/skin-cancer-facts

EPA. (n.d.). UV *index*. Retrieved from http://www2.epa.gov/sunwise /uv-index

Gonzaga, E. R. (2009, January). Role of UV light in photodamage, skin aging, and skin cancer. *American Journal of Clinical Dermatology 10*(S1), 19–24. Retrieved from Academic Search Premier.

Lin, J. S., Eder, M., & Weinmann, S. (2011, February). Behavioral counseling to prevent skin cancer: A systematic review for the U.S. Preventive Services Task Force. *Annals of Internal Medicine 154*(3), 190–201. Retrieved from Academic Search Premier.

Mayo Clinic. (2012). *Sunburn: Risk factors*. Retrieved from http://www .mayoclinic.com/health/sunburn/DS00964/DSECTION=risk-factors)

National Library of Medicine. (2011, May 13). *Sunburn*. Retrieved from www.nlm.nih.gov/medlineplus/ency/article/003227.htm

LearningCurve can help you review! Go to **bedfordstmartins.com /choicesconnections**.

CHAPTER (14) REVIEW

CHAPTER RECAP

- Your **speech thesis** will guide the structure of your speech. Evolving from your *specific purpose statement*, it will inform your audience of your position on the topic and provide insight into your main points.
- The *body* of your speech contains your **main points,** which are backed up by your *supporting materials*.
- The *organizational pattern* you choose (**topical, chronological, spatial, cause-effect,** or **problem-solution**) will help your audience understand and follow your speech's main points.
- Both the *introduction* and the *conclusion* serve important purposes in a speech. These are moments when you have the opportunity to gain listeners' attention, disclose your thesis, establish credibility, connect to your audience, preview and summarize your main points, prepare listeners for the end of your speech, and make a final impression.
- Developing **preparation** and **delivery outlines** helps you plan the flow and logic of your speech and keep you on task during the actual presentation, making you a more successful speaker.

LAUNCHPAD

LaunchPad for *Choices & Connections* offers unique video scenarios and encourages self-assessment through adaptive quizzing. Go to **bedfordstmartins.com /choicesconnections** to get access.

 LearningCurve adaptive quizzes

 How to Communicate video scenarios

 Video clips that illustrate key concepts

KEY TERMS

1️⃣ Which of the following is *not* a requirement of a speech thesis?

   a. It includes all your main points.

   b. It is one sentence.

   c. It is stated during your speech.

   d. It alerts the audience to your position.

2️⃣ When using statistics, it is important to _____.

   a. give precise and detailed numbers

   b. put them in a meaningful context

   c. use multiple examples each time

   d. include them throughout the speech

3️⃣ If you are giving a speech on how Web sites like Kickstarter have changed how small businesses raise funds, a _____ would be the best way to structure your main points.

   a. spatial pattern   **c.** problem-solution pattern

   b. topical pattern   **d.** cause-effect pattern

4️⃣ What is the best way to engage your listeners if they are already familiar with the information you are presenting?

   a. Include unrelated stories and jokes for a touch of humor.

   b. Spend more time on your visual aids than on your supporting materials.

   c. Forgo any introduction, and get right to the body of the speech.

   d. Look for additional sources that present new testimony or examples.

5️⃣ Why might you create several drafts of your delivery outline?

   a. To include time codes to monitor pacing

   b. To eliminate any internal summaries

   c. To allow for revisions after practicing your speech

   d. To replace the organizational pattern

ACTIVITIES

1️⃣ **Speech Analysis**

Find a professional speech that interests you. Try a TED talk (available at www .ted.com/talks), or search databases like Gifts of Speech (http://gos.sbc.edu) or American Rhetoric (www.americanrhetoric.com). In a brief paper, identify the speech thesis, its main points, and the organizational pattern. Additionally, analyze how well the speaker engages listeners through novelty, humor, stories, and presentation media.

2️⃣ **Introduction Redo**

Review the attention-getter used in the speech outline for "Protect the Largest Organ in Your Life" by Jessica Bordonaro on page 364. Working with a group of classmates, brainstorm additional ways to gain the listeners' attention if you were giving this speech. Choose one of the alternatives and present it to the class, explaining why you selected that one over other ideas.

15

Delivering Your Speech

(F) ive-year-old kids don't usually give speeches. It's even less likely they would speak to a professional baseball team. But Josh Sacco is no ordinary five-year-old. Standing on the field at Fenway Park before the 2010 Opening Day game of the Boston Red Sox, Josh addressed the players and a sell-out crowd of over 36,000 fans, projecting the confidence and authority of a seasoned coach:

> Great moments are born from great opportunity.
> And that's what you have here tonight, boys.
> That's what you've earned here, tonight.
> One game.
> If we played 'em ten times, they might win nine.
> But not this game. Not tonight.

Josh delivered a rousing message to the Red Sox that night: beat your longtime rivals, the New York Yankees.

How did Josh end up giving a speech at Fenway Park? Dedicated practice. Josh had become quite skilled at reenacting a speech delivered by Kurt Russell in the movie *Miracle*, which chronicles the U.S. Olympic hockey team's historic victory over the Soviet Union in the 1980 Winter Olympic Games. In the movie, Russell plays the determined U.S. hockey coach Herb Brooks. A pivotal moment occurs when Brooks addresses the U.S. team in the locker room before their semifinal game against the Soviet Union. The U.S. team is considered the underdog and given no chance to beat the Soviets, who are enjoying a 21-game winning streak. Sensing a low morale, Brooks delivers a brief yet compelling speech convincing his team that they can win. And they do. Prevailing in a 4–3 victory, the Americans end the Soviets' winning streak and go on to capture the gold medal.

Josh, a die-hard hockey fan, watched *Miracle* more than 100 times, carefully practicing Brooks's "Great Moments" speech. Impressed by Josh's mastery of the speech, his father, Jim, recorded Josh's performance and posted it on YouTube for relatives

Bruce Kluckhohn/NHLI via Getty Images

to view. The video went viral, leading to national television and blog coverage, as well as an appearance on the *Ellen DeGeneres Show*. DeGeneres even paid for Josh to attend the 2010 Winter Olympic Games, where he gave his rendition of the speech to the U.S. Olympic hockey team before their game against Canada. Just two months later, he delivered the speech to the Red Sox—who went on to beat the Yankees in a 9–7 victory that night.

Although Josh memorized a speech that he did not compose himself (remember, he was only five years old!), his story highlights an essential lesson for people wanting to improve their public-speaking skills: practice pays off. The many hours Josh spent viewing and practicing the movie speech imprinted in his memory the language, gestures, and vocal rhythms that excited and inspired his listeners. Given the considerable time you put into each step of the speech preparation process—*thinking* about your audience and specific speech purpose, *investigating* or researching your topic, and carefully *composing* the presentation—your speech will fall flat if you don't practice. That's why steps 4 and 5—*rehearse* and *revise*—are important elements of your speech preparation. Only through rehearsing and revising can you get a sense of how to improve both your speech's content and your verbal and nonverbal skills in delivering it. (See Table 15.1 for the Five Steps in Speech Preparation.) Such practice is key to engaging your audience during your speech delivery. In this chapter, you'll learn:

- How to deliver a speech effectively
- Ways to connect with your audience
- Ideas for managing speech anxiety
- The process for selecting and using presentation aids
- How to evaluate others' speeches and use feedback to improve your own presentation skills

✔️ **LearningCurve** can help you review! Go to **bedfordstmartins.com /choicesconnections**.

Speech Delivery Modes

You can start Step 4: Rehearse by considering how you will actually give your speech. Will you have time to adequately prepare? How heavily (if at all) will you rely on notes? Will factors such as the setting, situation, or audience influence your presentation? Answering questions like these will help you determine your delivery style.

When preparing a presentation, there are three primary modes of delivery. You might have to deliver your message when you have little to no time for preparation (impromptu); you might write out and then read or memorize an entire script (manuscript); or you might have a combination of both, in which you prepare your research and notes but do not plan every word you'll say in advance (extemporaneous).

Impromptu Speaking

Imagine that just as you arrive at a 25th anniversary dinner for your favorite aunt and uncle, your mother asks if you'll "say a few words" about the couple after dessert is served. You scan the room of more than 50 guests and

TABLE 15.1

FIVE STEPS IN SPEECH PREPARATION

1 THINK	**2** INVESTIGATE	**3** COMPOSE	**4** REHEARSE	**5** REVISE
Choose your topic, adapt to your audience	Plan your strategy, conduct your research, evaluate your sources	Develop your speech structure and support material, prepare your visual aids	Create speaking notes, practice aloud, work on delivery	Process feedback from others and self-reflection, write a final outline and speaking notes

nervously agree to do it. Responding to your mom's request requires **impromptu speaking**—making public remarks with little or no time for preparation or rehearsal.

Although daunting, there are ways you can handle impromptu speaking situations. First, anticipate as much as possible occasions where you might be asked to say something. If you know people will be making speeches at the anniversary dinner and you are especially close with your aunt and uncle, might you be expected to say a few words? Second, keep your message brief, and don't apologize for being unprepared. Third, identify a central point you want to make, and provide two or three illustrative points or facts to back you up. Fourth, restate your central point as your conclusion. If you have the time, compose a brief speaking outline to help keep you focused. For most impromptu situations, providing a small amount of information should satisfy your audience. No one expects you to give a long, detailed speech on a moment's notice.

Because it's almost impossible to rehearse impromptu speeches, you can practice this type of speaking in other ways. Take advantage of opportunities that allow you to present your ideas in front of large groups, such as contributing to class discussions or work meetings. You'll gain experience thinking quickly on your feet, and grow more comfortable speaking on a moment's notice. Additionally, the How to Communicate feature in Chapter 14 (pp. 356–357) will help you develop your skills with a special type of impromptu speech known as an elevator speech.

Manuscript speaking allows you to correctly state more intricate, emotional language and phrases, like Martin Luther King Jr. did in his "I Have a Dream" speech. When might you want to use a manuscript for your speeches?

Hulton-Deutsch Collection/Corbis

Manuscript Speaking

Some occasions require **manuscript speaking,** in which your speech is based on a written text that you either read word for word or commit to memory—like Josh Sacco at Fenway Park. For Josh, it was important that he reenact the speech as it was given in the movie *Miracle*, which meant he had to memorize it. Other times, manuscript speaking is used when exact word choice is critical. World leaders, for example, often speak from prepared texts in public. This helps them avoid saying something that could be misunderstood by listeners.

Manuscript speaking is best used in formal situations, such as political speeches, commencement addresses, and ceremonies. Such occasions usually require a speaker to carefully craft a message using language that is finely polished, even poetic. This can be easier to do if the speech is written out in advance. Consider the following excerpt from Martin Luther King Jr.'s (1963) historic "I Have a Dream" speech:

> In a sense we have come to our nation's capital to cash a check. When the architects of our Republic wrote the magnificent words of the Constitution and the Declaration of Independence, they were signing a promissory note to which every American was to fall heir. This note was a promise that all

men would be guaranteed the inalienable rights of life, liberty, and the pursuit of happiness.

Rather than using plain words to call for racial equality, Dr. King used vivid imagery ("we have come to our nation's capital to cash a check") to communicate America's responsibility for ending racial discrimination. Bringing that powerful image to his listeners' minds would have been more difficult if Dr. King hadn't written out those exact words in advance. When using poetic language, constructing intricate metaphors, or delving into complicated matters, manuscript speaking can allow you to get the details right.

But manuscript speaking also has drawbacks. For one thing, if you focus on a written text, you have less time to make eye contact with your listeners. Or, if you memorize your manuscript so you can maintain more eye contact with your audience, you might sound stilted or lose your place, leading to embarrassing pauses or mistakes. Finally, using a manuscript can make it difficult to adapt to your audience. If you sense your listeners need an additional example to understand a point you're making, you might find it hard to deviate from your script and provide that example. Using a manuscript to read or memorize a speech should be reserved for formal occasions. For many classroom speeches, the extemporaneous delivery style is more appropriate.

Extemporaneous Speaking

Extemporaneous speaking includes elements of both manuscript and impromptu speaking. In this case, you create a structured preparation outline for your speech ahead of time, mapping out what you plan to cover (like manuscript speaking). Then you reduce your preparation outline to a delivery outline that allows you to add or eliminate information as needed during your presentation (like impromptu speaking). The resulting speech sounds more conversational than it would if you read from or memorized a manuscript. A *conversational tone* is similar to a casual conversation; it uses a natural, spoken language style rather than a formal, written language style, and the speaker exudes emotion and passion for the topic (Doetkott & Motley, 2009).

In most settings, an extemporaneous style of speaking is a great way to connect with your listeners. A well-prepared delivery outline allows you to focus on using familiar language, eye contact, gestures, and an engaging conversational style. Of course, these same qualities can be achieved in impromptu or manuscript speaking, but it can be challenging if you're speaking with little preparation, reciting a speech from memory, or reading from paper or a screen. With the extemporaneous mode, your speech will be a little bit different each time you deliver it. But if you've gone through the five steps of speech preparation beforehand, you can be confident that your speech will be successful each time.

Managing Your Speech Delivery

> Step 4: Rehearse isn't just about the delivery mode you will use. Practicing your delivery will help you feel more comfortable and confident, fostering a sense of closeness with your listeners and gaining their respect.

With a select crowd of media, family, and friends seated in the room, Tiger Woods looked straight into the television camera and apologized for the sordid sex scandal that ended his marriage and jeopardized his golf career. Reading from a manuscript, Woods took over 13 minutes to apologize for his marital infidelity, state that he was getting professional counseling, and beg for privacy as his family struggled to repair their shattered lives. Although Woods said all the right things—"I am deeply sorry for my irresponsible and selfish behavior I engaged in" (CNN, 2010)—and used gestures known to engage audiences, such as eye contact and erect posture, the news media questioned the authenticity of his public apology. One editorial noted that "Tiger Woods' public apology . . . had all of the fingerprints of practiced public relations advisers," and that although the speech was smart, it was also empty— Woods never acknowledged the harm he caused to those outside his family and kept the focus on himself ("Tiger," 2010). Others thought his speech appeared overly rehearsed, calculating, and lacking genuine emotion. The most caustic critics saw the speech as a ploy to win back the corporate sponsors who had dumped Woods after news of the scandal broke.

Woods's delivery created skepticism in his listeners because his speech lacked two key elements: immediacy and a powerful speech style. **Immediacy** is a sense of closeness that your audience feels toward you as a speaker (Mehrabian, 1972). You create immediacy by using familiar language and engaging nonverbal behaviors. Communicators who show immediacy are often described as warm and approachable (Richmond, McCroskey, & Johnson, 2003). The other important element in speech delivery is the ability to present yourself and your message confidently. Known as a **powerful**

The uncomfortable and hollow delivery of Tiger Woods's apology speech caused viewers to feel uncertain about his remorse. How do you think he could have demonstrated more immediacy and a powerful speaking style to better connect with the audience?

Lori Moffett/Bloomberg/Getty Images

speech style, these verbal and nonverbal behaviors gain the respect of your listeners (Fragale, 2006; Hosman, Huebner, & Siltanen, 2002). Woods's failure to convey these two elements is why people in the audience distrusted his message. To avoid a similar fate, you'll want to convey immediacy and project a powerful speech style in your presentations while also managing any speech anxiety you may feel.

Conveying Immediacy

You can create a sense of immediacy by adopting an **oral style**—language that's similar to how people talk—when delivering your speech. An oral style differs radically from a **written style,** which is usually more formal and detailed. Consider the following examples:

> *Written style:* "Although the word *sustainability* denotes a wide variety of concerns, many people restrict its meaning to the green movement. However, it is imperative that a broader meaning be embraced."

> *Oral style:* "If you're like me, when you hear the word *sustainability*, you only think of things like energy conservation and recycling. But the word means so much more."

A written style often results from composing a manuscript speech or writing an overly detailed delivery outline. Why? Because when people write out a speech, they typically use formal language and complex sentences. This results in a spoken presentation that may sound like a written paper. But listeners prefer the oral style over the more formal tone of the written style (Doetkott & Motley, 2009). This was one of the mistakes Tiger Woods made. By composing and delivering from a manuscript, he was unable to present his message in a natural, conversational manner and therefore failed to create a sense of immediacy with his audience.

However, immediacy isn't achieved through an oral style alone. You also connect with your audience through *nonverbal behaviors*, such as vocal characteristics, eye contact, facial expressions, gestures, and body posture.

Vocal Characteristics. Your voice creates a sense of either closeness or distance with the audience. When delivering your speech, consider how these three features will help you connect with listeners. First, your **vocal pitch** is the high and low registers of your voice. In ordinary conversation, your vocal pitch varies with your emotions. When you're excited, your pitch rises; when you're serious, your pitch lowers. While practicing your speech, mark sections of your delivery outline to show where your voice needs to convey emotion, such as when telling an illustrative story or to emphasize an especially important statistic. This will help you vary your vocal pitch and give your audience a sense of how you feel about your topic.

As founder of Girls Who Code, an organization that aims to close the gender gap in computing fields, lawyer and politician Reshma Sanjuani often speaks to groups large and small about the causes she believes in. Whether to inform her audience about issues related to women in software development or to persuade donors to fund her nonprofit, using consistent eye contact helps Sanjuani connect with her audience and project confidence as a speaker.

John Minchillo/Invision/AP Images

Second, **vocal tone**—the richness and sound quality of your voice—also varies during natural conversations. For instance, your tone sounds different when you're discouraged than when you're optimistic. People who don't vary their vocal pitch and vocal tone during a conversation or public presentation are speaking in a **monotone**—which doesn't create a sense of immediacy. A monotone delivery bores an audience, giving the impression you don't care about what you are saying. Woods made this mistake in his apology speech.

Third, **vocal rate**—how rapidly you speak—also determines immediacy. Woods spoke at a slow rate, averaging about 112 words per minute in his speech. Speaking at such a rate can cause the audience to quickly lose interest in what you are saying. Ideally, speakers deliver their ideas at 140–175 words per minute. Don't worry too much about those exact numbers or counting your words. The real lesson is this: If you speak too rapidly, your listeners may miss something or feel exhausted trying to keep up. But if you speak too slowly, your audience's attention can begin to wander.

Eye Contact. In our discussion of nonverbal communication in Chapter 6, we explain how eye contact shows attention, interest, affection, and even aggression. During a presentation, eye contact signals your interest and desire to connect with your audience. You can do this by spending two to three seconds looking at listeners in one section of your audience, then spending the same amount of time looking at listeners in another section, and so on, throughout your speech. Be sure to make random eye contact so it feels natural and spontaneous. If you simply scan the room back and forth, it feels staged and diminishes the sense of closeness.

When managing your eye contact during a speech, watch out for two common mistakes: not making enough eye contact because you are too focused on reading your notes, or making eye contact with only those listeners who are the most interested and supportive. In both instances, listeners who don't receive eye contact will feel ignored. Finally, if you are delivering an online presentation and no audience is physically present with you in the room, look straight at the camera, as though you were talking to a close friend.

Facial Expressions. Your audience can tell how strongly you feel about your message by observing your facial expressions. For example, you might smile with expressive eyes when making a humorous point. On the other hand, you would probably smile less and project a solemn look when telling a tragic story. In both cases, facial expressions reinforce your feelings about the message, strengthening the connection with your audience.

Facial expressions should naturally arise from your feelings about specific points you're making in the speech. As you compose your speech, take time to *critically self-reflect* (see Chapter 2) about your feelings related to the topic. This can help you become facially expressive as you deliver specific points during your speech. Keep in mind that a lack of facial expressiveness on your part—or worse, overly rehearsed or exaggerated expressions—will come across as insincere, unbelievable, or both.

Gestures and Body Posture. Your gestures and posture also reveal the intensity of your involvement with your topic and thus affect the degree of immediacy your audience feels. In everyday conversation, you naturally use your hands and move your body to help you describe something or tell a story. However, when you give a speech, nervousness can cause your gestures to be awkward, stilted, or even nonexistent. Or you may attempt to manage your nervousness through **adaptive gestures,** such as fidgeting, twirling your hair, or fiddling with your jewelry. Even your posture is more likely to become stiff. Any of these changes can block you from creating a sense of immediacy with your audience. For example, folding your arms across your body or jingling your pocket change sends the message that you're not engaged with your topic or your audience. Slumping over a lectern suggests that you're bored or tired—further eroding immediacy. Carefully monitor your gestures and posture to make sure you are producing *congruent messages.* As Chapter 6 explains, this happens when your verbal communication and nonverbal communication match. When rehearsing your speech, focus on proper posture and practice specific gestures, such as pointing, to emphasize main points or to reinforce your visual aids.

Projecting a Powerful Speech Style

During a presentation, your choice of language and other nonverbal behaviors can gain or lose the respect of your audience. When speaking publicly, you want to influence your audience to listen by using a powerful speech style. Audiences will pay more attention if they respect you and will lose motivation to listen if they don't. You achieve a powerful speech style through the words you choose and the way you use your voice. Additionally, your dress and physical appearance will affect how the audience regards you and your message.

Language. A common mistake speakers make is to use **powerless language** during a speech—words that suggest they're uncertain about their message or themselves. Examples of powerless language include **hedging,** or words that lessen a message's impact, such as *sorta, kinda,* and *somewhat.* Such words can confuse an audience and suggest you're holding something back. **Disclaimers**—phrases that remove responsibility for the statement you're making—are another example. For instance, saying "I'm not an expert, but . . ." or "I could be wrong about this, but . . ." reduces your power. A final example is using unnecessary words—known as **intensifiers**—to overempha-size a point ("It was a *really, really* good movie" or "The decision to increase tuition was *totally* wrong"). If you use a lot of powerless language while delivering a speech, you might be viewed as unlikable and fail to earn the respect of your audience (Holtgraves & Lasky, 1999).

Vocal Delivery. Your voice also projects confidence—or uncertainty—and influences how your audience perceives you. Consider your **vocal volume,** or how loudly or quietly you speak. Speaking too softly can make it hard for listeners to hear you and may cause them to doubt your confidence and cred-ibility. Conversely, if you speak too loudly, your audience may see you as overbearing. You want to talk just loudly enough for people sitting in the back row to hear you.

Poor **articulation** can further erode how you are viewed, because it can cause your audience to misunderstand what you're saying. Don't run through words ("Whaddayougonnado?" rather than "What are you going to do?") or drop the endings of words ("How's it goin'?" rather than "How's it going?"). Likewise, pay attention to your **pronunciation,** or the way you say words. Poor pronunciation—for example, saying "ambalance" instead of "ambulance"—may cause your audience to question your credibility.

Finally, avoid overusing **vocalized pauses and fillers** (*um, ah, you know*). Since these are common in ordinary conversation, your audience can toler-ate occasional use of them. But researchers have found that frequent occur-rence of such hesitations in a presentation leads to a negative impression of a speaker (Johnson & Vinson, 1990). If you need time to collect your thoughts about what you're going to say next, just pause briefly.

Dress and Physical Appearance. How you dress and your physical appear-ance can build or undermine the impression you make on an audience. If you want your audience to take you seriously, you should look the part. In addi-tion to being properly groomed, this may mean not dressing as though you're headed to the beach, to sleep, or to the dance club. You'll also want to avoid chewing gum or wearing "noisy" jewelry, sunglasses, flip-flops, or a baseball cap during your presentation. In short, there should be nothing about your

DOUBLE TAKE

PROPER (VS) IMPROPER CLOTHING

What you wear when delivering a speech is more important than you might initially think. Improper dress risks being distracting, or sending the message that you don't care. Of the students below, which one displays confidence and is more likely to capture an audience's attention?

Image Source/Corbis

Tom Carter/Photo Edit

appearance that distracts the audience from listening to your speech. Instead, you'll want to look your best.

Start by matching your dress to what is appropriate for the occasion and your audience. In some situations, you may need to dress formally, whereas in others, a more casual appearance will be appropriate. For example, you might wear business attire when giving a presentation to college alumni at a fund-raising event, but you might choose more casual attire for delivering a speech in your communication class. A general rule of thumb is that you should dress slightly more formally than you expect your audience to dress.

MAKING COMMUNICATION CHOICES

THIS IS HOW I TALK

1

CONSIDER THE DILEMMA

Raised in the rural South, Mike never thought much about how he spoke, but enrolling at a university in the Midwest changed all that. Soon after moving to campus, Mike's roommates started teasing him about his southern accent, calling him "hick" and "redneck." Although Mike laughed it off, he became increasingly self-conscious about his accent. Afraid of being stereotyped, he rarely spoke up in class, and he dreaded having to give presentations. But Mike's biggest concern was that he wanted to be a lawyer, and attorneys do a lot of public speaking.

As you're leaving your political science class one day, Dr. Brenner calls you over to a conversation he's having with Mike about joining the college's mock trial team—a competitive activity in which students simulate trial lawyers by delivering opening statements, questioning witnesses, and presenting closing statements. Dr. Brenner introduces you as a team member who

has grown immensely by participating in mock trial competitions. Nodding in agreement, you tell Mike, "It's great preparation for law school. You learn how to think under pressure and present a court case in front of others. You get a lot of constructive criticism, too."

"That's not something I could do," Mike says. "I don't like talking in front of people around here." When Dr. Brenner asks why, Mike replies, "People think I'm stupid 'cause of the way I talk." Upon Dr. Brenner's suggestion that Mike enroll in a voice and diction class if he is concerned about his accent, Mike responds, "I don't think it's right to change who I am. It'd be like disrespecting my family. Anyway, I'll probably just wind up going to law school back home and practicing law there. I gotta run. See you next week."

After Mike leaves the classroom, Dr. Brenner turns to you and says, "Will you talk to him again to see if he'll reconsider?"

2

CONNECT THE RESEARCH

Accents are a common basis for stereotypes. U.S. citizens consistently rate the South as a place where accented speech portrays residents as backward or uneducated (Preston 1999; Preston, 2002). Even when a southern accent is perceived as friendly or polite, listeners may still question the speaker's competence or ability. Such judgments aren't reserved solely for southerners, however; many non-native English speakers are also stereotyped as unintelligent if they have heavily accented speech (Burlage, Marafka, Parsons, & Milaski, 2004).

Although such judgments are clearly wrong, they persist because accents signal cultural difference. In fact, accents may be more

important than appearance in marking others as cultural *outgroupers* (Rakić, Steffens, & Mummendey, 2011). This is an important distinction, because people feel less certain about and uncomfortable around those whom they judge as culturally dissimilar.

However, unfavorable judgments about accents don't always stem from stereotypes. Heavy accents can make it difficult to understand messages, leading listeners to question the speaker's credibility (Lev-Ari & Keysar, 2010). When an accent becomes a hindrance to being understood by others, pursuing a class or training to reduce these effects might be appropriate.

Before making a communication choice, consider the facts of the situation, and think about the research on accented speech. Also, reflect on what you've learned so far about conveying immediacy (pp. 379–381) and projecting a powerful speech style (pp. 381–385). Then answer these questions:

1 What other factors about his cultural background and career goals should Mike consider in deciding whether to modify his accent?

2 When you talk to Mike, will you repeat Dr. Brenner's suggestion that he enroll in a voice and diction class? Why or why not?

3 What other advice could you give Mike to make him feel more comfortable making presentations?

Another consideration for determining how to dress is the speech topic. Shorts and a T-shirt could be proper attire for an informative speech about setting up a weekend campsite but would be completely inappropriate to wear for a persuasive speech about donating time to visit the elderly. Check with your instructor when in doubt about any special dress requirements for class assignments.

Managing Your Delivery in Online Speeches

As you progress through your college education and work life, you will increasingly face situations in which you will need to deliver an online presentation. For example, your sociology professor may require a video podcast, or your job may involve video conferences with employees located around the world. In these and other situations, you want to ensure that your audience stays tuned in to your message by conveying immediacy and projecting a powerful speech style. How? In addition to relying on the same language and nonverbal elements previously discussed, there are some specific things to keep in mind for online presentations.

Whether you are recording a video to post or streaming in real time, you'll want to make sure the camera is properly adjusted. Focus the lens to a medium close-up shot, which captures your upper torso and head. By doing so, your viewers will experience a more personal connection than they would if your image were too close or too far away. You should also keep your background free of visual distractions. Something as simple as a clock or painting on the wall behind you can be distracting to listeners.

Be expressive with your face, eyes, and voice. Although this is clearly important at presentations where your audience will see you, it is also important for podcasts or any narrations you may do. Even if your audience can't see your facial expressions, using your nonverbal communication will help

When delivering a speech online, paying close attention to your surroundings, outside noise, and the camera angle is as important as your appearance and other delivery skills. Consider what aspects this speaker set up well for his online presentation and how he could improve.

Engaged facial expressions will convey nonverbal meaning to viewers.

Appropriate clothing helps establish credibility.

Check to make sure your head and upper torso appear on screen. You don't want to seem too far from audiences.

Could art on the walls behind him distract listeners?

Even if an area isn't seen, having a messy work surface could create noise during the speech.

your vocal expressiveness. If your audience can see you, avoid excessive gesturing and body movements that could be distracting.

To help keep your audience engaged, use presentation software and other visual aids. Well-designed and meaningfully integrated slides, for example, can help your audience understand complex ideas, especially statistical information. We cover more on how to use such software on page 391.

Of course, you'll still need to practice. Whether it's face-to-face or online, a key part of any successful presentation is practice. It is especially important that you practice with any technology you might use to make sure you know how it works and are comfortable with it. Recording your practice also allows you to check and revise your camera setup, expressiveness, sound levels, and lighting quality.

Managing Speech Anxiety

All the time you spend rehearsing can be undermined if your nerves take over once you're in front of an audience. But being nervous about speaking in public, or **speech anxiety,** is a common experience for many people, because no one wants to lose face or become embarrassed in a public setting (Buss, 1980). Potentially adding to that fear are your own negative thoughts. As Chapter 2 discusses, *self-fulfilling prophecies* are predictions you make about interactions that lead you to communicate in ways that make those predictions come true. This can happen in any communication context, whether group, interpersonal, or public speaking. Studies have shown that people who experience high levels of anxiety about giving a speech often have thoughts such as "I'm really going to blow this!" (Ayres, 1988). If you think like this, it is more likely to happen.

Finding remedies for speech anxiety has long been a focus of research (McCroskey, 2009; Smith, Sawyer, & Behnke, 2005). Although there is no "magic pill" cure, there are several strategies to help reduce the nervousness associated with public speaking. If you experience speech anxiety, here are some suggestions to try:

- *Look for opportunities to speak up in large groups.* Make comments and ask questions whenever you're in a large group, such as a classroom, a forum, or a meeting. These experiences will gradually help reduce your feelings of self-consciousness when speaking in front of large groups.

- *Choose speech topics that matter to you.* If you can choose your speech topics, select subjects that you find interesting or important. This way, you'll be more focused on your message than on yourself, so you'll feel less nervous (Motley, 1990).

- *Create a situational analysis.* During the rehearsal step of your speech preparation, spend some time learning about your speech setting and equipment needs. You will feel more comfortable and confident if you are familiar with the room setup. Trying to find a power outlet for your laptop just moments before the actual presentation will waste time and cause nervousness. Conduct a situational analysis by thinking about and planning for your physical settings before the actual presentation day (see Table 15.2).

- *Expect the unexpected.* Even if you conduct a thorough situational analysis, you can still be met with a last-minute surprise. Having to adapt to such surprises can magnify speech anxiety because you'll suddenly feel stressed. For example, how would you handle losing the USB drive containing your PowerPoint slides? Try to plan ahead for things that might go wrong so you won't have to make last-minute, under-pressure decisions (e.g., putting your slides in more than one place). Being prepared for such "unexpected" events will help boost your confidence overall.

- *Know your introduction.* During the first few minutes of a speech, your nervousness peaks, since this is the time when your audience is the most attentive to you (Buss, 1980). Take time to rehearse exactly what your first few words are going to be as you greet your audience and begin your presentation.

- *Use visualization techniques.* If you've ever been involved in competitive sports, you know it can be helpful before a competition to quiet your mind and body and imagine yourself succeeding. Visualization is just as effective in reducing pre-speech jitters (Ayres & Ayres, 2003; Ayres & Hopf, 1987). To visualize a successful presentation, follow these steps:

(1) relax your body through deep, concentrated breathing; (2) develop a vivid image of yourself confidently moving through your day; (3) imagine yourself successfully presenting; and (4) visualize yourself getting praise from your audience and others after the speech (Ayres & Hopf, 1987). You can also watch videos of successful speakers and then substitute your own image for those speakers in a visualization session (Ayres, 2005).

- *Practice.* Students who have an intense fear of public speaking spend less time practicing and more time preparing their notes (Ayres, 1996). Prepared notes, however, won't improve your delivery; only practice can do that. But just standing before a mirror reciting your speech isn't practice. Later in this chapter we discuss more about practicing and getting feedback on your speech. Taking time to practice will relieve a lot of speech anxiety.

Finally, your enrollment in this class will provide experiences with public speaking. This will reduce its novelty and help you feel more confident when presenting.

TABLE 15.2

SITUATIONAL ANALYSIS

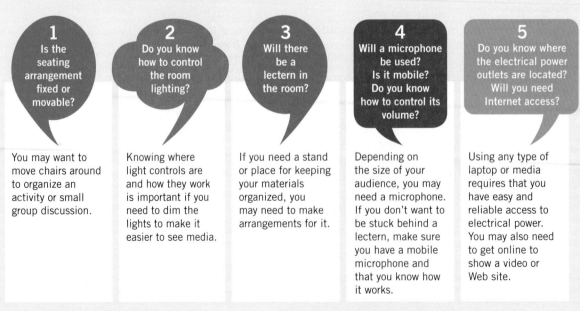

1	2	3	4	5
Is the seating arrangement fixed or movable?	Do you know how to control the room lighting?	Will there be a lectern in the room?	Will a microphone be used? Is it mobile? Do you know how to control its volume?	Do you know where the electrical power outlets are located? Will you need Internet access?
You may want to move chairs around to organize an activity or small group discussion.	Knowing where light controls are and how they work is important if you need to dim the lights to make it easier to see media.	If you need a stand or place for keeping your materials organized, you may need to make arrangements for it.	Depending on the size of your audience, you may need a microphone. If you don't want to be stuck behind a lectern, make sure you have a mobile microphone and that you know how it works.	Using any type of laptop or media requires that you have easy and reliable access to electrical power. You may also need to get online to show a video or Web site.

Choosing and Using Presentation Aids

> Incorporating visual support for your ideas will enhance your speech. These aids not only help you keep your audience's attention but also help your audience understand complex points. But not just any image or slide will do. Selecting the right visuals and rehearsing with them is key to improving your delivery.

Adding visuals or media (graphs, charts, physical objects, videos, and photographs) to your speech can make it more interesting for your listeners. For example, neuroscientist Jill Bolte Taylor captivates her audiences when she brings out an actual human brain, with an attached spinal cord, in her presentations about the brain's remarkable capability to recover from certain injuries. But this display is no gimmick. Instead, Dr. Taylor uses this physical object to illustrate part of her powerful story about recovering from a massive stroke at the age of 37. (You can view Dr. Taylor's talk at www.ted.com /talks.) In your own speeches, you'll also want to use **presentation aids**—tools used to display the visuals you've selected—to help explain or illustrate your points.

Types of Presentation Aids

In addition to common forms of presentation software, such as PowerPoint, Keynote, and Prezi, you can use whiteboards and flip charts, handouts, physical objects, posters, and video to present your speech's visual elements.

Whiteboards and Flip Charts. A whiteboard or flip chart allows you to write or show key ideas while you deliver your speech. For example, if you're describing a chemical formula, you can write it on a whiteboard or flip chart. Or if you solicit feedback from your audience—for example, asking them to call out the costs associated with renting an apartment as part of a real estate seminar—you can jot down their responses on a whiteboard or flip chart. The flexibility of creating your visual aid as you present allows you to address a specific audience's needs or create a record of their responses. However, these tools have a few drawbacks. First, your writing must be neat and visible. It will frustrate your audience if they can't read your writing because it's messy or too small. Second, while writing, you have to turn away from your listeners, breaking eye contact and reducing immediacy. To minimize the impact of this, stop talking while you're writing, then address your audience immediately after. This way, you can make eye contact while you are talking, and the audience can always hear you.

Handouts. Suppose you're listening to a college official talk about how to apply for a particular scholarship on your campus. Wouldn't it be helpful if you had a handout of the steps to follow or the actual form that you need to complete? Handouts can help your listeners follow steps in a process or remember important information. But handouts can also present a major distraction during a presentation. For example, if you distribute handouts of your PowerPoint slides just as you begin your speech, your listeners will probably start flipping through the handouts and may miss the opening of your presentation. If you decide to use handouts, give careful thought to how much information to put on them, and consider distributing them after your speech.

Physical Objects. Sometimes it is easier to show your audience a prop, or a physical object that represents an idea in your speech. An advantage of using physical objects is that they can have more visual impact than a two-dimensional diagram or photograph. For example, the real human brain used by Dr. Taylor has greater impact than would diagrams alone. Physical objects provide a novel experience for your audience, giving them something to focus on beyond your words. If you decide to use physical objects, be sure to consider your presentation space. Will everyone be able to see your prop? Since passing an object around the room can be distracting, consider other options for displaying a small object. Can you walk it through the audience? Is a document camera available for projecting an image of the object on a screen? Of course, in a classroom setting, be sure to check with your instructor before bringing anything in. Most schools prohibit certain items on campus (weapons, alcohol, animals), and there may be other considerations that limit what you can display (such as students with allergies to specific foods or plants).

Posters. Though increasingly rare in our digital age, posters are another form of presentation aid. (Students, however, are likely to still use posters for classroom speeches, especially if an instructor doesn't allow the use of PowerPoint.) The main advantage of using posters is that you're not dependent on electrical or technical support for your presentation—all you need is an easel or a wall for displaying them. Posters are usually best for displaying charts, graphs, or other visual information. If you choose to use posters in a speech, remember two things: First, make sure any information on the poster is large enough for the entire audience to see. Second, your poster should look as neat and professional as possible. Be sure to use legible handwriting, or if possible, use computer software to design the content, so it is colorful and clear. Depending on the context of your speech, you may even consider having a print shop produce your poster.

Video. Speakers commonly include video clips in their presentations—either from Web sites like YouTube, Hulu, and Vimeo or from content they create themselves. For example, some of our students shot video of their service-learning experiences at a Salvation Army family shelter and then used that as part of their group presentation. A major benefit of video is that—much like physical objects—it will grab your audience's attention. Yet effectively integrating video clips takes planning and practice. You must be sure that you can quickly access the required video clip. Few things create more of a distraction in a speech than when an audience has to watch a speaker try to locate a video on the Web, fumble with equipment, or attempt to find the exact starting point on a video. Also, if you are using a clip that is streaming online, have a backup plan in case you lose Internet access during your speech. Finally, make sure any clips you use are brief. A video can help you illustrate a point, but it shouldn't make the point for you.

Presentation Software. Although Power-Point has its critics, it is still widely used in academic, business, and even military presentations. That's because presentation software—such as PowerPoint, Keynote, or Prezi—makes it easy to import graphics and achieve a highly professional, polished look on your slides. It can also help the audience follow your presentation by providing key points or summary information. But you want to avoid letting presentation slides come between you and your listeners and thus undermining your immediacy or powerful speech style. The How to Communicate: Delivering a Speech feature on pages 392–393 gives insight on how to successfully present with slides.

Another common pitfall with presentation software is poor design. Do not bombard your audience with a steady stream of slides containing small text, hard-to-read fonts, too many bullet points, or overwhelming colors and images. Instead, use as few slides as possible; provide concise text; and include relevant visuals, such as charts, graphs, or photos. For more tips on using presentation software, go to **bedfordstmartins.com/choicesconnections** for the How-to Guide for Using PowerPoint tutorial.

After seeing Al Gore's slide show on global warming, film producer Laurie David was so inspired she immediately contacted Gore to start a project that would eventually become the Academy Award–winning documentary *An Inconvenient Truth*. Have you ever seen a presentation where the visuals enhanced the presentation and inspired you?

VALERY HACHE/AFP/Getty Images

Tips for Using Presentation Aids

No matter what presentation aids you decide to use, keep the following tips in mind while preparing, rehearsing, and delivering your speech:

- *Know how to use your aids.* While composing and rehearsing your speech, spend time with the presentation visuals you're going to be using— ideally, in the same setting where you'll be giving your presentation. You

DELIVERING A SPEECH

 One way to improve your presentation is by rehearsing in front of other people. Learn how to manage your speech delivery by going to LaunchPad at **bedfordstmartins.com /choicesconnections** and completing the **How to Communicate video scenario** for Chapter 15 to practice your skills.

CONSIDER THIS:
You and two classmates are working together on a presentation for your food science class. The group splits the work into three sections, and your portion will cover nutrition and fast food. Now, you are practicing your delivery together for the first time, and you want to make a good impression.

WHAT WOULD YOU DO?
The following advice illustrates how you can convey immediacy and a powerful speech style and best use presentation aids in your rehearsal. As you watch the video, consider how various verbal, nonverbal, and listening concepts influence your delivery style. Then, test your knowledge of key skills, and create your own responses to the **What if? video prompts**.

① **CONVEY IMMEDIACY.** Use an oral style of language and create a conversational tone with your voice. Make eye contact with your audience and use expressive gestures and facial expressions. See pages 379–381.

(2) CONVEY POWER.

Avoid powerless language, hedging, and disclaimers. Practice your pronunciation and minimize your use of vocalized pauses and fillers. Dress appropriately for the occasion. See pages 381–385.

"In a 2010 article posted on WebMD.com, medical writer Daniel DeNoon claims that 9 out of 10 Americans consume too much salt daily."

(3) KNOW HOW TO USE YOUR PRESENTATION AIDS.

When presenting with slides, use a clicker and laser pointer so you aren't stuck behind a computer. Move around purposefully, staying focused on your audience, not your presentation media.

"Switch the slides right before the DeNoon quote so the audience can see the graphic. Gesture to, but don't stare at, the slide."

 WHAT IF? But what if things don't work out as shown? Test your ability to adapt your communication by watching the What if? videos and making a plan for each situation.

1. If you speak very quickly and use vocal fillers ("Okay. There's a medical writer, Daniel DeNoon, who says that . . . um . . . 9 out of 10 Americans . . ."), what steps would you take to improve your next practice session?

2. How could you improve your delivery if your slides distract you from the audience?

can damage your credibility by fumbling with your slides or not knowing how to properly handle any physical objects you've brought.

- *Prepare your audience for what they're about to see or hear.* Take time to introduce any slide or handout you present—especially if it contains complex information. For example, you should explain what a graph shows: "As this next graph will demonstrate, the number of students in federal subsidized school lunch programs has doubled over the past five years."

- *Thoroughly explain the information on a presentation aid.* Whether you're introducing a slide, a poster, or a video, don't rush your listeners through it. Take time to discuss the idea conveyed by the presentation aid.

- *Talk to your audience, not the medium.* Remember that you need to convey immediacy with your audience for them to pay attention. Don't talk with your back to your audience, for example, while writing on a whiteboard or changing PowerPoint slides. Such behaviors will make your audience feel disconnected.

- *Remove the presentation aid once you're done with it.* After you've made your point with a presentation aid, cover it up, remove it from the screen, or erase the image. You want your audience attending to *you* as you move to your next point, not mulling over a previous graph or image left up on the screen.

- *Have a backup plan.* You can never account for everything that might happen during your speech, but you should prepare alternatives in case your presentation aids fail. For example, what if a lightbulb in the projector burns out? Or your computer crashes? Or your marker runs out of ink? You always need to have a backup plan.

Evaluating Speeches and Managing Feedback

Rehearsing your speech is not a solitary activity. Getting feedback from others about your speech and delivery provides vital information you can use to complete the last part of your speech preparation—Step 5: Revise. You'll use feedback to make any necessary changes to the presentation, as well as to improve your public-speaking skills over the long term.

On an episode of *The Office*, Dwight Schrute is named Dunder Mifflin Paper Salesman of the Year, and learns he must give an acceptance speech at the company sales convention. Terrified of public speaking, Dwight turns to his bumbling boss, Michael Scott, for suggestions about how to approach the speech. Dwight's initial plan is to simply thank as many people as possible during his speech. But Michael advises, "These are salesmen, Dwight; salesmen expect to be entertained," and proceeds to coach Dwight on the finer points of public speaking. Michael orders other Dunder Mifflin employees into the conference room so Dwight can practice in front of an audience and get their feedback. But Dwight claims the setup isn't helpful because he's not nervous in front of his coworkers, since they are his subordinates—not actual salespeople. Jim Halpert, a coworker and salesman, counters that argument by pointing out that Dwight has no authority over anyone in the room. Michael agrees. Completely frustrated with the "practice session," Dwight throws his note cards on the floor and stomps out of the room. In a last-ditch effort to provide advice, Michael calls out, "Confidence, Dwight."

Although Dwight's practice session failed, at least Michael tried to get him feedback from other people. Most of you will not have a conference room full of coworkers to use for practice, but you can enlist family, friends, or fellow classmates to help you rehearse and to provide feedback on your speech. Students who practice in front of a small audience are more likely to receive higher evaluations on their actual speech performance than those who practice alone or in front of a mirror (Smith & Frymier, 2006). By practicing in front of others, you can get feedback about your speech structure, content, and delivery. Using this information to make necessary changes to your speech outline and delivery is an important part of Step Five: Revise. But not all feedback is helpful. Feedback that is overly general ("That was great!") or broadly critical ("Confidence, Dwight") lacks details about what's working and what communication behaviors need to change. Knowing how to give others useful feedback and how to base your own revisions on the feedback others give you completes your speech preparation.

Giving Effective Feedback

Whether in your communication class, at work, or as a favor to a friend, you may be asked to give oral or written feedback on other people's presentations. Actively listening to and evaluating other speakers will help you improve your own public-speaking skills. But what should you listen for? Consider the checklist of elements regarding effective speech structure, content, and delivery in Figure 15.1. These elements will help you give useful feedback while evaluating someone else's speech, as well as receive and use feedback from others on your own speeches.

Feedback is most useful when it's delivered soon after a rehearsal or the actual presentation and is specific—whether it's praise or criticism. Examples of useful feedback would include comments like "You maintained good eye contact with everyone in the audience" or "I would have been able to follow your ideas more easily if you had half the number of slides." When providing feedback to others, keep the following guidelines in mind:

1. *Make sure the recipient is ready to hear what you have to say.* Timing is everything when giving feedback. If a speaker has just finished a presentation (whether a rehearsal or real), the person may need a few minutes to

FIGURE 15.1

GENERAL SPEECH CRITIQUE*

For each element, rate the speaker's use of the element on a scale of **1–3** as defined below:

3 = Element was evident and very effective
2 = Element was there but could be revised for greater impact
1 = Element was not evident or ineffective

INTRODUCTION

When starting the speech, did the speaker   **Comments:**

____ **1.** gain attention through an interesting question, story, or some other creative means?
____ **2.** provide appropriate background to the topic—including relevant definitions?
____ **3.** take steps to establish credibility?
____ **4.** clearly state the speech thesis and briefly preview the main points?

BODY

In developing the body of the speech, did the speaker   **Comments:**

____ **1.** identify and organize main points in a manner that was easy to follow?
____ **2.** use well-chosen examples, testimony, statistics, and other forms of support for main points?
____ **3.** integrate outside references, orally citing sources when appropriate?
____ **4.** choose appropriate and clear language; avoid unnecessary jargon?

CONCLUSION

When moving to the finish of the speech, did the speaker   **Comments:**

____ **1.** clearly indicate the speech was concluding by providing summary statements?
____ **2.** provide a final appeal or make a general point about the subject?
____ **3.** end the speech with a memorable statement?

PRESENTATION AIDS

When using presentation aids, did the speaker   **Comments:**

____ **1.** incorporate relevant and well-designed visual support (e.g., graphs and charts)?
____ **2.** effectively handle presentation aids, avoiding any distraction?

DELIVERY

During the speech, did the speaker   **Comments:**

____ **1.** use voice in a way appropriate to the topic by varying inflection, tone, and volume?
____ **2.** speak words clearly with proper pronunciation and grammar?
____ **3.** physically move and gesture with purpose, avoiding distracting mannerisms?
____ **4.** establish and maintain eye contact with all areas of the room while making appropriate use of notes?
____ **5.** appear confident, poised, and in control of the situation; didn't rush?

OVERALL EVALUATION

Considering the speech as a whole, did the speaker   **Comments:**

____ **1.** choose an appropriate topic and specific purpose statement?
____ **2.** adapt the topic to the audience throughout the speech?
____ **3.** meet the assignment requirements, including specified time limits?

*Note: This is just one example of a critique. Your instructor may use something different. This sample is meant to provide you with a sense of things to think about when evaluating your own or someone else's speech.

collect his or her thoughts or take care of physical needs (e.g., getting a glass of water) before listening to what you have to say.

2. *Start with positive comments.* Find something good to say in order to create some rapport with the speaker. This lays the groundwork for any constructive criticism that may follow.

3. *Use descriptive language.* Abstract language creates misunderstanding ("You did a great job!"). It is usually best to point out specific things you saw and heard ("The story in your opener had vivid images that helped me see the people you were describing"). Although it's not easy to do, you will often need to point out problems with a speech to help the speaker improve. You'll especially want to use descriptive language when offering any *constructive criticism* ("You were pacing back and forth and it was distracting" or "I didn't hear a preview of your main points").

4. *Don't overload the person with information.* People have a limit on how much they can process at a given time. Pick out the two or three things that are most important to say, and leave it at that.

5. *End on a positive note.* It's important to leave on good terms with the person. Find something to say that gives hope or encouragement.

LearningCurve can help you review! Go to **bedfordstmartins.com /choicesconnections**.

Using Feedback to Improve Your Speech Performance

Feedback is helpful during your speech rehearsal and after you have delivered your actual presentation. When practicing your speech, feedback will guide your revisions to the speech outline or your delivery. Making such changes is key to ensuring that your presentation is well received by the audience. Seeking out feedback after the actual presentation—perhaps from classmates or from your instructor—will support your growth and development as a public speaker for your next classroom speech and throughout your life.

Of course, feedback is wasted if you don't act on it. But not all feedback will be useful. Seriously consider what advice you should take and what can be ignored. For example, does your introduction really need more punch? Is there a point where a graph would be more informative than a long list of statistics? Should you speak more slowly when telling a compelling story? Do you need to get out from behind the lectern more often during your talk? Make the changes you think need to be made prior to delivering your speech when it really counts.

After you've given the actual speech, ask for feedback from audience members or a trusted friend or colleague who sat in on the presentation. Their input can help you plan and practice for your next speech. If you video-record the speech, use the General Speech Critique form in Figure 15.1 to evaluate the recording and gather additional insights into how you can deliver a better speech the next time.

CHAPTER (15) REVIEW

CHAPTER RECAP

- There are three primary modes for delivering a speech: **impromptu, manuscript,** and **extemporaneous speaking.**
- Conveying **immediacy** and projecting a **powerful speech style** are ways to connect with your audience. Understanding these elements will help you with everything from adopting an **oral style** of language and using appropriate nonverbal behaviors to choosing effective language, vocal delivery, and attire.
- **Speech anxiety** is a common experience, but you can manage it through a variety of ways, such as conducting a situational analysis and rehearsing your delivery style.
- It is important to know how to use your **presentation aids,** to have a backup plan in case any technology fails, and to explain to the audience what they are about to see or hear.
- Learning how to give and receive competent feedback on public speeches will help you better prepare, rehearse, revise, and deliver your own presentations.

LAUNCHPAD

LaunchPad for *Choices & Connections* offers unique video scenarios and encourages self-assessment through adaptive quizzing. Go to **bedfordstmartins.com /choicesconnections** to get access.

 LearningCurve adaptive quizzes

 How to Communicate video scenarios

 Video clips that illustrate key concepts

KEY TERMS

Impromptu speaking, p. 375
Manuscript speaking, p. 376
Extemporaneous speaking, p. 377
Immediacy, p. 378
Powerful speech style, p. 379
Oral style, p. 379
Written style, p. 379
Vocal pitch, p. 379
Vocal tone, p. 380
Monotone, p. 380
Vocal rate, p. 380

Adaptive gestures, p. 381
Powerless language, p. 382
Hedging, p. 382
Disclaimers, p. 382
Intensifiers, p. 382
Vocal volume, p. 382
Articulation, p. 382
Pronunciation, p. 382
Vocalized pauses and fillers, p. 382
Speech anxiety, p. 386
Presentation aids, p. 389

1 Whether you memorize a speech or read from a written version, manuscript speaking has several drawbacks, including _____.

a. lack of preparation time

b. prioritizing a conversational tone

c. difficulty adapting to your audience

d. a depleted vocal rate

2 Why do audience members prefer speakers to use an oral style of language?

a. It sounds more like a written paper.

b. It emphasizes nonverbal behaviors.

c. It is more casual and conversational.

d. It provides more detailed information.

3 Using a lot of over-the-top descriptions, such as "the absolutely best ever," is an example of _____.

a. disclaimers   **c.** hedging

b. intensifiers   **d.** vocalized pauses and fillers

4 When you imagine yourself competently presenting and receiving praise, which strategy are you using to manage speech anxiety?

a. Visualization techniques

b. Creating a situational analysis

c. Choosing topics that matter to you

d. Knowing your introduction

5 Which of the following is *not* suggested as a guideline for providing speech feedback to others?

a. Don't overload the person with information.

b. Start with positive comments.

c. Provide as much detailed information as possible.

d. Make sure the participant is ready.

ACTIVITIES

1 **Slide Show**

Choose a TED talk (available at www.ted.com/talks) on a subject that interests you. As you watch, note specific examples of presentation aids used by the speaker. Evaluate the speaker's use of presentation aids and how effectively the aids support the message. Share your findings with the class.

2 **Practice, Feedback, Repeat**

Arrange to rehearse your speech with a group of classmates (either in person or via video-recorded rehearsals). Using the General Speech Critique form in Figure 15.1, give feedback on the group's speeches. Then use the group's feedback to revise your own speech, and discuss your plan with the group.

16

Informative Speeches

Sitting in a village café drinking *malwa*, a local homemade brew, a group of Ugandan men are attending a lecture.[1] A health worker is explaining that women are more susceptible to malaria during pregnancy because their immune system is weakened. If a pregnant woman is infected with malaria—spread through the bite of mosquitoes—she and her child could become seriously ill and even die (World Health Organization, 2003). Though the village health clinics make this information available, most of the men don't know these facts. Why? As Christine Munduru of the Open Society Initiative for East Africa (OSIEA) explains, "When special meetings are held to educate

people on health issues, the men don't go because they think health is something only the women should deal with" (Cumberland, 2010).

This practice prompted local scientists and health care workers to think of alternative ways to get important information distributed in the village. They decided to go where the village men *do* gather: the local bar. They began holding a series of casual discussions—known as Café Scientifique—to educate the men about health issues, as well as topics like agriculture and domestic violence. Conducted in the local language, the talks were a hit from the start. "It was amazing," says Munduru. "Nobody wanted to miss out. . . . We let the community take charge and choose the topics, although we guide them to make sure that they are balanced. We empower them with information then leave them to make their own decisions" (Cumberland, 2010).

While the Café Scientifique sessions are prospering in Uganda, the concept actually began in a wine bar in Leeds, England. Worried that people didn't know enough about modern scientific advancements, British television producer Duncan Dallas planned an informal session about Darwinism—a theory about how species evolve. Almost 50 people showed up and inspired Dallas to transform Café Scientifique into a

[1]Drawn from Cumberland (2010).

worldwide movement. Also known as "science cafes," the idea is to provide "a place where, for the price of a cup of coffee or a glass of wine, anyone can come to explore the latest ideas in science and technology" (www.cafescientifique.org).

No matter where Café Scientifique events take place, the format is fairly consistent. Most talks are conducted in coffee shops, bars, or restaurants (like the one shown here in Germany). A local scientist or technologist speaks for about 20 minutes about a topic of interest to listeners. Speakers focus their talks on simple main points, using everyday language that audience members can understand—even those with no scientific background (Dallas, 2006). After a talk, the speaker takes questions from the audience for about an hour. According to John Cohen, immunology professor at the University of Colorado and founder of a Café Scientifique in Denver, people can ask questions or just listen to scientists in a relaxed setting and learn something new (Sink, 2006). But the presenters also benefit— they learn how to competently communicate their research and ideas to the general public.

The Café Scientifique presentations can also have unexpected outcomes. After listening to the malaria presentation, many Ugandan men—who ordinarily sleep alone under mosquito nets—gave the nets to their pregnant wives to protect them against mosquito bites.

✓ **LearningCurve** can help you review! Go to **bedfordstmartins.com /choicesconnections**.

Informative speaking happens in a lot of different everyday settings. For example, in a college class, while at work, or elsewhere in your community, you could be asked to give a talk that's aimed at informing and enlightening an audience. Maybe you'll offer insights about a particular topic (why pregnant women are more susceptible to malaria), show how to do something (how to stain a piece of furniture), talk about an event or a person of interest (the story of Steve Jobs and Apple), or explain the differences and similarities between several ideas or things (the distinguishing features of film versus digital photography). When delivering an informative speech, you'll still follow the five steps for speech preparation that we discuss in Chapters 13, 14, and 15: think, investigate, compose, rehearse, and revise (see Table 16.1). In addition, you'll consider the unique aspects of informative speeches. In this chapter, you'll learn:

- The functions and specific purposes of informative speeches
- Key differences between informative and persuasive speaking
- Four major types of informative speeches
- Guidelines for preparing informative speeches

What Is Informative Speaking?

Whenever you want to help your audience better understand a topic, you are speaking to inform. As a student, many of the course lectures you attend (in person or online) fall into this category. But informative presentations also happen in other places, such as meetings at work, "how-to" demonstrations on YouTube, and even during storytelling events or poetry readings.

Informative speeches educate your audience about a topic, demonstrate how something works, tell stories about events or people, or explain similarities and differences between things or ideas. The health care worker at the Ugandan village Café Scientifique gave an informative presentation that educated the audience about the risks of malaria during pregnancy.

Regardless of where you're delivering an informative speech (a local bar, a classroom, or a corporate boardroom) and how you're delivering it (face-to-face, via a podcast, or on YouTube), your first step is to *think* about how you'll adapt the talk to your audience. This includes determining your speech's function and specific purpose, and knowing how informative speeches differ from persuasive ones.

Functions of Informative Speeches

Informative presentations serve one of two functions. One function is to raise awareness about a topic for listeners (Rowan, 2003). For instance, suppose you're the treasurer of a youth soccer league. At monthly meetings, you might give a routine financial report on the costs of running the league. Since board

TABLE 16.1

FIVE STEPS IN SPEECH PREPARATION

THINK	INVESTIGATE	COMPOSE	REHEARSE	REVISE
Choose your topic, adapt to your audience	Plan your strategy, conduct your research, evaluate your sources	Develop your speech structure and support material, prepare your visual aids	Create speaking notes, practice aloud, work on delivery	Process feedback from others and self-reflection, write a final outline and speaking notes

edel/Shutterstock

members are already familiar with these costs, your presentation simply functions to keep them up to date.

A second and different function for informative speeches is to provide an in-depth explanation of a topic (Rowan, 2003). Imagine that the soccer league received a large monetary donation. In this case, you'd probably prepare a presentation that gives board members detailed information about the gift—such as options for spending the money or investing it.

As you prepare an informative talk, ask yourself, Do I just want to raise my listeners' awareness about a topic? Or should I provide a deeper explanation so that they can better understand the issue? Your answer will depend on what you discover about your listeners' information needs during your audience analysis. As Chapter 13 explains, an *audience analysis* is the process of identifying important characteristics about your listeners, and using this information to prepare your speech. Understanding your listeners' prior knowledge about the topic and other characteristics about them—such as their demographics and their attitudes, beliefs, and values—will help you determine your specific purpose.

Specific Purposes for Informative Speeches

After determining the information needs of your audience, it's time to write out your *specific purpose statement*, which is one complete sentence that summarizes your goal for the speech. As with any presentation, your specific purpose statement for an informative talk helps you narrow your topic. It also keeps you focused as you research and compose your speech. It will eventually form the basis for your *speech thesis*—the sentence that identifies the central idea of your presentation for your audience.

As you write your specific purpose statement, keep in mind what your audience already knows about your speech topic. By targeting your specific purpose to the audience's level of knowledge, you avoid **information overload,** which happens when the amount and nature of material exceeds listeners' ability to process it. For example, the health care workers in Uganda keep presentations about malaria at a basic level and avoid overwhelming the villagers with unnecessary medical jargon. Similarly, when preparing your own speeches, use audience analysis to adapt your specific purpose statement to meet the information needs of your listeners.

You'll also want to focus the specific purpose statement on one central idea. Suppose you're assigned a 10-minute presentation on the Bauhaus movement for your art history class. Trying to cover the movement's impact on typography, architecture, and other art forms would be difficult to do in the assigned time. Instead, it would be better to narrow the topic to cover the movement's impact on just one area.

Whenever you're preparing an informative speech, start by writing a specific purpose statement appropriate to the audience and situation. Table 16.2 shows examples of specific purpose statements for a wide range of informative speech situations. A specific purpose statement brings clarity to your speech preparation. But sticking to the general purpose of informing rather than persuading an audience can be tricky if you don't understand how they differ.

Informative versus Persuasive Speaking

When you're developing your specific purpose statement, it can be easy to confuse informative speaking with persuasive speaking. Although both types of speeches are developed using the five steps in speech preparation, there are important differences between the two.

First, informative and persuasive speaking have different goals. When informing an audience, you want your listeners to understand the topic better. When you're giving a persuasive speech, the goal is to reinforce or change your listeners' attitudes—maybe even motivate them to take a particular action. Getting listeners to take an action or change their attitudes is not a goal of an informative speech.

Second, when preparing an informative talk, you must keep a neutral point of view as you *investigate* and *compose* your presentation. Suppose you are preparing an informative speech about animal testing in biomedical research. In this case, you would pull together information about the pros and cons of such research without taking a stand on the topic. But if you wanted to give a persuasive speech about animal testing in biomedical research, you would not only analyze the pros and cons but also take a position on the issue.

Maintaining a neutral stance when you're speaking informatively can be challenging—especially if your presentation is going to cover a controversial

TABLE 16.2

SPECIFIC PURPOSE STATEMENTS FOR INFORMATIVE SPEECHES

ART HISTORY COURSE

General Assignment: Develop an oral presentation on an important movement in art history

Specific Purpose Statement: To inform my class on the impact of Bauhaus on typography.

SCOUT MEETING

General Assignment: Describe fund-raising responsibilities

Specific Purpose Statement: To explain who will do what to prepare for and conduct Saturday's Jamboree event.

EMPLOYEE MEETING

General Assignment: Update employees on changes to their health benefits

Specific Purpose Statement: To explain two major changes in the company's health benefits program.

RESEARCH CONFERENCE

General Assignment: Share your latest research findings with your colleagues

Specific Purpose Statement: To tell my listeners about the design and findings of my vaccine study.

INTRODUCTORY STATISTICS COURSE

General Assignment: Show class members that you understand the concept of standard deviation

Specific Purpose Statement: To demonstrate how to calculate a standard deviation.

CITY COUNCIL MEETING

General Assignment: Represent neighbors' views about traffic

Specific Purpose Statement: To identify five major concerns neighbors are expressing about traffic in our city.

issue that you feel strongly about. One way to remain neutral is to avoid making *motivational appeals* to your listeners' emotions, such as "If you care about cute, helpless, and innocent puppies, . . ." This does not mean you shouldn't try to connect with your audience by using interesting supporting materials. Instead, just keep reminding yourself that your purpose is to inform, not persuade. (Chapter 17 explains more about motivational appeals for persuasive speeches.)

Even though informative and persuasive presentations have distinct differences, they also have some similarities. For instance, when you're speaking to inform, you thoroughly *investigate* your topic and present the information in a balanced, neutral way. However, you still need to convince your audience that you're providing objective and credible information. Likewise, in persuasive speeches, you need to inform your listeners about the topic before you can try to persuade them to change their attitudes or practices. Given these similarities, the important thing to remember is to stay true to your speech's general purpose: informing or persuading.

Types of Informative Speeches

> When determining your topic and specific purpose for an informative speech, you should also consider an additional aspect: your approach. Not all informative presentations work in the same way. Sometimes you may want to explain something or demonstrate how it works. Other times, you'll share a story about an event or draw comparisons between things.

Faced with an informative speech assignment in her communication course, Cheryl decided to talk about her Ta Moko. Often mistaken for a tattoo, a Ta Moko (or moko) is a permanent facial or body marking common to the Maori tribal people of New Zealand. Having traveled to New Zealand three summers in a row, Cheryl developed an appreciation and affection for Maori culture. On her third trip, she had an artist create a Ta Moko on her right forearm. In *composing* her speech, Cheryl determined that her specific

Whether you're speaking about a cultural practice, like the body markings of the Maori tribe, or another informative topic, identifying what type of speech you'll give can help guide your work in the investigate and compose steps. As you consider your topic, think about if you will focus on one type or if, like Cheryl, you will combine types.

Tim Graham/Getty Images

purpose was to inform her class about how a Ta Moko differs from a tattoo. To do this, she first defined the meaning of Ta Moko and explained its spiritual significance in Maori culture. She then compared and contrasted a Ta Moko and a tattoo. Finally, she explained the design and personal meaning of her own moko. During her six-minute presentation, Cheryl defined an important term (Ta Moko), described an object (the moko), compared it to a similar and well-known object (tattoo), and told a personal story.

Whether it's a classroom assignment or a work situation, there are various ways of making an informative presentation. Knowing what these are can help you make sound choices when you start *investigating* and *composing* an informative speech. In this chapter, we focus on the four most common types: expository, process or demonstration, narrative, and comparison/contrast. You might use one of these types as a primary way of presenting the information in your speech. For example, perhaps your instructor has asked you to develop an informative speech focused on demonstrating a particular process. However, in most informative speaking situations outside of the classroom, you may find yourself combining several or all four types—as Cheryl did—to achieve your specific purpose.

Expository Presentations

When you *define* a term, *explain* a concept, or *describe* an object or a place to your audience, you are making an **expository presentation**. For instance, a museum docent enriches visitors' understanding of the art by defining relevant terms and describing painting techniques. In a meeting about salary increases, a manager defines "interest-based negotiation" and explains how it relates to pay raises. (See Table 16.3 for examples of expository speech topics.)

When you're *composing* an expository presentation, you will apply many of the practices associated with this step of speech preparation, including choosing an appropriate organization pattern for your main points, and developing an introduction and a conclusion. A topical pattern is the most common way expository presentations are organized. You may recall from Chapter 14 that this organizational pattern breaks down main points into specific categories or subtopics. For example, if you're giving a speech about autism, you might organize the presentation like this:

Speech thesis: Scientific research is changing misconceptions about autism.

Main points:

I. Autism is a general term that reflects a range of pervasive developmental disorders, known as autism spectrum disorders (ASDs).

II. ASDs are characterized by abnormal social and communication behaviors.

III. Current research sheds some light on possible causes of ASDs.

You'll also want to use clear, straightforward language in expository presentations. For instance, if you're going to be talking about a complex, technical subject that's unfamiliar to your audience, don't use a lot of specialized vocabulary or acronyms. Also, remember that word meanings can vary widely. Try to stick to commonly accepted definitions of words (*denotative meanings*) rather than using terms that have personal meaning or relevance (*connotative meanings*). Use your audience analysis to determine which words and types of examples would best help your listeners understand your points.

Process or Demonstration Presentations

In a **process or demonstration presentation,** you either explain how something works or show your audience how to do something. For example, an engineer explains how fuel cells work. Or a training manager shows employees how to use the company's new web conferencing system. (Table 16.3 includes additional examples of process or demonstration presentations.)

Since processes and activities take place over time, a chronological pattern is often the best organizational structure for this type of presentation. The audience is better able to follow the sequence if you make frequent use of *signposts*, such as *First, Next,* and *The last step.* Here's an example of a process presentation organization:

Speech thesis: Creating a compost pile involves easy steps, using common household waste materials.

Main points:

I. First, select and prepare the right location in your yard for the compost pile.

II. Second, determine the types of household waste materials appropriate for composting.

III. Third, begin creating the compost pile by layering the waste materials to encourage proper decomposition.

IV. Fourth, be prepared to quickly address common problems in compost piles.

V. Finally, identify when the compost is ready for use.

In process or demonstration presentations, many speakers make the mistake of moving too quickly through each step. To avoid this, slow down the pace of your delivery by using *internal summaries* ("So as you can see, most materials that wind up in your kitchen garbage disposal or recycle bin can be used in the compost pile"). This type of repetition also supports your listeners' ability to *remember* the information later (see Chapter 7 for a discussion of the listening process). Visual aids, such as diagrams and props, can further help your audience understand the steps you're describing. For example, a diagram showing how to choose a good location for your compost pile would enhance your verbal explanation. Finally, as with expository presentations, take the time to define unfamiliar terms and jargon so you don't confuse your audience.

Whenever you give a speech, listeners may have follow-up questions for you—asking for more information or wanting to further discuss or dispute a point. This type of question-and-answer session is common after a demonstration speech, when audience members may want clarification. For ideas on how to handle such situations, see the How to Communicate: Responding to Audience Questions feature on pages 412–413.

Narrative Presentations

When you're describing an event or telling a story about a person, you're giving a **narrative presentation**. For example, you might report on your campus's annual Oktoberfest celebration to fulfill an oral presentation requirement for your history class. Or you might share a story about specific people you know, such as recounting childhood pranks you and your cousins played at family reunions. (See Table 16.3 for additional examples of narrative presentations.)

The best narrative presentations tell a good story that captures and holds listeners' interest and attention. A chronological pattern of organization usually works best for this kind of speech because it enables you to lay out a sequence of events. For example, suppose you're giving a speech about the Coachella Valley Music and Arts Festival. To provide an account of this event, you'd want to use vivid language while describing the people, the

Perhaps even more compelling than all of the Harry Potter novels is the story of J. K. Rowling's rise from poverty to international success. Rowling's narrative speeches inform her audiences about her personal struggles, and can inspire them to believe in their abilities regardless of how dismal their circumstances may seem.

John Phillips/UK Press via Getty Images

intensity of the musical performances, and the depth of emotion you experienced at the festival. Here's how your outline of main points might look:

> *Speech thesis:* Convincing my friends to stay at the Coachella festival paid off with an amazing technological surprise.
>
> *Main points:*
>
> I. Coachella is one of the largest three-day music festivals in the world.
>
> II. After three exhausting days, my friends were ready to leave Sunday afternoon, but I convinced them to stay for the Dr. Dre and Snoop Dogg evening performance.
>
> III. Imagine our surprise to see the late Tupac Shakur join Dr. Dre and Snoop Dogg onstage.
>
> IV. Thanks to the miracle of hologram technology, we experienced an amazing set of classical rap music.

You'll also want to use language that draws your listeners into the sights, sounds, and emotions of the story ("exhausting," "imagine," "surprise," "miracle"). The right nonverbal communication can further help you capture and hold your listeners' attention. Just observe the nonverbal skills of good storytellers, like those found on the Moth (http://themoth.org/stories). Their animated gestures and facial expressions, along with appropriate changes in vocal tone, pitch, and volume, engage listeners with the stories they're telling. Practice these same nonverbal skills when *rehearsing* your speech, and seek feedback to improve your delivery.

Comparison/Contrast Presentations

In some speaking situations, you'll be called on to present the similarities and differences between ideas, things, events, or people. In these cases, you'll be making a **comparison/contrast presentation**. For example, if you volunteer at the local science museum, you might explain the differences and similarities between the bacterial and viral infections to visiting school groups. Or as the president of your parent-teacher organization, you might spell out the implications of purchasing new playground equipment or a new photocopier with the revenue generated from a recent fund-raiser.

When preparing this type of speech, start by identifying what you'll be comparing or contrasting. Stick to just a few things, so your audience can keep track of the comparisons. For example, at the science museum, you wouldn't want to compare and contrast 10 different types of bacteria and viruses. Instead, you would want to compare and contrast general differences and similarities.

A topical pattern of organization works well for most comparison/contrast speeches, because it helps you focus on how the features or characteristics of the things you're comparing are similar and different. Consider the following outline for the speech examining the similarities and differences between bacterial and viral infections:

> *Speech thesis:* Bacterial and viral infections have some similarities, but they also have important differences.

Main points:

I. Bacteria and viruses are spread in similar ways.

II. Both result in diseases of varying severity.

III. Bacteria are structurally different from viruses.

IV. Some bacteria are actually helpful to the body.

V. Treatments for bacterial and viral infections are different.

Other ways to compare and contrast are by talking about costs and benefits, advantages and disadvantages, or pros and cons related to different items. Table 16.3 shows more examples of comparison/contrast presentations.

TABLE 16.3

EXAMPLES OF INFORMATIVE PRESENTATIONS

- Defining feng shui
- Explaining open source computing
- Explaining Stockholm syndrome
- Describing mezuzah

EXPOSITORY PRESENTATIONS

- Using an automatic external defibrillator
- Demonstrating basic personal defense
- Playing Sabakiball
- Using FinalCut Pro for video editing

PROCESS OR DEMONSTRATION PRESENTATIONS

- Volunteering for hospice
- Life and work of J. K. Rowling
- Raising a service animal
- A day at NASCAR

NARRATIVE PRESENTATIONS

- Differences of internships and externships
- Pros and cons of various e-readers
- Similarities in families on *Downton Abbey* and *Breaking Bad*

COMPARISON/CONTRAST PRESENTATIONS

Introwiz1/Shutterstock

RESPONDING TO AUDIENCE QUESTIONS

 One way to improve your public-speaking skills is by adapting to different audience behaviors. Learn how to handle questions from listeners by going to LaunchPad at **bedfordstmartins.com/choicesconnections** and completing the **How to Communicate video scenario** for Chapter 16 to practice your skills.

CONSIDER THIS: You are giving an informative speech to your communication class. Drawing on social science research, you explain why some online videos posted by ordinary people go viral and are seen by millions. After concluding your speech, you have time to answer questions from the audience.

WHAT WOULD YOU DO? A question-and-answer period is a chance to connect interpersonally with your audience while engaging them further in the speech topic. As part of your speech preparation, anticipate possible questions that may come up. While watching the video, consider how communication skills like active listening, perception, and immediacy can help you competently manage audience interaction. Then, test your knowledge of key skills, and create your own responses to the **What if? video prompts**.

"One question I had while researching this topic was whether you need to buy a high-quality video camera to produce good video."

1 HAVE A FEW QUESTIONS PREPARED. To deal with any awkward silence when you open for questions, have a few questions ready to ask (and answer) yourself to get things started. Taking this first step can encourage a quiet audience to open up.

2 ACTIVELY LISTEN TO QUESTIONS. Repeat questions to ensure you understand them, and for the benefit of others in the audience who may not have heard them. Avoid evaluations ("That's a really good question") as they may imply that some questions are better than others.

3 INVOLVE YOUR AUDIENCE. Make eye contact with the person asking the question, but address your response to the entire audience. You don't want to talk one-on-one with the questioner, causing others to feel excluded.

④ BE BRIEF AND COMPLETE WITH YOUR ANSWERS. Look for opportunities to refer back to key points in your speech. If you don't know the answer to a question, say so.

"As I pointed out earlier, television shows—like *Late Night with Jimmy Fallon* and *The Ellen DeGeneres Show*—have a place for posting fan videos on their Web sites. That's how some viral videos first get noticed."

"That's all the time we have. Let me close by saying what a pleasure it has been . . ."

⑤ STICK TO A TIME LIMIT. Give the audience your contact information in case they want to follow up with additional questions. Have a prepared closing remark that ends the question-and-answer period on a positive note.

 WHAT IF? But what if things don't work out as shown? After all, audiences are unpredictable. Test your ability to adapt your communication by watching the What if? videos and planning a response for each situation.

1. When a listener takes over and keeps asking questions, how would you handle it? "I also want to ask if you need some kind of legal permission to post a video. Also, what if I get a store's name in the scene? Or what about . . . ?"

2. When an audience member questions the sources cited during your speech ("You said there's 'research' that predicts which videos are likely to go viral, right? . . . I don't believe it"), how can you respond competently?

Guidelines for Informative Speaking

> The type of informative speech you prepare is determined by the situation, your specific purpose, and the information needs of the audience. Although the type may vary, there are common guidelines competent speakers apply when preparing informative presentations.

While attending a leadership seminar taught by the renowned management consultant Stephen R. Covey (author of *The Seven Habits of Highly Effective People*), Joe and 200 other audience members participated in a brief activity. They were asked to close their eyes and use a hand to point north. Covey then told them to open their eyes and look around. The audience erupted in laughter as everyone saw 200 hands pointing in different directions. Covey then pulled out a compass to verify which direction was truly north. This activity expressed his speech thesis: effective leaders use sound principles ("true north") to guide their followers; otherwise, chaos breaks out. But the demonstration also provides a great example of how presenters can engage an audience during an informative speech and make their messages memorable. Years later, Joe still remembers learning the principle of "true north" at Covey's seminar.

After Hurricane Katrina destroyed hundreds of homes in New Orleans, Brad Pitt and William McDonough founded Make It Right in order to build energy-efficient, affordable homes for displaced families. To spread the word on the need for safe and habitable living spaces, both men speak passionately about their work and the good it can do. Now, Make It Right has built and converted homes not only in New Orleans but also in New Jersey and Kansas. How can you translate your passions into an exciting speech?

Matthew HINTON/AFP/Getty Images

As you prepare your own informative presentations, following the guidelines discussed in this section will keep your listeners engaged and help them remember your message for years to come.

Choose a Topic You Care About

When you have the freedom to choose your own topic for an informative speech, pick something that reflects your interests and experiences. Consider talking about a favorite hobby (how to make beaded jewelry), presenting a narrative about a vacation (best beaches to visit during spring break in Cancun), or explaining a concept or process you learned in another college course (the role of lie detectors in the criminal justice system). Picking a topic you care about keeps you motivated as you prepare your speech. (For more on how to choose a speech topic, see Chapter 13, pp. 316–320.) It also helps you come across as more animated and passionate in your speech delivery. When you care about your topic, it shows. If you seem bored by your topic, your audience will be, too.

Capture—and Hold—Your Listeners' Attention

Research on perception and listening reveals that people are highly selective in how they focus their attention. We tend to pay attention to messages that relate to our own needs and interests rather than messages we deem unimportant (Fiske & Taylor, 1991). For example, if you're like most students, you perk up during a class lecture if your teacher says, "Listen up, people: what I'm covering now will be on the midterm." After all, it is in your best interest to do well on the midterm. But how, exactly, do you create messages that connect with your listeners' interests?

Start with a compelling introduction to your speech, explaining how your audience will benefit from the information you're about to share ("Knowing the differences between face-to-face and online classes can help you decide which class format is better for you"). People will pay closer attention to your message when they know what's in it for them.

However, capturing your audience's attention during the introduction of your speech isn't all you need to do; you also need to maintain it during the rest of your presentation. Develop your ideas by using supporting materials—such as interesting and relevant examples or stories—that relate to your audience members' lives and priorities. As you *compose* each main point of your speech, keep the following question in mind: How can I relate this point to my audience's physical, emotional, intellectual, or social priorities?

Use Everyday Language

Using an *oral style of language* can make your informative presentation more engaging. This style is similar to how people talk in everyday life instead of the more formal language you use in many written assignments. As Chapter 15

MAKING COMMUNICATION CHOICES
SOME THINGS ARE BETTER LEFT UNSAID

① **CONSIDER THE DILEMMA**

As an active member of your campus community, you belong to several clubs and serve as a student representative to the college dean's advisory council. You also volunteer as a peer mentor. In this role, you help guide first-year students in their academic and social adjustment to college. Given your academic standing and your popularity as a mentor, Dr. Dawkins—the college dean—asks you to present a session called Academic Survival Skills for Your First Semester during new-student orientation.

Though you are honored, you are also nervous, and you share your concerns with your friend Jack: "I'm not sure how I can keep the students interested in academic survival skills. Dr. Dawkins wants me to present for 15 to 20 minutes."

"Just tell them about your first semester and what worked for you," Jack advises.

"I can't do that," you reply. "My first semester was a disaster. I almost quit school." When Jack asks you what happened, you reluctantly explain, "Well, it's pretty embarrassing, but I was accused of plagiarizing a paper in my intro psych class. I didn't give proper credit for my sources. It's not that I didn't want to; I just didn't know how."

"So, did you fail the class?" Jack asks.

"No," you answer. "I got an F on the paper. But I learned to ask for help instead of making assumptions about how to do something. The professor took me under her wing. I ended up passing the course, and I actually changed my major to psychology."

"Wow! That's a powerful lesson. Why don't you tell the students that story?" Jack suggests.

"Are you kidding me? Dr. Dawkins will be there. I don't want him knowing that. Besides, I'm supposed to be teaching these students how to avoid getting into that kind of trouble."

② **CONNECT THE RESEARCH**

Self-disclosure occurs in speeches when you share information about yourself that wouldn't ordinarily be known by listeners. Speakers often do this to bond with their listeners. In educational settings—like a new-student orientation—appropriate self-disclosure increases student motivation and liking for the instructor (Hill, Ah Yn, & Lindsey, 2008). Additionally, researchers have found that learning is promoted through the use of self-disclosure and stories to illustrate concepts (Downs, Javidi, & Nussbaum, 1988).

However, the kind of personal information you share matters. Researchers Pamela Lannutti and Elena Strauman (2006) found that students give high positive evaluations to teachers who self-disclose information that is positive and relevant to the lesson ("During my first week of college, I was so hyped that I was up and dressed by six o'clock every morning"). Such revelations help students see instructors as human. But there is a limit. Self-disclosing negative information (personal flaws, bad habits) or talking excessively about themselves causes students to view presenters unfavorably (Downs et al., 1988).

Before making a communication choice, consider the facts of the situation, and the research on self-disclosure in academic settings. Also, reflect on what you've learned so far about informative speech preparation (pp. 402–406), narrative presentations (pp. 409–410), and the guidelines for informative speaking (pp. 414–419). Then answer these questions:

1 How might the new students benefit from your personal story?

2 What risks do you take by including your personal narrative in the presentation? If you do not disclose the experience, how else might you engage your audience?

3 What will you say in your speech?

explains, adopting an oral style of language helps you create a sense of immediacy with your audience. It helps people quickly understand what you're saying, and it makes your message more appealing. Consider the differences in the language of this main point for a speech on common chemicals found in the home:

> *Written style:* "Biohazardous material exists in the kitchen cabinets of most U.S. households."

> *Oral style:* "If you look in your kitchen cabinets tonight, you'll likely find some common biohazardous material."

Most audiences prefer to listen to an oral style of language because it is more active, interesting, and common than a written style. In addition to being easier on listeners' ears, an oral style of language helps you come across as more personable and authentic to your audience.

Make Your Speech Understandable

When you're communicating ideas that are unfamiliar to your audience, it helps to connect those ideas to concepts or things that *are* familiar to listeners. For example, when Joe's children were preschoolers, he couldn't tell them he'd be home from work by four o'clock. They didn't know how to tell time yet, so "four o'clock" had no meaning for them. Instead, he'd say, "I'll be home when *Reading Rainbow* is over." Since *Reading Rainbow* was their favorite television program, this reference made a familiar connection in their minds. Similarly, you can use examples and illustrative stories to connect difficult concepts to your listeners' experiences and thus make those concepts easier to understand. Think of how educators, presenters, and even TV show hosts do this. Astrophysicist Dr. Neil deGrasse Tyson is well-known

FIGURE 16.1

HELP YOUR AUDIENCE REMEMBER YOUR MESSAGE

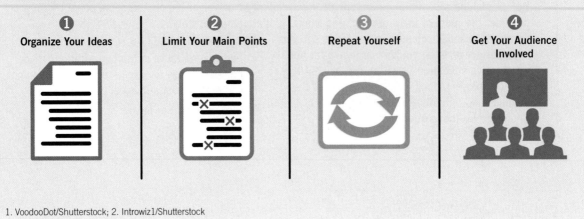

1
Organize Your Ideas

2
Limit Your Main Points

3
Repeat Yourself

4
Get Your Audience Involved

for using this technique. For example, when pointing out the many facets of carbon, Dr. Tyson explains this way:

> You might think of carbon as a kind of unpleasant little element. After all, it's the active ingredient in soot. It's also the stuff left over after you burn your toast. But it's actually quite distinguished among elements. Carbon has the highest melting point. Pure carbon can become graphite—one of the softest materials around—used every time you write with a pencil. . . . But carbon's greatest distinction of all is that it's the building block for the molecules of life.[2]

Through the use of familiar examples (toast, pencils), demonstrations, and stories, Tyson explains complex scientific principles to general audiences on his TV show *NOVA ScienceNOW* as well as to people who attend his lectures and speeches.

Help Your Audience Remember Your Message

One measure of an informative speech's success is whether your listeners remember it. However, a lot of things can interfere with an audience's ability to pay attention to—and thus retain—the information you share with them. For example, listeners may get distracted by outside *noise* during the speech—such as a phone ringing or someone talking nearby. An overly warm or cool temperature in the room can be just as intrusive. Or listeners can simply get lost in their own thoughts or get sidetracked by other Web sites

---

[2]Hayden Planetarium (2009).

or apps, especially if they are watching your speech online. To help your audience pay attention and remember your message, try the following strategies:

LearningCurve can help you review! Go to bedfordstmartins.com /choicesconnections.

- *Organize your ideas.* When you show listeners how ideas go together, they'll be more likely to remember them. Consider this group of letters: PBSCBSESPNNBC. If you were to read these out loud to an audience, your listeners would find it difficult to remember them. But if you organized the letters into groupings that made sense to your audience—PBS, CBS, ESPN, NBC—the letters would become meaningful, and listeners would more easily retain them. Using *connectives* (*First, Next*) in your speech can further help your audience see how your main points are related.

- *Limit your main points.* As Chapter 14 discusses, *main points* are the key statements or principles that support the speech thesis (see pp. 343–349). As you prepare your informative speech, try to limit your main points to between three and five. Too many more, and the audience (and you!) might have trouble following and remembering your line of thinking.

- *Repeat yourself.* Repeating information helps people retain it. While studying for a test, you probably go over the information several times to commit it to memory. Help your audience remember your main ideas by using the same basic principle of repetition. However, don't just say the same words over and over. Instead, illustrate a main point through different means. For instance, you can use a preview statement to introduce the point, increase the volume of your voice when explaining the point, reinforce the point through a visual aid, and then remind the audience of the point in your summary statement.

- *Get your audience involved.* People tend to remember things that they participate in. Think about your college classes. Which ones do you remember the most—the classes in which the teacher lectured in a monotone, or those that had lots of discussion and group work? Even with a large group, it's possible to still involve your audience. Stephen Covey managed to get 200 listeners to try to indicate north as a way of illustrating a point. To involve your listeners during an informative speech, ask for a volunteer to take part in a simple demonstration or have listeners answer a simple question. These kinds of positive disruptions break up your speech and help your audience pay closer attention to your point—which makes it more likely that they'll remember your message.

To see how the principles and guidelines of informative speeches can come together, look over the transcript for the speech "Social Media, Social Identity, and Social Causes" by Anna Davis on pages 420–423. A video of the speech is available online at **bedfordstmartins.com/choicesconnections**.

Sample Informative Speech

SOCIAL MEDIA, SOCIAL IDENTITY, AND SOCIAL CAUSES

By Anna Davis

● ⊙ *To watch a video of this speech and see Anna's preparation and delivery outlines, go to bedfordstmartins.com /choicesconnections.*

● *Anna makes her attention-getter relevant to the audience by referencing the social media tools that nearly everyone in her class will be familiar with.*

● *Anna's personal example helps establish her credibility. It also relates to her speech thesis, which deals with how social media helps everyone answer the question, "Who am I?"*

● *Anna's preview statement organizes her speech. Each section is briefly highlighted so that listeners can anticipate what is coming.*

● *By defining technical terms here, Anna can use them later in the speech with the assurance that the audience will understand precisely what she means. What other examples of everyday language do you see Anna using throughout the speech?*

Anna wears appropriate clothing and begins her speech with a warm greeting and a personal story to connect with her listeners.

Just before my first year of college, I was excited and nervous about meeting other new students on campus. As soon as dorm assignments were announced, we all began friending each other on Facebook and following each other on Twitter. ● This is how I found out that my roommate was an obsessive soccer fan and had seen all of Quentin Tarantino's movies. The school also sponsored online forums, allowing me to learn about different student groups and to find like-minded people across campus. For example, I connected immediately with students who share my interest in animal rescue and adoption. These online connections and groups helped my college friendships develop quickly and meaningfully, and gave me a sense of belonging on campus before I even arrived. ●

Today I'd like to share with you how social media is being used, not only to help students connect but also as a powerful tool to advance social causes and motivate us to act on their behalf. We'll start by looking at a compelling theory of why social media is so uniquely suited to forging connections. Next, I'll review some data on social media's meteoric rise. Finally, we'll see how today's activists are harnessing social media to support an array of social causes to make life better for us all. ●

Let's begin our conversation about these intriguing developments in communication by considering the underlying reasons why we want to use social media in the first place. What is it that drives us to connect through social media with like-minded people and groups?

Social identity theory offers a compelling answer to this question. First, let me define the concept of social identity. Social identity refers to how you understand yourself in relation to your group memberships. ● Michael Hogg, a professor of social psychology at Claremont University, focuses on social identity research. In his 2006 book on contemporary social psychological theories, Hogg explains that group affiliations provide us with an important source of identity, and we therefore want our groups to be valued positively in relation to other groups. ● By "affiliations" I simply mean the groups that we join and perhaps link to online.

Social psychologist Henry Tajfel—one of the founders of social identity theory—spent years considering how we form our social identities. Tajfel believes that the groups to which we attach ourselves, both online and off, help answer the very important question, Who am I? According to Tajfel's • 1979 book *The Social Psychology of Intergroup Relations*, we associate with certain groups to help resolve the anxiety brought about by this fundamental question of identity. By selecting certain groups and not others, we define who we are and develop a sense of belonging in the social world. •

A quick pause to check her notes helps Anna keep her speech focused and ensures she hits all her main points and examples.

Social media sites such as Facebook provide a platform for this type of social identity formation by offering participants certain tools, such as the ability to "friend" people, groups, and even brands, and to "like" certain posts. The simple act of friending, for example, promotes social affiliation between two individuals, and our Facebook friends are collectively a source of social identity. Because we are proclaiming something important to our groups, announcing that we are in a serious relationship takes on great social significance. As we all know, it's not official until it's "Facebook official."

As you can see, social identity theory gives us insight into the reasons behind the popularity of social media sites: they let us proclaim to ourselves and the world, "This is who I am." • Even so, the near miraculous rate of growth of these sites over the past decade is surprising.

A simple graphic helps the audience understand how quickly social media took off.

According to Marcia Clemmit's 2010 *CQ Researcher* article on social networking, Facebook had over 1 million members in 2005—just one year after its launch. This growth from zero to a million in one year was quite an impressive feat. Today, according to a May 2013 article on the number of active Facebook users published by the Associated Press, Facebook harbors over 1.16 billion members. • That's almost four times the population of the United States. Like Facebook, Twitter's growth has also been astronomical. Shea Bennett, editor of the Mediabistro-sponsored blog *AllTwitter*, reports in an October 2013 article that Twitter had 218 million active users at the end of June 2013. Like Facebook, its success can be largely attributed to the demand for virtual communities that enable users to connect with one another.

As the data clearly show, people around the world are defining themselves socially and answering the question, "Who am I?" through the use of social media sites. • And social movement organizations have taken note. Organizations of all kinds are using social media to get their messages across to global consumers and spur their members into action.

• By paraphrasing an expert in the field, Anna helps establish credibility for her speech. Does Anna give sufficient background about her sources?

• This transition helps listeners prepare for the next main point of Anna's speech.

• Anna provides an internal summary as she transitions to the next part of her speech. This connective helps her audience listen to and remember her main points.

• To help her audience understand the large numbers she quotes, Anna relates the number of facebook users to the population of the United States, so the audience can get a sense of just how big 1.16 billion people really is.

• The subtle repetition of the question, "Who am I?" relates this main point back to the speech thesis.

Social movements, defined by Princeton.edu as "a group of people with a common ideology who try together to achieve certain general goals," range across the political and social spectrum. Consider Occupy Wall Street and the Tea Party. Both of these organizations communicate their messages and build support through social media sites. • For example, they use Facebook to announce events and link to petitions. In fact, a nonprofit organization called Social Movement Technologies created a Facebook page to help individual social movement organizations get out their message.

But social media is not just being used as a platform for informing the public of a group's mission and activities, or even merely to get people to sign petitions. Increasingly, activists are deploying social media to motivate like-minded people to get into the fight.

To get a sense of what this means, consider the recent efforts of a seventeen-year-old skateboarder from St. Cloud, Minnesota. •

For three years, Austin Lee found himself struggling to get support for a skate park in his local community. But when he decided to use Facebook for his cause, things changed nearly overnight. Lee's posting attracted 1,085 members, and even drew a portion of those members to city council meetings on behalf of his cause. In 2010, David Unze of *USA Today* reported that Lee won the approval—and $500,000—for his skate park.

To properly introduce a new slide, Anna gestures to it but keeps her attention focused on her audience.

• And it all happened within one day of Lee's original posting on Facebook.

As you can see, if you can use social media to convince people to identify with what you want to accomplish, success is possible. Lee's accomplishment shows us that we not only identify and affiliate ourselves with groups but also are willing to actively work toward accomplishing their goals.

Today I hope I've shown that the skyrocketing use of social media sites over the past decade is no accident. The human desire to develop a positive sense of social identity through group affiliation is one reason for this phenomenon. Capitalizing on this universal psychological drive, social movement organizations are harnessing these technologies to accomplish their goals. Social media sites allow us to communicate, express, and identify with one another in ways that encourage affiliation as well as action. Whether it's a major political movement or a teenager's desire for a local skate park, social media technologies are powerful.

So as you tweet about new groups or see the next "Facebook official" status update, think about what groups you like, whom you have friended, and what those affiliations may be able to do for you. •

• Since she's speaking to inform rather than persuade, Anna uses examples that are well balanced and do not express a bias.

• By telling Austin's story, Anna keeps the audience engaged, while providing a real example to support her claims. How well does Austin's story capture your interest? What suggestions—if any—do you have to improve Anna's use of the story?

• Anna mentions several sources throughout her speech. How effectively does she orally cite each of these sources?

• To make her final words count, Anna's concluding statement is memorable, succinct, and summarizes her thesis.

REFERENCES

Associated Press. (2013, May 1). Number of active users at Facebook over the years. *Yahoo! News*. Retrieved from http://news.yahoo.com /number-active-users-facebook-over-230449748.html

Bennett, S. (2013, October 4). How many active users does Twitter have, and how fast is it growing? [Web log post]. Retrieved from http://www .mediabistro.com/alltwitter/tag/twitter-active-users

Clemmitt, M. (2010, September 17). Social networking. *CQ Researcher, 20*(32). Retrieved from http://www.cqpress.com/product/Researcher -Social-Networking-v20-32.html

Hogg, M. (2006). Social identity theory. In P. J. Burke (Ed.), *Contemporary social psychological theories* (pp. 111–136). Palo Alto, CA: Stanford University Press.

Madden, M., Lenhart, A., Cortesi, S., Gasser, U., Duggan, M., Smith, A., & Beaton, M. (2013, May 21). Teens, social media, and privacy. *Pew Internet and American Life Project*. Retrieved from http://www.pewinternet.org/Reports /2013/Teens-Social-Media-And-Privacy.aspx

Social movement. (n.d.). *Wordnetweb.Princeton.edu*. Retrieved from http://wordnetweb.princeton.edu/perl/webwn?s=social%20movement

Social Movement Technologies. (n.d.). In *Facebook* [Group page]. Retrieved from http://www.facebook.com/SocialMovementTechnologies

Tajfel, H., & Turner, J. C. (1979). An integrative theory of intergroup conflict. *The social psychology of intergroup relations*, v. 33, p. 47.

Unze, D. (2010, March 26). Facebook helps spark movements. *USA Today*. Retrieved from http://usatoday30.usatoday.com/news/nation /2010-03-25-facebook_N.htm

SAMPLE SPEECH RESOURCES

 There is a lot more to Anna's speech than the transcript above. See how the whole speech came together by going to **bedfordstmartins.com/choicesconnections** and accessing the **Sample Speech Resources** for Chapter 16. There you will find:

1 Video of Anna's speech "Social Media, Social Identity, and Social Causes"

2 The preparation outline for Anna's speech

3 The delivery outline for Anna's speech

4 Anna's PowerPoint slides

5 A rehearsal clip of Anna practicing her speech

CHAPTER ⑯ REVIEW

CHAPTER RECAP

- **Informative speeches** allow you to raise awareness about a topic or provide an in-depth explanation of a topic. Avoid **information overload** for your audience by considering how much information is possible to share with them.
- To maintain a focus on informing (instead of persuading), keep in mind your general purpose, and maintain a neutral point of view when preparing your presentation.
- The four most common types of informative speeches are **expository, process or demonstration, narrative,** and **comparison/contrast.** You may use one or more types to achieve your speech thesis.
- Delivering a successful informative speech includes following the five steps of speech preparation, but it is also important to focus on making your speech understandable and helping your audience remember key points.

LAUNCHPAD

LaunchPad for *Choices & Connections* offers unique video scenarios and encourages self-assessment through adaptive quizzing. Go to **bedfordstmartins.com /choicesconnections** to get access.

 LearningCurve adaptive quizzes

 How to Communicate video scenarios

 Video clips that illustrate key concepts

 Sample speech resources

KEY TERMS

1 If you are giving an informative speech about how to apply to the social work program on your campus, what function of informative speaking are you fulfilling?

a. In-depth explanation   **c.** Audience analysis

b. Raising awareness   **d.** Specific purpose

2 Which of the following is *not* a goal of informative speaking?

a. Improving listeners' understanding

b. Keeping a neutral point of view

c. Avoiding motivational appeals

d. Changing listeners' attitudes

3 Giving a speech about the different eras in Internet development is an example of a(n) _____ presentation.

a. expository   **c.** process or demonstration

b. narrative   **d.** comparison/contrast

4 Using an oral style of language allows you to _____ when giving an informative speech.

a. be memorable   **c.** create immediacy

b. target listeners' interests   **d.** use connotative meanings

5 Using connectives in your speech will help you _____ and therefore help your audience remember your message.

a. limit your main points   **c.** stay on message

b. organize your ideas   **d.** involve your listeners

ACTIVITIES

1 Show and Analyze

Watch a cooking show on the Food Network—like Rachael Ray's *30 Minute Meals* or Sunny Anderson's *Cooking for Real* (you can find episodes at www.foodnetwork .com, or use any how-to show you like). In a brief paper, identify specific strategies the host uses to explain the process of preparing a meal. Also, make note of how the guidelines for informative speaking are evident in the program.

2 Sharing Your Story

Identify a small object that has personal meaning for you (a photograph, a tattoo, a piece of jewelry, a family heirloom). Prepare a two- to three-minute narrative presentation that tells the story of the item's significance. Rehearse your presentation with a classmate, and get feedback to help you revise it. Then deliver the revised speech to your class, or video-record it for the course Web site.

17

Persuasive Speeches

It's the thing that no parent ever wants to experience, but it happens; it happened to Jan Withers. In a 2012 speech to traffic safety professionals in Orlando, Florida, she explained what happened on the worst day of her life:

> It started with my husband receiving a phone call that Alisa had been in an accident—that is what he called it at that time. Of course, as it turns out, it wasn't an accident at all. The truth is, someone made a choice—a tragic choice—to drive drunk.
>
> Nobody thinks that it can happen to them. Even in that moment, as my husband told me that we needed to go to the hospital immediately, it never crossed my mind that she would die. Never. But she did.[1]

Alisa was 15 years old.

Not wanting others to face the same tragedy, Jan turned her loss into action by joining Mothers Against Drunk Driving (MADD), eventually becoming its national president. A grassroots organization, MADD advocates for families and victims who have suffered injury or loss at the hands of a driver impaired by alcohol or drugs. Through persuasive communication—speeches to parents and school assemblies, meetings with lawmakers, and social media campaigns—MADD volunteers speak out for tougher laws aimed at reducing impaired driving. Since its founding in 1980, more than 1,000 such laws have been passed at the state and federal levels, including legislation raising the minimum drinking age and establishing sobriety checkpoints (El-Guebaly, 2005).

One reason MADD volunteers are so persuasive is that they translate abstract statistics into personal stories their listeners can relate to. In her 2012 speech, Jan Withers pointed out how this approach contributes to MADD's success:

> In the nearly 20 years since [Alisa's] death, MADD has changed the national culture on drunk driving specifically and traffic safety generally. We put a face and a name with the numbers. We got legislators, government agencies, and the media

[1]Speech excerpts in this section from Withers (2012).

AP Photo/The New Mexican, Clyde Mueller

to understand that it was possible to do something about the human element of the traffic safety problem. Most of all, we helped Americans realize that drunk driving isn't something that we have to live with.

Guided by a vision of a future free of drunk driving, MADD volunteers make presentations and create other types of communication messages to raise awareness about the human toll of drunk driving. So whether it's through a persuasive speech, a blog post, or a tweet, MADD emphasizes a clear and simple message: don't drink and drive. Without question, the organization's persuasive communication tactics work. MADD has helped change attitudes, behaviors, and laws about driving while impaired.

Life Lost
Could Be
YOURS

MADD
Activism | Victim Services | Education

✓ **LearningCurve** can help you review! Go to **bedfordstmartins.com /choicesconnections**.

Think about your everyday communication and how often you try to influence others' attitudes, behaviors, and actions. For instance, on your way to work, you call up a friend and try to persuade her to see the movie you want to see. At your job, you convince a coworker to cover your shift. Persuasive communications like these happen in a wide range of settings. In this chapter, however, we focus on **persuasive speeches**—those that reinforce or change listeners' attitudes and beliefs and possibly even motivate them to take action.

Persuasive speaking is notably different from coercion. **Coercion** involves using threats, manipulation, and even violence to force others to do something against their will. Any use of coercion is unethical. Instead, when you speak to persuade others, you provide your audience with accurate and honest information, giving them the freedom to choose whether to accept your message or not. In this chapter, you'll learn:

- The different types of persuasive speeches
- The importance of credibility in persuasive speaking
- How to organize a persuasive speech and support your claims
- Strategies for appealing to your audience's needs and emotions
- General guidelines for persuasive speaking

What Is Persuasive Speaking?

> Persuasive speeches are unique because their goal is to change the audience's beliefs or behavior. When preparing such a presentation, consider the type of persuasive speech you'll give, what your specific purpose will be, and—most importantly—how to get your audience to believe what you have to say.

Throughout your academic, social, and professional life, you will be called on to prepare persuasive presentations. Your most immediate need, of course, is probably for this communication class. Luckily, you are already familiar with how to start any speech assignment. To deliver a persuasive speech, follow the five steps for speech preparation discussed in Chapters 13, 14, and 15: think, investigate, compose, rehearse, and revise. (See Table 17.1.) In addition, there are factors specific to persuasive speaking to keep in mind as you prepare.

Types of Persuasive Speeches

When *thinking* about the topic of your presentation, you will want to consider what kind of persuasive speech you want to give. There are three types:

1. A **speech of fact** establishes whether something is true or not ("Chocolate can reduce the onset of heart disease") or whether an event will or won't happen ("The polarity of the earth will be reversed by the year 3000").

TABLE 17.1

FIVE STEPS IN SPEECH PREPARATION

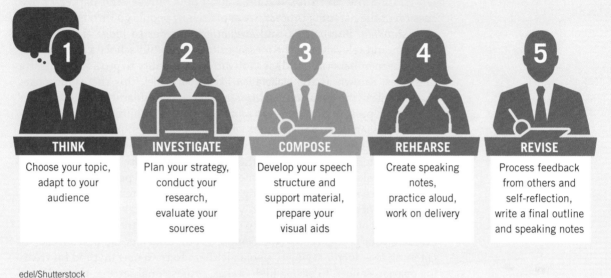

THINK	INVESTIGATE	COMPOSE	REHEARSE	REVISE
Choose your topic, adapt to your audience	Plan your strategy, conduct your research, evaluate your sources	Develop your speech structure and support material, prepare your visual aids	Create speaking notes, practice aloud, work on delivery	Process feedback from others and self-reflection, write a final outline and speaking notes

edel/Shutterstock

2. A **speech of value** proposes a judgment on a topic ("Euthanasia is morally wrong") or explains why something is good or bad ("Here is why the Batman movies are better films than the Superman franchise").

3. A **speech of policy** argues about whether an action should or should not be taken ("First-year students should be required to live on campus").

Choosing which type of persuasive speech you'll give helps you develop your speech thesis during the *composing* step of your preparation.

Audience Analysis for Persuasive Speeches

After determining your persuasive speech type and your topic, the next part of the *thinking* step includes analyzing the attitudes your audience may have about your message. As Chapter 13 discusses, *audience analysis* is the process of identifying important characteristics about your listeners, and using this information to prepare your speech. Although you always want to know as much as possible about your audience, paying special attention to any strongly held *attitudes*, *beliefs*, and *values* is especially helpful when preparing a persuasive speech. Will the audience have favorable views toward your topic? Will they strongly oppose your position? Will they be undecided or uncommitted on the issue? Consider the answers to these questions while researching your topic and composing your speech; it will help you create persuasive main points and present your message ethically.

There is one more factor to consider about your listeners when preparing a persuasive speech: How motivated will they be to pay attention?

Understanding the Elaboration Likelihood Model. In Chapter 7's discussion of the listening process, we explain how people go through stages of *understanding, interpreting,* and *evaluating* in order to judge the accuracy, interest, and relevance of the messages they hear. But scholars suggest that audience members vary in their motivation and ability to process persuasive messages. Known as the **elaboration likelihood model,** this theory proposes that listeners who are intensely interested in your topic and can easily understand your presentation will put more effort into thinking about your persuasive message than will listeners who don't care about or don't understand your speech topic. Knowing how your audience will process your message will help when you're *composing* the presentation. There are two routes listeners can take when processing messages: central and peripheral.

Audience members who are highly motivated to listen and who have the knowledge needed to understand your message will take a **central route** to processing your speech—meaning they'll pay more attention and carefully evaluate your points (Petty & Cacioppo, 1986). Consider medical specialists listening to a doctor trying to persuade them to try a new method for treating ovarian cancer. In such a high-stakes, professional setting, the audience members are highly motivated to pay attention, and they'll be comfortable with the complex information being presented. In this case, the doctor would want to emphasize current research, compose detailed supporting points for his or her main ideas, and plan time for audience questions.

Audiences who are less motivated about the topic or who don't have the time or knowledge needed to understand the information might take a **peripheral route** to processing your message (Petty & Cacioppo, 1986). This means they are not fully engaged with the speech. They may *selectively listen* for items of personal interest but miss your larger message and therefore not fully understand your thesis. Their attention may wane, or they may get easily distracted. Listeners who take a peripheral route to processing messages can be easily influenced by a speaker's expertise or emotional appeals, but any changes in attitudes and behaviors are often short lived (Petty, Barden, & Wheeler, 2002). For example, they might give a few dollars to a charity immediately after listening to an emotional appeal but not become regular contributors.

Using the Elaboration Likelihood Model. If your audience analysis indicates that listeners may take a peripheral route to processing your message, there are ways to encourage them to use a central route. Suppose you're giving a presentation to persuade your classmates to embrace proper nutrition in their daily diet. But most of your classmates don't see proper nutrition as important and don't know a lot about the technical details related to nutrition (such as how it affects the body or long-term health consequences). Listeners are more likely to give considerable thought to a message when the topic is made personally relevant to them (Petty et al., 2002). Your speech introduction is the place to start building this awareness. As Chapter 14 explains, one function of the speech introduction is to *connect the topic to the*

Including the audience in your speech is a sure way to make sure they stay connected and attentive. Using personal pronouns—like "you" and "we"—instead of making general statements lets your audience know that your topic is being presented specifically to their interests. What other techniques could you use to encourage the central route to processing in your listeners?

needs and interest of your audience. When introducing your speech, tell the audience how they will benefit from what you are about to say.

After the speech introduction, you can continue motivating the audience to use central route processing by composing a main point on the positive outcomes of accepting your speech thesis. For example, you could list the advantages of proper nutrition ("By eating healthier, you'll not only look better but also set a great example for your friends and family"). Additionally, you will want to tell them what highly credible experts have said about the issue, so that they understand why it is important or something they should care about ("The National Institutes of Health points out that poor nutrition is a contributing factor in obesity, heart disease, and diabetes"). If you present personally relevant, logical, and well-supported messages, your listeners are more likely to thoughtfully process your message (Wagner & Petty, 2011). Later in this chapter, we'll cover more about how to organize and use logical reasoning in a persuasive speech.

Finally, researchers Wagner and Petty (2011) suggest that even small changes in language help listeners thoughtfully process persuasive messages. For example, using familiar words rather than technical words makes it easier to listen to a speech. Audience members become distracted and tune out when speakers use language that is hard to understand. Additionally, relying on personal pronouns ("*You* will feel great when *you* eat well") instead of impersonal pronouns ("*People* feel great when *they* eat well") encourages listeners to feel personally connected to your message and thus to take a central route in processing your speech (Wagner & Petty, 2011).

Specific Purposes for Persuasive Speeches. When it comes time to write the specific purpose statement for your persuasive speech, keep in mind that most persuasive presentations focus on one of three desired outcomes. First, your speech could *reinforce your audience's existing attitudes and beliefs*. Much like the inspiring and rousing speeches given at pep rallies ("This year we win it all!"), this focus is most effective when your listeners already support your position, and your specific purpose is to persuade them to "keep the faith." In this case, your specific purpose might be "To persuade my audience that we are the best team in the conference."

Second, if your listeners are uncommitted about your speech topic or if their attitudes and beliefs about the topic differ from yours, your desired outcome might be to *change your audience's attitudes and beliefs*. Let's say you're talking to an audience that doesn't care that much about sports, and you want to convince your listeners that your school's sports program matters. In this case, your specific purpose might be "To convince my audience that a successful sports team is good for student morale." Since some attitudes and beliefs are at the core of people's self-concept, such as religious and lifestyle choices, one speech won't likely change them. In this case, look for other attitudes and beliefs less central to your audience's identity that you might use to engage them.

A third possible desired outcome is to *motivate your audience to take some action*. This could include taking up a charitable cause, making different choices, or participating in a political action. If your audience is already convinced that successful sports teams improve student morale, your specific purpose could be "To persuade my audience to donate time or supplies to fund-raising efforts for new team uniforms."

Credibility in Persuasive Speeches. As a pediatrician and co-inventor of the rotavirus vaccine, Dr. Paul Offit spends a lot of time talking with audiences about why it's important to vaccinate children against certain diseases. During such occasions, he often meets people who disagree with his claim, usually because they believe that childhood vaccines may have unintended consequences—such as causing autism—and should therefore be avoided. Raging for more than a decade, this controversy has passionate proponents on both sides.

Even though Offit believes that scientific research has shown no link between vaccinations and autism, he knows that some parents believe there's a connection. They place a lot of confidence in other sources, such as what they read online or hear other parents say about their own experiences. With so much competing information available, his audience members will have a range of existing knowledge about vaccines and possibly strong attitudes about the topic. Fully aware of the challenge, Offit carefully plans his speeches in order to persuade parents to vaccinate their children.

A critical step for Offit is making sure his listeners find him credible. **Credibility** is an audience's perception of a speaker's trustworthiness and the validity of the information provided in the speech. If your listeners think you're credible, they are more likely to believe you. If they don't think you're credible, you won't have much luck persuading them. The importance of credibility in persuasive speaking can be traced all the way back to the ancient Greek philosopher Aristotle, who pointed out that a speaker's **ethos** (credibility) determines whether he or she can influence listeners (Cooper, 1960).

Certainly, a speaker needs more than credibility, or ethos, to be persuasive. According to Aristotle, speakers should also present the audience with good logical reasons (he called this *logos*) and make appeals to their emotions (or *pathos*). These three elements—ethos, logos, and pathos—are known as **rhetorical proofs** (Cooper, 1960). Ethical and competent persuasive speeches will include all three forms of rhetorical proof. Later in the chapter we consider principles and skills for using logical reasoning and emotional appeals in composing your speech.

But let's first look at ethos, or credibility. How exactly do listeners decide whether you're credible? They consider the three Cs: your character, competence, and charisma.

As the cofounder of the organization Water.org, which aims to bring safe water and sanitation to developing countries, actor Matt Damon spends a lot of time influencing audiences to support his cause. Part of his success is due to his ability to connect with audiences on a humane and passionate level, without relying on his celebrity status. How does someone's general character influence how you listen to them?

Todd Williamson/Invision for Water.org/AP Images

Character. You demonstrate **character** by showing your audience that you understand their needs, have their best interests in mind, and genuinely believe in your topic. This communicates that you are trustworthy. Another way to show character is by making it clear to your listeners what they stand to gain by hearing you out. How can you do all this? Determine what you and your audience have in common, and work that into your speech. Building this bridge to your audience conveys the message that you are all in this together.

Competence. When it comes to credibility, **competence** is the degree of expertise your audience thinks you have regarding your speech topic. Even if you're not an expert on the subject, you can still convey competence by thoroughly researching it.

One way to demonstrate competence is by only using information from resources that pass the evaluation requirements discussed in Chapter 13. Your research sources should be highly credible, reliable (objective), and current. In addition, work any personal knowledge or experience you have regarding the topic into your speech. For example, if you want to persuade your listeners to get certified in cardiopulmonary resuscitation (CPR), tell them about your own CPR training experience. Finally, carefully organize and prepare your speech. Even the most knowledgeable, reputable speakers have a hard time looking competent if their material doesn't follow a logical sequence or if they jump around from point to point.

Charisma. Your **charisma** stems from how much warmth, personality, and dynamism your audience sees in you. Charismatic speakers engage their audience, even when presenting on topics that don't initially appeal to listeners. Although some people are more naturally outgoing and personable, anyone can work on strengthening their charisma. Even if you're usually more reserved, you can still practice behaviors that will help you engage with your audience and come across as charismatic. For instance, try varying the volume and pitch of your voice, establishing eye contact with audience members, and moving from behind the lectern and among your listeners if possible. As Chapter 15 describes, using such nonverbal communication skills in your delivery creates *immediacy*, or a sense of closeness, with your audience. This means they are more likely to view you as warm and approachable and be engaged by your presentation.

Organizing and Supporting Persuasive Speeches

Taking steps to establish credibility with your audience is important. But you can't rely only on your credibility to achieve your specific purpose. You also need to organize your points in a way that makes sense and give listeners evidence to support your claims.

The Kobal Collection/Walt Disney Pictures

Successful persuasive speeches have a clear organization and use logical reasoning to prove points. Without these two elements, you risk leaving audiences feeling as confused as Alice when she falls into Wonderland. How can you keep your audiences from feeling like they've entered another dimension?

Shortly after falling down a rabbit hole in the classic story *Alice in Wonderland*, Alice finds herself talking to the Cheshire Cat as she tries to make sense of the strange world she has found herself in:

> "What sort of people live about here?"
>
> "In *that* direction," the Cat said, waving its right paw round, "lives a Hatter: and in *that* direction," waving the other paw, "lives a March Hare. Visit either you like; they're both mad."
>
> "But I don't want to go among mad people," Alice remarked.
>
> "Oh, you can't help that," said the Cat: "we're all mad here. I'm mad. You're mad."
>
> "How do you know I'm mad?" said Alice.
>
> "You must be," said the Cat, "or you wouldn't have come here."
>
> Alice didn't think that proved it at all.
>
> —Lewis Carroll, *Alice in Wonderland*[2]

Alice's encounter with the Cheshire Cat is just one of many conversations she has with unusual characters who pull her into loops of confusing logic. Though these characters try to get her to play by the absurd rules of their world, Alice demands stronger proof about why she should believe them.

If you want to be successful in persuading others, you must avoid twisted logic that leaves your listeners feeling like Alice. Even if you have a lot of credibility with your listeners, if you don't provide them with a clearly organized presentation and solid evidence, they may not accept what you have to say. The development of logical reasons for your position is what Aristotle referred to as **logos.**

---

[2]Excerpted from Carroll (2013), p. 49.

Organizing Persuasive Speeches

Chapter 14 discusses the five most common organizational patterns for composing a speech: topical, chronological, spatial, cause-effect, and problem-solution. These structures are useful for organizing both informative and persuasive speeches. In addition, one pattern is unique to persuasive presentations. The **motivated sequence** is a five-step method for organizing a persuasive speech about a problem (Gronbeck, McKerrow, Ehninger, & Monroe, 1990). Consider using this pattern when delivering a *speech of policy* (you want the audience to take some action on your topic).

To see how the motivated sequence can help you organize a persuasive speech, let's walk through the process using the following specific purpose: to persuade my audience to enroll in a Cardiopulmonary Resuscitation (CPR) course.

Step 1: Attention. Introduce the topic to your audience, and give them a reason to listen. Recall from the discussion of the elaboration likelihood model that relating the topic to the needs and interests of the audience can help with this. Use the guidelines in Chapter 14 to compose an effective speech introduction that engages your listeners, discloses your speech thesis, establishes your credibility, and connects the topic to the audience. For example, "When I was hiking in Colorado last summer with my Uncle Bill, he suddenly collapsed. Thanks to my cardiopulmonary resuscitation (or CPR) training, I was able to help. This experience made me realize how important it is for all of us to know CPR; a situation like mine could happen to any of

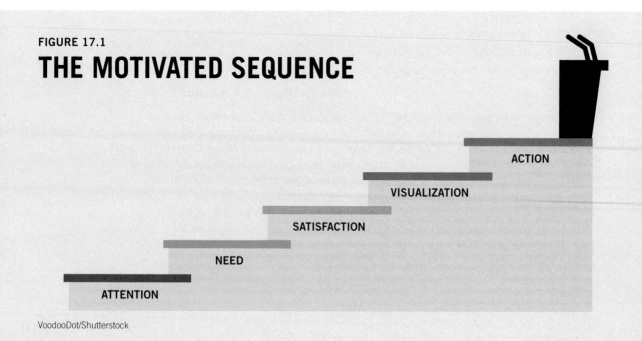

FIGURE 17.1

THE MOTIVATED SEQUENCE

ATTENTION

NEED

SATISFACTION

VISUALIZATION

ACTION

VoodooDot/Shutterstock

you." You can then preview the main points of the presentation as a transition to the body of the speech.

Step 2: Need. Clearly state the problem you want the audience to be concerned about as a main point. To highlight why knowing CPR is critical, you could say something like, "People die needlessly every year from cardiac arrest in the United States." Then use your research (statistical information, testimony, and other supporting materials) to show the audience why they should be concerned about the problem. Be sure that you're drawing from highly credible sources in your research.

Step 3: Satisfaction. Show the audience that the plan you are recommending is reasonable and that by supporting it, they can help solve or prevent the problem. For example, "CPR training is relatively easy to complete either here on campus or at other organizations, such as hospitals, fire departments, and your local Red Cross." You could go on to explain the specifics of CPR training, including locations, costs, and what the training is like.

If you're taking on a large-scale problem in your speech that calls for complex solutions, focus on specific things your audience can do to help. When discussing inner-city deterioration, for example, you may try to persuade your audience to do one thing to help prevent it, such as eating at downtown restaurants instead of suburban restaurants. Don't just detail big problems without offering solutions.

Step 4: Visualization. Get your listeners to imagine the good things that can happen if the problem is fixed or the negative consequences if nothing is done. How you approach this step depends on what you've learned about your listeners through audience analysis. If you believe the audience will generally favor your position, focus on the positive results of taking action: "Learning CPR has many benefits, not the least of which is potentially saving lives."

If you think your audience is mostly uncommitted or undecided about your topic, you could focus on the negative consequences if listeners don't do anything about the problem: "If you're not CPR certified, you'll be unprepared to help if someone—your child, a colleague, a friend—goes into cardiac arrest." Alternatively, if you have time, you can emphasize the positive results of acting as well as the negative impact of doing nothing.

Step 5: Action. Summarize your main points, and challenge the audience to make a specific commitment. End your speech with a concise, powerful thought that leaves listeners reflecting about your overall message. You could close with a story, a rhetorical question, or a quotation, such as "Learn CPR. Save lives."

Reasoning for Persuasive Speeches

In addition to providing your audience with a clear structure for your speech, you need to develop a logical basis for each of your main points. During the *investigation* step of your speech preparation, you collect facts, expert

MAKING COMMUNICATION CHOICES
DO OR DIE: USING SCARE TACTICS TO PERSUADE OTHERS

1 CONSIDER THE DILEMMA

As a service-learning project, your life science class is organizing a health screening day on your campus. Medical professionals will be offering blood pressure checks, cholesterol and diabetes screening, and vaccinations. Students can complete a full health screening in about 15 minutes. Your instructor, Professor Griswold, created several student teams to support the event. Since you are majoring in public relations, you joined the event-promotion team.

Your team wants to develop a slogan to market the event. This tagline will help tie together all the promotional efforts, whether posted on Facebook, Twitter, or campus bulletin boards; printed on flyers; or passed on through face-to-face interactions. During your first team meeting, one member suggests that playing on fear is a good way to motivate students, saying, "I think we need to have a message that scares people. Something like, 'Don't be a zombie. Dying young is no joke. Attend the Health Screening Fair.'" Two other group members immediately vocalize their enthusiasm for the idea.

But you see it differently. Since your sophomore year of high school, you have had an annual physical exam. Your mother encouraged you and your sister to have regular checkups for peace of mind. In fact, one routine test showed a heart abnormality in your sister that was easily treated. This personal experience makes you believe the slogan should emphasize the positive benefits of health screenings instead of relying on scare tactics.

2 CONNECT THE RESEARCH

Whether television commercials, printed brochures, or social media campaigns, there are lots of persuasive messages designed to motivate you to take care of your health. These messages are so plentiful that communication scholars even study how health professionals develop messages to maximize persuasive effect.

One line of research looks at how the choice of positive or negative language in health messages influences receivers. Specifically, *gain-framed messages* use language that points out the benefits of taking care of your health (O'Keefe & Jensen, 2009). For example, a gain-framed message about getting a health screening would be, "If you have regular health checkups, you will enjoy peace of mind." On the other hand, health messages using language that emphasizes the cost of not following good health practices are known as *loss-framed messages* (O'Keefe & Jensen, 2009). A loss-framed message about getting a health screening would be, "If you don't have regular health checkups, you could die from a terminal disease that could've been treated if it was caught earlier."

Several factors determine which approach is the better one to use. When you want to influence others to take preventive action to maintain good health, such as flossing daily, wearing sunscreen, or exercising regularly, gain-framed messages may be the most persuasive (Rothman, Bartels, Wlaschin, & Salovey, 2006). However, if your motivation is to convince others that routine tests—such as blood pressure checks, mammograms, or STD testing—will detect and lessen the impact of potential health problems, a loss-framed message may be best. In this case, you would want the health message to detail the risks of doing nothing (Rothman et al., 2006).

Additionally, the success of either type of message frame is affected by individual differences. Receivers will respond differently to these appeals depending on their personality characteristics, motivation and interests, health history, and confidence in their own ability to follow health recommendations (Covey, 2012).

Before making a communication choice, consider the facts of the situation, and think about the research on gain-framed and loss-framed health messages. Also, reflect on what you've learned so far about the elaboration likelihood model (pp. 430–431), the motivated sequence (pp. 436–437), and credibility (pp. 432–433). Then answer these questions:

❶ What ethical considerations must you keep in mind when choosing how to persuade others—especially if you are using fear?

❷ What particular features about your audience (age, reliance on social media, life experiences) make it challenging to determine whether to use a gain- or a loss-framed approach for the slogan? Which challenge is most important to keep in mind when preparing the slogan?

❸ What are you going to suggest to your team?

testimony, and specific examples. To turn all that material into the logical basis for your speech, first identify patterns in your supporting materials, and then summarize those patterns into arguments that become the main points of your speech. This process is known as **reasoning.** So if your thesis is "Playing the right video games can enhance your brainpower," one of your main points (or arguments) might be, "Video gaming strengthens spatial skills." Of course, it's not enough to just state the point; your audience expects you to prove it. This is where your research comes in. Use your research findings to back up your claim by citing studies and expert testimony that illustrate how video gaming improves students' spatial skills in educational settings.

There are many ways to use reasoning to support your ideas, but let's focus on the four most common ones: deductive, inductive, analogical, and cause-effect.

Deductive Reasoning. When you start with a generally held principle and then show how a specific instance relates to that principle, you're using **deductive reasoning.** Deductive reasoning typically has three elements: the **major premise,** or general statement you believe your audience will accept as true ("Honor students have disciplined study habits"); a **minor premise,** or specific instance of the general claim ("Ella is an honor student"); and a **conclusion** about the relationship between the two ideas ("Therefore, Ella must have disciplined study habits").

Of course, your audience may not readily accept a major premise that's very broad: "*All* honor students have disciplined study habits." It might be more realistic and believable to say that *most* honor students have disciplined study habits. Words like *most, probably,* and *likely* are **qualifiers**—language that indicates how certain you are about your major premise (Toulmin, 1958). Your audience will be more likely to consider your broader claims when you use qualifiers and provide additional evidence to support them.

TABLE 17.2

USING REASONING TO SUPPORT YOUR IDEAS

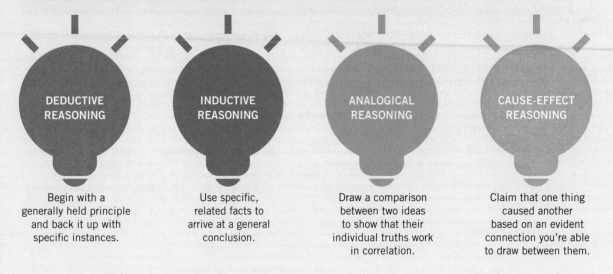

DEDUCTIVE REASONING	INDUCTIVE REASONING	ANALOGICAL REASONING	CAUSE-EFFECT REASONING
Begin with a generally held principle and back it up with specific instances.	Use specific, related facts to arrive at a general conclusion.	Draw a comparison between two ideas to show that their individual truths work in correlation.	Claim that one thing caused another based on an evident connection you're able to draw between them.

popcic/Shutterstock

Inductive Reasoning. When you connect a set of specific, related facts to arrive at a more general conclusion, you're using **inductive reasoning.** For example, if a new friend is late meeting you for an evening out, you probably think nothing of it. But if it happens the next four or five times you get together, you'll probably conclude that your friend isn't capable of being on time. In a speech, you can use facts based on your personal observations or from the research you've compiled to arrive at a general conclusion.

When you're using inductive reasoning, avoid outdated or limited examples. For instance, suppose a speaker said, "I will never eat at that restaurant again, and you shouldn't either. Four years ago, they served me a soggy salad." If you heard this, you might think to yourself, "Well, that was four years ago. Things might have changed a lot at the restaurant since then. I'm not sure this person knows what he's talking about." Your audience is likely to recognize when you don't have enough adequate evidence to support your claim.

Analogical Reasoning. In Chapter 14, we discuss that when *composing* your speech, you can use *analogies*—comparisons of two unlike items—to support your points. Similarly, **analogical reasoning** is when you support a claim by drawing a comparison between two ideas or situations to show that what's true for one could be true for the other: "By following the town of Springfield's example of a comprehensive recycling program, we, too, could make our streets and alleys cleaner." Particularly for a speech of policy, this form of reasoning can demonstrate how your proposed solution has been successfully implemented elsewhere.

To use analogical reasoning, you'll need to show that the two things you're comparing have significant similarities. Making false or unrealistic comparisons is not ethical. To gauge similarities in the recycling example, you would want to ask yourself questions like, Is the population of Springfield similar to that of our city? Are the financial resources similar? Are citizens similarly interested in participating in a recycling program? If the things you're comparing are too different, you'll find it harder to convince your audience that your claim makes sense.

Cause-Effect Reasoning. When you use **cause-effect reasoning**, you draw a connection between two events or things and claim that one produced the other. You can claim that effect Y was caused by X. For example, "An unnecessary number of human lives were lost [*effect*] during Hurricane Katrina because of a lack of timely and substantial response by the federal government [*cause*]." To reason from an effect to its cause, you have to work back in time. This type of claim is best suited for explaining why something occurred.

You can also claim that specific events or things will cause a particular effect in the future: "The use of performance-enhancing drugs can put someone at increased risk for cancer."

When using cause-effect reasoning, make sure your claims are based on causal relationships supported by the evidence found during the *investigation* step. You don't want to suggest a causal link when there isn't any solid evidence showing that such a link exists. For example, stating "It's going to rain tomorrow because I washed my car" is faulty causal reasoning. Cleaning your car doesn't *cause* rain. Reasoning errors like this are known as fallacies.

Avoiding Fallacies

One sure way to undermine your speech's organization and reasoning is by failing—much like the Cheshire Cat—to provide your listeners with a logical connection between the claims you're making and the facts. **Fallacies** are false claims—those that aren't true or are based on inadequate or inaccurate evidence. If you make false claims, not only will your listeners question your credibility but you will violate the ethical principle that says you're responsible for providing your audience with solid reasons to consider your position. Common fallacies you should avoid include the following:

- *Ad hominem arguments.* You attack a person rather than an idea: "Stephens is a college dropout. It's no wonder he's made such an insane proposal."

- *Hasty generalizations.* You make a bold claim based on limited evidence: "Four-wheeling is a safe sport. I ride a few times a year, and I've never had an accident."

- *Bandwagon appeals.* You claim that if others are doing what you're recommending, then it's a good course of action: "Many other colleges no longer place high priority on SAT or ACT scores for admission, so our college should do the same."

- *Straw person claims.* You oversimplify or misrepresent the other side of a controversial topic to make your own case stronger: "Anyone who supports this proposed legislation has no respect for the U.S. Constitution."

To present a fallacy-free speech, thoroughly research and carefully compose your presentation. In addition, rehearse your presentation in front of others, and then ask them for feedback on the validity of your claims. If you think your claims may contain fallacies, conduct additional research to find evidence that strengthens your reasoning. Your listeners will ultimately decide whether to accept what you have to say, but if you provide them with well-developed reasons, they can make an informed choice.

Appealing to Your Audience's Needs and Emotions

Persuasion is more than just credibility and reasoning. Appealing to your listeners' emotions and encouraging them to experience strong feelings about your issue make it more likely that they will agree with you and follow your suggestions.

Imagine that you're watching your favorite show when a commercial for Save the Children comes on. There's a photo of an emaciated young girl, and a narrator says, "Only seven years old, Rokia lives a life of poverty and malnourishment in Mali, Africa. She isn't likely to see her 12th birthday. But you can be the difference in Rokia's life. Your contribution to Save the Children, an organization that helps children like Rokia, will ensure that she is well fed, is educated, and receives proper medical care." How persuasive would you find that argument? What about this one: imagine that there was no picture of Rokia, and the narrator said nothing about her life, only that "there are millions of African children who are victims of food shortage and disease." Which of the two announcements would be more likely to compel you to send money to Save the Children?

In a research study, participants who were given Rokia's personal story, along with her photograph, donated more money than those who had only received general information about what Save the Children does in Africa (Small, Loewenstein, & Slovic, 2007). What explains the difference? Simply put, it's easier to feel a sense of personal connection when you hear and see the specific struggles of a single person. Broad appeals and abstract language ("millions of African children need your help") often fail to make people feel the same kind of emotional connection and, as a result, are less persuasive.

Well-reasoned claims get your audience thinking about your message, but you also want them feeling something about your topic. Do you want them to experience compassion? Concern about their future well-being? A sense of urgency about solving a problem? During the *composing* step of your speech preparation, consider the needs of your listeners and the emotions you want them to experience. Then develop **motivational appeals**—explicit statements (examples, testimony, stories) that speak to these needs and feelings. Using motivational appeals in your speech encourages your audience to connect personally with your topic. As discussed earlier in this chapter, such appeals are what Aristotle called **pathos.**

Although motivational appeals enhance your persuasive message, remember to combine them with logical reasons for supporting your position. If your listeners think you're playing too heavily on their emotions, they may feel they're being manipulated, and you could lose credibility.

Connecting to Your Audience's Needs

According to psychologist Abraham Maslow, much of human behavior is motivated by the desire to meet basic life needs, known as the **hierarchy of needs** (Maslow, 1943). If you're extremely hungry or tired, nothing matters to you except food or rest. Maslow suggested that such *physical needs* form the base of the hierarchy. Only after you've met your physical needs do you turn your attention to higher-level concerns—namely, *security needs* (avoiding harm and uncertainty), *social needs* (forming bonds with others), *ego needs* (having respect and admiration from others), and *self-actualization needs* (realizing your full potential).

Maslow's framework is useful for planning motivational appeals for your speech. If you show your listeners how certain needs are in danger or how specific needs could be satisfied if they follow your call to action, you'll likely capture their attention. For example, suppose your presentation is encouraging your classmates to get a flu shot. To provide a motivational appeal, ask them, "Do you really want to get the flu just when you have to study for finals? If not, take a minute to get the shot—it won't take long, and it'll give you peace of mind." This would appeal to their security needs.

FIGURE 17.2

MASLOW'S HIERARCHY OF NEEDS

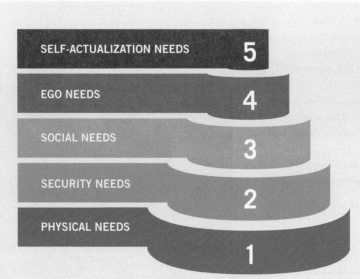

SELF-ACTUALIZATION NEEDS 5

EGO NEEDS 4

SOCIAL NEEDS 3

SECURITY NEEDS 2

PHYSICAL NEEDS 1

Naeblys/Shutterstock

Providing Testimony and Stories

As the study about Save the Children and the story of Rokia shows, listeners will pay more attention to a persuasive speech when you present relevant testimony from a person they can relate to or tell a compelling story about your topic. In composing your speech, consider how you can incorporate *testimony* (the words or experiences of others) or a personal story to make an emotional connection with your audience. In Chapter 14, we discuss how using such stories can help you capture and hold your audience's interest and attention while delivering your speech. A well-chosen story can also evoke powerful feelings in your listeners—such as pride, fear, anger, or hope. What feelings do you experience when reading this excerpt from a speech by NASA astronaut Mae Carol Jemison (2012)?

> When I was growing up in the 1960's on the south side of Chicago, I remember being so excited about space exploration! I wanted to be involved! But, there was always just one type of person in earth orbit or in Mission Control. And they did not look like me. Even though, as a country, we would proudly rally and root for the Space Program, so many of us felt as though we were left out. When I did finally fly in space, the first thing I saw from earth orbit was Chicago, my hometown. I was working on the middeck where there aren't many windows, and as we passed over Chicago, the commander called me up to the flight deck. It was such a significant moment, because ever since I was a little girl I had always assumed I would go into space. Looking out the window of that Space Shuttle, I thought if that little girl growing up in Chicago could see her older self now, she would have a huge grin on her face.

Inspiring personal stories like astronaut Mae Carol Jemison's keep listeners engaged and wanting to know more. They can also inspire hope and motivation in audiences. What kinds of stories do you find the most powerful? How can you work them into your own speeches?

Brendan Hoffman/Getty Images

As that of the first African American woman in space, Dr. Jemison's story usually stirs a sense of optimism and hope in listeners: that they can overcome obstacles and achieve their dreams just like she did.

Using Descriptive Language

In Chapter 5 on verbal communication, we discuss how to use the *cooperative principle* to produce understandable messages. This means using language that is as informative, honest, relevant, and clear as required for a particular situation. When composing your speech, you want to use the cooperative principle to ensure that your audience comprehends what you are saying. In addition, you can make an emotional connection with your listeners by using language that's powerfully descriptive. For example, suppose you attend a presentation in which the speaker says, "There is poverty in the United States." This matter-of-fact statement doesn't make the idea of poverty personal or real to you—or to any of the other listeners. Now look at this passage from a speech delivered by former New York governor Mario Cuomo (1984) on the same topic:

> In this part of the city, there are more poor than ever, more families in trouble, more and more people who need help but can't find it. Even worse: There are elderly people who tremble in the basements of the houses there. And there are people who sleep in the city streets, in the gutter, where the glitter doesn't show. There are ghettos where thousands of young people, without a job or an education, give their lives away to drug dealers every day.

In this speech, Cuomo took an abstract term—poverty—and transformed it into vivid images. Picturing the families, elderly people, homeless, and city youth described in the speech made his audience eager to help eradicate poverty. As you compose your speech, think about how you, too, can use descriptive language to create compelling images in your listeners' minds. The How to Communicate feature on pages 446–447 provides specific steps for developing emotional appeals in your speeches.

Guidelines for Persuasive Speaking

There's no doubt that persuading an audience is challenging. But careful preparation can lead to success. While preparing, composing, and delivering your speech, it is important to be realistic about what you're trying to accomplish and to maintain high ethical standards by giving your audience fair and objective information.

The unique goals of persuasive speeches—reinforcing or changing listeners' attitudes and beliefs, and possibly motivating them to take action—require that you keep in mind specific guidelines when preparing your presentation.

EMOTIONAL APPEALS

Adapting your persuasive speech to your audience's needs and emotions can help you succeed. Learn how to make emotional appeals competently by going to LaunchPad at **bedfordstmartins.com/choicesconnections** and completing the **How to Communicate video scenario** for Chapter 17 to practice your skills.

CONSIDER THIS: Your final speech assignment is a persuasive one, and you decide to encourage your classmates to shop at local businesses. Since your parents own their own bakery, you feel very strongly about this issue. In addition to the arguments you developed from your research on the issue, you want to inspire your audience to feel as passionate about local shopping as you do yourself.

WHAT WOULD YOU DO? The following advice illustrates how you can make emotional appeals without overplaying your examples. As you watch the video, consider how your supporting materials, language style, and nonverbal behaviors influence the success of emotional appeals. Then, test your knowledge of key skills, and create your own responses to the **What if? video prompts**.

(1) LIST THE EMOTIONAL RESPONSES you want your audience to experience. Do this after writing your specific purpose statement. Depending on your topic, these might be negative emotions (anger, guilt, shame) or positive emotions (happiness, hope, pride).

"Shopping locally preserves the special character of a city and instills pride in its residents."

(2) SELECT APPROPRIATE SUPPORTING MATERIALS. When investigating your speech, look for stories, examples, and images that reflect the depth of emotion associated with the topic.

"In their book *Better Together: Restoring the American Community*, Robert Putnam and Lewis Feldstein state . . ."

③ CAREFULLY CHOOSE where to make your emotional appeals. When composing your speech, match your stories, examples, and images to places where they will have impact—such as gaining attention in your introduction or supporting a main point. Be sure to have a mix of evidence and emotional appeals.

"Some local business owners may have been in your neighborhood for years and know a lot about the area. Consider the story of Frank Catalfumo . . ."

④ ENHANCE YOUR DELIVERY. When making your appeals, pay particular attention to using your voice, face, and gestures to express emotion as you tell a story, share an example, or explain an image.

WHAT IF? But what if things don't work out as shown? Using emotional appeals can be tricky, as there is a fine line between too much and too little. Test your ability to adapt your communication by watching the What if? videos and planning a course of action for each situation.

1. When you overly rely on your personal story ("This would never happen in our bakery. After two or three visits, you'll be greeted by name. You become a part of the family"), how can you maintain your credibility with the audience?
2. What can you do if you don't actually feel the emotion you want your audience to feel?

Establish Goodwill with Your Audience

When you show your listeners that you're genuinely concerned about their welfare, you're demonstrating *goodwill*. One way to demonstrate goodwill is to note in your speech's introduction how your topic relates to your audience ("I'm sure we are all concerned about the recent crime spree"). You can also show goodwill through the sincere expression of *empathy*—acknowledging emotions your audience may be experiencing ("I know that most of you are very worried, and some of you are outraged, by the increase in muggings"). When you clearly demonstrate that you care about them, your listeners are more likely to pay attention to your message.

If you are talking about a controversial issue, goodwill will be evident if you stay objective when preparing the speech. During your research phase, investigate all sides of the issue. This will give you a broad perspective on the topic. Not only will this help you compose your speech in a fair and informed way, but you'll also be able to anticipate and respond to questions from audience members. This shows goodwill because you can prove how you've thought about and prepared for your audience's reaction.

Keep Your Specific Purpose Realistic

Remember that you won't be able to change the world with one presentation. This is especially true with speeches of value and policy. People don't easily change their deep-seated values or behaviors just by listening to a single presentation. Keep this in mind as you're developing your specific purpose. You might get better results by using the **foot-in-the-door technique:** asking your audience to agree to a small action in the hope that you'll gain their compliance over time (Burger, 1999). For instance, rather than telling your listeners that they should eliminate all fast food from their diet, you may want to define a more realistic specific purpose: to persuade the audience to make healthy choices when ordering fast food.

Decide How to Present Your Issue

Many persuasive speeches center on controversial issues for which there are multiple valid viewpoints. If you choose such a topic for your speech, decide how you're going to deal with points of view that differ from your own. Will you acknowledge these opposing viewpoints in your speech, or ignore them? Consider two things when answering this question.

First, think about how much time you have for your presentation. If discussing opposing views about your topic means that you'll have to cut relevant arguments in support of your position, don't do it. Second, ask yourself if your audience will already be familiar with the opposing views. If not, introduce a main point that compares and contrasts the opposing views about your topic. When you expose your audience to opposing views, they are more likely to resist future attempts by others to change their minds (Banas & Rains, 2010).

ESTABLISHING GOODWILL

Showing that you care about and can empathize with your audience creates a bond that keeps listeners focused on your message. This is important when delivering a speech in any context—whether amongst peers at work, at a fund-raising event, or in the classroom. How do you express to others that you have their best interest in mind?

(Clockwise from top left) Jon Feingersh/Blend Images/Corbis; KARIM SAHIB/AFP/Getty Images/Newscom; Adam Crowley/Blend Images/Corbis

Maintain High Ethical Standards

As in all communication situations, observe the highest ethical standards in preparing and delivering a persuasive message. How? Give your listeners valid and reliable information based on sound research. If you distort, withhold, or misrepresent the facts, you deprive listeners of the information they need to freely accept or reject your message. That's unethical and therefore incompetent. Instead, you can choose to prepare an ethical speech that achieves your persuasive goals. Jan Withers had nothing to gain personally by getting involved with MADD. She had already suffered the unimaginable loss of a child. Instead, she directed her efforts toward changing the social attitudes of her audiences and the laws related to drinking and driving so that people around her and future generations could benefit. To see how the principles and guidelines of persuasive speeches can come together, look over the transcript for the speech "Becoming a Socially Conscious Consumer" by Jacob Hahn on pages 450–453. A video of the speech is available online at **bedfordstmartins.com/choicesconnections**.

LearningCurve can help you review! Go to **bedfordstmartins.com /choicesconnections**.

Sample Persuasive Speech

BECOMING A SOCIALLY CONSCIOUS CONSUMER •

By Jacob Hahn

Through descriptive language and concerned facial expressions, Jacob conveys the emotional aspect of his speech topic.

It started with a few cracks in the wall. • But then, on April 24, 2013, it became the worst disaster in the history of the garment industry. According to BBC News, on that day the Rana Plaza garment factory in Dhaka, Bangladesh, completely collapsed, leading to the deaths of over 1,100 people.

Along with the bodies, bricks, and garments left in the rubble, questions remained about who was to blame for the tragedy. • Sure, there were the obvious culprits—the plaza owner, the construction company. But, there were other suspects too. What about the companies whose goods were manufactured there? As Emran Hossain and Dave Jamieson pointed out in their May 2, 2013, *Huffington Post* article, garment industry insiders partially blame Western retailers for the tragedy. They claim that it is retailer demand for low-priced labor that creates these poorly constructed and unsafe work factories, which then leads to disasters like the factory collapse.

The thousands of miles that separate us from tragedies like this can make them seem unrelated to our everyday lives. But what if they are not? What if, by purchasing the products these companies make, individuals such as you and me are also somewhat responsible for what happened? •

As we'll see today, there is evidence to support the idea that consumers and companies share a responsibility to ensure safer conditions for factory workers. This is why I encourage all of you to become socially conscious consumers and help convince companies to adopt ethical manufacturing standards. Being a socially conscious consumer means being aware of the issues communities face worldwide and actively trying to correct them. •

To emphasize his point about the goods at the center of this issue, Jacob refers to the common types of clothing made in the factories.

Why would companies do business with factories that allow dangerous working conditions? • It's actually quite simple: Corporations want bigger profit margins. The cheaper the production costs, the more money they make when the product sells. And since consumers show more interest in buying lower-priced

---

• ▶ To watch a video of this speech and see Jacob's preparation and delivery outlines, go to bedfordstmartins.com /choicesconnections.

• Jacob uses a recent event that gained a lot of media attention to immediately engage his audience. He also orally cites the source of his data to help build credibility. How else does Jacob demonstrate credibility throughout the speech?

• Jacob is using the motivated sequence to organize his speech. This section represents the Attention step, in which he gives his audience a reason to listen.

• To make this topic relevant to his listeners, Jacob directly states how it relates to them. This enhances their interest and encourages them to take the central route to processing the speech message.

• Jacob's straightforward thesis statement tells his audience exactly what he wants them to take away from the speech.

• This is where Jacob begins the Need step of the motivated sequence.

products than in thinking about how such items are produced, the pressure is on to provide inexpensive goods. The only way to do this and still make money is to make the goods at the lowest cost possible.

But there is a way to break this cycle of cheap labor and deadly working conditions. You, me, all of us as consumers, must be willing to step up and take an active role in the system. ● We can do this in two ways: First, we can pressure companies to improve working conditions for factory laborers, and second, we can pay fairer prices. ● Some consumer groups are now signaling their willingness to do this, and corporations are responding.

The force behind this new kind of partnership is called "cause-related marketing." According to the *Financial Times*, *cause-related marketing* is when a company and a charity (or a consumer group) tackle a social or an environmental problem and create business value for the company at the same time. ● In March 2012, the global marketing firm Nielsen conducted a worldwide study on consumer responses to cause-related marketing. The poll found that two-thirds of consumers around the world say they prefer to buy products and services from companies that give back to society. Nearly 50 percent of consumers said that they were, and I'm quoting here, "willing to pay more for goods and services from companies that are giving back."

To connect with his audience, Jacob looks to different parts of the room throughout his speech, making sure that each listener feels included.

The fact that large numbers of consumers are concerned enough about fairness to pay more for products is key to solving the problems that surround the ethical manufacture of clothing. Corporations can appeal to this group of socially conscious consumers, as they are called, by addressing concerns about ethical manufacturing. What do corporations gain by meeting these concerns? It allows them to charge more for their products while also raising their profit margins and improving their brand image. This means that as socially conscious consumers, we can set the standards that corporations must meet if they wish to maximize their profit from our purchasing power.

You may find yourself asking, Can this actually work? ● The answer is a simple yes. In both the food and apparel industries, calls for changes in working conditions led to the now widely known nonprofit organization Fair Trade USA. According to its Web site, Fair Trade USA is an organization that seeks "to inspire the rise of the [socially] Conscious Consumer and eliminate exploitation" worldwide. ● If products are stamped with the Fair Trade logo, it means the farmers and workers who created those products were fairly treated and justly compensated through an internationally established price.

● Throughout the speech, Jacob uses personal pronouns to build goodwill with his audience. Using simple and familiar language also makes it easier to listen to his speech.

● As part of the Satisfaction step in the motivated sequence, Jacob explains how he plans to meet the needs discussed earlier.

● Jacob introduces a new term by clearly defining it and orally citing a credible source for the definition.

● This brief question serves as a transitional phrase to the Visualization step of the motivated sequence, which helps the audience see how change is possible.

● Jacob uses analogic reasoning by providing a similar example of how well the fair Trade model has worked in the coffee and chocolate industry.

Fair Trade USA made its mark in the food industry through its relationship to coffee production in third-world nations. Its success helped major companies such as Starbucks and Whole Foods recognize the strength of cause-related marketing: If you appeal to the high ethical standards of socially conscious consumers, they will pay more for your product. ●

- *From his audience analysis, Jacob learned that many of his classmates shop at and respect these two businesses. Thus, this example is very familiar to the listeners.*

Appealing to high ethical standards is often directly related to preventing tragedies like the one that occurred in Bangladesh. After the factory collapsed, the major apparel sellers faced intense criticism over their lax labor practices. In response, these companies are now much more interested in establishing their products as Fair Trade to meet socially conscious consumer standards. For example, as Jason Burke, Saad Hammadi, and Simon Neville report in the May 13, 2013, edition of the *Guardian*, major fashion chains like H&M, Zara, C&A, Tesco, and Primark have pledged to help raise the standards for working conditions. ● According to the article, they will be helping to "finance fire safety and building improvements in the factories they use in Bangladesh."

- *Jacob uses a direct quote here to support his point that things can change. The repetition of the opening example also makes the speech more coherent.*

So, what exactly can you do to help bring about ethical labor practices within the clothing industry? The two steps I encourage you to take are these: become informed, and ask questions about what you're buying—whether it's shoes, a T-shirt, or any other type of apparel. ●

- *The Action step is the most important aspect of the motivated sequence. Jacob provides two clear ways his audience can participate and create actual change. Do you think he is proposing realistic actions for his audience to take? What other actions could he suggest?*

Simple gestures, like counting off the two ways listeners can become socially conscious consumers, can help audience members follow along with the speech structure.

To be informed, go to Web sites such as fairtradeusa.org, thirdworldtraveler.com, and tenthousandvillages.com, which list and sell products from clothing manufacturers who have worked to meet the Fair Trade conditions. This list grows monthly, and by supporting these companies through your purchases, you can become a socially conscious consumer.

Additionally, ask questions of other retailers. Whether you shop online or at local retail stores, ask direct questions before purchasing clothes—for example, Where are your products made? Do you have proof of fair-trade practices? Where can I find this information before I make my purchase? Such questions define the socially conscious consumer, and they ensure that you will not be directly contributing to unsafe and unfair labor practices. ●

- *Jacob appeals to the ego needs of his audience by explaining how they can show concern for others when making purchases.*

Although several factors contributed to the tragedy in Bangladesh, there is one clear way to help prevent future disasters: become a socially conscious consumer. By being informed and asking questions, you, too, can make a difference in the lives of workers around the world.

REFERENCES

BBC News. (2013, May 23). Bangladesh factory collapse probe uncovers abuses. *BBC*. Retrieved from www.bbc.co.uk/news/world-asia-22635409

Burke, J., Hammadi, S., & Neville, S. (2013, May 13). Fashion chains sign accord to help finance safety in Bangladesh factories. *The Guardian*. Retrieved from www.innovations.harvard.edu/news/2798331.html?p=1

Cheng, A. (2013, June 20). *MarketWatch: Fair trade fashion gaining momentum after Bangladesh incidents*. Retrieved from www.fairtradeusa.org/press-room/in_the_news/marketwatch-fair-trade-fashion-gaining-momentum-after-bangladesh-incidents

Coffee. (n.d.). Retrieved from www.fairtradeusa.org/products-partners/coffee

"Fair Trade" helps "free trade" work for the poor. (n.d.). Retrieved from www.fairtradeusa.org/about-fair-trade-usa

Financial Times Lexicon. (n.d.). *Cause-related marketing*. Retrieved from http://lexicon.ft.com/Term?term=cause_related-marketing

Hossain, E., & Jamieson, D. (2013, May 2). Bangladesh garment industry leader says blame for tragedies lies with western retailers. *Huffington Post*. Retrieved from www.huffingtonpost.com/2013/05/02/bangladesh-garment-blame-retailers_n_3204245.html

Moore, B. (2011, November 1). Has campaigning for an ethical fashion industry had any impact? *The Guardian*. Retrieved from www.theguardian.com/environment/green-living-blog/2011/nov/01/campaigning-ethical-fashion-industry

Nielsen. (2012, June 27). *Successful brands care: The case for cause marketing*. Retrieved from www.nielsen.com/us/en/newswire/2012/successful-brands-care-the-case-for-cause-marketing.html

Nielsen. (2012, March 27). *The global, socially conscious consumer*. Retrieved from www.nielsen.com/us/en/newswire/2012/the-global-socially-conscious-consumer.html

SAMPLE SPEECH RESOURCES

There is a lot more to Jacob's speech than the transcript above. See how the whole speech came together by going to **bedfordstmartins.com/choicesconnections** and accessing the **Sample Speech Resources** for Chapter 17. There you will find:

1   Video of Jacob's speech "Becoming a Socially Conscious Consumer"

2   The preparation outline for Jacob's speech

3   The delivery outline for Jacob's speech

4   A rehearsal clip of Jacob practicing his speech

CHAPTER ⑰ REVIEW

CHAPTER RECAP

- There are three types of **persuasive speeches—speeches of fact, value,** and **policy**—which you can use to reinforce or change listeners' attitudes and beliefs, or encourage them to take action.
- Your **ethos,** or **credibility,** is what determines whether an audience views you as trustworthy. Failure to properly display your **character, competence,** and **charisma** can result in an ineffective speech.
- Using the **motivated sequence** will help you form a logical structure to your persuasive argument, but if you lack sound **reasoning,** listeners are less likely to believe your claims.
- **Motivational appeals** connect with an audience's needs and feelings. Also known as **pathos,** this is how you can get an audience emotionally involved with your topic.
- Considering the risk of **coercion,** it is especially important to maintain high ethical standards in persuasive speeches and to establish *goodwill* with your audience.

LAUNCHPAD

LaunchPad for *Choices & Connections* offers unique video scenarios and encourages self-assessment through adaptive quizzing. Go to **bedfordstmartins.com /choicesconnections** to get access.

 LearningCurve adaptive quizzes

 How to Communicate video scenarios

 Video clips that illustrate key concepts

 Sample speech resources

KEY TERMS

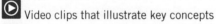

1 For persuasive presentations, a speech of _____ argues for a specific action—for example, persuading your audience to exercise at least three hours a week.

a. fact
b. policy
c. value
d. ethics

2 According to the elaboration likelihood model, listeners are more likely to take a _____ to processing your message if they already understand the content.

a. peripheral route
b. connected route
c. central route
d. direct route

3 When establishing ethos with an audience, creating a sense of immediacy can help with your _____.

a. credibility
b. charisma
c. competence
d. closeness

4 Which of the following fallacies occurs if you argue that you deserve a Friday night off because a coworker also has it off?

a. Hasty generalization
b. Straw person claim
c. Ad hominem argument
d. Bandwagon appeal

5 Before convincing your audience to regularly volunteer at a local food bank, you may start by asking them to make a small donation or visit the Web site to learn more about the operation. This is known as _____.

a. the foot-in-the door technique
b. a motivational appeal
c. the hierarchy of needs
d. displaying goodwill

ACTIVITIES

1 Identifying Rhetorical Proof

Find a persuasive speech online. This could be from a politician, a TED talk (www.ted.com), a commencement address, or even one of your own classmates. While listening to the speech, note effective uses of *ethos*, *logos*, and *pathos*, or times when they could have been used more effectively. Write a brief paper explaining the speech's thesis, your findings, and whether you found the speech persuasive.

2 As Seen on TV

Working in groups, use the motivated sequence on pages 436–437 to plan a two- to three-minute infomercial selling an imaginary service to your classmates. Base the infomercial on a service that college students might actually use (dating Web site, tutoring business, personal trainer, dog-sitting service). After preparing and rehearsing the infomercial, perform it in front of your class, or make a video and post it to the class Web site. Be prepared to explain how you incorporated each step in the motivated sequence.

Appendix
Interviewing

"What was the best mistake you made on the job? Why was it the best?"[1]

"On a scale of 1–10, how weird are you?"

If you ever interview for a job with Zappos—the online shoe, clothing, and accessories company—brace yourself for questions like these. Known for a unique culture that encourages workers to "create fun and a little weirdness," Zappos seeks to hire employees who embody the company's core values ("Zappos," n.d.). These include delivering WOW through service, embracing and driving change, and being passionate and determined ("Zappos," n.d.).

To identify prospective employees who personify these values, Zappos hiring teams conduct two types of interviews. In the initial interview—usually on the phone or at a job fair—the teams evaluate candidates' job experience and skills, asking about work history, job-relevant abilities, and salary requirements. They also ask standard interview questions, such as, "What is your greatest strength?" and "Would you say you're more or less creative than the average person? Can you give me an example?"

People who make a good impression during the first interview are invited to Zappos's headquarters in Henderson, Nevada, for a second type of interview. At this point, the hiring team is interested in whether a candidate is a good fit for Zappos's company culture. They ask questions that explore the person's values and self-awareness, such as, "What would you say is the biggest misperception that people have of you?" (Bryant, 2010). Zappos CEO Tony Hsieh explains that such questions give interviewers a sense of how self-aware candidates are and of their honesty levels (Bryant, 2010).

But as with any interview, there's more to a Zappos meeting than just answering questions. The hiring team also pays attention to how candidates treat others and handle unexpected events, like meeting an employee who is wearing pajamas or bunny ears. That's typical at Zappos, where employees are known to be

Brad Swonetz/Redux Pictures

---

[1]This quote and subsequent material for this opening story based on Hsieh (2010).

quirky. The team wants to know that new hires can adapt to such situations and that they don't take themselves too seriously (Gurchiek, 2011). Preparing for either interview type can be tricky, especially since you never know what you'll be asked or whom you will run into. But when interviews are well planned and have clear goals—like the ones at Zappos—they can be very useful and even surprisingly fun for both interviewers and interviewees.

✓ **LearningCurve** can
help you review! Go to
**bedfordstmartins.com
/choicesconnections**.

Whether it's to get a job with Zappos or a job with any other company, developing competent interviewing skills will help you achieve your professional goals. But interviews aren't just for finding employment; you will use these skills in other communication situations—for example, interviewing someone as research for a presentation, as a way to explore a potential career path, or even to correspond with the public if you work in fields such as journalism or public relations. In this appendix, you'll learn:

- The different types of interviews
- Ways to plan interview topics and interview questions
- How to communicate competently during interviews
- Steps for preparing for and managing information and employment selection interviews
- Strategies for writing a résumé and cover letter

What Is Interviewing?

> An interview is like a good conversation, filled with thoughtful questions and interesting answers. But an interview also has a structure and a defined purpose. Its success often depends on how carefully you plan it, including anticipating the topics that will be covered and the questions that will be asked.

Think about different situations in which you ask questions to get information from others. For example, to prepare a speech, you chat with an expert as part of your research on the topic. To write an article for the school paper, you meet with a school administrator. To make a hiring decision, you talk with a number of job applicants. In each of these situations, you are thoughtfully questioning, or interviewing, others. **Interviewing** is a planned and structured conversation between two or more persons that uses questions and answers to meet a specific purpose.

An interview is planned and structured because the participants have clearly defined roles and responsibilities. The **interviewer** determines the interview purpose, plans the questions, and manages the flow of the conversation. The success of an interview can depend on how well an interviewer prepares in advance. For example, before interviewing a school administrator for an article you're writing, you think about the topics you want to discuss and create a list of relevant questions to ask.

The **interviewee** is the person answering the questions. However, this is not a passive activity. Interviewees must actively participate in the interview, too. If the school administrator responds to your questions with one-word answers or shows little interest in being interviewed, you won't get the information you need for the article you're writing.

Many interviews are dyadic—that is, they involve two people. But some take place in small groups. For example, during a job interview, four team

DIFFERENT TYPES OF INTERVIEWS

Interviews are not limited to employment prospects. You may interview a grandparent to learn about your family history, collect information from witnesses, or talk to participants at a rally. All of these situations require you to ask questions in a succinct and thoughtful manner. When you have interviewed others, how did you plan for the interview purpose and protocol?

(Clockwise from top left) Konstantin Sutyagin/ShutterStock; ZUMA Press, Inc./Alamy; Richard Lord/The Image Works

members might ask questions to one interviewee. Or, a journalist may conduct a small group interview—meeting with multiple interviewees at the same time. Interviews can also occur in face-to-face settings or through mediated communication (such as by telephone or videoconferencing).

Types of Interviews

Although there are a large variety of ways that interviews occur in public, personal, and professional settings, the two types you are most likely to encounter are information interviews and employment interviews.

Information interviews generate knowledge or understanding about a particular topic. For instance, marketing consultants use *focus groups* to interview customers about their experiences using a product or a service. Doctors ask their patients questions to learn about their medical histories. Information interviews can also help you prepare a speech. Interviewing other people about your topic helps you gather testimony and examples to use in your speech.

Employment interviews manage an organization's personnel. There are three kinds of employment interviews. **Selection interviews** determine whether applicants have the education, experience, and proper attitude required for a job. Once a person is hired, employers use **performance or appraisal interviews** to evaluate his or her work and to set new goals. This kind of interview typically occurs once a year. Organizations use **exit interviews** to identify why an employee is leaving a job, and use the resulting insights to improve management practices.

Because these two types of interviews are used for different reasons, they require interviewers to approach them in different ways. In this appendix, you'll learn skills for communicating competently during both types of interviews. But the first step for both types is the same: preparation.

Preparing for an Interview

Preparing for an interview entails a number of steps, including defining the purpose of the interview, developing an interview protocol, and determining what questions to ask.

Defining Your Purpose. To prepare for an interview you'll be conducting, start by defining your purpose. This helps you identify what topics to cover. Imagine that you're preparing a persuasive speech about your school's spring break volunteer program. You might arrange to interview the dean of students to find out about volunteer opportunities, program requirements, and the benefits of doing community service. If you're interviewing job applicants, your purpose is to find the best candidate by exploring such topics as each applicant's work history and relevant experience (see Table A.1). Having a clear purpose for the interview gives focus and structure to the topics that will be discussed.

If you're going to be interviewed, you should also take time beforehand to consider what topics might be covered. That way, you can be prepared to answer questions. For instance, if you're going to be interviewed for a job, you'll want to be ready to talk about how you've successfully applied your skills in previous work settings.

Developing an Interview Protocol. When preparing to conduct an interview, you should also develop an **interview protocol**—a list of questions, written in a logical order, that guide the interview. Like a preparation outline for a speech, preparing an interview protocol in advance will show whether you are including all the topics you need and arranging them in a way that makes sense. For example, if you are interviewing a job candidate, you may want to start with general questions ("Tell me about your work history") before moving to more specific questions ("What project did you find most challenging?").

If you plan on asking highly specific or difficult questions, think about when to bring those up. Asking them too early in an interview could make

POSSIBLE INTERVIEW TOPICS

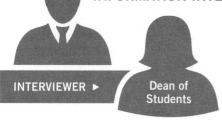

INFORMATION INTERVIEW

Purpose: To gather information for a speech about the spring break volunteer program

Possible Topics:
Types of agencies
Finding the right opportunity
How to apply
Benefits of participating
Success stories

INTERVIEWER ▶ Dean of Students

EMPLOYMENT SELECTION INTERVIEW

Purpose: To find the best candidate to join our project team

Possible Topics:
Interest in position
Work history and academic background
Technical problem-solving skills
Communication and leadership skills
Ability to work in teams and under pressure

INTERVIEWER ▶ Applicant

VoodooDot/Shutterstock

the interviewee uncomfortable or confused. Depending on the type of interview, that could make it difficult to get the information you need. It's usually easier to start with less personal, or "safe," questions ("What did you like most about your last job?"), and then move on to questions about emotional or difficult topics ("What was your biggest mistake?").

Determining Questions to Ask. Questions are the heart of any interview. But not all questions are the same. You can use questions to introduce a new topic, get clarification, or ask for additional details. Even the way you phrase a question influences the answers you get. So when you're developing your interview protocol, consider the different types of questions you can ask.

You can introduce topics or new areas within a topic by using **primary questions.** These questions guide the conversation and are written into the interview protocol. For example, "Dr. Ghent, let's talk about volunteer service and leadership. How does volunteering help students develop their leadership skills?"

You can follow up on answers given by an interviewee with **secondary questions.** These questions aren't usually written into the interview protocol; instead, they evolve out of the conversation. A secondary question can help you clarify vague answers ("When you say 'students increase their social intelligence,' what do you mean?") or probe further into a response ("Tell me more about your summer work as a lifeguard"). Often a secondary question is nothing more than a brief comment to encourage the interviewee to continue answering the question ("Go on" or "Then what happened?"). To use secondary questions successfully, use *active listening skills* to ensure you understand the interviewee's answers. If you're preoccupied or distracted, you'll miss opportunities to clarify or probe answers further.

How you phrase a question can also affect the way interviewees answer. **Open questions** give interviewees a lot of freedom in formulating their responses. For example, "How do students benefit by volunteering during their spring break?" could be answered in any number of ways. On the other hand, **closed questions** usually require only a yes or no response, which limits the range of possible answers. For instance, "Can you operate a forklift?" Use open questions when you want to generate more detailed responses. Closed questions help you move quickly through topics during the interview and swiftly determine whether you've gathered critical information. To illustrate, if someone applying for a job as a forklift operator can't operate the equipment, you'd want to know that immediately.

To find out what the interviewee really thinks or feels about a topic, you can use **neutral questions** ("What do you think of the new bonus policy?"). **Leading questions** point the respondent to an answer you prefer ("Don't you think the new bonus policy is a great idea?"). For that reason, leading questions are generally less useful for finding out what an interviewee really thinks. Table A.2 provides examples of neutral and leading questions.

Essential Communication Skills for Interviewing

> Regardless of your role—interviewer or interviewee—you create a relationship every time you take part in an interview. Just like any interpersonal interaction you partake in, the success of the interview depends on how well you communicate with your partner.

Although information and employment interviews have different purposes, you need the same essential communication skills to successfully manage either type. These include being an active listener; building rapport and demonstrating cooperation; and, if required, using mediated communication technologies competently.

Being an Active Listener

A successful interview requires both the interviewer and the interviewee to carefully listen to what is being said. As Chapter 7 explains, *listening* involves

TABLE A.2

NEUTRAL AND LEADING QUESTIONS

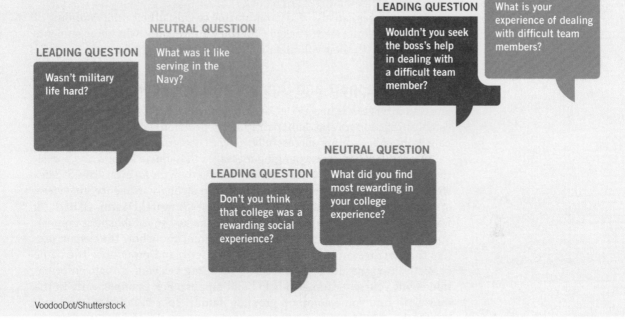

LEADING QUESTION

Wasn't military life hard?

NEUTRAL QUESTION

What was it like serving in the Navy?

LEADING QUESTION

Wouldn't you seek the boss's help in dealing with a difficult team member?

NEUTRAL QUESTION

What is your experience of dealing with difficult team members?

LEADING QUESTION

Don't you think that college was a rewarding social experience?

NEUTRAL QUESTION

What did you find most rewarding in your college experience?

VoodooDot/Shutterstock

hearing, understanding, interpreting, evaluating, remembering, and responding to others' communication. In addition, during interviews, you can show that you are mentally and physically ready to listen by practicing **attending skills.** You can demonstrate these skills in several ways.

First, choose a quiet location with few distractions, such as an office or another room that allows you some privacy during the interview. This is true whether you are conducting the interview in person, on the phone, or via web conference. Prevent disruptions by silencing your phone and not multitasking during the interview. Second, use nonverbal communication to promote *immediacy*, or a sense of closeness and involvement between you and your interview partner. For instance, make eye contact, face the other person, smile, use an engaged vocal tone, and occasionally lean toward him or her.

Your verbal responses can also confirm that you are listening. One way to do this is by **paraphrasing**—restating in your own words what you think the person said. Paraphrasing is most helpful when the interviewee has given a long and detailed answer, because it helps you check your understanding of the response. When you paraphrase, you give the other person a chance to correct any misunderstandings and to provide additional details if needed. Here's an example:

> *Interviewer:* "So you believe the project was a success because the weekly status meetings held everyone accountable; is that right?"

Interviewee: "Yes, the status meetings were one reason, but I also believe it was successful because . . ."

Interviewees can also use paraphrasing to check their understanding of something the interviewer asked ("So you want to know why some students aren't happy with their volunteer experience; is that right?").

Building Rapport and Demonstrating Cooperation

Since an interview is like a relationship, using interpersonal skills—such as establishing rapport and demonstrating cooperation—can help you participate in interviews more successfully.

Rapport building, or exchanging messages that create a bond and a positive first impression, helps you quickly set the tone for an interview. Studies show that even your opening handshake can strongly influence interviewers' impression of you during job interviews (Stewart, Dustin, Barrick, & Darnold, 2008). A friendly, upbeat greeting is key to establishing rapport. You'll also want to use the other person's name, know how the person prefers to be addressed (Dr. Franklin, Ms. Watson), and pronounce the name correctly. Appropriate *self-disclosure*—revealing relevant private information about yourself—can also help build rapport. For example, early in the interview, find some common ground—family, sports, hobbies—and talk briefly about it. But keep these topics noncontroversial and appropriate.

In addition to building rapport, demonstrate cooperation. As Chapter 5 explains, applying Grice's *cooperative principle* means you make messages understandable by being informative, honest, relevant, and clear. Table A.3 explains how to use this principle during interviews.

Using Mediated Communication during Interviews

Many businesses use mediated communication technologies—such as videoconferencing or Skype—to conduct employment selection interviews. These technologies can help save time and travel costs, but they can also present special challenges for interview participants. To ensure that your interview achieves its purpose, consider how to best use these technologies.

There are two forms of video interviews. *Synchronous video interviews* are done in real time, using Skype or other videoconferencing systems. In *asynchronous video interviews*, applicants record answers to questions provided to them in advance. The recorded video is then uploaded to a secure Web site, where employers can quickly view a number of applicants and determine whom to interview further. Organizations commonly use this tactic to reduce the cost and time of handling first-round interviews (Kiger, 2010).

With synchronous and asynchronous video interviews, following certain steps will help you competently conduct or participate in the conversation. First, make sure you know how to use whatever equipment is involved. Take time to learn how the camera operates and how to use the related videoconferencing software. Second, test the equipment in the actual setting

USING GRICE'S COOPERATIVE PRINCIPLE IN AN INTERVIEW

Cooperative Principle	BE INFORMATIVE	BE HONEST	BE RELEVANT	BE CLEAR
Interviewer	Prepare an interview protocol. Clearly introduce yourself and identify the interview purpose.	Ask secondary questions to clarify areas of confusion. Avoid asking leading questions.	Keep questions focused on the interview purpose.	Use appropriate and understandable language. Define jargon or specialized terms that the interviewee may not know.
Interviewee	Answer questions completely. Give specific examples to illustrate your points.	Provide truthful responses. Don't exaggerate or make false statements.	Give the necessary answers to questions. Avoid long-winded responses.	Use specific language in responding. Avoid vague or ambiguous words.

sellingpix/Shutterstock

where you'll be conducting or recording the interview. Confirm that you have sufficient lighting and that the background is free of any visual or sound distractions. Third, practice your video delivery. Focus the camera to a medium close-up shot, so that you capture your upper torso and head. Dress appropriately, and remember to maintain eye contact with the camera and vary your vocal expressiveness. In addition, minimize distracting gestures and adopt appropriate facial expressions. Finally, spend time rehearsing and recording yourself on video. Use the resulting feedback to adjust your delivery or appearance to create a good impression.

Information Interviewing

You may conduct information interviews for a variety of reasons: talking to an expert as research for a speech, or reaching out to a local nonprofit as part of a service-learning project. Or you might meet with someone who works at a company you want to learn more about. Careful preparation will help you get the most from these experiences.

When asked about her life, Kay Wang didn't want to share many details.[2] But as her son and granddaughter prodded her, she told tales of her adventures.

---

[2]Information about Kay Wang from http://storycorps.org/animation/no-more-questions.

DOUBLE TAKE

PROPER (VS) IMPROPER VIDEO INTERVIEWS

When you are interviewing via online videos, your dress, posture, facial expressions, and even the room in the background can all greatly impact the perceptions others have of you. Consider how seemingly "small" things make a big difference in the video interviews depicted below.

Bad posture

Improper dress

Unstable surface for computer

Warm facial expression

Proper dress

Stable surface for computer

Elena Yakusheva/Shutterstock

MJTH/Shutterstock

Born and raised in China, she admits to being a disobedient child who often lied to cut class and spend time with her boyfriends. After moving to the United States, her escapades continued. She worked as a detective for Bloomingdale's department store, catching shoplifters—including an unnamed famous designer. She was also a nurse and met her husband at a hospital where he was a patient.

How do we know all this about Kay? Her family took her to a StoryCorps booth, where they could interview her and preserve the stories she told. StoryCorps is a nonprofit organization with permanent and mobile recording booths throughout the United States (http://storycorps.org). Within these booths, people tell the ordinary and extraordinary stories of their lives. As one of the largest oral history projects in the United States, StoryCorps has a simple motto: "Ask great questions. Share great stories."

StoryCorps encourages friends, family members, coworkers, and romantic partners to interview each other. The goal of these conversations is to share and record the stories that participants consider important. To help them do that, StoryCorps provides participants with a trained facilitator who offers guidance on the types of questions to ask. Participants also receive instruction on how to listen, show respect to their interview partner, and take notes. Completed interviews are archived at the American Folklife Center at the Library of Congress. Some are even featured on NPR's *Morning Edition* or turned into animated shorts for the StoryCorps Web site.

Whether you're conducting an interview for StoryCorps or for your own interests, you will get the most out of an information interview if you carefully prepare for and manage it, like Kay Wang's family did.

Preparing for an Information Interview

Information interviews are conducted to gain knowledge or understanding about a particular topic. When you decide that you need to conduct an information interview—whether as part of your job hunt, for a speech, or to even explore certain interests—you can't just wing it. To prepare, start by conducting background research, identifying your purpose, and developing your interview protocol. Then you can actually set up the interview.

Conduct Background Research. Deciding whom you want to interview isn't always as easy as it sounds. The key is to select someone who has the relevant experience and knowledge to provide the information you need. For example, suppose your university recently introduced new mechanisms to enhance campus security. This includes a new text-message and e-mail system for broadcasting all-campus alerts in the event of threats. You are preparing an informative speech to describe how the alert system works. At first, you consider interviewing a campus police officer, since the campus police normally enforce security protocols. However, the head of the university's information technology (IT) department might be an even better

storycorps.org

Through an animated version of Kay Wang's interview that StoryCorps created, you can hear the stories and memories that Kay shared with her son and granddaughter. Both the audio and animated copies of the interview provide her family with a lasting record of her life and allow the rest of us a glimpse at her fiesty spirit. You can watch the animation of Kay's interview online at http://storycorps.org/animation/no-more-questions.

source of information, since she selected the new system and will be in charge of implementing, operating, and maintaining it.

Identify Your Purpose. After conducting background research and selecting an individual to interview, it's time to identify your purpose: Why do you want to interview this particular person? What information are you hoping to gain? Framing your purpose in a focused rather than vague way will help you ask more specific questions, which will be more likely to get you the information you need. Consider the differences between the following information interview purposes:

- Vague: "I want to find out about the new campus-alert system."
- Focused: "I want to determine why the new system is better than the old one; how students and faculty can sign up for alerts; and how alerts are communicated to outside groups, such as students' parents and the media."

Imagine meeting with the head of the IT department and saying, "So, what can you tell me about the new campus-alert system?" She may respond with a lot of interesting information, and some of it may be just what you need. But some of it may *not* be what you need because you've asked a vague question. By having a focused purpose, you can ask specific questions, such as, "How is the new system better than the one we've been using?" which more likely gets you the information needed to fulfill your purpose.

Prepare Your Interview Protocol. As discussed earlier, an interview protocol is a written plan for the questions you will ask during the interview. Without a protocol, you could end up wasting your own and the interviewee's time.

Develop a protocol by coming up with a set of primary questions to introduce major topics and related areas. Write *open questions* that will lead to insightful and quality information ("What are the costs and advantages of the new system?"). Make limited use of *closed questions* ("Do you think the new system is better?").

Request the Interview. Contact the person to request a meeting. Usually, e-mail is the best way to do this, but you can also follow up with a phone call if necessary. Explain your purpose and how much time you will need to conduct the interview. Decide on a mutually agreeable date and time to meet, one that's convenient for the interviewee. Don't forget to confirm details, such as location (if meeting in person), telephone number (if phone based), or screen name and application (if Web based). Most important, on the day of the interview, arrive/log in 5–10 minutes early, have your interview protocol in hand, and stick to the agreed-upon time frame.

Managing an Information Interview

Once you've been granted an information interview, you can manage it competently by building rapport, being engaged, and ending on a productive note.

Build Rapport. Open the interview by building rapport. Unless you're already well acquainted with the person, it's natural to be nervous. Chatting informally at first will help both of you feel more comfortable. During this time, provide the person with background about the interview purpose. If you want to video- or audio-record the session, ask for permission to do so.

Be Engaged. Apply *active listening skills* by asking follow-up questions to clarify the person's meaning or to get more information. Paraphrase lengthy answers to ensure that you understand what the interviewee has said. Take accurate notes, and capture any statement that you may later want to quote as part of a speech or a written document.

End on a Productive Note. The process of ending an interview is known as **leave-taking.** Much like the conclusion to a speech, leave-taking indicates that the interview is about to finish. You can signal this through your final question, such as, "Is there anything I didn't ask about that you think I should know?" Or make a summary statement, such as, "I very much appreciate your help. I now understand how the new system works." Making such summarizing questions and statements helps the person identify whether any important information has been left out, or whether some details need correcting. You can also use leave-taking to ask permission to get back in touch with any additional questions that might come up ("If I need to follow up, can I contact you at this number?"). Be sure to thank the person for his or her time, and follow up with a thank-you note.

Employment Selection Interviewing

> Your best chance of getting the job of your dreams is to make an excellent impression during the employment selection interview. To do that, you'll need to prepare carefully for the interview and then skillfully manage the communication that unfolds during the interview.

It seems unimaginable, but it happens: in the middle of an interview, a job candidate responds to a text message. Equally shocking: a job applicant tells the interviewer that he doesn't like to get up early. Another candidate calls in sick to her current employer during the interview, faking an illness. In a survey of more than 2,600 hiring managers, these are just a few of the mistakes applicants make while interviewing for a job (Chulik, 2013). While these missteps may be funny to read about, they probably cost the applicants the jobs.

How you present yourself and communicate during a job interview can make or break your chances of getting hired. Following are some strategies for competently preparing for and managing an employment selection interview.

Preparing for an Employment Selection Interview

Whether you are looking for your first job or internship, seeking a promotion, applying to a different company, or considering changing careers, you will need to prepare for employment selection interviews. This includes researching potential employers, developing your résumé and cover letter, reviewing your social media image, and planning your own questions for the interviewer. To learn even more about how to prepare for a job interview, check out sites like monster.com or careerbuilder.com, or visit your school's career services department.

Research Potential Employers. Learn as much as you can about the company that is interviewing you. Recruiters and hiring managers favor applicants who know something about the organization. This includes understanding what the enterprise does (what it produces and what industry it's in) and having a sense of how the job you're interviewing for fits into the company as a whole. Armed with this knowledge, you can speak more intelligently about how your experience and skills are a good fit for the job (Joyce, 2008).

If you saw the job listing in an advertisement or on the company's Web site, the posting probably included a job description. If the description is vague, try to get more details—for example, by calling the company's human resources department. The more you understand the nature of the job, the better sense you'll have of whether you're a good fit for the position. The job description will also help you write a compelling cover letter and adapt your résumé (see pp. A-14 to A-18).

By researching the company, you can also prepare answers to questions that may come up during an interview. For example, the interviewer will likely ask you why you're interested in the job. "I just need a job" is not an acceptable answer; you need to explain why you are a good fit for *that* job. (See Table A.4 for additional interview questions you should be ready to answer.) Also, think about what job-specific questions might come up during the interview. For instance, if you're interviewing for a programming position, the interviewer might ask you to describe your experience troubleshooting coding problems. Reviewing the job description will help you anticipate these questions and prepare responses.

Develop Your Résumé and Cover Letter. When you apply for a job, you typically submit a résumé. A **résumé** is a written summary of your education, work experience, and skills. Most employers require one of two types of résumés. The first type is the **chronological résumé**, which details the history of your education and work experience, starting with the most recent. The second type is the **functional résumé,** which focuses on how your skills and experiences relate to the specific job you're applying for. This information is not in chronological order. See Figures A.1 and A.2 for samples of a chronological and a functional résumé. These samples show the basic categories and types of information résumés often include. However, there are a lot of varying opinions on what detailed content should be covered. Some

(Continued on page A-18)

COMMONLY ASKED INTERVIEW QUESTIONS

- What behaviors or traits in coworkers do you find most difficult? How do you handle these?
- Give an example of a conflict you had with a coworker or boss. How did you handle it? What was the result?
- What educational and professional accomplishments do you hope to achieve in the next five years?

- What strengths and skills would you bring to this company?
- Describe a situation when you've demonstrated competent leadership.
- Tell me about a time when something did not turn out well. What happened? Why do you think it happened? What did you learn from it?
- Why do you want to work for us?

- What makes you a good candidate for this job?
- What have you done to improve your knowledge and/or skills in the past year?
- What should I know about you that I cannot learn from reading your résumé?
- Provide an example of your work on a team. What was your role? What would others on the team say about your contribution?

- What would your coworkers say about what it's like to work with you?
- What would you describe as your biggest educational or work mistake? What happened? What did you learn from it?
- How do you manage stress?
- What is your greatest weakness?
- What has been your proudest accomplishment?

CHRONOLOGICAL RÉSUMÉ

Jessica Garcia

124 Central Ave., Elgin, TX   (512) 555-4621   JessieMGarcia@email.com

Objective   *To use my digital media experience and skills to support the digital marketing goals of a business organization.*

Experience   *Silver Onion Media,* Austin, TX   (January 2015–Present)
Social Media Intern

- Maintain daily updates to company's Facebook and Twitter accounts to help build brand awareness and customer loyalty.
- Create surveys and polls to gauge customer interest in relevant trends and topics. Report results to company's Marketing Director.

Bootstrap Youth Mentoring Project, Austin, TX   (November 2013–Present)
Volunteer, Web Content Consultant

- Write articles and shoot video about program events.

The Accent, Austin TX   (September 2011–May 2013)
Reporter (Student Newspaper at Austin Community College)

- Wrote weekly articles on campus life, conducted interviews with faculty, staff, and students.
- Managed social events calendar in print edition and online version.
- Trained new reporters in the publication process.

Skills & Interests   Maintain a personal blog documenting my travels and volunteer work: jessiesmarvels.blogspot.com; fluent in English and Spanish; proficient with Microsoft Office, Adobe Dreamweaver, InDesign, social media platforms

Education   University of Texas, Austin, Bachelor of Arts, Anticipated May 2015
Anticipated Summa Cum Laude honors
Major: Communication
Austin Community College, Associate Degree, 2013

References supplied upon request

FUNCTIONAL RÉSUMÉ

Jessica Garcia

124 Central Ave., Elgin, TX   (512) 555-4621   JessieMGarcia@email.com

Summary of Skills

Social Media Development

- Ability to apply communication theory in developing Facebook and Twitter presence for increasing brand awareness and customer loyalty.
- Maintain personal travel blog documenting travels and charitable work (jessiesmarvels.blogspot.com).

Digital Media and Survey Skills

- Proficient with Adobe Photoshop, Dreamweaver, InDesign, Zoomerang, and Survey Monkey. Portfolio of team-based web design projects available.
- Ability to write survey questions gauging customer interest in relevant trends.
- Knowledge of Microsoft Excel for conducting descriptive data analysis.

Journalism and Creative Writing Skills

- Competent writer for both print and online publication. Recognized for feature story writing. Trained student reporters for community college newspaper.

Communication and Team Skills

- Collaborate with others in developing web content for school and internships.
- Leader of service learning project for nonprofit public relations course.
- Fluent in English and Spanish.

Summary of Work Experience

Silver Onion Media, Austin, TX   (January 2015–Present)
- Social Media Intern

Bootstrap Youth Mentoring Project, Austin, TX   (November 2013–Present)
- Volunteer, Web Content Consultant

The Accent, Austin TX   (September 2011–May 2013)
- Reporter (Student Newspaper at Austin Community College)

Education

University of Texas, Austin, Bachelor of Arts, Anticipated May 2015
Anticipated Summa Cum Laude honors
Major: Communication
Austin Community College, Associate Degree, 2013

References supplied upon request

recruiters say an objective statement is no longer necessary. Some advocate for disclosing a high GPA, while others say never to include one at all. When putting together your own résumés, research what is the acceptable standard in the industry to which you are applying.

Which type of résumé is more appropriate? We recommend preparing both types. Then you can decide which one to submit depending on the job application requirements and your work history. For example, for employers that ask for a detailed work history, a chronological résumé is better. If you have a limited work history, a functional résumé may be the right choice because it helps you emphasize job-relevant skills you've gained through your academic experience.

Many employers now expect you to submit your résumé electronically, either as an e-mail attachment (PDF) or uploaded to a Web site. This enables companies to scan résumés into a database and conduct keyword searches to quickly identify applicants with desirable experiences and skills. For this reason, you will want to develop a searchable résumé. Finally, some employers will allow or require you to submit other application materials, such as work samples, videos, or a portfolio of related classwork. In such cases, guidelines on formats, sizes, and submissions are likely to be provided. All these materials should be as carefully composed as any traditional résumé.

There are many good resources online that can help you create résumés, including monster.com and jobsearch.about.com. You can also seek support at your college's career services department. Use these sources as well as your own research to carefully craft your application materials.

Résumés are often accompanied by a **cover letter,** which introduces you and highlights your qualifications for the job in question. Think of the cover letter as a persuasive message that expresses how your work experience and skills meet the employer's needs. Use vivid and descriptive language to direct the reader to key areas of your résumé that showcase your qualifications. Write different cover letters for each job you apply for, tailoring each letter to the position's specific needs. Conclude your cover letter by requesting an interview.

Remember that your résumé and cover letter are the first impression an employer will get of you as a potential employee. Make sure these documents truly convey your qualifications for the job. Ensure that they look good, too. Employers will spend just a few minutes reviewing them, so create professional-looking documents with clean, crisp formats. Use a readable font, such as Arial or Helvetica, and use active rather than passive voice to maintain readers' interest. Proofread carefully for proper spelling and grammar—careless mistakes will quickly place you in the rejection pile. Most important, keep both documents brief; each should be no more than one page long.

Review Your Social Media Image. If potential employers saw your Facebook profile, Twitter feed, or Tumblr account, what impressions would they form about you? Would they conclude that you're a serious, hardworking type, or that you mostly play paintball and hang out at the beach?

COVER LETTER

McKinney's Restaurant Group
Attn: Ms. Marianne Burton, Director of Marketing
2727 E. Rose Blvd., Suite 24B
Fort Worth, TX 76102

Dear Ms. Burton:

In response to your current posting on monster.com, I am writing to apply for the position of digital marketing specialist with McKinney's Restaurant Group. I will be graduating this May from the University of Texas at Austin with a degree in Communication. Given the outstanding reputation of your restaurants in the Dallas-Forth Worth area, I would be delighted to contribute my digital media skills to your team of marketing professionals.

Your job posting expressed a desire to develop a greater social media presence with young adults and families. I believe that I can help you meet this objective. Currently as a social media intern for Silver Onion Media, I maintain its Facebook and Twitter accounts. Since starting in January, I have increased Facebook followings by 15% and Twitter followings by 22%. By using web analytics, I am identifying potential new audiences and opportunities to increase the online visibility of Silver Onion. Let me also add that I am fluent in Spanish, which can support social media outreach to your Spanish-speaking customers in the Dallas-Forth Worth area.

Additionally, my writing experience is particularly notable. While attending Austin Community College, I was a reporter for the student newspaper. Although I started by writing weekly articles, I increasingly gained responsibility for managing the social events calendar and training other student reporters. Among my proudest achievements is receiving the Texas Community College Journalism Association's 2013 Best Feature Story award for my article "Homeless Scholar: The Real Education of Maya Rose."

Finally, your posting also states a desire for a candidate who can collaborate with others in developing web content. I am proficient with Adobe Photoshop, Dreamweaver, and InDesign. In my courses and internship, I regularly work with others to develop content and solve difficult design challenges. I would be happy to share with you my portfolio of web content created from these experiences.

Enclosed is my résumé, including my contact address and phone number. I look forward to an opportunity to interview with you soon.

Respectfully,

Jessica Garcia

MAKING COMMUNICATION CHOICES

WELL . . . TO BE TOTALLY HONEST WITH YOU

1 CONSIDER THE DILEMMA

It's your chance for a dream job after you graduate in May. As a sports marketing major, you know how hard it is to land a job with a professional team. Most graduates begin their careers with college programs, taking years to advance to the big leagues. Sitting in the reception lounge of the team's Oklahoma City headquarters, you count yourself lucky to have an interview for an entry-level position in special events promotions.

As you wait, you mentally rehearse answers to possible interview questions: What makes you a good candidate for this position? Give an example of a time you had difficulty working on a team project. How did you handle it?

Victoria Mines, special events coordinator, soon approaches, greets you enthusiastically, and invites you into her office. As you make small talk, you feel an immediate connection with her, especially when you learn that you both graduated from the same

university. You talk about professors you had in common and the football team's season. After quickly reviewing your résumé, Victoria begins asking some of the exact questions for which you had prepared. She appears interested in each response, nodding approvingly and smiling.

Then Victoria asks the question you hadn't anticipated: "I notice on your résumé that you interned in special events one summer for the Beaumont Scorpions. Will you describe how that experience has helped you prepare for this position?"

Filled with dread, you consider how to answer the question. You don't want to ruin the positive vibe in the interview, but that internship was the worst. You answered telephones, ran errands for the stadium manager, and worked in the box office. Frustrated by the lack of any meaningful marketing experiences, you quit mid-season.

2 CONNECT THE RESEARCH

During an employment interview, you want to project a positive *face*, or view of yourself. As Chapter 2 explains, your *face* is actively created and presented through your communication with others. You create your face during interviews in one of three ways.

First, interviewees may *self-promote* by truthfully describing past work experiences using positive language ("I delivered outstanding customer service through sales and problem solving for guests"). Employers expect interviewees to use self-promotion when talking about past work experiences, achievements, and job-relevant skills (Swider, Barrick, Harris, & Stoverink, 2011). Second, interviewees may engage in slight *image creation*, which involves exaggerating or modifying some truth about past work experience. For example, saying "I coordinated ticket sales for the Scorpions" exaggerates your role working in the ticket booth.

Third, job candidates may try to maintain positive face by creating a *false image* ("I planned an appreciation day for local firefighters"). Unlike slight image creation, which has some element of truth, false image creation is lying (Swider et al., 2011).

Scholars found that interviewers give high ratings to applicants who use self-promotion in interviews (Swider et al., 2011). But slight or false image creation can be costly. Exaggerating or creating a false face means that interviewees must pay careful attention to other answers in order to avoid contradicting them. This concentration often results in interviewees giving low-quality and less specific answers to questions in order to keep up the act. Such answers can cause poor interview ratings, which may lead to not getting hired (Swider et al., 2011).

Before making a communication choice, consider the facts of the situation, and think about the research on managing impressions in an interview. Also, reflect on what you've learned so far about creating résumés (pp. A-14 to A-18), communication skills in interviewing (pp. A-6 to A-9), and managing yourself in an employment selection interview (pp. A-21 to A-23). Then answer these questions:

1 What role does the immediate connection you feel with Victoria Mines play in encouraging self-disclosure about the internship experience?

2 What are the benefits and risks of choosing to maintain a positive face through self-promotion, exaggerating, or misrepresenting your internship?

3 How will you respond to Victoria's question?

As Chapter 3 on mediated communication points out, you create your *online face* through your social media activity: your posts, your e-mail and screen names, and the comments others make about you.

Some employers check Google, LinkedIn, and social media sites to gather additional information about job applicants. They will more likely view you favorably if the images on these sites show you in a respectable setting (e.g., playing tennis rather than drinking at a party) and if others post positive comments about you (Hong, Tandoc Jr., Kim, Kim, & Wise, 2012). Your e-mail and screen names will also influence their impressions of you. If you don't already have at least one e-mail address that includes your full name, set one up and use it to correspond with potential employers. (For more on maintaining a positive online face, see Chapter 3, pp. 65–70.)

Develop Your Own Questions. Most employment selection interviewers conclude the interview by inviting the applicant to ask questions. This is another opportunity for you to demonstrate what you know about the company. Rather than saying "I can't think of anything," be prepared with a few questions. For example, you could ask about opportunities for advancement within the company, or inquire about some detail in the job description that wasn't covered during the interview. Avoid questions that you could easily answer by looking at the employer's Web site or other published material.

Managing an Employment Selection Interview

In addition to carefully preparing for a job interview, you'll make a good impression by communicating skillfully during the interview. Keys to successfully managing a job interview include dressing appropriately, understanding every question posed to you, dealing competently with any un-lawful questions that arise, demonstrating positivity and optimism, and following up promptly and appreciatively.

Dress Appropriately. It may seem unfair, but interviewers will judge you by your clothes, hairstyle, body art, and other nonverbal behaviors. In one study of applicants for a university research-assistant position, students who dressed professionally for the interview were rated higher in social skills and considered more desirable for employment than those who were informally dressed (Gifford, Ng, & Wilkinson, 1985).

Because your appearance strongly influences how a prospective employer judges your abilities, you'll want to carefully plan your wardrobe for a selection interview—even if the interview will be conducted online or through video. If possible, visit the potential employer's work site or Web site to see how employees dress. You can also ask someone who's familiar with the business or someone in the company's human resources department. However, the standard rule is to dress in a professional manner.

Understand Every Question. Even when interviewers have prepared for the meeting, they may ask confusing or assumptive questions. Rather than just spouting out a response you are unsure of, take the time to clarify the question first. It is better to make sure you understand the question than give an answer the interviewer thinks doesn't make sense. If the interviewer asks you a question that's unclear, ask him or her to repeat it or to clarify it.

You can also show that you understand a question by restating it or repeating a few key words in your response. For example:

> *Interviewer:* In this job, you will encounter demanding hotel guests who have little patience. What experience do you have dealing with difficult people?
>
> *You:* My experience in dealing with difficult people can be illustrated in three ways . . .

Deal Competently with Unlawful Questions. Federal and state laws exist to protect citizens from discrimination when applying for a job. It is illegal for employers to ask job applicants about things that are not relevant to the job, such as their age, sex, ethnicity, national origin, and religion. For example, an interviewer should not ask you any of the following questions:

- Where were you born?
- When were you born?
- What is your native language?
- Are you married?
- Do you have or plan to have children?
- Do you have reliable child care?
- Do you have any disabilities?
- Will you need to take time off for religious observances?

Employers *may* ask a question about religion, gender, age, or national origin if it relates to a **bona fide occupational qualification**—a characteristic essential to operating the business. For example, it's legal to ask "Are you over 21?" for a job that involves selling alcohol, "What languages do you speak?" if the job requires interacting with suppliers or consumers in specific languages, or "Can you lift a 50-pound box?" if the job calls for physical strength.

If you believe a question is unlawful, you'll need to decide how to respond. First, consider the motive behind the question. Is it an innocent mistake or malicious in intent? Second, think about how much you want the job. Though not legal or even fair, know that it might be risky to point out that a question is unlawful.

With these factors in mind, you could respond in a number of ways. You could answer briefly without elaborating. Thus, if the interviewer asks, "Is English your native language?" you may simply respond, "No." Or you could direct your answer to something that's relevant to the job. For instance, "I believe my Spanish-speaking skills would be an asset in serving many of your clients in South Texas." Finally, you could refuse to answer any question that you believe is unlawful or inappropriate. You can do this in a way that's assertive but polite. For example, "I don't believe my native language is important to my ability to do this job effectively."

Demonstrate Positivity and Optimism. During a job interview, you want to put your best foot forward. Interviewers expect you to do some self-promotion, including describing your job-related experiences positively, without misrepresenting your accomplishments (Swider et al., 2011). Focus on strengths you bring to the position. Your aim is to sell yourself by demonstrating how your experience and skills can meet the employer's needs.

Don't downplay or cover up negative work experiences. Instead, talk about what you learned from those experiences. If you had a bad experience with a previous boss or job, be as diplomatic as possible in describing it. Criticizing your last boss will only make *you* look bad. Also anticipate questions about your weaknesses. When interviewers ask these types of questions, they are looking to see if you are self-aware and trying to improve. There may be times, however, when these types of questions may seem aggressive or overly stressful; the How to Communicate feature on pages A-24 to A-25 considers additional skills necessary for responding competently.

Follow Up Promptly. Even after an interview, you'll need to continue making a positive impression as you follow up. For instance, if the interviewer asks for a list of references, send it within 24 hours. In addition to expressing appreciation at the end of the interview, send a note thanking the person for his or her time. A gracious thank-you note also includes specific details from the interview, such as why you continue to be interested in the job and why you might be a good fit. If the hiring manager is trying to decide between you and another applicant, a skillfully crafted thank-you note will make you more memorable and could tip the scales in your favor. Even if you ultimately don't get the job, a follow-up note may leave the door open for future interview opportunities at that company.

☑ **LearningCurve** can help you review! Go to **bedfordstmartins.com /choicesconnections**.

MANAGING STRESS QUESTIONS

 One way to improve your interviewing skills is by adapting to interviewers' behaviors. Learn how to handle stress questions by going to LaunchPad at **bedfordstmartins.com /choicesconnections** and completing the **How to Communicate video scenario** for the Appendix to practice your skills.

CONSIDER THIS: During a job interview, the recruiter glares at you and asks, "What do you dislike about your current job?" in an accusatory tone. As you begin telling her that you're looking for a position with growth opportunity, she interrupts and says, "C'mon. Stick to the question. What don't you like about the job you have now?"

WHAT WOULD YOU DO? Employers may use stress questions (or stress interviews) to see how applicants handle pressure or uncomfortable situations. Interviewers create the stress by interrupting, appearing uninterested, asking irrelevant questions, or aggressively challenging interviewees' answers. As you watch the video, consider how competent communication skills can help you handle the pressure. Then, test your knowledge of key skills, and create your own responses to the **What if? video prompts**.

---

1 **REMAIN CALM.** Breathe deeply, and resist any urge to respond with aggressive language or nonverbal behavior.

2 **PARAPHRASE THE INTERVIEWER'S QUESTION** or remarks to clarify the intended meaning. Avoid commenting on the interviewer's tone or behavior.

"You want me to identify specific challenges of my current job, is that right?"

③ USE POSITIVE LANGUAGE

and take your time answering the question. Stay focused on the interviewer's question or remark.

"One challenge I have is with coworkers who don't follow through on tasks. From this I have learned . . ."

④ MAINTAIN POSITIVE NONVERBAL BEHAVIORS,

such as smiling, direct eye contact, and calm vocal tone, and eliminate adaptive gestures (for example, touching your face or playing with a pen in your hand).

WHAT IF? But what if things don't work out as shown? Even if you are handling the stressful interview questions well, the employer may try other tactics. Test your ability to adapt your communication by watching the *What if?* videos and planning a response for each situation.

1. When the interviewer maintains a long silence after you have answered a question how do you react?

2. When the interviewer questions whether you have been truthful with an answer ("You make it sound like everyone on your team thinks you're just swell. I don't believe that"), what would you say?

APPENDIX REVIEW

APPENDIX RECAP

- Whereas **employment interviews** are focused exclusively on workplace interactions, you can use **information interviews** in a variety of personal, school, and work situations.
- Developing an **interview protocol** will help you plan what topics to cover, what questions to ask, and the proper order for your questions. **Open questions** and **neutral questions** will help you get detailed responses.
- Using your **attending skills,** engaging in **rapport building,** demonstrating cooperation, and properly using mediated communication technologies will help you communicate competently during interviews.
- Some of the best things you can do to prepare for and manage information and employment interviews include doing your research, dressing appropriately, being engaged in the conversation, demonstrating positivity and optimism, and following up appropriately.
- When composing **résumés** and **cover letters** for **selection interviews,** craft each one to specifically highlight how your work experience and skills meet the employer's needs.

LAUNCHPAD

LaunchPad for *Choices & Connections* offers unique video scenarios and encourages self-assessment through adaptive quizzing. Go to **bedfordstmartins.com /choicesconnections** to get access.

 LearningCurve adaptive quizzes

 How to Communicate video scenarios

KEY TERMS

1 Before starting a new job, your previous employer asks you to meet and discuss why you are changing jobs. This is an example of a(n) _____ interview.

a. information

c. appraisal

b. selection

d. exit

2 If you are interviewing a local artist for a research project and ask her "How long have you been painting?" you've just asked a(n) _____ question.

a. open

c. leading

b. closed

d. secondary

3 One way to demonstrate your attending skills in any interview is to _____ so that you can check your understanding of what was said.

a. use paraphrasing

c. build rapport

b. promote immediacy

d. be informative

4 If you don't have a lot of paid work experience but want to highlight your course and volunteer work, what type of résumé is best to use?

a. Functional résumé

c. Scannable résumé

b. Chronological résumé

d. Digital résumé

5 Which of the following is an example of a bona fide occupational qualification question?

a. What is your date of birth?

b. Do you have reliable child care?

c. Are you available to work at night?

d. What is your political affiliation?

ACTIVITIES

1 **Job Search Basics**

Using a career Web site (monster.com or careerbuilder.com) or a specific company Web site, find an entry-level job posting that interests you, making sure it is appropriate for your work experience and qualifications. Then write a résumé and a cover letter for the position. Exchange your résumé and cover letter with a classmate, and get feedback on your documents.

2 **What to Wear**

Working in groups, use Google images (or a similar image search engine) to find examples of appropriate dress and appearance for an employment selection interview in a professional setting. Based on your findings, develop a list of recommendations for both men and women of appropriate employment interview attire and appearance. Share your results with the class.

Glossary

accommodation: (p. 193) Managing conflict by abandoning your own goals or actions and giving in to others' desires.

action-oriented listeners: (p. 172) Those who like focused and organized information and want clear, to-the-point messages from others. Also known as *task-oriented listeners*.

actor-observer effect: (p. 44) The tendency to make external attributions regarding your own behaviors.

adaptive gestures: (p. 381) Movements that attempt to manage nervousness, such as fidgeting, twirling your hair, or fiddling with your jewelry.

adaptors: (p. 142) Touching gestures that serve a physical or psychological purpose, such as rubbing your chin when thinking about a tough question.

adjourning: (p. 266) The group developmental phase where members take time to evaluate and reflect on how well they accomplished the task and the quality of their relationships.

affect displays: (p. 151) Intentional or unintentional behaviors that depict actual or feigned emotion.

affective conflict: (p. 298) Disagreements stemming from interpersonal or cultural differences between members, power struggles, or simply bad feelings.

aggressive listening: (p. 177) Attending to what others say solely to find an opportunity to attack or criticize (also known as *ambushing*).

algebraic impressions: (p. 47) Impressions formed by analyzing the positive and negative things you learn about someone to calculate an overall impression, then updating this impression as you learn new information.

analogical reasoning: (p. 440) Supporting a claim by drawing a comparison between two ideas or situations to show that what's true for one could be true for the other.

analogy: (p. 348) A comparison between something familiar to your audience and an idea that is not familiar to them, but that you want them to understand.

appropriateness: (p. 19) The degree to which your communication matches expectations regarding how people should communicate.

argumentativeness: (p. 276) A group member's willingness to take a stance on controversial issues and verbally refute others who disagree.

articulation: (p. 382) Presenting information clearly so that the audience can understand what you're saying.

artifacts: (p. 146) Objects you possess that influence how you see yourself and that you use to express your identity to others.

assurances: (p. 252) Messages that emphasize how much your relationship partners mean to you, point out how important the relationships are to you, and show that you see a secure future together.

asynchronous communication: (p. 62) Communication in which a time lapse exists between a message sent (as in e-mail, voice mail, or a post to a forum), and a response, if there is a response at all.

attending skills: (p. A-7) In an interview setting, the ability to show that you are mentally and physically ready to listen—choosing a quiet location with few distractions and using nonverbal communication to promote immediacy between you and your interview partner.

attitude: (p. 322) An evaluation that makes a person respond favorably or unfavorably toward an issue, situation, or person.

attributional complexity: (p. 105) The ability to acknowledge that other people's behaviors have complex causes.

attributions: (p. 43) Rationales you create to explain the comments or behaviors of others.

audience analysis: (p. 321) A process of identifying important characteristics about your listeners, and using this information to prepare your speech.

autocratic leadership style: (p. 290) A leadership style in which the leader directs others, telling them what to do.

avoidance: (p. 191) Approaching a conflict by ignoring it and not managing it.

avoiding: (p. 233) A stage in the coming apart phase of a relationship when one or both partners decide that they can no longer be around each other and begin distancing themselves physically.

beautiful-is-good effect: (p. 218) The phenomenon that attractive people are often assumed to offer other valued resources, like competent communication skills, intelligence, and well-adjusted personalities.

belief: (p. 323) A conviction regarding what is true and untrue.

birds-of-a-feather effect: (p. 217) The notion that people seek romantic partnerships, close family involvements, friendships, and coworker relationships with those they see as similar to themselves.

bona fide occupational qualification: (p. A-22) A characteristic essential to operating a particular business, such as being of legal age to work in a store that sells alcohol.

bonding: (p. 229) In a relationship, a public ritual that announces to the world that you and your romantic partner have made a commitment to each other.

brainstorming: (p. 318) A creative problem-solving strategy that involves coming up with as many ideas as possible in a defined period of time.

butler lies: (p. 74) The type of deception people use to avoid conversation, prevent embarrassment, or simply be polite.

captive audience: (p. 323) Listeners who are required to attend the presentation.

cause-effect pattern: (p. 352) An organizational pattern that shows how events or forces will lead to (or did lead to) specific outcomes.

cause-effect reasoning: (p. 441) Drawing a connection between two events or things and claiming that one produced the other.

central route: (p. 430) The way audience members who are highly motivated to listen and who have the knowledge needed to understand your message will process your speech. These audience members pay more attention and carefully evaluate your points.

channel: (p. 6) The sensory dimension (sound, sight, or touch) along which communicators transmit information.

character: (p. 434) Showing your audience that you understand their needs, have their best interests in mind, and genuinely believe in your topic.

charisma: (p. 434) In speech delivery, the warmth, personality, and dynamism your audience sees in you.

chronological pattern: (p. 352) A pattern that organizes main points by time sequence or in a series of steps.

chronological résumé: (p. A-14) A résumé that details the history of your education and work experience, starting with the most recent.

closed questions: (p. A-6) Questions that require a yes or no response, that limit the range of possible answers.

co-cultural communication theory: (p. 87) The idea that the people who have more power within a society determine the dominant culture because they get to decide the prevailing views, values, and traditions of the society.

co-cultures: (p. 88) Members of a society who don't conform to the language, values, lifestyle, or even physical appearance of the dominant culture.

coercion: (p. 428) Communication that involves using threats, manipulation, and or even violence to force others to do something against their will.

cohesive group: (p. 272) A group setting where members like each other and have a sense of camaraderie.

collaboration: (p. 195) A way of approaching conflict by treating it as a mutual problem-solving challenge.

collectivistic culture: (pp. 37, 94) A culture that values the needs and goals of the community or group above an individual's. Collectivistic cultures also value the importance of belonging to groups that look after you in exchange for loyalty.

communication: (p. 5) The process through which people use messages to generate meanings within and across contexts, cultures, channels, and media.

communication accommodation theory: (p. 106) The idea that people are especially motivated to adapt their communication when they seek social approval, wish to establish relationships with others, and view others' language use as appropriate.

communication apprehension: (p. 275) The fear or anxiety associated with real or anticipated communication with others.

communication climate: (p. 294) The emotional tone established within a group.

communication competence: (p. 19) The process of consistently communicating in ways that are appropriate, effective, and ethical.

Communication Privacy Management Theory: (p. 245) The idea that individuals create informational boundaries by choosing carefully the kind of private information they reveal and the people with whom they share it.

communication rules: (p. 246) Conditions governing what people can (and can't) talk about, how they can discuss such topics, and who else should have access to this information.

communication skills: (p. 24) Repeatable goal-directed behaviors and behavioral patterns that enable you to improve the quality of your interpersonal encounters and relationships.

companionate love: (p. 221) An intense form of liking defined by emotional investment and the close intertwining of two people's lives.

comparison/contrast presentation: (p. 410) A speech that presents the similarities and differences between ideas, things, events, or people.

competence: (p. 434) During public speeches, the degree of expertise your audience thinks you have regarding your speech topic.

competition: (p. 194) Confronting others and pursuing your own goals to the exclusion of theirs.

compose: (p. 342) The third step in the process of preparing a speech, in which you develop your speech structure and main ideas, arranging them into a coherent and engaging presentation, and plan any visual aids.

compromise: (p. 201) What happens when the parties involved in a conflict change their goals and actions to make them compatible.

concept map: (p. 318) A drawing showing connections among related ideas that helps you expand on one idea with more specific topics.

conclusion: (p. 439) The third element in deductive reasoning, in which you show the relationship between your general (or major) premise and your specific (or minor) premise.

conflict: (p. 188) A communication process between people who perceive incompatible goals or interference in achieving their objective.

congruent messages: (p. 135) Messages in which the sender's verbal and nonverbal behaviors match.

connectives: (p. 353) Words and phrases that link your ideas together in a speech.

connotative meanings: (p. 113) The meanings you associate with words based on your life experiences.

consensual validation: (p. 336) In evaluating your sources for a speech, this occurs when other sources agree with or use the same information you're considering using.

consensus: (p. 306) What occurs when all group members support a given course of action on a decision.

constitutive rules: (p. 113) Guidelines that define word meaning according to a particular language's vocabulary.

content-oriented listeners: (p. 172) Those who prefer to be intellectually challenged by messages. They enjoy hearing all sides of an argument and prefer complex, detailed information.

contexts: (p. 6) Situations in which communication occurs. Context includes the physical locations, backgrounds, genders, ages, moods, and relationships of the communicators, as well as the time of day.

cooperative principle: (p. 116) The idea that you should make your verbal messages informative, honest, and relevant, given what the situation requires.

cover letter: (p. A-18) A statement written by a job applicant that introduces him- or herself and highlights qualifications for the job in question.

credibility: (p. 432) An audience's perception of a speaker's trustworthiness and the validity of the information provided in the speech.

critical self-reflection: (p. 33) A special kind of self-awareness that focuses on evaluating and improving your communication.

cues-filtered-out model: (p. 62) Mediation communication in which many of the cues vital for making sense of messages (facial expressions, tone of voice) are not available, which makes mediated communication more difficult to understand than face-to-face communication.

culture: (pp. 36, 84) The established, coherent set of beliefs, attitudes, values, and practices shared by a large group of people.

cumulative annoyance: (p. 191) A result of avoiding conflict in which your repressed resentment grows as your mental list of complaints about other people builds up.

cyberbullying: (pp. 76, 125) Persistent online harassment to exert power, cause social embarrassment, inflict emotional pain, or damage a person's reputation.

deception: (p. 127) The deliberate use of uninformative, untruthful, irrelevant, or vague language for the purpose of misleading others.

decision making: (p. 305) The process of making choices among alternatives.

deductive reasoning: (p. 439) The process of starting with a generally held principle and then showing how a specific instance relates to that principle.

defamation: (p. 129) Intentionally false communication that harms a person's reputation.

delivery outline: (p. 362) A set of notes that helps you keep track of your ideas while you're presenting your speech to an audience.

democratic leadership style: (p. 290) A leadership style in which the leader invites input from group members and encourages shared decision making.

demographics: (p. 321) Categorical groupings that make it easier to target people depending on their age, sex, education level, group memberships (religious or political associations), socioeconomic status, family status (single, married, divorced, partnered, with children or without), and cultural background.

denotative meanings: (p. 113) The literal, or dictionary, definitions of words as agreed upon by members of a culture.

dialects: (p. 114) Variations on language shared by large groups of people or in particular regions.

differentiating: (p. 229) In the first stage of coming apart in a relationship, the point at which the beliefs, attitudes, and values that distinguish you from your partner dominate your thoughts and communications.

digital deception: (p. 74) The act of sending messages that intentionally mislead or create a false belief in recipients.

direct quotation: (p. 349) In a speech, repeating the exact words a person said or wrote in order to make a point.

dirty secrets: (p. 206) Messages that are honest in content but have been kept hidden to protect someone's feelings.

disclaimers: (p. 382) Phrases that remove responsibility for the statement you're making.

display rules: (pp. 96, 137) Guidelines for when, where, and how to appropriately express emotion.

dominance: (p. 153) Interpersonal behaviors used to exert power or influence over others.

domination: (p. 200) What happens when one person or group of people get their way by influencing others to accommodate and abandon their goals.

dyadic: (p. 212) Involving pairs of people, or dyads.

effectiveness: (p. 20) The ability to use communication to accomplish self-presentation, instrumental, and relationship goals.

egocentric roles: (p. 269) Roles that occur when one team member's communication disrupts the group's efforts.

elaboration likelihood model: (p. 430) A theory that proposes that listeners who are intensely interested in your topic and can easily understand your presentation will put more effort into thinking about your persuasive message than listeners who don't care about or understand your speech topic.

embarrassment: (p. 39) Feelings of shame, humiliation, and sadness that come when we lose face.

emblems: (p. 142) Gestures that symbolize a specific verbal meaning within a given culture, such as the "thumbs up" or the "V for victory" sign.

empathy: (p. 53) Understanding of another person's perspective and awareness of his or her feelings in an attempt to identify with that individual.

empathy deficits: (p. 74) The dramatic reduction in your ability to experience the other person's feelings.

employment interviews: (p. A-4) Interviews that manage an organization's personnel.

escalation: (p. 194) A dramatic rise in emotional intensity and unproductive communication.

ethics: (p. 20) The set of moral principles that guide your behavior toward others. Ethical communication consistently displays respect, kindness, and compassion.

ethnocentrism: (p. 105) The belief that your own cultural beliefs, attitudes, values, and practices are superior to those of all other cultures.

ethos: (p. 433) A speaker's credibility, which, according to Greek philosopher Aristotle, determines whether he or she can influence listeners.

evaluating: (p. 164) Comparing newly received information against your past knowledge to check its accuracy and validity.

examples: (p. 347) Specific references that illustrate ideas.

exit interviews: (p. A-4) Interviews to identify why an employee is leaving a job. Resulting insights are used to improve management practices.

experimenting: (p. 228) A stage of coming together with someone that involves exchanging demographic information (e.g., names, college majors, hometowns).

expository presentation: (p. 407) A presentation that defines what a term means, explains a concept, or describes an object or place to your audience.

extemporaneous speaking: (p. 377) Composing a preparation outline ahead of time (as in *manuscript speaking*) and then reducing your preparation outline to a brief speaking outline that allows you to add or eliminate information as needed during your presentation (as in *impromptu speaking*).

face: (p. 38) The positive self you want others to see and believe.

fallacies: (p. 441) Claims that aren't true or are based on inadequate or inaccurate evidence.

family: (p. 221) A network of people who share their lives over long periods of time and are bound by marriage, blood, or commitment; who consider themselves a family; and who share a significant history and anticipated future of functioning in a family relationship.

feedback: (p. 9) The verbal and nonverbal messages coming from recipients in response to messages from senders.

fields of experience: (p. 9) The beliefs, attitudes, values, and experiences that each participant brings to a communication event.

flaming: (p. 75) Saying vicious and aggressive things online that you would never say in person.

foot-in-the-door technique: (p. 448) A persuasive technique that involves asking your audience to agree to a small action in the hope that you'll gain their compliance over time.

formal roles: (p. 268) Assigned positions that members take on by appointment or election.

forming: (p. 265) The group developmental phase where members become acquainted with each other and seek to understand the task.

friendships: (p. 223) Voluntary interpersonal relationships characterized by intimacy and liking.

functional résumé: (p. A-14) Focuses on how your skills and experiences relate to the specific job you're applying for.

functional view of leadership: (p. 292) Considers the types of communication behaviors that help a group work toward its goal. For example, if you volunteer to put together the slide deck for a group project presentation, you are providing useful task leadership.

fundamental attribution error: (p. 44) The tendency to attribute others' behaviors to internal rather than external forces.

gender: (p. 37) The set of social, psychological, and cultural attributes that characterize a person as male or female.

general purpose: (p. 317) When preparing a speech, your reason for giving the presentation.

Gestalt: (p. 46) A general impression of a person that's either positive or negative.

group brainstorming: (p. 302) Occurs when a team focuses on generating as many ideas as possible to solve a defined problem, often integrated with step three of the structured problem-solving process.

group roles: (p. 268) Also known as *informal roles*, these are specific patterns of behavior and communication that members of a group develop from interacting over time.

groupthink: (p. 298) A phenomenon that occurs when group members want to maintain harmony more than anything else and so avoid challenging one another's ideas.

halo effect: (p. 47) A tendency to positively interpret the behavior of a person for whom you have formed a positive Gestalt.

haptics: (p. 144) A nonverbal code that represents messages conveyed through touch.

hearing: (p. 162) Physically processing the sound that others have produced, and mentally focusing your attention on it.

hedging: (p. 382) Using words that lessen a message's impact, such as *sorta*, *kinda*, and *somewhat*.

hierarchy of needs: (p. 443) A theory developed by psychologist Abraham Maslow which posits that much of human behavior is motivated by the desire to meet basic life needs.

high-contact cultures: (p. 137) Cultures that prefer frequent touching, shared gaze, close physical proximity, and direct body orientation (facing each other while talking).

high-context cultures: (p. 95) Cultures in which people use relatively vague and ambiguous language, and even silence, to convey important meanings. They talk indirectly, using hints or suggestions, and therefore don't feel the need to provide a lot of explicit information.

honesty: (p. 117) Sharing information you're certain about and never presenting information as true when you know it's false.

horn effect: (p. 47) A tendency to negatively interpret the behavior of a person for whom you have formed a negative Gestalt.

I-It: (p. 214) An interpersonal communication approach in which you regard people as objects to observe, and that are there to be manipulated and exploited.

"I" language: (p. 119) Phrases that emphasize ownership of your feelings, opinions, and beliefs.

I-Thou: (p. 214) An interpersonal communication approach in which you consider an individual with an open mind, giving the person the same attention and respect you expect for yourself.

identity-based digital deception: (p. 74) The act of falsely misrepresenting an identity or gender by exaggerating or enhancing aspects of your identity online.

illustrators: (p. 142) Gestures used to accent or illustrate a verbal message.

immediacy: (p. 378) A sense of closeness that your audience feels toward you as a speaker.

impersonal communication: (p. 215) Exchanges that have a negligible perceived impact on your thoughts, emotions, behaviors, and relationships.

impressions: (p. 45) Mental images of who people are and how you feel about them.

impromptu speaking: (p. 375) The act of making public remarks with little or no time for preparation or rehearsal.

incongruent messages: (p. 135) Messages in which the sender's verbal and nonverbal behaviors contradict one another.

individualistic culture: (pp. 36, 93) A culture that values independence and personal goals over group goals.

inductive reasoning: (p. 440) Connecting a set of specific, related facts to arrive at a more general conclusion.

information interview: (pp. 335, A-3) A meeting in which you ask questions to gain knowledge or understanding about a particular topic.

information overload: (p. 404) What happens when the amount and nature of material exceeds a listener's ability to process it.

informative speeches: (pp. 317, 402) Speeches that educate your audience about a topic, demonstrate how something works, tell stories about events or people, or explain similarities and differences between things or ideas.

ingroupers: (p. 89) People you consider fundamentally similar to you because they share your interests, beliefs, attitudes, and values.

initiating: (p. 227) A stage of coming together when you size up a new person to decide whether you want to get to know that person better.

instrumental goals: (p. 7) Practical objectives you want to achieve or tasks you want to accomplish.

integrating: (p. 228) A stage of coming together when your and your partner's personalities seem to blend.

integrative agreements: (p. 201) Creative solutions that enable all sides to keep and reach their original goals.

intensifiers: (p. 382) Unnecessary words that overemphasize a point, such as *really* and *totally*.

intensifying: (p. 228) A stage of coming together when you find yourself feeling strongly attracted to or interested in another person.

interaction: (p. 6) The result of a series of messages exchanged between people, whether face-to-face or online.

interactive communication model: (p. 9) A model that views communication as a process involving senders and receivers that is influenced by two additional factors: *feedback* and *fields of experience*.

intercultural competence: (p. 103) The ability to communicate appropriately, effectively, and ethically with people from diverse backgrounds.

internal previews: (p. 353) Statements that tell your audience what you are going to tell them before you actually do.

internal summaries: (p. 353) A short review of information that you've discussed within a section of the speech.

interpersonal communication: (pp. 16, 212) A dynamic form of communication between two people in which the messages exchanged significantly influence their thoughts, emotions, behaviors, and relationships.

interpersonal relationships: (p. 216) The emotional, mental, and physical involvements that you forge with others through communication.

interpretation: (p. 43) The third step of the perception process, in which you assign meaning to the information you have selected.

interpreting: (p. 164) Identifying any implications (or connotative meanings) suggested in the person's words and considering what action the person is trying to perform.

interviewee: (p. A-2) The person at the interview who answers the questions.

interviewer: (p. A-2) The person at the interview who determines the interview purpose, plans the questions, and manages the flow of the conversation.

interviewing: (p. A-2) A planned and structured conversation between two or more persons that uses questions and answers to meet a specific purpose.

interview protocol: (p. A-4) A list of questions, written in a logical order, which guide the interview.

intimacy: (p. 153) A feeling of closeness and bonding that exists between us and our relationship partners.

investigate: (p. 314) The second step in preparing a speech, in which you plan a research strategy, conduct research, and evaluate the resources found.

kinesics: (p. 139) Body movement communication that encompasses most of the cues people typically think of as nonverbal communication: facial expressions, eye contact, gestures, and posture.

kitchen-sinking: (p. 195) A form of escalation in which combatants in a conflict hurl assorted accusations at each other that have little to do with the disagreement at hand.

laissez-faire leadership style: (p. 290) A leadership style in which the leader provides little direction or structure, leaving the group to maintain control of what happens.

leadership: (p. 288) The ability to influence and direct others to meet group goals.

leading questions: (p. A-6) Questions that point the respondent to an answer you prefer.

leave-taking: (p. A-13) The process of ending an interview, often signaled by asking the final question.

liking: (p. 220) A feeling of affection and respect that we often have for our friends, extended family members, and coworkers.

linear communication model: (p. 8) A depiction of communication as an activity in which information flows in one direction, from a starting point to an end point.

listening: (p. 162) The six-stage process of hearing, understanding, interpreting, evaluating, remembering, and responding to others' communication.

listening functions: (p. 167) The five general purposes that listening serves: to comprehend, to discern, to analyze, to appreciate, and to provide support.

listening style: (p. 172) An individual's habitual pattern of listening behaviors, which reflects one's attitudes, beliefs, and predispositions about listening.

logos: (p. 435) The development of logical reasons for your position.

loving: (p. 220) A more intense emotional connection consisting of intimacy, caring, and attachment.

low-contact cultures: (p. 137) Cultures that prefer infrequent touching, little shared gaze, larger physical distance, and indirect body orientation.

low-context cultures: (p. 95) Cultures that are often individualistic, in which people tend not to presume that others share their beliefs, attitudes, and values. They strive to be informative, clear, and direct in their communication, and they openly express their views and try to persuade others to accept them.

main points: (p. 344) The key statements or principles that support your speech thesis and help your audience understand your message.

maintenance roles: (p. 268) When group members communicate to build trusting and appreciative interpersonal relationships.

major premise: (p. 439) The general statement you believe your audience will accept as true.

manuscript speaking: (p. 376) A public speech that is based on a written text that you either read word for word or commit to memory.

mask: (p. 38) The public self designed to strategically veil the private self.

mass media: (p. 59) Mediated communication vehicles that involve the sending of messages from content creators to huge, relatively anonymous audiences.

media: (p. 6) Tools used to exchange messages, including texting, tweeting, posting, e-mailing, making a phone call, or talking face-to-face.

mediated communication: (pp. 16, 58) Communication in which the communicators are separated, or "mediated," by some type of technological device.

meeting agenda: (p. 308) A structured, written outline that guides communication among meeting participants by showing which topics will be discussed, in what order, and (often) for how long.

meeting minutes: (p. 309) A written record of the discussion, actions, and decisions sent to everyone who attended, and to anyone who did not attend but needs to know what happened.

mere exposure effect: (p. 216) The phenomenon that you're more likely to pursue relationships with people with whom you have frequent contact, whether face-to-face or online.

message: (p. 6) The "package" of information transported during communication.

message-based digital deception: (p. 74) The manipulation of information with the intent of misleading recipients.

minor premise: (p. 439) A specific instance of a general claim.

misunderstanding: (p. 118) Misperceiving the meaning of another's verbal communication.

mnemonics: (p. 165) Devices that aid memory.

monochronic time orientation: (p. 98) A cultural orientation toward time as a precious resource.

monotone: (p. 380) An unvarying vocal pitch and tone in conversation or public presentation.

motivated sequence: (p. 436) A five-step method for organizing a persuasive speech about a problem which appeals to an audience's attention, need to be concerned, satisfaction, ability to visualize the argument, and desire to take action.

motivational appeals: (p. 442) Explicit statements (examples, testimony, stories) that speak to the needs and feelings of your audience.

M-time orientation: (p. 147) For "monochronic time," a cultural orientation toward time as a precious resource that can be saved, spent, wasted, lost, made up, or can run out. Those who have this orientation put a premium on careful scheduling and time management.

multitask: (p. 168) Shifting attention back and forth between many different tasks at once.

narrative presentation: (p. 409) A presentation that describes an event or tells a story about a person.

negative feedback: (p. 166) Using verbal and nonverbal cues to show that you're not listening to a speaker.

neutral questions: (p. A-6) During an interview, inquiries used to find out what the interviewee really thinks or feels about a topic.

noise: (p. 8) Distractions that change how the message is received. Noise may originate outside the communicators, as in poor phone reception.

nonverbal communication: (p. 134) The intentional or unintentional transmission of meaning through an individual's nonspoken physical and behavioral cues.

norming: (p. 266) The group developmental phase where members agree about the plans for working toward the goal and who will do what.

norms: (p. 272) The expectations about behavior within a group.

online disinhibition: (p. 71) The ability to feel comfortable saying things—good and bad—that you would never say to someone face-to-face.

online harassment: (p. 75) Mediated messages perceived by the recipient as disturbing, threatening, or obsessive.

open questions: (p. A-6) Questions that give interviewees a lot of freedom in formulating their responses.

oral style: (p. 379) Using language that is similar to how people talk.

organization: (p. 43) The second step of the perception process, in which you structure the information you've received through your senses into a coherent pattern in your mind.

outgroupers: (p. 89) People you consider fundamentally different from you because of their beliefs, attitudes, and values.

paraphrasing: (pp. 349, A-7) Providing your own summary of another person's words or experience.

passionate love: (p. 221) A state of intense emotional and physical longing for union with another person.

pathos: (p. 443) Appeals to the audience's emotions, allowing them to connect personally with your topic.

people-oriented listeners: (p. 172) Those who view listening as an opportunity to establish commonalities between themselves and others.

perception: (p. 42) The process of selecting, organizing, and interpreting information from your senses.

perception-checking: (p. 49) A five-step process to test your impressions of someone and to avoid errors in judgment. It involves reviewing your knowledge of the person, assessing attributions you've made, questioning your impressions, and sharing and checking your impressions with the person.

performance or appraisal interviews: (p. A-4) Usually annual reviews of an employee to evaluate his or her work and to set new goals.

performing: (p. 266) The group developmental phase where members actually make the required contributions for completing the task. At this phase, group members' efforts are well coordinated and directed to achieving the goal.

peripheral route: (p. 430) The way audiences who are less motivated about the topic or who don't have the time or knowledge needed to understand the information may process your speech. They may selectively listen and are easily distracted.

persuasive speeches: (pp. 317, 428) Speeches that reinforce or change listeners' attitudes and beliefs and may motivate them to take action.

plagiarism: (p. 329) The misrepresentation of others' works as your own, commonly occurring when you use someone else's exact words or summarize a unique idea without crediting the source.

polychronic time orientation: (p. 99) A cultural orientation toward time, where it is not viewed as a resource to be spent, saved, or guarded.

positive feedback: (p. 166) Using verbal and nonverbal cues to show that you're listening and are comprehending specific comments.

positivity: (p. 250) A tactic in sustaining a healthy relationship by communicating in a cheerful and optimistic fashion, doing unsolicited favors, and giving unexpected gifts.

power: (pp. 87, 193) The ability to influence or control important resources, events, and people.

power distance: (p. 98) The degree to which people in a particular culture view the unequal distribution of power as acceptable.

powerful speech style: (p. 378) Using verbal and nonverbal behaviors to present yourself and your message confidently and thus gain the respect of your listeners.

powerless language: (p. 382) Words suggesting you're uncertain about your message or yourself.

prejudice: (p. 91) Stereotypes that reflect rigid attitudes, positive or negative, toward groups and their members.

prejudiced language: (p. 124) Speech that displays contempt, dislike, or disdain for a group or its members.

preparation outline: (p. 362) Details your presentation's overall structure and helps you plan the order, flow, and logic of your speech, ensuring there are no weaknesses or missing elements.

presentation aids: (p. 389) Tools used to display the visuals you've selected to help explain or illustrate your points.

primary groups: (p. 264) The individuals who meet your basic life, psychological, and social needs.

primary questions: (p. A-5) Questions that guide the conversation and are written into the interview protocol.

primary resources: (p. 331) Direct accounts, straight from the original source, such as scientific reports, firsthand descriptions of events, diary writings, photographs of events, congressional-hearing transcripts, and speech manuscripts.

principle of subordination: (p. 363) A practice in composing a preparation outline that ensures that you're making valid arguments and that your claims are well supported and logical.

problem-solution pattern: (p. 353) An organizational pattern that allows you to describe a problem and then present a solution that will help you motivate listeners to take action to address a challenge.

process or demonstration presentation: (p. 408) A presentation that explains how something works or shows the audience how to do something.

pronunciation: (p. 382) The way you say words.

proxemics: (p. 145) How close or far away you position yourself from others while communicating.

pseudo-conflict: (p. 192) The perception that there's a conflict between you and others when there really isn't.

pseudo-listening: (p. 177) Behaving as if you're paying attention though you're really not.

P-time orientation: (p. 147) For "polychronic time," a cultural orientation toward time that values interpersonal interaction and doesn't view time as a resource to be spent, saved, or guarded.

public communication: (p. 16) The process of preparing and delivering a message to an audience to achieve a specific purpose (also known as public speaking).

qualifiers: (p. 439) Language that indicates how certain you are about your major premise.

race: (p. 90) A classification of people based on common ancestry or descent that is judged almost exclusively by a person's physical features.

rapport building: (p. A-8) Exchanging messages that create a bond and a positive first impression that help you quickly set the tone for an interview.

reasoning: (p. 439) The act of turning all the material you've gathered into the logical basis for your speech, identifying patterns in your support materials, and summarizing those patterns into arguments that become the main points of your speech.

receiver: (p. 8) The person for whom a message is intended or to whom it is delivered.

reciprocal liking: (p. 218) When someone you're interested in makes it clear that he or she is also interested in you.

regulative rules: (p. 113) Guidelines that control how you use language.

regulators: (p. 142) Gestures used to help control turn taking during interpersonal encounters—for example, averting eye contact to avoid someone or zipping up

book bags as a class to signal to a professor that the lecture should end.

rehearse: (p. 315) The fourth step in the process of preparing a speech, in which you practice a presentation on your own and in front of others, inviting feedback for improvements.

relational dialectics: (p. 245) Competing impulses and tensions that arise between ourselves and relational partners.

relational maintenance: (p. 250) Efforts that partners make to keep their relationship strong and ensure satisfaction from the relationship. They may show devotion by making time to talk, spending time together, and offering help or support to each other.

relationship goals: (p. 7) Building, maintaining, or terminating bonds with others through interpersonal communication.

remembering: (p. 165) Recalling stored information back into your conscious mind.

resources: (p. 216) The valued qualities people possess that compel us to pursue relationships with others.

responding: (p. 166) Communicating your attention and comprehension to the speaker.

résumé: (p. A-14) A written summary of your education, work experience, and skills.

revise: (p. 315) The fifth step in the process of preparing a speech, in which you adapt the speech based on the feedback you received while rehearsing.

rhetoric: (p. 13) The theory and practice of persuading others through speech.

rhetorical proofs: (p. 433) The three elements of a speech that make it persuasive to an audience: credibility (ethos), good logical reasons (logos), and appeals to their emotions (pathos).

romantic relationships: (p. 219) Interpersonal involvements in which the participants perceive the bond as romantic.

secondary groups: (p. 264) People with whom you want to achieve specific goals or perform tasks, such as an event.

secondary questions: (p. A-5) Questions in an interview that evolve out of the conversation and can help you clarify vague answers.

secondary resources: (p. 331) Works that analyze and interpret primary resources, such as magazine articles, biographies, textbooks, and newspaper articles.

selection: (p. 42) The first step of *perception* that requires you to focus your attention on certain sights, sounds, tastes, touches, or smells in your environment.

selection interviews: (p. A-4) The kind of interviews that employers use to determine whether applicants have the education, experience, and proper attitude required for a job.

selective listening: (p. 176) Listening only to parts of a message (those that are the most interesting to the listener) and dismissing the rest.

self: (p. 32) The evolving blend of who you are, including your self-awareness, self-concept, and self-esteem.

self-awareness: (p. 32) The ability to view yourself as a unique person distinct from your surrounding environment and to reflect on your thoughts, feelings, and behaviors.

self-concept: (p. 33) Your overall idea of who you are based on the beliefs, attitudes, and values you have about yourself.

self-disclosure: (p. 239) Revealing private information about yourself to others.

Self-Discrepancy Theory: (p. 35) The idea that your self-esteem results from comparing two mental standards: your *ideal* self (the qualities you want to possess) and your *ought* self (the person you think others want you to be).

self-esteem: (p. 35) The overall value you assign to yourself.

self-fulfilling prophecies: (p. 34) Predictions you make about interactions that cause you to communicate in ways that make those predictions come true.

self-presentation goals: (p. 7) In interpersonal encounters, presenting yourself in certain ways so that others perceive you as you want them to.

self-serving bias: (p. 45) A tendency to credit yourself for successes by making an internal attribution.

Self-Verification Theory: (p. 33) The idea that you often choose your relational partners based on how well they support your self-concept.

sender: (p. 8) The individual who generates the information to be communicated, packages it into a message, and chooses one or more channels for sending it.

separation: (p. 200) What happens when one or more of the people involved in a conflict terminate communication.

shared leadership: (p. 288) Each group member having the capacity to influence and direct the group in achieving its goals.

signposts: (p. 354) Brief words—often numbers—that quickly introduce a new idea.

situational view of leadership: (p. 290) A view that maintains that effective leadership is determined by the group's readiness to take on a task, including its motivation and group members' experience and knowledge.

small group: (p. 262) Three or more interdependent persons who share a common identity and who communicate to achieve common goals or purposes.

small group communication: (p. 16) Communication that involves three or more interdependent persons who share a common identity (such as membership on a team) and who communicate to achieve common goals or purposes.

sniping: (p. 205) Communicating in a negative way and then leaving the encounter.

social bookmarking: (p. 329) Free Web-based services that let you save, organize, and keep brief notes about your online resources.

social comparison: (p. 32) Observing and assigning meaning to others' behaviors and then comparing their behaviors to your own.

social exchange theory: (p. 216) The idea that you'll feel drawn to individuals who offer you substantial benefits (positive things you like and want) with few costs (negative things demanded of you in return).

social information processing theory: (p. 62) The idea that people communicating through social media compensate for the lack of nonverbal feedback by taking more care with choosing their words.

social loafing: (p. 269) A common egocentric group role where one teammate relies on other members to do all the work.

social media: (p. 59) Communication vehicles that allow communicators to send and receive messages in real time or across time intervals.

social penetration theory: (p. 239) A model that suggests that you reveal information about yourself to others by peeling back, or penetrating, layers of yourself.

spatial pattern: (p. 352) An organizational pattern that shows listeners how things are related within a physical space.

special-occasion speeches: (p. 317) Speeches intended to entertain, celebrate, commemorate, or inspire. These include introducing someone at an event, accepting or giving an award, commemorating an event or person, or giving a toast.

specific purpose statement: (p. 326) One complete sentence summarizing the goal of your speech.

speech anxiety: (p. 386) Being nervous about speaking in public.

speech of fact: (p. 428) Establishes whether something is true or not or whether an event will or won't happen.

speech of policy: (p. 429) Argues about whether an action should or should not be taken.

speech of value: (p. 429) Proposes a judgment on a topic or explains why something is good or bad.

speech thesis: (p. 342) One complete sentence that identifies the central idea of your presentation for your audience.

speech topic: (p. 317) The specific content you will present.

stagnating: (p. 232) The stage of coming apart in a relationship when communication between partners comes to a standstill because there are few safe topics to talk about.

statistic: (p. 347) A number that summarizes a formal observation about a phenomenon.

Stereotype Content Model: (p. 91) The idea that prejudice centers on two judgments made about others: how warm and friendly they are, and how competent they are. These judgments create two possible kinds of prejudice: benevolent and hostile.

stereotyping: (p. 48) Categorizing people into a social group and then evaluating them based on information you have related to the group.

storming: (p. 266) The group developmental phase when members express different ideas about how to approach the task and who will take on leadership roles.

structural improvements: (p. 202) Clarifying rules that parties involved in a conflict use to change their relationship and improve the balance of power to prevent further disputes.

structured problem-solving approach: (p. 301) A problem-solving approach in which teams collect information on the nature and scope of the problem facing them, then systematically search for a solution.

style view of leadership: (p. 290) Focuses on the behaviors that leaders use to influence others.

submissiveness: (p. 154) The willingness to allow others to exert power over you.

subpoints: (p. 345) Specific principles derived from breaking down and further dividing main points in order to help you explain an idea more clearly.

substantive conflict: (p. 298) Disagreements about the group's tasks, procedures, or decision options.

sudden-death statements: (p. 205) Spontaneous declarations that the relationship is over, even though the people involved did not consider termination a possibility before the conflict.

supportive communication: (p. 256) Sharing messages that express emotional support and that offer personal assistance, such as telling a person of your sympathy or listening to someone without judging.

symbols: (p. 113) Items used to represent other things, ideas, or events.

synchronous communication: (p. 61) A back-and-forth exchange of messages that occurs in real time (by phone or Skype, for example), best for communicating difficult or complicated messages.

task roles: (p. 268) Exchanging information about duties or goals important to your group.

terminating: (p. 233) The stage in ending a relationship when the partners come together for a final encounter to give a sense of closure and resolution.

testimony: (p. 348) A means of supporting a main point that relies on the words or experiences of others.

think: (p. 314) The first step in preparing a speech, in which you determine the purpose of your speech, choose the topic, and consider how to adapt it to your audience.

time-oriented listeners: (p. 172) Those who prefer brief, concise messages to save time.

topical pattern: (p. 351) A pattern that organizes main points into categories or subtopics.

traits view of leadership: (p. 289) The assumption that all talented leaders share certain personal and physical characteristics.

transactional communication model: (p. 10) A depiction of communication in which participants mutually influence one another's communication behavior.

transitional phrases: (p. 354) Phrases that indicate that you're shifting to another point or idea.

trolling: (p. 75) Posting flame messages on purpose to start arguments online.

uncertainty avoidance: (p. 95) The degree to which a culture tolerates and accepts unpredictability.

understanding: (p. 164) Recognizing the literal (or denotative) meaning of the words the other person has said.

values: (p. 323) Strongly held beliefs that guide our behaviors.

verbal aggression: (p. 125) Using language to attack others' self-concepts—their appearance, behavior, or character—rather than their positions.

verbal communication: (p. 112) The use of spoken or written language to interact with others.

virtual small group: (p. 264) Any team of individuals who communicate primarily through technology to achieve common goals.

vocalics: (p. 142) Vocal characteristics used to communicate nonverbal messages, such as volume, pitch, rate, tone, vocalized sounds, and silence.

vocalized pauses and fillers: (p. 382) Words such as *um*, *ah*, and *you know* that create hesitations in the flow of your speech.

vocal pitch: (p. 379) The high and low registers of your voice.

vocal rate: (p. 380) How rapidly you speak.

vocal tone: (p. 380) The richness and sound quality of your voice.

vocal volume: (p. 382) How loudly or quietly you speak.

voluntary audience: (p. 325) Listeners who attend a presentation out of self-interest or to fulfill some personal need.

warranting value: (p. 65) The degree to which online information is supported by other people and outside evidence.

"we" language: (p. 119) Phrases that emphasize inclusion and enhance feelings of connection and similarity.

workplace relationships: (p. 224) Affiliations you have with professional peers, supervisors, subordinates, or mentors.

world-mindedness: (p. 103) The ability to practice and demonstrate acceptance and respect toward other cultures' beliefs, values, and customs.

written style: (p. 379) Language that is more formal and detailed than an oral speech style.

"you" language: (p. 119) Phrases that place the focus of attention and blame on others.

Pop Quiz Answers

Chapter 1

1. B (p. 5)
2. C (p. 7)
3. A (p. 10)
4. B (p. 19)
5. A (p. 24)

Chapter 2

1. A (p. 35)
2. B (p. 38)
3. D (p. 44)
4. C (p. 47)
5. B (p. 49)

Chapter 3

1. B (p. 61)
2. D (p. 65)
3. C (p. 72)
4. A (p. 75)
5. D (p. 58)

Chapter 4

1. D (p. 87)
2. C (p. 89)
3. B (p. 95)
4. B (p. 95)
5. B (p. 102)

Chapter 5

1. C (p. 113)
2. B (p. 116)
3. A (p. 119)
4. D (p. 126)
5. D (p. 127)

Chapter 6

1. D (p. 137)
2. A (p. 142)
3. A (p. 146)
4. C (p. 153)
5. B (p. 157)

Chapter 7

1. A (p. 164)
2. C (p. 167)
3. D (p. 168)
4. C (p. 172)
5. A (p. 177)

Chapter 8

1. A (p. 192)
2. D (p. 195)
3. B (p. 201)
4. B (p. 206)
5. C (p. 207)

Chapter 9

1. C (p. 214)
2. D (p. 218)
3. A (p. 222)
4. A (p. 224)
5. B (p. 228)

Chapter 10

1. B (p. 242)
2. A (p. 246)
3. C (p. 248)
4. C (p. 251)
5. D (p. 257)

Chapter 11

1. B (p. 266)
2. C (p. 268)
3. A (p. 272)
4. C (p. 278)
5. D (p. 281)

Chapter 12

1. C (p. 288)
2. C (p. 292)
3. B (p. 294)
4. D (p. 301)
5. A (p. 305)

Chapter 13

1. D (p. 315)
2. C (p. 322)
3. A (p. 326)
4. D (p. 327)
5. B (p. 336)

Chapter 14

1. A (p. 342)
2. B (p. 347)
3. D (p. 352)
4. D (p. 354)
5. C (p. 363)

Chapter 15

1. C (p. 377)
2. D (p. 379)
3. B (p. 382)
4. A (p. 387)
5. C (p. 395)

Chapter 16

1. A (p. 403)
2. D (p. 404)
3. A (p. 407)
4. C (p. 417)
5. B (p. 419)

Chapter 17

1. B (p. 429)
2. C (p. 430)
3. B (p. 434)
4. D (p. 441)
5. A (p. 448)

Appendix

1. A (p. A-3)
2. A (p. A-6)
3. A (p. A-7)
4. A (p. A-14)
5. A (p. A-22)

References

Academy of Achievement. (1991, February 21). *Oprah Winfrey Interview: America's Beloved Best Friend.* Retrieved from http://www.achievement.org/autodoc/page/win0int-1

Afifi, T. D., & Steuber, K. (2010). The cycle of concealment model. *Journal of Social and Personal Relationships, 27*(8), 1019–1034.

Afifi, T. D., McManus, T., Hutchinson, S., & Baker, B. (2007). Inappropriate parental divorce disclosures, the factors that prompt them, and their impact on parents' and adolescents' well-being. *Communication Monographs, 74*(1), pp. 78–102.

Afifi, T. D., McManus, T., Steuber, K., & Coho, A. (2009). Verbal avoidance and dissatisfaction in intimate conflict situations. *Human Communication Research, 35,* 357–383.

Allport, G. W. (1954). *The nature of prejudice.* Cambridge, MA: Addison-Wesley.

Altman, I., & Taylor, D. A. (1973). *Social penetration: The development of interpersonal relationships.* New York, NY: Holt, Rinehart & Winston.

Anderson, C. M., & Martin, M. M. (1999). The relationship of argumentativeness and verbal aggression to cohesion, consensus, and satisfaction in small groups. *Communication Reports, 12,* 21–31.

Anderson, N. H. (1981). *Foundations of information integration theory.* Orlando, FL: Academic Press.

Arasaratnam, L. A. (2006). Further testing of a new model of intercultural communication competence. *Communication Research Reports, 23,* 93–99.

Arasaratnam, L. A., & Banerjee, S. C. (2007). Ethnocentrism and sensation seeking as variables that influence intercultural contact-seeking behavior: A path analysis. *Communication Research Reports, 24*(4), 303–310.

Aron, A., Fisher, H., Strong, G., Acevedo, B., Riela, S., & Tsapelas, I. (2008). Falling in love. In S. Sprecher, A. Wenzel, & J. Harvey (Eds.), *Handbook of relationship initiation* (pp. 315–336). New York, NY: Psychology Press.

Aubert, B. A., & Kelsey, B. L. (2003). Further understanding of trust and performance in virtual teams. *Small Group Research, 34,* 575–618.

Ayres, J. (1988). Coping with speech anxiety: The power of positive thinking. *Communication Education, 37,* 289–296.

Ayres, J. (1996). Speech preparation processes and speech apprehension. *Communication Education, 45,* 228–235.

Ayres, J. (2005). Performance visualization and behavioral disruption: A clarification. *Communication Reports, 18,* 55–63.

Ayres, J., & Ayres, T. A. (2003). Using images to enhance the impact of visualization. *Communication Reports, 16,* 47–55.

Ayres, J., & Hopf, T. S. (1987). Visualization, systematic desensitization, and rational emotive therapy: A comparative evaluation. *Communication Education, 36,* 236–240.

Back, M. D., Stopfer, J. M., Vazire, S., Gaddis, S., Schmukle, S. C., Egloff, B., & Gosling, S. D. (2010). Facebook profiles reflect actual personality, not self-idealization. *Psychological Science, 21*(3), 372–374.

Baer, M. (2010). Cyberstalking and the Internet landscape we have constructed. *Virginia Journal of Law & Technology, 15,* 154–172.

Bailenson, J. N., Beall, A. C., Loomis, J., Blascovich, J., & Turk, M. (2005). Transformed social interaction, augmented gaze, and social influence in immersive virtual environments. *Human Communication Research, 31*(4), 511–537.

Banas, J. A., & Rains, S. A. (2010). A meta-analysis of research on inoculation theory. *Communication Monographs, 77,* 281–311.

Barker, L. L., & Watson, K. W. (2000). *Listen up.* New York, NY: St. Martin's Press.

Barker, V., & Ota, H. (2011). Mixi diary versus Facebook photos: Social networking site use among Japanese and Caucasian American females. *Journal of Intercultural Communication Research, 40*(1), 39–63.

Barnlund, D. C. (1975). *Private and public self in Japan and the United States.* Tokyo, Japan: Simul Press.

Baumeister, R. F., & Leary, M. R. (1995). The need to belong: Desire for interpersonal attachments as a fundamental human motivation. *Psychological Bulletin, 117,* 497–529.

Baxter, L. A. (1990). Dialectical contradictions in relationship development. *Journal of Social and Personal Relationships, 7,* 69–88.

Baym, N. K. (2010). *Personal connections in the digital age.* Digital Media and Society Series. Malden, MA: Polity Press.

Bazelon, E. (2010, July 20). What really happened to Phoebe Prince? *Slate.* Retrieved from www.slate.com

Beall, M. L. (2010). Perspectives on intercultural listening. In A. D. Wolvin (Ed.), *Listening and human communication in the 21st century* (pp. 225–238). Oxford, England: Blackwell.

Bell, B. S., & Kozlowski, S. W. J. (2002). A typology of virtual teams: Implications for effective leadership. *Group & Organization Management, 27,* 14–49.

Benoit, P. J., & Benoit, W. E. (1990). To argue or not to argue. In R. Trapp & J. Schuetz (Eds.), *Perspectives on argumentation: Essays in honor of Wayne Brockriede* (pp. 55–72). Prospect Heights, IL: Waveland Press.

Berger, C. R., & Bradac, J. J. (1982). *Language and social knowledge: Uncertainty in interpersonal relations.* London, England: Edward Arnold.

Berger, C. R., & Calabrese, R. J. (1975). Some explorations in initial interaction and beyond: Toward a developmental theory of interpersonal communication. *Human Communication Research, 1*, 99–112. doi:10.1111/j.1468-2958.1975.tb00258.x

Berscheid, E. (2002). Emotion. In H. H. Kelley et al. (Eds.), *Close relationships* (2nd ed., pp. 110–168). Clinton Corners, NY: Percheron Press.

Berscheid, E., & Regan, P. (2005). *The psychology of interpersonal relationships*. Upper Saddle River, NJ: Pearson Education.

Berscheid, E., & Walster, E. (1978). *Interpersonal attraction* (2nd ed.). Reading, MA: Addison-Wesley.

Bianconi, L. (2002). *Culture and identity: Issues of authenticity in another value system*. Paper presented at the XII Sietar-EU Conference, Vienna Austria.

Bill & Melinda Gates Foundation. (2010). University of Washington Commencement Address. Retrieved from www .gatesfoundation.org/speeches-commentary/Pages /william-gates-sr-2010-uw-commencement-100612.aspx

Birdwhistell, R. L. (1970). *Kinesics and context: Essays on body motion communication*. Philadelphia: University of Pennsylvania Press.

Bochner, S., & Hesketh, B. (1994). Power distance, individualism /collectivism, and job related attitudes in a culturally diverse work group. *Journal of Cross-Cultural Psychology, 25*, 233–257.

Bodenhausen, G. V., Macrae, C. N., & Sherman, J. W. (1999). On the dialectics of discrimination: Dual processes in social stereotyping. In S. Chaiken & Y. Trope (Eds.), *Dual process theories in social psychology* (pp. 271–290). New York, NY: Guilford Press.

Bodie, G. D., & Fitch-Hauser, M. (2010). Quantitative research in listening: Explication and overview. In A. D. Wolvin (Ed.), *Listening and human communication in the 21st century* (pp. 46–93). Oxford, England: Blackwell.

Bodie, G. D., & Worthington, D. L. (2010). Revisiting the Listening Styles Profile (LSP-16): A confirmatory factor analytic approach to scale validation and reliability estimation. *The International Journal of Listening, 24*, 69–88.

Boon, S. D., Deveau, V. L., & Alibhai, A. M. (2009). Payback: The parameters of revenge in romantic relationships. *Journal of Social and Personal Relationships, 26*(6–7), 747–768.

Bornstein, R. F. (1989). Exposure and affect: Overview and meta-analysis of research, 1968–1987. *Psychological Bulletin, 106*, 265–289.

boyd, d. (2007, May 13). Social network sites: Public, private, or what? *Knowledge Tree*. Retrieved from http://www.danah .org/papers/KnowledgeTree.pdf

Braithwaite, D. O., Bach, B. W., Baxter, L. A., DiVerniero, R., Hammonds, J. R., Hosek, A. M., & Wolfe, B. M. (2010). Constructing family: A typology of voluntary kin. *Journal of Social and Personal Relationships, 27*(3), 388–407.

Brewer, M. B. (1999). The psychology of prejudice: Ingroup love or outgroup hate? *Journal of Social Issues, 55*, 429–444.

Brewer, M. B., & Campbell, D. T. (1976). *Ethnocentrism and intergroup attitudes: East African evidence*. Beverly Hills, CA: Sage.

Brigman, G., Lane, D., Lane, D., Lawrence, R., & Switzer, D. (1999). Teaching children school success skills. *The Journal of Educational Research, 92*(6), 323–329.

Brown, V. R., & Paulus, P. B. (2002). Making group brainstorming more effective: Recommendations from an associative memory perspective. *Current Directions in Psychological Science, 11*, 208–212.

Bryant, A. (2010, January 9). On a scale of 1 to 10, how weird are you? *The New York Times*. Retrieved from www .nytimes.com

Bryant, G. A., & Fox Tree, J. E. (2005). Is there an ironic tone of voice? *Language and Speech, 48*, 257–277.

Brym, R. J., & Lenton, R. L. (2001). *Love online: A report on digital dating in Canada*. Retrieved from http://www.nelson.com /nelson/harcourt/sociology/newsociety3e/loveonline.pdf

Buber, M. (1965). *The knowledge of man: A philosophy of the interhuman*. New York, NY: Harper & Row.

Burger, J. M. (1999). The foot-in-the-door compliance procedure: A multiple-process analysis and review. *Personality and Social Psychology Review, 3*, 303–325.

Burgoon, J. K., & Dunbar, N. E. (2000). An interactionist perspective on dominance-submission: Interpersonal dominance as a dynamic, situationally contingent social skill. *Communication Monographs, 67*, 96–121.

Burgoon, J. K., & Hoobler, G. D. (2002). Nonverbal signals. In M. L. Knapp & J. A. Daly (Eds.), *Handbook of interpersonal communication* (3rd ed., pp. 240–299). Thousand Oaks, CA: Sage.

Burgoon, J. K., Buller, D. B., & Woodall, W. G. (1996). *Nonverbal communication: The unspoken dialogue* (2nd ed.). New York, NY: McGraw-Hill.

Burgoon, M. (1995). A kinder, gentler discipline: Feeling good about being mediocre. In B. R. Burleson (Ed.), *Communication yearbook* (Vol. 18, pp. 464–479). Thousand Oaks, CA: Sage.

Buriel, R., & De Ment, T. (1997). Immigration and sociocultural change in Mexican, Chinese, and Vietnamese American families. In A. Booth, A. C. Crouter, & N. Landale (Eds.), *Immigration and the family: Research and policy on U.S. immigrants* (pp. 165–200). Mahwah, NJ: Erlbaum.

Burlage, K., Marafka, J., Parsons, M., & Milaski, J. (2004). *Perception of speakers based on accent*. Paper presented at the 53rd annual convention of the International Communication Association, New Orleans, LA.

Burleson, B. R., & MacGeorge, E. L. (2002). Supportive communication. In M. L. Knapp & J. A. Daly (Eds.), *Handbook of interpersonal communication* (pp. 374–422). Thousand Oaks, CA: Sage.

Burleson, B. R., Metts, S., & Kirch, M. W. (2000). Communication in close relationships. In C. Hendrick & S. S. Hendrick (Eds.), *Close relationships: A sourcebook* (pp. 244–258). Thousand Oaks, CA: Sage.

Bushe, G. R., & Coetzer, G. H. (2007). Group development and team effectiveness: Using cognitive representations to measure group development and predict task performance and group viability. *The Journal of Applied Behavioral Science, 43*, 184–212. doi:10.1177/0021886306298892

Buss, A. H. (1980). *Self-consciousness and social anxiety*. San Francisco, CA: W. H. Freeman.

California Department of Education (n.d.). *Cesar E. Chavez*. Retrieved from http://chavez.cde.ca.gov

Cameron, D. (2009). *The myth of Venus and Mars: Do men and women really speak different languages?* New York, NY: Oxford University Press.

Campany, N., Dubinsky, R., Druskat, V. U., Mangino, M., & Flynn, E. (2007). What makes good teams work better: Research-based strategies that distinguish top-performing cross-functional drug development teams. *Organizational Development Journal, 25*, 179–186.

Campbell, R. G., & Babrow, A. S. (2004). The role of empathy in responses to persuasive risk communication: Overcoming resistance to HIV prevention messages. *Health Communication, 16*, 159–182.

Canary, D. J., Emmers-Sommer, T. M., & Faulkner, S. (1997). *Sex and gender differences in personal relationships*. New York, NY: Guilford Press.

Carr, N. (2010). *The shallows: What the Internet is doing to our brains*. New York, NY: Norton.

Carroll, Lewis. (2013). *Alice in Wonderland* (3rd ed.) (D. J. Gray, Ed.). New York, NY: Norton.

Carton, J. S., Kessler, E. A., & Pape, C. L. (1999). Nonverbal decoding skills and relationship well-being in adults. *Journal of Nonverbal Behavior, 23*, 91–100.

Castelli, L., Tomelleri, S., & Zogmaister, C. (2008). Implicit ingroup metafavoritism: Subtle preference for ingroup members displaying ingroup bias. *Personality and Social Psychology Bulletin, 34*(6), 807–818.

Catmull, E. (2008, September). How Pixar fosters collective creativity. *Harvard Business Review, 86*(9), 64–72.

Caughlin, J., & Golish, T. (2002). An analysis of the association between topic avoidance and dissatisfaction: Comparing perceptual and interpersonal explanations. *Communication Monographs, 69*, 275–296.

Caughlin, J. P., & Vangelisti, A. L. (2000). An individual difference explanation of why married couples engage in demand/withdraw patterns of conflict. *Journal of Social and Personal Relationships, 17*, 523–551.

Chaffee, S. H., & Metzger, M. J. (2001). The end of mass communication? *Mass Communication & Society, 4*, 365–379.

Chen, G.-M., & Starosta, W. J. (1998). *Foundation of intercultural communication*. Boston: Allyn and Bacon.

Chen, G.-M., & Starosta, W. J. (2005). *Foundation of intercultural communication*. Boston: Allyn and Bacon.

Chesebro, J. L. (1999). The relationship between listening styles and conversational sensitivity. *Communication Research Reports, 16*, 233–238.

Chulik, A. (2013, January 9). "Hey honey, what are we having for dinner?" Job candidates' biggest interview blunders. Retrieved from http://thehiringsite.careerbuilder.com /2013/01/09/biggest-interview-blunders

Clark, R. A., & Delia, J. (1979). Topoi and rhetorical competence. *Quarterly Journal of Speech, 65*, 187–206.

Clarke, M. L. (1953). *Rhetoric at Rome: A historical survey*. London, England: Cohen and West.

Cleveland, J. N., Stockdale, M., & Murphy, K. R. (2000). *Women and men in organizations: Sex and gender issues at work*. Mahwah, NJ: Erlbaum.

CNN (2010). Tiger Wood's full apology speech. Retrieved from www.youtube.com/watch?v=Xs8nseNP4s0

Conquergood, D. (1994). Homeboys and hoods: Gang communication and cultural space. In L. R. Frey (Ed.), *Group communication in context: Studies of natural groups* (pp. 23–55). Hillsdale, NJ: Lawrence Erlbaum.

Cooley, C. H. (1902). *Human nature and the social order*. New York, NY: Scribner.

Cooper, L. (1960). *The rhetoric of Aristotle: An expanded translation with supplementary examples for students of composition and public speaking*. Englewood Cliffs, NJ: Prentice Hall.

Costanzo, F. S., Markel, N. N., & Costanzo, R. R. (1969). Voice quality profile and perceived emotion. *Journal of Counseling Psychology, 16*, 267–270.

County of Los Angeles Public Library (n.d.). *About César E. Chávez*. Retrieved from http://www.colapublib.org/chavez /about.html

Coupland, N., Giles, H., & Wiemann, J. M. (Eds.). (1991). *Miscommunication and problematic talk*. Newbury Park, CA: Sage.

Covey, J. (2012, August 27). The role of dispositional factors in moderating message framing effects. *Health Psychology*. doi:10.1037/a0029305

Crosnoe, R., & Cavanagh, S. E. (2010). Families with children and adolescents: A review, critique, and future agenda. *Journal of Marriage and Family, 72*, 594–611.

Cross, S. E., & Madson, L. (1997). Models of the self: Self-construals and gender. *Psychological Bulletin, 122*, 5–37.

Culnan, M. J., & Markus, M. L. (1987). Information technologies. In F. M. Jablin, L. L. Putnam, K. H. Roberts, & L. W. Porter (Eds.), *Handbook of organizational communication: An interdisciplinary perspective* (pp. 420–443). Newbury Park, CA: Sage.

Cumberland, S. (2010). Life-saving learning around the drinking pot. *Bulletin of the World Health Organization, 88*, 721–722. doi:10.2471/BLT.10.011010

Cuomo, M. M. (1984, July 16). *1984 Democratic National Convention keynote address*. Retrieved from www.americanrhetoric .com/speeches/mariocuomo1984dnc.htm

Dainton, M., & Stafford, L. (1993). Routine maintenance behaviors: A comparison of relationship type, partner similarity and sex differences. *Journal of Social and Personal Relationships, 10*, 255–271.

Dainton, M., Zelley, E., & Langan, E. (2003). Maintaining friendships throughout the lifespan. In D. J. Canary & M. Dainton (Eds.), *Maintaining relationships through communication: Relational, contextual, and cultural variations* (pp. 79–102). Mahwah, NJ: Erlbaum.

Dallas, D. (2006, July 28). Café Scientifique—Déjà vu. *Cell, 126*(2), 227–229. doi:10.1016/j.cell.2006.07.006

Davis, K. E., & Todd, M. L. (1985). Assessing friendship: Prototypes, paradigm cases, and relationship description. In S. Duck & D. Perlman (Eds.), *Understanding personal relationships: An interdisciplinary approach* (pp. 17–38). London, England: Sage.

Davis, M. H. (1994). *Empathy: A social psychological approach.* Madison, WI: Brown & Benchmark Publishers.

Delgado-Gaitan, C. (1993). Parenting in two generations of Mexican American families. *International Journal of Behavioral Development, 16,* 409–427.

Delia, J. G. (1972). Dialects and the effects of stereotypes on interpersonal attraction and cognitive processes in impression formation. *Quarterly Journal of Speech, 58,* 285–297.

Demerjian, D. (2008, March). Hustle & flow. *Fast Company.* Retrieved from www.fastcompany.com/magazine/123 /hustle-and-flow.html

DePaulo, B. M., Kirkendol, S. E., Kashy, D. A., Wyer, M. M., & Epstein, J. A. (1996). Lying in everyday life. *Journal of Personality and Social Psychology, 70,* 979–995.

DePaulo, B. M., Lindsay, J. J., Malone, B. E., Muhlenbruck, L., Charlton, K., & Cooper, H. (2003). Cues to deception. *Psychological Bulletin, 129*(1), 74–118.

Devine, P. G. (1989). Stereotypes and prejudice: Their automatic and controlled components. *Journal of Personality and Social Psychology, 56,* 5–18.

Dewey, J. (1933). *How we think: A restatement of the relation of reflective thinking to the educative process* (Rev. ed.). Boston, MA: D. C. Heath.

Dey, R. (2010, October 18). *Leadership is key to success.* Retrieved from www.army.mil/-news/2010/10/18/46689-leadership -is-key-to-success/

Dindia, K., & Allen, M. (1992). Sex differences in self-disclosure: A meta-analysis. *Psychological Bulletin, 112,* 106–124.

Doetkott, R., and Motley, M. (2009, November 11). *Public speaking delivery styles: Audience preference and recollection.* Paper presented at the annual meeting of the NCA 95th Annual Convention, Chicago Hilton & Towers, Chicago, IL.

Donath, J. (1999). Identity and deception in the virtual community. In M. A. Smith & P. Kollock (Eds.), *Communities in cyberspace* (pp. 29–59). London, England: Routledge.

Donath, J., & boyd, d. (2004). Public displays of connection. *BT Technology Journal, 22,* 71–82.

Donohue, W. A., & Kolt, R. (1992). *Managing interpersonal conflict.* Newbury Park, CA: Sage.

Downs, V. C., Javidi, M. M., & Nussbaum, J. F. (1988). An analysis of teachers' verbal communication within the college classroom: Use of humor, self-disclosure, and narratives. *Communication Education, 37,* 127–141.

Dream Share Project (2011, January 3). The founder of SXSW Festival. [Audio interview]. Retrieved from http://thedreamshareproject.com/blog/2011/01/03 /the-founder-of-sxsw-festival/

Druskat, V., & Wolff, S. B. (2001). Building the emotional intelligence of groups. *Harvard Business Review, 79*(3), 81–90.

Duan, C., & Hill, C. E. (1996). The current state of empathy research. *Journal of Counseling Psychology, 43,* 261–274.

Duarte, N. (2008). *Slide:ology: The art and science of creating great presentations.* Sebastopol CA: O'Reilly Media.

Dues, M., & Brown, M. (2004). *Boxing Plato's shadow: An introduction to the study of human communication.* Boston, MA: McGraw-Hill.

Duran, R. L., Kelly, L., & Rotaru, T. (2011). Mobile phones in romantic relationships and the dialectic of autonomy versus connection. *Communication Quarterly, 59,* 19–36.

Eagly, A. H., Ashmore, R. D., Makhijani, M. G., & Longo, L. C. (1991). What is beautiful is good, but . . . : A meta-analytic review of research on the physical attractiveness stereotype. *Psychological Bulletin, 110,* 109–128.

Educause (2007, June 7). 7 Things you should know about Wikipedia. Retrieved from www.educause.edu/ELI /7ThingsYouShouldKnowAboutWikip/161666

Eisterhold, J., Attardo, S., & Boxer, D. (2006). Reactions to irony in discourse: Evidence for the least disruption principle. *Journal of Pragmatics, 38,* 1239–1256.

Ekman, P. (2003). *Emotions revealed. Recognizing faces and feelings to improve communication and emotional life.* New York, NY: Times Books.

Ekman, P., & Friesen, W. V. (1975). Unmasking the face: A guide to recognizing emotions from facial clues. Englewood Cliffs, NJ: Prentice Hall.

El-Guebaly, N. (2005). Don't drink and drive: The successful message of Mothers Against Drunk Driving (MADD). *World Psychiatry, 4*(1), 35–36.

Ellison, N. B., Heino, R. D., & Gibbs, J. L. (2006). Managing impressions online: Self-presentation processes in the online dating environment. *Journal of Computer-Mediated Communication, 11*(2), 415–441.

Ellison, N. B., Steinfield, C., & Lampe, C. (2007). The benefits of Facebook "friends": Social capital and college students' use of online social network sites. *Journal of Computer-Mediated Communication, 12*(4), 1143–1168. Retrieved from http:// onlinelibrary.wiley.com/doi/10.1111/j.1083-6101.2007 .00367.x/full

Englehardt, E. E. (2001). Introduction to ethics in interpersonal communication. In E. E. Englehardt (Ed.), *Ethical issues in interpersonal communication: Friends, intimates, sexuality, marriage, and family* (pp. 1–27). Orlando, FL: Harcourt College.

Evangelist, M. (2006, January 4). Behind the magic curtain. *The Guardian.* Retrieved from www.guardian.co.uk/technology /2006/jan/05/newmedia.media1

Farrell, R. (2011, August 3). 23 traits of good leaders. *CNN.com.* Retrieved from www.cnn.com/2011/LIVING/08/03 /good.leader.traits.cb/index.html

Febbraro, A. R., McKee, B., & Riedel, S. L. (2008, November). *Multinational military operations and intercultural factors*

(NATO RTO Technical Report). Retrieved from http://ftp.rta.nato.int/public//PubFullText/RTO/TR/RTO-TR-HFM-120///$$TR-HFM-120-ALL.pdf

Felmlee, D., Orzechowicz, D., & Fortes, C. (2010). Fairy tales: Attraction and stereotypes in same-gender relationships. *Sex Roles, 62*, 226–240.

Felps, W., Mitchell, T. R., & Byington, E. (2006). How, when, and why bad apples spoil the barrel: Negative group members and dysfunctional groups. In B. M. Shaw (Ed.), *Research in organizational behavior: An annual series of analytical essays and critical reviews* (Vol. 27, pp. 175–222). Amsterdam, Netherlands: Elsevier.

Fenigstein, A., Scheier, M. F., & Buss, A. H. (1975). Public and private self-consciousness: Assessment and theory. *Journal of Consulting and Clinical Psychology, 43*, 522–527.

Fiske, S. T., & Taylor, S. E. (1991). *Social cognition* (2nd ed.). New York, NY: McGraw-Hill.

Fiske, S. T., Cuddy, A. J. C., Glick, P., & Xu, J. (2002). A model of (often mixed) stereotype content: Competence and warmth respectively follow from perceived status and competition. *Journal of Personality and Social Psychology, 82*, 878–902.

Floyd, K. (1999). All touches are not created equal: Effects of form and duration on observers' interpretations of an embrace. *Journal of Nonverbal Behavior, 23*, 283–299.

Floyd, K., & Burgoon, J. K. (1999). Reacting to nonverbal expressions of liking: A test of interaction adaptation theory. *Communication Monographs, 66*, 219–239.

Floyd, K., & Morman, M. T. (1999). The measurement of affectionate communication. *Communication Quarterly, 46*, 144–162.

Forward, G. L., Czech, K., & Lee, C. M. (2011). Assessing Gibb's supportive and defensive communication climate: An examination of measurement and construct validity. *Communication Research Reports, 28*, 1–15.

Foss, S. K., Foss, K. A., & Trapp, R. (1991). *Contemporary perspectives in rhetoric* (2nd ed.). Prospect Heights, IL: Waveland Press.

Fox, K. R. (1992). Physical education and development of self-esteem in children. In N. Armstrong (Ed.), *New directions in physical education: Vol. 2. Towards a national curriculum* (pp. 33–54). Champaign, IL: Human Kinetics.

Fox, K. R. (1997). The physical self and processes in self-esteem development. In K. Fox (Ed.), *The physical self* (pp. 111–139). Champaign, IL: Human Kinetics.

Fragale, A. R. (2006). The power of powerless speech: The effects of speech style and task interdependence on status conferral. *Organizational Behavior and Human Decision Processes, 101*, 243–261.

France, L. R. (2009, September 14). Anger over West's disruption at MTV Awards. *CNN Entertainment.* Retrieved from http://articles.cnn.com/2009-09-14/entertainment/kanye.west.reaction_1_taylor-swift-mtv-video-music-awards-vma?_s=PM:SHOWBIZ

Franklin, J. (2011). *33 Men: Inside the miraculous survival and dramatic rescue of the Chilean miners.* New York, NY: Putnam.

Frisby, B. N., & Westerman, D. (2010). Rational actors: Channel selection and rational choices in romantic conflict episodes. *Journal of Social and Personal Relationships, 27*, 970–981.

Gallow, C. (2012, March 8). 7 ways Tim Cook gave a Steve Jobs–like presentation. *Forbes.com.* Retrieved from www.forbes.com/sites/carminegallo/2012/03/08/7-ways-tim-cook-gave-a-steve-jobs-like-presentation

Galvin, K. M., Brommel, B. J., & Bylund, C. L. (2004). *Family communication: Cohesion and change* (6th ed.). New York, NY: Pearson.

Garamone, J. (2011, January 3). *Mullen: Leaders key to nation's, military's future.* Retrieved from www.defense.gov/News/NewsArticle.aspx?ID=62303

Garber, M. (2012, March 20). Would you give job interviewers your Facebook password? Because they might ask. *The Atlantic.* Retrieved from http://www.theatlantic.com

Gardner, A. (2010, October 18). Surgery mix-ups surprisingly common. *CNN.com.* Retrieved from www.cnn.com/2010/HEALTH/10/18/health.surgery.mixups.common/

Giannakakis, A. E., & Fritsche, I. (2011). Social identities, group norms, and threat: On the malleability of ingroup bias. *Personality and Social Psychology Bulletin, 37*(1), 82–93.

Gibb, J. (1961). Defensive communications. *Journal of Communication, 11*, 141–148.

Gibbs, J. L., Ellison, N. B., & Heino, R. D. (2006). Self-presentation in online personals: The role of anticipated future interaction, self-disclosure, and perceived success in Internet dating. *Communication Research, 33*, 1–26.

Gifford, R., Ng, C. F., & Wilkinson, M. (1985). Nonverbal cues in the employment interview: Links between applicant qualities and interviewer judgments. *Journal of Applied Psychology, 70*, 729–736.

Giles, H., Coupland, N., & Coupland, J. (Eds.). (1991). *Contexts of accommodation: Developments in applied linguistics.* Cambridge, England: Cambridge University Press.

Gleason, L. B. (1989). *The development of language.* Columbus, OH: Merrill.

Glenn, D. (2010, February 28). *Divided attention.* Retrieved from http://chronicle.com/article/Scholars-Turn-Their-Attention/63746/

Global Deception Research Team. (2006). A world of lies. *Journal of Cross-Cultural Psychology, 37*, 60–74.

Goffman, E. (1955). On facework: An analysis of ritual elements in social interaction. *Psychiatry, 18*, 319–345.

Goleman, D. (2006). *Social intelligence: The new science of human relationships.* New York, NY: Bantam Dell.

Goleman, D. (2007, February 20). Flame first, think later: New clues to e-mail misbehavior. *The New York Times.* Retrieved from http://www.nytimes.com

Golish, T. D. (2000). Changes in closeness between adult children and their parents: A turning point analysis. *Communication Reports, 13*, 79–97.

Goodwin, C. (1981). *Conversational organization: Interactions between speakers and hearers.* New York: Academic Press.

Gosling, S. D., Gaddis, S., & Vazire, S. (2007, March). *Personality impressions based on Facebook profiles.* Paper presented at the International Conference on Weblogs and Social Media, Boulder, CO.

Gottman, J. M. & Silver, N. (1999). *The seven principles for making marriage work.* New York, NY: Three Rivers Press.

Greene, L. (2008, May 29). Wrong patient almost gets cardiac catheterization at Tampa General Hospital. *St. Petersburg Times.* Retrieved from www.tampabay.com/news/health /medicine/wrong-patient-almost-gets-cardiac-catheterization -at-tampa-general-hospital/530118

Grice, H. P. (1989). *Studies in the way of words.* Cambridge, MA: Harvard University Press.

Gronbeck, B. E., McKerrow, R. E., Ehninger, D., & Monroe, A. H. (1990). *Principles and types of speech communication* (11th ed.). Glenview, IL: Scott, Foresman/Little, Brown Higher Education.

Gruner, C. R. (1985). Advice to the beginning speaker on using humor—what the research tells us. *Communication Education, 34*, 142–147.

Gudykunst, W. B., & Kim, Y. Y. (2003). *Communicating with strangers: An approach to intercultural communication* (4th ed.). New York, NY: McGraw-Hill.

Gurchiek, K. (2011, June 21). Delivering HR at Zappos. Retrieved from www.weknownext.com/workplace /delivering-hr-at-zappos-hr-magazine-june-2011

Haas, S. M., & Stafford, L. (2005). Maintenance behaviors in same-sex and marital relationships: A matched sample comparison. *Journal of Family Communication, 5*, 43–60.

Hall, E. T. (1963). A system for the notation of proxemic behavior. *American Anthropologist, 65*, 1003–1026.

Hall, E. T. (1976). *Beyond culture.* New York, NY: Doubleday.

Hall, E. T. (1981). *The silent language.* New York, NY: Anchor/ Doubleday.

Hall, E. T. (1983). *The dance of life: The other dimension of time.* New York, NY: Doubleday.

Hall, E. T. (1997a). Context and meaning. In L. A. Samovar & R. E. Porter (Eds.), *Intercultural communication: A reader* (8th ed., pp. 45–53). Belmont, CA: Wadsworth.

Hall, E. T. (1997b). Monochronic and polychronic time. In L. A. Samovar & R. E. Porter (Eds.), *Intercultural communication: A reader* (8th ed., pp. 277–284). Belmont, CA: Wadsworth.

Hall, E. T., & Hall, M. R. (1987). *Understanding cultural differences.* Yarmouth, ME: Intercultural Press.

Hall, J. A. (1998). How big are nonverbal sex differences? The case of smiling and sensitivity to nonverbal cues. In D. J. Canary & K. Dindia (Eds.), *Sex differences and similarities in communication: Critical essays and empirical investigations of sex and gender in interaction* (pp. 155–178). Mahwah, NJ: Erlbaum.

Hall, J. A., Carter, J. D., & Horgan, T. G. (2000). Gender differences in nonverbal communication of emotion. In A. H. Fischer (Ed.), *Gender and emotion: Social psychological perspectives* (pp. 97–117). Cambridge, England: Cambridge University Press.

Hall, J. A., Park, N., Song, H., & Cody, M. J. (2010). Strategic misrepresentation in online dating: The effects of gender, self-monitoring, and personality traits. *Journal of Social and Personal Relationships, 27*(1), 117–135.

Hammer, M. R., Bennett, M. J., & Wiseman, R. (2003). Measuring intercultural sensitivity: The intercultural development inventory. *International Journal of Intercultural Relations, 27*, 421–443.

Hancock, J. T. (2007). Digital deception: When, where and how people lie online. In K. McKenna, T. Postmes, U. Reips, & A. N. Joinson (Eds.), *Oxford handbook of Internet psychology* (pp. 287–301). Oxford, England: Oxford University Press.

Hancock, J. T., & Toma, C. L. (2009). Putting your best face forward: The accuracy of online dating photographs. *Journal of Communication, 59*, 367–386. doi:10.1111/j.1460-2466 .2009.01420.x

Hansen, J. (2010). Patient safety: What can we do? *Vital Speeches of the Day, 76*(4), 158–162. Retrieved from Academic Search Premier.

Harkins, S. G. (1987). Social loafing and social facilitation. *Journal of Experimental Social Psychology, 23*, 1–18.

Hatfield, E. E., & Sprecher, S. (1986). *Mirror, mirror . . . the importance of looks in everyday life.* Albany: State University of New York Press.

Hayden Planetarium (2009, June 30). Carbon: The chemistry of carbon and how it contributes to the formation of life. Retrieved from www.haydenplanetarium.org/tyson /watch/2009/06/30/carbon

Hayes, J. G., & Metts, S. (2008). Managing the expression of emotion. *Western Journal of Communication, 72*, 374–396.

Hays, R. B. (1988). Friendship. In S. Duck (Ed.), *Handbook of personal relationships: Theory, research, and interventions* (pp. 391–408). Chichester, England: Wiley.

Healy, G. B. (2008, January 8). Ending medical errors with airline industry's help. *Boston.com.* Retrieved from www.boston .com/news/health/articles/2008/01/08/ending_medical _errors_with_airline_industrys_help/

Heffernan, V. (2009, January). Confessions of a TED addict. *New York Times Magazine,* 13–14. Retrieved from ProQuest National Newspapers Core (Document ID: 1634754151)

Heider, F. (1958). *The psychology of interpersonal relations.* New York, NY: Wiley.

Heino, R. D., Ellison, N. B., & Gibbs, J. L. (2010). Relation-shopping: Investigating the market metaphor in online dating. *Journal of Social and Personal Relationships, 27*(4), 427–447.

Hemmings, K. H. (2011). *The Descendants.* New York, NY: Random House.

Hendrick, S. S., & Hendrick, C. (1992). *Romantic love.* Thousand Oaks, CA: Sage.

Hersey, P., & Blanchard, K. H. (1988). *Management and organizational behavior.* Englewood Cliffs, NJ: Prentice Hall.

Heslin, R. (1974, May). *Steps toward a taxonomy of touching.* Paper presented at the annual meeting of the Midwestern Psychological Association, Chicago, IL.

Higgins, E. T. (1987). Self-discrepancy: A theory relating self and affect. *Psychological Review, 94*, 319–340.

Hill, J., Ah Yn, K., & Lindsey, L. (2008). The interaction effect of teacher self-disclosure valence and relevance on student motivation, teacher liking, and teacher immediacy. Conference Papers—National Communication Association, 1.

Hodgins, H. S., & Belch, C. (2000). Interparental violence and nonverbal abilities. *Journal of Nonverbal Behavior, 24*, 3–24.

Hofstede, G. (1991). *Cultures and organizations.* London, England: McGraw-Hill.

Hofstede, G. (1998). I, we, they. In J. N. Martin, T. K. Naka-yama, & L. A. Flores (Eds.), *Readings in cultural contexts* (pp. 345–357). Mountain View, CA: Mayfield.

Hofstede, G. (2001). Culture's consequences: Comparing values, behaviors, institutions, and organizations across nations (2nd ed., pp. 79–123). Thousand Oaks, CA: Sage.

Hofstede, G. (2009a). *The Hofstede Center, dimensions, uncertainty avoidance.* Retrieved from http://geert-hofstede.com /dimensions.html

Hofstede, G. (2009b). *The Hofstede Center, national cultural dimensions.* Retrieved from http://geert-hofstede.com /national-culture.html

Hofstede, G., Hofstede, G. J., & Minkov, M. (2010). *Cultures and organizations: Software for the mind* (3rd ed.). New York, NY: McGraw-Hill.

Holtgraves, T., & Lasky, B. (1999). Linguistic power and persuasion. *Journal of Language and Social Psychology, 18*, 196–205.

Honeycutt, J. M. (1999). Typological differences in predicting marital happiness from oral history behaviors and imagined interactions. *Communication Monographs, 66*, 276–291.

Hong, S., Tandoc Jr., E., Kim, E. A., Kim, B., and Wise, K. (2012). The real you? The role of visual cues and comment congruence in perceptions of social attractiveness from Facebook profiles. *Cyberpsychology, Behavior, and Social Networking, 15*, 339–344. doi:10.1089/cyber.2011.0511

Horne, C. F. (1917). *The sacred books and early literature of the east: Vol. 2. Egypt.* New York, NY: Parke, Austin, & Lipscomb.

Hosek, A. M., & Thompson, J. (2009). Communication privacy management and college instruction: Exploring the rules and boundaries that frame instructor private disclosures. *Communication Education, 58*, 327–349.

Hosman, L. A., Huebner, T. M., & Siltanen, S. A. (2002). The impact of power-of-speech style, argument strength, and need for cognition on impression formation, cognitive responses, and persuasion. *Journal of Language and Social Psychology, 21*, 361–379.

Hsieh, T. (2010). *Delivering happiness: A path to profits, passions, and purpose.* New York, NY: Business Plus.

Hyde, J. S. (2005). The gender similarities hypothesis. *American Psychologist, 60*, 581–592.

Infante, D. (1995). Teaching students to understand and control verbal aggression. *Communication Education, 44*, 51–63.

Infante, D. A. (1987). Aggressiveness. In J. C. McCroskey & J. A. Daly (Eds.), *Personality and interpersonal communication* (pp. 157–192). Newbury Park, CA: Sage.

Infante, D. A., & Rancer, A. S. (1982). A conceptualization and measure of argumentativeness. *Journal of Personality Assessment, 46*, 72–80.

Infante, D. A., & Wigley, C. J. (1986). Verbal aggressiveness: An interpersonal model and measure. *Communication Monographs, 53*, 61–69.

Infante, D. A., Chandler, T. A., & Rudd, J. E. (1989). Test of an argumentative skill deficiency model of interspousal violence. *Communication Monographs, 56*, 163–177.

Ingram, M. (2013, March 11). The future of online etiquette is already here—it's just unevenly distributed. Retrieved from http://gigaom.com/2013/03/11/the-future-of-online -etiquette-is-already-here-its-just-unevenly-distributed/

Institute of International Education. (2011, November 14). *Open doors 2011: Report on international education exchange.* Retrieved from www.iie.org/Research-and-Publications /~/media/Files/Corporate/Open-Doors/Open-Doors -2011-Briefing-Presentation.ashx

Jackson, M. (2008). *Distracted: The erosion of attention and the coming dark age.* Amherst, NY: Prometheus Books.

Jacobs, S., Dawson, E. J., & Brashers, D. (1996). Information manipulation theory: A replication and assessment. *Communication Monographs, 63*, 70–82.

Jalongo, M. R. (2008). *Learning to listen, listening to learn: Building essential skills in young children.* Washington, DC: National Association for the Education of Young Children.

Janis, I. L. (1982). *Groupthink: Psychological studies of policy decisions and fiascoes* (2nd ed.). Boston, MA: Houghton Mifflin.

Janusik, L. A. (2002). Teaching listening: What do we do? What should we do? *The International Journal of Listening, 16*, 5–39.

Jemison, M. C. (2012). If Title IX achieves its full potential. *Vital Speeches of the Day, 78*(9), 276.

Jimenez, V. & McCornack, S. A. (2011, August). *Cross-cultural differences in immediacy behaviors of female friends.* Paper presented at the annual MSU McNair Fellowship conference, East Lansing, MI.

Johnson, A. J., Wittenberg, E., Villagran, M. M., Mazur, M., & Villagran, P. (2003). Relational progression as a dialectic: Examining turning points in communication among friends. *Communication Monographs, 70*(3), 230–249.

Johnson, C., & Vinson, L. (1990). Placement and frequency of powerless talk and impression formation. *Communication Quarterly, 38*, 325–333.

Johnson, D. W., & Johnson, F. P. (2008). *Joining together: Group theory and group skills* (10th ed.). New York, NY: Pearson.

Johnston, M. K. (2007). The influence of communication on group attraction during team activities. *Journal of Organizational Culture, Communication, and Conflict, 11*, 43–48.

Joinson, A. N. (2001, March/April). Self-disclosure in computer-mediated communication: The role of self-awareness and visual anonymity. *European Journal of Social Psychology, 31*, 177–192.

Jones-DeWeever, A. (2007). Women and Katrina. *Vital Speeches of the Day, 73*(10), 446–449. Retrieved from Academic Search Premier.

Jones, S. E., & LeBaron, C. D. (2002). Research on the relationship between verbal and nonverbal communication: Emerging integrations. *Journal of Communication, 52,* 499–521.

Jones, W., Bruce, H., Foxley, A., & Munat, C. F. (2006, November). *Planning personal projects and organizing personal information.* Paper presented at the Association for Information Science and Technology 2006 Annual Meeting, Austin, TX. Retrieved from http://kftf.ischool.washington .edu/docs/asist06.pdf

Jordan, L. (2011, January 16). The man behind Storycorps. Retrieved from http://therumpus.net/2011/01/the-man -behind-storycorps

Jourard, S. M. (1964). *The transparent self.* New York, NY: Van Nostrand Reinhold.

Joyce, M. P. (2008). Interviewing techniques used in selected organizations today. *Business Communication Quarterly, 71,* 376–380. doi:10.1177/1080569908321427

JR. (2011). *The 2011 TED acceptance speech.* Retrieved from www.ted.com/talks/lang/en/jr_s_ted_prize_wish_use_art _to_turn_the_world_inside_out.html

Judge, T. A., Ilies, R., Bono, J. E., & Gerhardt, M. W. (2002). Personality and leadership: A qualitative and quantitative review. *Journal of Applied Psychology, 87,* 765–780.

Kagawa, N., & McCornack, S. A. (2004, November). *Collectivistic Americans and individualistic Japanese: A cross-cultural comparison of parental understanding.* Paper presented at the annual meeting of the National Communication Association, Chicago, IL.

Keck, K. L., & Samp, J. A. (2007). The dynamic nature of goals and message production as revealed in a sequential analysis of conflict interactions. *Human Communication Research, 33,* 27–47.

Keesing, R. M. (1974). Theories of culture. *Annual Review of Anthropology, 3,* 73–97.

Kellermann, K. (1989). The negativity effect in interaction: It's all in your point of view. *Human Communication Research, 16,* 147–183.

Kelley, H. H., & Thibaut, J. W. (1978). *Interpersonal relations: A theory of interdependence.* New York, NY: Wiley.

Kelley, T. & Littman, J. (2001). *The art of innovation: Lessons in creativity from IDEO, America's leading design firm.* New York, NY: Doubleday.

Kelly, A. E., & McKillop, K. J. (1996). Consequences of revealing personal secrets. *Psychological Bulletin, 120,* 450–465.

Kennedy, G. A. (1999). *Classical rhetoric and its Christian and secular tradition from ancient to modern times.* Chapel Hill: University of North Carolina Press.

Khatchadourian, R. (2011). In the picture: An artist's global experiment to help people be seen. *The New Yorker.* Retrieved from www.newyorker.com/reporting/2011/11/28 /111128fa_fact_khatchadourian#ixzz1x18s3xLj

Kiger, P. J. (2010, January 12). Webcam job interviews: How to survive and thrive. Retrieved from www.fastcompany.com /1508932/webcam-job-interviews-how-survive -and-thrive

King, M. L. (1963). *I have a dream* . . . Speech transcript from www.archives.gov/press/exhibits/dream-speech.pdf

Kingsley Westerman, C., & Westerman, D. (2010). Supervisor impression management: Message content and channel effects on impressions. *Communication Studies, 61,* 585–601.

Kirkman, B. L., Rosen, B., Gibson, C. B., Tesluk, P. E., & McPherson, S. O. (2002). Five challenges to virtual team success: Lessons from Sabre, Inc. *Academy of Management.* Retrieved from www.jstor.org/stable/4165869

Kirkpatrick, S. A., & Locke, E. A. (1991). Leadership: Do traits matter? *Academy of Management Executive, 5*(2), 48–60.

Klopf, D. W. (2001*). Intercultural encounters: The fundamentals of intercultural communication* (5th ed.). Englewood, CO: Morton.

Knapp, M. (1984). *Interpersonal communication and human relationships.* Boston, MA: Allyn and Bacon.

Knapp, M. L., & Hall, J. A. (2002). *Nonverbal communication in human interaction* (5th ed.). Belmont, CA: Wadsworth/ Thomson Learning.

Knapp, M. L., Daly, J. A., Albada, K. F., & Miller, G. R. (2002). Background and current trends in the study of interpersonal communication. In M. L. Knapp & J. A. Daly (Eds.), *Handbook of interpersonal communication* (3rd ed., pp. 3–20). Thousand Oaks, CA: Sage.

Kozlowski, S. W. J., & Bell, B. S. (2003). Work groups and teams in organizations. In W. C. Brown, D. R. Ilgen, & R. J. Klimoski (Eds.), *Handbook of psychology: Industrial and organizational psychology* (Vol. 12, pp. 333–375). London, England: Wiley.

Kramer, M. W. (2006). Shared leadership in a community theater group: Filling the leadership role. *Journal of Applied Communication Research, 34,* 141–162.

Krause, J. (2001). *Properties of naturally produced clear speech at normal rates and implications for intelligibility enhancement* (Unpublished doctoral dissertation). Massachusetts Institute of Technology, Cambridge, MA.

Kruger, J., Epley, N., Parker, J., & Ng, Z. (2005). Egocentrism over e-mail: Can we communicate as well as we think? *Journal of Personality and Social Psychology, 89,* 925–936.

Kubany, E. S., Richard, D. C., Bauer, G. B., & Muraoka, M. Y. (1992). Impact of assertive and accusatory communication of distress and anger: A verbal component analysis. *Aggressive Behavior, 18,* 337–347.

Kudoh, T., & Matsumoto, D. (1985). Cross-cultural examination of the semantic dimensions of body postures. *Journal of Personality and Social Psychology, 48,* 1440–1446.

Kuhn, J. L. (2001). Toward an ecological humanistic psychology. *Journal of Humanistic Psychology, 41,* 9–24.

LaFollette, H., & Graham, G. (1986). Honesty and intimacy. *Journal of Social and Personal Relationships, 3,* 3–18.

LaGesse, D. (2005, October 31). Heeding her own voice. *U.S. News and World Report.* Retrieved from www.usnews.com /usnews/news/articles/051031/31winfrey.htm

Langdridge, D., & Butt, T. (2004). The fundamental attribution error: A phenomenological critique. *British Journal of Social Psychology, 43*, 357–369.

Lannutti, P. J., & Strauman, E. C. (2006). Classroom communication: The influence of instructor self-disclosure on student evaluations. *Communication Quarterly, 54*, 89–99.

Lasswell, H. D. (1927). *Propaganda technique in the world war.* New York, NY: Knopf.

Lea, M. & Spears, R. (1992). Paralanguage and social perception in computer-mediated communication. *Journal of Organizational Computing, 2*, 321–341.

Lehrer, J. (2010, June). Animating a blockbuster: Inside Pixar's creative magic. *Wired.* Retrieved from www.wired.com

Lehrer, J. (2011, October 7). Steve Jobs: "Technology alone is not enough." *The New Yorker.* Retrieved from www.newyorker.com

Lev-Ari, S., & Keysar, B. (2010). Why don't we believe non-native speakers? The influence of accent on credibility. *Journal of Experimental Social Psychology, 46*, 1093–1096. doi:10.1016/j.jesp.2010.05.025

Limon, M. S., & La France, B. H. (2005). Communication traits and leadership emergence: Examining the impact of argumentativeness, communication apprehension, and verbal aggressiveness in work groups. *Southern Communication Journal, 70*, 123–133.

Lippa, R. A. (2002). *Gender, nature, and nurture.* Mahwah, NJ: Erlbaum.

Littlejohn, S. W., & Foss, K. A. (2010). *Theories of human communication* (10th ed.). Long Grove, IL: Waveland Press.

Logan, L. (2013). The Innovator: Jack Dorsey. *60 Minutes.* Interview transcript. Retrieved from http://www.cbsnews.com/8301-18560_162-57574758/the-innovator-jack-dorsey/

Luft, J. (1970). *Group processes: An introduction to group dynamics* (2nd ed.). Palo Alto, CA: National Press Books.

Lustig, M. W., & Koester, J. (2006). *Intercultural competence: Interpersonal communication across cultures* (5th ed.). Boston, MA: Allyn and Bacon.

Lynch, O. (2002). Humorous communication: Finding a place for humor in communication research. *Communication Theory, 12*, 423–445.

Malis, R. S., & Roloff, M. E. (2006). Demand/withdraw patterns in serial arguments: Implications for well-being. *Human Communication Research, 32*, 198–216.

Mashek, D. J., & Aron, A. (2004). *Handbook of closeness and intimacy.* Mahwah, NJ: Erlbaum.

Maslow, A. H. (1943). A theory of human motivation. *Psychological Review, 50*, 370–396.

Matsumoto, D. (2006). Culture and nonverbal behavior. In V. Manusov & M. Patterson (Eds.), *Handbook of nonverbal communication.* Thousand Oaks, CA: Sage.

Matsumoto, D., Takeuchi, S., Andayani, S., Kouznetsova, N., & Krupp, D. (1998). The contribution of individualism-collectivism to cross-national differences in display rules. *Asian Journal of Social Psychology, 1*, 147–165.

Mattioli, D. (2008, June 10). Next on the agenda: Kisses from Honey Bunny. *WSJ.com.* Retrieved from http://online.wsj.com

McCornack, S. A. (2008). Information manipulation theory: Explaining how deception works. In L. A. Baxter & D. O. Braithwaite (Eds.), *Engaging theories in interpersonal communication: Multiple perspectives.* Thousand Oaks, CA: Sage.

McCornack, S. A., & Levine, T. R. (1990). When lies are uncovered: Emotional and relational outcomes of discovered deception. *Communication Monographs, 57*, 119–138.

McCroskey, J. C. (2009). Communication apprehension: What have we learned in the last four decades. *Human Communication, 12*, 157–171.

McCroskey, J. C. (2008). Communication apprehension: What have we learned in the last four decades? *Human Communication, 12*, 179–187.

McCroskey, J. C., & Andersen, J. F. (1976). The relationship between communication apprehension and academic achievement among college students. *Human Communication Research, 3*, 73–81.

McCroskey, J. C., & Teven, J. J. (1999). Goodwill: A reexamination of the construct and its measurement. *Communication Monographs, 66*, 90–103.

McCroskey, J. C., Daly, J. A., & Sorensen, G. (1976). Personality correlates of communication apprehension: A research note. *Human Communication Research, 2*, 376–380.

McEwan, B., Babin Gallagher, B., & Farinelli, L. (2008, November). *The end of a friendship: Friendship dissolution reasons and methods.* Paper presented at the annual meeting of the National Communication Association, San Diego, CA.

McGonigal, J. (June, 2012). *The game that can give you 10 extra years of life.* Presented at TED Global 2012 in Edinburgh, Scotland. Retrieved from www.ted.com/talks/jane_mcgonigal_the_game_that_can_give_you_10_extra_years_of_life.html

Medina, J. (2008). Brain rules: 12 principles for surviving and thriving at work, home, and school. Seattle, WA: Pear Press.

Mehrabian, A. (1972). *Nonverbal communication.* Chicago, IL: Aldine-Atherton.

Menegatos, L., Lederman, L. C., & Hess, A. (2010). Friends don't let Jane hook up drunk: A qualitative analysis of participation in a simulation of college drinking-related decisions. *Communication Education, 59*, 374–388.

Miller, G. R., & Steinberg, M. (1975). *Between people: A new analysis of interpersonal communication.* Chicago, IL: Science Research Associates.

Miller, L., Hefner, V., & Scott, A. (2007, May). *Turning points in dyadic friendship development and termination.* Paper presented at the annual meeting of the International Communication Association, San Francisco, CA.

Miller-Ott, A. E., Kelly, L., & Duran, R. L. (2012). The effects of cell phone usage rules on satisfaction in romantic relationships. *Communication Quarterly, 60*, 17–34.

Milne, A. A. (1926). *Winnie-the-Pooh.* New York, NY: E.P. Dutton.

Milne, A. A. (1928). *The house at Pooh Corner.* New York, NY: E.P. Dutton.

Milne, J. (2007). *The page at Pooh Corner*. Retrieved from www .pooh-corner.org/index.shtml

Morgeson, F. P., DeRue, D. S., & Karam, E. P. (2010). Leadership in teams: A functional approach to understanding leadership structures and processes. *Journal of Management, 36*, 5–39. doi:10.1177/0149206309347376

Motley, M. T. (1990). Public speaking anxiety qua performance anxiety: A revised model and an alternative therapy. *Journal of Social Behavior & Personality, 5*, 85–104.

MTV.com. (2011, March 10). Gym, tan, find out who Sammi is texting [Television series episode]. *Jersey Shore*. Retrieved from www.mtv.com/videos/jersey-shore-season-2-ep -24-gym-tan-find-out-who-sammi-is-texting/1659569 /playlist.jhtml

Mulac, A., Bradac, J. J., & Mann, S. K. (1985). Male/female language differences and attributional consequences in children's television. *Human Communication Research, 11*, 481–506.

Mulac, A., Incontro, C. R., & James, M. R. (1985). Comparison of the gender-linked language effect and sex role stereotypes. *Journal of Personality and Social Psychology, 49*, 1098–1109.

Munro, K. (2002). Conflict in cyberspace: How to resolve conflict online. In J. Suler (Ed.), *The psychology of cyberspace*. Retrieved from http://www-usr.rider.edu/~suler/psycyber /conflict.html

Myers, D. G. (2000). Wealth, well-being, and the new American dream. *Center for a New American Dream*. Retrieved from www.davidmyers.org/Brix?pageID=49

Myers, D. G. (2002). *The pursuit of happiness: Discovering the pathway to fulfillment, well-being, and enduring personal joy*. New York, NY: HarperCollins.

Myers, D. G. (2004, Summer). The secret to happiness. *Yes!* 13–16.

Myers, D. G. (2013). Happiness. Excerpted from *Psychology* (10th ed.). New York, NY: Worth Publishers.

Myers, S. A., & Anderson, C. M. (2008). *The fundamentals of small group communication*. Thousand Oaks, CA: Sage.

National Communication Association. (1999). *NCA credo for ethical communication*. Retrieved from http://www.natcom.org

National Communication Association. (2002). *What is communication?* Retrieved from http://www.natcom.org/Tertiary .aspx?id=236

Neimeyer, R. A., & Mitchell, K. A. (1988). Similarity and attraction: A longitudinal study. *Journal of Social and Personal Relationships, 5*, 131–148.

Nelson, J. (2006). Leadership. *Vital Speeches of the Day, 72*(8), 239–242. Retrieved from Academic Search Premier.

Neuliep, J. W., & McCroskey, J. C. (1997). The development of a U.S. and generalized ethnocentrism scale. *Communication Research Reports, 14*, 385–398.

Nosko, A., Wood, E., & Molema, S. (2010). All about me: Disclosure in online social networking profiles: The case of FACEBOOK. *Computers in Human Behavior, 26*, 406–418.

NPR Staff (2012, March 19). *How creativity works*: It's all in your imagination [Audio file]. *NPR*. Retrieved from www.npr .org/2012/03/19/148777350/how-creativity-works-its -all-in-your-imagination

Nunamaker, J. F., Jr., Reinig, B. A., & Briggs, R. O. (2009). Principles for effective virtual teamwork. *Communications of the ACM, 52*(4), 113–117.

Oetzel, J. G., & Ting-Toomey, S. (2003). Face concerns in interpersonal conflict: A cross-cultural empirical test of the face negotiation theory. *Communication Research, 30*, 599–624. doi:10.1177/0093650203257841

Oetzel, J., Ting-Toomey, S., Matsumoto, T., Yokochi, Y., Pan, X., Takai, J., & Wilcox, R. (2001). Face and facework in conflict: A cross-cultural comparison of China, Germany, Japan, and the United States. *Communication Monographs, 68*, 235–258.

Ohbuchi, K., & Sato, K. (1994). Children's reactions to mitigating accounts: Apologies, excuses, and intentionality of harm. *Journal of Social Psychology, 134*, 5–17.

O'Keefe, D. J., & Jensen, J. D. (2009). The relative persuasiveness of gain-framed and loss-framed messages for encouraging disease detection behaviors: A meta-analytic review. *Journal of Communication, 59*, 296–316.

Ophir, E., Nass, C. I., & Wagner, A. D. (2012). Cognitive control in media multitaskers. *Proceedings of the National Academy of Sciences.*

Orbe, M. P. (1998). *Constructing co-cultural theory: An explication of culture, power, and communication*. Thousand Oaks, CA: Sage.

Osborn, A. F. (1953). *Applied imagination: Principles and procedures of creative thinking*. New York, NY: Charles Scribner's Sons.

Park, H. S. & Guan, X. (2006). The effects of national culture and face concerns on intention to apologize: A comparison of the USA and China. *Journal of Intercultural Communication Research, 35*(3), 183–204.

Parks, M. R. (1994). Communicative competence and interpersonal control. In M. L. Knapp & G. R. Miller (Eds.), *Handbook of interpersonal communication* (2nd ed., pp. 589–620). Beverly Hills, CA: Sage.

Parks, M. R., & Adelman, M. B. (1983). Communication networks and the development of romantic relationships: An expansion of uncertainty reduction theory. *Human Communication Research, 10*, 55–79.

Parks, M. R., & Floyd, K. (1996). Making friends in cyberspace. *Journal of Communication, 46*, 80–97.

Patterson, M. L. (1983). *Nonverbal behavior: A functional perspective*. New York, NY: Springer-Verlag.

Patterson, M. L. (1988). Functions of nonverbal behavior in close relationships. In S. W. Duck (Ed.), *Handbook of personal relationships* (pp. 41–56). New York, NY: Wiley.

Patterson, M. L. (1995). A parallel process model of nonverbal communication. *Journal of Nonverbal Behavior, 19*, 3–29.

Paul, E. L., McManus, B., & Hayes, A. (2000). "Hookups": Characteristics and correlates of college students' spontaneous and anonymous sexual experiences. *The Journal of Sex Research, 37*, 76–88.

Payne, M. J., & Sabourin, T. C. (1990). Argumentative skill deficiency and its relationship to quality of marriage. *Communication Research Reports, 7*, 121–124.

Pearce, C. L., & Conger, J. A. (Eds.). (2002). *Shared leadership: Reframing the hows and whys of leadership*. Thousand Oaks, CA: Sage.

Pennebaker, J. W. (1997). *Opening up: The healing power of expressing emotions*. New York, NY: Guilford Press.

Peterson, D. R. (2002). Conflict. In H. H. Kelley et al. (Eds.), *Close relationships* (2nd ed., pp. 360–396). Clinton Corners, NY: Percheron Press.

Petronio, S. (2000). The boundaries of privacy: Praxis of everyday life. In S. Petronio (Ed.), *Balancing the secrets of private disclosures* (pp. 37–49). Mahwah, NJ: Erlbaum.

Petronio, S., & Caughlin, J. P. (2006). Communication privacy management theory: Understanding families. In D. O. Braithwaite & L. A. Baxter (Eds.), *Engaging theories in family communication: Multiple perspectives* (pp. 35–49). Thousand Oaks, CA: Sage.

Petty, R. E., & Cacioppo, J. T. (1986). The elaboration likelihood model of persuasion. In L. Berkowitz (Ed.), *Advances in experimental social psychology* (Vol. 19, pp. 123–205). New York, NY: Academic Press.

Petty, R. E., Barden, J., & Wheeler, S. E. (2002). The elaboration likelihood model of persuasion: Health promotions that yield sustained behavior change. In R. J. DiClemente, R. A. Crosby, & M. C. Kegler (Eds.), *Emerging theories in health promotion practice* (pp. 71–99). San Francisco, CA: Jossey-Bass.

Piaget, J. (1926). *Language and thought of the child* (M. Gabain, Trans.). London, England: Routledge & Kegan Paul.

Planalp, S., & Honeycutt, J. M. (1985). Events that increase uncertainty in personal relationships. *Human Communication Research, 11*, 593–604.

Preston, D. R. (1999). Language myth #17: They speak really bad English Down South and in New York City. In L. Bauer & P. Trudgill (Eds.), *Language myths* (pp. 139–149). New York, NY: Penguin Books.

Preston, D. R. (2002). Language with an attitude. In J. K. Chambers, P. Trudgill, & N. Schilling-Estes (Eds.), *The handbook of language variation and change* (pp. 40–66). Oxford, England: Blackwell.

Pruitt, D. G., & Carnevale, P. J. (1993). *Negotiation in social conflict*. Monterey, CA: Brooks-Cole.

Purdy, M., & Newman, N. (1999, March). *Listening and gender: Characteristics of good and poor listeners*. Paper presented to the International Listening Association, Albuquerque, NM.

Quan-Haase, A., & Young, A. L. (2010). Uses and gratifications of social media: A comparison of Facebook and instant messaging. *Bulletin of Science Technology & Society, 30*, 350–361.

Rahim, M. A. (2002). Toward a theory of managing organizational conflict. *International Journal of Conflict Management, 13*, 206–235.

Rainey, V. P. (2000, December). The potential for miscommunication using email as a source of communications. *Transactions of the Society for Design and Process Science, 4*, 21–43.

Rainie, L., & Tancer, B. (2007, April 24). *Wikipedia users*. Retrieved from http://pewinternet.org/Reports/2007/Wikipedia-users.aspx

Rakić, T., Steffens, M. C., & Mummendey, A. (2011). Blinded by the accent! The minor role of looks in ethnic categorization. *Journal of Personality and Social Psychology, 100*, 16–29. doi:10.1037/a0021522

Ramasubramanian, S. (2010). Testing the cognitive-affective consistency model of intercultural attitudes: Do stereotypical perceptions influence prejudicial feelings? *Journal of Intercultural Communication Research, 39*(2), 105–121.

Ramirez-Sanchez, R. (2008). Marginalization from within: Expanding co-cultural theory through the experience of the Afro punk. *The Howard Journal of Communications, 19*, 89–104.

Rawlins, W. K. (1992). *Friendship matters: Communication, dialectics, and the life course*. New York, NY: Aldine de Gruyter.

Reik, T. (1972). *A psychologist looks at love*. New York, NY: Lancer.

Reis, H. T., & Patrick, B. C. (1996). Attachment and intimacy: Component processes. In E. T. Higgins & A. W. Kruglanski (Eds.), *Social psychology: Handbook of basic principles* (pp. 523–563). New York, NY: Guilford Press.

Reis, H. T., & Shaver, P. (1988). Intimacy as an interpersonal process. In S. W. Duck (Ed.), *Handbook of personal relationships* (pp. 367–389). New York, NY: Wiley.

Rice, L. (2011, March 15). *The Bachelor* creator on his long-running franchise: "The romance space is ours." *Entertainment Weekly*. Retrieved from http://insidetv.ew.com/2011/03/15/the-bachelor-creator-ashley-h/

Richmond, V. P., McCroskey, J. C., & Johnson, A. D. (2003). Development of the nonverbal immediacy scale (NIS): Measures of self- and other-perceived nonverbal immediacy. *Communication Quarterly, 51*, 504–517.

Ridge, R. D., & Berscheid, E. (1989, May). *On loving and being in love: A necessary distinction*. Paper presented at the annual convention of the Midwestern Psychological Association, Chicago, IL.

Riela, S., Rodriguez, G., Aron, A., Xu, X., & Acevedo, B. P. (2010). Experiences of falling in love: Investigating culture, ethnicity, gender, and speed. *Journal of Social and Personal Relationships, 27*, 473–493.

Riggio, R. E. (2006). Nonverbal skills and abilities. In V. Manusov & M. Patterson (Eds.), *Handbook of nonverbal communication*. Thousand Oaks, CA: Sage.

Rochat, P. (2003). Five levels of self-awareness as they unfold early in life. *Consciousness and Cognition, 12*, 717–731.

Roethlisberger, F. J., & Dickson, W. J. (1939). *Management and the worker*. Cambridge, MA: Harvard University Press.

Roloff, M. E., & Soule, K. P. (2002). Interpersonal conflict: A review. In M. L. Knapp & J. A. Daly (Eds.), *Handbook of interpersonal communication* (3rd ed., pp. 475–528). Thousand Oaks, CA: Sage.

Romano, N. C., Jr., & Nunamaker, J. F., Jr. (2001). Meeting analysis: Findings from research and practice. In *Proceedings of the 34th annual Hawaii international conference on system sciences*. Retrieved from www.computer.org/csdl/proceedings/hicss/2001/0981/01/index.html

Rothman, A. J., Bartels, R. D., Wlaschin, J., & Salovey, P. (2006). The strategic use of gain- and loss-framed messages to promote healthy behavior: How theory can inform practice. *Journal of Communication, 56*, S202–S220.

Rowan, K. (2003). Informing and explaining skills: Theory and research on informative communication. In J. O. Green and B. R. Burleson (Eds.), *Handbook of Communication and Social Interaction* (pp. 403–438). Mahwah, NJ: Lawrence Erlbaum.

Rubin, Z. (1973). *Liking and loving: An invitation to social psychology.* New York: Holt, Rinehart & Winston.

Rubin, Z. (1973). *Liking and loving: An invitation to social psychology.* New York, NY: Holt, Rinehart & Winston.

Sager, K. L., & Gastil, J. (1999). Reaching consensus on consensus: A study of the relationships between individual decision-making styles and use of the consensus decision rule. *Communication Quarterly, 47*, 67–79.

Sager, K. L., & Gastil, J. (2006). The origins and consequences of consensus decision making: A test of the social consensus model. *Southern Communication Journal, 71*, 1–24.

Sawyer, K. (2007). *Group genius: The creative power of collaboration.* New York, NY: Basic Books.

Schramm, W. (Ed.). (1954). *The process and effects of mass communication.* Urbana: University of Illinois Press.

Schutz, A. (1999). It was your fault! Self-serving biases in autobiographical accounts of conflicts in married couples. *Journal of Social and Personal Relationships, 16*, 193–208.

Searle, J. (1965). What is a speech act? In M. Black (Ed.), *Philosophy in America* (pp. 221–239). Ithaca, NY: Cornell University Press.

Seattle Poetry Slam. (2013). *Ed Mabrey.* Retrieved from http://seattlepoetryslam.org/?p=598

Seider, B. H., Hirschberger, G., Nelson, K. L., & Levenson, R. W. (2009). We can work it out: Age differences in relational pronouns, physiology, and behavior in marital conflict. *Psychology and Aging, 24*(3), 604–613.

Shannon, C. E., & Weaver, W. (1949). *The mathematical theory of communication.* Urbana: University of Illinois Press.

Shedletsky, L. J., & Aitken, J. E. (2004). *Human communication on the Internet.* Boston, MA: Pearson Education/Allyn and Bacon.

Shelton, J. N., Trail, T. E., West, T. V., & Bergsieker, H. B. (2010). From strangers to friends: The interpersonal process model of intimacy in developing interracial friendships. *Journal of Social and Personal Relationships, 27*(1), 71–90.

Shenk, J. W. (2005). *Lincoln's melancholy: How depression challenged a president and fueled his greatness.* New York, NY: Houghton Mifflin.

Sherr, L. (2010, December 26). Oprah Winfrey: Everybody just wants to be heard. *Parade.* Retrieved from www.parade.com/celebrity/celebrity-parade/2010/1222-oprah-biggest-dream-ever.html

Shin, H. B., & Kominski, R. A. (2010). Language use in the United States: 2007 (American community survey reports, ACS-12). Washington, DC: U.S. Census Bureau.

Sias, P. M., & Cahill, D. J. (1998). From co-workers to friends: The development of peer friendships in the workplace. *Western Journal of Communication, 62*, 273–300.

Sias, P. M., & Perry, T. (2004). Disengaging from workplace relationships: A research note. *Human Communication Research, 30*, 589–602.

Sias, P. M., Drzewiecka, J. A., Meares, M., Bent, R., Konomi, Y., Ortega, M., & White, C. (2008). Intercultural friendship development. *Communication Reports, 21*(1), 1–13.

Siebdrat, F., Hoegl, M., & Ernst, H. (2009). How to manage virtual teams. *MIT Sloan Management Review, 50*(4), 63–68.

Sillars, A. L. (1980). Attributions and communication in roommate conflicts. *Communication Monographs, 47*, 180–200.

Sillars, A., Roberts, L. J., Leonard, K. E., & Dun, T. (2000). Cognition during marital conflict: The relationship of thought and talk. *Journal of Social and Personal Relationships, 17*, 479–502.

Silverstein, M., & Giarrusso, R. (2010). Aging and family life: A decade review. *Journal of Marriage and Family, 72*, 1039–1058.

Silvia, P. (2008). Interest—the curious emotion. *Current Directions in Psychological Science, 17*, 57–60.

Sink, M. (2006, February 21). Science comes to the masses (you want fries with that?). *New York Times* (Late Edition [East Coast]), p. F3. Retrieved from ProQuest National Newspapers Core (Document ID: 990692051)

Small, D. A., Loewenstein, G., & Slovic, P. (2007). Sympathy and callousness: The impact of deliberative thought on donations to identifiable and statistical victims. *Organizational Behavior and Human Decision Processes, 102*, 143–153.

Smith, C. D., Sawyer, C. R., & Behnke, R. R. (2005). Physical symptoms of discomfort associated with worry about giving a public speech. *Communication Reports, 18*, 31–41.

Smith, G., & Anderson, K. J. (2005). Students' ratings of professors: The teaching style contingency for Latino/a professors. *Journal of Latinos and Education, 4*, 115–136.

Smith, T. E., & Frymier, A. B. (2006). Get 'real': Does practicing speeches before an audience improve performance? *Communication Quarterly, 54*, 111–125.

Socha, T. J. (1997). Group communication across the life span. In L. R. Frey & J. K. Barge (Eds.), *Managing group life: Communicating in decision-making groups* (pp. 3–28). Boston, MA: Houghton Mifflin.

Sommer, R. (1965). Further studies of small group ecology. *Sociometry, 28*, 337–348.

Soto, J. A., Levenson, R. W., & Ebling, R. (2005). Cultures of moderation and expression: Emotional experience, behavior, and physiology in Chinese Americans and Mexican Americans. *Emotion, 5*, 154–165.

Spears, R., Postmes, T., Lea, M., & Watt, S. E. (2001). A SIDE view of social influence. In J. P. Forgas & K. D. Williams (Eds.), *Social influence: Direct and indirect processes* (pp. 331–350). Philadelphia, PA: Psychology Press/Taylor and Francis Group.

Spender, D. (1990). *Man made language*. London, England: Pandora Press.

Spitzberg, B. H., & Cupach, W. R. (1984). *Interpersonal communication competence*. Beverly Hills, CA: Sage.

Spitzberg, B. H., & Cupach, W. R. (2002). Interpersonal skills. In M. L. Knapp & J. A. Daly (Eds.), *Handbook of interpersonal communication* (3rd ed., pp. 564–611). Thousand Oaks, CA: Sage.

Sporer, S. L., & Schwandt, B. (2006). Paraverbal indicators of deception: A meta-analytic synthesis. *Applied Cognitive Psychology, 20*(4), 421–446.

Sprecher, S. (2001). A comparison of emotional consequences of and changes in equity over time using global and domain-specific measures of equity. *Journal of Social and Personal Relationships, 18*, 477–501.

Stafford, L. (2010). Measuring relationship maintenance behaviors: Critique and development of the revised relationship maintenance behavior scale. *Journal of Social and Personal Relationships, 28*, 278–303.

Stafford, L., Dainton, M., & Haas, S. (2000). Measuring routine and strategic relational maintenance: Scale revision, sex versus gender roles, and the prediction of relational characteristics. *Communication Monographs, 67*, 306–323.

Stern, J. (2009). Making smarter movies. *Vital Speeches of the Day, 75*(8), 347–352. Retrieved from Academic Search Premier.

Stewart, G. L., Dustin, S. L., Barrick, M. R., & Darnold, T. C. (2008). Exploring the handshake in employment interviews. *Journal of Applied Psychology, 93*, 1139–1146.

Stiff, J. B., Dillard, J. P., Somera, L., Kim, H., & Sleight, C. (1988). Empathy, communication, and prosocial behavior. *Communication Monographs, 55*, 198–213.

Stockett, K. (2009). *The Help*. New York, NY: Penguin Group.

Streek, J. (1980). Speech acts in interaction: A critique of Searle. *Discourse Processes, 3*, 133–154.

Suler, J. (2004). The online disinhibition effect. *Cyberpsychology & Behavior, 7*, 321–326.

Sumner, William G. (1906). *Folkways*. Boston, MA: Ginn.

Swann, W. B., Jr., & Pelham, B. W. (2002). Who wants out when the going gets good? Psychological investment and preference for self-verifying college roommates. *Journal of Self and Identity, 1*, 219–233.

Swann, W. B., Jr., Chang-Schneider, C., & Angulo, S. (2007). Self-verification in relationships as an adaptive process. In J. Wood, A. Tesser, & J. Holmes (Eds.), *Self and Relationships*. New York, NY: Psychology Press.

Swann, W. B., Jr., Hixon, J. G., & De La Ronde, C. (1992). Embracing the bitter truth: Negative self-concepts and marital commitment. *Psychological Science, 3*, 118–121.

Swider, B. W., Barrick, M. R., Harris, T. B., & Stoverink, A. C. (2011). Managing and creating an image in the interview: The role of interviewee initial impressions. *Journal of Applied Psychology, 96*, 1275–1288.

Tardy, C. H. (2000). Self-disclosure and health: Revising Sidney Jourard's hypothesis. In S. Petronio (Ed.), *Balancing the secrets of private disclosures* (pp. 111–122). Mahwah, NJ: Erlbaum.

Tardy, C., & Dindia, K. (1997). Self-disclosure. In O. Hargie (Ed.), *The handbook of communication skills*. London, England: Routledge.

Taylor Swift speaks out on Kanye incident. (2009, September 14). *US Weekly*. Retrieved from www.usmagazine.com /celebritynews/news/taylor-swift-2009149

TED.com (n.d.) *About TED*. Retrieved from www.ted.com/pages /about

TED.com (n.d.). *The TED Prize*. Retrieved from www.ted.com /prize

Teo, T. M. S. (2005). *Cross-cultural leadership: A military perspective (NSSC7)*. Kingston, Ontario, Canada: Canadian Forces College.

Teven, J. J. (2008). An examination of perceived credibility of the 2008 presidential candidates: Relationships with believability, likeability, and deceptiveness. *Human Communication, 11*, 383–400.

Teven, J. J., & Hanson, T. L. (2004). The impact of teacher immediacy and perceived caring on teacher competence and trustworthiness. *Communication Quarterly, 52*, 39–53.

The Walt Disney Company (n.d.). Our Businesses: The Walt Disney Studios: Pixar. Retrieved from http:// thewaltdisneycompany.com/disney-companies/studio -entertainment

Thomas, L. T., & Levine, T. R. (1994). Disentangling listening and verbal recall: Related but separate constructs? *Human Communication Research, 21*, 103–127.

Tiger: Speaking from a smart, but empty, script [Editorial]. (2010, February 20). *The Boston Globe*. Retrieved from www .boston.com/bostonglobe/editorial_opinion/editorials /articles/2010/02/20/tiger_speaking_from_a_smart_but _empty_scriptTing-Toomey, S. (1997). Managing intercultural conflicts effectively. In L. A. Samovar & R. E. Porter (Eds.), *Intercultural communication: A reader* (pp. 392–403). Belmont, CA: Wadsworth.

Ting-Toomey, S. (1999). *Communicating across cultures*. New York, NY: Guilford Press.

Ting-Toomey, S. (2005). The matrix of face: An updated face-negotiation theory. In W. B. Gudykunst (Ed.), *Theorizing about intercultural communication* (pp. 211–234). Thousand Oaks, CA: Sage.

Tolkien, J. R. R. (1994). *The Fellowship of the Ring: Being the First Part of The Lord of the Rings*. Boston, MA: Houghton Mifflin. (Original work published 1954)

Tong, S. T., Van Der Heide, B., Langwell, L., & Walther, J. B. (2008). Too much of a good thing? The relationship between number of friends and interpersonal impressions on Facebook. *Journal of Computer-Mediated Communication, 13,* 531–549.

Toulmin, S. (1958). *The uses of argument.* Cambridge, England: Cambridge University Press.

Tovares, A. V. (2010). All in the family: Small stories and narrative construction of a shared family identity that includes pets. *Narrative Inquiry, 20*(1), 1–19.

Triandis, H. (1988). Collectivism v. individualism: A reconceptualisation of a basic concept in cross-cultural social psychology. In G. K. Verma & C. Bagley (Eds.), *Cross-cultural studies of personality, attitudes and cognition* (pp. 60–95). New York, NY: St. Martin's Press.

Tsai, J. L., & Levenson, R. W. (1997). Cultural influences of emotional responding: Chinese American and European American dating couples during interpersonal conflict. *Journal of Cross-Cultural Psychology, 28,* 600–625.

T Screen Test Films: Tyra Banks. (2008). *The New York Times/T Magazine.* Retrieved from www.youtube.com/watch?feature =player_embedded&v=aINaHOxZN_4

Tuckman, B. (1965). Developmental sequence in small groups. *Psychological Bulletin, 63,* 384–399.

Tuckman, B. W., & Jensen, M. A. C. (1977). Stages of small-group development revisited. *Group & Organization Studies, 2*(4), 419–427.

Turkle, S. (2008). Always-on/always-on-you: The tethered self. In J. E. Katz (Ed.), *The handbook of mobile communication studies* (pp. 121–138). Cambridge, MA: MIT Press.

Turner, J. C., Hogg, M. A., Oakes, P. J., Reicher, S. D., & Wetherell, M. S. (1987). *Rediscovering the social group: A self-categorization theory.* Cambridge, MA: Basil Blackwell.

U.S. Census Bureau (2012, May 17). *Most children younger than age 1 are minorities, census bureau reports.* Retrieved from www.census.gov/newsroom/releases/archives/population /cb12-90.html

Valdes, M. (2007, August 10). Alaska Airlines, Sea-Tac Airport look to streamline check-in. *The Seattle Times.* Retrieved from http://community.seattletimes.nwsource.com/archive/?date =20070810&slug=alaskaairweb10

Vazire, S., & Gosling, S. D. (2004). E-Perceptions: Personality impressions based on personal websites. *Journal of Personality and Social Psychology, 87,* 123–132.

Wagner, B. C., & Petty, R. E. (2011). The elaboration likelihood model of persuasion: Thoughtful and non-thoughtful social influence. In D. Chadee (Ed.), *Theories in social psychology* (pp. 96–116). Oxford, England: Wiley-Blackwell.

Walker, C. M., Sockman, B. R., & Koehn, S. (2011). An exploratory study of cyberbullying with undergraduate university students. *TechTrends, 55*(2), 31–38.

Wallace, P. (1999). *The psychology of the Internet.* Cambridge, England: Cambridge University Press.

Wallace, W. (2008). Coaching character. *Vital Speeches of the Day, 74*(3), 119–121. Retrieved from Academic Search Premier.

Walther, J. B. (1992). Interpersonal effects in computer-mediated interaction: A relational perspective. *Communication Research, 19,* 52–90.

Walther, J. B., & Parks, M. R. (2002). Cues filtered out, cues filtered in: Computer-mediated communication and relationships. In M. L. Knapp & J. A. Daly (Eds.), *Handbook of interpersonal communication* (pp. 529–563). Thousand Oaks, CA: Sage.

Walther, J. B., Van Der Heide, B., Kim, S. Y., Westerman, D., & Tong, S. T. (2008). The role of friends' appearance and behavior on evaluations of individuals on Facebook: Are we known by the company we keep? *Human Communication Research, 34,* 28–49.

Walther, J., Van Der Heide, B., Hamel, L. M., & Shulman, H. C. (2009). Self-generated versus other-generated statements and impressions in computer-mediated communication: A test of warranting theory using Facebook. *Communication Research, 36,* 229–253.

Walther, J., Van Der Heide, B., Kim S., Westerman, D., & Tong, S. T. (2008). The role of friends' appearance and behavior on evaluations of individuals on Facebook: Are we known by the company we keep? *Human Communication Research, 34,* 28–49.

Watercutter, A. (2013, February 4). How Oreo won the marketing super bowl with a timely blackout ad on Twitter. *Wired.* Retrieved from www.wired.com/underwire/2013/02 /oreo-twitter-super-bowl/

Waterman, A. (1984). *The psychology of individualism.* New York, NY: Praeger.

Watzlawick, P., Beavin, J. H., & Jackson, D. D. (1967). *Pragmatics of human communication: A study of interactional patterns, pathologies, and paradoxes.* New York, NY: Norton.

Weisz, C., & Wood, L. F. (2005). Social identity support and friendship outcomes: A longitudinal study predicting who will be friends and best friends 4 years later. *Journal of Social and Personal Relationships, 22*(3), 416–432.

Whalen, J. M., Pexman, P. M., & Gill, A. J. (2009). "Should Be Fun—Not!" Incidence and marking of nonliteral language in e-mail. *Journal of Language and Social Psychology, 28,* 263–280.

Wheeless, L. R. (1978). A follow-up study of the relationships among trust, disclosure, and interpersonal solidarity. *Human Communication Research, 4,* 143–145.

White, J. (2010, September 28). Workplace bullying: Recognize and prevent it. *CIO insight.* Retrieved from http://www .cioinsight.com/c/a/Latest-News/Workplace-Bullying -Recognize-and-Prevent-It-884670/

Whitty, M. T., & Buchanan, T. (2010). What's in a screen name? Attractiveness of different types of screen names used by online daters. *International Journal of Internet Science, 5,* 5–19.

Whorf, B. L. (1952). *Collected papers on metalinguistics*. Washington, DC: Department of State, Foreign Service Institute.

Wiemann, J. M. (1977). Explication and test of a model of communicative competence. *Human Communication Research, 3*, 195–213.

Wilmot, W. W., & Hocker, J. L. (2010). *Interpersonal conflict* (8th ed.). Boston, MA: McGraw-Hill.

Wilson, T. D. (2002). Strangers to ourselves: Discovering the adaptive unconscious. Cambridge, MA: Harvard University Press.

Withers, J. (2012, June 14). Speech presented at the 2012 Lifesavers Conference on Highway Safety Priorities, Orlando, FL. Speech transcript retrieved from www.madd.org/media-center/2012-lifesavers-speech.html

Wolak, J., Mitchell, K., & Finkelhor, D. (2006). *Online victimization of youth: Five years later*. Alexandria, VA: National Center for Missing and Exploited Children.

World Health Organization (2003). *Lives at risk: malaria in pregnancy*. Retrieved from www.who.int/features/2003/04b/en

Wu, D. Y. H., & Tseng, W. (1985). Introduction: The characteristics of Chinese culture. In W. Tseng & D. Y. H. Wu (Eds.), *Chinese culture and mental health* (pp. 3–13). Orlando, FL: Academic Press.

Yoshimura, S. (2007). Goals and emotional outcomes of revenge activities in interpersonal relationships. *Journal of Social and Personal Relationships, 24*(1): 87–98.

Zacchilli, T. L., Hendrick, C., & Hendrick, S. S. (2009). The romantic partner conflict scale: A new scale to measure relationship conflict. *Journal of Social and Personal Relationships, 26*, 1073–1096.

Zappos family core values. (n.d.). Retrieved from http://about.zappos.com/our-unique-culture/zappos-core-values

Index

Your Video Choices

bedfordstmartins.com/choicesconnections

LaunchPad offers Bedford/St. Martin's superior video content organized to work seamlessly with the printed textbook. Go to LaunchPad for *Choices & Connections* to find the **How to Communicate** video scenarios, **Key Term Videos** including full-length speeches, and **Sample Speech Resources** that complement the book content. Here is a list of the videos and where their concepts appear in the text.